VAIN GLORY

CHAPMAN, Guy Patterson, ed. Vain Glory: a Miscellany of the Great War, 1914–1918; Written by Those Who Fought in It on Each Side and on All Fronts. Cassell (dist. by Dufour), 1969 (orig. pub. in 1937). 762p 68-139997. 7.95

CHOICE NOV. '69 History, Geography & Travel

This reissue of the forerunner of Desmond Flower and James Reeves' *The War, 1939–1945* (called in the U.S. *The Taste of Courage*, 1960) is more than welcome for it carries within its appendices a hefty bibliography of the World War I. More than this, the selections of what it was like by one who was intimately engaged is not nearly so likely to be recreated by a modern anthologist. For libraries which do not have much on the 1914–18 conflict, this is a book which they should add. There are some unfortunate features, however, in the reissue. The original preface has been removed, rather than being left as a historical document. Modern editorial notes would have been most helpful as there are places and persons mentioned which are no longer familiar. Though there are no illustrations, these can be found in Taylor's *Illustrated History of the First World War* (CHOICE, July–August 1964). Table of contents proper is at the end.

VAIN GLORY

A miscellany of the Great War 1914–1918
written by those who fought in it on
each side and on all fronts

EDITED WITH AN INTRODUCTION

BY

GUY CHAPMAN

O.B.E., M.C.

Cur mundus militat sub vana gloria
Jacopone da Todi

CASSELL · LONDON

CASSELL & COMPANY LTD
35 Red Lion Square, London WC1
Melbourne, Sydney, Toronto
Johannesburg, Auckland

This edition © Cassell & Co. Ltd 1968

S.B.N. 304 92580 1

First published 1937
Second edition March 1968
Second edition, second impression August 1968

Printed in Great Britain by
Cox & Wyman Ltd, London, Fakenham and Reading
668

CONTENTS

INTRODUCTION

I

THIS book had its origin in the mind of Mr. Desmond Flower of Cassell and Company, who invited me to devise and compile such a book as this is, not an anthology but a collection of actualities, if possible in the words of actors or eye-witnesses. Of our conversation I remember little, but it has stuck in my mind that the incident which had gripped Mr. Flower's imagination was "The Taxis of the Marne", which has as vividly remained a popular legend in France. In 1914, the accounts of the incident stirred all of us, the thought of hundreds of French taxis filled with French red-trousered infantry rushing across country to a triumphal counter-attack. Coming at the end of those ten frightful days of the retreat from Mons and Charleroi, it was intoxicating, and passed easily into legend. Did not M. Jean Dutourd summon them to help in his denunciation of the defeat of 1940, *les fantômes cahotants aux formes asseᵹ antiques pour n'être plus ridicules?*

Romantic legends are not invariably accurate, and when I came to search for a quotable account it was not to be had: official reports have no weakness for the enthusiasms of spectators. Colonel Lyet's *Joffre et Galliéni à la Marne*, which contains the official reports of the organizers, had not yet been published. All I could find was the brief scene in Lintier's *Ma Pièce* (page 71), of a gunner subaltern standing in the dark at the side of the road watching a column of Paris taxis jolting up a country road, taxis filled with sleeping *fantassins*. "Who are you?"—"Seventh Division. Going into the line." I incline to think that short exchange of words conveys more than any elaborate account, much more than the precise phrases of the officers who organized the affair.

These taxis were one of my earliest obstacles. There were many more. In so large a collection much depended on the size of the fees which would have to be paid to authors. On the whole they were not greedy, except an American firm which controlled Barbusse's rights and demanded a sum for a passage which would have absorbed a tenth of the money at my disposal. So Barbusse does not appear. There was also a brilliant diarist—it was, I think, the Master of Belhaven—who refused unless he was guaranteed that there would be no pacifist nonsense, a guarantee that could scarcely be given.

The real trouble was the planning. People in every walk of life were involved, not only the soldiers, sailors and airmen, but everyone from capitalist to mill-hand. It involved a dozen European countries, and allies and enemies had to be accommodated. It covered many areas in three continents. And it had signposts all along the way, few of which could be by-passed. It must begin with the murder of the Archduke and it must end with both sides of the armistice, the winners and the losers. For the rest, there were the obvious milestones: Liège, Mons, le Cateau, the Marne, First Ypres, the first gas attack, Jutland, the first day of the Somme, etc. Even so, there were all kinds of gaps. For the Somme there are innumerable accounts, for Third Ypres many. Of Arras, a short and bloody battle, possibly for daily average the highest casualty record, very few.

There was also the problem of the eye-witness. Could one include history? One passage from the Official History was included simply because it was so vivid as to convince me that General Edmonds had been there himself. It is the passage describing the warm April afternoon in 1915 on which the first gas attack was made. There was the problem of excerpts from novels. In some cases I happened to know the author, or of the author, and was prepared to bet that he was quoting his own experience. It is, of course, well known that Frederick Manning had served in the ranks of the King's Shropshire Light Infantry, but even had one not known it one could swear that the return to the battalion transport lines after battle was an actual experience, even to the snob's: "They can say what they like, but we're a f——g fine mob." (Page 317.) Manning I never met, but there is a passage from an unpublished novel (pages 315–19) by my old friend Daniel George, who assured me of its authenticity: it was of the ghastly mess that occurred at Gommecourt on 1 July 1916. Similarly, passages from the late Edward Thompson's two novels are transmutations of experience in Mesopotamia and Palestine: Edward Thompson was perhaps the most honest man I ever met.

There are two pieces I was very glad to rescue from the common grave of the ephemeral press, the first the recollection of 1 July 1916, by N.C.O., 22nd Manchester Regiment, (pages 319–25) the second "The Reflections of a Soldier" (page 377). Both these were written by the late Professor R. H. Tawney, one of our finest writers of classical prose. Typical of the man, he served in the ranks.

On looking through the book again, I incline to think that most of it is pretty authentic. There are moments of pellucid vividness caught by narrators. One I have already mentioned: the first gas attack. There is another of equal clarity, the short passage by Captain Brownlow of the breaking off of the engagement of le Cateau, with the infantry coming down from the ridge by Caudry (page 43). I don't think there are any faked pieces. (I have a faint recollection of a letter in *The Times Literary Supplement* many years ago, from Mr. Robert Graves, who asserted that the more incredible an account the more likely it was to be true.) There are errors of taste on my part, which I regret, and also of charity. I particularly regret the short piece about Joffre. Mr. Corelli Barnett, in his admirable *The Desert Generals*, quotes the opinion of General Sir Richard O'Connor. After the unbelievable victory at Beda Fomm in January 1941, he was asked what it felt like to be a completely successful commander. He replied: "I would never consider a commander completely successful until he had restored the situation after a serious defeat and a long retreat." Joffre suffered a scalding defeat in August 1914, along almost the whole front of the battle from Mulhouse to Charleroi. The armies reeled back, with Joffre all the time striving to build up a force on the left of the British to outflank von Kluck. But it was not until 4 September that the opportunity was at last offered which led to the counter-offensive two days later, and began the battle of the Marne. Even that story has its dramatic moments, of which the acme is the moment on the morning of 4 September when the officers of the 3rd Bureau realize that von Kluck has mistakenly exposed his flank, and young Major Gamelin has the Commander-in-Chief fetched to argue. It is said that Joffre once remarked that he did not know who had won the battle of the Marne but, had it been lost, it would have been he who had lost it.

A number of books were published after this appeared from which I would gladly have borrowed. There is Lord Chandos's autobiography, which has a vivid account of the fighting round Vieux Berquin in April 1918, the moment when a sweating Irish Guardsman, calling on all the saints in Paradise, presents a short message from Lieutenant-Colonel the Hon. H. R. L. Alexander (today Lord Alexander of Tunis) which runs: "Dear Oliver, I am running very short of soldiers, Alex." An incident which I would have liked to include is a pendant to the curious episode at St. Quentin (pages 46–9). It is the story of the other half of the battalion. It had been cut off at le Cateau and under the Second-in-Command marched by night between the German advance screen and the main body of Germans until it could rejoin the 4th Division. One of the subalterns with this party became in due course Field-Marshal Viscount Montgomery. Alas, in his memoirs he squeezes this remarkable performance into six lines.

2

I realize that, to a generation which is thirty years from the original publication and fifty from its genesis in the First World War, parts may be unintelligible. In 1937, when this book appeared, a great number of the participants in the war were still alive, would recognize the incidents and understand the scenes, would feel the mud, and recall the stenches. The names of battles, the names of places, were strands in the fibre of our existence. Moreover, unlike 1939–45, the war had been largely and almost immoveably concentrated in one area. Not less than eighty-five per cent of the army fought in France at one time or another, and inside a very limited area. Most men would have known something of places such as Clapham Junction, Stirling Castle, Hill 60, Spoil Bank, the Duck's Bill, the Brickstacks, the Hohenzollern, the Double Crassier, Stuff Trench, High Wood and so on. Those names were as familiar as Leicester Square or Whitechapel Road were to a Londoner.

There is one aspect of these four years which should be underlined. They were a revolutionary period, both militarily and socially. There is one brief battle, of which a brilliant account comes in Major-General Sir Edward Spears's first book, *Liaison 1914*, the battle at Guise on 29 August, when Franchet d'Esperey refused to engage his infantry in support of two other corps until his artillery was in position. Then, with the first shells of 120 guns bursting, he mounted his charger and rode at the head of the 2nd Division, which went into action with bands playing and the colours uncased. "The long lines of skirmishers went forward in a victorious wave, the men frantic with joy at the new and longed for sensation after a week of retreat." The French artillery observers reported that the enemy was running back to the Oise bridges and the German batteries limbering up. But, wrote

Spears, the gunners were almost the only soldiers to catch sight of the German infantry all day: the French infantry did not. So, on 29 August 1914, the armies of the nineteenth century went out with bands playing and colours unfurled and the Corps Commander and his staff riding towards the battlefield as in 1870. But the day closed in the twentieth century with an artillery battle.

We were all pretty unsophisticated. There was still something of the belief that it was all a game. Christmas 1914 (see pages 100–3) has no replica between 1939 and 1945. But in 1915, in case the infantry were foolish enough to repeat the 1914 exercise, G.H.Q. ordered a slow bombardment during the day. There was still every now and then a hark back to something of the spirit of Fontenoy. To the trooper who brought in an officer-prisoner, his squadron commander said: "Why didn't you run him through?" and received the reply: "The gentleman wasn't looking, sir."

Behind the superficial aspect of the war as a period of wounds, death, and heroism or its reverse, there is another and more profound characteristic. The four years were years of social revolution, of which the consequences are visible today. Up to 1914, the army was a class institution, almost part of a caste system. The war came unexpectedly and with dramatic swiftness—in six weeks. (The war of 1939–45 had six years' gestation.) In 1914 there had been no preparations; everything had to be improvised. Nobody except Kitchener believed it could last. "It will be over in six weeks," said one of my uncles. "Rothschilds will see to that." Perhaps Kitchener's most serious claim to fame is his forecast of a long war. "Kitchener's Armies" were enlisted for "three years or the duration". There had never been anything in English history like the "First Hundred Thousand", and the "Second" and the "Third".

"Democracy," wrote some cynical Frenchman whose name I have forgotten, "is the name we give the people when we need them." These mobs of volunteers needed officers. They were needed all the more urgently from the hour it was perceived that Kitchener had been right, that there was no evidence, no Pisgah-sight, for its conclusion. The officers of the small Regular Army (including the Brigade of Guards, it had in all 156 infantry battalions, nearly half of them overseas) were being killed and wounded in France at a rate undreamed of. And already the Territorial battalions were being sent out piecemeal. Hence, within a very short time, there began the granting of temporary commissions to men who had been in officers' training corps or, possibly, had served in some irregular yeomanry regiment in the South African War. This, of course, came as an unpleasant shock to those brought up in the tradition of "an officer and a gentleman" in His Majesty's services who was bound to possess private means. "Temporary gentlemen" was the common sneer of the early days. On the other hand, many of the temporary gentlemen were better educated, more experienced, and more worldly wise than officers who had spent long periods in garrisons overseas and knew little outside military society. Thus began the melting of the class structure of 1914, and the army began to move towards a professional virtuosity of which the outcome is to be seen in the advertisements in the newspapers today.

We were also affected by the presence of the Imperial troops, from Canada, Australia, New Zealand, and South Africa, who to some extent suspected us of wanting to revive an eighteenth-century attitude and were always ready with derogatory comments, especially the Australians (that "hardened refractory and terrible people", as Defoe said of the Scots), who despised us—"Another Tommy officer who didn't know he'd won"—and who were much better paid than we were. The Canadians, too, had their little ways. At the tail of the March retreat in 1918, a brigade from the Guards Division was put into the line on the flank of a Canadian Division. The Canadians promptly set every man jack available to dig a defensive switch just in case the Guards gave way.

3

The introduction I wrote in 1937 contained a certain amount of nattering about morale which, in view of what the citizens of London, Bristol, Plymouth, Hull, and other cities stood up to in 1940–1 seems to me jejune. Morale is one of those fine indefinite abstractions to which appeal is made, often after some disaster brought about by higher incompetence. In actual warfare men are not dismayed by casualties, but by muddle and indifference. If men and women believe they are fighting for themselves and their like, they will continue to fight even in disaster. Their beliefs and feelings are those of the Shropshire men whose conversation is printed on pages 350–3.[1] The French trouble

---

[1] "Our armies swore terribly in Flanders". In the social ambience of 1937 certain words were still taboo, and in the passages from Manning's *Middle Parts of Fortune* I excised the monotonous monosyllable which I am told is permissible today.

ACKNOWLEDGMENTS

THE Editor and Publishers wish to acknowledge the courtesy of the authors, publishers and other holders of copyright who have permitted the inclusion in this anthology of extracts from books and other sources. The list which follows necessarily gives the original sources from which *Vain Glory* was compiled, but a number of the books named have since been reissued by different publishers, while some of the listed publishers are no longer in existence. Readers wishing to follow up any of the extracts in *Vain Glory* by further reading are advised to seek the help of their bookseller or librarian in finding whether the required book is still in print and if so under whose imprint.

George Allen & Unwin, Ltd., *Falsehood in Wartime*, Lord Ponsonby ; *A Fatalist at War*, Rudolf Binding ; *Britain Holds On*, C. E. Playne ; *Students Make their Lives*, W. Wilkinson.

Angus & Robertson (Sydney), *Jacka's Mob*, E. J. Rule ; *The Desert Column*, I. L. Idriess ; *The Gallant Company*, H. L. Williams ; *Official History of the A.I.F.* ; *Memoir of A. C. Stephen*.

The Editor, *The Army Quarterly*.

Edward Arnold & Co., *From Day to Day*, Lord Sandhurst ; *Gallipoli Diary* Sir Ian Hamilton.

Arthur Barker, Ltd., *The Land-locked Lake*, A. A. Hanbury-Sparrow ; *The Invisible Army*, Desmond Ryan.

Captain A. F. Behrend, *Nine Days*.

George Bell & Sons, Ltd., *Steady Drummer*, Stanley Casson.

J. & H. Bell, Ltd., *The Sherwood Foresters in the Great War, 1914–18*, W. Coape Oates.

Ernest Benn, Ltd., *From Chauffeur to Brigadier*, Brig.-Gen. C. B. Baker-Carr.

Paul Bewsher, *Green Balls*.

William Blackwood & Sons, *Wounded and a Prisoner of War*, An Exchanged Officer ; *History of the 13th Hussars*, Sir Mortimer Durand ; *Green Balls*, Paul Bewsher ; *The Tank in Action*, D. G. Browne.

Geoffrey Bles, Ltd., *French Head-quarters*, J. de Pierrefeu ; *Fusilier Bluff*.

Vera Brittain, *Testament of Youth* ; *Poems*.

Cambridge University Press, *Letters of Charles Sorley.*

Jonathan Cape, Ltd., *Cry Havoc!* Beverley Nichols; *A Brass Hat in No Man's Land*, Brig.-Gen. F. P. Crozier; *Winged Victory*, V. M. Yeates; *The Outlaws*, Ernst von Salomon; *Seven Pillars of Wisdom*, T. E. Lawrence.

Carroll Carstairs, *A Generation Missing.*

Cassell & Co., Ltd., *Goodbye to all that*, Robert Graves.

Brig.-Gen. John Charteris, *At G.H.Q.*

Chatto & Windus, *Black Monastery*, A. Kuncz; *Poems*, Wilfred Owen; *Unknown Warriors*, K. E. Luard; *Storm of Steel*, Ernst Junger; *The Spanish Farm Trilogy*, R. H. Mottram; *Disenchantment*, C. E. Montague; *The Right Place*, C. E. Montague; *C. E. Montague, A Memoir*, Oliver Elton.

Clarendon Press, Oxford, *The War in the Air.*

R. Cobden-Sanderson, Ltd., *Undertones of War*, Edmund Blunden ; *Other Ranks*, W. V. Tilsley.

W. Collins, Sons & Co., Ltd., *Life of Patrick Shaw-Stewart*, R. A. Knox.

Constable & Co., Ltd., *Poems*, Alan Seeger ; *Pushed and the Return Push*, " Quex " ; *Little Brother goes Soldiering*, R. H. Kiernan ; *U-Boat Stories*, K. Neureuther ; *Lord Carnock*, H. Nicolson ; *Peacemaking 1919*, H. Nicolson ; *Memoirs of Prince Max of Baden.*

Peter Davies, Ltd., *The Advance from Mons, 1914*, Walter Bloem, Captain 12th Brandenburg Grenadiers (Tr. from the German by G. C. Wynne. With a Foreword by Brig.-Gen. Sir J. E. Edmonds) ; *My Seventy-Five, Journal of a French Gunner, Aug.–Sept. 1914*, Paul Lintier (Tr. from the French by P.D. With a Foreword by Marshal Joffre) ; *Coronel and After*, Lloyd Hurst, Pay.-Com., R.N. (retired). With a Preface by Admiral Sir Herbert W. Richmond ; *A Subaltern's War*, Charles Edmonds ; *Her Privates We*, Private 19022 (Frederick Manning).

J. M. Dent & Sons, Ltd., *Everyman at War ; A Subaltern on the Somme*, Mark VII.

M. Diaz-Retg, *L'Assaut contre Verdun.*

Noel Douglas, Ltd., *Generals Die in Bed*, C. Y. Harrison.

Gerald Duckworth & Co., Ltd., *Time Stood Still*, P. Cohen-Portheim ; *Into the Blue*, Norman Macmillan.

John Easton, *Broadchalk.*

The Editor of the *Economist.*

Eyre and Spottiswoode, Ltd., and Lady Wester Wemyss, *The Life and Letters of Admiral of the Fleet, Lord Wester Wemyss.*

Faber & Faber, Ltd., *Unwilling Passenger*, Lt.-Col. Arthur Osburn ; *The Kaiser's Coolies*, Theodor Plivier ; *Haig*, Duff Cooper ; *A Soldier's Diary of the Great War ; Up to Mametz*, Ll. Wyn Griffith ; *Memoirs of an Infantry Officer*, Siegfried Sassoon ; *Trekking On*, Lt. Col. Deneys Reitz ; *The End of a War*, Herbert Read ; *The Wet Flanders Plain*, H. Williamson.

Negley Farson, *The Way of a Transgressor.*

Daniel George, *Gommecourt.*

Victor Gollancz, Ltd., *The Way of a Transgressor*, Negley Farson ; *War is War*, in 1917, of which a glimpse is given on pages 414–17, was partly due to exasperation at repeated failures, especially the failure of the attack in April 1917 on the Chemin des Dames. Though part of the trouble was bred and fostered in the back areas, it would not have been effective had there been even a modest success. The real cause was frustration. Not fighting in their own country, the British never had to withstand the frustration of having their country occupied. At no time, so far as I know, did it ever cross our minds that we could possibly not win the war, and we never knew how near we came to not winning it.

4

All wars have their controversial episodes and their legends. Without wishing to evoke the Angels of Mons, there are two comments of beliefs written by the late General Sir Harold Franklyn, who served in France for the better part of the 1914–18 war and commanded the 5th Division in France in 1939–40. In his brief account of May 1940 he says: "The British Army fought magnificently under the most trying circumstances which were none of its making. . . . In 1914, the Mons Star was awarded for the retreat from Belgium when only one corps of three divisions was seriously engaged. In my opinion there was more fighting by many more men in the retreat to Dunkirk than in the retreat from Mons."

His second comment is about the Dunkirk bridgehead, "where I spent forty-eight hours. A great deal of nonsense has been written about the bridgehead; there was very little shelling, much the same as Armentières on a quiet day in 1915 or 1916." Old soldiers will know what that means.

I should like to offer my thanks to Mr. Arthur L. Hayward, whose guidance and counsel have been of the greatest assistance to me, and who moreover carried out the thankless task of adding the connecting passages between groups of pieces.

GUY CHAPMAN

PRELIMINARIES

SARAJEVO

H.B.M. Consul in Sarajevo to Sir Edward Grey, Secretary of
State for Foreign Affairs : Telegram, 28th June, 12.30 p.m.

ACCORDING to news received here heir apparent and his consort
assassinated this morning by means of an explosive nature.

British Documents on the Origins of the War, XI.

NO NEWS

28*th June.* . . . that very evening the catch was made. The
image of St. Anthony was rowed out to meet the triumphant boat
full of anchovies, in the prow of which, silver-laden, he solemnly and
benignly returned. There would be fireworks two days later. . . .
We sat on the crescent beach, with a young yellow moon hanging
over Monte San Costanzo to westward and in the old *palazzo* where
we slept, the yellow candlelight winking under the lea of the eastward horn of the land. . . . Down through the dusky olive-grove
came Vincenzo with the evening's provisions and the newspaper.

" What news ? " we asked.

" No news," he said. " The fireworks cannot be set off for three
days, and some Austrian Duke has been killed somewhere. *Ecco
il giornale !* "

Compton Mackenzie.

3

THE OUTBREAK

IMPRESSIONS

By July 26th, events had assumed so serious an aspect that I was recalled from leave in Brittany, and on the morning of July 27th, I arrived at my head-quarters at Nancy.

General Foch.

So engrossed was I in work . . . that I did not notice the course of world affairs. . . . On Thursday, July 30th, we went to Hohenlinden to visit a newly married couple. . . . It was dusk when we returned to the station, and there the station master told us of strange and amazing rumours he had heard. . . . The following morning we scanned the headlines. . . . There it was in black and white—the rumours were true.

Capt. Walter Bloem.

The song and guitar were busy in Neumagen all that night (1st Aug.). "When you get back to England," said the fatherly policeman to me, "you tell them that Germany doesn't sleep." But what the lights of the street had hid, the light of next morning showed us. . . . The children who seemed to scent disaster were crying—all of those I saw. The women were mostly snuffling and gulping, which is worse. And the men, the singers of the night before, with drawn faces and forced smiles, were trying to seek comfort from their long drooping pipes and envying those who need not rejoin their barracks till Tuesday. It was Sunday, and the wailing notes of an intercession service on a bad organ were exuded from the church in the background. I have never seen a sight more miserable. . . .

Charles Sorley.

1*st Aug.* . . . We sat down to dine. I had uncorked a bottle of old Bordeaux, when Le Mée grasped my arm. "Listen!"

A loud murmur rose from the street through the open window. At the same moment, something magnetic, not to be put into words, yet very definite, passed through each of us. . . .

"It's come."

"Yes," nodded Le Mée, "it has come." We ran to the window. Down below in the street, moving towards the barracks, we saw a rolling wave of heads. Every face wore the same expression of blank stupor and distraction; in all the eyes was the same strange phosphorescent gleam. There came a hoarse strangled sound of women's voices.

"Well, Le Mée, here's health to you. And may we crack a bottle again together a few months hence."

"Here's to us."

And picking up our swords we ran back to barracks.

Paul Lintier.

3rd Aug. . . . I went by tram from Vauxhall Bridge Road to the Oval to see Surrey play Notts. Hobbs made the highest score of his career—226. . . . During the day, frequent editions of the papers were brought round the ground with the latest news about the war. . . . One of the newsvendors was calling out: " Mobilization of the Fleet, sir. Sprechen Sie Deutsch? Germany in the North Sea, sir."

Victor Smith.

3rd Aug. An hour later Sir Edward Grey returned to the Foreign Office. Nicolson went upstairs to see him. The Secretary of State was leaning gloomily by the window. Nicolson congratulated him on the success of his speech. Sir Edward did not answer. He moved to the centre of the room and raised his hands with clenched fists above his head. He brought his fists with a crash upon the table. "I hate war," he groaned, "I hate war."

Hon. Harold Nicolson.

4th Aug. I found the Chancellor very agitated. His Excellency at once began a harangue, which lasted for about twenty minutes. He said that the step taken by His Majesty's Government was terrible to a degree; just for a word—" neutrality," a word which in war time had so often been disregarded—just for a scrap of paper Great Britain was going to make war on a kindred nation who desired nothing better than to be friends with her. All his efforts in that direction had been rendered useless by this last terrible step, and the policy to which, as I knew, he had devoted himself since his accession to office had tumbled down like a house of cards. What we had done was unthinkable; it was like striking a man from behind while he was fighting for his life against two assailants. He held Great Britain responsible for all the terrible events that might happen. I protested strongly against that statement, and said that, in the same way as he and Herr von Jagow wished me to understand that for strategical reasons it was a matter of life and death to Germany to advance through Belgium and violate the latter's neutrality, so I would wish him to understand that it was, so to speak, a matter of " life and death " for the honour of Great Britain that she should keep her solemn engagement to do her utmost to defend Belgium's neutrality if attacked. That solemn compact simply had to be kept, or what confidence could anyone have in engagements given by Great Britain in the future ? The Chancellor said, " But at what price will that compact have been kept. Has the British Government thought of that ? "

Sir E. Goschen (*British Ambassador in Berlin*) *to*
Sir Edward Grey.

THE FIRST BLUNDER

4th Aug. It was expected that the German Government would return no reply to this ultimatum and that a state of war would arise at 11 p.m. A communication was thus prepared for delivery to Prince Lichnowsky when the ultimatum expired. . . . While they were so engaged, one of the private secretaries dashed in to say that Germany had declared war on England. It was then 9.40 p.m. and the Note prepared for Prince Lichnowsky was hurriedly re-drafted and typed. The amended version began with the words : " The German Empire having declared war upon Great Britain, I have the honour, etc." The passports were enclosed in this amended letter and Mr. Lancelot Oliphant, at that time assistant in the Eastern Department, was despatched to Prince Lichnowsky. He returned at 10.15. A few minutes later an urgent telegram arrived *en clair* from Sir Edward Goschen at Berlin. It reported that the Chancellor had informed him by telephone that Germany would not reply to the ultimatum, and that therefore, to his infinite regret, a state of war would arise by midnight.

The Foreign Office were appalled by this intimation. Immediate enquiries were made as to how the previous information had been received to the effect that Germany had taken the initiative in declaring war. It was ascertained that this information was based on an intercepted wireless message by which German shipping were warned that war with England was imminent. It was the Admiralty who had made the mistake. The Foreign Office then realized with acute horror that they had handed to Prince Lichnowsky an incorrect declaration of war. It was decided that at any cost this document must be retrieved and the right one substituted. It was decided also that the youngest member of the staff should be selected for this invidious mission, and the choice therefore fell upon Nicolson's youngest son.

Grasping the correct declaration in a nervous hand, he walked across the Horse Guards Parade and rang the bell at the side-door of the Embassy which gives on the Duke of York's steps. It was by then some five minutes after eleven. After much ringing a footman appeared. He stated that Prince Lichnowsky had gone to bed. The bearer of the missive insisted on seeing His Excellency and advised the footman to summon the butler. The latter appeared and stated that His Highness had given instructions that he was in no circumstances to be disturbed. The Foreign Office clerk stated that he was the bearer of a communication of the utmost importance from Sir Edward Grey. The butler, at that, opened the door and left young Nicolson in the basement. He was absent for five minutes. On his return he asked Sir Edward Grey's emissary to follow him and walked majestically towards the lift. They rose silently together to the third floor and then proceeded along a pile-carpeted passage. The butler knocked at a door. There was a screen behind the door and behind the screen a brass bedstead on which the Ambassador was reclining in pyjamas. The Foreign Office clerk stated that there had been a slight error in the document previously delivered and that he had come to substitute for it another, and more correct, version. Prince Lichnowsky indicated the writing table in the window. "You will find it there," he said. The envelope had been but half-opened, and the passports protruded. It did not appear that the Ambassador had read the communication or opened the letter in which the passports had been enclosed. He must have guessed its significance from the feel of the passports and have cast it on his table in despair. A receipt had to be demanded and signed. The blotting pad was brought across to the bed, and the pen dipped in the ink. While the Ambassador was signing, the sound of shouting came up from the Mall below, and the strains of the Marseillaise. The crowds were streaming back from Buckingham Palace. Prince Lichnowsky turned out the pink lamp beside his bed, and then feeling he had perhaps been uncivil, he again lighted it. " Give my best regards," he said, " to your father. I shall not in all probability see him before my departure."

Hon. Harold Nicolson.

EVENTS

5th Aug. Owing to the summary rejection by the German Government of the request made by His Majesty's Government for assurance that the neutrality of Belgium will be respected, His Majesty's Ambassador at Berlin has received his passports and His Majesty's Government have declared to the German Government that a state of war exists between Great Britain and Germany as from 11 p.m. on the 4th August.

Foreign Office Statement.

On August 4th, England declared war ; on August 5th, an order was published from which I discovered that I was now an " enemy alien."

P. Cohen-Portheim.

I was at Harlech when war was declared ; I decided to enlist a day or two later. . . . I forgot my pacifism—I was ready to believe the worst of Germans. . . .

Robert Graves.

11th Aug. Surrey beat Kent at Lord's yesterday by 8 wickets, and so improved still further their position at the head of the Championship table. . . . 7,040 people paid for admission.

" The Times."

12th Aug. My regiment left Wellington Barracks at seven in the morning. . . . It was very quiet in the streets. . . . On the march the wives and relations of men said good-bye to them at intervals. . . . We left Southampton without much delay. . . .

Hon. Aubrey Herbert.

Away back in the third week of August, 1914, I found myself marching just after midnight out from the walled city of Yarkand through the desert of Takla Makan, straight into the North Star. Sometimes my Pathan henchman and I marched and trotted over the hard track of the gravel plain, and sometimes floundered through the soft sands of the dunes. In the morning, before the first dawn, my little caravan had settled down for the night on the plastered earthen shelves that serve for beds in Turkistan. I woke up in full daylight, and, walking out into the little muddy courtyard, was surprised by the sight of the khaki blouse and the blue breeches with the broad sky-blue stripe of the Orenburg Cossacks. This was a patrol under a young Sotnik, a troop leader. We breakfasted together, and haltingly and with great difficulty in scrappy Russian I learnt a vague rumour that some great war was impending in Europe. This was indeed news, but we still had no idea about whom the bickering was between. The Sotnik had an idea that Germany and Russia were going to be the principal participants.

Two days later I reached Kashgar, and on the road met a *jigit*, a mounted messenger, sent out by Sir George Macartney to confirm the news of the war; but still there was no mention of a British participation, though that was anticipated. Instead of marching on northward and north-eastward across the desert to Maralbashi and Aksu to the Tian-Shan, the objective I had marked out for myself, I waited three days in Kashgar for more news from Europe. Sure enough, two days later, another *jigit* arrived from Irkeshtam, the telegraph office on the Russian frontier, with his great leathern saddle-bags bulging with newspapers, telegrams and despatches. This, indeed, was the Great War.

That night I was the guest of the two sotnias of the Orenburg Cossacks, and the event was celebrated till well after the milk came round in the morning. That same morning after a very few hours' sleep I packed off my young Khatak orderly, Ghulam Ali, giving him a pony and telling him to march southward the forty or fifty days' march over the Pamirs to the Punjab. I little guessed that the next time I should see him would be in the bight of a blood-clotted stretcher in the Salient. I myself marched on through the Southern Tian-Shan to the Russian railhead at Andijan.

Capt. L. V. S. Blacker (The Guides).

CROWDS

BERLIN

On the evening of July 31 I started for Berlin. Down the midnight Channel the searchlights were turning and streaming in long, white wedges. Passing into Germany, we at once met trains full of working men in horse-trucks decked with flowers, and scribbled over with chalk inscriptions: "*Nach Paris*," "*Nach Petersburg*," but none so far "*Nach London*." They were cheering and singing, as people always cheer and sing when war is coming. We were only six hours late in Berlin, but my luggage was lost in the chaos of crowds rushing home from their summer holidays, and I never recovered it, though in the middle of the War I received a postcard that had somehow arrived through Holland, telling me that the porter, with whom I had left the "Schein," or registration ticket, had found the luggage, and what would I like done with it? A fine example of international honesty.

For two days I waited and watched. Up and down the wide road of Unter den Linden crowds paced incessantly by day and night, singing the German war songs: "*Was blasen die Trompeten?*" which is the finest; "*Deutschland, Deutschland ueber Alles*," which comes next, and "*Die Wacht am Rhein*," which was the most popular, because most clearly defensive against the secular enemy. As I walked to and fro among the patriot crowd, I came to know many of the circling and returning faces by sight, and I still have clearly in mind the face of one young working-woman who, with mouth that opened like a cavern, and with the rapt devotion of an ecstatic saint, was continuously chanting:

> "*Lieb Vaterland kann ruhig sein!* (*bis*)
> *Fest steht und treu die Wacht,*
> *Die Wacht am Rhein.*"

So she passed me by. So the interminable crowds went past,

a-tiptoe for war, because they had never known it. Sometimes a company of infantry, sometimes a squadron of horse went down the road westward, wearing the new grey uniforms in place of the familiar " Prussian blue." They passed to probable death amid cheering, handshaking, gifts of flowers and of food. Sometimes the Kaiser in full uniform swept along in his fine motor, the chauffeur clearing the way by perpetually sounding the four notes which wicked Socialists interpreted as saying " *Das Volk bezahlt !* " (" The People pays ! "). Cheered he was certainly, but everyone believed or knew that the Kaiser himself had never wished for war. He claimed the title of " Friedens-Kaiser," just as many have chosen to call our Edward VII " The Peace-Maker." The most mighty storm of cheering was reserved for the Crown Prince, known to be at variance with his father in longing to test his imagined genius on the field. Him the people cheered, for they had never known war.

Henry W. Nevinson.

PETERSBURG

There was a crowd in front of a newspaper office. Every few minutes a momentous phrase scribbled in charcoal appeared in the window :

ENGLAND GIVES UP PEACE NEGOTIATIONS

GERMANY INVADES BELGIUM

Mobilization progressing with Great Enthusiasm

and at 7.50 p.m. :

GERMANY DECLARES WAR ON RUSSIA

Spontaneously the crowd started singing the national anthem. The little pimply clerk who had pasted up the irrevocable announcement was still standing in the window, enjoying his vicarious importance. The people were staring at the sprawling words, as if trying to understand what they actually meant as far as each personal little life was concerned.

Then the edges of the crowd started breaking off and drifting in one direction, up the Nevsky Prospect. I heard the phrase " German Embassy " repeated several times. I walked slowly that way.

The mob pulled an officer from his cab and carried him in triumph.

I went into a telephone-box and called up Stana.

" Yes, it's been declared . . . I don't know what I am going to do yet . . . All right, I'll be over about midnight."

I did not like the way her receiver clicked ; there seemed to be contempt in it.

When I got to the St. Isaac Square it was swarming with people. It must have been about nine o'clock, for it was pretty light yet— the enervating, exciting twilight of the northern nights.

The great greystone monstrosity of the German Embassy was facing the red granite of St. Isaac's Cathedral. The crowds were pressing around, waiting for something to happen. I was watching a young naval officer being pawed by an over-patriotic group when the steady hammering of axes on metal made me look up at the Embassy roof, which was decorated with colossal figures of overfed German warriors holding bloated cart-horses. A flagstaff supported a bronze eagle with spread wings.

Several men were busily hammering at the feet of the Teutons. The very first strokes pitched the mob to a frenzy : the heroic figures were hollow !

" They are empty ! . . . A good omen ! . . . Another German bluff ! . . . We'll show them ! . . . Hack them all down ! . . . No, leave the horses standing ! . . . The national anthem ! . . . Lord, save Thy People ! "

The axes were hammering faster and faster. At last one warrior swayed, pitched forward, and crashed to the pavement one hundred feet below. A tremendous howl went up, scaring a flock of crows off the gilded dome of St. Isaac's. The turn of the eagle came ; the bird came hurtling down, and the battered remains were immediately drowned in the near-by Moika river.

But obviously the destruction of the symbols was not enough. A quickly organized gang smashed a side-door of the Embassy.

I could see flashlights and torches moving inside, flitting to the upper stories. A big window opened and spat a great portrait of the Kaiser at the crowd below. When it reached the cobble-stones, there was just about enough left to start a good bonfire. A rosewood grand piano followed, exploding like a bomb ; the moan of the broken strings vibrated in the air for a second and was drowned :

too many people were trying to outshout their own terror of the future.

"Deploy ! . . . Trot ! . . . Ma-a-arch ! "

A troop of mounted *gendarmes* was approaching from the other end of the square. The crowd opened up like the Red Sea for the Israelites. A new crowd carrying the portrait of the Emperor and singing a hymn was advancing slowly towards the *gendarmes*. Their officer halted the men and stiffened at the salute ; this was the only thing he did towards restoring order. The bonfire was being fed by the furniture, books, pictures, and papers which came hurtling through the windows of the Embassy.

The emblazoned crockery of state came crashing, and the shattering sound whipped the crowd into a new wave of hysteria.

A woman tore her dress at the collar, fell on her knees with a shriek, and pressed her naked breasts against the dusty boots of a young officer in campaign uniform.

"Take me ! Right here, before these people ! Poor boy . . . you will give your life . . . for God . . . for the Tsar . . . for Russia ! "

Another shriek, and she fainted. Men and women were running aimlessly around the bonfire . . . Is it an effect of light and shadow, or do I really see high cheek-bones, slanting eyes, and the conic fur caps of Aladin Mirza's horde ?

Whew ! . . . I let out the breath I had been holding unconsciously during the entire bacchanal.

Sergei Kournakoff.

MORLAIX, FINISTERRE

It was Saturday afternoon. [2nd August.] Everybody was waiting in the streets. The beach was empty. At midday the news had already gone round that the order for mobilization would arrive any moment. I went once more to the post office to enquire. The five hundred francs which that morning had been despatched by wire from Budapest did not arrive.

About half-past two the clerk of the Mairie arrived on a bicycle, with ceaseless bell-ringing, from the direction of Morlaix. He was hugging a black portfolio under his arm. The mobilization order.

c

At three o'clock the tocsin shrieked. The senseless clanging of the village church bell was a worthy heralding of the world's gloomy change of scenery. To feverish imagination everything was now a play-acting or the pictures of a dream.

Old women in black with white head-dresses came hurrying. Suddenly they were all over the space round the platform which had been set up in front of the church, like big, white-crested, black birds. Then the men, as many of them as were at home, arrived in their Sunday clothes.

The holiday-makers silently made way for the assembling villagers. They had first right to hear the news.

In deathly silence the mayor read out the order for general mobilization.

Then petrified dumbness. Not a voice applauded. Someone sobbed, once, and the crowd stirred, and everyone went their various ways home.

In the hotel there was a never-ceasing buzz of excitement. The men were looking at time-tables. The father, husband and three brothers of the hotel proprietress set off to join their units. For the rest there were few Frenchmen among the holiday-makers. They should have arrived by the Saturday evening train from the neighbouring towns, but now they did not come, nor even later.

We—Orbok, Jeanette, a Russian sculptor and his mistress, and I—held a despairing council of action in the drawing-room of the Bon Accueil. None of us had any money, but we had somehow to reach Paris, and it was said that not even the evening express from Morlaix was to leave. But if it went it would undoubtedly be the last train to Paris.

We should have to go to Morlaix by the motor-bus. Even by that means it took a good three-quarters of an hour.

I decided to ask the hotel proprietress for money for the journey. But she, poor thing, was beside herself with grief. It was quite useless rattling at her door or trying to open it. From inside only her despairing sobbing came in answer.

Meanwhile the bus had gone.

We were already discussing walking all the way to Paris when a clean-shaven, knickerbockered man in the lounge addressed us in German and asked us, if we were going to Paris would we take him with us. He had heard we were Hungarians. He was German, he could not speak French and he was afraid he might meet with unpleasantness on the way.

"Haben Sie Geld?" we shouted at him all together.

"Das schon," the Prussian said, grinning, and pulled out a handful of gold from his pocket.

We all provided ourselves with money and agreed that we should meet within a quarter of an hour in front of the hotel and from there set off on foot in all haste for Morlaix. The Russian sculptor and his mistress also helped themselves from the gold on the Prussian's palm, but, probably on the woman's advice, they thought it better not to come with us. . . .

I arrived panting in my room. From the next room came the rattle of sewing-machines, and singing. The sewing-girls sang:

> "*Allons, partons, belles,*
> *Partons pour la guerre,*
> *Partons, il est temps . . .*"

I listened unconsciously as I hurriedly packed together a change of linen, stuffed my toilet necessities into my bag. . . . It was six o'clock in the evening. We had two hours and a half to cover a distance which usually required four hours to walk.

We set off running. The holiday-makers, still clustered in groups, made way for us with hostile stares. The Bretons standing in front of their low houses glowered at us. No one waved us good-bye.

Aladar Kuncz.

LONDON

Then came the declaration of war, most dramatically. Tuesday night, five minutes after the ultimatum had expired, the Admiralty telegraphed to the fleet " Go." In a few minutes the answer came back " Off." Soldiers began to march through the city going to the railway stations. An indescribable crowd so blocked the streets about the Admiralty, the War Office, and the Foreign Office, that at one o'clock in the morning I had to drive in my car by other streets to get home.

The next day the German Embassy was turned over to me. I went to see the German Ambassador at three o'clock in the afternoon. He came down in his pyjamas, a crazy man. I feared he might literally go mad. He is of the anti-war party and he had done his best and utterly failed. This interview was one of the most pathetic experiences of my life. The poor man had not slept for several nights. Then came the crowds of frightened Germans, afraid that they would be arrested. They besieged the German Embassy and our Embassy. I put one of our naval officers in the German Embassy, put the United States seal on the door to protect it, and we began business there, too. Our naval officer has moved in—sleeps there. He has an assistant, a stenographer, a messenger: and I gave him the German automobile and chauffeur and two English servants that were left there. . . . All London has been awake for a week. Soldiers are marching day and night; immense throngs block the streets about the government offices. But they are all very orderly. Every day Germans are arrested on suspicion; and several of them have committed suicide. Yesterday one poor American woman yielded to the excitement and cut her throat. I find it hard to get about much. People stop me on the street, follow me to luncheon, grab me as I come out of any committee meeting— to know my opinion of this or that—how can they get home? Will such-and-such a boat fly the American flag? Why did I take the German Embassy? I have to fight my way about and rush to an automobile. I have had to buy me a second one to keep up the racket. Buy?—no—only bargain for it, for I have not any money. But everybody is considerate, and that makes no matter for the moment. . . .

I shall never forget Sir Edward Grey's telling me of the ultimatum —while he wept; nor the poor German Ambassador who has lost in his high game—almost a demented man ; nor the King as he declaimed at me for half an hour and threw up his hands and said, " My God, Mr. Page, what else could we do ? " Nor the Austrian Ambassador's wringing his hands and weeping and crying out, " My dear Colleague, my dear Colleague."

Walter H. Page (U.S. Ambassador).

LIÉGE

A BELGIAN GUNNER OFFICER'S VIEW— 3RD BELGIAN DIVISION

6th Aug. Barchon. Dawn began to break. An order reached us, word to put ourselves at the disposal of the brigade commander behind Fort Boncelles. Vague information trickled through ; the gap between Forts Evegnée and Fléron had been forced, and the Germans had possession of Queue du Bois. The valley was no longer secure. The break-in had been made on both banks. Some said Bressoux might be occupied. Still that had to be our route.

We left La Xhavée, and time enough. As we crossed the little square, a hail of bullets smashed on the walls. Our group descended the hill, its head at Jupille. A hospitable household offered us a cup of coffee and a crust. Then a more urgent order arrived. " Move to Sart-Tilman, quickly ; situation critical."

The major shouted : " Mount. Trot." We had to get there at all costs as quickly as we could and in as great strength as possible. We moved off at the trot, the guns and limbers jolting along the pavé with a clatter of iron, and the houses at the roadside echoing and re-echoing the din. As we reached the level-crossing at Bressoux, *Zim . . . boom*, the first shell. It was obvious we had been seen. But from where ? It was a mystery.

A shudder ran through us ; we grew feverish, cold in the back and burning gusts in the head. We had to control ourselves not to yell ; all we shouted was : " Forward, forward ! "

At the Cornillon level-crossing, as we swept by the steep streets, at each shells came, sometimes at the head of the column, sometimes at the rear. Walls were smashed, glass flew into splinters : windows were flung up, and we saw women with clasped hands. The streets were deserted. At one corner we saw a Civil Guard post. On the Quai de Boverie, a civilian running beside our trotting horses told us about the attack of which General Leman had just been the victim. Two German officers and six soldiers, pretending to be English, had thrust their way into head-quarters. Commandant M—— had been shot; but the staff fortunately had resisted, the general had been rescued, and the Germans had payed dearly for their rash attempt.

We went along the Quai de Mativa. By now the horses were scarcely able to trot. We had got to get there. Using our spurs and our whips, we tried to mend their pace. They were covered with sweat, and the bits were white with foam. For ourselves, we did not know whether we were hot or cold. It was as if we had been electrified, and we were shaking all over. We reached the end of Sart-Tilman on foot. An aid-post, which already seemed quite full, gave us a glimpse of a busy crowd. We passed at the walk, for the hill was beginning. It was a horrible, terrifying sight. On both sides of the winding road, bodies lay in the ditch. A little chasseur, quite a child, not yet twenty, was among them, almost kneeling on the bank, with his head hanging down, so that he looked as if he was sobbing. Opposite him lay a man of the reserve class, with grey hair and clutching hands. All along, it was the same spectacle. Bodies; still more bodies. On their backs, their arms crossed, mouths open, eyes closed, their skulls smashed, their hands bleeding. I remember one man who had put his elbows on the edge of the ditch to die and whose fixed eyes watched us curiously as we passed. We were overwhelmed; our hearts contracted; we fell silent with horror, crushed. We shouted at the men to keep their eyes up the hill. But even we had difficulty in turning our heads away from those dreadful eyes.

Through this army of the dead, wounded were coming back. I recall a man who staggered from this side of the road to that, one hand grappled to his chest, the other feeling in space for support; his face and his wandering eyes showed the depth of his suffering. On hand-carts, on chance stretchers, on ladders, all the time, wounded in close waves. A private of the 9th Infantry, supported by two comrades, staggered along; his open tunic and his torn shirt let us see a scarlet chest with a small black hole in the middle from which trickled thick blood. A battalion commander, crouched over a bicycle, was being led along by a stretcher-bearer. Priests with their cassocks trussed up were carrying stretchers. From one, an officer was shouting : " Put me down. Go and look for the men. Leave me to die in the ditch."

We went to get our orders from the general. " Where do you want me to put you ? " he asked : " I can't use you here. Stand by." We were, indeed, in the middle of a wood, with, except to the rear, no sky-line. As for the enemy, their position was not known. Bullets whined through the leaves, and a shell burst in the branches. Our vet, once a private in the 11th Infantry, picked up a rifle, and, without a word, went off, slowly and deliberately, straight to the front. We were never to see him again.

An order was passed to us. " Keep a look-out to the left towards Fort d'Embourg. The French are coming up in support. Don't mistake them for Germans." Infantry companies, pale, haggard, with thinned ranks were retiring. " What's up ? Why, they're too many and they keep coming on. The fort's surrounded and we've had 75 per cent. casualties." We gave them all the encouragement we could. " Well, we're here ; tell us where they are. The French are coming up too." But they shook their heads sadly, as if to say : " It's too late."

Then we heard sounds in the distance. The musketry fire slackened. The deep note of the guns in the forts boomed at intervals. The infantry groups grew fewer and fewer. Worn-out infantrymen came by, one by one. And here we were, still in column along the road. Our enthusiasm had faded to silence ; an indefinable disquiet took us by the throat. The men stood at their horses' heads, silent as ourselves. In vain, we looked at the sky-line. The so-much-promised French were not to come. We gathered round our major, waiting for his decision. A group of chasseurs, Major L. at their head, came back. " It's all over," they told us : " we're the last ; there's nothing behind."

We consulted together. Stay on the road ? Impossible. We should be pursued and surrounded. In the sunken road where we were, we could not even turn round. The major suggested that we should get into action front, a little back, and make a stand to the end. Quite mad, but sublime. " We will die with you," exclaimed the chasseurs ; and they hastily began to rally odd men, the last remnants of their battalion, to give us infantry support. They were no more than 25 in all, of whom half were officers.

With difficulty we made a half-wheel and took up position two or three hundred yards back in a patch of broom and tree-stumps. We had a field of fire of four to five hundred yards with the Meuse valley on our right and the woods on our left. The tiniest enemy patrol could have turned our position and coolly shot us down one by one from the shelter of the trees. Not one of us had the smallest doubt about the fate which would be ours ; just death.

. . . Half an hour slipped by, slow as a century. The rifle fire had completely died away. Not a sound rose from the valley. We were alone and the solitude worried us. Why was the enemy not advancing ? The sacrifice was prepared ; we awaited it firmly and would sell our lives dearly.

Another quarter of an hour went by. Not a voice ; not a whisper ; everywhere silence. Where were we ? What had become of our brigade ? They had forgotten us, and we were alone. Well, honour was satisfied ; since nothing threatened us, we could withdraw. Pessimistic rumours began to spread. Several of the gaps between the forts had been broken through, the forts were now only replying feebly, Liége was in the hands of the enemy, the position was turned. From the dead men as we had imagined ourselves to be, we had become prisoners.

Back we went down the long winding road to Sart-Tilman, between the rigid corpses. We no longer felt the fever of the morning ; fierce anguish gripped us ; infinite despair, profound distress took us by the throat, crushed our hearts. . . . Prisoners after five days of war ! The aid-post at the foot of the hill had disappeared. We met the general and his A.D.C. alone. " Wait for orders by the Angleur bridge." Once more we halted, once more we waited. An orderly arrived. We were to push on to the plateau d'Ans. But the town, was the town really entered ? We had to move. The group broke up with orders to rendezvous on the plateau d'Ans. We went by the outer districts and reached the boulevards. The streets were deserted ; all the shutters were closed. The boulevard was gloomy and empty. Here and there at wide intervals stood a picquet or two of civil guards. A few friends ran up to shake our hands. " It's all over ? " they muttered : and we, unable to answer " yes," nodded as we passed.

At the Place Saint-Lambert, a battery rejoined us at the trot. They had had great difficulty in crossing the Maghin bridge which was being shelled. We climbed up towards the plateau d'Ans.

Soldiers were flocking in from all sides. Was Liége after all not yet entered that they had let us escape so easily ? By this reckoning, the Germans were not past Herstal.

On the Waremme road on the plateau there was indescribable confusion. Infantry, batteries, ammunition columns, baggage and ration wagons, supply columns and spare horses were all mixed together. Cavalry patrols declared that the Waremme road, our last hope, was cut. Liége was surrounded. This time it was all over. Someone said that there was not much hope of escape, but nevertheless, when a little order had been restored, an attempt would be made to break through the German curtain in front of us. The prospect of action lifted our despondency. Our courage picked up. A breath of hope swept over us ; the soldier slung on his pack, the trooper held up his head. Forward.

We passed Fort de Loncin. The little order we had been able to make in the column had disappeared. The artillery marched anyhow in the middle of the infantry. On both sides of the road, the auxiliary horse column trotted. The riders, all men of the reserve classes, in every kind of uniform representing all arms, were without saddles or bridles. Some had put ropes through their horses' mouths, others had sacks for saddles and string for stirrups.

Scouts pushed forward to explore the nearer hills. A few uhlans appeared in the distance, but made no attempt to approach. Exhausted soldiers flung themselves down in the ditch and were with great difficulty roused. We were now long past Awans, and began to think we should not be disturbed. Then reaction set in. For three days we had neither slept nor eaten except for a crust picked up here and there at a doorway. We could no longer stay on our horses and we suffered horribly from hunger. Infinite lassitude crept over us. It needed all our energy to resist the desire to imitate the soldiers who after having fought so bravely were now falling into ditches saying : " Let me be. I must sleep." Night fell and we still went on. A comrade dozed in the saddle. Roused, he dropped off again at once, and his nose swayed down to his horse's ears. He only kept his seat by a miracle of balance.

It was now pitch dark. At a turning, a staff officer directed us to Villers-le-Peuplier. There was no moon. We were unable to distinguish our whereabouts in this unknown country. Suddenly we seemed to see a shadow across the road. " Who goes there ? "

There was no answer but a mad galloping which died away in the night. After a halt and the return of the scouts we had sent out to left and right, we set off once more. A few shots broke out. Another halt. We turned on to the fields, made a half-wheel and came back to the road. I could see nothing. At last, how I do not know, we reached Villers-le-Peuplier. It was two in the morning. We woke up the inhabitants. Someone showed us a little house. Nothing but a loft to sleep in, but there was straw. Oh magnificent bed! While we arranged things, the major sat down on the stairs, and, worn out, at once fell fast asleep. And asleep ourselves we tumbled down anyhow on the straw.

Capt.-Comm. Robert de Wilde (Belgian Artillery).

THE GERMAN SIDE

The advance brigades had, indeed, a difficult task to accomplish at Liége. It was certainly an extraordinarily bold plan to penetrate the girdle of forts right into the heart of a modern fortress. The troops felt nervous ; from conversations with the officers, I gathered that their faith in the success of this undertaking was only slight.

In the night of the 5th–6th August the advance on Liége, through its fortifications, began. . . . About one o'clock the advance began. It was to take us north of Fort Fléron via Retinne through the line of forts, and then on to the heights of La Chartreuse, on the outskirts of the town. We were due there early in the morning. The other brigades which were to break through the girdle of forts at other points were to reach the town at the same hour.

General von Emmich's Staff was almost at the end of the column. Suddenly there was a longish halt. I pushed my way to the front. There was no apparent reason for the halt, which proved to have been due to a most regrettable misunderstanding of the situation. I myself was really only a spectator, and had no authority to give orders. It was my duty only to report the events at Liége when I met my General later on, and also to co-ordinate General von Emmich's plans with General von Bulow's probable disposition. I put the column in motion again and remained at its head. In the meantime, we had lost touch with the troops in front. We had considerable trouble in finding our way in the pitch darkness, but at length reached Retinne. We were still out of touch with the others. I started out from the village at the head of the column, and took the wrong road. We were immediately fired at, and men fell right and left. I shall never forget hearing the thud of bullets striking human bodies. We made some rushes at the invisible enemy, but the firing became more intense. It was not easy to take our bearings in the dark, but there was no doubt that we had gone astray. The essential thing was to get out of range, and this was unfortunate, because the men could only think that I was afraid. But there was nothing else to be done—higher things were at stake. I crept back and gave my men the order to follow me to the outskirts of the village.

Once back at Retinne, I found the right road. Here I saw General von Wussow's orderly with his horses. He thought that the General had fallen. With a handful of men I took the right road, the high road leading to Queue du Bois. Suddenly there was firing ahead. Machine-gun bullets swept the road but did not harm us. A little further on we came across a heap of dead and wounded German soldiers, who proved to be some of the advance party with General von Wussow. They must have run into machine-gun fire earlier on. I collected some men of the 4th Jäger Battalion and the 27th Infantry Regiment who were gradually arriving and decided to take over the command of the brigade. The first thing was to destroy the enemy's machine-guns firing down the road. Captains von Harbou and Brinckmann, of the General Staff, pushed their way, with a few brave men, through the hedges and farms on both sides of the road, and fell upon the guns. The strong gun-team surrendered and the road was clear.

We continued on our way and soon were engaged in heavy house-to-house fighting in Queue du Bois. Gradually it became light. I went on ahead with a few men. . . . A field howitzer was brought up ; then a second. They fired right and left into the houses and so cleared the streets. Little by little we advanced. The men were reluctant to proceed and I was often compelled to exhort them not to leave me to go on alone. At last the village lay behind us. The inhabitants had fled, and it was now a question of fighting the regular Belgian Army. . . .

We had successfully broken through the girdle of forts. The 165th Infantry Regiment, under its distinguished Commanding

Officer, the then Colonel von Oven, pushed on in close order. General von Emmich arrived, and the advance on La Chartreuse was continued.

General von Emmich placed at my disposal other parts of the 11th Infantry Brigade, who were further south, in the belief that they also had broken through. Our advance continued without incident.

We could see the works on the north side of Liége as we climbed out of the Meuse valley to the heights east of La Chartreuse. It was about two o'clock when the brigade arrived there. Guns were at once trained on the town, and a shot was fired now and again, partly as a signal to the other brigades, partly to intimidate the Governor of the fortress and the inhabitants. But I had to be exceedingly sparing of the ammunition, for we were very short. The troops were exhausted and much weakened by the hard fighting ; officers had lost their horses, and the field kitchens had been left behind. I rested the brigade and provided for them as best I could by commandeering supplies from the neighbouring houses. General von Emmich soon rejoined us.

From the heights east of La Chartreuse we had a fine view of the town lying at our feet. The citadel on the far bank of the Meuse stood out prominently. Suddenly white flags fluttered from it. General von Emmich wanted to send an officer with a flag of truce. I proposed waiting for the enemy's envoy, but the General adhered to his decision, and Captain von Harbou rode into the town. He returned at seven p.m., and reported that the white flag had been flown against the Governor's will. It was then too late to advance into the town. We had a heavy night ahead of us. Meanwhile I had let the brigade take up a position. Our situation was exceedingly serious. No news reached us from the other brigades, not even from the 11th, and no despatch-riders got through. It became increasingly clear that the brigade was isolated within the circle of forts, cut off from the outer world. We had to reckon with hostile attacks. The thousand-odd Belgian prisoners we had with us increased our difficulties. When we found out that the old work of La Chartreuse, just below us, was unoccupied, I sent a company there with these prisoners. The company commander must have doubted my sanity.

As darkness fell, the nervousness of the troops increased. I went round the front, exhorting them to keep steady and hold fast. The assurance, " We shall be in Liége to-morrow," restored their spirits. . . .

I shall never forget the night of the 6th–7th August. It was cold and as I had left my kit behind, Major von Marcard gave me his cloak. I was very anxious and listened feverishly for the sound of fighting. I still hoped that at least one brigade had broken through the girdle of forts. But all was quiet, though every half-hour or so a howitzer shell fell into the town. The suspense was unbearable. About ten p.m. I ordered Captain Ott, with a Jäger company, to seize the bridges over the Meuse, in order to make them available for our further advance, and also give us advanced posts. The captain looked at me—and went. The company reached its objective without any fighting, but no reports came back.

Morning broke. I went to General von Emmich, and discussed the situation with him. We still adhered to our decision to enter the town, but the General would not at that moment fix the time. His order to me to enter the town reached me soon after, whilst I was doing something to improve the position of the brigade, and trying to reach the road by which the 11th Brigade would come up. Colonel von Oven was in charge of the advance guard ; the rest of the brigade, with the prisoners, followed at a certain distance, headed by General von Emmich with his Staff and myself with the Brigade Staff. As we entered, many scattered Belgian soldiers surrendered.

Colonel von Oven was to occupy the citadel. As a result of the reports he received, he decided not to do this, but to take the road towards Fort Loncin, on the north-west side of the town, and take up a position at that exit from Liége. Thinking that Colonel von Oven was in possession of the citadel, I went there with the Brigade Adjutant in a Belgian car which I had commandeered. When I arrived no German soldier was to be seen and the citadel was still in the hands of the enemy. I banged on the gates, which were locked. They were opened from inside. The few hundred Belgians who were there surrendered at my summons.

The brigade now came up and took possession of the citadel, which I immediately put in a state of defence.

Gen. Ludendorff.

WAR AIMS

RT. HON. H. H. ASQUITH, IN THE HOUSE OF COMMONS

8th Aug. IF I am asked what we are fighting for I reply in two sentences. In the first place, to fulfil a solemn international obligation, an obligation which, if it had been entered into between private persons in the ordinary concerns of life, would have been regarded as an obligation not only of law but of honour, which no self-respecting man could possibly have repudiated. I say, secondly, we are fighting to vindicate the principle which, in these days when force, material force, sometimes seems to be the dominant influence and factor in the development of mankind, we are fighting to vindicate the principle that small nationalities are not to be crushed, in defiance of international good faith, by the arbitrary will of a strong and overmastering Power.

I do not believe any nation ever entered into a great controversy —and this is one of the greatest history will ever know—with a clearer conscience and a stronger conviction that it is fighting, not for aggression, not for the maintenance even of its own selfish interest, but that it is fighting in defence of principles the maintenance of which is vital to the civilization of the world. With a full conviction, not only of the wisdom and justice, but of the obligations which lay upon us to challenge this great issue, we are entering into the struggle.

Parliamentary Debates. Commons.

AS WE LOOKED TO A FRENCHMAN

THIS country woke up late to the war. The realization of it came from outside—in seeing the German Jews of the Commercial Road putting up their shutters, those of the West End hiding their pictures, the fall of Consols, the weakness of wool on Sydney, the flight of the Americans in their nickel-plated cars, and Gold even more timid ; by learning that arthritic diplomats were leaving the waters with their cures incomplete, that kings were running back to their capitals, and that the neutral countries were bolting fast their frontiers. Then there were the departures of the French hairdressers and chefs who marched to the stations under a banner.

They saw the warships leave Portsmouth as they had every year, for Cowes ; but the guns were uncovered and the German yachts had not arrived. The sea reacted first, then the coast-line where the reserve coast-guards went to the signal stations with their kit in green canvas bags. And the fever spread at last from the edges to the centre.

All this happened insensibly. England never experienced that *nuit blanche* when millions of men kissed their wives with dry lips and burned their letters. She knew nothing of that confusion, did not close her port-holes or cut the cable.

All she did was to put a Bobby on duty in front of the German Embassy.

Paul Morand.

ENGLAND, AWAKE !

Your King and Country
Need You

A CALL TO ARMS

An addition of 100,000 men to his
Majesty's Regular Army is immediately
necessary in the present grave National
Emergency

Full information can be obtained at any
Post Office in the Kingdom or at any
Military Depot

GOD SAVE THE KING

Advertisement.

The Motto for Patriots

BUSINESS AS USUAL

(But please pay Cash)
From a letter to " The Times.'

THE LANDING

13th Aug. We arrived very early at Le Havre in a blazing sun. As we came in, the French soldiers tumbled out of their barracks and came to cheer us. Our men had never seen foreign uniforms before, and roared with laughter at their colours. Stephen Burton of the Coldstream Guards rebuked his men. He said: "These French troops are our Allies; they are going to fight with us against the Germans." Whereupon one man said: "Poor chaps, they deserve to be encouraged," and took off his cap and waved it and shouted "Vive l'Empereur!" He was a bit behind the times. I believe if the Germans beat us and invaded England they would still be laughed at in the villages as ridiculous foreigners. . . .

The French had been very hospitable. They had given the men, where they had been able to do so free of observation, wine, coffee and beer. The result was distressing. About twenty of the men collapsed at the top of the hill in a ditch, some of them unconscious, seeming almost dying, like fish out of water. The French behaved very well, especially the women, and stopped giving them spirits. I got hold of cars and carried the men off to their various camps. . . .

. . . About 10.30 we moved off. It was a warm night with faint moonlight. Coming into the town the effect was operatic. As we marched or were halted all the windows opened and the people put their heads out to try and talk to us. At about half-past eleven it began to rain, but the men whistled the Marseillaise and "It's a long way to Tipperary." The people came out of the houses, trying to catch the hands of the men and walking along beside them. We were halted in front of the station, and waited endlessly in the rain.

Hon. Aubrey Herbert.

THE FIRST CONFLICT

GENERALS FRENCH AND LANREZAC

17th Aug. Sir John stepped out of his car looking very spick and span. He was a good deal shorter than General Lanrezac, who came out to greet him. The two men stood for a moment in strong contrast to each other, Lanrezac large, swarthy, revealing his creole origin (he was born in Guadeloupe), Sir John ruddy-faced, his white moustache drooping over the corners of his mouth. His clear penetrating blue eyes, his very upright bearing and quick movements, made him infinitely the more attractive personality, and gave him the appearance of being by far the more soldierly of the two. You had only to look at him to see that he was a brave, determined man.

At that time I did not know him, but later it fell to my lot to see him often, and at times when he was being as highly tried as any individual could be. I learnt to love and to admire the man who never lost his head, and on whom danger had the effect it has on the wild boar : he would become morose, furious for a time, harsh, but he would face up and never shirk. He knew only one way of dealing with a difficulty, and that was to tackle it. When everything seemed to crumble about him he stood his ground undismayed.

I was told a story of him, I think by General Foch, of how during the bad days at Ypres he once arrived at the latter's head-quarters and said : " I have no more reserves. The only men I have left are the sentries at my gates. I will take them with me to where the line is broken, and the last of the English will be killed fighting."

If he had once lost confidence in a man, justly or unjustly, that man could do no right in his eyes. He was as bad an enemy as he was a good friend, and that is saying a great deal. He was deeply attached to the French nation, and after the War, being unable to live in his place in Ireland, which had been sacked, he lived in France from choice. But he judged both French and British by the same standards, and when, at the time of Mons, he came to the conclusion that General Lanrezac was not playing the game with him, it was finished. Once he had lost confidence in the Commander of the Fifth Army he ignored him and acted as if he and his Army did not exist.

To-day all was still well.

The two men walked into General Lanrezac's sanctum together, the one short, brisk, taking long strides out of proportion to his size, the other big, bulky, heavy, moving with short steps as if his body were too heavy for his legs. . . .

. . . We knew that Lanrezac spoke no English, and Sir John, though he understood a little French, at that time could hardly speak it at all. . . .

. . . Sir John, stepping up to a map in the 3me Bureau, took out his glasses, located a place with his finger, and said to Lanrezac : " Mon Général, est-ce-que——" His French then gave out, and turning to one of his staff, he asked : " How do you say ' to cross the river ' in French ? " He was told, and proceeded : " Est-ce-que les Allemands vont traverser la Meuse à——à——" Then he fumbled over the pronunciation of the name. " Huy " was the place, unfortunately one of the most difficult words imaginable to pronounce, the " u " having practically to be whistled. It was quite beyond Sir John. " Hoy," he said at last, triumphantly. " What does he say ? What does he say ? " exclaimed Lanrezac. Somebody explained that the Marshal wanted to know whether in his opinion the Germans were going to cross the river at Huy ? Lanrezac shrugged his shoulders impatiently. " Tell the Marshal," he said curtly, " that in my opinion the Germans have merely gone to the Meuse to fish." This story gives some idea of Lanrezac's mentality and manners. Evidently his conversation with Sir John had put him out of temper, and he did not hesitate to show it by being deliberately rude. . . .

The staffs of both armies were not slow to realize that the two men had not taken to each other. General Lanrezac did not disguise from his entourage his feelings towards Sir John, and I learnt a few days later at Le Cateau that Sir John had not liked Lanrezac.

The interview had resulted in a complete fiasco.

Brig.-Gen. E. L. Spears.

THE FIRST BRUSH

By August 21 the concentration of the British forces was sufficiently complete for them to go into action, and an advance was begun in the direction of Mons, which was reached on the following day.

4TH DRAGOON GUARDS

22nd Aug. . . . On the Saturday, Hornby with a half-squadron had got as far as Soignies where, from the church tower, the field of Waterloo was just visible. They had pursued and charged some German cavalry : Bavarian ploughboys in German uniforms—that was all they really were. These boys carried long metal lances, like lengths of gas piping, they could not manage. Some of these lads had been killed and three or four wounded and captured. Fair resolute, genial and a keen soldier, Hornby with his troop, magnificently mounted—as indeed we all were—yelling at full charge, their long straight swords a glittering row of steely points, would have put fear into far more hardened soldiers. I was not surprised, when I saw them, that several of these young Bavarians had turned tail. I could speak a few words of German and as I dressed their wounds I asked them what they thought of the War. They said they did not know what to make of it, nor what it was all about. They had, they said, been called up for military training only a few weeks before the War broke out. Apparently they had nearly all shown very little fight; some of our men pursuing them had refrained at first from running two of them through—because their " backs were turned " ! This chivalry and gallantry was not to last very long. Hornby's sword had been already blooded. He showed it to me—about four inches of the blade near the tip was smeared with blood. I asked one of the prisoners for a button, which he cut off—my first souvenir ! Rather tearfully he insisted that his brother had been shot at Munich for refusing to join up, and that he himself was very pleased he had been taken prisoner.

Lt.-Col. Arthur Osburn (R.A.M.C.)

MONS

AT THE CANAL

23rd Aug. We had no sooner left the edge of the wood than a volley of bullets whistled past our noses and cracked into the trees behind. Five or six cries near me, five or six of my grey lads collapsed on the grass. Damn it ! this was serious. The firing seemed at long range and half-left.

"Forward !" I shouted, taking my place with three of my "staff" ten paces in front of the section leader, Holder-Egger, and the section in well-extended formation ten paces behind him again. Here we were, advancing as if on a parade ground. Huitt, huitt, srr, srr, srr ! about our ears, away in front a sharp, rapid hammering sound, then a pause, then more rapid hammering—machine-guns. Over to our left, about Tertre, the rifle and machine-gun fire was even more intense, the roar of guns and bursting shells increasing. . . .

"Line the bank in front," I ordered, and in a few short rushes we were there, lying flat against the grass bank and looking cautiously over the top. Where was the enemy ? Not the faintest sign of him anywhere, nothing except the cows that had become restless and were gadding about. One, as I watched, rose on its hind legs, and then collapsed in a heap on the ground. And still the bullets kept coming, over our heads and all about us.

I searched through my glasses. Yes, there among the buildings away at the far end of the meadow was a faint haze of smoke. Then in God's name let us get closer.

"Forward again—at the double !" We crossed the track, jumped the broad dyke full of stagnant water on the far side, and then on across the squelching meadow. Tack, tack, tack, tack, tack !—srr—srr—huitt—tschiu—tschiu—tschirr !—cries—more lads falling.

"Down ! Open fire—far end of meadow—range 1,000 yards !"

33

And so we went on, gradually working forward by rushes of a hundred, later fifty, and then about thirty yards towards the invisible enemy. At every rush a few more fell, but one could do nothing for them. On, on, that was the only solution. Easier said than done, however, for not only was the meadow horribly swampy, filling our boots with water, but it was intersected by broad, water-logged drains and barbed-wire fences that had to be cut through.

Where was the rest of the battalion? Nothing to be seen of them. Yes, there, a hundred yards to our left, a section of Grenadiers was working forward like us by short rushes, its leader, in front at every rush, taking giant strides. Why, it's the long-legged Fritz-Dietrich Gräser, he who sang the "*Krone am Rhein*" so well that evening at Weisweiler when we sat listening to the band with the old lady and her pretty niece. I'd known him for two years now, and a charming fellow he was. Now they were down again, this time along another broad water-drain with a barbed-wire fence along the enemy's side of it. And what was Gräser doing? Sure enough, he was running along the whole front of his section cutting the wire fence himself, in the middle of a burst of rifle and machine-gun fire. Plucky young devil ! . . .

From our new line I again searched the front through my glasses. Still no sign of the enemy. Only the unfortunate cows, now just ahead of us, and being between the two firing lines they were in a bad way, bellowing desperately, one after the other collapsing. To right and left, a cry here, a cry there : " I'm hit, sir ! O God ! Oh, mother ! I'm done for ! "

" I'm dying, sir ! " said another near me. " I can't help you, my young man, we must go on—come, give me your hand."

Gräser's clear voice again : " On again—double ! " On we went.

Behind us the whole meadow was dotted with little grey heaps. The hundred and sixty men that left the wood with me had shrunk to less than a hundred. But Grabert's section at my signal had now worked forward and prolonged our line to the right. He, too, had lost heavily, nevertheless there was still quite a respectable crowd of us gradually moving on, wave by wave, closer and closer to the invisible enemy. We officers had some time previously taken a rifle from a dead or wounded man, filled our pockets with cartridges, and were firing away into the haze of smoke at the far end of the meadow.

I felt, however, that these continuous rushes were telling on the men, and that they must have a breathing space.

"Stop for a bit!" I shouted down the line. "No further advance without my orders!" . . .

We were now about 500 yards from the canal bank. A few paces in front lay some of the miserable cows in horrible death agonies. . . .

From now on the English fire gradually weakened, almost ceased. No hail of bullets greeted each rush forward, and we were able to get within 150 yards of the canal bank. I said to Gräser: "Now we'll do one more 30-yard rush, all together, then fix bayonets and charge the houses and the canal banks."

The enemy must have been waiting for this moment to get us all together at close range, for immediately the line rose it was as if the hounds of hell had been loosed at us, yelling, barking, hammering as a mass of lead swept in among us.

"Down!" I shouted, and on my left I heard through the din Gräser's voice repeating it. Voluntarily and in many cases involuntarily, we all collapsed flat on the grass as if swept by a scythe.

Previously after each rush Gräser had brightened us up with a commentary of curses and cheery chatter, but now there was a noticeable silence on my left.

"Gräser!" I called out. No answer. "Where is Lieutenant Gräser?" And then from among the cries and groans all round came a low-voiced reply: "Lieutenant Gräser is dead, sir, just this moment. Shot through the head and heart as he fell. He's here." . . .

From now on matters went from bad to worse. Wherever I looked, right or left, were dead or wounded, quivering in convulsions, groaning terribly, blood oozing from fresh wounds. The worst was that the heaviest firing now began to come on us from the strip of wood that jutted out into the meadow to our right rear. It must be our own men, I thought, who could not imagine we had got on so far and now evidently took us for the enemy. Luckily we had a way of stopping that: "Who has the red flag?" Grenadier Just produced it, and lying on his back waved it wildly. No result; in fact the fire from the right rear became even heavier. . . .

The fire began again from the front—srr—srr—tschiu—tschuitt! all among us. One of the wounded men was hit a second time, another unwounded got hit through the head and just relaxed dead. . . .

All this time the rifle-fire was continuing from the canal bank, but so long as we kept flat and our heads well down the bullets passed just over us.   The sky was beginning to redden in the west; if only night would come quickly.   I looked back for any sign of reinforcements or ammunition being sent up.   Nothing coming, nothing.   Yes, one man.   It was Pohlenz.   Brave lad, I'd given him up some time since as dead.   But there he was, fired at from all directions, and he cared not; still a cigarette between the narrow lips of his happy-go-lucky, gutter-snipe face.   He lay down beside me and took out of his pockets four packets of cartridges : " The major says we are to stay where we are, and the battalion will soon be coming up to us bringing ammunition with them.   And here's a little to carry on with."   He opened the packets and threw the chargefuls to left and right, eager hands reaching out for them.   " And here's a regimental order."

I unrolled the scrap of paper from a field note-book.   " According, to orders from Brigade Head-quarters a general attack will be made on the bridges at 6.30 p.m."   On the bridges !   Of course, the canal bridges.   The map showed a thing like a bridge near the group of houses half-right called Les Herbières.   Good !   when the others come up we'll go on with them.   To go on alone now would be idiotic.   I looked at my watch.   The attack was to be at 6.30.   It was already 7 p.m.

" What's happening back there ? " I asked Pohlenz.

" The battalion is three or four hundred yards behind us."

" Many losses ? "

Pohlenz beat the air with his hands two or three times.   " Grey corpses lying all over the meadow."

" Have all the companies had losses ? "

" All of them, sir." . . .

It must have been some hours, it seemed an eternity, before gradually the dusk came, terribly slowly, but at last it began to cover us. . . .

Walter Bloem (12th *Brandenburg Grenadiers*).

THE REALITY OF WAR

All through the 23rd Sir John French, whose men had withstood the assaults of three German Army Corps, held on, but as night fell he knew that the position was untenable, and early next morning the British began to retreat and the Germans to advance.

THE ROAD

23rd Aug. The main street, a continuation of the great chaussée up which Napoleon's IV Corps had marched to Waterloo, led into Philippeville from the north. It ran along one side of the place, and was packed with people, all going in one direction, their backs to the north. A grey mob, grey because the black clothes most of them wore were covered with dust, was filing endlessly by; they occupied the whole width of the road, pouring past like a crowd returning from a race meeting, but in absolute silence, the only sound being that of very tired feet dragging on the pavés. Each individual in that slowly-moving mass looked the embodiment of a personal tragedy; men and women with set staring faces, carrying heavy bundles, moving on they knew not where, formed a background of grim despair to this or that group or individual whose more vivid suffering seemed to illuminate that drab flow of desolation.

I can still see a couple of young girls, sisters perhaps, helping each other, hardly able to drag themselves along, the blood from their torn feet oozing through their low silk shoes: a very sick woman, who looked as if she were dying, balanced somehow on a perambulator; a paralytic old man in a wheelbarrow, pushed by his sturdy daughter; a very old, very respectable couple, who for years had probably done no more than walk arm-in-arm round a small garden, now, still arm-in-arm, were helping each other in utter bewilderment of mind and exhaustion of body down the long meaningless road. I remember, too, a small boy playing the man and encouraging his mother, and an exhausted woman sinking under the weight of her two babies.

37

And none might stop : the gendarmes pounced on any who tarried and shoved them forward. The mass of refugees must be kept on the move. If they halted they would hopelessly block the communications they were already so seriously encumbering. Later, perhaps, it would become necessary to drive them off the roads into the fields, to clear the way for the troops, so on they had to stagger, men and tired cattle together, with here and there a huge cart drawn by oxen, packed with children. Some of these carts must have contained the entire infant population of a village thrown in pell-mell. Were their parents trudging behind, or had they fallen by the way ? The column of civilians must go endlessly on, whoever might drop out or get left behind, on and on and on, a wretched, racked, miserable mass of humanity, whose motive power was fear, and whose urge was a sound, the dull rumble of guns, ominously near, growling ceaselessly to the north.

Whenever there came a particularly sharp burst of artillery fire rending the air like a sudden thunder-clap, the whole miserable column trembled and staggered forward, all but the oxen moving faster for a moment, then relapsing into the former slow drag.

Brig.-Gen. E. L. Spears.

COCK O' THE NORTH

24th Aug. I met the 1st Battalion of the Gordons marching into the village (Quévy-le-Petit). Owing to the narrowness of the road and to the crush of troops, I was obliged to stop until the battalion had marched by. With interest and admiration, I watched these Scottish soldiers tramp past in the swirling dust, big-boned, brawny men, with faces brick-red from exertion and heat, and with tunics unbuttoned at the neck. In front of me was a staff officer in a car, who was also held up by the jam of traffic. As the Gordons passed, he said : " Jove, they're magnificent ! I'd give a fortune to see them get into the enemy with the bayonet ! " Little did he know the strange fate the next few days held for these men.

Capt. C. A. L. Brownlow, R.A.

A COMMENT

25th Aug.   The bitterest incident of all was when passing through a little village, we trod underfoot a strip of cloth which had hung in greeting across the street, and which bore the words : " Welcome to our saviours, the British ! "

ibid.

LE CATEAU

THE DECISION

26th Aug. However, some of the fog was cleared away by the arrival of General Allenby, accompanied by his G.S.O.I. Colonel J. Vaughan (now Major-General, C.B., C.M.G., D.S.O.) at my head-quarters at 2 a.m. . . . . He wanted to know what I was going to do, saying that unless I could move at once and get away in the dark, the enemy were so close that I should be forced to fight at daylight. I then sent for Major-General Hubert Hamilton, the Com-mander of the 3rd Division, whose head-quarters were close by, and asked him whether his troops could move off at once or at any rate before daylight, and his reply was very definite that the 3rd Division could not move before 9 a.m. The 5th Division were, if possible, in a worse plight, being more scattered, whilst of the 4th Division . . . there was no news, except that they had last been seen after dark still in their positions south of Solesmes, covering the retire-ment of masses of transport and fugitives jammed up in the roads.

The following arguments passed through my mind :

(*a*) It must be a long time after daylight before the whole force covered by rearguards can get on the move.

(*b*) The enemy are in force close to our billets (for such Allenby had impressed on me).

(*c*) To turn our backs on them in broad daylight with worn-out men suffering from sore feet will leave us a prey to hostile cavalry supported by infantry in motors.

(*d*) The roads are encumbered with military transport and civilian fugitives and carts, some still on the enemy side of our position, and time to allow them to clear off is essential.

(*e*) The I Corps is reported to be engaged some miles north-east of us and to retire would expose their flank to the full brunt of Von Kluck's troops.

(*f*) The Cavalry Division can be of little help in covering our retreat, for this Allenby had told me.

(*g*) Our infantry have proved their staunchness and astounding accuracy with the rifle, our gunners are a marvel, and if Allenby and Snow will act under me, and Sordet will guard my west flank, we should be successful in giving the enemy a stopping blow, under cover of which we could retire.

Well do I remember the dead silence in the little room at Bertry when I was rapidly considering these points and the sigh of relief when, on my asking Allenby if he would accept orders from me, and he replied in the affirmative, I remarked : " Very well, gentlemen, we will fight, and I will ask General Snow to act under me as well."

Gen. Sir Horace Smith-Dorrien.

THE BATTLEFIELD

26th Aug. Topping the crest of a rise, the whole scene of the struggle was suddenly spread in a panorama before me.

In the foreground, tucked in a hollow, was the little village of Montigny, from whose church tower hung a Red Cross flag ; beyond the ground rose in a low ridge or swell of land on which were the villages of Beauvois, Caudry, Audencourt, Beaumont, with the tops of the houses of Troisvilles showing on the right. Just below those villages running clean across the landscape and shutting out all further view, was the avenue of pollarded trees which marked the Cambrai road and which looked like a gigantic ruler lying athwart the countryside.

The infantry were hastily entrenching along a line which connected up these villages and which was roughly parallel to and about a thousand yards from the great road. The crest of the ridge, however, hid them from my view, but, though the infantry were invisible, I could see our artillery. On the southern slopes of the ridge, some fully and some partially concealed from the enemy, our batteries stretched in an irregular line from right to left. The guns and wagons and detachments stood dark and distinct, though diminished through distance to minute weapons and tiny figures. Every gun was firing, and countless flashes of light scintillated against the gold and green sweep of country. The whole of the scene was flecked with the white and yellow smoke-clouds of enemy shrapnel and high explosive, the nearer of which appeared tongued with cruel yellow flames. I could see the bursting shell smashing and crumpling the villages, sweeping the batteries with a hail of death and searching the valleys and hidden approaches.

And all the while the thunder of the guns rolled and reverberated in deep-toned waves of sound which spread and spread in ever growing circles, striking the ear of many a distant listener and making him wonder what that sinister noise could forbode.

Capt. C. A. L. Brownlow, R.A.

THE RETREAT

THE RETREAT BEGINS

SUDDENLY about 3 p.m. a staff officer, mounted on a horse whose nostrils were dilated with exertion, cantered hard up the road, drew rein and leaning forward in his saddle spoke to the Captain in a tense voice.

" The right has gone—we've got to retire. Take your column back at once. The road Clary–Elincourt–Malincourt–Beaurevoir." " Clary–Elincourt–Malincourt–Beaurevoir," he repeated, and then clapping his spurs to his horse, he was away down the road to warn others.

At these words something seemed to happen along the whole front. Down every road far and near, which had been white and nearly deserted, there now appeared dark streams of troops, moving southwards. The wall of flesh and blood which had barred the way to the enemy for so many hours began to crumble and disappear.

Capt. C. A. L. Brownlow, R.A.

THE ATTACK ON THE 1ST GORDONS

The Gordons did not get the order to retreat. They held their ground and only retired after nightfall, when they were surrounded, and after an hour's struggle, captured by two German regiments.

26th Aug. The German infantry first came into view crossing the beetroot fields on top of the hill on our right front, where the telegraph poles acted as the 1,200 yards' mark. Through these fields they advanced in close formation until disturbed by the attentions of a machine-gun either of ours or of the Royal Scots (who were holding the other side of the village of Audencourt). It was not long before we had a chance of getting rid of some ammunition. German troops, debouching from the little wood where the cows had taken refuge earlier in the day, now advanced across the stubble field on top of the hill, moving to their left flank across our front. My glasses showed they were extended to not more than two paces, keeping a very bad line, evidently very weary and marching in the hot sun with manifest disgust.

The command, " Five rounds rapid at the stubble field 900 yards," produced a cinematographic picture in my field-glasses. The Germans hopped into cover like rabbits. Some threw themselves flat behind the corn-stooks, and when the firing ceased got up and bolted back to the wood. Two or three who had also appeared to fling themselves down, remained motionless.

The enemy, having discovered that we could be dangerous even at 900 yards, then successfully crossed the stubble-field in two short rushes without losing a man, and reinforced their men who were advancing through the beetroot fields on our right.

Great numbers of troops now began to appear on the ridge between Bethencourt and the little wood. They advanced in three or four lines of sections of ten to fifteen men extended to two paces. Their line of advance was direct on the village of Audencourt and on the low plateau on our right, so that we were able to pour upon them an enfilade fire. They were advancing in short rushes across pasture-land which provided no cover whatever, and they offered a clearly visible target even when lying down. Although our men were nearly all first-class shots, they did not often hit the target. This was owing to the unpleasant fact that the German gunners kept up a steady stream of shrapnel, which burst just in front of our trenches and broke over the top like a wave. Shooting at the advancing enemy had to be timed by the bursting shell.

We adopted the plan of firing two rounds and then ducking down at intervals, which were determined as far as could be arranged for by the arrival of the shell. But the shooting of the battalion was good enough to delay the enemy's advance. From the 900-yard mark they took more than an hour to reach their first objective, which was the Route Nationale, 400 yards from our nearest trench. Here they were able to concentrate in great numbers, as the road runs along an embankment behind which nothing but artillery could reach them. This was the situation on our front at about three o'clock in the afternoon. I happened to look down the line and saw Captain Lumsden looking rather anxiously to the rear. I then saw that a number of our people were retiring. There was not much time to think about what this might mean, as the enemy were beginning to cross the road ; we had fixed bayonets, and I thought we would have little chance against the large number of Germans who had concentrated behind the embankment. For a long time, for nearly an hour, the British guns had been silent, but they had not all retired. With a white star-shaped flash two shells burst right over the road behind which the Germans were massed. Those two shells must have knocked out forty or fifty men. The enemy fled right back up the hill up to the 900-yard mark, followed by rapid fire and loud cheering from all along the line.

The Germans were now re-forming on the hillside, and a machine-gun hidden in the village of Bethencourt began to play up and down our trench.

The bullets began to spray too close to my left ear, and laying my glasses on the parapet I was about to sit down for a few minutes rest, and indeed had got half-way to the sitting position, when the machine-gun found its target.

Recollections of what passed through my mind at that moment is very clear. I knew instantly what had happened. The blow might have come from a sledge-hammer, except that it seemed to carry with it an impression of speed. I saw for one instant in my mind's eye the battlefield at which I had been gazing through my glasses the whole day. Then the vision was hidden by a scarlet circle, and a voice said, " Mr. H. has got it." Through the red mist of the scarlet circle I looked at my watch (the movement to do so had begun in my mind before I was hit) ; it was spattered with blood ; the hands showed five minutes to four.

An Exchanged Officer.

26–27*th Aug.* Of the rest of the night I have no clear recollection ; it remains in my mind as a blurred nightmare, in which shadowy figures slept as they rode or slept as they walked, in which phantom teams halted in sleep, checking for miles a ghostly stream of men and in which the will to move ever wrestled with the desire to sleep.

Capt. C. A. L. Brownlow, R.A.

THE EPISODE OF ST. QUENTIN

27th Aug. As we turned into the Grande Place at St. Quentin on that late August afternoon not a single German was to be seen. The whole square was thronged with British infantrymen standing in groups or wandering about in an aimless fashion, most of them without either packs or rifles. Scores had gone to sleep sitting on the pavement, their backs against the fronts of the shops. Many exhausted lay at full length on the pavement. Some few, obviously intoxicated, wandered about firing in the air at real or imaginary German aeroplanes. The great majority were not only without their arms but had apparently either lost or thrown away their belts, water-bottles and other equipment.

There must have been several hundred men in the square, and more in the side streets ; yet apparently they were without officers —anyway, no offiᴄers were to be seen. On the road down to the station we found Major Tom Bridges with part of his squadron and a few Lancers, horse-gunners and other stragglers who had attached themselves to his command. We followed him down to the station. Apparently some hours before our arrival the last train that was to leave St. Quentin—Paris-wards—for several years, had steamed out, carrying with it most of the British General Staff. A mob of disorganized soldiery had collected at the station, and I was told some had booed and cheered ironically these senior Staff officers as the Staff train steamed out. Certainly many of these infantrymen appeared to be in a queer, rather truculent, mood. Bridges, who had sized up the situation, harangued this disorganized mob that only a few hours before had represented at least two famous regiments of the 4th Division.

Dismounted and standing far back in the crowd I could not hear what he said, but his words of encouragement and exhortation were received with sullen disapproval and murmurs by the bulk of those around him. One man shouted out : " Our old man (his Colonel) has surrendered to the Germans, and we'll stick to him. *We don't want any bloody cavalry interfering !* " and he pointed his rifle at Bridges. I failed at first to understand how all these English soldiers could have surrendered to the Germans whom we had left several miles outside the city. But I was tired and hungry and I didn't much care what happened. Losing interest in what was taking place at the station I rode back up to the Grande Place, hoping I should find some food and a sofa on which I could lie down. As I rode up from the station many of the men in the street stared at me disdainfully, their arms folded ; scarcely one saluted—I was for them only " one of the bloody interfering cavalry officers."

When I awoke it was dusk, and two or three officers of the 4th Dragoon Guards were in the square with Bridges. Apparently, Bridges was having an interview with some official—I believe, the Mayor of St. Quentin—urging him to provide horses and carts to take those of our men who were too sore-footed to be able to march out of the town. I walked over to listen. As far as I could understand, the official—Mayor or whoever he was—was very indignant ; he kept saying :

" You understand, m'sieur le Majeur, it is now too late. These men have surrendered to the Germans ? "

" How ? The Germans are not here ! "

" Their colonel and officers have signed a paper giving me the numbers of the men of each regiment and the names of the officers who are prepared to surrender, and I have sent a copy of this out under a white flag to the Commander of the approaching German Army ! "

" But you have no business, m'sieur, as a loyal Frenchman, to assist allied troops to surrender ! "

" What else ? " urged the Mayor. " Consider, m'sieur le Majeur, the alternatives. The German Army is at Gricourt ? Very well, I, representing the inhabitants of St. Quentin, who do not want our beautiful town unnecessarily destroyed by shell-fire because it happens to be full of English troops, have said to your colonels, and your men : ' Will you please go out and fight the German Army *outside* St. Quentin,' but your men they say : ' No ! We cannot fight ! We have lost nearly all our officers, our Staff have gone away by train, we do not know where to. Also, we have no artillery, most of us have neither rifles nor ammunition, and we are all so very tired ! ' Then, m'sieur le Majeur, I say to them : ' Then please if you will not fight will you please *go right away*, and presently the Germans will enter St. Quentin peacefully ; so the inhabitants will be glad to be tranquil, and not killed, and all our good shops not burnt.' But they reply to me : ' No, we cannot go away ! We are terribly, terribly tired. We have had no proper food nor rest for many days, and yesterday we fought a great battle. We have not got any maps, and we do not even know where to go to. So we will stay in St. Quentin and have a little rest ! ' Then I say to them : ' Since you will neither fight nor go away, then please you must surrender.' So I send out a list of those who surrender to the German Commander, and now all is properly arranged ! ' "

Arranged ! Yet the logic of this argument was irresistible— but for one point, which Bridges had quickly seized upon. The men *could* be got away if every horse and cart in St. Quentin was collected for those men too tired to march ; his cavalrymen would escort them out of the town. So the shops and streets would be cleared of tired and drunken men, and there would be no more firing off of rifles ; but there was to be no more of this wine, only tea or coffee and bread.

So eventually it was arranged ; Bridges had saved the situation which though bad was understandable. Disorganized stragglers had arrived by the hundred, many out of sheer fatigue having thrown away their packs and rifles. They had tramped beneath the blazing August sun with empty stomachs, dispirited and utterly weary ; many had received quantities of wine from kindly French peasants to revive them in those dusty lanes. Literally, in many cases their bellies were full of wine and their boots were half full of blood ; that I saw myself. The English soldier's feet like his head, but unlike his heart, are not his strong point. . . .

Bridges asked me to count the men who were collecting in the Square and get them into fours. I counted one hundred and ten fours—that is to say four hundred and forty men. Then he asked me to do something else, I forget what it was. A few men had whistles and Jew's harps, perhaps they had them in their haversacks as soldiers often do, and they formed a sort of band. We persuaded one of the colonels to march in front of his men. My recollection is that he looked very pale, entirely dazed, had no Sam Browne belt, and leant heavily on his stick, apparently so exhausted with fatigue and the heat that he could scarcely have known what he was doing. Some of his men called to him encouraging words, affectionate and familiar, but not meant insolently—such as : " Buck up, sir ! Cheer up, Daddy ! Now we shan't be long ! We are all going back to ' Hang-le-Tear ' ! "

Actually I saw him saluting one of his own corporals who did not even look surprised. What with fatigue, heat, drink and the demoralization of defeat, many hardly knew what they were doing. I was so tired myself that I went to sleep on my horse almost immediately after I remounted, and nearly fell off, much to the amusement of some of the infantry who supposed I was as drunk with white wine as some of their comrades.

It was nearly half-past twelve before we left St. Quentin. The sultry August day had passed to leave a thick summer mist. Our small army was at last collected. Every kind of vehicle had been filled with men with blistered feet. In front of them, on foot, were several hundred infantry, mostly of two regiments, but containing representatives of nearly every unit in the 4th Division, and behind, to form the rearguard to this extraordinary cavalcade, Tom Bridges' mounted column—the gallant little band of 4th Dragoon Guards with driblets of Lancers, Hussars, Irish Horse, Signallers and the rest of the stragglers. In front of all rode a liaison officer and a guide sent by the Mayor, and I think Tom Bridges. By his side, walking, armed with a walking stick, was one of the two colonels —a thick-set man—who had surrendered. (The other had disappeared.) And immediately behind them the miscellaneous " band " of Jew's harps and penny whistles. So through the darkness and the thick shrouding fog of that summer night we marched out, literally feeling our way through the countryside, so thick was the mist. At about two in the morning we had reached the villages of Savy and Roupy. Just as we started to leave St. Quentin I woke up to the fact that my precious map-case was missing, and I had to return to look for it in the now deserted Grande Place. As for a moment I sat on my horse alone there, taking a last look round, I heard an ominous sound—the metallic rattle on the cobbles, of cavalry in formation entering the town through one of the darkened side-streets that led into the Grande Place.

The Germans must have entered St. Quentin but a few minutes after the tail of our queer little column disappeared westward through the fog towards Savy.

Lt.-Col. Arthur Osburn (R.A.M.C. attached 4th Dragoon Guards).

CHARLES PÉGUY

28*th Aug.* Leaving the road, each of us tried to find a little shade and stretched himself under the apple-trees. On the command to fall in, there was an obvious slackness, resulting from fatigue. " Come on, the 19th ; up you get," shouted Péguy. Some scarcely stirred, and a drawling Parisian voice in an ironic whine, called : " There ain't no 19th left ! "—" So that's what you think," quickly answered Péguy to the unknown interrupter ; " so long as I am here, my man, there will be a 19th. Come on, children, forward." And he led off.

Victor Boudon.

THE BATTLE OF HELIGOLAND BIGHT

In the early hours of August 28 a force of British destroyers and submarines penetrated into Heligoland Bight, and by eight o'clock German destroyers hastened out to meet them. Fighting went on throughout the morning, with losses to both sides, but when the British fleet turned away, shortly after one o'clock, they had inflicted losses on the Germans that had a marked psychological effect on their maritime policy for the rest of the War.

28th Aug. For three hours now *Ariadne* has been at full speed. The look-out is strengthened by an extra hand. . . .

" See anything ? "

" Nothing." . . .

It gets a little lighter. A gap appears in the gigantic " laundry," but round them the damp mist continues to rise.

" Do you see that ? "

" Yes, right ahead."

" Ship right ahead," reports the look-out on the bridge below.

" She's heading straight for us."

" Three funnels. That's *Köln*."

" She's being fired on."

" She's running."

Another vessel emerges from the well of fog, a gigantic grey colossus. From the searchlight platform of *Ariadne* is flashed the recognition signal. No answer from the ship.

" A battle cruiser."

" She's English . . ."

Ariadne is a bundle of nerves. Below, at the ventilator shafts and ammunition hoists are tense upturned faces. " What's up on deck ? " ask voices from bunkers, engine-room and stokehold.

" A big Englishman."

" Four turrets 13·5."

" Flagship *Lion*."

" And our ships ? "

" Not in sight yet."

A second battle-cruiser of the same class comes into view. *Tiger.*
Sixteen heavy turret-guns are trained on the little *Ariadne*. . . .

Ariadne swings round, attempting to withdraw at full speed under
cover of the mist. *Lion* opens fire with her foremost turret. Smoke
belches from the muzzle of the guns. . . . A second and a half.

Two fountains rise from the sea a few hundred yards from the
ship.

" Six thousand," announces the fire control for the benefit of his
own guns.

" Six thousand," repeat the men at the gun telephone.

" Salvo—fire."

The gun-layer at the starboard gun pulls back the trigger lever.
A deafening crash. Thirty-two pounds of iron from each gun.
Against the thick armour plate of the battle-cruisers they are mere
peas that bounce off without effect. The five men serving *Ariadne's*
guns are out on the open deck. The eighty men of each British
turret-gun behind thick walls of steel.

The next shots fall astern. The enemy has got his bracket
correct, has found the range. Now a ring of flame flashes out round
the two armoured ships. The brown cordite smoke of their charges
rises like a wall.

Köln has vanished in the mist. *Ariadne* has turned her stern to
the battle-cruisers and offers only a small target. The shells fall
close to the ship. Columns of water, green, translucent, rise high
in the air, like crystal cupolas, then collapse over the deck. . . .

Thirty-two pounds of iron from each gun. Each broadside a
hundred and sixty pounds. *Lion and Tiger* are firing at long intervals, but with each salvo they hurl six tons of steel and explosive
through the air. . . .

Ammunition carriers, look-out men, blackened faces of the gun
crews all again stare eastward whence the heavy ships must come
to their deliverance. And every living being ducks again as the
approaching metal thunders through the air.

That's the concussion. There's nothing to be done against
that. . . .

The shell had gone through the deck and exploded in the bows.

A rush of air howls through the hole it has made. Coal-dust. Smoke. The dust subsides, a sparkling black cloud.

The smoke rises high, a heavy ochre brown. Through passages, manholes, at last even through the shot-hole itself streams a flood of half-naked black bodies. The stokers. They are leaving the lower decks. The coal bunkers are on fire, the stokeholds are full of smoke. Five boilers are out of action. *Ariadne* can only steam half-speed.

At the bow-gun all the gear has been destroyed—telephones, telescope, sights swept away. P.O. Weiss takes his sights along the barrel and the report of his gun is only a little later than the others.

Salvo—fire.

Behind the smoke of the discharge they cower, five at each gun. A handful of men on the bridge, the signal bridge and the search-light platform. At the foot of the bridge and round the bases of the funnels, in huddled heaps, the stokers who have left their posts. Everywhere hands clutching each other, jaws set so tight that the bones show white through their cheeks.

The after-gun can get no more ammunition. The shaft of the hoist has been driven in. The after-magazine is in darkness. . . .

The shells are coming now with a flat trajectory and tear the sides out of the ship. From every pore and hole steam boils up, black smoke-clouds pour. Now the light has failed in the after-boiler-rooms. Compartments are smoked out, decks swept clear. All who can still move leave the stern. The wounded are taken forward. Bridges, funnels, masts are invisible, enveloped in a thick screen of smoke which drags astern of the riddled ship in a wide awake.

The sky, which for half an hour has hung over ship and crew like an enormous rumbling sheet of metal, suddenly stops vibrating and is quiet again. *Lion* and *Tiger* have ceased fire. They cannot see anything through the smoke.

Two of the boats are still seaworthy . . . they are lowered. Then the wounded are let down by lines. Stumps of limbs are temporarily bandaged. A leg hanging by a shred of flesh is severed with a knife.

All that remains of the crew is in the bows. Bloodshot eyes, hoarse voices. On Armoured Decks I and II there are still men. In the after-magazines, too ! The magazines are under water.

What about those on the armoured deck ?   P.O. Weiss has gone with a couple of men to get them.   Hundreds of eyes stare aft in the direction of the boilers.

The charges and shells by the guns explode.   The lower part of the ship is one glowing furnace.   The thin armoured decks under their feet gets hotter and hotter.   Standing on it becomes unbearable. . . .

A shadow breaks through the red tinted chaos, a huddled clump of figures, supporting each other, dragging each other forward.   Paul Weiss and his men.   Driven back, exhausted, they come towards the bow.   The men from the armoured deck are not with them. The captain gives the order : " On life-belts !   Abandon ship."

Theodor Plivier.

GEMÜTLICHKEIT

THE GERMANS WELCOME THEIR PRISONERS

AT Douai I was detained on the square in front of the Hôtel de Ville with a sentry over me, and was subjected to continual abuse and revilement. On the arrival of the other prisoners we were all confined in a large shed for the night. No food, except a little provided by the French Red Cross Society, was given, also no straw, and we spent a terrible night there, men being obliged to walk about all night to keep warm, as their greatcoats had been taken from them.

On the 17th October, in the morning, the French Red Cross people appeared to be sympathetic and sorry for us; but they were able to do little or nothing to protect us.

Up to this time I had managed to retain my overcoat, but it was now forcibly taken from me by an officer at a few stations further on.

On reaching the German-Belgian frontier the French prisoners were given some potato soup. The people in charge of it told us that none was for us, but that if any was left over after the French had been fed we should get what remained. This is in accordance with the general treatment of British prisoners by the Germans, who always endeavour to attend to our necessities last, and to put us to as much inconvenience and ill-treatment as possible. We subsequently got a little soup and a few slices of bread amongst twenty-five British prisoners in the same wagon with me.

On the 18th October, early, we arrived at Cologne, and the four officers and myself were removed from the wagon, and after some delay sent on to Crefeld.

I said that fifty-two prisoners were in the wagon with me when we left Douai. These were: (*here follows the names of four officers*), myself, fifteen English soldiers, and thirty-two French civilians of all grades of society. It is difficult to indicate or give a proper idea of the indescribably wretched condition which we were in after being starved and confined in the manner stated for three days and three nights. As is well known, one of these wagons is considered to be able to accommodate six horses or forty men, and this only with the doors open so as to admit of ventilation. What with the filth of the interior, the number of people confined in it, and the absence of ventilation, it seemed to recall something of what one has read of the Black Hole of Calcutta. To give an idea of the state of mind to which we have been reduced, I got one of the better-class French prisoners to secrete a letter to my wife in the hope that he might be able to get it out to her when he reached his destination, as these French civilian prisoners were being treated better than ourselves. They all expressed great pity for the way in which we were being treated.

I found out that the wagon in front of us was full up with English soldiers. This particular wagon had no ventilation slit of any sort or description, and men were crowded into this even worse than they were in the wagon in which I was. They banged away continually on the wooden sides of the van, and finally, as I supposed the Germans thought that they might be suffocated, a carpenter was got, who cut a small round hole in one of the sides.

At the station we were driven into closed-in wagons, from which horses had just been removed, fifty-two men being crowded into the one in which the other four officers and myself were. So tight were we packed that there was only room for some of us to sit down on the floor. This floor was covered fully three inches deep in fresh manure, and the stench of horse urine was almost asphyxiating. We were boxed up in this foul wagon, with practically no ventilation, for thirty hours, with no food, and no opportunity of attending to purposes of nature. All along the line we were cursed by officers and soldiers alike at the various stations, and at Mons Bergen I was pulled out in front of the wagon by the order of the officer in charge of the station, and, after cursing me in filthy language for some ten minutes, he ordered one of his soldiers to kick me back into the wagon, which he did, sending me sprawling into the filthy mess at the bottom of the wagon. I should like to mention here that I am thoroughly conversant with German, and understood everything that was said. Only at one station on the road was any attempt made on the part of German officers to interfere and stop their men from cursing us. This officer appeared to be sorry for the sad plight which we were in. I should also like to mention that two men of the German guard also gave us what they could in food, and did their very best, in spite of opposition from the Germans. At about 2 p.m. on the same day we were all marched off to the railway station, being reviled at and cursed all the way by German officers, as well as by German soldiers. One of our officers was spat on by a German officer.

Major Vandaleur (Scottish Rifles).[1]

[1] *Quoted in Parliamentary Papers. Report on the Transport of British Prisoners of War to Germany, Aug.–Dec., 1914.*

THE RETREAT GOES ON

SEVENTY-FIVES

31*st Aug.* " Into line, right wheel ! "

Moving across fields up a steep slope, we took up a position on the heights commanding the Beauclair gap and the road we had just left.

A spur ran down between this position and Tailly, hiding all of the latter except the weathercock on the church, which seemed to rise out of the ground.

Through the V-shaped gap in the hills overlooking the Meuse the enemy could see us without difficulty. And we in turn had a view of the woods and meadows beyond Beauclair which he occupied, and which a French battery in front of us, but under cover of another spur, was bombarding with shrapnel.

In the distance the German infantry began debouching across the fields from the woods, looking like an army of black insects on a smooth green lawn. We at once opened fire, and the enemy hastily withdrew back into the woods, which we continued to bombard.

It looked as if the battle as a whole was going in our favour. More French batteries went forward along the Beauclair road and unlimbered in the gap itself. Others moving into position at various points on the hills round about us, and still others farther away on the heights directly overlooking the Meuse, thundered without respite. Clouds of dust and flashes of flame here and there in the green landscape revealed the existence of invisible guns at many points. So violent was the bombardment from this formidable position that the air gradually became thick. An acrid fog of dust and powder floated across the valley ; crashing echoes reverberated from side to side and went rolling round the hills ; a vast, deafening roar drummed in our ears, overwhelmed us, made us drowsy.

" Cease fire ! "

At once all was absolutely still round the guns. It was about midday.

Suddenly, without any preliminary ranging, the enemy began a heavy bombardment of Tailly and the fir woods immediately above our position. Some artillery wagons which had been drawn up at the edge of these woods since morning cleared off at a gallop. A section of infantry emerged out of the smoke of a big high-explosive shell.

"Take cover !" came Captain de Brisoult's word of command.

The fire of the French batteries little by little died down.

Higher up the valley, where our own wagons were waiting, a salvo of shrapnel burst : a fuse went droning loudly through the air. No one seemed to be hit. The wagons still stood there, a motionless dark rectangle on the green grass.

The enemy found the exact range of a battery on the far side of a fir plantation just below us. We watched them getting their guns away one by one through the wood under an inferno of shelling.

Hutin, who was crouching behind the shield, suddenly got up and looked ahead. He stood with folded arms.

"It's begun !" he growled between clenched teeth.

"What's begun ? Get down !"

I pulled his sleeve.

"It's begun ! The retreat ! Ah, bon Dieu de bon Dieu !"

I stood up too. He was right. We could see sections of infantry coming back over the crest.

Brejard shouted at us :

"Get down under cover, you two !"

A shell burst close by ; the pieces whizzed through the air, and a shower of clods and stones spattered the ground all round us. I crouched down instinctively ; Hutin never moved, being too pre-occupied with the spectacle of the retiring infantry, who were appearing in greater numbers every moment.

"Ah, I thought as much !" he said ; "here comes a staff officer ; we'll be off too, in a moment . . . Good God, if we're always going to be retiring like this we might as well take the train while we're about it !"

He was right again : the officer brought us orders to retire at once.

Paul Lintier (44th Art. Reg.).

THE IRISH GUARDS AT VILLERS-COTTERÊTS

1st Sept. Desmond, the Colonel and I rode back into the big, green wood. It was very peaceful. The sun was shining through the beech-trees, and for a bit the whole thing seemed unreal. The C.O. talked to the men, telling them to reserve their fire till the Germans were close on them. " Then you will kill them and they won't get up again." That made them laugh. The German advance began very rapidly. The Coldstreamers must have begun falling back about this time. The Germans came up in front and on our left flank. There was a tremendous fire. The leaves, branches, etc., rained upon one. One's face was constantly fanned by the wind from their bullets. This showed how bad their fire was. My regiment took cover very well, and after the first minute or two fired pretty carefully. Moonshine was startled to begin with by the fire, but afterwards remained very still and confidential. Desmond did not get off his horse ; he told me to lead my horse back into the wood and then come back to the firing line. The Colonel then told me to gallop up to the Brigadier to say that the retreat was being effectively carried out; that there were two squadrons advancing and he did not know what force of infantry. In this estimate he was very much out, as subsequent events proved. Eric, now at home wounded, said to me : " The Germans seemed hardly to have an advance guard ; it was an army rolling over us." When I found the Brigadier he wanted to know if the C.O. seemed happy about things. I said I thought on the whole he did. There were bullets everywhere and men falling, but the fire was still too high. One bullet in about half a million must have hit a man. I returned to the Colonel. Our men had then begun to retire down the main road to Rond de la Reine. A galloper came up and, as far as I heard, said that we were to hang on and not retreat yet. This officer was, I think, killed immediately after giving his message. The Colonel said that the Coldstreamers had already begun to retreat, that we couldn't hold on there, but must go back to the position we had left. We were ordered to resume the position which Hubert had been told to leave. The Germans were by this time about 250 yards away, firing on us with machine-guns and rifles. The noise was perfectly awful. In a lull the C.O. said to the men : " Do you hear that ? Do you know what they are doing that for ? They are doing that to frighten you." I said to him : "If that's all, they might as well stop. As far as I am concerned, they have succeeded, two hours ago."

The men were ordered to charge, but the order was not heard in the noise, and after we had held this position for some minutes a command was given to retreat. Another galloper brought it, who also, I think, was shot. Guernsey, whom I met with his company, asked me to gallop back and tell Valentine he must retire his platoon ; he had not received the order. I found Valentine and got off my horse and walked him some yards down the road, the Germans following. He, like everybody else, was very pleased at the calm way the men were behaving.

I mounted and galloped after the Colonel, who said : " If only we could get at them with the bayonet I believe one of our men is as good as three of theirs." He started in the direction of the Brigadier. Men were now falling fast. I happened to see one man drop with a bayonet in his hand a few yards off, and reined in my horse to see if I could help him, but the C.O. called me and I followed him. The man whom I had seen was Hubert, though I did not know it at the time. The C.O. said : " It is impossible now to rescue wounded men ; we have all we can do." He had a charmed life. He raced from one place to another through the wood ; cheering the men and chaffing them, and talking to me ; smoking cigarette after cigarette. Under ordinary conditions one would have thought it mad to ride at the ridiculous pace we did over the very broken ground, but the bullets made everything else irrelevant. At about 1 o'clock we went up to the Brigadier at the corner of the road. The fighting there was pretty hot. One of the men told the Colonel that Hubert was killed. The Colonel said : " Are you sure ? " The man said : " Well, I can't swear." I was sent back to see. The man said he was about 400 yards away, and as I galloped as hard as I could, G. called to me : " To the right and then to the left." As I raced through the wood there was a cessation of the firing, though a number of shots came from both sides. They snapped very close. I found Hubert in the road we had been holding. I jumped off my horse and put my hand on his shoulder and spoke to him. He must have been killed at once, and looked absolutely peaceful. He cannot have suffered at all. I leant over to see if he had letters in his pocket, when I heard a whistle 25 or 30 yards behind me in the wood. I stood up and called: "If that is an Englishman, get outside the wood and up to the corner like hell; you will be shot if you try and join the rest through the wood. The Germans are between us." I bent over to pick up Hubert's bayonet, when again a whistle came and the sound of low voices, talking German. I then thought the sooner I was away the better. As I swung into the saddle a shot came from just behind me, missing me. I rode back as fast as Moonshine could go. The lull in the firing had ceased, and the Germans were all round us. One could see them in the wood, and they were shooting quite close. The man who finally got me was about 15 to 20 yards away; his bullet must have passed through a tree or through Bron's greatcoat, because it came into my side broken up. It was like a tremendous punch. I galloped straight on to my regiment and told the Colonel that Hubert was dead. He said: "I am sorry, and I am sorry that you are hit. I am going to charge." He had told me earlier that he meant to if he got the chance.

I got off and asked them to take on my horse. Then I lay down on the ground and a R.A.M.C. man dressed me. The Red Cross men gave a loud whistle when they saw my wound, and said the bullet had gone through me. The fire was frightfully hot. The men who were helping me were crouching down, lying on the ground. While he was dressing me a horse—his, I suppose—was shot just behind us. I asked them to go, as they could do me no good and would only get killed or taken themselves. The doctor gave me some morphia, and I gave them my revolver. They put me on a stretcher, leaving another empty stretcher beside me. This was hit several times. Shots came from all directions, and the fire seemed to be lower than earlier in the day. The bullets were just above me and my stretcher. I lost consciousness for a bit; then I heard my regiment charging. There were loud cries and little spurts of spasmodic shooting; then everything was quiet and a deep peace fell upon the wood. It was very dreamlike.

Hon. Aubrey Herbert.

ORBAIS

2nd Sept. At about 5 p.m., H.Q. left for Orbais. I well remember the poignant sadness of abandoning the beautiful rich valley of the Marne, so typical of France, to the enemy, and the shame of seeing some girls by the bridge over the river shaking their fists at us. There, too, I saw an elderly woman trembling with rage as our car went by. She must have been a woman of education, for, parodying a celebrated line, she screamed " La Garde ne se bat pas ! "

Brig.-Gen. E. L. Spears.

MAPS

3rd Sept. The prospect of the retreat being continued was depressing to all of us, and especially exasperating to Commandant Lamotte, the efficient little officer in charge of the distribution of maps for the Army. With the Army moving at such a rate, to supply all units with the vast quantity of maps required was no light task. Lamotte kept dashing off to Paris to exhort the map-printing department, already working day and night, to even greater efforts. Maps of France, always more maps of France, were called for, whilst vast quantities of maps of Germany, carefully prepared for a successful offensive, filled the vaults, never to be disturbed.

At Orbais the special grievance of our little cartographer was that people would insist on fighting battles at the junction of two maps, thereby thoughtlessly and wastefully using two sheets where one should have sufficed.

Brig.-Gen. E. L. Spears.

SERBIA

SCHWARMEREI

Aug. In a meadow, close to the river, on the left bank of the Yadar, just below the inn of Krivaia, I saw the following spectacle :

A group of children, girls, women, and men, 15 in all, were lying dead, tied together by their hands. Most of them had been bayoneted. One young girl had been bayoneted below the jaw, on the left, and the point of the weapon had come out through the right cheek-bone. Many of the corpses had no teeth left. On the back of an old woman who was lying on her face, there was some coagulated blood, and in this were found some teeth. This old woman was lying beside the girl whose wound has been described above. It would appear that the old woman was killed first, and the young girl immediately afterwards, so that the teeth of the latter were scattered on the back of the old woman. The chemises of the little girls and young women were blood-stained, which seems to indicate that they had been violated before being killed. Near this group, apart, lay the dead bodies of three men who had been bayoneted in the head, throat, and cheek.

Colonel Dokitch (commanding 20th Serbian Infantry Regiment) in Report on Atrocities committed by the Austro-Hungarian Army.

TANNENBERG

Hindenburg and his chief of staff, Ludendorff, took over command of the East Prussian front on August 23 and immediately began a vigorous policy of attack against the advancing Russian armies under Samsonov. Between August 26 and 30 the two armies were in constant battle, and Hindenburg's triumph was such that, at the end, he had crushed two Russian armies, and captured over 100,000 prisoners and 500 guns.

NIEDENBURG, 25*th Aug*. The XVth Corps was halting to-day, though firing ceased at 9 a.m. yesterday. Nothing is known of the position of the XIIIth and VIth Corps to-night. Things will have to move more quickly for the Russians to do any good in the preliminary campaign in East Prussia, the object of which should be to annihilate the two or three German corps here together with their reserve divisions before they can be reinforced.

26*th Aug*. There was bad staff work in starting. The Automobile Colonel—a delightful fellow to talk to—was quite unable to read a map, so we went three miles on the wrong road, and the heavy cars had to turn to the right about on a sandy track. It did not occur to him that he should have reconnoitred the road in his light car while the transport cars were taking in petrol at Niedenburg. Yet the Russians seem to muddle through in a happy-go-lucky way....

There was a dramatic incident in the middle of the meal. An officer brought in a telegram for the C. of S. and said that the G.O.C. Ist Corps wished to speak on the telephone with the Army Commander or the Chief of Staff. He said he was hotly engaged. General Postovski put on his pince-nez, read the telegram, and he and General Samsonov buckled on their swords, said good-bye to the Commandant, and left at once.

It appears that this attack on the Ist Corps was not unexpected. This corps is at Usdau, and was known to be faced by a German corps which was reinforced to-day. I tried to induce Anders to start off for the Ist Corps, but without effect. . . .

Ostrolenka, 28*th Aug*. I arrived at Niedenburg at 8.30 and

found Samsonov had gone on. I followed with a colonel of the General Staff along the route running north-east to Jedwabno. Every few hundred yards we stopped to question stragglers, who always had the same story—that they had lost their way through no fault of their own. Samsonov said two days ago that Jewish soldiers skulked in the woods and so avoided fighting, but many of the men we saw to-day were certainly not Jews. We found Samsonov sitting on the ground poring over maps and surrounded with his staff. I stood aside. Suddenly he stood up and ordered eight of the men of the sotnia of Cossacks that was with us to dismount and give up their animals. I prepared to go off too, but he beckoned to me and took me aside. He said that he considered it his duty to tell me that the position was very critical. His place and duty was with the army, but he advised me to return while there was time, as my duty was to send in " valuable " reports to my Government. He said that the Ist Corps, the 2nd Division and the XVth Corps had been forced back on his left. He had just heard that the VIth Corps had been driven back yesterday afternoon[1] in disorder on his right. He was sending back all his automobiles *via* Willenberg to Ostrolenka, as Niedenburg and the Niedenburg–Mlava route were no longer safe.

He concluded that he did not know what was going to happen, but even if the worst happened, it would not affect the ultimate result of the War.

It was my duty to keep in touch with my Government, and I knew enough of the Russian character to understand that the presence of a foreigner at a time so critical would increase the nerve-strain of the staff, so I said good-bye, and Samsonov, with his seven staff

---

[1] According to German accounts, the disaster to the VIth Corps took place on the evening of the 26th, and not of the 27th. Samsonov only learned of it at 9.30 a.m. on the 28th.

Nearly three years afterwards I met an officer who had served on the staff of the VIth Corps. He said that it had marched thirteen days without a halt, without proper transport and most of the time without bread. The 4th Division was attacked by a German corps and the 16th Division " wavered." The corps commander received an order to march on Allenstein but retreated through Ortelsburg when he should have fought. Though in the fighting only one regiment suffered severely, the corps was cut off from direct communication with the Staff of the Army and had no idea what enemy forces were on its flanks. The German heavy artillery " made a bad impression " on the Russian rank and file.

officers, mounted the Cossack horses and rode north-west, followed by the remainder of the squadron. Both he and his staff were as calm as possible; they said : " The enemy has luck one day, we will have luck another." They told me he was going to the XVth Corps, which was suffering from hunger as well as from heavy loss in a four-days' battle, and that he was going to collect what he could to drive the Germans back. . . .

Warsaw, 31st Aug. A telephone message came at 8.30 a.m. to say that the train of the G.O.C. 2nd Army was at the St. P. station. I went down and retrieved my servant Maxim. I was told that the best thing I could do would be to return to Ostrolenka and I would find out everything there. No one had any idea where Samsonov was. (He had been dead over thirty hours.) . . .

Ostrov, 1st Sept. I arrived at Ostrolenka at 9.30 a.m., to find the staff train had gone to Ostrov. I asked the railway transport officer if he could direct me to Samsonov. He shook his head, and as I pressed for a reply, he drew his hand significantly across his throat. Samsonov has been routed and has shot himself. . . .

The main German attack from Gilgenburg on Niedenburg and Willenberg seems to have completely cut off the XIIIth as well as the XVth Corps. Only odd men of both corps are now coming into Ostrolenka. All the guns and transport have been lost. . . .

Ostrov, 2nd Sept. . . . The Staff of the Army followed the remnants of the XVth Corps in the retreat of the 29th, having been cut off from all communication with the Ist Corps since the morning of the 28th, and with the VIth and XIIIth Corps since the evening of the same day. They soon became isolated, Samsonov having told the Cossack escort, who had suffered severely in charging a machine-gun party, to shift for themselves. All the night of the 29th–30th they stumbled through the woods that fringe the north of the railway from Niedenburg to Willenberg, moving hand-in-hand to avoid losing one another in the darkness. Samsonov said repeatedly that the disgrace of such a defeat was more than he could bear. " The Emperor trusted me. How can I face him after such a disaster ? " He went aside and his staff heard a shot. They searched for his body without success, but all are convinced that he shot himself. The Chief of Staff and other officers managed to reach Russian territory, having covered forty miles on foot. . . .

Major-Gen. Sir Alfred Knox.

THE PAST

THE DEATH OF CHARLES PÉGUY IN FRONT OF VILLEROY

5*th Sept.* Climbing the bank, rifle in hand, bent almost double to offer the smallest possible target, tripping over beets and clods of earth, we advanced to the assault. . . . A rush, and then a second carried us 200 yards forward. For the moment to go forward, in a single wave without supports, over ground where the forward slope and our conspicuous uniforms made us magnificent targets, with only 150 rounds per man and no chance of more, was madness, a certain and complete massacre. Not a dozen of us would get there.

"Down," yelled Péguy; "Independent fire." But himself, he remained standing, his glasses in his hand, directing our fire, heroic in this hell. . . . We fired like madmen, blackened with powder, the rifles scorching our fingers, and between rounds thrusting our hands into the earth to fling up a miserable shelter. On all sides, cries, screams and groans. How many dead? We could no longer count. . . .

Péguy remained standing in spite of our shouts of "Lie down."

Many of us had lost our packs at Ravenel, and at this moment a pack would have been welcome cover. Our lieutenant's voice went on shouting with furious energy: "Shoot, shoot, *nom de Dieu.*"

Someone cried: "We haven't our packs; we shall all get it in the neck."

"Doesn't matter," returned Péguy; "I haven't a pack either. Go on. Keep on firing." He drew himself up as if in challenge to the storm of bullets, as it were to summon the death he had glorified in his verse. At that moment a bullet pierced his noble forehead. He fell on the hillside without a cry, having seen at last clearly that ultimate vision of the longed-for victory. When, some yards farther on, frantically leaping forward, I glanced behind me, I saw stretched on the hot dusty earth, among the broad green leaves, a black and scarlet stain in the midst of so many others, the body of our beloved brave lieutenant.

Victor Boudon.

THE MARNE

It was on September 3 that General Galliéni learned that Von Kluck was making a flank march to the east of Paris. He instantly got into touch with Joffre, pressing him to start an offensive, and on the following day the Fifth army crossed the Marne and began to press back the Germans.

GALLIÉNI, COMMANDER OF THE FORTIFIED CAMP OF PARIS, THINKS

ON 3rd Sept., and even on the morning of 4th, i.e. at the moment when the march of the German First Army towards the south-east was being confirmed, I had to make the decision to safeguard above all the interests of the capital which had been entrusted to my care. At that moment, our armies, including the British force, had received orders to retreat behind the Seine, and the C.-in-C. was stressing the fact that this movement should be carried out as quickly as possible. From my point of view, this retirement was bad because (1) it uncovered the Fortified Camp of Paris, (2) it took no account of the enemy, (3) it could not be carried out in time, for the heads of the German columns would certainly be at Pont-sur-Yonne, Nogent-sur-Seine, etc. by the time the English and French troops got there . . . (4) it ruined all ideas of an immediate offensive. . . . In every operation of war, is it not one's first duty to scrutinize the enemy, to see what objective is to be reached and to be in a position to destroy him ? In the circumstances, the situation presented itself to my eyes in the simplest manner, at least so far as concerned the Fortified Camp of Paris, from the Ourcq to the Marne. A German army was advancing at a great pace southwards against the Anglo-French forces, which had been in retreat for several days. But, on the other hand, this German army in its march was offering a flank and uncovering even its communications to a French army advancing from the west. . . . Was it not then the duty of the commander of the French army without losing an instant to fall on the German army which had been rash enough to make this flank march in disdain of the western army ?

General Galliéni.

GALLIÉNI ACTS

4th Sept. 9.1 *a.m.*
Secret Order No. 11.
    From General Galliéni, commanding the Armies of Paris, to General Maunoury, commanding the Sixth Army at Le Raincy.

As a result of the movement of the German Armies, who appear to be passing forward from our front towards the south-east, it is my intention to move your army against their flank, i.e. eastward, in touch with the British forces.

I will indicate your line of march as soon as I know that of the British Army. But on receipt of this, make your dispositions that your troops may be ready to move this afternoon and to undertake to-morrow a general movement eastward from the Entrenched Camp.

You will immediately push forward your cavalry patrols over the whole sector between the Chantilly road and the Marne.

On receipt of this order, the 45th division will come under your orders. You will report to me in person to confer as soon as possible.

Galliéni.

JOFFRE TALKS

6th Sept. 7.30 *a.m.* At the moment when the battle on which the fate of the country hangs, is about to open, it is necessary to remind all ranks that it is no longer the moment to look to the rear. Every effort must be made to attack and throw back the enemy. A unit which can no longer advance, must at all costs retain the ground it has gained, and rather than retire, be killed on the spot. In the present circumstances, no weakness can be tolerated.

Joffre's Order of the Day.

THE CYNIC COMMENTS

One evening at G.Q.G. at Chantilly I was shown the famous order of the Marne, which directed that a stand should be made towards the north, written entirely in Colonel Gamelin's writing and signed by Joffre. A magnificent piece of history, inscribed on red paper. . . . Cruel deception ! The famous order bore three different dates, written one over the other.

Jean de Pierrefeu.

GALLIÉNI'S TAXIS

7th Sept. A block had brought me momentarily to a halt against the boundary wall of a château, when a car with its lights extinguished, ploughing its way through the throng, forced a confused wave of men and beasts against me, the weight of which flattened me against the wall. . . .

Another car followed in its wake, then others and still others, in endless, silent, succession.

The moon had risen, and its rays shone reflected on the shiny peaks of taxi-drivers' caps. Inside the cabs, one could make out the bent heads of sleeping soldiers.

Someone asked, " Wounded ? " And a passing voice replied : " No. Seventh Division. From Paris. Going into the line. . . ."

Paul Lintier.

9TH ROYAL LANCERS AND 1ST GUARD DRAGOON REGIMENT OF BERLIN

7th Sept. Behind a friendly stone wall, I stopped and took out my glasses. The stubble stretched away towards a line of woods. Diagonally, across the broad road that led north from the village, came a line of horsemen.

Magnificent in the morning sun they rode, a solid line, rising and falling with regular cadence, as though mechanically propelled. The 1st Garde Dragoner Regiment of Berlin, of the Garde Kavallerie Division of the Garde Korps, the proudest, finest cavalry of the German Army—over one hundred of them, seeming double the number to me—were charging across the fields.   On they came like machine-made waves on a machine-made ocean.

Then from the left shot other horsemen, one well ahead, another not far back, and a scattered scurrying bunch of two score behind, riding like mad, full tilt at the ranks of German pride and might bearing down upon them.   The Germans quickened appreciably, and their lances waved downwards to the rest.   Their pace was slow compared with the whirlwind rush of the smaller band.   Crash ! went the 9th into the Garde.   Colonel Campbell and Captain Reynolds were down, and horses reared and staggered. . . .   Not one horse refused.

The 9th scored heavily off their more numerous foes.   A few fell, but more than double the number of Germans bit the dust. . . . Galloping on, the 9th circled round the village and away to the rear.

The Germans stopped and many of them dismounted.   One of them went coolly through the pockets of Reynolds, lying with an aluminium lance through his side.   A farrier-sergeant lay dead near a pond at the village end.   The Germans knocked in his head and tossed his body into the pool. . . .

By this time Colonel Burnett of the 18th Hussars with a dismounted squadron, had worked round to the left with a machine-gun.   When he opened on them, the Germans mounted and swung by him into the full line of fire. . . .   The result was a field strewn with many German dead.   The rest galloped away, leaving their wounded behind them.[1]

Frederick Coleman.

ADVANCE OF THE 2ND DIVISION

7th Sept.   How or where we spent the night has passed out of memory, but early next morning we have debouched from Haute Vesnes and are moving on a country lane down a small valley that is shut in by two spurs.   These spurs, which jut out from the Haute Vesnes ridge, descend to a larger valley along which a road runs. Beyond this valley the ground again rises in a fold parallel to the

[1] Actually the charge was made by one troop, about 30 strong, under Col. Campbell, which overwhelmed that part of the German squadron (120) which it struck.   Further, it was a different squadron (4th) of the same German regiment which the 18th Hussars annihilated, only three escaping.   (See *Official History, Vol. I.*)

Haute Vesnes ridge. Thus the little re-entrant we are in runs, so to speak, across the grain of the countryside, and our view is shut in by the blinkers of the foothills on either side.

We are marching at some speed with the two leading platoons deployed, for a message has just come in from the neighbouring French Fifth Army to say that fifty-six heavy guns are ahead, jammed on the road by masses of retreating transport. We, in a state of mingled eagerness and trepidation, are going out for this prize, when almost simultaneously two things happen. The first is the sight of the scouting officer tumbling down the right-hand spur with the startling news that a column of German infantry is just over the far side, marching parallel to ourselves, and the second the sudden appar-ition of two German cyclists on the valley road only a hundred yards in front. Their approach has been masked by the spur, and they are as surprised to see us as we them. Even as our vanguard is flinging itself down to open fire, they bend over the handle-bars and pedal for life—ten yards—twenty yards—the first bullet smacks past them, thirty yards—the whole platoon is firing, forty yards——Go on, brave hearts, you'll win through ! Forty-five yards—they're off, all in a heap. Alas ! Alas ! But it was bound to be. My God ! They've not been touched ! They're behind a milestone, and firing back, one on either side. By the Lord Harry, they're stout fellows, but did you ever see anything like the shooting of our men ?

For half a minute the unequal fight continued. Then, to our amazed admiration, the one on the right-hand side—as we looked at it—of the milestone jumped up and, standing sideways to us, semaphored to someone we couldn't see. Flick, flick, flick went his hands faster than we could read, his elbows never straight. Our men can't hit him, though there are forty, and they are professional soldiers, firing. It's absurd, ridiculous. Their officer, who is standing up, is cursing them. " Look at you ! Good shots, aren't you ? " he jeers in mocking indignation.

The German is down. Has he hurled himself or been hurled by a bullet to the ground ? You can't tell from the way he fell. But there is a sudden silence.

Next minute the order comes to fall back to Haute Vesnes. You shake yourself out of the awe into which this short-lived drama has plunged you, turn your platoon about, and march back. As you enter the village, you look over your shoulder just in time to see a scurry of field-greys swarm up the opposing ridge and disappear half-way up into a sunken lane that climbs diagonally across its front.

Once more we deploy. Whatever the military reason of our withdrawal, there can be no doubt it was very sporting, for it has allowed the enemy to start fair. Both sides are now in position and commence an infantry fire fight at fifteen hundred yards. The bullets sigh their treacherous songs over our heads. The overture lasts a full hour; nobody advances, and if we are waiting for superiority of fire we shall stop here all day from the look of it. We're not hitting any more than they are, and after a while you order your platoon to cease fire, for to go on is merely to waste ammunition. You are sick of these dolorous whistles that terminate in such unexpectedly vicious smacks as the bullets hit the ground. But what, meanwhile, of the fifty-six guns?

At last, however, after what has seemed an interminable delay, one of our batteries opens and soon has its shrapnel bursting into the lane. You order your platoon to reopen fire.

A white flag appears. "Go on shooting, don't stop," for we hold that the German is as notoriously treacherous as the tiger, and whilst we feel no moral indignation about this characteristic, we are resolved not to be caught by his siren song of the white flag. A second white flag appears, then a third; in two or three minutes there are a dozen stuck up along his front. He stops firing; we continue; so, pulling down one or two, he resumes. "Cease fire," you order your men, for this long-range firing is useless, and they are still not shooting when the advance starts by rushes. The officer commanding the next platoon, which belongs to another battalion, curses you for not giving him covering fire. Very well, if he wants it, he can have it, though you feel certain it is quite useless.

Now it is your turn to rush. On your way you pass two men of the next regiment who are on their hands and knees in a small hollow. You curse them and tell them to go on. They reply indignantly they've been hit. Have they? It seems incredible, for the soft wail of the bullets is lost in the jangle of equipment of running men. But you suddenly realize your own men feel you a brute for going for these fellows and your mind is sharply illuminated by the knowledge that to them a wound, no matter how slight, terminates all moral obligation to go on. In a flash you grasp the truth that discipline cannot go farther than public opinion allows, and full of chagrin, uncertain whether the two men have made a fool of you, or you of yourself, you hurry your men forward.

Line after line is rushing down the hill and collecting in the dead ground at the bottom. There have been no more casualties and, indeed, the Germans seem to have stopped firing. Reforming your platoon on the road, you are on the point of advancing straight forward up the bank when you become aware that the whole line is moving off to the right, evidently with the intention of taking the enemy in the flank. You follow, angry with yourself for not having thought of such a manœuvre. You wonder who did. You appreciate the unknown is a better tactician and feel vaguely jealous.

Presently the line forms half left with yourself somewhere in the centre, and the advance is resumed. Your heart is beating hard, for there will be a charge, and the thought fills you with dread. You'll have to lead and you neither want to be killed nor to kill anybody. Officers, you feel, shouldn't engage in the rough-and-tumble—that's for the men ; theirs is the thinking part. But the men won't charge unless you charge too—you've seen enough already to realize that —and if you lead, will the men follow ? In craven mistrust you fear the worst, and your heart goes thump, thump, thump with apprehension, but at the same time you are frightfully inquisitive to find out what a charge is really like.

But before the critical moment can come, there's a small plantation to be gone through ; a few of them may be in that. Revolver in hand, you start to force your way through the thick undergrowth and brushwood, then, prig and poseur that you are, put it back in your holster and draw your sword instead. You do this because you want to show everybody what a well-schooled and careful shot you are—to carry a loaded revolver through such dense scrub really isn't safe, and you want everyone to see you appreciate the fact. However, if everybody is in the same plight as yourself, totally unable to keep open their eyes through these slashing and lashing twigs, for, try as you will, you haven't the will-power, your model action has probably passed unobserved. Head down, you burst your way through the far edge, look up in agonized apprehension and——

Glory ! Glory ! Alleluia ! They're surrendering. They're crossing the odd hundred yards between ourselves and the lane, walking wisely. That is to say, their gait and gestures command us to control our excitement and withhold from massacre. Numerically far the weaker, yet at this moment their will is the stronger.

The sudden reaction from inner tension has left your mind in a state of limpid clarity. You rally your scattered platoon—as far as you can see you are about the only officer that does—and fall them into fours. Higher up the hill a large bunch of prisoners—perhaps a hundred—are being plundered by a disorderly mob of men, the Germans actually assisting their captors in their spoliation. With your formed platoon you drive off the looters and recover some of the public and private property, including a pair of exquisite little field-glasses—there were a lot of them about—which you annex for yourself. (Easy come is easy go—the R.A.M.C. stole them from you six weeks later.) Then, looking round for an officer of theirs, you perceive a tall sergeant-major of the Jaegers, and succeed in making him realize you want the prisoners fallen into fours. He gets them into line and gives the order. It is slackly obeyed, and then he lets fly. You and your men have the interesting experience of hearing a Prussian sergeant-major really telling off his men. It is impressive, and although you know your own men don't know German any more than you, yet you are glad they are hearing this torrent of savage abuse. You hope somehow they'll apply it to themselves, for after all this Jaeger is saying no more than you would often like to say, and they must realize that. Is he calling them Bastards ? " You can call your men anything except that," you had once been told " for that goes home too often."

The reprimand's finished. An order : " Guttural-Gut ! " Click, click of their heels, like guardsmen. " Quick march ! " Yes, but where ?

For, having got them on the move, you don't know what to do with them. In your exhilaration you'd forgotten all about those fifty-six guns. Of course the advance will be resumed instantly and your company will be where it was when the day started, in the van. And where will you be ? In the rear, if you don't look out, guarding prisoners. You could kick yourself for your beastly officiousness, which as a just retribution will deprive you of the chance of honour.

But there was no need for apprehension. The advance is stopped for the day. We are all, victors and prisoners alike, to fall back to Haute Vesnes—the third time we shall have seen that blasted village this day.

Lt.-Col. A. A. Hanbury-Sparrow (R. Berkshire Regt.).

WAITING FOR RESCUE

Friday, September 11*th.* Our English prisoners were marched off this morning. We are full of speculation as to what has really happened. Valentine, Buddy and I are well.

10.10 *a.m.* There are machine-guns about four miles away.

10.30 *a.m.* There is a heavy rifle fire within a mile. It is very trying lying here in bed. We have nothing to read except *The Rajah's Heir* which V. sent to me and which has become known as the treasure-house of fun. It is a sort of mixture of Hymns Ancient and Modern and the *Fairchild Family*.

2 *p.m.* There is a Maxim within a few hundred yards of the house. Rifle volleys outside in the garden. A rising wind and rain threatening.

3 *p.m.* Heavy rain. The French are visible, advancing.

3.10 *p.m.* The French are here. They came in in fine style, like conquerors; one man first, riding, his hand on his hip. The German sentries who had been posted to protect us wounded walked down and surrendered their bayonets. The German doctors came to us for help. I offered to go, but W. went. The French infantry and cavalry came streaming through. Our wounded went out into the pouring rain to cheer them. They got water from our men, whose hands they kissed. The German guns are on the skyline. The Germans are in full retreat, and said to be cut off by the English.

5 *p.m.* A heavy bombardment of the German guns began from here. I have come upstairs to a long low garret with skylights, in order to leave Valentine and Buddy more room. Through the sky-light one can see every flash of the French and German guns. The doctors all come up here to watch with their field-glasses through my skylights.

Hon. Aubrey Herbert.

A PALADIN

12*th Sept.* General de Maud'huy had just been roused from sleep on the straw of a shed and was standing in the street, when a little group of unmistakable purport came round the corner. Twelve soldiers and an N.C.O., a firing party, a couple of gendarmes, and between them an unarmed soldier. My heart sank and a feeling of horror overcame me. An execution was about to take place. General de Maud'huy gave a look, then held up his hand so that the party halted, and with his characteristic quick step went up to the doomed man. He asked what he had been condemned for. It was for abandoning his post. The General then began to talk to the man. Quite simply he explained discipline to him. Abandoning your post was letting down your pals, more, it was letting down your country that looked to you to defend her. He spoke of the necessity of example, how some could do their duty without prompting but others, less strong, had to know and understand the supreme cost of failure. He told the condemned man that his crime was not venial, not low, and that he must die as an example, so that others should not fail. Surprisingly the wretch agreed, nodded his head. The burden of infamy was lifted from his shoulders. He saw a glimmer of something, redemption in his own eyes, a real hope, though he knew he was to die.

Maud'huy went on, carrying the man with him to comprehension that any sacrifice was worth while if it helped France ever so little. What did anything matter if he knew this?

Finally de Maud'huy held out his hand : " Yours also is a way of dying for France," he said. The procession started again, but now the victim was a willing one.

The sound of a volley in the distance announced that all was over. General de Maud'huy wiped the beads of perspiration from his brow, and for the first time perhaps his hand trembled as he lit his pipe.

Brig.-Gen. E. L. Spears.

THE AISNE

2ND LANCASHIRE FUSILIERS AND 2ND ESSEX REGIMENT

13*th Sept.* . . . A long strip of wood separated us from the Chivres valley and partly hid us from the enemy. We piled arms here and awaited the final order to entrench. Meanwhile the enemy's artillery had opened along the whole front, but uncertain of our actual positions he was firing at random over a wide area. Shortly after, the battalion adjutant came up and said the major wished to see me. We went through the strip of wood and found the major, Captain von Bülow, and the few remaining officers of the battalion standing in a clearing from which a grand view could be had across the valley. We could not see the Aisne itself, but a line of willows away on the far side marked its course, with here and there groups of houses and church-towers along its green banks. Stretched out across the broad expanse of meadows between us and the river was a long line of dots wide apart, and looking through glasses one saw that these dots were infantry advancing, widely extended : English infantry, too, unmistakably.[1] A field battery on our left had spotted them, and we watched their shrapnel bursting over the advancing line. Soon a second line of dots emerged from the willows along the river-bank, at least ten paces apart, and began to advance. More of our batteries came into action ; but it was noticed that a shell, however well aimed, seldom killed more than one man, the lines being so well and widely

[1] This refers to the attack by the 12th Infantry Brigade (2nd Lancashire Fusiliers and the 2nd Essex Regiment) ; they had crossed the Aisne by the damaged bridge at Venizel, and thence attacked at the Chivres spur and west of it. On their left the 1st Rifle Brigade (11th Brigade) had occupied the woods above St. Marguerite, west of the Chivres valley, earlier in the day, having crossed the river during the night by the Venizel bridge, filing across the central girder which alone remained intact.

extended. The front line had taken cover when the shelling began, running behind any hedges or buildings near by, but this second line kept steadily on, while a third and fourth line now appeared from the river-bank, each keeping about two hundred yards distance from the line in front. Our guns now fired like mad, but it did not stop the movement : a fifth and a sixth line came on, all with the same wide intervals between men and the same distance apart. It was magnificently done.

The whole wide expanse of flat meadow-land beneath us was now dotted with tiny brown-grey men pushing on closer and closer, their attack obviously making for the position of the corps on our immediate right, from which rifle-fire was already hammering into the advancing lines. Nevertheless they still moved forwards, line after line of them, and gradually disappeared from our view behind the wooded slopes at the southern end of the Chivres valley.

Walter Bloem (12*th Brandenburg Grenadiers*).

THE PUNDITS

13th Sept. Berthelot asked me when I thought we should cross into Germany, and I replied that unless we made some serious blunder we ought to be at Elsenborn in 4 weeks. He thought 3 weeks.

Field-Marshal Sir Henry Wilson.

Col. Pénélon suggested to Joffre some form of helmet or breastplate for the troops. " My friend," he replied, " we shall not have time to make them. I shall tear up the Boches within two months."

Jean de Pierrefeu.

" THEY ORDER, SAID I, THIS MATTER BETTER IN FRANCE——"

14th Sept. I had a conversation with one of the officers connected with the court martial that condemned these people, and shudderingly remarked that the evidence was slight, the accusation often improbable, and how could guilt be established in such cases without the possibility of error? His answer made a profound impression on me. " You English don't know what war is. The existence of France is at stake. A single spy may cause such harm as to imperil the fate of the nation. Justice has little to do with it. Our duty is to see that no spy escapes whatever the cost may be. If a proportion of those who are executed to-day are guilty, even one or two, we have every reason to be satisfied that our duty to the country has been done."

Brig.-Gen. E. L. Spears.

REFUGEES

THIS chilly, misty evening, it is my privilege to entertain the Vandenberger family—or, rather, what remains of the Vandenberger family—in a corner of one of the refreshment-rooms of Waterloo Station. Five days have elapsed since they arrived in London from a ruined Belgian village. London, during those five days, has taken good care of the Vandenbergers. And this evening, in half an hour's time, they are to travel to Exeter, as the guests of an English lady and her husband and daughter, in their calm, charming, old-fashioned country-house.

Four Vandenbergers: the mother, a son aged fourteen, and two little girls of seven and nine. The father is "missing." Also a grandfather is "missing." Also a daughter is "missing." Also Madame Vandenberger's old mother is "missing." In fact, although the entire Vandenberger family fled their village side by side, only four of them wretchedly reached London. How, or where, or when they became separated, Madame Vandenberger cannot tell. At all events, somewhere or other, in the frantic rush to the Belgian coast, the stricken and distracted Vandenberger party was broken up.

A typical, sturdy peasant woman, Madame Vandenberger. Forty years of age, but her face, previously weather-stained by hard work in the open fields, now further ravaged by distress and despair. Her fourteen-year-old son, brown of skin, lanky, restless and awkward. The two little girls—well, each clasps a doll tightly under her arm and a stick of chocolate in one hand, and there are blue ribbons in their hair, blonde hair that has been streaked and tarnished from past rural exposure to the fierce Belgian sun. So do the Vandenbergers sit in the refreshment-room at Waterloo (more shades of Belgium!) waiting for the Exeter train, eating sandwiches and chocolates and drinking *café au lait*. Coffee is the Belgian refugee's chief consolation. Since kindly English people have been sending our stricken visitors parcels of tea, I should like to quote the following warning from a letter that I have received from a distinguished Belgian lady : " Faites moi le plaisir de dire en toute occasion qu'on leur donne toujours du café au lait, et pas de thé—car c'est leur réconfort et la base de leur soutien moral et physique, et le thé leur est une vraie drogue." Shades of dear, devastated Belgium again ! Among her peasantry, tea (as my correspondent points out) has ever been regarded as a strong dangerous medicine ; a " drug." In villages, even in small towns, it was only procurable from the chemist. And the cautious chemist placed his tea high up on a shelf, in an ominous glass jar, amidst other sinister poisons.

So, coffee and milk (three large cups of it all round) for my guests in this corner of Waterloo Station. As they speak little French, and my own knowledge of Flemish is deplorable, conversation is difficult. Nor, I feel sure, is Madame Vandenberger in the least degree inclined to talk. The frantic flight from her village—the desperate exodus to Antwerp—the arrival at foreign Folkestone— then London—and now Exeter ; all these agonies, all these sudden, startling vicissitudes have left her dizzy and dazed. Here she sits at Waterloo, bareheaded, wrapped up in a shawl, with two bundles at her feet—silent and expressionless. Smaller bundles by the side of the son and the two little girls. Exeter ! I have assured Madame Vandenberger that she and her children will receive the most sympathetic of welcomes from the charming English lady, and her open-hearted husband, and their delightful children—and I know it well.

Exeter ! But what can Exeter, with all its hospitality and beauty, signify at the present moment, in Waterloo Station, to a dazed, broken Belgian peasant woman who has scarcely ever moved out of her own primitive native village ? Exeter—another journey, another long step into the unknown, farther and farther away from " missing " old Mother Vandenberger, and " missing," shaky Grandfather Van-denberger, and the " missing " seventeen-year-old daughter Vanden-berger, and——

" Give me a kiss," says an English lady to the Vandenberger little girls, as she comes up into our corner and presents the blonde and stricken small sisters with a handsome box of chocolates. More gifts of chocolates follow. A stout gentleman presses half a sovereign into the limp, roughened hands of the mother. After that, a parcel of buns. After that . . . to the train. And there, on the cold, misty platform, I help bareheaded and ravaged Madame Vandenberger, and the tired young Vandenbergers, and their toys, chocolates and bundles into an empty third-class carriage, and the guard gives the signal, and the train leaves for Exeter.

As a result of the bombardment of Antwerp, behold Folkestone invaded every day by further contingents of homeless Belgians. A few hours later, picture scores of the new refugees established, with their bundles and their tired, brown-faced babies and children, in the innumerable halls, rooms and corridors of the vast, rambling Alexandra Palace. This afternoon it shelters over a thousand stricken Belgians. This afternoon, too, the palace is eagerly approached by dozens of other visitors, also laden with parcels and bundles, but none of them is allowed to proceed farther than the lodge that stands at the entrance to the grounds.

"Can't let anyone pass without a permit," states the lodge-keeper.

Appeals, protests, exhortations from the visitors, but the lodge-keeper remains inflexible. Finally, the bundles and parcels are delivered into his charge, and the visitors turn away.

"People are very kind," the lodgekeeper informs me. "All day long they come up wanting to see the refugees, and nearly everyone brings a parcel. Clothes, boots, food, toys—I couldn't say what else. Apart from the presents, can't they do something to help? Yes, there's no mistake about it, people are very kind."

Mainly ladies, the visitors. Nor did the lodgekeeper exaggerate when he states that they and their kindly offerings "came up all day long." One visitor after another, some of them arrived from distant places. For instance, this grey-haired lady, with three parcels of clothing, *and* the hospitable intimation that she would "like" to take in and care for no fewer than six Belgian children, in her country-house at Woking. A less prosperous lady—indeed, shabby and frail—anxious to help the Belgian mothers in "any way I can." And then, delightful apparition, a radiant English girl of eighteen, who informs the lodgekeeper that she wants to give the Belgian babies their nightly baths.

"What, all of them!" exclaims the lodgekeeper, at once admiringly and humorously.

"I can come every day from five o'clock to eight," says the charming girl. "Shall I bring towels?"

I should have liked to know it was settled! But the dear girl and the lady from Woking are referred to the Belgian Refugee Society in London.

John F. Macdonald.

NEWS

Sept. They telegraphed out that they wanted stories of atrocities. Well, there weren't any atrocities at that time. So then they telegraphed out that they wanted stories of refugees. So I said to myself, "That's fine. I won't have to move." There was a little town outside Brussels where one went to get dinner—a very good dinner, too. I heard the Hun had been there. I supposed there must have been a baby there. So I wrote a heart-rending story about the baby of Combeel Loo being rescued from the Hun in the light of the burning homesteads.

The next day they telegraphed out to me to send the baby along, as they had about five thousand letters offering to adopt it. The day after that baby clothes began to pour into the office. Even Queen Alexandra wired her sympathy and sent some clothes. Well, I couldn't wire back to them there wasn't a baby. So I finally arranged with the doctor that took care of the refugees that the blessed baby died of some very contagious disease, so it couldn't even have a public burial.

And a crèche was started with all the baby clothes.

Lord Ponsonby (quoting a War Correspondent).

FIRST YPRES

Early in October the British army was moved north to Flanders,
where it arrived just after the fall of Antwerp and the retreat of the
Belgian army.

GHELUVELT

31*st Oct.* Shall I ever forget this day ? It will be indelibly stamped
on my memory. How anyone survived to tell the story is a mystery
to me, but I must write the events as they occurred.

As usual the Huns commenced to shell us early in the morning and
concentrated an overwhelming number of batteries on Gheluvelt
and the surrounding area. After about two hours' bombardment,
they launch an infantry attack which sweeps over our troops in the
front line, who were killed or captured to a man, and swarming on
in masses, they reach the outskirts of Gheluvelt. From our two
companies in the front line we can get no news, and fear they have
been cut off with the others. At about 11 o'clock we are called on
to counter-attack with our two remaining companies, and leaving
our trenches, we move forward to try to carry out our task. The
ground all round is literally alive with bursting shells, and about a
score of men are struck down as they leave the trenches. However,
on we go, in extended order, and push into the village which is still
burning and German shells are bursting against the houses, throwing
bricks and dust in all directions. Riley is killed quite soon, and I
am once more in command of the company. During the advance
I receive a blow near my hip which almost knocks me down, and
thinking I am hit, I look down and discover that a bullet had entered
my compass case, cleared it out and passed on without doing me
any harm. On reaching the centre of the village, we are unable
to make any further progress as the Huns have firmly established
themselves in the houses in front of us, and in spite of the fact that

Prince joins me with A company, all we can do is to lie down and engage the enemy with our rifles. This is too one-sided to last for long, and we receive orders from Major Carter to withdraw and seek shelter in the trenches we have just left. Back we go. More khaki figures are left on the ground dead and dying, and those fortunate enough to escape unhurt regain the trenches.

After remaining there for another half-hour, we get orders to abandon our position and retire to Hooge, as we are told that the Germans have completely broken our front line beyond repair. The 2nd K.R.R.C. on our left are to conform to our movement. Seizing a favourable moment we commence to retire, and move back widely extended, pursued by the German shells, to which are now added the nerve-racking machine-gun and rifle fire.

Crossing the Menin road we make a detour through a thick wood, and proceed in the direction of Hooge. On the way we pass a battery limbering up, and they soon move back at a gallop. As they do so, the German gunners get their range and smother the guns and teams in bursting shrapnel. We are struck dumb with horror and expect to see nothing but their mangled remains, but much to our joy not a man or horse is hit, and they gallop off back to a new position. . . . Soon after leaving our trenches we fell in with the Gordons and Royal Scots Fusiliers of the 7th Division, who are also retiring to conform to the general backward movement.

On arrival at Hooge we find staff officers very busy halting all troops, and fresh orders are issued to turn round in conjunction with other units, to advance and counter-attack, and at all costs stop the Germans from advancing any nearer to Ypres.

By now we are sadly reduced in numbers, and only five officers Major Carter, the commanding officer, Captains Allen, Prince and Lieut. Ker and myself and about 125 other ranks are left. Just as we are about to advance, our transport arrives under Lieut. Wilkinson, and roping in some twenty-five transport drivers, we move forward with our left on the Menin road.

After going about 400 yards, we strike the leading German infantry, and a real soldiers' battle commences. So confident are they that they have broken through that they come on in massed formation, without taking any protective precautions, and we soon make holes in their ranks. In one instance I note German mounted officers leading troops forward in formation of fours, and, calling on the men nearest me to fire at this splendid target, we very soon shot down the officer, horse and a great number of men.

As each body of Germans is destroyed, we surge forward and take on the next, shooting and charging alternately, bayoneting the survivors until by sheer exhaustion and losses we come to a standstill. The Worcester Regiment and other troops on our left recapture Gheluvelt in a glorious charge which sweeps all before them, and most of the ground lost during the day is regained, although unfortunately, at an awful price. Wilkinson is killed in a most gallant manner, serving an abandoned machine-gun which he acquired, and he must have accounted for scores of Germans before he was killed. Our numbers are reduced to about ninety.

The shadows of night are now closing in, and we all set to work to dig in and consolidate the ground we stand on, but owing to our exhausted condition make very little progress. The units of the 1st and 7th Divisions are inconceivably mixed, and a good deal of time is spent sorting out the men and reorganizing in preparation for the next day. Every man, such as spare transport men and Royal Engineers, is in the firing line, and we have literally no reserves should the Germans attempt another break through. . . . During the night several attempts on the part of the Germans to break our line at a number of points are easily repulsed without loss to ourselves. Many stragglers join up and by morning the strength of the battalion has increased to nearly 150 officers and men.

November 1st brings about a renewal of the fighting and all day, long the Germans try to force us back. . . . On our particular sector we easily hold back the enemy infantry, but have fewer men left by the end of the day, mostly hit by shell fire which never ceases for a moment throughout the entire day.

. . . It is a sad thing to realize that during the last three days' desperate fighting, the 25 officers and 900 men who went into action on 30th are now reduced to five officers and 150 men, which practically means that for the time being we have ceased to exist as a battalion.

Capt. J. G. W. Hyndson (1st Loyal Regiment).

CORONEL AND THE FALKLANDS

On November 1, Admiral Cradock, who had been coasting up the Chile shores, encountered the German squadron under von Spee off Coronel. The battle opened as the sun was sinking, about 6.20 p.m., and by an hour later the three British vessels were crippled and making for the westward. The Germans pursued, and at 8.58 the "Monmouth" went down with Cradock's flag flying.

Five weeks later, on December 8, Admiral Sturdee was lying in wait at the Falkland Islands when von Spee was sighted shortly after 8 a.m. Sturdee stood out after him and after a hard-fought battle entirely destroyed the German squadron with the exception of the " Dresden "

1*st Nov.* As viewed from the enemy's line, the sun was setting immediately behind us, thus dazzling their gunlayers and giving us light on our target ; but as soon as the orb dipped below the horizon, shortly before 7 p.m., the conditions were completely reversed. We were now silhouetted against the afterglow, with a clear horizon behind to show up splashes from falling shells, while their ships to us were smudged into low black shapes scarcely discernible against the background of gathering night clouds. Ranges became increasingly difficult to take, and it now was apparent that the enemy were no longer avoiding action ; at 7.0 p.m. their line, now only 12,500 yards distant, opened fire, which we immediately returned. The speed of 17 knots into a heavy head was sending showers of spray over our forecastle, which dimmed the glasses of the gun telescopes, and *Glasgow's* gunlayers, firing from eight feet above the waterline, could hardly see their target. While our control-officers reported that the results of our shooting could not be corrected, as no splashes were visible in the failing light, *Leipzig* and *Dresden* had got *Glasgow's* range exactly, and *Scharnhorst* and *Gneisenau* were able to apply early and simultaneously their whole gun-power on *Good Hope* and

Monmouth respectively. At least one shot of the third salvo from *Scharnhorst* sent up a heavy burst of flame on the fore-part of *Good Hope*, and after this salvo the curious effect of a continuous sheet of flame appeared along the sides of *Good Hope* and *Monmouth*, on which flame the heavy sea seemed to have no effect. The fore-turret of *Monmouth* was also enveloped in flames and continued to burn for some minutes. As all the paint had been scraped from it, this must have been the cordite charges burning round the gun. Both ships, however, continued to fight some guns, and were rewarded with a few hits on the topsides of *Scharnhorst* and *Gneisenau*.

At 7.14 p.m. *Monmouth*, after being hit several times, sheered off to starboard, and *Glasgow*, which continued to follow in the wake of *Good Hope*, had to ease down to avoid masking *Monmouth's* fire. Firing was not at its hottest ; the enemy had the range perfectly and all their salvoes straddled our lines. The scene ahead was appalling and absorbed the attention of those not actively engaged in directing our fire far more than the enemy's scarcely distinguishable line.

Good Hope and *Monmouth* were now on either bow of *Glasgow*, and the smoke from their funnels was reddened by the dull glare of the deck-fires below. On the far side the " overs " showed high white splashes against the darkening sky, and the columns of water thrown up by the " shorts " were yellowed by the discharges from our guns. Frequently either ship flashed into a vivid orange as a lyddite shell detonated against her upperworks.

Ears had become deafened by the roar of our guns and almost insensible to the shriek of fragments flying overhead from the shells which burst short. The enemy's ships were no longer visible, and the gunlayers, when the motion of the ship allowed them, could aim only through the zone of splashes between the lines at the flashes of the enemy's guns.

Both *Good Hope* and *Monmouth*, under the sustained fire of their opponents, were now obviously in distress.

Monmouth again yawed off to starboard, burning furiously and heeling slightly, and we had again to reduce speed to avoid entering the hail of projectiles meant for her.

Good Hope, after three-quarters of an hour in action, was keeping up a desultory firing from only a few of her guns. The fires on board were increasing their brilliance, and soon she dropped back more on our port bow and towards the enemy. At 7.50 p.m. there was a terrific explosion on board between her mainmast and her aftermost funnel, and the gush of flames, reaching a height of over 200 feet, lighted up a cloud of debris that was flung still higher in the air.

Those that lived through the explosion must undoubtedly have been stunned ; her fire then ceased, as did also that of *Scharnhorst* upon her, and she lay between the lines, a low black hull, gutted of her upperworks, and only lighted by a dull red glare which shortly disappeared. Although no one on board *Glasgow* actually saw her founder, she could not have survived such a shock many minutes.

Scharnhorst now began firing on *Monmouth*, and *Gneisenau* directed her fire upon *Glasgow*, which had been from the start under a rain of shells from *Leipzig* and *Dresden* and had been firing at *Leipzig* in return. This latter ship suddenly ceased fire, shortly before the explosion in *Good Hope*, and dropping back, her place was taken by *Dresden*, but *Leipzig* was soon able to rejoin the line as fourth ship.

Glasgow meanwhile had been shifting her fire to *Gneisenau*, and we undoubtedly got one hit at least with our fore 6-inch gun on her afterpart, causing a slight fire.

Scharnhorst and *Gneisenau* both had had small fires at intervals, but not so serious as those in our leading ships.

The rising moon, shining fitfully through the clouds, gave us an occasional glimpse of the enemy ships, and fire was shifted continually to any ship thus shown up. Firing had now ceased in *Monmouth* and the enemy were firing only at our flashes, so that every shot from *Glasgow's* guns drew three replies, and at 8.5 p.m. *Glasgow* also ceased fire.

Monmouth now turned away from the line to starboard, badly down by the bows, listed to port and with the glow of her ignited interior brightening the port-holes below her quarter-deck. *Glasgow* closed to her port quarter and enquired by flashing lamp, " Are you all right ? " and received in reply " I want to get stern to sea. I am making water badly forward." She still continued to turn and was now heading north-east. The enemy, thinking no doubt that we had continued on our course longer than we did, now realized that we had turned, and the four ships approached in line abreast. Some observers state that a fifth cruiser, *Nürnberg*, was by then in their line, but of this we could not be certain. *Monmouth* was asked at 8.20 p.m., " Can you steer N.W. ?   The enemy are following us astern," to which she gave no answer.

The moon was now clear of the clouds, and it was obvious that *Monmouth* could neither fight nor fly ; so our Captain had to decide whether to share her fate, without being able to render any adequate assistance, or to attempt to escape the enemy.   We had maintained our place in the line for over an hour, under fire from two ships, and although we had been struck several times, we had sustained no vital injury.

It was essential that there should be a survivor of the action to turn *Canopus*, which was hurrying at her best speed to join up, and if surprised alone by four or five ships, however gallantly she fought, must have finally shared the fate of the other ships.

Monmouth was therefore reluctantly left, and when last seen, was bravely facing the oncoming enemy.   *Glasgow* then increased to full speed and soon left the enemy astern, losing sight of them about 8.50 p.m.   Half an hour later, a searchlight flickered below the horizon, as though searching for us, and seventy-five flashes of the firing against *Monmouth* were counted, and then silence !

We worked gradually round to a southward course and managed to do 24 knots against a head sea, reducing later to 20 knots and running for the Magellan Straits before the enemy could intercept us there.   Throughout the action the enemy had been jamming ceaselessly all W/T communication and we had been unable to get any messages through ; but as we drew farther away, their jamming had less effect and we succeeded in turning *Canopus*.

Pay. Com. Lloyd Hurst, R.N.

A MIDSHIPMAN'S NARRATIVE

8th Dec.   At 9.50 we had action sounded off and went to quarters. We got everything ready, guns loaded, etc.   At about eleven a " stand easy " was sounded off, and we had an opportunity to see what was going on.   About noon, the right-hand ship of the line, the *Nürnberg*, came round across the line to the left (to us), or front (to them), to the *Scharnhorst*.   We could not make out the reason for this, but think it must have been for orders from von Spee.   At about one o'clock the battle-cruisers opened fire on the enemy with their twelve-inch. The range was about 18,000 to 20,000 yards (eleven or twelve miles). They fired first on the *Nürnberg*, and found the range with their third salvo. The *Nürnberg* caught fire and went away to the (our) right again, in the rear of the German squadron. She then managed to get the fire under. At about two o'clock the land observation station signalled the presence of colliers on the other side of the island. We suspected armed liners to be present, and sent the *Bristol* and *Macedonia*, our rear ships, to deal with them. It is believed that an armed liner was present, but escaped before the arrival of the *Bristol* and *Macedonia*. The colliers were sunk. When the enemy saw the battle-cruisers they had the surprise of their lives. Survivors say that they had no idea they were there. The light cruisers made off to the right (their rear). The *Glasgow*, *Kent*, and *Cornwall* went in pursuit. All this time the enemy was on the starboard bow. At one o'clock we again went to action stations, but could not get in range. The enemy's armoured cruisers, in spite of the very heavy odds against them, fired magnificently, and hit both the battle-cruisers, causing fires. At two o'clock both sides drew off to repair damages. We had another stand easy. By this time the light cruisers and their pursuers were out of sight on the starboard beam. We went to quarters again at three o'clock, and again engaged the enemy. The battle-cruisers were hitting the flagship *Scharnhorst* well. We closed in on her and reduced the range to ten thousand yards. Her third funnel was shot away about four o'clock. She soon had a heavy list to port, and the *Gneisenau* took her place. B. turret put the finishing touch to her, hitting her aft. At 4.16 the *Scharnhorst* sank. She had fought magnificently to the last against great odds. We continued firing at the *Gneisenau*, and it was splendid to see the way they fought three big ships. Several shells passed near and over us, but we were not hit at all. (A sea has just come into the gun-room splashing all over the letter. Please excuse this.) At about a quarter to six one of her funnels went, and she got a heavy list to starboard. One by one her guns were knocked out, but she continued firing to the last and went down at 6.2 blazing. A pall of smoke hung over the spot where she sank. We lowered what boats we had (two small cutters and one whaler) as fast as we could. I went away in the third cutter. It was slightly rough and very cold. It was an hour before the ship had got to the scene of the sinking and had lowered her boats. We saved about a hundred and fifty. It was horrible, so I will say no more. I got one officer and about sixteen men into my boat. There were none left struggling in the water when we returned. All the *Scharnhorst's* were killed or went down with their ship. One of the officers saved was a first cousin of our admiral's (Stoddart). He is a strong chap and quite a good fellow. He had an extraordinary experience. Half the *Gneisenau's* men were killed by shell fire alone. He was in an 8·2 turret as second torpedo officer. The turret was knocked out and he was the sole survivor. He then went to a casemate gun, which was also knocked out and practically all the crew killed. He went to a third (another casemate), which was also knocked out, and he was again practically the sole survivor. He went to another gun and the ship was then sunk. He remained in icy water for nearly one and a quarter hours, and was picked up by one of our cutters. He was rather dazed, but cool and collected in the boat. After lying shivering in the bottom of a cutter for half an hour he was hauled up by a bowline into one of his enemy's ships. When he got on board he said, " I believe I have a first cousin in one of your ships. His name is Stoddart." Then to find him as admiral in the ship that picked him up ! He went into the admiral's quarters, and is now none the worse for his experience.

Lieut.-Com. A. C. Jelf.

NARRATIVE OF THE CAPTAIN OF S.M.S. " GNEISENAU "

8th Dec. Towards three o'clock in the afternoon the enemy made another attempt to get out of the way of the wind, and wheeled round to the larboard. If we had continued on our course, the result would have been a circular battle, which would have robbed us of the advantage of our position. Count Spee, therefore, imitated the evolution of the enemy and a short time afterwards reversed to larboard, so that both lines again confronted each other on a south-westerly course. The targets were then in reverse positions ; the *Gneisenau* facing the flagship and the *Scharnhorst* facing the second battle-cruiser.

As we passed the *Scharnhorst* during this movement, we noticed that she lay deeper than usual and heeled slightly to the larboard. There was a large hole in the fore end and a similar one in the quarter-deck. Her funnels had been reversed, smoke was rising from the ship and flames were visible in the interior through shell-holes and port-holes. But her guns thundered incessantly; the starboard batteries now came into action and brought fresh force into the fray. But it looked as if her fate were sealed. She moved more slowly in the water and suffered considerably under the hail of enemy shells. The Admiral must have felt that his ship was nearing her end. Just as he had previously sacrificed his armoured cruisers to save his light cruisers, so he purposed to sacrifice the *Scharnhorst* to save the *Gneisenau*. Determined to get the last ounce out of his resources and to fight as long as he could float, and in this way facilitate the escape of our ship, he swung round to the enemy on the starboard, in the hope of damaging him by firing torpedoes ! A grave but splendid decision ! In staking his own person, Admiral Spee repaid his squadron a hundredfold the absolute confidence which the squadron had always placed in him, even when in ignorance of his plans. We again passed by the *Scharnhorst*. The water had now risen to the fore upper deck. Fires were raging fore and aft, but the Admiral's flag floated proudly from the after-mast and the gaff. The *Scharnhorst* gradually heeled over to larboard, and her bows became more and more submerged. Her fore turret was about $6\frac{1}{2}$ feet above the water when it fired its last shot, then—the screws revolved in the air and the ship swiftly slid head first into the abyss, a few thousand yards behind us. A thick cloud of smoke, produced by the boilers and the guns, spurted above her grave as high as our masts. It seemed to be telling us : " *Scharnhorst* awaits *Gneisenau*." A feeling of utter loneliness, as if one had lost his best friend, came over everybody who had witnessed the end, and the same feeling gripped me when, in reply to my enquiry from the central station, " What is the *Scharnhorst* doing ? " the answer came from the bridge : " She is sinking."—" She is sinking," softly repeated the boatswain's mate at my side. Not " she seems to have sunk," or " she has perhaps sunk," but the stark fact, advised in three precise words, which left no room for hope. In our narrow compartment not a word was said. Each of us could read in the eyes of the others how this news affected them, but each continued doing his duty as before, with a stronger renunciation of life. " Three-quarters to starboard," ordered the Commander. He could not accept the Admiral's heroic sacrifice, because we had already suffered too much ourselves. He therefore made towards the enemy, in order to decrease the distance and improve the chances of our guns.

Henceforward we had against us two battle-cruisers, as well as a third adversary, which announced its arrival with clamour and hooting; it was an armoured-cruiser of the *Hampshire* type, and it fired 7·4 inch shells into us from behind, as if the other two had not been sufficient. One of the big cruisers separated from her sister and after describing wide circles got on our flank. One after another our starboard guns were put out of action. The armour-plate of the 9-inch casemate was pierced, and when the smoke had cleared away, the men were all found dead and the gun out of action. Another shell exploded on the upper deck just above the bed of the 8-inch fore gun; it swept the men away as if they had been bundles of clothes; hurling some of them into the 6-inch casement below, where it also killed nearly all the men at one blow. The battery chief and his young lieutenant, who were both near the spot where the shell exploded, escaped death by a miracle. Wounded and covered with blood, the former was hurled under a heap of corpses and was brought to consciousness by streams of cold water. What he saw around him is too horrible to be described.

Our ship's resistance capacity was slowly diminishing, as I ascertained from an inspection of the lower compartments which I made at this time. Debris and corpses were accumulating, icy water dripped in one place and in another gushed in streams through panels and shell-holes, extinguishing fires and drenching the men to the bone. Wherever it was possible to do so, efforts were made to man guns. Appeal was made to the reservists to make good the losses; ammunition was passed from hand to hand when wagons were lacking. At this moment, the *Gneisenau*, whose damaged engines were no longer capable of much speed, began to turn slowly over on her starboard, owing to a shattered helm caused by the fire from the rear. Thick smoke clung to the ship and prevented us from seeing the enemy flagship. But we could see the others, and as many of our larboard guns as could fire at all were trained upon them, until these guns in their turn were silenced. The after turret had long been jammed; only the fore turret remaining intact and continuing to fire all alone as long as its ammunition lasted. But the ammunition was beginning to give out, and to fetch supplies from other batteries through shattered gangways was a dangerous and protracted undertaking. So silence fell upon the ship, for the enemy likewise ceased firing, probably thinking that we were vanquished. Again the forecastle flashed angrily ; the last shot they were able to charge left the fore-turret and, as we were later to learn, buried itself deeply in the hull of the *Invincible*. The enemy retorted in kind, his shell hit the dressing-station and smashed the fore bulwark. The distance having now become very close, every shot must tell, for the hounds having run the fox to earth were now approaching cautiously to finish him off. The cannonade gradually died down, the bloody work was done ; it was now up to us not to let the floating ship fall into the enemy's hands and to preserve as many survivors as possible for the Fatherland. The crew were ordered to go on deck and provide themselves with lifebuoys. The men left their stations in perfect order and the wounded comrades were carried above. Hardly any staircases and ladders were left, but the sheet-iron crumpled up in numerous places offered a support sufficient for climbing on deck through the breaches.

I wanted to be the last to leave the central station, but the second torpedo officer remained there behind me, explaining to me that it had not yet been reported to him that all his men had received instructions to evacuate the torpedo rooms. Loyalty of officers and men, even in the foundering ship ! It goes without saying in the navy, but it is fine to see it in operation. I therefore left the officer behind me, telling him to follow me as quickly as possible, and climbed into daylight through the dark and narrow shaft. The blockhouse and the bridge were intact, the helmsmen and the sentries were in full muster at their stations, awaiting fresh orders. But a glance over the ship, which was heeled over, revealed what had happened above. The fore-funnel was bent towards the starboard ; the other three showed holes, blotches and red stains where the grey paint had peeled off. The wireless rod had slid down the mast as far as the truck and torn the flag to ribbons. The battle flag on the fore-mast had been shot away, but the black balls were still just under the yard in the position for " Full speed ahead." Broken tackle hung from the rigging, loose flag cords fluttered in the slight breeze. The shattered guns of the light artillery pointed their muzzles in the air and shrapnel lay all about. Through gaping holes in the deck and the bulwarks men were climbing out of the ship, coal-blackened from bunkers and fire-boxes, inflamed by the battle as if they had come from the guns, but all quiet and efficient as if they were parading. Some officers stood in the shattered boats, distributing buoys and spars, others at the railing supervised the distribution of hammocks. The men scrambled forward as best they could, as the ship was being slowly submerged, in an endeavour to reach the highest side of her, whence they could climb down to the corbelling and be ready to leave the ship. The English were approaching from three different sides. Many fists were shaken at them from the crowd of men, whose anger found vent in vigorous sailors' curses. The Commander, who with habitual calmness had given his clear orders to the last, gave three cheers for " His Majesty the Emperor " and for " Our good and brave *Gneisenau !* " and began to make preparations for sinking our ship. Our crew, who had really performed prodigies of valour and endurance, joined in with enthusiasm, and " *Deutschland, Deutschland über Alles,*" rang out in stentorian tones over the ship, and afterwards the song of the black, white and red flag, which, all tattered and torn, still floated from the mainmast and gaff.

Capt. Pochhammer.

CHRISTMAS

25th Dec. At 8.30 a.m. I was looking out, and saw four Germans leave their trenches and come towards us; I told two of my men to go and meet them, *unarmed* (as the Germans were unarmed), and to see that they did not pass the half-way line. We were 350–400 yards apart at this point. My fellows were not very keen, not knowing what was up, so I went out alone, and met Barry, one of our ensigns, also coming out from another part of the line. By the time we got to them, they were three quarters of the way over, and much too near our barbed wire, so I moved them back. They were three private soldiers and a stretcher-bearer, and their spokesman started off by saying that he thought it only right to come over and wish us a happy Christmas, and trusted us implicitly to keep the truce. He came from Suffolk, where he had left his best girl and a 3½ h.p. motor-bike ! He told me that he could not get a letter to the girl, and wanted to send one through me. I made him write out a post card in front of me, in English, and I sent it off that night. I told him that she probably would not be a bit keen to see him again. We then entered on a long discussion on every sort of thing. I was dressed in an old stocking-cap and a man's overcoat, and they took me for a corporal, a thing which I did not discourage, as I had an eye to going as near their lines as possible. I asked them what orders they had from their officers as to coming over to us, and they said *none*; they had just come over out of goodwill. . . .

I kept it up for half an hour, and then escorted them back as far as their barbed wire, having a jolly good look round all the time, and picking up various little bits of information which I had not had an opportunity of doing under fire ! I left instructions with them that if any of them came out later they must not come over the half-way line, and appointed a ditch as the meeting-place. We parted after an exchange of Albany cigarettes and German cigars, and I went straight to H.-qrs. to report.

On my return at 10 a.m. I was surprised to hear a hell of a din going on, and not a single man left in my trenches; they were completely denuded (against my orders), and nothing lived! I heard strains of *Tipperary* floating down the breeze, swiftly followed by a tremendous burst of *Deutschland über Alles*, and as I got to my own Coy. H.-qrs. dug-out, I saw, to my amazement, not only a crowd of about 150 British and Germans at the half-way house which I had appointed opposite my lines, but six or seven such crowds, all the way down our lines, extending towards the 8th Division on our right. I bustled out and asked if there were any German officers in my crowd, and the noise died down (as this time I was myself in my own cap and badges of rank).

I found two, but had to talk to them through an interpreter, as they could neither talk English nor French. . . . I explained to them that strict orders must be maintained as to meeting half-way, and everyone unarmed; and we both agreed not to fire until the other did, thereby creating a complete deadlock and armistice (if strictly observed). . . .

Meanwhile Scots and Huns were fraternizing in the most genuine possible manner. Every sort of souvenir was exchanged, addresses given and received, photos of families shown, etc. One of our fellows offered a German a cigarette; the German said, " Virginian ? " Our fellow said, " Aye, straight-cut " : the German said, " No thanks, I only smoke Turkish ! " (Sort of 10/- a 100 me !) It gave us all a good laugh.

A German N.C.O. with the Iron Cross—gained, he told me, for conspicuous skill in sniping—started his fellows off on some marching tune. When they had done I set the note for " *The Boys of Bonnie Scotland, where the heather and the bluebells grow,*" and so we went on, singing everything from " *Good King Wenceslaus* " down to the ordinary Tommies' song, and ended up with " *Auld Lang Syne,*" which we all, English, Scots, Irish, Prussians, Wurtembergers, etc., joined in. It was absolutely astounding, and if I had seen it on a cinematograph film I should have sworn that it was faked ! . . .

Just after we had finished " *Auld Lang Syne* " an old hare started up, and seeing so many of us about in an unwonted spot—did not know which way to go. I gave one loud " View Holloa," and one and all, British and Germans, rushed about giving chase, slipping up on the frozen plough, falling about, and after a hot two minutes we killed in the open, a German and one of our fellows falling together heavily upon the completely baffled hare. Shortly afterwards we saw four more hares, and killed one again ; both were good heavy weight and had evidently been out between the two rows of trenches for the last two months, well-fed on the cabbage patches, etc., many of which are untouched on the " no-man's land." The enemy kept one and we kept the other. It was now 11.30 a.m. and at this moment George Paynter arrived on the scene, with a hearty " Well, my lads, a Merry Christmas to you ! This is d——d comic, isn't it ? " . . . George told them that he thought it only right that we should show that we could desist from hostilities on a day which was so important in both countries ; and he then said, " Well, my boys, I've brought you over something to celebrate this funny show with," and he produced from his pocket a large bottle of rum (not ration rum, but the proper stuff). One large shout went up, and the nasty little spokesman uncorked it, and in a heavy ceremonious manner, drank our healths, in the name of his " camaraden " ; the bottle was then passed on and polished off before you could say knife. . . .

During the afternoon the same extraordinary scene was enacted between the lines, and one of the enemy told me that he was long-ing to get back to London : I assured him that " So was I." He said that he was sick of the war, and I told him that when the truce was ended, any of his friends would be welcome in our trenches, and would be well-received, fed, and given a free passage to the Isle of Man ! Another coursing meeting took place, with no result, and at 4.30 p.m. we agreed to keep in our respective trenches, and told them that the truce was ended. . . .

The Border Regiment were occupying this section on Christmas Day, and Giles Loder, our Adjutant, went down there with a party that morning on hearing of the friendly demonstrations in front of my Coy., to see if he could come to an agreement about our dead, who were still lying out between the trenches. The trenches are so close at this point, that of course each side had to be far stricter. Well, he found an extremely pleasant and superior stamp of German officer, who arranged to bring all our dead to the half-way line. We took them over there, and buried 29 exactly half-way between the two lines. Giles collected all personal effects, pay-books and iden-tity discs, but was stopped by the Germans when he told some men to bring in the rifles ; all rifles lying on their side of the half-way line they kept carefully ! . . .

They apparently treated our prisoners well, and did all they could for our wounded. This officer kept on pointing to our dead and saying, " *Les braves, c'est bien dommage.*"

When George heard of it he went down to that section and talked to the nice officer and gave him a scarf. That same evening a German orderly came to the half-way line, and brought a pair of warm, woolly gloves as a present in return for George.

Captain Sir Edward Hulse, Bart. (2nd Scots Guards).

THE NEW YEAR

NEW YEAR'S RESOLUTION BY THE ROYAL HOUSEHOLD

31*st Dec.* I heard from Lord Steward that after consultation with Stamfordham, he was to drop from his List of Warrant Holders all Holders residing in Germany and Austria.

Lord Sandhurst.

THE FIRST FOOT IN THE HOUSE

31*st Dec.* I had warned all my sentries as usual and had succeeded in getting about three-quarters of an hour's sleep when the platoon Sergeant of No. 12 burst in and informed me most laconically, "German to see you, sir!"

I struck a light and tumbled out, and heard a voice outside saying, "Offizier? Hauptmann?" and found a little fellow, fairly clean and fairly superior to the average German private, being well hustled and pushed between two fixed bayonets. The minute he saw me he came up, saluted, covered in smiles and awfully pleased with himself, said "Nach London? Nach London?" I replied, "No, my lad, Nach the Isle of Man," on which the escort burst into guffaws. . . . I went rapidly through his pockets which were bulging on every side, and found no papers or anything of value, but an incredible amount of every kind of food and comestibles. He had come fully provided for the journey and was annoyingly pleased with himself.

Capt. Sir Edward Hulse, Bart. (Scots Guards).

VOICES—1914-15

CAVALRY SONG

DRÜBEN am Wiesenrand,
hocken zwei Dohlen—
Fall' ich am Donaustrand?
Sterb' ich in Polen?
Was liegt daran?
Eh' sie meine Seele holen,
kämpf ich als Reitersmann.
. . . .

Drüben im Abendrot
fliegen zwei Krähen—
Wann kommt der Schnitter Tod,
um uns zu mähen?
Es ist nicht schad'!
Seh' ich nur unsere Fahnen wehen
auf Belgerad!

Hugo Zuckermann.

Out on the meadow's edge
two daws are perching—
Shall I fall on Danube's bank?
Lie slain in Poland?
What does it matter?
If I fight as a horseman
Ere they fetch my soul away.

Out in the sunset's glow
two crows are flying—

When will come Reaper Death
through our ranks scything ?
Nought to be sorry for
If I but see our flag
O'er Belgrade flying !

THE BRITISH SOLDIER

15th Aug. We entrain to-day at 1 p.m. and hope to reach France to-night. We leave very quietly as if marching to manœuvres, but a more magnificent regiment never moved out of barracks for war. Everyone is full of enthusiasm. . . . So far I have been the luckiest man alive. I have had the happiest possible life, and have always been working for war, and have just got into the biggest in the prime of life for a soldier.

Capt. Francis Grenfell, V.C.

THE GERMAN VOLUNTEER

Our march to the station was a gripping and uplifting experience ! Such a march is hallowed by its background of significance and danger. Both those who were leaving and those who remained behind were beset by the same thoughts and feelings. It seemed as if one lived through as much in that hour as ordinarily in months and years. Such enthusiasm !—the whole battalion with helmets and tunics decked with flowers—handkerchiefs waving untiringly— cheers on every side—and over and over again the ever fresh and wonderful reassurance from the soldiers : *fest steht und treu die Wacht am Rhein !* The hour is one such as seldom strikes in the life of a nation, and it is so marvellous and moving as to be in itself sufficient compensation for many sufferings and sacrifices.

Walter Limmer.

SACRIFICE TO THE PAST

17th September, 1914. (*Before leaving for his regiment.*) So I will end this book. All my longing and all my desire I poured out to the gods yesterday, in a prayer prouder and humbler than any before. I am setting out in great joy and expectation, not in search of adventure and the spurious excitement of unknown experiences, but in the firm belief and hope that I shall become manly and firm, fully developed, broadminded, full of power and strength, in readiness for the great life which will be waiting for me later on.

That on my return from battle and victory, honourably endured, I may find my parents with many hopes fulfilled and happy in new work, that I may find myself again, well and strong and ready for anything the world may offer, that I may find my country again, grown prouder and yet more modest, stronger and more courageous, pregnant with the rising form of the new era—in spite of the conflicts and the raging storms of the yet unredeemed future ; that I may play my part in helping to create this new era in the spirit of the still sleeping godhead ; this, oh, ye ruling powers, I hope for, I implore, nay I demand, of you.

Otto Braun (aged 17).

1915

SEASIDE TOWN

Jany. We knocked at one of the sea-front boarding-houses. The woman who opened to us was weary and dishevelled as though she had spent the night out in the storm. She gazed at us, startled and hostile, when we asked for a lodging. When we urged that we had come from London and understood she was accustomed to let, she hesitated suspiciously, then reluctantly explained that she had promised to hold herself in readiness to receive any shipwrecked seamen who might be saved from drowning. " I've been up with them all night—some of 'em's gone, some of 'em's still here. We have to put 'em in hot blankets as soon as they're carried in."

" But there won't be another wreck to-night ! " we essayed, rather feebly, to rally her.

" There were three lots brought in here yesterday, and two the day before," she answered mournfully, and pointed to the many craft out in the bay, telling us they were all minesweepers engaged in the perilous work of clearing away explosive mines laid by the German warships and daily causing the loss of many vessels.

This was an aspect of the German visit not recorded in the Press. In our ignorance of war, we heard her with shocked surprise.

She agreed at last that we should stay with her, on condition that we would leave at once if another party of shipwrecked mariners were brought in. Barely an hour had passed when her daughter flung open our door :

" Another boat's blown up ! You'll have to go ! "

. . . He told us, as others in the town had done, that the German battleships came so close to the shore that the people (believing them British) feared they would run aground. He was at the window when the firing began, and he called to his wife : "It's no good, lass, the Germans have come !"

Then he told her to go next door and help their neighbour to pacify her children. She was running to the back door, but he locked it and said : " I'm an Englishman and a Yorkshireman, and they'll not make us go the back way !" He walked to the end of the terrace and stood facing the battleships. He was not hit, but he showed us a big bit of shell which had fallen beside him. Believing, like everyone else, that the Germans intended landing, he looked around for our soldiers. They were nowhere to be seen. After the bombardment ceased they got into their trenches and sang a hymn. "They were no better than wooden soldiers !" he cried indignantly. His wife reproved him, with a timid glance at us : " What use would it have been for our British soldiers to come out to be killed ? "

Turning to the new town, we found much damage, and especially in the neighbourhood of the wireless station. A shell had fallen and burst before a lofty building, boring a great hole in the ground ; and almost to the roof, the walls were splashed with mud thrown up by the impact and scarred by shrapnel. In a small house with a side wall down, and two great holes in front, a mother and all her children had been killed—only her husband was left to mourn them. Three out of four rooms had been wrecked in a house near by, and within a stone's-throw the shattering of a classic portico had killed the postman and the housemaid at the front door. No street here had escaped ; in some streets house after house was conspicuously battered ; in others it seemed that only the windows had been broken—till from another angle one saw roofs broken in and walls with gaping holes.

Returning to our lodging we learnt that yet another boat had been blown up. It was bitterly cold ; the wind howled fiercely. We huddled by the fire, saddened and chilled. A girl ran past the window sobbing and wailing. A few minutes later she passed again. As I heard her coming a third time I went out to her, and saw that she was about sixteen years of age, hatless and poorly dressed. In abandonment of grief, she flung herself now against the wall, now leaned her head for a moment upon a window-sill, crying : " Dad ! Dad ! Oh, Dad !" As I came up with her two women met her. They knew her and understood what she muttered between her sobs

better than I.   They told me that her father was on one of the minesweepers out in the bay.   She shrank into trembling reserve and,
faltering nervously that she must go to her mother, fled from us in
the dusk.

Sylvia Pankhurst.

KITCHENER'S ARMY

Who of all those who were in camp at that time, and still are alive, will not remember until he dies the second boyhood that he had in the late frosts and then in the swiftly filling and bursting spring and early summer of 1915? The awakening bird-notes of Réveille at dawn, the two-mile run through auroral mists breaking over a still inviolate England, the men's smoking breath and the swish of their feet brushing the dew from the tips of the June grass and printing their track of darker green on the pearly-grey turf; the long, intent morning parades under the gummy shine of chestnut buds in the deepening meadows; the peace of the tranquil hours on guard at some sequestered post, alone with the sylvester midnight, the wheeling stars and the quiet breathing of the earth in its sleep, when time, to the sentry's sense, fleets on unexpectedly fast and life seems much too short because day has slipped into day without the night-long sleeper's false sense of a pause; and then jocund days of marching and digging trenches in the sun; the silly little songs on the road that seemed, then, to have tunes most human, pretty, and jolly; the dinners of haversack rations you ate as you sat on the road-makers' heaps of chopped stones or lay back among buttercups.

When you think of the youth that you have lost, the times when it seems to you now that life was most poignantly good may not be the ones when everything seemed at the time to go well with your plans, and the world, as they say, to be at your feet; rather some few unaccountable moments when nothing took place that was out of the way and yet some word of a friend's, or a look on the face of the sky, the taste of a glass of spring water, the plash of laughter and oars heard across midsummer meadows at night raised the soul of enjoyment within you to strangely higher powers of itself. That spirit bloweth and is still: it will not rise for our whistling nor keep a time-table; no wine that we know can give us anything more than a fugitive caricature of its ecstasies. When it has blown free we remember it always, and know, without proof, that while the rapture was there we were not drunk, but wise ; that for a moment some intervening darkness had thinned and we were seeing further than we can see now into the heart of life.

C. E. Montague.

ARMENTIÈRES

In December, 1914, one mill started work again. Others followed. Then a new type of combat in the history of war began ; the cannon against the factory, the gunner against the workman. In March, 1915, 16 factories were at work with a personnel of 2,900. To the no-man's-land between the industrious town and the front line came factory hands, when their day's work was over, to dig in their gardens. They could hear the rifle shots from the trenches two thousand yards away. The population adapted itself to living in the shadow of death as if to bad weather. They hoped the German batteries would soon be pushed back. The hands discussed it over their usual mug of beer, the masters over a hand at bridge.

They sleep in the cellars. The night, sometimes roaring with explosions, glitters with constellations of flares. The supply columns start at the blackest hour of night, when one can see only the length of one's arm between the walls of the houses. Relieving troops march by whistling but invisible. Then a vast silence falls on the streets, creeping out from the shadows in which man has ceased from killing. In the town where lights and movement are forbidden, there is the nothingness of a dead planet. Striking across this vast peace, as Massacre draws its breath, a machine-gun starts once more to stutter in the obstinate tones of a tongue searching for a word impossible to pronounce. At daylight, the workers appear in the streets of this town at war. They meet lines of soldiers, muddy from their night's duty in the wet, shell-torn earth. They call good day and good luck greeting each other by name, for the soldier is billetted on the worker. They cling to the same values ; the decency of the job, to do what the moment bids ; hold your trench, go to your mill. " Time's up," says the soldier. " *Il est temps*," says the workman ; and he goes past the burnt-out houses of the rue des Murets and the rue d'Ypres, for beyond lie the factories, whose activity can only be recognized by their smoke. No longer do the whistles call ; and the staff comes on time. This town whose mornings once echoed with summonses to work, to-day labours in secret. Only the rumble of guns here has its freedom. It echoes while women and children clear away the ruins to get to their work. . . .

The linen mill of Charles Jeanson is to-day the nearest one at work to the firing line. In front, hidden by the wall of the yard, an English battery replies to the German. The flax carts as they are pushed across the yard crush bits of broken glass, and tip up over fragments of shell. There is damage, but no disorder. The book-keeper day by day sticks to his books. These folk do not think about shells, they think about work. Bare-armed girls have stuck flowers on the frames they work at. The factory has its sentry just like the trenches. He hears the gun-fire, the whisper of the shell, and says : " That one's over ; it wasn't meant for us." He stands on tip-toe to see whereabouts in the town it has fallen. If the explosions draw nearer, the sentry warns the engineer who shuts off the steam of the driving power. The staff wrapped up in the concentration and clatter of the work only learn of the danger because the machines stop. They go down to the basement. When they come up again, the stink of explosive fills the factory. The workers say that after a shell they need a drink, because the nitrous gases make the throat raw. It is getting more difficult to keep a good look-out. The English military authorities have forbidden climbing on the roofs. Eyes must be kept fixed on the belfry of St. Charles's church close by. When the black smoke of the German shells breaks out round it, it is time to knock off and smoke one's pipe in the cellar. " If it wasn't for that tower," say the workers, " we'd be left in peace." The Germans often aim at it, miss it and hit the factory : and that means hours lost.

On Wednesday, 30th June, 1915, at 12.45, six spinners were going along together for the one-o'clock shift. Shells were falling on the road they must take. No one told them that they ought to be prudent and take cover in a cellar. It was the time to push on. They trudged on along their usual way in the middle of the explosions. Three hundred yards from the factory, a shell burst on them. Valentine Vandenbussche, aged 22, was killed outright. Her two sisters were wounded. Their three companions, who were not touched, became medical orderlies, and helped to pick them up. At the beginning of the shift, 550 out of 556 women were at their frames. Only

Valentine Vandenbussche, her two sisters and their three friends were missing. On the following Thursday, at 6.30 a.m., the three were back at the factory. . . .

This town has invented a heroism which no earlier war has known; industry in battle, with the workers at their job behind walls hit by bullets. The factory hears the battle, the soldier hears the spinning. There are two victories; to prevent the enemy breaking through, to prevent the industry dying. The German gunner dominates both bivouac and workshop, weapons and tools. The rattle of shuttles at 21 beats to the minute and the rattle of machine-guns accompany each other. The explosions of the neighbouring battery shake the wall on one side of which the n.c.o. shouts "Fire!" and on the other the foreman says to the spinner "Mend." The war goes on, the job goes on, one within the other. When they leave the factory at nightfall, the workers go back to their cellars to sleep. They never have enough candles or oil. Deprived of light, they say, to put heart into their children frightened by the explosions: "One's better off at home;" for those who have been evacuated write that they would rather endure the danger in their own country where they are known, than the life of refugees in places where there is no beer. Wine does not quench the thirst but makes you drunk; no one appreciates them and they have lost everything but what they can carry on their backs. . . .

As soon as the smoke of an engine appeared over the station, the Germans used to shoot it up. The hotel next door lost all its windows. The strong mirrors of the coffee-room which remained upright, are cracked by long winding, crooked fissures like sabre blades. The train service has had to be withdrawn to the sidings on the plain. The station-master alone remains at the station by the telephone. As he comes across the rails in front of the principal building, he sees the trucks which the Germans have derailed beneath the bridge at the next station, Perenchies.

The proprietress of the hotel is to-day less worried by the guns. She is five-and-twenty. Her husband took this house six months before the War began. But he has been called up, and so that she may run the house without being distracted from the business side, she has sent her child to the care of her relatives. Business is not so bad. The English n.c.o.'s have formed a club in the big dining-room. Every evening they come in from 6 to 8, start the mechanical

piano and drink their beer. They make an enormous equable noise ;
all shout the same words together. Then they drink copiously.
Their strong jaws close on the thick glasses and they empty them
in a couple of gulps.

The chairman announces the next singer. A heavy-handed man
pounds the piano. The proprietress and her two elderly servants
are sweating with supplying the orders of these big soldiers, each
one of whom wears his hair parted and has the back of his neck
close-cropped. We must do honour to her trade. If, at the mobilization, she had closed the hotel on which only a quarter of the pur-
chase price had been paid, she would have risked ruin. She had
carefully calculated her takings after the arrival and departure of the
frequent peace-time trains. She knew how many litres she must
sell at each blast of the engine whistle starting from the 4.58 a.m.
But the station clock has stopped at 11.33 on a day of which no
one can recall the date. The pavé in the square is checkered with
grass. There are no more profitable travellers thirsty with the
arrival or departure, but this army drinks heavily enough. . . .

Pierre Hamp.

ALLIED SONG

Après la guerre fini,
Tous les soldats partis,
Mademoiselle avec piccanini
Souvenir des Anglais.

GEMÜTLICHKEIT

PRISON CAMP AT WITTENBERG

THE arrival of the British medical officers at the camp came about in the following way. From the month of November, 1914, thirteen English doctors had been detained at Halle. They were none of them required for attendance upon their own men, and it is difficult to understand how, consistently with the Geneva Convention, their continued detention was justifiable. Indeed, in direct defiance of the provisions of that Convention, these doctors were treated as ordinary prisoners of war, and the Committee cannot resist the suspicion that they were deliberately detained by the German authorities so that they might be made available, if need be, for work of danger in relief of their own staff. Be that as it may, after three months' wrongful detention these doctors were, on the 10th February, 1915, informed that they were to be distributed amongst the other German camps, and particularly that six were required for the camp at Wittenberg. By arrangement amongst themselves the six sent there were Major Fry, Major Priestley, Captain Sutcliffe, Captain Field, Captain Vidal, and Captain—then Lieutenant—Lauder. No reason was given for the order that they should go to Wittenberg, and it was from the guard on the train that they first heard of typhus there.

On arrival at Wittenberg they were marched to the camp. They visited the different compounds. They were received in apathetic silence. The rooms were unlighted ; the men were aimlessly marching up and down ; some were lying on the floor, probably sickening for typhus. When they got into the open air again Major Fry broke down. The horror of it all was more than he could for the moment bear. Later in the evening Major Priestley and Captain Vidal were directed to go to two temporary hospitals outside the camp, Major Priestley to the Kronprinz Hospital, and Captain Vidal to the Elbarfin Hospital. There were no infectious diseases at either hospital, and the general conditions at each were satisfactory. These officers were kept there until the 7th March, 1915.

Of the four officers left on the 11th February at the camp itself, Captain Lauder alone survives, and the conditions as he describes them during the period between the 11th February and the 7th March are full of horror. The wonder is that any prisoner escaped infection.

Captain Lauder found, for instance, that while in the bungalows there was normally one mattress to three men, in the improvised hospital there were no mattresses at all. This, of course, was known throughout the camp, and in consequence there were many typhus patients scattered over the compounds who were determined not to come into the hospital if they could help it. In one compound alone Captain Lauder discovered fifty hidden cases of typhus. Further, when a patient was brought from the compound to the hospital, either the mattress on which he had lain was brought with him or it was left behind in his bungalow. If it was brought with him his former companions were left without anything to sleep on ; if it was left behind his still uninfected companions were left to sleep upon the infected mattress, and it was almost inevitable that they should catch the disease. Again, in the absence of stretchers, all the typhus cases had to be carried down to the hospital on the tables on which the men ate their food, and there was no possibility of washing these tables because, as above stated, there was practically no soap in the camp. Moreover, the German authorities at first refused to allow the whole of compound No. 8 to be used for typhus patients. They required that these should be mixed with other sufferers, a regulation for which it seems impossible to suggest any justification. The result simply was to spread the infection to those already afflicted in some other way.

During the first month the food ration for each patient was half a *petit pain* and half a cup of milk each day. The only soup to be got was from the camp kitchen, but that came up in a wooden tub without a cover, and it arrived at the hospital—so one of the prisoners says—full of dust and dirt. It was hopeless diet for patients in a fever. In truth the ration was not a ration at all, it was a pretence. It was not even possible to give the patients warm water with their milk.

The camp conditions were too much for each of the four medical officers who were left there ; two of them, Major Fry and Captain

Sutcliffe, very soon sickened, and they died of typhus about a month after their arrival. Captain Field was attacked later by the disease and also died. There is no doubt in the minds of the committee that the condition to which the camp authorities had reduced the camp and the prisoners they had abandoned was directly responsible for the deaths of these devoted men. Lieutenant Lauder was finally stricken with the disease on the 7th March, after having for three days with a temperature due to typhus stuck to his work, there being no one then to take his place. He alone of the officers attacked finally recovered. When convalescent he bravely resumed his duty.

On the 7th March Major Priestley and Captain Vidal were directed to return to the main camp. They were met there by Captain Field. Major Fry and Captain Sutcliffe were then dying. Lieutenant Lauder, as above explained, was in the early stages of typhus.

Two Russian medical generals were in command in the hospital. There were then about 1,000 cases of typhus in the camp, and fresh cases were coming in at the rate of about 50, and sometimes more, a day. There were at that time about 150 British cases.

The British sick were lying scattered amongst the French and the Russians, both in the compound No. 8 and in the other compounds of the camp. Being sometimes dressed in French, Belgian, or Russian uniforms, they were difficult to recognize. They were lying in their clothes on the floor, or on the straw mattresses above described. In the beginning there were no beds in compound No. 8 ; there were not even, as has been shown, mattresses for all. Major Priestley saw delirious men waving arms brown to the elbow with fæcal matter. The patients were alive with vermin ; in the half light he attempted to brush what he took to be an accumulation of dust from the folds of a patient's clothes, and he discovered it to be a moving mass of lice. In one room in compound No. 8 the patients lay so close to one another on the floor that he had to stand straddle-legged across them to examine them.

Captain Vidal's description is even more appalling. It was impossible, he says, to obtain bedpans for the British patients, and consequently in cases of delirium, and even in less serious cases, the state of the mattress was indescribable. Even such a thing as paper for sanitary purposes was almost unprocurable.

The difficulty in the way of obtaining sufficient drugs and dressings was for a long time extreme. Camphorated oil, Captain Lauder

says, could never at Wittenberg, contrary to his experience in other
German camps, be secured in adequate quantity, yet this was practically the only stimulant available.   Day after day a list of medical
requisites would be sent out, and only a third of the things requested
would be supplied.   Bed sores were common.   In several cases toes
or whole feet became gangrenous, and sufficient bandages were not
available to dress them.   One of the patients now returned to this
country.   Private Lutwyche of the 1st Battalion Royal Scots Fusiliers,
had in May to have one leg amputated below the knee, and in July
the other leg amputated at the same place, in both cases owing to
gangrene.   Had dressings at the proper time been available both
feet would in all probability have been saved.   And his case does not
stand alone.   The officers are quite satisfied that the *post*-typhus
gangrene, which was so common, was largely due to the fact that
for so many patients there were neither socks nor anything else to
keep their feet warm.

In the earlier stages of the epidemic there was practically no
hospital clothing available for the British prisoners.   There was only
a small sulphur chamber for disinfecting purposes.   When a patient's
outer clothing was taken off to be sent to the disinfector he had to
be left in his shirt, as no other clothing or shirts were supplied.   Each
patient brought his blankets from the camp with him, and as no
covering could be provided for him while disinfection was taking
place it was impossible adequately to disinfect his clothing unless he
was to be left naked.

As regards the washing of patients in hospital, this was entirely
out of the question.   Until a supply of soap was obtained by Captain
Vidal's efforts from England at a later date there was no soap forthcoming.   The only supply was a small quantity secured from the
officers' canteen, and that was kept for the very worst cases.

It was to Major Priestley's great powers of organization, the
devoted labours and strong personality of Captain Vidal and, after
his recovery, the splendid work of Captain Lauder, that gradual
improvement in the conditions was due.   An observation ward was
instituted in compound No. 8 and placed in charge of Captain Lauder.
Major Priestley took over the treatment of typhus in the hospital,
and Captain Vidal, in addition to other duties, was placed in charge
of the surgical ward.   Major Priestley at length obtained permission
to collect, and he did collect, all the British typhus patients in one

bungalow of that compound. He secured for his patients what bedding, hospital clothing, urinals, etc., he could as these filtered daily from the hands of the Germans outside into the storeroom. He arranged that the milk and the soup should arrive in special vessels before the bungalow ; he obtained for each patient about three cupfuls of milk per day, and for the convalescents a thin soup and some white rolls. Clothing, beds, and bedding, were gradually collected, so that the patients could at least be put into clean clothes, and their own were disinfected in a movable steam disinfector that after a time was working. As the cases decreased in number the appalling overcrowding of the hospital in the beginning at length disappeared.

In all this work Major Priestley, Captain Vidal, and Captain Lauder were splendidly supported by the many English prisoners who volunteered as nurses. Many of these devoted men caught the infection and died of the fever.

On one occasion only during the whole course of the epidemic did Dr. Aschenbach enter the hospital, or even the camp. His visit took place about four weeks after Major Priestley's arrival, and after some kind of order had been evolved. He came attired in a complete suit of protective clothing, including a mask and rubber gloves. His inspection was brief and rapid.

For his services in combating the epidemic, Dr. Aschenbach, the Committee understand, has been awarded the Iron Cross.

Some of the German guards outside the camp were infected by prisoners to whom, contrary to orders, they persisted in selling things. These men were placed by the Germans in a hospital outside the camp, and one of the German medical staff, an Alsatian as it happened, was sent to attend them. At a later stage in the outbreak this young man came to the hospital, but simply to take bacteriological specimens for research work at Magdeburg. He helped in no way.

With these exceptions no visit was paid to the camp during the whole outbreak by any member of the German Medical Service.

The dead were buried in a cemetery formed out of a part of the camp. The Germans sent in a certain number of coffins every day, into which the bodies of the dead were put and carried out by their comrades through a gate in the barbed wire. There was not sufficient room for burial of so many, and the coffins were piled one upon another, but the Committee do not think there was any special danger in the arrangement. What the prisoners found hardest to bear in this matter were the jeers with which the coffins were frequently greeted by the inhabitants of Wittenberg, who stood outside the wire and were permitted to insult their dead. . . .

The cruelty of the administration at Wittenberg Camp from the very commencement has become notorious. Savage dogs were habitually employed to terrorize the prisoners ; flogging with a rubber whip was frequent ; men were struck with little or no provocation, and were tied to posts with their arms above their heads for hours. Captain Lauder reports that many of these men went so far as to look upon the typhus, with all its horrors, as a godsend ; they preferred it to the presence of the German guards.

And the callousness during the outbreak even of so prominent an officer as Dr. Aschenbach is illustrated by an incident related by Captain Lauder. Shortly after their arrival at the camp, Major Fry, with Captain Lauder, was begging Dr. Aschenbach, standing outside the entanglements, for some medical requisite urgently required. One of his staff with Dr. Aschenbach was apparently favourably inclined towards the request, but it was curtly refused by Dr. Aschenbach, who turned away with the words " Schweine Engländer."

Parliamentary Paper (*Report on the Prison Camp*
at Wittenberg.)

THEY SAY

WHAT SAY THEY?

Mr. W. H. Anderson . . . the condition of the women and girls who are employed by Messrs. Armstrong and Whitworth at their Elswick works. The girls there work twelve hours per day with one and a half hours break for meals, Sundays as well. They are working two shifts at present and girls are working all night. They have been working three shifts, but the girls were half-dead and they found they had to stop it. Girls of 17 get 8 shillings a week, girls of 18, 9 shillings a week, girls of 19, 10 shillings a week, and girls of 20 11 shillings a week, and in addition to this there is a bonus which seems largely to be used for the purpose of speeding up the girls. The average wage is low, and the girls have to put in work at a very high rate of speed. The bonus rate is: Sundays, $4\frac{1}{2}d$. an hour, ordinary times, $3d$. an hour. Some of the girls say they have worked twenty hours at a stretch since the War broke out. Many times they have worked 95 hours a week. . . .

Hansard, March 15, 1915.

LET THEM SAY:

Rates of Dividend on Ordinary Capital.

Percentages—	1914.	1915.	1916.	1917.	1918.
Iron, Coal and Steel . .	6·3	6	12·1	14·9	13·4
Motor and Cycle . .	5·2	5·7	6·6	10·2	16·5
Rubber	5·7	5·7	18·7	13·2	5·9
	inc. Tea				
Shipping	4·3	4·6	10·5	16·4	17·9
Textiles . . .				24·5	24·5
Oil					33·8

From the annual reports of the " Economist."

THE SCHOOLBOY AND WAR

22nd Mar. For the benefit of future generations let me state how the War affects Harrow School. Yesterday a German aeroplane indulged in a little harmless bombdropping not many miles away. But to all intents and purposes the War might be non-existent. Though brothers and fathers are fighting, Harrovians behave as usual and eat as much as usual, if not more. Ned Hodge's brother is missing, but that does not prevent him from ragging Sam all day long. Men die and ships sink and hearts break, and the world rolls on the same as ever. To-night we had the time of our lives. Alister and I contrived an enormous and simply terrifying ghost and placed it near the door in his room. After lights out, Sam, Ned, Nick, Foley as well as Alister and myself hid ourselves under beds, tables, chairs and curtains. The fire was low. Then Wheeler came along. He *was* alarmed ! One by one we appeared after much ghostliness, and eventually we shut Wheeler up in the bed. . . . It was a very jolly day, and I hope things will go on in this way.

" *Twenty Years On,*" in " *Life and Letters.*"

NIGHT CLUB IN WAR TIME

HERE we all are reunited round a table at Murray's for our common pleasure, which is hers. Clarisse dominates us from her height: she has more brilliance than the women, more self-assurance than the men. The *maître d'hôtel* naturally gravitates to her. We group ourselves round her, happy to be in this comfortable cellar, this quilted catacomb, in which pleasure officiates. The women of this subterrain have their nails polished and their faces painted; and their armpits are for all to see. Couples are dancing, rolling round an imaginary axis, twisting the waltz like a straw-plait from which the music trickles down. The men of the subterrain have their arms in slings, their heads bandaged; the negro music worries their heads a little, takes them back to the ineffaceable memory of the trench where they were hit, of the first glass of water. The waiters, as they serve, stumble over the crutches lying along the floor.

There are, too, others, fatter, more florid, drinking Pommery out of cider bottles; for it is after ten o'clock—the neutrals. These are the Scandinavians, the Dutchmen and the Americans. They exchange understanding glances; and beneath the tablecloth offer two hundred thousand Mausers for immediate delivery on the high seas off Barcelona, or bring out of their hip pockets samples of all the uniform fabrics of the belligerents. With complete good humour they buy back rejected cargoes (after all, the Russians will take anything) and contracts in arrears. All the squalls of machine-gun fire which one day will be unloosed against mankind, emerge from here. Tom shouts with laughter at the sight: " Absolutely the last word," he says; " last word of the crucified." Then he holds out a shrapnel bullet, recently extracted from his head, to one of them: " If that's any use to you again . . . ?

Paul Morand.

DEBOUT LES MORTS !

AT the beginning of April, at the time of the big attacks on the Bois d'Ailly, I was ordered to make a diversion at the Bois Brulé . . . I was then an *adjutant* . . . No. 7 platoon, mine, with three others from different companies, was ordered to attack the German line. The fight was bitter ; we had many dead and wounded. All night long bombing scraps went on under torrents of rain, which soaked us to the skin. But we held on to the trench, and I felt an immense exultation. I was keyed up to an astonishing intensity of vitality, and a desire to laugh always in my mouth. Twice I was knocked over by trench-mortar shells, covered with earth and debris, and picked myself up laughing as if I'd seen a joke. Next morning we were relieved . . . and went back to the second line where we tried to sleep. At midday we were hastily roused. The Boche had just counter-attacked with bombs and trench mortars. They pushed us back ; and then there was a panic. Not only did they recapture their own front line, but even reached ours. Already men were hurrying down the communication trenches, shouting, " The Boches ! The Boches ! " I forced a passage through a crowd of fugitives, and while I elbowed my way through, I shouted, " No, no. The Boches aren't there. They've gone back. They've beat it," and that kind of thing which, blown from mouth to mouth, stopped the retirement a little. A few volunteers joined me and I rushed forward. My bombers sprayed the Boches, and they ran back. I climbed out of the French trench. I was as certain that I was as good as dead as I was of the sunlight. But what serenity was mine, the serenity of a man dying in a state of grace. . . .

Still throwing bombs, we reached the enemy trench. We got back our own bit, and I had a block of sandbags thrown up in the C.T. between the first and second German lines. I breathed again.

On the left, however, the Germans were still fighting in our front line, and on the right, the trench was unoccupied, neither our men

nor the Boches having come up.   We were only a handful, completely
isolated, and a hail of bombs was coming at our heads from in front.
If the Boches had only known how few we were . . .   Suddenly I
realized the precariousness of our position.   I grew frightened.   I
threw myself down behind a pile of sandbags.   But Pte. Benoit
didn't care.   He went on fighting like a lion against God knows
how many.

His example shamed me.   I got a grip of myself.   A few of our
own men reached us, and night fell.   We could not remain where
we were.   To the right there was still nobody.   I could see the
trench for some thirty yards ending in a gigantic traverse.   Should
I go and see what was happening there ?   By an effort of will, I made
my decision.

The trench was full of French corpses.   There was blood everywhere.   At first I went with great circumspection, with little assurance.
I was alone with all these dead ! . . .   Then little by little I grew
bolder.   I dared to look at the bodies and it seemed to me as if they
returned my stare.   From our own point behind me, my men watched
me with fear in their eyes in which I read : " He's going to get himself
killed."   It was true that in the shelter of the C.T. the Boches were
redoubling their efforts.   Their bombs came whirling over, and the
avalanche was again rapidly approaching.   I turned toward the
bodies at my feet.   I thought : " Is their sacrifice then to be useless ?
Have they died in vain ?   Will the Boches come back and rob our
dead ? "   I was seized with anger.   I have no clear recollection of
what I did or said.   I only know that I shouted something like this :
" You there, stand up !   What are you mucking about on the ground
for ?   Get up ! and help us pitch these bloody swine out."—" Up
the dead."   Was it lunacy ?   No.   *For the dead answered me.*   They
said, " We'll follow."   And rising to my summons, their souls
mingled with mine and formed a mass of fire, a huge river of metal.
Nothing now could astonish me, nothing could stop me.   I had the
faith which moveth mountains.   My voice, harsh and worn with
shouting orders for two days and a night, came back to me clear
and strong.

What happened then ?   I only want to tell you what I remember,
leaving out what they told me afterwards.   I must frankly admit I
don't know.   There is a blank in my memory ; the action has swallowed it up.   I have only a vague idea of a crazy attack.   There

were two, three or four of us against a multitude; but that was a fountain of pride and encouragement. One of my platoon, wounded in the arm, went on throwing bombs dripping with blood. For myself, I had the impression that my body had grown and swollen beyond all measure, a giant's body with superabundant strength, an amazing clarity of thought which allowed me to have my eyes in all directions at once, to shout an order to one man, while I waved a command to a second, firing a rifle and dodging the bomb which threatened me. . . .

Twice we ran out of bombs, and both times we found a sack full at our feet, mixed up with the sandbags. The whole day we had walked over them without seeing them. It was the dead who put them there. . . .

At last the Boches grew quieter. We were able to consolidate our forward bomb block in the C.T. Again we were masters of the position.

Lieut. Jacques Péricard.

PRIMITIVE WARFARE

15th April. The first time I ever encountered a German machine in the air, both the pilot (Harvey-Kelly) and myself were completely unarmed. Our machine had not been climbing well, and as I was considered somewhat heavy for an observer, Harvey-Kelly told me to leave behind all unnecessary gear. I therefore left behind my carbine and ammunition. We were taking photographs of the trench system to the north of Neuve Chapelle when I suddenly espied a German two-seater about 100 yards away and just below us. The German observer did not appear to be shooting at us. There was nothing to be done. We waved a hand to the enemy and proceeded with our task. The enemy did likewise. At the time this did not appear to me in any way ridiculous—there is a bond of sympathy between all who fly, even between enemies. But afterwards just for safety's sake I always carried a carbine with me in the air. In the ensuing two or three months I had an occasional shot at a German machine. But these encounters can hardly be dignified with the name of "fights." If we saw an enemy machine nearby, we would fly over towards it, and fire at it some half a dozen rounds. We scarcely expected to shoot the enemy down ; but it was a pleasant break in the monotony of reconnaissance and artillery observation. I remember being surprised one day to hear that an observer of another squadron (his name, Lascelles, sticks in my memory to this day, though I never met him), had shot down a German machine in our lines with a rifle.

Wing-Commander W. S. Douglas.

"THE DOZEN WHITE LOUSES DO BECOME AN OLD COAT WELL"

20th April. The section is in a bad way. Last time we were up, there were only five of us. Three have gone down with jaundice, pleurisy, and piles, and several of the remainder are far from fit.

Apart from my foot, I keep wonderfully well and have learnt to take care of myself. Lanoline cured my hands, and frequent dressings of Harrison's Pomade keep down a " certain liveliness." Luckily I don't suffer in that way so badly as many of us do. To some extent, also, one has learnt what to carry, or rather what not to carry. A single piece of soap lasts for ever, when one can only wash three days in the week, and with the warmer weather one does not need woollens. I discarded my goatskin some time ago, but one likes a spare shirt and vest. Someone sent me out a beautiful vest, soft and lined with a sort of cotton wool, but it turned out to be a regular nest for vermin. I received a shirt also, but the good lady who made it had either run short of material, or had forgotten the tails entirely. At any rate, it only reached to the waist.

H. S. Clapham (H.A.C.).

DEATH AT SCYROS

21st April. Here, next day, Charles and I wandered all over the south half of the island in brilliant sunshine and sweet smelling air : we were fed on milk and goat's cheese by a magnificent islander—whom we identified with Eumaeus—in his completely Homeric steading, were rowed back to our ship by another sturdy Greek fisherman and his still sturdier wife, and were greeted over the ship's side with slight sarcasm by Rupert, who had taken our watches and suffered endless boredom to enable us to overstay our scheduled time without dire consequences. Here we floundered about on precipitous perfumed hill-sides packed with spring flowers and sharp stones, in the throes of Battalion and Divisional Field Days more bewildering, unexpected, and exhausting than any we had previously dreed on the Dorsetshire downs, till Rupert, who would not be left behind, felt tired and went to bed early while we still sat and smoked and talked after dinner. Here, one day after, we knew that the germ of pneumonia had attacked him, weak as he was, in the lip, and I was frightened to see him so motionless and fevered just before he was shifted—lowered over the side in a couch from the *Grantully* to a French hospital ship—and here, after one day more, Charles commanded the burial-party and I the firing-party, when we buried him among the olives of Scyros the night before we sailed for the Peninsula. . . .

Lt.-Com. Patrick Shaw-Stewart, R.N.V.R.

THE FIRST GAS-ATTACK

THE VIEW

THE 22nd April was a glorious spring day. Air reconnaissance in the morning had disclosed considerable liveliness behind the German lines and some activity in the Houthulst Forest (2 miles north of Langemarck), where a column was seen on the march, though it tried to evade observation; but there was nothing abnormal in this. In the forenoon there was considerable shelling of Ypres by 17-inch and 8-inch howitzers and lighter guns, and towards midday, of the roads leading into the town; but this gradually ceased and all was quiet again.

Suddenly, at 5 p.m., a new and furious bombardment of Ypres by heavy howitzers was recommenced. The villages in front of Ypres, almost untouched until then, were also heavily shelled, and simultaneously French field-guns to the north-east of Ypres began a somewhat rapid fire, although the German field artillery was silent. At first some officers who heard the firing surmised that the newly arrived Algerian Division was " shooting itself in "; but those who were on points of vantage saw two curious greenish-yellow clouds on the ground on either side of Langemarck in front of the German line. These clouds spread laterally, joined up, and, moving before a light wind, became a bluish-white mist, such as is seen over water meadows on a frosty night. Behind the mist the enemy, by the sound of his rifle fire, was advancing. Soon, even as far off as the V Corps report centre at " Goldfish Chateau " (2,000 yards west of Ypres railway station and five miles from Langemarck) a peculiar smell was noticed, accompanied by smarting of the eyes and tingling of the nose and the throat. It was some little time, however, before it was realized that the yellow clouds were due to the gas about which warnings had been received, and almost simultaneously French coloured troops, without officers, began drifting down the roads through the back areas of the V Corps. Soon afterwards French Territorial troops were seen hurriedly crossing the bridges over the canal north of Ypres. It was impossible to understand what the Africans said, but from the way they coughed and pointed to their throats, it was evident that, if not suffering from the effects of gas, they were thoroughly scared. Teams and wagons of the French field artillery next appeared retiring, and the throng of fugitives soon became thicker and more disordered, some individuals running and continuing to run until they reached Vlamertinghe and beyond. Although the " seventy-fives " were firing regularly, it was obvious that something very serious had happened, and this was emphasized when, about 7 p.m., the French guns suddenly ceased fire.

Brig.-Gen. Sir J. E. Edmonds.

COUNTER-ATTACK

It was Thursday evening, April 22nd, 1915. In a meadow of the Poperinghe-Ypres road, the men of the Queen Victoria Rifles were taking their ease. We had just fought our first big action in the fight for Hill 60. We had had a gruelling time, and had left many of our comrades on its slopes. We survivors were utterly spent and weary ; but we felt in good heart, for only an hour ago we had been personally congratulated by Sir John French, also the Army Commander, General Smith-Dorrien.

Now some of us were stretched out asleep on the grass, others making preparations for a much-needed toilet. Our cooks were preparing a meal, and on our right a squad of Sappers were busily erecting huts in which we were to sleep. Alas ! we never used them ! As the sun was beginning to sink, this peaceful atmosphere was shattered by the noise of heavy shell-fire coming from the north-west, which increased every minute in volume, while a mile away on our right a 42-cm. shell burst in the heart of the stricken city of Ypres.

As we gazed in the direction of the bombardment, where our line joined the French, six miles away, we could see in the failing light the flash of shrapnel with here and there the light of a rocket. But more curious than anything else was a low cloud of yellow-grey smoke or vapour, and, underlying everything, a dull confused murmuring.

Suddenly down the road from the Yser Canal came a galloping team of horses, the riders goading on their mounts in a frenzied way; then another and another, till the road became a seething mass with a pall of dust over all.

Plainly something terrible was happening. What was it? Officers, and Staff Officers too, stood gazing at the scene, awestruck and dumbfounded; for in the northerly breeze there came a pungent nauseating smell that tickled the throat and made our eyes smart. The horses and men were still pouring down the road, two or three on a horse, I saw, while over the fields streamed mobs of infantry, the dusky warriors of French Africa; away went their rifles, equipment, even their tunics that they might run the faster. One man came stumbling through our lines. An officer of ours held him up with levelled revolver, "What's the matter, you bloody lot of cowards?" says he. The Zouave was frothing at the mouth, his eyes started from their sockets, and he fell writhing at the officer's feet. "Fall in!" Ah! we expected that cry; and soon we moved across the fields in the direction of the line for about a mile. The battalion is formed into line, and we dig ourselves in.

It is quite dark now, and water is being brought round, and we hear how the Germans have, by the use of poison gas, driven a French army corps out of the line, creating a huge gap which the Canadians have closed *pro tem.* A cheer goes up at this bald statement, though little we knew at what a cost those gallant souls were holding on.

About midnight we withdrew from our temporary trenches and marched about for the rest of the night, till at dawn we were permitted to snatch what sleep we could under a hedge. About the middle of the morning we were on the move again, to the north, and were soon swinging along through Vlamertinghe. About two miles out of that town we halted in a field. By this time we had joined up with the remainder of our Brigade, the 13th, and, after a meal had been served, we were ordered to dump our packs and fall in by companies. Here our company commander, Captain Flemming, addressed us. "We are," he said, "tired and weary men who would like to rest; however, there are men more weary than we who need our help. We may not have to do much; we may have to do a great deal. Whatever happens, fight like hell. I shall at any rate." A few moments more—then off we go again towards that incessant bombardment, which seemed to come closer every minute.

The Scottish Borderers led the Brigade, followed by the Royal West Kents, then ourselves—all with bayonets fixed, for we were told to be prepared to meet the Germans anywhere on the road.

We were now in the area of the ill-fated French Colonial Corps. Ambulances were everywhere, and the village of Brielen, through which we passed, was choked with wounded and gassed men. We were very mystified about this gas, and had no protection whatever against it.

Shortly after passing through Brielen we turned to the left down a road which led to the Canal, along the south side of which ran a steep soil bank, and, as the head of our battalion reached this, we halted. We could see nothing of what went on on the other side, but knew by the rattle of musketry that there was something doing. So there was, for when we finally crossed the pontoon we found that the Jocks had met the Germans on the north bank and had bundled them helter-skelter up the slope to Pilckem. This saved us any dirty work for that day, so we spent the rest of it till midnight in carrying supplies and ammunition to the Jocks and Kents, and afterwards lay in reserve on the Canal bank. It froze hard that night, and after the sweating fatigue of carrying boxes of S.A.A. all night we were literally aching with cold.

All night there seemed to be a spasmodic bombardment all round the salient.

Next morning about 12 o'clock the Adjutant, Captain Culme-Seymour, was chatting to Captain Flemming a few paces away from where I was lying, when up rushed a breathless despatch rider and handed him a message, which he read aloud to Flemming. I caught three words, "Things are critical." In about five minutes the Colonel had the battalion on the move. We moved off in double file by companies, our company leading; as we did so a big shell burst in the midst of " D " Company, making a fearful mess. We moved on quickly, like a gigantic serpent, with short halts now and then. As we skirted Ypres there was a roar of swift-moving thunder and a 17-inch shell, which seemed to be falling on top of us, burst a quarter of a mile away, covering us with dirt.

Over meadows and fields green with young crops which would

never be harvested, past cows peacefully grazing that had had their last milking, we went, passing curiously unperturbed peasants, who watched us from the farms and cottages.

As we crossed the Roulers road a lone cavalryman came galloping down it, hatless and rolling in his saddle as though drunk. Some wag throws a ribald jest at him. He turns his ashy face towards us, and his saddle it seems is a mass of blood. Above us a Taube appears and, hovering over us, lets fall a cascade of glittering silver, like petals. A few moments more and shells begin to fall about us in quantities, and gaps begin to appear in our snakelike line.

We pass a field battery; it is not firing, as it has nothing to fire, and its commander sits weeping on the trail of one of his useless guns. We quicken our pace, but the shelling gets heavier. It seems to us to be raining shrapnel. Captain Flemming falls, but struggles to his feet and waves us on with encouraging words. We double across a field, and in a few moments come on to the road again. Here was action indeed, for barely had we reached the road and started to work our way towards St. Julien, than we found ourselves amongst a crowd of Canadians of all regiments jumbled up anyhow, and apparently fighting a desperate rear-guard action. They nearly all appeared to be wounded and were firing as hard as they could. A machine-gun played down the road. Then comes an order: "Dig in on the roadside." We all scrambled into the ditch, which, like all Flanders ditches, was full of black, liquid mud, and started to work with entrenching tools—a hopeless job. A woman was bringing jugs of water from a cottage a few yards away; evidently she had just completed her week's washing, for a line of garments fluttered in the garden.

"Dig! Dig, for your lives!" shouts an officer. But, dig! How can we? 'Tis balers we need.

A detonation like thunder, and I inhale the filthy fumes of a 5·9 as I cringe against the muddy bank. The German heavies have got the road taped to an inch. Their last shell has pitched on our two M.G. teams, sheltering in the ditch on the other side of the road. They disappear, and all we can hear are groans so terrible they will haunt me for ever. Kennison, their officer, stares dazed, looking at a mass of blood and earth. Another crash and the woman and her cottage and water-jars vanish and her pitiful washing hangs in a mocking way from her sagging clothes-line. A bunch of telephone wires falls about us. To my bemused brain this is a catastrophe in itself, and I curse a Canadian sapper beside me for not attempting to mend them. He eyes me vacantly, for he is dead. More and more of these huge shells, two of them right in our midst. Shrieks of agony and groans all round me. I am splashed with blood. Surely I am hit, for my head feels as though a battering-ram has struck it. But no, I appear not to be, though all about me are bits of men and ghastly mixtures of khaki and blood.

Anthony R. Hossack (Queen Victoria Rifles).

HOLDING ON

26th April. When dawn broke in our battered support trench it was evident enough that we were all in the hollow of a great bowl, with the Germans sitting on the rim and shooting at us. We spent three days here continuously on the alert, for we had orders to stand by to be sent in support in any direction. Our little battalion was serving the purpose of reserve for a whole Army Corps, for we were short of men and the line was thinly held. But we had a superb view of the long line of battle. In effect it was an isosceles triangle which was being attacked along the whole length of its long sides. The short base was Ypres itself. At night we could see the flares and star-shells running almost all round us. The main road, along which all the traffic of reinforcement and supply went, bisected the base of the triangle and ended at its point. Some cynic remarked, truly enough, that if you walked from Ypres along this road you could be hit from almost every possible angle except from directly behind, so that the only invulnerable part of your body would be a long thin line down the spine.

Around us at intervals strange things happened. A small farm barely two hundred yards away sheltered some guns. Suddenly the German observers found the target and in a trice great salvoes of heavy shells came swirling over, and the farm in a few minutes was a waving forest of red smokeless flame. It burned for an hour and what happened to the gunners there I do not know. It was in any case none of our business, and we watched it with the detachment that only infantry can show for gunners, or gunners for infantry.

We were on a small eminence and away towards the village of St. Julien we could look down over our own and the German lines.

Just about sunset on a calm evening I was looking in this direction when slowly the brown line of trenches and earth began to change to a dull luminous green. Looking intently I saw great clouds of greenish-yellow vapour creeping across from the German lines, and all clearly issuing from one or two fixed points. We had heard talk of gas, and we had once or twice detected the smell of strange chemical odours, but here was a gas-attack, a mile away, which I could see in action with my own eyes. It was, in fact, one of the last attempts of the Germans at this time to use chlorine and, like its predecessors, which had occurred before we moved up, it failed.

The men had already shown signs of nervousness of gas, a nervousness based only on the wild stories that runners had brought. But here it was for me to see without breathing, to look at impartially so that I could be prepared when I met it. The other signs of battle had filled me with a curious elation. The shells that burst so close, the line ahead of us that we might fill at any moment, gave me a strange pleasure. The gas, with its green paralysis, changed my mood. I was angry rather than frightened, angry as the dog that snaps at the unaccustomed.

Our seniors were alarmed and waited for advice, for they saw that at any moment we might be called upon to deal with a situation that neither they nor we had ever been trained to meet. Unexpectedly help came. A parcel was delivered for each company labelled, " Gas Masks, Type I." Unpacked, the parcel revealed bundles of small squares of blue flannel, just large enough to cover the mouth, with a tape on each side to tie round behind the head. Whatever benign personage contrived these amiable death-traps I do not know. But anything more futile could never have been devised by the simplicity of man. On the whole we preferred to resort to the face-towels dipped in our own urine, which an earlier order had suggested would be a temporary palliative. Nor was our confidence restored a day later by the arrival of " Gas Masks, Type II," which was to replace the first. On unpacking my particular bundle I found that the new masks consisted of large pieces of hairy Harris tweed about three feet long and one in width, again with tapes nattily fixed to the sides. With much laughter the men tried to don their new masks. But at the bottom of the parcel I found a small printed label briefly entitled " BODY BELTS." So without further enquiries I ordered my men to put them to whatever use seemed best to them. To a man they placed them round their long-suffering stomachs.

I have often wondered what inspired genius was at work away back in England to give us these gifts. I have been told since that Gas Mask Type I was invented by the fertile brain of a Cabinet Minister. I feel tempted to attribute Type II to the Archbishop of Canterbury.

But local genius did more. The authorities on the spot with incredible and commendable speed bought up hundreds of vine-growers' sprays. These we had for use in the trenches, and filled them with chemicals fitted to neutralize chlorine.

At last our time for action came. On the final day in the trenches the fire along the line became intense. As we waited and watched suddenly over the sky-line ahead of us ran two distraught figures. They flopped into our trenches exhausted, without rifles or equipment. " We are the last of the Buffs, sir," cried one. " The Germans have attacked and the regiment is wiped out." I gave them some rum and found them rifles and equipment, comforted them and told them to get ready for more fighting. A moment later a signaller came running madly down to us : " The Germans are coming over in their thousands, sir," he said, panting. " They have broken through." We all got ready, fixed our bayonets and looked martial, when a group of four more men came tumbling over. " We are the last of the Buffs, sir," they cried. This was too much for my witty Lancashiremen, and we all roared with laughter. " Come and meet some of your friends," I said and took them along to the first pair. They began to look foolish and then they also laughed. Indeed we all enjoyed ourselves quite a lot. And of Germans " in their thousands " there was no trace. Actually a small trench had been lost to the enemy and these men had managed to get away. But it was a lesson in how a stampede starts. For the line was as strong as a rock and there was no general attack. I kept the men with me, and in half an hour they were as ready as the rest to move up again when wanted. The dramatic touch amused me. I suppose the title of " Buffs " leads to clichés. The men had done too much reading of the newspapers in quiet trenches. They could hardly help coining the phrase, for in their ears it must have sounded heroic. There was something distinguished in being " the last of the Buffs " but the distinction was becoming too popular and their sense of humour saved them at last.

But the battle was being pressed in earnest and the position in the salient had become impossible, for the long triangle was being whittled down to a thinness almost impossible for habitation. It is one thing to hold the front against the enemy but another to be shot in the back from the enemy on the other side of the triangle —and that was what was happening. Our trenches in some places could be fired at from behind by German artillery south of Ypres. The Higher Command took a wise decision. We were told that day that the Salient was to be abandoned, except for a stump that was to be held around the city of Ypres. The great spearhead was to be cut off. Our part was to go up at night to the trenches and man them, while their occupants withdrew. We were to stay there an hour or so and then leave ourselves, selecting a score of men and officers to stay behind and fire at intervals to disguise the fact that the trenches were abandoned. These in turn were to depart at dawn and find their way back.

Now at last was some kind of positive action which would defeat the aims of the enemy. We rejoiced. No one for a moment felt that, in resigning the ridiculous triangle of battered ground to the Germans, we were retreating or giving away anything to his advantage. That he should have ultimately to cross the area he had destroyed and then come up against a happily consolidated army of soldiers who were, for once, angry and full of hate, seemed to us to be entirely satisfactory. For the temper of the men was roused after the gas-attacks : they were amazed that so little had resulted from them, but anxious to prevent any further exploitation of successes of this kind. For the first time I saw the British Army animated as a unity with one single feeling. I have read often enough since the War of the dogged good-will of the men, and their lack of hate of the enemy, of their knowledge that they were pawns in a great game of politics, just waiting to be butchered. However true this may have been of the troops later on, after successive slaughters and failures like Loos and the Somme, it was not so now. We all knew that the Germans were anxious to kill as many of us as possible ; that every individual was animated by the same idea ; that Germany had her tail up ; and we all to a man felt that we should ourselves kill as many Germans as we could in return. It

was war in its simplest form, perhaps in its only attractive form—
a battle of wills and a conflict of determination. I felt relieved that
the uncertainty was at an end. That strange pursuit in single file
through shadowy Ypres where we sought we knew not what, and
ended we knew not where, was over. I can still recollect the emptiness of our minds as we halted on the road near Zonnebeke : we had
no idea whether we were to attack or defend : whether we were to
stay there or go further ; as we waited by a ghostly row of shattered
elms, I remember how suddenly out of the flat moonlight drifted a
long weary column of strange dusky men, broken and drooping,
with their tall lank forms hardly perceptible at first, and marching
with padded feet like a battalion of exhausted leopards. These were
the remnants of the Lahore Division, poor untutored Pathans, transferred from their happy hills to this marshy bog, to be blown slowly
to bits by high explosive. Inconsequently they had drifted past us,
and we, as inconsequently, drifted forward to the place they had left.

But now all that uncertainty and vague surmise was over. We
formed up at dusk, and marched over broken ground into trenches
that led us to a sloping hill with the vague outlines of trees near it.
As we neared, silence was ordered, and, unexpectedly, we found
ourselves filling a trench that was already crammed with those whom
we relieved. But they were battered and broken and, as we filled
up the narrow trench that we were to occupy for barely a few hours,
we could not help treading as we went on wounded and dying men.
To this day I shall remember those cries of the wounded as they
begged us not to leave them behind when we went. As I turned
a bend I trod unintending on a figure heaped up in a shadow. He
cried out in agony. I could think of nothing that could conceiv-
ably be said to him, for in such a case there is nothing to say. And
I had to press on, for the Germans were hardly seventy yards away,
and such was the confusion of the relief that, had they turned machine-
guns on the trenches, we should have been shot like rabbits. It was
a matter of life and death to us all, and the wounded had to give
way to the prime consideration of the whole and the living. We
did indeed attempt to get back all the wounded we could, but, any
hint to the Germans that we were abandoning the salient, and a
storm of artillery would have torn up the roads and caught us all
in the open. There was no moon yet, and we finally took up our
fire-stations in the trench, firing actively, so as to give no hint of

the coming retreat. In due course our orders came, and all but the
percentage of officers and men who were to be left behind as a skeleton garrison, moved out into the open ground behind the trenches
and formed up into column. There was a deathly silence from the
German side, and at any moment we expected attack, or at least to
be swept by rifle fire and guns. But nothing happened and, strung
up to the highest tension, we marched off towards the spinal road
of the salient that would take us back behind the new lines which,
we were told, were already held and manned, ready for the German
advance which would take place on the morrow. We reached the
road simultaneously with other columns and a pack of men, here
and there ten abreast, units confused, companies mixed, and officers
searching for their men like lost spirits, filled up the whole surface.
At intervals ambulances, packed beyond their capacity, pushed doggedly through the moving column. And over all was a soft and
velvety darkness. There was, indeed, confusion, and yet it took
but little trouble when at last we crossed the canal at Ypres to get
ourselves sorted out. I knew my destination, and at a point about
a mile from where we started, I moved my small platoon across
open country with the aid of a night-compass. I had never done
this before except in barrack-squares and had never dreamed that it
would ever come in handy. . . .

We had a long and rough march. For the first night, as if by
some providence, the Germans neglected to shell the roads. It was
the one night when their harvest would have been a rich one. At
last we came to the canal and the outskirts of battered Ypres. We
passed through the new lines and heard the cheerful shouts of those
who were manning it, and were waiting for the dawn when they
would be able to pick off Germans as they advanced to the new
position. We shouted back, bandied a joke or two and went on.
Belgians near the Canal waved to us and at last we reached the village of Elverdinghe. Dawn was now well up and, as the sun rose,
we filed into the delightful garden of an old castle, with an orna-
mental lake. But it was raining hard and we found shelter under
trees and hedges. Food appeared in due course, but the Germans
were shelling every thicket and every copse, and it was not long
before we were moved off to shelter farther back in a wood. There
we had a magnificent rest, sprawling in the sun, washing in streams
and resting to our hearts' content. Fragments of the armies of our

allies appeared among the trees—Moroccans with high turbans, French cuirassiers with brass helmets like London firemen, and coloured Zouaves. The men foregathered with all alike, talking unaffectedly in the lingua franca of the Low Countries that all Englishmen have always talked when fighting in Flanders.

That night I slept the solid sleep of the healthily exhausted, wrapped in a blanket under a small oak-tree. At intervals I awoke to watch the stars and was greeted by the singing of a nightingale in wild bursts of song, a music as lovely as was that of the lark repellent.

Stanley Casson (Lancashire Fusiliers).

THE GERMAN VIEW

24th April. The effects of the successful gas-attack were horrible. I am not pleased with the idea of poisoning men. Of course, the entire world will rage about it first and then imitate us. All the dead lie on their backs, with clenched fists ; the whole field is yellow. They say that Ypres must fall now. One can see it burning—not without a pang for the beautiful city. Langemarck is a heap of rubbish, and all rubbish-heaps look alike ; there is no sense in describing one. All that remains of the church is the doorway with the date " 1620." . . .

27th April. After fresh attacks a sleeping army lies in front of one of our brigades ; they rest in good order, man by man, and will never wake again—Canadian divisions. The enemy's losses are enormous.

The battlefield is fearful. One is overcome by a peculiar sour, heavy, and penetrating smell of corpses. Rising over a plank bridge you find that its middle is supported only by the body of a long-dead horse. Men that were killed last October lie half in swamp and half in the yellow-sprouting beet-fields. The legs of an Englishman, still encased in puttees, stick out into a trench, the corpse being built into the parapet ; a soldier hangs his rifle on them. A little brook runs through the trench, and everyone uses the water for drinking and washing ; it is the only water they have. Nobody minds the pale Englishman who is rotting away a few steps farther up. In Langemarck cemetery a hecatomb had been piled up ; for the dead must have lain above ground-level. German shells falling into it started a horrible resurrection.   At one point I saw twenty-two dead horses, still harnessed, accompanied by a few dead drivers. Cattle and pigs lie about, half-rotten ; broken trees, drives razed to the ground ; crater upon crater in the roads and in the fields.   Such is a six-months'-old battlefield.

Rudolf Binding.

GALLIPOLI

The need of the Allies to open up communication between the Mediterranean and the Black Sea, for the purpose of aiding Russia, necessitated the Dardanelles Campaign. Five Divisions—two from the United Kingdom, two of Australian and New Zealand troops, and one of French colonial troops, were detailed for the campaign. The expedition was concentrated in Mudros Bay, Lemnos, under the command of Sir Ian Hamilton, and thence made the landings on the Peninsula.

THE LANDING

25th April. When we got to " X " Beach the foreshore and cliffs had been made good without much loss in the first instance, we were told, though there is a hot fight going on just south of it. But fresh troops will soon be landing :—so far so good. Further round, at " W " Beach, another lodgment had been effected ; very desperate and bloody, we are told by the Naval Beachmaster ; and indeed we can see some of the dead, but the Lancashire Fusiliers hold the beach though we don't seem yet to have penetrated inland. By Sedd-el-Bahr, where we hove to about 6.45, the light was very baffling ; land wrapped in haze, sun full in our eyes. Here we watched as best we could over the fight being put up by the Turks against our forlorn hope on the *River Clyde*. Very soon it became clear that we were being held. Through our glasses we could quite clearly watch the sea being whipped up all along the beach and about the *River Clyde* by a pelting storm of rifle bullets. We could see also how a number of our dare-devils were up to their necks in this tormented water trying to struggle on to land from the barges linking the *River Clyde* to the shore. There was a line of men lying flat down under cover of a little sandbank in the centre of the beach. They were so held under by fire they dared not, evidently, stir. Watching these gallant souls from the safety of a battleship gave me a hateful feeling : Roger Keyes said to me he simply could not bear it. Often a commander may have to watch tragedies from a post of safety. That is all right. I have had my share of the hair's-breadth business and now it becomes the turn of the youngsters. But, from the battleship, you are outside the frame of the picture. The thing becomes monstrous ; too cold-blooded ; like looking on at gladiators from the dress circle. The moment we became satisfied that none of our men had made their way further than a few feet above sea-level, the *Queen* opened a heavy fire from her 6-inch batteries upon the Castle, the village and the high steep ground ringing round the beach in a semi-circle. The enemy lay very low somewhere underground. At times the *River Clyde* signalled that the worst fire came from the old Fort and Sedd-el-Bahr ; at times that these bullets were pouring out from about the second highest rung of seats on the West of that amphitheatre in which we were striving to take our places. Ashore the machine-guns and rifles never ceased —tic-tac, tic-tac, b-r-r—tic-tac, tic-tac, b-r-r-r-r. . . . Drowned every few seconds by our tremendous salvoes, this more nervous noise crept back insistently into our ears in the interval. As men fixed in the grip of nightmare, we were powerless—unable to do anything but wait.

When we saw our covering party fairly hung up under fire from the Castle and its outworks, it became a question of issuing fresh orders to the main body who had not yet been committed to that attack. There was no use throwing them ashore to increase the number of targets on the beach. Roger Keyes started the notion that these troops might well be diverted to " Y " where they could land unopposed and whence they might be able to help their advance guard at " V " more effectively than by direct reinforcement if they threatened to cut the Turkish line of retreat from Sedd-el-Bahr. Braithwaite was rather dubious from the orthodox General Staff point of view as to whether it was sound for G.H.Q. to barge into Hunter-Weston's plans, seeing he was executive Commander of the whole of this southern invasion. But to me the idea seemed simple common sense. If it did not suit Hunter-Weston's book, he had only to say so. Certainly Hunter-Weston was in closer touch with all these landings than we were ; it was not for me to force his hand : there was no question of that : so at 9.15 I wirelessed as follows :

" G.O.C. in C. to G.O.C. *Euryalus.*

" Would you like to get some more men ashore on ' Y ' beach ? If so, trawlers are available."

Three-quarters of an hour passed ; the state of affairs at Sedd-el-Bahr was no better, and in an attack if you don't get better you get worse ; the supports were not being landed ; no answer had come to hand. So I repeated my signal to Hunter-Weston, making it this time personal from me to him and ordering him to acknowledge receipt. (Lord Bobs's wrinkle) :

" General Hamilton to General Hunter-Weston, *Euryalus.*

" Do you want any more men landed at ' Y ' ? There are trawlers available. Acknowledge the signal."

At 11 a.m. I got this answer :

" From General Hunter-Weston to G.O.C., *Queen Elizabeth.*

" Admiral Wemyss and Principal Naval Transport Officer state that to interfere with present arrangements and try to land men at ' Y ' Beach would delay disembarkation."

About noon, a Naval Officer (Lieutenant Smith), a fine fellow, came off to get some more small-arm ammunition for the machine-guns on the *River Clyde*. He said the state of things on and around that ship was " awful," a word which carried twenty-fold weight owing to the fact that it was spoken by a youth never very emotional, I am sure, and now on his mettle to make his report with indifference and calm. The whole landing-place at " V " Beach is ringed round with fire. The shots from our naval guns, smashing as their impact appears, might as well be confetti for all the effect they have upon the Turkish trenches. The *River Clyde* is commanded and swept not only by rifles at 100 yards' range, but by pom-poms and field-guns. Her own double battery of machine-guns mounted in a sandbag revetment in her bows are to some extent forcing the enemy to keep their heads down and preventing them from actually rushing the little party of our men who are crouching behind the sand-bank. But these same men of ours cannot raise head or hand one inch beyond that lucky ledge of sand by the water's brink. And the bay at Sedd-el-Bahr, so the last messengers have told us, had turned red. The *River Clyde* so far saves the situation. She was only ready two days before we plunged. . . .

At two o'clock a large number of our wounded who had taken

refuge under the base of the arches of the old fort at Sedd-el-Bahr began to signal for help. The *Queen Elizabeth* sent away a picket boat which passed through the bullet storm and most gallantly brought off the best part of them.

Soon after two o'clock we were cheered by sighting our own brave fellows making a push from the direction of " W." We reckon they must be Worcesters and Essex men moving up to support and Royal Fusiliers and the Lancashire Fusiliers, who have been struggling unaided against the bulk of the Turkish troops. The new lot came along by rushes from the Westwards, across from " X " to " W " towards Sedd-el-Bahr, and we prayed God very fervently they might be able to press on so as to strike the right rear of the enemy troops encircling " V " Beach. At 3.10 the leading heroes—we were amazed at their daring—actually stood up in order the better to cut through a broad belt of wire entanglement. One by one the men passed through and fought their way to within a few yards of a redoubt dominating the hill between Beaches " W " and " V." This belt of wire ran perpendicularly, not parallel, to the coastline and had evidently been fixed up precisely to prevent what we were now about to attempt. To watch V.C.'s being won by wire cutting; to see the very figure and attitude of the hero; to be safe oneself except from the offchance of a shell—was like being stretched upon the rack ! All day we hung *vis-à-vis* this inferno. With so great loss and with so desperate a situation the white flag would have gone up in the South African War but there was no idea of it to-day and I don't feel afraid of it even now, in the dark of a moonless night, where evil thoughts are given most power over the mind.

Nor does Hunter-Weston. We had a hurried dinner, de Robeck, Keyes, Braithwaite, Godfrey, Hope and I, in the signal office under the bridge. As we were finishing Hunter-Weston came on board. After he had told us his story, breathlessly and listened to with breathless interest, I asked him what about our troops at " Y " ? He thought they were now in touch with our troops at " X " but that they had been through some hard fighting to get there. His last message had been that they were being hard pressed but as he had heard nothing more since then he assumed they were all right —— ! Anyway, he was cheery, stout-hearted, quite a good tonic and—on the whole—his news is good.

Gen. Sir Ian Hamilton.

THE SINKING OF THE *LUSITANIA*

The Cunard liner " Lusitania " was on her homeward voyage from New York when she was met by the German submarine U20 off the Old Head of Kinsale, May 7, 1915. Having fired a torpedo, U20 rose to the surface, 300 yards away from the sinking ship, and stood by stolidly while 1,198 men, women and children met their death by drowning. Germany celebrated this naval victory by striking a special medal, and awarding the Commander the Pour le Mérite medal, the highest honour any officer could receive.

On Saturday, May 1st (the day on which the *Lusitania* was to sail), in order that there might be no mistake as to German intentions, the German Embassy at Washington issued a warning to passengers couched in general terms, which was printed in the New York morning papers directly under the notice of the sailing of the *Lusitania*. The first-class passengers, who were not due on board till about ten o'clock, had still time after reading the warning, unmistakable in form and position, to cancel their passage if they chose. For the third-class passengers it came too late. As a matter of fact, I believe that no British and scarcely any American passengers acted on the warning, but we were most of us very fully conscious of the risk we were running. A number of people wrote farewell letters to their home folk and posted them in New York to follow on another vessel. . . .

We were due to arrive in Liverpool on Saturday, May 8th, and we had all imagined that the attempts would be made in the Irish Sea during our last night. We were wrong. On the Friday after-noon, at about two o'clock, we were off the south-west coast of Ireland, the Old Head of Kinsale was visible in the distance ; my father and I had just come out of the dining-room after lunching and were strolling into the lift on " D " deck. " I think we might stay up on deck to-night to see if we get our thrill," he said. I had no time to answer. There was a dull, thud-like, not very loud but unmistakable explosion. It seemed to come from a little below us and about the middle of the vessel on the port side, that was the side towards the land. I turned and came out of the lift ; somehow, the stairs seemed safer. My father walked over to look out of a port-hole. I did not wait. I had days before made up my mind that if anything happened one's instinct would be to make straight for the boat-deck (it is a horrible feeling to stay under cover even for a few moments in a boat that may be sinking), but that one must control that and go straight to one's cabin to fetch one's life-belt and then on to the boat-deck. As I ran up the stairs, the boat was already heeling over. As I ran, I thought, " I wonder I'm not more frightened," and then, " I'm beginning to get frightened, but I mustn't let myself."

I collected my life-belt, the " Boddy " belt provided by the Cunard Company. On my way back I ran into my father's cabin and took out one of his belts, fearing that he might be occupied with his papers and forget to fetch one for himself. Then I went up on to " A " deck (the boat-deck). Here there was, of course, a choice of sides. I chose the starboard side, feeling that it would somehow be safer to be as far away from the submarine as possible. The side farther from the submarine was also the higher out of the water, as the boat had listed over towards the side on which she had been hit and the deck was now slanting at a considerable angle ; and to be as high as possible out of the water felt safer too.

As I came out into the sunlight, I saw standing together the American doctor, Dr. F——, and his sister-in-law, Miss C——. I asked if I might stay beside them until I caught sight of my father, which I made sure of doing soon. I put on my own life-belt and held the other in my hand. Just after I reached the deck a stream of steerage passengers came rushing up from below and fought their way into the boat nearest us, which was being lowered. They were white-faced and terrified ; I think they were shrieking ; there was no kind of order—the strongest got there first, the weak were pushed aside. Here and there a man had his arm round a woman's waist and bore her along with him ; but there were no children to be seen ; no children could have lived in that throng. They rushed a boat before it was ready for them. A ship's officer made some feeble attempt to prevent them, but there was no real attempt at order or discipline. As we watched, I turned to the American girl . . . " I always thought a shipwreck was a well-organized affair."—" So did I," said she, " but I've learnt a devil of a lot in the last five minutes." Two seamen began to lower the boat, which was full to overflowing, but no one was in command of them. One man lowered his end quickly, the other lowered his end slowly ; the boat was in an almost perpendicular position when it reached the water. Half the people fell out, but the boat did not capsize, and I think most of them scrambled back afterwards. I do not know. We turned away and did not look. It was not safe to look at horrible things just then. Curious that it never for a moment struck any of us as possible to attempt to get into the boat ourselves. Even at that moment death would have seemed better than to make part of that terror-infected crowd. I remember regretfully thinking something of this sort.

That was the last boat I saw lowered. It became impossible to lower any more from our side owing to the list on the ship. No one else except that white-faced stream seemed to lose control. A number of people were moving about the deck, gently and vaguely. They reminded one of a swarm of bees who do not know where the queen has gone. Presently Dr. F—— decided to go down and fetch life-belts for himself and his sister-in-law. Whilst he was away, the vessel righted herself perceptibly, and word was passed round that the bulkheads had been closed and the danger was over. We laughed and shook hands, and I said, " Well, you've had your thrill all right."—" I never want another," she answered. Soon after, the doctor returned bearing two life-belts. He said he had had to wade through deep water down below to get them.

Whilst we were standing, I unhooked my skirt so that it should come straight off and not impede me in the water. The list on the ship soon got worse again, and, indeed, became very bad. Presently Dr. F—— said he thought we had better jump into the sea. (We had thought of doing so before, but word had been passed round from the captain that it was better to stay where we were.) Dr. F—— and Miss C—— moved towards the edge of the deck where the boat had been and there was no railing. I followed them, feeling frightened at the idea of jumping so far (it was, I believe, some sixty feet normally from " A " deck to the sea), and telling myself how ridiculous I was to have physical fear of the jump when we stood in such grave danger as we did. I think others must have had the same fear, for a little crowd stood hesitating on the brink and kept me back. And then, suddenly, I saw that the water had come over on to the deck. We were not, as I had thought, sixty feet above the sea ; we were already under the sea. I saw the water green just about up to my knees. I do not remember its coming up farther ; that must all have happened in a second. The ship sank and I was sucked right down with her.

The next thing I can remember was being deep down under the water. It was very dark, nearly black. I fought to come up. I was terrified of being caught on some part of the ship and kept down. That was the worst moment of terror, the only moment of acute terror, that I knew. My wrist did catch on a rope. I was scarcely aware of it at the time, but I have the mark on me to this day. At first I swallowed a lot of water ; then I remembered that I had read that one should not swallow water, so I shut my mouth. Something bothered me in my right hand and prevented me striking out with it ; I discovered that it was the life-belt I had been holding for my father. As I reached the surface I grasped a little bit of board, quite thin, a few inches wide and perhaps two or three feet long. I thought this was keeping me afloat. I was wrong. My most excellent life-belt was doing that. But everything that happened after I had been submerged was a little misty and vague ; I was slightly stupefied from then on.

When I came to the surface I found that I formed part of a large, round, floating island composed of people and debris of all sorts, lying so close together that at first there was not very much water noticeable in between. People, boats, hen-coops, chairs, rafts, boards and goodness knows what besides, all floating cheek by jowl. A man with a white face and yellow moustache came and held on to the other end of my board. I did not quite like it, for I felt it was not large enough for two, but I did not feel justified in objecting. Every now and again he would try and move round towards my end of the board. This frightened me ; I scarcely knew why at the time (I was probably quite right to be frightened ; it is likely enough that he wanted to hold on to me). I summoned up my strength— to speak was an effort—and told him to go back to his own end, so that we might keep the board properly balanced. He said nothing and just meekly went back. After a while I noticed that he had disappeared. I don't know what had happened to him. He may have gone off to a hen-coop which was floating near by. I don't know whether he had a lifebelt on or not. Somehow I think not.

Many people were praying aloud in a curious, unemotional monotone ; others were shouting for help in much the same slow, impersonal chant : " Bo-at . . . bo-at . . . bo-at . . ." I shouted for a minute or two, but it was obvious that there was no chance of any boat responding, so I soon desisted. One or two boats were visible, but they were a long way from where I was, and clearly had all they could do to pick up the people close beside them. So far as I could see, they did not appear to be moving much. By and by my legs got bitterly cold, and I decided to try to swim to a boat so as to get them out of the cold water, but it was a big effort swimming (I could normally swim a hundred yards or so, but I am not an expert swimmer). I only swam a few strokes and almost immediately gave up the attempt, because I did not see how I could get along without letting go of my piece of board, which nothing would have induced me to abandon.

There was no acute feeling of fear whilst one was floating in the water. I can remember feeling thankful that I had not been drowned underneath, but had reached the surface safely, and thinking that even if the worst happened there could be nothing unbearable to go through now that my head was above the water. The life-belt held one up in a comfortable sitting position, with one's head lying rather back, as if one were in a hammock. One was a little dazed and rather stupid and vague. I doubt whether any of the people in the water were acutely frightened or in any consciously unbearable agony of mind. When Death is as close as he was then the sharp agony of fear is not there ; the thing is too overwhelming and stunning for that. One has the sense of something taking care of one—I don't mean in the sense of protecting one from death ; rather of death itself being a benignant power. At moments I wondered whether the whole thing was perhaps a nightmare from which I should wake, and once—half laughing, I think—I wondered, looking round on the sun and pale blue sky and calm sea, whether I had reached heaven without knowing it—and devoutly hoped I hadn't.

One was acutely uncomfortable, no more than that. A discomfort mainly due to the intense cold, but further—at least so far as I was concerned—to the fact that, being a very bad sailor, when presently a little swell got up, I was sea-sick. I remember, as I sat in the water, I thought out an improvement which I considered should be adopted for all life-belts. There should be, I thought, a little bottle of chloroform strapped into each belt, so that one could inhale it and lose consciousness when one wished to. I must have been exceedingly uncomfortable before I thought of that.

The swell of the sea had the effect of causing the close-packed island of wreckage and people to drift apart. Presently I was a hundred yards or more away from anyone else. I looked up at the sun, which was high in the sky, and wished that I might lose consciousness. I don't know how long after that I did lose it, but that is the last thing I remember in the water.

The next thing I remember is lying naked between blankets on a deck in the dark. (I was, I discovered later, on a tiny patrol steamer named the *Bluebell.*) Every now and again a sailor came and looked at me and said, " That's better." I had a vague idea that something had happened, but I thought that I was still on the deck of the *Lusitania,* and I was vaguely annoyed that some unknown sailor should be attending to me instead of my own stewardess. Gradually memory came back. The sailor offered me a cup of lukewarm tea, which I drank (we were on a teetotal vessel). There did not seem much wrong with me except that my whole body was shaking violently and my teeth were chattering like castanets, as I had never supposed teeth could chatter, and that I had a violent pain in the small of my back, which I suppose was rheumatism. The sailor said he thought I had better go below, as it would be warmer. " We left you up here to begin with," he explained, " as we thought you were dead, and it did not seem worth while cumbering up the cabin with you." There was some discussion as to how to get me down the cabin stairs. " It took three men to lift you on board," someone explained. I said that I thought I could walk ; so, supported on either arm and with a third man holding back my dripping hair, I managed to get down. I was put into the captain's bunk, whence someone rather further recovered was ejected to make room for me. The warmth below was delicious ; it seemed to make one almost delirious. I should say that almost all of us down there (I do not know how many rescued were on board ; I can remember noticing five or six, but probably there were thirty or forty) were a little drunk with the heat and the light and the joy of knowing ourselves to be alive. We were talking at the tops of our voices and laughing a great deal. At one time I was talking and laughing with some woman when a sailor came in and asked us if we had lost anyone in the wreck. I can remember the sudden sobering with which we answered. I did not then know what had happened to my father ; she was almost sure that her husband was drowned. He was, she had already told me (there are no veils just after a shipwreck), all she had in the world. It seemed that his loss probably meant the breaking up of her whole life, yet at that moment she was full of cheerfulness and laughter.

I can remember two exceptions to the general merriment. The captain of the *Lusitania* was amongst those rescued on our little boat, but I never heard him speak. The other exception was a woman, who sat silent in the outer cabin. Presently she began to speak. Quietly, gently, in a low, rather monotonous voice, she described how she had lost her child. She had, so far as I can recollect, been made to place him on a raft, which, owing to some mismanagement, had capsized. She considered that his death had been unnecessary ; that it had been due to the lack of organization and discipline on board, and gently, dispassionately, she said so to the captain of the *Lusitania*. She further stated her intention of saying so publicly later. It seemed to me, fresh from the incompetent muddle on the *Lusitania's* deck, that she entirely proved her case. A sailor who came in to attend to me suggested that she was hysterical. She appeared to me to be the one person on board who was not. . . .

We got into Queenstown Harbour about eleven. A man (the steward who had waited at our table on the *Lusitania*) came on board and told me that my father had been rescued and was already on shore. When we came alongside, the captain of the *Bluebell* came in and asked if I could go ashore, as he wanted to move on again. I said certainly, but not wrapped in one tiny blanket. Modesty, which had been completely absent for some hours, was beginning faintly to return. I said I could do it if only I had a couple of safety-pins to fasten the thing together ; but it was a man's ship, and the idea of safety-pins produced hoots of laughter. Finally someone went ashore and borrowed a " British Warm " from one of the soldiers on the quay. Clad in this, with the blanket tucked round my waist underneath it, and wearing the captain's carpet slippers, I started for the shore. The gangway was a difficult obstacle. It was so placed that it meant stepping up eighteen inches or possibly a couple of feet. I must have been pretty weak, for I had to get down on to my hands and knees and crawl on to it.

At the other end of the gangway my father was waiting.

Viscountess Rhondda.

ARCADIA

5th May. This day began for me about midnight, as I lay in my dug-out in the breastwork watching the Plough swing slowly round. I shall remember that night; there was a heavy thunder-shower in the evening, but when we marched down it cleared away for a warm still summer night; still, that is, except for the snipers' rifles, and the rattle of the machine-guns, and sometimes the boom of a big gun far away, coming so long after the flash that you had almost forgotten to expect it. The breastwork which we held ran through an orchard and along some hedgerows. There was a sweet smell of wet earth and wet grass after the rain, and since I could not sleep, I wandered about among the ghostly cherry trees all in white, and watched the star-shells rising and falling to north and south. Presently a misty moon came up, and a nightingale began to sing. I have only heard him once before, in the daytime, near Farley Mount, at Winchester; but, of course, I knew him at once, and it was strange to stand there and listen, for the song seemed to come all the more sweetly and clearly in the quiet intervals between the bursts of firing. There was something infinitely sweet and sad about it, as if the country-side were singing gently to itself, in the midst of all our noise and confusion and muddy work. . . . So I stood there, and thought of all the men and women who had listened to that song, just as for the first few weeks after Tom was killed I found myself thinking perpetually of all the men who had been killed in battle—Hector and Achilles and all the heroes of long ago, who were once so strong and active, and now are so quiet. Gradually the night wore on, until day began to break, and I could see clearly the daisies and buttercups in the long grass about my feet. Then I gathered my platoon together, and marched back past the silent farms to our billets.

Alexander Douglas Gillespie (Argyll and Sutherland
Highlanders).

IN THE GOLDEN HORN

25th May. The rumour was already abroad in Constantinople that eleven British submarines were operating in the Sea of Marmora when E 11 herself arrived in the harbour. She was the first enemy of any description to intrude on the sacred precincts of the Golden Horn in the five hundred years the Turks had held the city. Nasmith's own account is a classic of maddening brevity. " So," he wrote, " we dived unobserved into Constantinople." The word " so " refers to the disgust the crew of E 11 felt when they could find nothing but small fry out in the open.

Nasmith raised periscope shortly after noon in the centre of the harbour, and immediately there occurred one of those incongruous, incidents which pleased him. " Our manœuvring," he used to say, " was rather difficult because of the cross-tides, the mud, and the current, but most particularly on account of a damn' fool of a fisherman who kept trying to grab the top of my periscope every time I raised it to take an observation. I don't think he had any idea what it was, but to get rid of him I gave him a chance to get a good hold on it. Then I ordered 'Down periscope quickly' and almost succeeded in capsizing his boat. When I looked at him a minute later he wore the most amazed and bewildered expression I ever hope to see."

The Arabian Nights Entertainment did not end with the adventure of E 11 and the modern Sinbad the Sailor. Rising close to the United States ship *Scorpion*, a good-sized vessel was seen close to the arsenal. Nasmith fired the port-bow tube. The torpedo developed a gyro-failure, which means that the gear which governed her direction failed, locking the rudder hard over.

Nasmith said that the torpedo went chasing around the harbour, acting like nothing so much as a hen with its head cut off. Round and round it went at a speed of forty-seven knots, and every few seconds it switched from hen to porpoise and jumped out of the water. "It was bound to hit something, and by the look of things it was just as likely to be us as anything else."

So he fired the starboard-bow tube. By this time the harbour was in an uproar, and if ever a submarine was in a delicate position it was E 11 at that moment. But Nasmith did a thing which I never heard equalled for sheer nerve. The moment he fired the torpedo at the ship loading by the arsenal wharf he put a small camera to the eyepiece of the periscope and took a picture of the munition ship blowing up. The first torpedo hit something and exploded at the same time.

" The enemy was given to issuing false reports about any successes we claimed," I have heard him explain. " They were experts at propaganda and counter-propaganda. So that we could reap the full moral effect of going into their precious harbour and blowing their ships to Hades as they lay moored safely inside, we tried taking some exposures with the camera lens close to the eyepiece of the periscope."

I saw the photograph. You could see the munition ship enveloped in a cloud of smoke with debris flying as high as the masthead. The sensitive film had also registered the cross wires and degree marks on the periscope lens which are used for judging distances and for taking bearings.

There was little question of the moral effect of E 11's astonishing exploit. Although the *Stambul* which she had sunk was an old ship, and was possibly beached before she sank, the city was thrown into a state of panic, troops were ordered off transports, and all sea traffic between Constantinople and the Peninsula was virtually stopped.

Getting out of Constantinople was infinitely more exciting than getting in there. Once certain of his kill, Nasmith gave the order to dive. Down she sank and then grounded heavily.

' Then we bounced thirty feet, if the depth indicators were to be believed," to recall Nasmith's own story again. " I went down and sat on the bottom. Then a strange thing happened. We looked at the compass to discover our best course, and we noticed we were altering course rapidly even though we were right on the bottom. We were swinging right round the compass card. We watched this happening with great interest. It was evident that we must be resting on the shoal under Leander Tower, judging by the depth, and were being turned by the current unless something had succeeded in hooking on to us and was towing us. This was a disquieting thought, so we started the motors and bumped our way gently off the shoal, sank into about eighty-five feet of water, and proceeded as requisite out of the harbour."

And when they were safely out of the harbour and out of the narrow waters of the Golden Horn they headed for the quieter reaches in the centre of the Sea of Marmora by Kalolimni. Here they rested the next day, charged their batteries, and washed and bathed. Nasmith told me, and I know from experience, what a godsend it was to bathe and change into clean clothes.

William Guy Carr.

COMMON FORM

May. I spent the rest of my watch in acquainting myself with the geography of the trench-section, finding how easy it was to get lost among culs-de-sac and disused alleys. Twice I overshot the company frontage and wandered among the Munsters on the left. Once I tripped and fell with a splash into deep mud. At last my watch was ended with the first signs of dawn. I passed the word along the line for the company to stand-to-arms. The N.C.O.s whispered hoarsely into the dug-outs : " Stand-to, stand-to," and out the men tumbled with their rifles in their hands. As I went towards company head-quarters to wake the officers I saw a man lying on his face in a machine-gun shelter. I stopped and said : " Stand-to, there." I flashed my torch on him and saw that his foot was bare. The machine-gunner beside him said : " No good talking to him, sir." I asked : " What's wrong ? What's he taken his boot and sock off for ? " I was ready for anything odd in the trenches. " Look for yourself, sir," he said. I shook the man by the arm and noticed suddenly that the back of his head was blown out. The first corpse that I saw in France was this suicide. He had taken off his boot and sock to pull the trigger of his rifle with his toe ; the muzzle was in his mouth. " Why did he do it ? " I said. " He was in the last push, sir and that sent him a bit queer, and on top of that, he got bad news from Limerick about his girl and another chap." He was not a Welshman, but belonged to the Munsters ; their machine-guns were at the extreme left of our company. The suicide had already been reported and two Irish officers came up. " We've had two or three of these lately," one of them told me. Then he said to the other : " While I remember, Callaghan, don't forget to write to his next-of-kin. Usual sort of letter, cheer them up, tell them he died a soldier's death, anything you like. I'm not going to report it as suicide."

Robert Graves (Royal Welch Fusiliers).

GALLIPOLI

ARMISTICE AT ANZAC

25th May. We walked from the sea and passed immediately up the hill, through a field of tall corn filled with poppies, then another cornfield ; then the fearful smell of death began as we came upon scattered bodies. We mounted over a plateau and down through gullies filled with thyme, where there lay about 4,000 Turkish dead. It was indescribable. One was grateful for the rain and the grey sky. . . . There were two wounded crying in that multitude of silence. . . . The Turkish Captain with me said : " At this spectacle even the most gentle must feel savage, and the most savage must weep." The dead fill acres of ground, mostly killed in the one big attack, but some recently. They fill the myrtle-grown gullies. One saw the result of machine-gun fire very clearly ; entire companies annihilated—not wounded, but killed, their heads doubled under them with the impetus of their rush and both hands clasping their bayonets. It was as if God had breathed in their faces. . . .

. . . A good deal of friction at first. The trenches were 10 to 15 yards apart. Each side was on the *qui vive* for treachery. In one gully the dead had got to be left unburied. It was impossible to bury them without one side seeing the position of the other. In the Turkish parapet there were many bodies buried. Fahreddin told Skeen he wanted to bury them, " but," he said, " we cannot take them out without putting something in their place." . . .

. . . I talked to the Turks, one of whom pointed to the graves. " That's politics," he said. Then he pointed to the dead bodies and said : " That's diplomacy. God pity all of us poor soldiers."

. . . Then Skeen came. He told me to get back as quickly as possible to Quinn's Post, as I said I was nervous at being away, and to retire the troops at 4 and the white-flag men at 4.15. . . .

. . . At 4 o'clock the Turks came to me for orders. I do not believe this could have happened anywhere else. I retired their troops and ours, walking along the line. At 4.7 I retired the white-flag men, making them shake hands with our men. Then I came to the upper end. About a dozen Turks came out. I chaffed them, and said that they would shoot me next day. They said, in a horrified chorus : " God forbid ! " The Albanians laughed and cheered, and said : " We will never shoot you." Then the Australians began coming up, and said : " Good-bye, old chap ; good luck ! " And the Turks said : " Oghur Ola gule gule gedejekseniz, gule gule gelejekseniz " (Smiling may you go and smiling come again). Then I told them all to get into their trenches, and unthinkingly went up to the Turkish trench and got a deep salaam from it.

Hon. Aubrey Herbert.

HOOGE

16th June. At 4.15 [a.m.] a whistle blew. The men in the front line went over the top, and we scrambled out and took their places in the front trench. In front of us was a small field, with grass knee-high, split diagonally by an old footpath. On the other side of the field was a belt of trees, known as Y Wood, in which lay the first Hun trench.

In a few moments flags went up there, to show that it had been captured and that the troops were going on. Another whistle, and we ourselves scrambled over the parapet and sprinted across the field. Personally I was so overweighted that I could only amble, and I remember being intensely amused at the sight of a little chap in front of me who seemed in even worse case than myself. Without thinking much about it, I took the diagonal path, as the line of least resistance, and most of my section did the same.

When I dropped into the Hun trench I found it a great place, only three feet wide, and at least eight deep, and beautifully made of white sand-bags, back and front. At that spot there was no sign of any damage by our shells, but a number of dead Huns lay in the bottom. There was a sniper's post just where I fell in, a comfortable little square hole, fitted with seats and shelves, bottles of beer, tinned meats, and a fine helmet hanging on a hook.

Our first duty was to change the wire, so, after annexing the helmet, I slipped off my pack, and, clambering out again, started to move the wire from what was now the rear, to the new front of the trench. It was rotten stuff, most of it loose coils, and the only knife-rests were not more than a couple of feet high. What there was movable of it, we got across without much difficulty, and we had just finished when we were ordered to move down the trench, as our diagonal advance had brought us too far to the right.

We moved down along the belt of woodland, which was only a few yards broad, to a spot where one of our companies was already hard at work digging a communication trench back to our old front line. Here there was really no trench at all. One or more of our own big shells had burst in the middle, filling it up for a distance of ten yards and practically destroying both parapet and parados. Some of us started building up the parapet with sandbags, and I saw the twins merrily at work hauling out dead Huns at least twice their own size.

There was a hedge along the back of the trench, so I scrambled through a hole in it, piled my pack, rifle, and other things, including the helmet, on the farther side, and started again on the wire. Hereabouts it was much better stuff, and it took us some time to get it across and pegged down. We had just got the last knife-rest across, when I saw a man who was placing sandbags on the parapet from the farther side swivel round, throw his legs into the trench, and collapse in a heap in the bottom. Several others were already lying there, and for the first time I realized that a regular hail of machine-gun bullets was sweeping over the trench.

I made a dive for my pack, but though I found that, my pet helmet had disappeared. Quite a string of wounded and masterless men had passed down the back of the hedge while I was working, and one of them must have thought it a good souvenir to take into hospital.

We all started to work at a feverish pace, digging out the trench and building up some sort of shelter in front. One chap, a very nice kid, was bowled over almost at once with a bullet in the groin, and lay in the trench, kicking and shrieking, while we worked.

The attacking battalions had carried several more trenches and we were told that two at least had been held, but our own orders were to consolidate and hold on to the trench we were in at all costs. We could see very little in front. There was a wide field of long grass, stretching gently upward to a low mound of earth several hundred yards away. This was the next line. Away on the right front was Bellewarde Wood and Hooge Château, both above us, but the latter was partly hidden by the corner of Y Wood.

I had just filled a sandbag and placed it on the top of the parapet when I happened to glance down, and saw a slight movement in the earth between my feet. I stooped and scraped away the soil with my fingers and found what seemed like palpitating flesh. It proved to be a man's cheek, and a few minutes' work uncovered his head.

I poured a little water down his throat, and two or three of us dug out the rest of him. He was undamaged except for his feet and ankles, which were a mass of pulp, and he recovered consciousness as we worked. The first thing he said was in English : " What Corps are you ? " He was a big man, and told us he was forty-five and had only been a soldier for a fortnight.

We dragged him out and laid him under the hedge. There was nothing else we could do for him. He had another drink later, but he must have died in the course of the day. I am afraid we forgot all about him, but nothing could have lived there until evening.

The Captain was the next to go. He insisted on standing on the parados, directing operations, and got a bullet in the lungs. He could walk, and two men were detailed to take him down to the dressing-station. One came back, to be killed later in the day, but the other stopped a bullet *en route*, and followed the Captain.

When we had got our big Hun out, he left a big hole in the ground, and we found a dead arm and hand projecting from the bottom. We dug about, but did not seem to be able to find the body, and when I seized the sleeve and pulled, the arm came out of the ground by itself. We had to dig deeper for our own sake, but there was nothing else left, except messy earth, which seemed to have been driven into the side of the trench. The man helping me turned sick, for it wasn't pretty work, but I claimed a substitute, and between us we carted out a barrowful in wetter sheets and dumped it under the hedge. After that I had had enough myself.

About 5.30 a.m. the Huns started shelling, and the new communication trench soon became a death-trap. A constant stream of wounded who had come down another trench from the north, passed along the rear. The Huns made a target of the two traverses (unluckily including our own), from which the communication trench opened, and numbers of the wounded were caught just behind us. The trench itself was soon choked with bodies, as it was easier and as safe to pass over the open above it.

The shelling got worse as the day wore on and several more of our men went down. They plastered us with crumps, shrapnel, and whizz-bangs. One of the latter took off a sandbag from the top of the parapet and landed it on my head. It nearly broke my neck and I felt ill for some time after.

It was grillingly hot and the air was full of dust, but although we were parched up, we dared not use much of our water.   One never knew how long it must last.   I came off better than most in that respect, for I had taken the precaution of carrying two water-bottles knowing that one would never last me.

The worst of it was the inaction.   Every minute several shells fell within a few yards and covered us with dust, and the smell of the explosives poisoned my mouth.   All I could do was to crouch against the parapet and pant for breath, expecting every moment to be my last.   And this went on for hours.   I began to long for the shell which would put an end to everything, but in time my nerves became almost numbed, and I lay like a log until roused.

I think it must have been midday when something happened. An alarm was given and we manned the parapet, to see some scores of men retreating at a run from the trench in front.   They ran right over us, men of half a dozen battalions, and many dropped on the way.   As they passed, something was said of gas, but it appeared that nearly all the officers in the two front trenches had been killed or wounded, someone had raised an alarm of gas, and the men had panicked and run.

A lot of the runaways insisted on gathering by the hedge just behind us, in spite of our warnings not to do so, and I saw at least twenty hit by shrapnel within a few yards of us.

The Brigade-Major arrived, cursing, and called upon some of our own men to advance and reoccupy the trench in front.   He led them himself, and they made a very fine dash across.   I do not think more than twenty fell, and they reoccupied the trench and, I believe, the third also, before the Huns realized that they were empty.

In connection with this attack a rather amusing incident happened amongst ourselves.   As soon as the man next me saw the attack commence, he yelled out: " They're our own men.   Come on, we can't let them go alone."   He was over the parapet in no time and dragged me half-way with him.   As soon as the " gallant lad " was seen, he was ordered back, and the order was repeated by nearly all the men who were manning the parapet.   He told me afterwards that it was the funniest of sights as he looked back, a dozen heads projecting over the sandbags, all with their mouths wide open, and all with one accord saying: " Come back, you silly ass ! "   He came back rather crestfallen.

The interlude was really a welcome one, and useful, too, for we realized then that nearly every rifle was clogged with dirt and entirely useless. We set to work cleaning at once, and this kept us occupied amidst the constant bursting of the shells. Our own guns were practically silent, and we supposed they were reserving ammunition, which was not too plentiful at the best of times.

Soon the runaways began to return. They had been turned back, in some cases, at the point of the revolver, but when their first panic had been overcome, they came back quite willingly, although they must have lost heavily in the process. They crowded into our trench, and there was hardly room to move a limb.

It was scorchingly hot and no one could eat, although I tried to do so. All day long—the longest day I ever spent—we were constantly covered with debris from the shell-bursts. Great pieces fell all about us, and, packed like herrings, we crowded in the bottom of the trench. Hardly anything could be done for the wounded. If their wounds were slight, they generally risked a dash to the rear. Every now and then we stood to in expectation of a counter-attack, but none developed.

About 6.0 p.m. the worst moment of the day came. The Huns started to bombard us with a shell which was quite new to us. It sounded like a gigantic fire-cracker, with two distinct explosions. These shells came over just above the parapet, in a flood, much more quickly than we could count them. After a quarter of an hour of this sort of thing, there was a sudden crash in the trench and ten feet of the parapet, just beyond me, was blown away and everyone around blinded by the dust. With my first glance I saw what looked like half a dozen bodies, mingled with sandbags, and then I smelt gas and realized that these were gas-shells. I had my respirator on in a hurry and most of our own men were as quick. The others were slower and suffered for it. One man was sick all over the sandbags and another was coughing his heart up. We pulled four men out of the debris unharmed. One man was unconscious, and died of gas later. Another was hopelessly smashed up and must have got it full in the chest.

We all thought that this was the end and almost hoped for it, but luckily the gas-shells stopped, and after a quarter of an hour we could take off our respirators. I started in at once to build up the parapet again, for we had been laid open to the world in front, but the gas lingered about the hole for hours, and I had to give up delving in the bottom for a time. As it was it made me feel very sick.

A counter-attack actually commenced as soon as the bombardment ceased, and we had to stand to again. My rifle had been broken in two pieces, but there were plenty of spare ones lying about now. I tried four, however, before I could get one to act at all. All were jammed, and that one was very stiff. As we leaned over the parapet, I saw the body of a Hun lying twenty yards out in front. It commenced to writhe and finally half-sat up. I suppose the gas had caught him. The man standing next me—a corporal in a county battalion—raised his rifle, and before I could stop him, sent a bullet into the body. It was a rotten thing to see, but I suppose it was really a merciful end for the poor chap, better than his own gas, at any rate.

The men in the front trenches had got it as badly as we had, and if the counter-attack was pressed, it did not seem humanly possible, in the condition we were in, to offer a successful defence. One man kept worrying us all by asking what we were to do if the Huns did us in, whether surrender or run ! Fortunately, our own guns started and apparently caught the Huns massing. The counter-attack accordingly crumpled up.

In the midst of it all, someone realized that the big gap in the parapet could not be manned, and four of us, including myself, were ordered to lie down behind what was left of the parados and cover the gap with our rifles. It was uncomfortable work, as the gas fumes were still very niffy and the place was a jumble of dead bodies. We could not stand up to clear them away, and in order to get a place at all, I had to lie across the body of a gigantic Hun.

As soon as things quietened down a bit, we had a chance to look around, Since the morning most of the branches of the trees in the wood had gone and many of the trunks had become mere splintered poles. Something else had changed also, and for a time I could not make out what it was. Then it suddenly flashed across my mind that the thick hedge at the back of the trench had entirely disappeared. It was right in the path of the storm of gas-shells and they had carried it away.

We managed to get some sort of parapet erected in the end. It was more or less bullet-proof, at any rate. At dusk some scores of men came back from the front line, wounded or gassed. They had to cross the open at a run or a shamble, but I did not see any hit. Then the Brigade-Major appeared, and cheered us by promising a relief that night. It still rained shells, although not so hard as before dusk, and we did not feel capable of standing much more of it.

As time wore on ·the shelling became more fitful, though it never actually ceased. It was comparatively cool again, and one could drink and even eat a little. My cap had gone in the general smash and I took another, which happened to fit.

No relief turned up, and about midnight two volunteers were asked for, to carry to the dressing-station a boy prisoner whose leg was smashed. There was considerable competition for the job, as we were told that the men selected could go on to the rear afterwards. A Fusilier and I were the lucky ones.

We managed to manufacture a sort of splint for the boy's leg and then tied his legs together. The Fusilier got him on his back and I took his legs. It was a rotten job, as the poor wretch started screaming, and screamed until he fainted. After hoisting him out of the trench, we had to cart him across the open, which was a wilderness of shell-holes. To make matters worse, I found I was as weak as a rabbit and could hardly carry myself. Just as we left the trench, a long line of dark figures passed us. They all wore the kilt, and we concluded that they were the expected relief.

We managed to get the boy as far as the old front-line, which was full of our own wounded, awaiting the doctor. There we found a hospital orderly, and he suggested we should leave our burden with him. We were thankful enough to do so, as the dressing-station was a full half-mile away.

H. S. Clapham (H.A.C.).

THE ORIGIN OF A LEGEND

28th June. We have a clerk here, Venables. He has got tired of writing, and, wanting to change the pen for the sword, borrowed a rifle and walked up to the front line at Quinn's Post. There he popped his head in and said : " Excuse me, is this a private trench, or may anyone fire out of it ? "

Hon. Aubrey Herbert.

VISION OF THE LINE

15th July. Meanwhile there is the usual evening sluggishness. Close by, a quickfirer is pounding away its allowance of a dozen shells a day. It is like a cow coughing. Eastward there begins a sound (all sounds begin at sundown and continue intermittently till midnight, reaching their zenith at about 9 p.m. and then dying away as sleepiness claims their makers)—a sound like a motor-cycle race —thousands of motor-cycles tearing round and round a track, with cut-outs out : it is really a pair of machine-guns firing. And now one sound awakens another. The old cow coughing has started the motor-bikes : and now at intervals of a few minutes come express trains in our direction : you can hear them rushing toward us ; they pass going straight for the town behind us : and you hear them begin to slow down as they reach the town : they will soon stop : but no, every time, just before they reach it, is a tremendous railway accident. At least, it must be a railway accident, there is so much noise, and you can see the dust that the wreckage scatters. Sometimes the train behind comes very close, but it too smashes on the wreckage of its forerunners. A tremendous cloud of dust, and then the groans. So many trains and accidents start the cow coughing again : only another cow this time, somewhere behind us, a tremendous-sized cow (wonderfully great), with awful whooping-cough. It must be a buffalo : this cough must burst its sides. And now someone starts sliding down the stairs on a tin tray, to soften the heart of the cow, make it laugh and cure its cough. The din he makes is appalling. He is beating the tray with a broom now, every two minutes a stroke : he has certainly stopped the cow by this time, probably killed it. He will leave off soon (thanks to the " shell tragedy ") : we know he can't last.

It is now almost dark : come out and see the fireworks. While waiting for them to begin you can notice how pale and white the corn is in the summer twilight : no wonder with all this whooping-cough about. And the motor-cycles: notice how all these races have at least a hundred entries: there is never a single cycle going. And why are there no birds coming back to roost? Where is the lark? I haven't heard him all to-day. He must have got whooping-cough as well, or be staying at home through fear of the cow. I think it will rain to-morrow, but there have been no swallows circling low, stroking their breasts on the full ears of corn. Anyhow, it is night now, but the circus does not close till twelve. Look! there is the first of them! The fireworks are beginning. Red flares shooting up high into the night, or skimming low over the ground, like the swallows that are not: and rockets bursting into stars. See how they illumine that patch of ground a mile in front. See it, it is deadly pale in their searching light: ghastly, I think, and featureless except for two big lines of eyebrows ashy white, parallel along it, raised a little from its surface. Eyebrows. Where are the eyes? Hush, there are no eyes. What those shooting flares illumine is a mole. A long thin mole. Burrowing by day, and shoving a timorous enquiring snout above the ground by night. Look, did you see it? No, you cannot see it from here. But were you a good deal nearer, you would see behind that snout a long and end-less row of sharp shining teeth. The rockets catch the light from these teeth and the teeth glitter: they are silently removed from the poison-spitting gums of the mole. For the mole's gums spit fire and, they say, send something more concrete than fire darting into the night. Even when its teeth are off. But you cannot see all this from here: you can only see the rockets and then for a moment the pale ground beneath. But it is quite dark now.

And now for the fun of the fair! You will hear soon the riding-master crack his whip—why, there it is. Listen, a thousand whips are cracking, whipping the horses round the ring. At last! The fun of the circus is begun. For the motor-cycle team race has started off again: and the whips are cracking all: and the wares-man starts again, beating his loud tin tray to attract the customers: and the cows in the cattle-show start coughing, coughing: and the firework display is at its best: and the circus specials come one after another bearing the merry-makers back to town, all to the inevitable crash, the inevitable accident. It can't last long: these accidents are so frequent, they'll all get soon killed off, I hope. Yes, it is diminishing. The train service is cancelled (and time too):

the cows have stopped coughing : and the cycle race is done. Only the kids who have bought new whips at the fair continue to crack them : and unused rockets that lie about the ground are still sent up occasionally. But now the children are being driven off to bed : only an occasional whip-crack now (perhaps the child is now the sufferer) : and the tired showmen going over the ground pick up the rocket-sticks and dead flares. At least I suppose this is what must be happening : for occasionally they still find one that has not yet gone off and send it up out of mere perversity. Else what silence !

It must be midnight now. Yes, it is midnight. But before you go to bed, bend down, put your ear against the ground. What do you hear ? " I hear an endless tapping and a tramping to and fro : both are muffled : but they come from everywhere. Tap, tap, tap : pick, pick, pick : tra-mp, tra-mp, tra-mp." So you see the circus-goers are not all gone to sleep. There is noise coming from the womb of earth, noise of men who tap and mine and dig and pass to and fro on their watch. What you have seen is the foam and froth of war : but underground is labour and throbbing and long watch. Which will one day bear their fruit. They will set the circus on fire. Then what pandemonium ! Let us hope it will not be to-morrow !

Charles Sorley (7th Suffolk Regt.).

POET IN ACTION

CHARLES SORLEY

4th Aug. We were holding trenches just to the south of Ploeg-steert wood. D Coy. were on the left of the Battalion, about 100 yards from the Germans. That opposite C.'s platoon was, I think, the most interesting part of our line, as the Germans were working on it from the day we took over till the day we left. They seemed to be making a redoubt of some kind, and, as those were the days when shells were scarce, we couldn't ask the gunners to blow it up . . . C. knew the ground in front of this better than anyone in the company : where the ditches and disused saps ran ; where the differ-ent shell-holes lay ; where the beetroot met the clover, and where the clover ended in a strip of long thin grass up to the enemy's wire. C. had been out crawling often before, just for the fun of the thing. . . . It was all planned out cleverly beforehand : C. and three other bombers to crawl up to within bombing distance, he leading and directing the show ; four riflemen were to come up on the flank and cover their retirement. . . . It was a dark night and everything went off splendidly up to the point when the bombs were to be thrown. . . . The pins had all been taken out and the second signal was just being passed when the third bomber dropped his infernal machine. I think the others heard it thud and tried to get clear ; at any rate he was stupid enough to fumble about in the long wet grass in an attempt to find it. There was a dreadful five-seconds' suspense : then the thing exploded right under him. In the con-fusion C. and one of the other men managed to throw their bombs, and that and the fire of the riflemen, who opened up a steady burst immediately, saved the party somewhat. C. crawled to the man who had dropped his bomb and dragged him into the shell-hole. . . . The shell-hole was his salvation. They had only just got into it when the Germans swept the ground with an absolute hail of rifle and machine-gun fire and lit all around with Véry lights. . . . When the Germans had quieted down a bit, some more men came out and helped to get the wounded in. The one with C. was in a very bad way and died soon after. C. said every bone in the upper part of his body must have been broken—it was like carrying a piece of living pulp—and he never forgot the curious inarticulate cry of the man as he picked him up. . . .

Next morning, a brilliant July day, I went round to pick up Intelligence and met C. on trench patrol. He had just come from breakfasting and was dressed in summer get-up ; gum boots, breeches, shirt-sleeves, sambrown belt and pistol. He had a bandage round his head, but only a very slight scratch from a fragment of bomb. He was walking along, reading from his German pocket edition of *Faust.* He told me the whole story of the raid : rather sorry that his plans had been let down just when they might have been so successful ; but he took it all in his happy careless fashion.

From an officer of the 7th Suffolk Regt.

GALLIPOLI

SUVLA BAY FROM THE SEA

6th August. Imbros. The sea was like glass—melted; blue-green with a dull red glow in it: the air seemed to have been boiled. Officers and men gave me the " feel " of being " for it " though over-serious for British soldiers who always in my previous experience, have been extraordinarily animated and gay when they are advancing " on a Koppje day." These new men seem subdued when I recall the blaze of enthusiasm in which the old lot started out of Mudros harbour on that April afternoon.

The *moral* of troops about to enter into battle supplies a splendid field of research for students of the human soul, for then the blind wall set in everyday intercourse between Commander and commanded seems to become brittle as crystal and as transparent. Only for a few moments—last moments for so many ? But, during those moments, the gesture of the General means so much—it strikes the attitude of his troops. It is up to Stopford and Hammersley to make those gestures. Stopford was not there, and is not the type; Hammersley is not that type either. How true it is that age, experience, wisdom count for less than youth, magnetism and love of danger when inexperience has to be heartened for the struggle.

Strolled back slowly along the beach, and, at 8.30, in the gathering dusk, saw the whole flotilla glide away and disappear ghostlike to the northwards. The empty harbour frightens me. Nothing in legend stranger or more terrible than the silent departure of this silent Army, K's new Corps, every mother's son of them, face to face with their fate. . . .

7th August. Imbros. Sitting in my hut after a night in the G.S. tent. One A.D.C. remains over there. As the cables come in he runs across with them. Freddie Maitland runs fast. I am watching to see his helmet top the ridge of sand that lies between.

The 9th Corps has got ashore; some scrapping along the beaches but no wire or hold-up like there was at Sedd-el-Bahr : that in itself is worth fifty million golden sovereigns. The surprise has come off ! . . .

8th August. Imbros. To-day's cables before I left were right from Helles ; splendid from Anzac and nothing further from Suvla.

Not another moment was to be lost, so Keyes took us both in his motor-boat to H.M.S. *Jonquil* to see Stopford. He (Stopford) seemed happy and said that everything was quite all right and going well. Mahon with some of his troops was pressing back the Turks along Kiretch Tepe Sirt. There had been a very stiff fight in the darkness at Lala Baba and next morning the Turks had fought so hard on a little mound called Hill 10 that he (Stopford) had been afraid we were not going to be able to take it at all. However, it had been taken, but there was great confusion and hours of delay in deploying for the attack of the foothills. They were easily carried in the end but by that time the men were so thirsty and tired that they did not follow up the beaten enemy.

" And where are they now ? " I asked.

" There," he replied, " along the foot of the hills," and he pointed out the line, north to south.

" But they held that line, more or less, yesterday," I said.

" Yes," said Stopford, and he went on to explain that the Brigadiers had been called upon to gain what ground they could without serious fighting but that, actually, they had not yet occupied any dominating tactical point. The men had been very tired ; he had not been able to get water up to them or land his guns as quickly as he had hoped. Therefore, he had decided to postpone the occupation of the ridge (which might lead to a regular battle) until next morning.

" A regular battle is just exactly what we are here for " was what I was inclined to say, but what I did say was that most of this was news to me ; that he should have instantly informed me of his decision that he could not obey my cabled order of yesterday afternoon to " push on rapidly." Stopford replied that he had only made up his mind within the past hour or so ; that he had just got back from the shore and was going to send me a full message when I arrived.

Now, what was to be done ? The Turks were so quiet it seemed to me certain they must have taken the knock-out. All along the beaches, and inland too, no end of our men were on the move, offering fine targets. The artillery which had so long annoyed Anzac used to fire from behind Ismail Oglu Tepe ; i.e., within point-blank range of where our men were now strolling about in crowds. Yet not a single shell was being fired. Either, the enemy's guns had been run back over the main ridge to save them ; or, the garrison of Ismail Oglu Tepe was so weak and shaken that they were avoiding any move which might precipitate a conflict.

I said to Stopford, " We must occupy the heights at once. It is imperative we get Ismail Oglu Tepe and Tekke Tepe *now* ! " To this he raised objections. He doubted whether the troops had got their water yet ; he and Reed were agreed we ought to get more guns ashore ; the combination of naval and military artillery was being worked out for the morning ; orders would all have to be re-written. He added that, whilst agreeing with me on principle as to the necessity for pushing on, there were many tactical reasons against it, especially the attitude of his Generals who had told him their men were too tired. I thought to myself of the many, many times Lord Bobs, French, every leader of note has had to fight that same *non possumus* ; of the old days when half the victory lay in the moral effort which could impel men half dead with hunger, thirst and sleeplessness to push along. A cruel, pitiless business but so is war itself. Was it not the greatest of soldiers who said his Marshals could always find ten good reasons for putting off an attack till next day ! . . .

9th August. Imbros. With the first streak of dawn I was up on the bridge with my glasses. The hills are so covered with scrub that it was hard to see what was going on in that uncertain light, but the heavyish shrapnel fire was a bad sign and the fact that the enemy's guns were firing from a knoll a few hundred yards East of Anafarta Sagir was proof that our troops were not holding Tekke Tepe. But the Officer of the Watch said that the small hours passed quietly ; no firing ashore during the hours of darkness. Could not make head or tail of it !

As the light grew stronger some of ours could be seen pushing up the western slopes of the long spur running out South-west from Anafarta. The scrub was so thick that they had to climb together and follow-my-leader along what appeared to be cattle-tracks up the hill. On our right all seemed going very well. Looking through naval telescopes we thought—we all thought—Ismail Oglu Tepe height was won. Very soon the shrapnel got on to those bunches of men on our left and there was something like a stampede from North to South. Looking closer we could see the enemy advancing behind their own bursting shrapnel and rolling up our line from the left on to the centre. Oh for the good *Queen Bess*, her high command, and her 15-inch shrapnel ! One broadside and these Turks would go scampering down to Gehenna. The enemy counter-attack was coming from the direction of Tekke Tepe and moving over the foothills and plain on Sulajik. Our centre made a convulsive effort (so it seemed) to throw back the steadily advancing Turks ; three or four companies (they looked like) moved out from the brush about Sulajik and tried to deploy. But the shrapnel got on to these fellows also and I lost sight of them. Then about 6 a.m. the whole lot seemed suddenly to collapse :—including the right ! Not only did they give ground but they came back—some of them—half-way to the sea. But others made a stand. The musketry fire got very heavy. The enemy were making a supreme effort. The Turkish shell fire grew hotter and hotter. The enemy's guns seemed now to be firing not only from round about Anafarta Sagir, but also from somewhere between 113 and 101, 2,500 yards or so South-west of Anafarta. Still these fellows of ours ; not more than a quarter of those on the ground at the outset—stuck it out. My heart has grown tough amidst the struggles of the Peninsula but the misery of this scene wellnigh broke it. What kept me going was the sight of Sari Bair—I could not keep my eyes off the Sari Bair ridge. Guns from all sides, sea and land, Turks and British, were turned on to it and enormous explosions were sending slices off the top of the high mountain to mix with the clouds in the sky. Under that canopy our men were fighting for dear life far above us !

Between 7.30 and 8.o the Turkish reinforcements at Suvla seemed to have got enough. They did not appear to be in any great strength : here and there they fell back : no more came up in support : evidently, they were being held : failure, not disaster, was the upshot : few things so bad they might not be worse. By 8.o the musketry and the shelling began to slacken down although there was a good deal of desultory shooting. We were holding our own ; the Welsh Division are coming in this morning ; but we have not sweated blood only to hold our own ; our occupation of the open key positions has been just too late ! The element of surprise—wasted ! The prime factor set aside for the sake of other factors ! Words are no use.

Looked at from the bridge of the *Triad*—not a bad observation station—the tendency of our men to get into little groups was very noticeable : as if they had not been trained in working under fire in the open. As to the general form of our attack against the hills on our right, it seemed to be what our French Allies call *décousu*. After a whole day's rest and preparing, there might have been more form and shape about the movement. Yet it was for the sake of this form and shape that the Turkish reinforcements have been given time to get on to the heights. Our stratagems worked well, but there is a time limit set to all make-believes ; the hour glass of fate was set at forty-eight hours, and now the sands have run out.

Gen. Sir Ian Hamilton.

SUVLA BAY FROM THE LAND

About 4.30 a.m. I was called to Essad Pasha, who informed me that the enemy had landed troops north of Ariburnu. Their aim was not yet clear. I was to occupy the Kodjadschemendagh–Djonk Bahir and wait there. My two infantry regiments, 25 and 64, with my battery, were at once given marching orders and I personally hurried ahead with my staff.

Stegemann pictures very dramatically in his well-known and first-class book how with drawn sword, at the head of my Division, I threw myself on the enemy who were already entrenching on the Djonk Bahir. I must say that it was unfortunately far from being as dramatic as he pictured it, or rather, Allah be praised ! that it was not so, because actually I reached the top before the English, and that was the chief point at the moment.

From a deep valley I saw before me the steep side of the Djonk Bahir whose high comb eventually merged in the near Kodjadschemendagh. We had to dismount from our horses and under the already burning rays of the sun (it was 6 a.m.) climb the sides of the Djonk Bahir, pulling ourselves slowly up by the help of small bushes and rough grass. On top was a long narrow plateau with an astonishingly far-reaching view over rough hilly country to the Ægean Sea.

Suvla Bay lay full of ships. We counted ten transports, six warships, and seven hospital ships. On land we saw a confused mass of troops like a disturbed ant-heap, and across the blinding white surface of the dried salt sea we saw a battery marching in a southerly direction. With our few revolvers we could do nothing against it.

All about us was peace and quiet—not a man to be seen and no enemy in front of us in the hills. With glasses I was able to pick out bit by bit Willmer's companies north of the Asmakdere on the east border of the flat country, and, on the flat, in certain places, entrenching. Nowhere was there fighting in progress.

I now began a reconnaissance of the country so as to be able to receive the approaching regiments with final orders. This was a long high ridge, which stretched from Abdurraham Bahir over Kodjadschemendagh–Djonk Bahir to the Dustepe, and to which the English gave the group name of Sari Bahir. My two regiments would be simply lost in this immense position if the enemy commenced the steep ascent from the valley immediately. A very limited field of fire. In front of us a confusion of valleys, nullahs and heights. It was impossible to find a post properly controlling the massive position as it was very broken up and covered with bush.

Very unpleasant for us was the Schahintepe which lay in front of the Djonk Bahir, somewhat to the south-west. This ought necessarily to have been included in the defence line if I had had time to make proper preparations.

It was now only possible to occupy the Djonk Bahir, as the key point of our position, with the reserves close behind, as the position had no depth. Additionally unpleasant was the fact that both wings were without support, and I had no troops to protect them. It was also impossible for the moment to find touch with the neighbouring 19th Division.

During this reconnaissance we found a Turkish battery whose battery commander I had to awaken, as he had no idea of the altered battlefront. He opened fire on the troops crossing the dried salt sea, but could only reach with high explosive. I also found a platoon of infantry of roughly twenty men covering the battery, which was at least something.

While I now dictated reports and orders to Hunussi Bey, who had first to translate these into Turkish, Zia Bey continually swept the country in front of us with my glasses, as it was essential to keep the English as far as possible away from us.

Suddenly the enemy infantry actually appeared in front of us at about 500 yards range. The English approached slowly, in single file, splendidly equipped and with white bands on their left arms, apparently very tired, and were crossing a hillside to our flank, emerging in continually increasing numbers from the valley below. I immediately sent an order to my infantry—this was the twenty-man-strong artillery-covering platoon—instantly to open fire. I received this answer : " We can only commence to fire when we receive the order of our battalion commander." This was too much for me altogether. I ran to the spot and threw myself among the troops who were lying in a small trench. What I said I cannot recollect, but they began to open fire and almost immediately the English laid down without answering our fire or apparently moving in any other way. They gave me the impression that they were glad to be spared further climbing.

Now I received unexpected reinforcement. From the direction of Dustepe I suddenly saw a Turkish column coming which was about to descend rearwards in the deep valley. It was two companies of the Infantry Regiment 72. My orders to halt immediately and come under my command had to be urgently repeated before they obeyed. At the same time the commander of the 1st Battalion of Infantry Regiment 14 reached the Kodjadschemendagh, and I took him with his companies under my orders.

Thus I was slowly able to establish a small firing front which I grouped in two wings, as the commanders of the Infantry Regiments 25 and 64 reported to me that their battalions would shortly be arriving. I had been successful in keeping this exceptionally important height in our hands and bringing the forward progress of the enemy to a halt.

An attack by the 5th and 6th Gurkha Battalions (it was probably these battalions which, with my twenty infantry I had opened fire on) failed. Nevertheless these Gurkhas succeeded in bringing a machine-gun into action on the Schahintepe which took the narrow ridge of Djonk Bahir under flanking fire. It was a very thin fire which did not disturb us much. Nevertheless I wanted to prevent my regiments, which were due to arrive at any moment, from being caught by this fire during their deployment. I therefore went over to the battery and ordered them to open fire with both guns of the left section on this machine-gun.

As I was starting back towards the left wing, which I considered endangered and which had still not found touch with the 19th Division—it was about 8 o'clock in the morning—I received from the machine-gun a shot through the breast. This was most annoying. Up to date I had escaped from many other worse positions without a scratch. Now I was forced to leave my brave Division just in this most critical moment. Zia Bey and Brandl sprang to my help immediately, but had to leave me lying as the machine-gun kept this point under continuous fire. After some time the fire slackened and both carried me behind the near protecting cliff. Brandl, who had studied medicine for six terms in Munich, found a bullet wound in the middle of the breast, close to the heart, and tied me up with a field dressing.

Maj.-Gen. Hans Kannengiesser.

NEW ZEALAND

10*th Aug.* . . . The N.Z. Infantry Brigade must have ceased to exist. Meanwhile the condition of the wounded is indescribable. They lie in the sand in rows upon rows, their faces caked with sand and blood; one murmur for water; no shelter from the sun; many of them in saps, with men passing all the time scattering more dust on them. There is hardly any possibility of transporting them. The fire zones are desperate, and the saps are blocked with ammunition transport and mules, also whinnying for water, carrying food, etc. Some unwounded men almost mad from thirst, cursing. . . .

. . . We have a terrible view here : lines of wounded creeping up from the hospital to the cemetery like a tide, and the cemetery is going like a live thing to meet the wounded. Between us and the sea is about 150 yards ; this space is now empty of men because of the sniping.

16*th Aug.* . . . The troops quartered in this fort were an Indian Field Battery and sixty-three New Zealanders, all that was left of their battalion. These men had been in the first landing. They had, every one of them, had dysentery or fever, and the great majority were still sick and over-ripe for hospital.

As time went on, and illness increased, one often heard men and officers say : " If we can't hold the trenches with sound men, we have got to hold them with sick men." When all was quiet, the sick-list grew daily. But when the men knew that there was to be an attack, they fought their sickness, to fight the Turk, and the stream to the hospitals shrank.

I admired nothing in the War more than the spirit of these sixty-three New Zealanders, who were soon to go to their last fight. When the day's work was over, and the sunset swept the sea, we used to lean upon the parapet and look up to where Chunuk Bair flamed, and talk. The great distance from their own country created an atmosphere of loneliness. This loneliness was emphasized by the fact that the New Zealanders rarely received the same recognition as the Australians in the Press, and many of their gallant deeds went unrecorded or were attributed to their greater neighbours. But they had a silent pride that put these things into proper perspective. The spirit of these men was unconquered and unconquerable. At night, when the great moon of the Dardanelles soared and all was quiet except the occasional whine of a bullet overhead, the voices of the tired men continually argued the merits of the Expedition, and there was always one end to these discussions : " Well, it may all be a —— mistake, but in a war of this size you will have mistakes of this size, and it doesn't matter a —— to us whether we are for it here or in France, for we came out to do one job, and it's nothing to us whether we finish in one place or another." The Turks were not the only fatalists in those days. . . .

Hon. Aubrey Herbert.

SOUAIN

24th Sept. We broke camp about 11 o'clock the night of the 24th, and marched up through ruined Souain to our place in one of the numerous *boyaux* where the *troupes d'attaque* were massed. The cannonade was pretty violent all that night, as it had been for several days previous, but toward dawn it reached an intensity unimaginable to anyone who has not seen a modern battle. A little before 9.15 the fire lessened suddenly, and the crackle of the fusillade between the reports of the cannon told us that the first wave of the assault had left and the attack begun. At the same time we received the order to advance. The German artillery had now begun to open upon us in earnest. Amid the most infernal roar of every kind of fire-arms, and through an atmosphere heavy with dust and smoke, we marched up through the *boyaux* to the *tranchées de départ*. At shallow places and over breaches that shells had made in the bank, we caught momentary glimpses of the blue lines sweeping up the hillside or silhouetted on the crest where they poured into the German trenches. When the last wave of the Colonial brigade had left we followed. *Bayonette au canon*, in lines of *tirailleurs*, we crossed the open space between the lines, over the barbed wire, where not so many of our men were lying as I had feared (thanks to the efficacy of the bombardment), and over the German trench, knocked to pieces and filled with their dead. In some places they still resisted in isolated groups. Opposite us, all was over, and the herds of prisoners were being already led down as we went up. We cheered, more in triumph than in hate ; but the poor devils, terror-stricken, help up their hands, begged for their lives, cried " Kamerad," " Bon Français," even " Vive la France." We advanced and lay down in columns by twos behind the second crest. Meanwhile, bridges had been thrown across trenches and *boyaux*, and the artillery, leaving the emplacements where they had been anchored a whole year, came across and took position in the open, a magnificent spectacle.

Squadrons of cavalry came up. Suddenly the long, unpicturesque *guerre de tranchées* was at an end, and the field really presented the aspect of the familiar battle pictures—the battalions in manœuvre, the officers, superbly indifferent to danger, galloping about on their chargers. But now the German guns, moved back, began to get our range, and the shells to burst over and around batteries and troops, many with admirable precision. Here my best comrade was struck down by shrapnel at my side—painfully but not mortally wounded.

I often envied him after that. For now our advanced troops were in contact with the German second-line defences, and these proved to be of a character so formidable that all further advance without a preliminary artillery preparation was out of the question. And our rôle, that of troops in reserve, was to lie passive in an open field under a shell-fire that every hour became more terrific, while aeroplanes and captive balloons, to which we were entirely exposed, regulated the fire.

That night we spent in the rain. With portable picks and shovels each man dug himself in as well as possible. The next day our concentrated artillery again began the bombardment, and again the fusillade announced the entrance of the infantry into action. But this time only the wounded appeared coming back, no prisoners. I went out and gave water to one of these, eager to get news. It was a young soldier, wounded in the hand. His face and voice bespoke the emotion of the experience he had been through in a way that I will never forget. " *Ah, les salauds !* " he cried, " they let us come right up to the barbed wire without firing. Then a hail of grenades and balls. My comrade fell, shot through the leg, got up, and the next moment had his head taken off by a grenade before my eyes."—" And the barbed wire, wasn't it cut down by the bombardment ? "—" Not at all in front of us." I congratulated him on having a *blessure heureuse* and being well out of the affair. But he thought only of his comrade, and went on down the road toward Souain nursing his mangled hand, with the stream of wounded seeking their *postes de secours.*

Alan Seeger.

LOOS

The battle of Loos was part of a general movement, the British attack being intended, in conjunction with a French attack on Vimy Ridge, to relieve the situation on the Russian front. The four-day offensive, preceded by four days of artillery bombardment, resulted in the capture of a stretch of the German front line, but it was found impossible to effect a break-through. The French attack in Artois similarly failed to take Vimy Ridge.

BEFORE LOOS

I REMINDED Gough that we shall win " Not by might nor by power, but by *My spirit*, saith the Lord of Hosts."

Sir Douglas Haig's Diary.

GAS

25*th Sept.* . . . There was not a breath of wind until 5 a.m., but before that Gold's reports had become pretty confident that the wind would be favourable. I went to D.H. at 2 a.m., when we had just received a report from a distant station that made Gold reasonably hopeful. Our own report from the line was that it was dead still. At 3, when the decision had to be made, I took Gold to Butler and then to D.H. Gold was then more confident and D.H. ordered zero hour for 5.50. Both at 2 and 3 D.H. was fast asleep, and had to be awakened to take the reports.

At 5 he came to our office with Fletcher. There was quite a faint breath of wind then, and Fletcher's cigarette smoke moved quite perceptibly towards the Germans. But it died away again in a few minutes, and a little later D.H. sent down a message from the tower to 1st Corps to enquire whether the attack could still be held up.

Gough replied that it was too late to change. I was with D.H. when the reply was brought in. He was very upset.

Brig.-Gen. John Charteris.

THE ATTACK ON THE VILLAGE

25th Sept. The moment had come when it was unwise to think. The country round Loos was like a sponge; the god of war had stamped with his foot on it, and thousands of men, armed, ready to kill, were squirted out on to the level, barren fields of danger. To dwell for a moment on the novel position of being standing where a thousand deaths swept by, missing you by a mere hair's breadth, would be sheer folly. There on the open field of death my life was out of my keeping, but the sensation of fear never entered my being. There was so much simplicity and so little effort in doing what I had done, in doing what eight hundred comrades had done, that I felt I could carry through the work before me with as much credit as my code of self-respect required. The maxims went crackle like dry brushwood under the feet of a marching host. A bullet passed very close to my face like a sharp, sudden breath; a second hit the ground in front, flicked up a little shower of dust, and ricochetted to the left, hitting the earth many times before it found a resting-place. The air was vicious with bullets; a million invisible birds flicked their wings very close to my face. Ahead the clouds of smoke, sluggish low-lying fog, and fumes of bursting shells, thick in volume, receded towards the German trenches, and formed a striking background for the soldiers who were marching up a low slope towards the enemy's parapet, which the smoke still hid from view. There was no haste in the forward move, every step was taken with regimental precision, and twice on the way across the Irish boys halted for a moment to correct their alignment. Only at a point on the right there was some confusion and a little irregularity. Were the men wavering? No fear! The boys on the right were dribbling the elusive football towards the German trench.

Raising the stretcher, my mate and I went forward. For the next few minutes I was conscious of many things. A slight rain was falling; the smoke and fumes I saw had drifted back, exposing a dark streak on the field of green, the enemy's trench. A little distance away from me three men hurried forward, and two of them carried a box of rifle ammunition. One of the bearers fell flat to earth, his two mates halted for a moment, looked at the stricken boy, and seemed to puzzle at something. Then they caught hold of the box hangers and rushed forward. The man on the ground raised himself on his elbow and looked after his mates, then sank down again to the wet ground. Another soldier came crawling towards us on his belly, looking for all the world like a gigantic lobster which had escaped from its basket. His lower lip was cut clean to the chin and hanging apart; blood welled through the muddy khaki trousers where they covered the hips.

I recognized the fellow.

" Much hurt, matey ? " I asked.

" I'll manage to get in," he said.

" Shall I put a dressing on ? " I enquired.

" I'll manage to get into our own trench," he stammered, spitting the blood from his lips. " There are others out at the wires. S—— has caught it bad. Try and get him in, Pat."

" Right, old man," I said, as he crawled off. " Good luck."

My cap was blown off my head as if by a violent gust of wind, and it dropped on the ground. I put it on again, and at that moment a shell burst near at hand and a dozen splinters sung by my ear. I walked forward with a steady step.

" What took my cap off ? " I asked myself. " It went away just as if it was caught in a breeze. God ! " I muttered, in a burst of realization, " it was that shell passing." I breathed very deeply, my blood rushed down to my toes and an airy sensation filled my body. Then the stretcher dragged.

" Lift the damned thing up," I called to my mate over my shoulder. There was no reply. I looked round to find him gone, either mixed up in a whooping rush of kilted Highlanders, who had lost their objective and were now charging parallel to their own trench, or perhaps he got killed. . . . How strange that the Highlanders could not charge in silence, I thought, and then recollected that most of my boyhood friends, Donegal lads, were in Scottish regiments. . . . I placed my stretcher on my shoulder, walked forward towards a bank of smoke which seemed to be standing stationary, and came across our platoon sergeant and part of his company.

" Are we going wrong, or are the Jocks wrong ? " he asked his men, then shouted, " Lie flat, boys, for a minute, until we see where we are. There's a big crucifix in Loos churchyard, and we've got to draw on that."

The men threw themselves flat; the sergeant went down on one knee and leant forward on his rifle, his hands on the bayonet standard, the fingers pointing upwards and the palms pressed close to the sword which was covered with rust. . . . How hard it would be to draw it from a dead body ! . . . The sergeant seemed to be kneeling in prayer. . . . In front the cloud cleared away, and the black crucifix standing over the graves of Loos became revealed.

" Advance, boys ! " said the sergeant. " Steady on to the foot of the Cross and rip the swine out of their trenches."

The Irish went forward . . .

Patrick MacGill (London Irish).

THE 19TH BRIGADE

25th Sept. What happened in the next few minutes is difficult for me now to sort out. It was more difficult still at the time. All we heard back there in the sidings was a distant cheer, confused crackle of rifle-fire, yells, heavy shelling on our front line, more shouts and yells and a continuous rattle of machine-guns. After a few minutes, lightly-wounded men of the Middlesex came stumbling down Maison Rouge Alley to the dressing-station. I was at the junction of the siding and the alley. " What's happened ? What's happened ? " I asked. " Bloody balls-up " was the most detailed answer I could get. Among the wounded were a number of men yellow-faced and choking, with their buttons tarnished green ; these were gas cases. Then came the stretcher cases. Maison Rouge Alley was narrow and the stretchers had difficulty in getting down. The Germans started shelling it with five-point-nines. Thomas went through the shelling to battalion head-quarters to ask for orders. It was the same place that I had visited on my first night in the trenches. This group of dug-outs in the reserve line showed very plainly from the air as battalion head-quarters, and should never have been occupied on the day of a battle. Just before Thomas arrived the Germans put five shells into it. The adjutant jumped one way, the colonel another, the regimental sergeant-major a third. One shell went into the signals dug-out and destroyed the telephone. The colonel had a slight wound on his hand ; he joined the stream of wounded and was carried as far as the base with it. The adjutant took charge. All this time A Company had been waiting in the siding for the rum to arrive ; the tradition of every attack was a double tot of rum beforehand. All the other companies got it except ours. The Actor was cursing : " Where the bloody hell's that storeman gone ? " We fixed bayonets in readiness to go up to the attack as soon as Thomas came back with orders. The Actor sent me along the siding to the other end of the company. The stream of wounded was continuous. At last Thomas's orderly appeared, saying : " Captain's orders, sir : A Company to move up to the front line." It seems that at that moment the storeman appeared with the rum. He was hugging the rum-bottle, without rifle or equipment, red-faced and retching. He staggered up to the Actor and said : " There you are, sir," then fell on his face in the thick mud of a sump-pit at the junction of the trench and the siding. The stopper of the bottle flew out and what was left of the three gallons bubbled on the ground. The Actor said nothing. It was a crime deserving the death-penalty. He put one foot on the store-man's neck, the other in the small of his back, and trod him into the mud. Then he gave the order " Company forward." The company went forward with a clatter of steel over the body, and that was the last heard of the storeman. . . .

The survivors of the first two companies of the Middlesex were lying in shell-craters close to the German wire, sniping and making the Germans keep their heads down. They had bombs to throw, but these were nearly all of a new type issued for the battle ; the fuses were lit on the match-and-matchbox principle and the rain had made them useless. The other two companies of the Middlesex soon followed in support. Machine-gun fire stopped them half-way. . . .

It was at this point that the Royal Welch Fusiliers came up in support. Maison Rouge Alley was a nightmare ; the Germans were shelling it with five-nines bursting with a black smoke and with lachrymatory shells. This caused a continual scramble backwards and forwards. There were cries and counter-cries : " Come on ! " " Get back, you bastards ! " " Gas turning on us ! " " Keep your heads, you men ! " " Back like hell, boys." " Whose orders ? " " What's happening ? " " Gas ! " " Back ! " " Come on ! " " Gas ! " " Back ! " Wounded men and stretcher-bearers were still trying to squeeze past. We were alternately putting on and taking off our gas-helmets and that made things worse. In many places the trench was filled in and we had to scramble over the top. Childe-Freeman got up to the front line with only fifty men of B Company ; the rest had lost their way in some abandoned trenches half-way up. The adjutant met him in the support line. "You ready to go over, Freeman ? " he asked. Freeman had to admit that he had lost most of his company. He felt this keenly as a disgrace ; it was the first time that he had commanded a company in battle. He decided to go over with his fifty men in support of the Middlesex. He blew his whistle and the company charged. They were stopped by machine-gun fire before they had passed our own entanglements. Freeman himself died, but of heart failure, as he stood on the parapet. After a few minutes C Company and the remainder of B reached the front line. The gas-cylinders were still whistling and the trench full of dying men. Samson decided to go over ; he would not have it said that the Royal Welch had let down the Middlesex. . . .

We went on up to the front line. It was full of dead and dying. The captain of the gas-company, who had kept his head and had a special oxygen respirator, had by now turned off the gas. Vermorel-sprayers had cleared out most of the gas, but we still had to wear our masks. We climbed up and crouched on the fire-step, where the gas was not so thick—gas was heavy stuff and kept low. Then Thomas arrived with the remainder of A Company and, with D, we waited for the whistle to follow the other two companies over. Fortunately at this moment the adjutant appeared. He told Thomas that he was now in command of the battalion and he didn't care a damn about orders ; he was going to cut his losses. He said he would not send A and D over until he got definite orders from brigade. He had sent a runner back because telephone communication was cut, and we must wait. Meanwhile the intense bombardment that was to follow the forty minutes' discharge of gas began. It concentrated on the German front trench and wire. A good deal of it was short and we had further casualties in our trenches. The survivors of the Middlesex and of our B and C Companies in craters in No Man's Land suffered heavily.

My mouth was dry, my eyes out of focus, and my legs quaking under me. I found a water-bottle full of rum and drank about half a pint; it quieted me and my head remained clear. Samson was lying wounded about twenty yards away from the front trench. Several attempts were made to get him in. He was very badly hit and groaning. Three men were killed in these attempts and two officers and two men wounded. Finally his own orderly managed to crawl out to him. Samson ordered him back, saying that he was riddled and not worth rescuing ; he sent his apologies to the company for making such a noise. We waited for about a couple of hours for the order to charge. The men were silent and depressed. Sergeant Townsend was making feeble, bitter jokes about the good old British army muddling through and how he thanked God we still had a navy. I shared the rest of the rum with him and he cheered up a little. Finally a runner came with a message that the attack was off for the present.

Robert Graves (Royal Welch Fus.).

COUNTER-ATTACK ON THE DUMP. 1ST ROYAL BERKSHIRE REGIMENT AND 12TH ROYAL FUSILIERS

27th Sept. It happened very suddenly, just as he was clutching at consciousness and fighting the black mists that descended upon his brain. A cheer from behind sent him spinning round, and simultaneously to his right a line of British dashed up cheering to the trenches, jumped them and sped on towards the Dump. We were attacking, then, as his instinct had forewarned him !

The Sussex major blew his whistle and waved his arm.

" Come on," Broadchalk shouted, and scrambled out of the trench. He had much ground to make up, for the company of the Berkshires—who had been pushed up to recapture the Dump—had a good start. He was only conscious that at last the tide had turned, that those hours of indecision were over : he must dash on and get in front : that was his place. He drew his revolver as he ran.

He saw the Sussex captain pitch forward on to his face and lie still : then he too pitched forward, and landed full on his stomach. For a moment he thought he was hit, but it was only a strand of wire that had coiled round his ankle. He had lost more ground, but he made it up and got into the front of the charge about twenty yards from the Dump. Where were they going ? where would they stop? The thought never came to him: he was just one of those three hundred men who had been chucked at the enemy and could only come to rest with their bayonets in their targets' bellies. There is no thought of repulse or successful opposition in the minds of a line of charging infantry: only a roar from each throat—parched and unparched—as they swept up the precipitous side of the slag heap.

Over the edge they found the machine-guns playing breast high and felt the sing of the bullets about their ears. The men each side of Broadchalk flung up their arms and toppled backwards like stormers in an old print, thrust down from a castle rampart.

They rallied on the slag heap and pushed forward again.

" Where are you, Sergeant-Major? "

" Here I am, sir ! " These were regulars, who had fought since the tail-end of the Aisne.

Wraiths in spiked helmets—the cloth covers shining white in the moonlight—were dashing for safety on all sides before them, like disturbed earwigs under a rotten tree-stump.

A roar went up from every throat; some fired their rifles, others shouted curses, called to the enemy to stand and face the music. There was a pause while they shouted in derision, then the whole line swept forward with a shout. . . .

" Half right, half left ! " shouted the Berkshire subaltern, " and line the edge of the Dump."

They split into two parties and wheeled, Trevor going to the left and Broadchalk to the right.

" Where are those bombers? Bloody Hell ! Where are those bombers? "

It was the sergeant-major: there was a catch in his voice as he realized that his bombers had been caught by the machine-guns, that the attack was doomed to failure.

The German guns had opened, the top of the Dump was one roaring furnace of bursting shrapnel and high explosive; snakes of smoke and coal writhed into the air as the gunners found their range; the machine-guns mowed the ground like scythes, raked it from side to side : men were falling fast; that band of three hundred men was reduced to a hundred in as many seconds—and still no further sign of the Germans.

They dashed forward to the edge of the Dump and flung themselves down in a firing-line. The sergeant-major doubled back in quest of his bombers.

In the trench running round the bottom of the Dump stood the Germans, firing from the shoulder at a target twenty feet above them : and no bombs ! Four bombers could have cleared those trenches in a few seconds ; now the infantry lay helpless, and, as a man thrust forward his head and shoulders to take aim at the enemy below, a bullet found him, fired at twenty feet. The hundred men were already fifty.

Over their heads, the height of a standing man's breast, the machine-gun bullets chattered ; in front and below lay certain death.

Broadchalk watched, fascinated. He kept his head over the edge, gazing at the Germans, firing with his revolver whenever he saw one take aim. He emptied all six chambers, and waited.

" Can't we charge them, sir ? "

" Lie still," shouted the Berkshire subaltern. He rose to his feet, and a bullet hit him : Broadchalk heard the gurgle of blood in his throat, heard the drumming of his heels and the last choke—then silence.

The fury burst out once more. The man next to Broadchalk was shot through the head, and rolled over on top of him : the man on his left was hit in the leg and started to whimper.

Broadchalk sat up, waiting for the shot that should end it all : there were only ten men alive.

A succession of crashes and bursts of flame in the line heralded a new danger : this was a new kind of shell to Broadchalk and at first his benumbed brain did not take in its significance.

" They're bombing us ! " shouted one of the survivors.

Broadchalk looked quickly over the edge : the Germans were thicker than ever and were shouting in excitement. He saw them lobbing bombs gently up towards him. A German shouted at the sight of him and threw a bomb. Broadchalk lay flat and it burst behind him.

" Get back twenty yards ! " he shouted. " Get into shell-holes."

They scurried back beyond range and lay in the shell-holes. There were four men with Broadchalk and they took it in turns to watch.

The shelling had died down, and the bombing had ceased : the Germans were waiting for dawn before they should collect their trophies. A long line of dead men hung like a fringe along the edge of the Dump. . . .

Desire for sleep, sleep at all costs, seized him once more : he struggled to evade it, but hadn't the power to resist any longer.

A shout at his side awoke him. " They're coming, sir ! " He opened his eyes wearily, and saw that the Dump was grey with the first streaks of dawn.

Men were shouting in German one to another beyond the edge of the slag heap. " Stand by ! " he called out, and loaded his revolver with the reserve six rounds from his pouch.

They waited in silence, their rifles trained on that edge of slag, that stood out black against the grey mist.

The shouts increased : spread from side to side, ran like a flame on a bonfire soaked in paraffin.

A burst of shouting in their rear and the clatter of running men. They turned and found a body of Germans not ten yards away, who had raised a yell at the sight of them.

Broadchalk saw a man rushing at him, saw his bayonet pointed full at his throat, lashed out with his ash stick and felt a crash on his head. Then a German from behind seized him by the arm and ran him down the slope.

John Easton (12*th Royal Fusiliers*).

THE LAST ATTACK

13*th October.* The attack is over : an utter failure. We were opposite a few mounds of rubble still known as the village of Hulluch, close to the famous Hohenzollern Redoubt.

There were two sand-bag barricades at the end of my trench. There were about 20 yards of No Man's Land between the barricades, and the trench beyond the second one was occupied by the enemy. D Company's job was to break down our barricade, rush with bombs the German one, scale it with ladders, and drive the enemy along, while the other companies attacked over the top.

Our artillery was well-ranged and fire was continuous for hours, but little real damage was done, as the enemy was in deep dug-outs, such as those captured a fortnight before. Still, there was an exciting whirlwind of shells, noise, and smoke, shells skimming over our heads with a scream and a whistle, crashing blackly on to the chalk parapets over the way. Just before zero hour our fellows put some gas over, but the wind shifted and I think the gas only added to the confusion. All this gas and bombardment gave the enemy the plainest possible idea of what to expect, and, in my opinion, our only chance would have been a surprise raid, preferably at night.

I was definitely ordered by the C.O. to remain at company head-quarters (a little scoop out of the side of the trench) to receive reports, so I had to put one of my subalterns, MacD., in charge of the bombing party. Though outwardly cheerful I felt sick when I told him. He looked grave, and stared far away over my head. Then he said " All right " quietly and resolutely, and went back to his men. I felt I loved him.

At last zero hour came, the bombardment lifted, and I knew that MacD. must have gone over the ruins of our barricade. I stayed back at my " head-quarters " tortured with anxiety. The arrange-ment was that he would send along a message as soon as he was in the German trench.

But nothing seemed to be happening and no word came. I guessed things had miscarried, and I pushed my way along the trench. Presently I met the bayonet men who were supposed to follow the bombers, edging back. They were mostly recruits, and were leaderless and much shaken. They cried out that the officer was killed by the barricade. Waving my revolver I scrambled past them, cursing them vigorously, but I could no more have hurt the dear lads than I could have shot my mother. I reached the spot where our barricade had been, caught one terrible glimpse of a heap of bodies, and, I remember, someone's hand neatly off at the wrist and grasping a bomb like a cricket ball, when a bomb shaped like a hairbrush came over the German barricade, and fell hissing at my feet. I swung round on my heel, and it exploded behind me, blowing me off my feet.

The shock was so severe that I really thought I was done for, and lay still for a few moments, but very soon I realized the spot was so unhealthy from falling bombs that I had better get out of it. I found I could crawl, and managed to get back to where our barricade had been, or rather a few yards behind that spot. There I thought I would try and stand up. I succeeded in doing so, and began to feel I wasn't so badly hurt after all. There was a group of grey-faced men some distance down the trench staring at me. I exhorted and implored them to come forward and rebuild the barricade, as it was obvious some defence had to be made. Our little show had failed, and for all I knew there might be a bombing counter-attack any minute. No one moved for a little while, they were all too shaken, but presently one of the survivors of the bombing party shouted, "I'm wi' ye, lad," and ran to me. We started to haul sand-bags into position, and then others trickled forward and they set to with a will. This stout fellow had no rifle, so I gave him my revolver.[1] I was feeling faint by this time, with my kilt in ribbons and my backside in a bloody mess, and a dull sick pain inside, so leaving him in charge temporarily, I went to find the other subaltern.

I found him sick and shaken by his first action, and sitting as though paralyzed, but I roused him, and left him in charge of the job (where I hear he did well) while I sought the M.O. to get the wound dressed. The Germans were shelling us now, and spurts of bullets broke and cracked all along the parapets. I saw one rip through the water-jacket of our Vickers gun as I limped along.

The M.O. seemed to think I could not be patched up in the trench, so he sent me down to the Casualty Clearing Station, in charge of two stretcher-bearers. The trenches were too narrow for a stretcher so I had to walk somehow. There was a lot of shelling, and the stretcher-bearers were risking their lives, and when we came to the open, I told them to go back and leave me. They refused, but eventually, as it seemed impossible to reach Lone Tree where the C.C.S. was, they assisted me down the steps of a deep dug-out and laid me down with the other wounded. They were fine fellows and did not care a damn for the shells; their only thought was for me. I would not let them come any farther, and had no desire whatever to go on myself!

I must have lost consciousness for many hours, for when I came-to the dug-out was dark and deserted. All the other wounded had gone, and possibly I had been left for dead. Anyway, I tried to call out, and at length attracted the attention of some men outside, who came down, helped me up, and over the open in the dark to the C.C.S. at Lone Tree. I vaguely remember the doctor recognizing me as an old schoolfellow, being put in a train, and into an ambulance car, in which the jolting was agonizing.

"A Soldier's Diary of the Great War."

[1] Which he kept for me for a year, until he was killed.

THE BAUCQ AND CAVELL CASE

Edith Cavell had been in Brussels some years before the War as matron of a nursing school. On August 5, 1915, she was arrested by the Germans and charged with harbouring refugees and helping them to escape with the aid of guides obtained through Philippe Baucq. On October 7 she was tried, sentenced to death on the 11th, and shot the following morning.

THE AMBASSADORS PLEAD

11th Oct. All this while Villalobar, Gibson, and de Leval were in the *salon* at the Ministry, the room of which I have spoken so often as the yellow *salon* because of the satin upholstery of its Louis XVI furniture of white lacquer—that bright, almost laughing little *salon*, all done in the gayest, lightest tones, where so many little dramas were played. All three of them were deeply moved and very anxious—the eternal contrast, as de Leval said, between sentiments and things. Lancken entered at last, very much surprised to find them ; he was accompanied by Count Harrach and by the young Baron von Falkenhausen.

" What is it, gentlemen ? " he said. " Has something serious happened ? "

They told him why they were there, and Lancken, raising his hands, said :

" Impossible ! "

He had vaguely heard that afternoon of a condemnation for " spying " [*sic*], but he did not know that it had anything to do with the case of Miss Cavell, and in any event it was impossible that they would put a woman to death that night.

" Who has given you this information ? For, really, to come and disturb me at such an hour you must have information from serious and trustworthy sources."

De Leval replied :

"Without doubt, I consider my information trustworthy, but I must refuse to tell you from whom I received it. Besides, what difference does it make? If the information is true our presence at this hour is justified; if is it not true I am ready to take the consequence of my mistake."

The Baron showed irritation.

"What!" he said, "it is because 'they say' that you come and disturb me at such an hour, me and these gentlemen? No, no, gentlemen, this news cannot be true; orders are never executed with such precipitation, especially when a woman is concerned. Come to see to-morrow."

He paused, and then added:

"Besides, how do you think that at this hour I can obtain any information. The Governor-General must certainly be sleeping."

Gibson, or one of them, suggested to him that a very simple way of finding out would be to telephone to the prison.

"Quite right," he said; "I had not thought of that."

He went out, was gone a few minutes, and came back embarrassed, so they said, even a little bit ashamed, for he said:

"You are right, gentlemen; I have learned by telephone that Miss Cavell has been condemned, and that she will be shot to-night."

Then de Leval drew out the letter that I had written to the Baron and gave it to him, and he read it in an undertone—with a little sarcastic smile, so de Leval said—and when he had finished he handed it back to de Leval and said:

"But it is necessary to have a plea for mercy at the same time . . ."

"Here it is," said de Leval, and he gave him the document. Then they all sat down.

I could see the scene—as it was described to me by Villalobar, by Gibson, by de Leval, in that pretty little *salon Louis seize* that I knew so well—Lancken giving way to an outburst of feeling against "that spy," as he called Miss Cavell, and Gibson and de Leval by turns pleading with him, the Marquis sitting by. It was not a question of spying, as they pointed out; it was a question of the life of a woman—a life that had been devoted to charity, to the service of others. She had nursed wounded soldiers, she had even nursed German wounded at the beginning of the War, and now she was accused of but one thing: of having helped British soldiers make their way toward Holland. She may have been imprudent, she may have acted against the laws of the occupying Power, but she was not a spy, she was not even accused of being a spy, she had not been convicted of spying, and she did not merit the death of a spy. They sat there pleading, Gibson and de Leval, bringing forth all the arguments that would occur to men of sense and sensibility. Gibson called Lancken's attention to their failure to inform the Legation of the sentence, of their failure to keep the word that Conrad had given. He argued that the offence charged against Miss Cavell had long since been accomplished, that as she had been for some weeks in prison a slight delay in carrying out the sentence could not endanger the German cause ; he even pointed out the effect such a deed as the summary execution of the death sentence against a woman would have on public opinion, not only in Belgium but in America and elsewhere ; he even spoke of the possibility of reprisals.

But it was all in vain. Baron von der Lancken explained to them that the Military Governor—that is, General von Sauberzweig—was the supreme authority in matters of this sort, that the Governor-General himself had no authority to intervene in such cases, and that under the provisions of German martial law it lay within the discretion of the Military Governor to accept or refuse an appeal for clemency. And then Villalobar suddenly cried out :

" Oh, come now ! It's a woman ; you can't shoot a woman like that ! "

The Baron paused, was evidently moved.

" Gentlemen, it is past eleven o'clock ; what can be done ? "

It was only von Sauberzweig who could act, he said, and they urged the Baron to go to see von Sauberzweig. Finally he consented. While he was gone, Villalobar, Gibson, and de Leval repeated to Harrach and von Falkenhausen all the arguments that might move them. Von Falkenhausen was young, he had been to Cambridge in England, and he was touched, though of course he was powerless. And de Leval says that when he gave signs of showing pity Harrach cast a glance at him, so that he said nothing more, and that then Harrach said :

" The life of one German soldier seems to us much more important than that of all these old English nurses. . . ."

At last Lancken returned and, standing there, announced :

"I am exceedingly sorry, but the Governor tells me that it is after due reflection that the execution was decided upon, and that he will not change his decision. . . . Making use of his prerogative, he even refuses to receive the plea for mercy. . . . Therefore, no one, not even the Emperor, can do anything for you."

With this he handed my letter and the *requête en grace* to Gibson. There was a moment of silence in the yellow *salon.* Then Villalobar sprang up, and seizing Lancken by the shoulder said to him in an energetic tone :

"Baron, I insist on speaking to you ! "

"*C'est inutile* . . ." began Lancken.

"*Je* veux *vous parler !* " the Marquis replied, giving categorical emphasis to the harsh imperative.

The old Spanish pride had been mounting in the Marquis, and he literally dragged the tall von der Lancken into a little room near by ; then voices were heard in sharp discussion, and even through the partition the voice of Villalobar :

"It is idiotic, this thing you are going to do ; you will have another Louvain ! "

A few moments later they came back—Villalobar in silent rage, Lancken very red. And, as de Leval said, without another word, dumb, in consternation, filled with an immense despair, they came away.

I heard the report, and they withdrew. A little while and I heard the street door open. The women who had waited all that night went out into the rain.

Brand Whitlock (U.S. Minister in Belgium).

THE LAST HOUR

On Monday evening, October 11, I was admitted by special passport from the German authorities to the prison of St. Gilles, where Miss Edith Cavell had been confined for ten weeks. The final sentence had been given early that afternoon.

To my astonishment and relief I found my friend perfectly calm and resigned. But this could not lessen the tenderness and intensity of feeling on either part during the last interview of almost an hour.

Her first words to me were upon a matter concerning herself personally, but the solemn asseveration which accompanied them was made expressedly in the light of God and eternity. She then added that she wished all her friends to know that she willingly gave her life for her country, and said : " I have no fear nor shrinking ; I have seen death so often that it is not strange or fearful to me." She further said : " I thank God for this ten weeks' quiet before the end. Life has always been hurried and full of difficulty. This time of rest has been a great mercy. They have all been very kind to to me here. But this I would say, standing as I do in view of God and eternity : I realize that patriotism is not enough. I must have no hatred or bitterness toward anyone."

We partook of the Holy Communion together, and she received the Gospel message of consolation with all her heart. At the close of the little service I began to repeat the words " Abide with me " and she joined softly in the end.

We sat quietly talking until it was time for me to go. She gave me parting messages for relations and friends. She spoke of her soul's needs at the moment and she received the assurance of God's word as only the Christian can do.

Then I said " Good-bye," and she smiled and said, " We shall meet again."

The German military chaplain was with her at the end and afterwards gave her Christian burial. He told me : " She was brave and bright to the last. She professed her Christian faith and that she was glad to die for her country. She died like a heroine."

H. Stirling T. Gahan (British Chaplain, Brussels).

THE AUSTRIANS CROSS THE DANUBE

Oct. . . . It was market day in Smederevo. The sun shone and the streets were full of life and bustle. Carts were drawn up round the market-place, laden some with grapes and some with shining gourds, yellow, green, and white, and as big as footballs. Groups of peasants gathered round the booths where hucksters were selling sweets and fairings. The white linen shirts of the women and their black aprons embroidered with red roses made a vivid pattern of chequers on the sunlit square. A continuous and cheerful squealing came from droves of pigs that kept passing hither and thither about the busy streets, and no scene could have been more human or more peaceful. After six months of quiet Smederevo seemed to have forgotten the War. We were buying cigarettes at a stall, when suddenly the squeal of a pig gone mad rose into a wild and deafening shriek, and exploded with a crash and a dying wail. A house a few yards up the street, jumped, collapsed, and clattered down in a cloud of dust. At once the market-place was full of crying and shouting. Everybody was running up the street and away from the river. " Whatever was that ? " I thought. Something wailed and crashed behind the great church. " I wonder if those can be shells," I thought. A short, sharp shriek jumped straight at us, and a house across the market-place crashed and crumbled. " Shells they are," I thought ; " the Huns are shelling the town," and I told Bullock of my discovery. He said that there was not a doubt of it. . . .

While I was thinking thus we were walking over to the public building in order to telephone to the admiral, and to tell him what was going on. As we entered the glass came flying from the windows, the plaster fell from the ceiling. The girl at the telephone said that the wires were all cut already ; she seemed to look upon it as a joke. The hall outside was full of townspeople. There was an old man who had a cut on his bald head, and a boy was bandaging it. We were going out again into the square when a shell burst in the street in front of us, and the blast of it or the surprise sent us stumbling back up the steps. Another shell fell on the corner of the building, shearing it off, and then there was a pause. We advised the folk inside to take refuge in the Grad, which was not being shelled, so far as we could hear, and we set out ourselves up the river road in order to join our party at the cottage. . . .

Arrived at the cottage, we gathered our party behind the screens on the terrace and looked across the river. Although some hundred heavy guns must have been firing in the plain below, their smoke and flashes were hidden by the trees, and there was nothing to be seen. A steady stream of 5.9-inch shells came whistling and whispering over our heads to burst upon the slopes above ; other shells of bigger size came with a shuffling noise and dropped in a place hidden from our view a few hundred yards down the river. Every now and then we heard four railway trains that followed close upon each other run past us on lines high up in the sky, and four dull thuds came from a hill a mile farther up the river. Clouds of earth could be seen jumping into the air up there and scattering and falling in a spray ; it was a battery of 11-inch howitzers shelling some suspected Serbian gun position. With a sudden volley of cracks a group of field batteries opened fire ; others followed quickly close below us on the far bank of the river, and soon the popping and thudding of the big guns was almost drowned by the smacking and cracking of dozens of little ones. The field-guns were firing small high-explosive shells at the Serbian trenches that ran along our bank of the river, and they were drenching our river road and the slopes above it with shrapnel. Their shells began to burst round the cottage, and the terrace was soon no longer a place in which to linger. We withdrew to a gully that ran down the hill near by, and we all sat down there under the shelter of a bank. Some peasant women with their children came hurrying down the gully and ran to us for protection, as people are wont to run to their kind, with however little reason, when they are in great fear. They sat down with us, and one of the women rocked herself and wept. She was holding something clasped to her, and wrapped in her shawl : it was her child, that had been killed by the fall of her house. Shrapnel began to burst higher up the gully, and, since there was no real shelter under our bank, we went down to the river road seeking for a safer place. On the way we found a bit of an old trench under a vineyard terrace which afforded good protection, and we put the women and their children there.   One of the seamen stole away when no one was looking, and ran back to the cottage.   He came back with a clean towel and wrapped it round the dead child.   The mother was dazed then, and took no notice, but afterwards, perhaps, the gentle act lightened a little for her the heavy memory of her loss.   After dark that evening the women stole away up the road, and we did not see them again.

Lt.-Com. E. Hilton Young (Lord Kennet).

THE FUTURE

MUSSOLINI, BERSAGLIERE

4th Nov, 1915. . . . About midnight, after six hours of rain and thunder, a great white silence falls. It is snow. We are buried in mud, and soaked to the bone. Simoni mutters to me : " I can't move the tips of my toes." And the snow goes on falling, slowly, slowly. We are white all over. The cold has eaten into our blood. We are forced to be absolutely motionless, for to move means the waking of an Austrian machine-gun.

Near me someone begins complaining. Lieut. Fanelli checks him in a low voice, but the bersagliere replies, and there is desperate supplication in his words. " I'm frozen, sir. I've no courage left."

He is a Southerner. But the lieutenant, who comes from Bari, is also in a critical state. In fact, soon afterwards, he calls Simoni and me and sends us to the captain to ask him to relieve us. It is now four in the morning. Our tour of duty should last for another fourteen hours.

I find the captain in his dug-out. He is not asleep, but watches. He is smoking. Lieutenants Raggi and Daidone are with him.

" Well ? "

" Lieutenant Fanelli has sent me, Sir, to say that the Bersaglieri can't hang on any longer. After six hours' rain and four hours' snow. . . ."

The captain asks me a few questions ; then turning to Raggi, says, " You will relieve them with a section of Number 3 platoon."

" Very good, sir. By the way, may I ask a favour ! A cigarette . . ."

I have gone back to my cubby-hole. I have found it still intact though many others have fallen in. Dawn breaks at last. This has been the hardest night of my two months in the trenches.

5th November. As soon as day is in ; " No. 1 section, packs on."

We go back to the position we previously occupied to dry ourselves a little. We are observed, as we go, by the Austrian sentries. *Ta-poum, ta-poum, ta-poum.* Seven men fall wounded one after the other. Only two are seriously injured. Reaching the place allotted to us, we light huge fires. Even the sun comes out to greet us. The calmness of the sky raises our spirits. The fire not only dries our muddy clothes, it cheers us up. Pietroantonio, from the Abruzzi, who came back as a volunteer from America to serve his country along with 2,000 other Italians, rattles off some highly interesting anecdotes about life among our overseas kinsmen. Our declaration of war against Austria was greeted with immense enthusiasm. Crowds of men besieged the consulates to be medically examined and get repatriated.

" I've seen some men," says Pietroantonio, " biting their lips with rage because they've been rejected."

That is intelligible. Millions and millions of Italians, and those from the South in particular, who have tramped the roads of the world for twenty years, know by bitter experience what it means to belong to a country of no political or military value.

Benito Mussolini.

THE PATRIOT GROCER

THE HOUSE OF LORDS

10*th Nov.* LORD DEVONPORT (Chairman, Kearley and Tonge, Ltd.). There was obviously a gross waste of public money in many directions for which the Government were responsible and into which they had gone with their eyes open. The question of separation allowances should be susceptible of reconsideration. Many families were now receiving week by week very much in excess of the income they were enjoying when the head of the family was at home and at work. He had not the slightest hesitation in saying that no family should receive more than they were receiving before the War. The Government ought certainly to review and recast the situation, and they would save the country from £20 million to £30 million a year. The naval and military pay lists should be most carefully overhauled, because he was certain such examination would reveal that there were men on them who were drawing pay who were of no fighting value or any other value whatever. There were shoals of men living on the public purse who were giving no adequate return for their services. . . . committee under official guidance in control would be a waste of time for business men, but he honestly believed that a committee of four or five business men, free from official control, and with power to report direct to Parliament, would reveal facts that would astonish the country.

Reported in " The Times " (Nov. 11, 1915).

WHAT A RETREAT MEANS

Nov. . . . Let me try, then, to tell what we saw that morning as we rode along the road to Pigsa. When we had ridden a few miles from the town we saw a crowd walking slowly to meet us. From a distance we recognized the Serbian uniform. "Here comes the vanguard of the army," we said; but when they came closer we wondered what sort of an army this could be. Here was no orderly march of troops; they came straggling by twos and threes. Here was none of the spring and swing of drilled men or of the seemliness of well-kept uniforms; they crawled at a snail's pace, staggering, bent to the ground, supporting themselves on sticks. Many were without caps or boots, and their clothes hung from them in rags and were caked deep in mud and filth; and when we came quite close we saw that looking at us from each of those forlorn figures was the same dreadful face that we had seen when we had raised the lad at the gate of the town—the same enormous black eyes with their unseeing stare, the same tragic suggestion that those faces which looked as if they had experienced centuries of suffering should really have been young. A haunting thing was that their faces were all exactly alike—one could not tell one from the other. Starvation had reduced them all to the same mask of pain. "What are they?" we asked the Serbian who accompanied us. He questioned one and told us that they were young recruits of the latest class, lads of from sixteen to eighteen, and that they had been sent on to Durazzo as unfit for service, while the fit men held the Bulgars back at Elbassan in order to cover the retreat southwards of the army at Scutari and Alessio. We were riding along the road for half the day, and all the time we were passing a continuous stream of these lads, exhausted and hungry, the sick, the dying, and the dead. Those with some resolution left had gathered together to march in groups of a dozen or so. Some of these bands had found a leader, some natural ruler of men with spirit higher than his fellows, who was keeping them together, encouraging them to go on walking and helping the weaker. Those more feeble and sick staggered on singly or in pairs. Many that were too weak to walk alone were being helped along by friends. For the most part they were sick and dying of sheer hunger, exposure, and fatigue, but there were many also in the last stage of dysentery, and there were some suffering from old wounds and from frostbite. If we left the road to ride amongst the bushes by its side we found here and there a huddled heap upon the ground, the body of some lad too weak to walk farther who had turned aside to die. Two that I saw were dead, and several were past help ; nor had we any real help to give them, and that for us was the most dreadful thing in that dreadful day. When we had distributed what food and money we had—the money to help them when they got to Durazzo—there was little or nothing more that we could do for them. If we found one in the bushes that we hoped might perhaps be still able to struggle on if he were helped, we could call to him the attention of some of the stronger ones and encourage them to look after him. Their exhaustion had made all but the very strongest so apathetic that of themselves they paid no attention to those that had fallen. But several of the fallen were past such help. They were in the stupor of death, and there was nothing that could be done for them but to leave them to die. I saw two boys (and this I set down for those that glorify war) that, too weak either of them to walk alone, were staggering along, each supported against the other. They were bent with the pains of dysentery, and the arm of the younger one had been broken, and having been left untended had set, projecting unnaturally. Every few steps these two stopped and lay down together by the roadside. Looking back at them after we had passed, I saw them stagger aside off the road and fall amongst the bushes. I rode back to them and found them lying side by side. The boy with the broken arm was at the point of death. The other spoke to me ; a few words were all he could manage, and I could not understand them, but I think that he was asking for help, for a brother or a friend. There was no help for me to give, and in a few minutes the younger boy died. One could not but be glad for him—the rest of death seemed so kindly a release from unimaginable pain and trouble.

Lt.-Com. E. Hilton-Young (Lord Kennet).

MESOPOTAMIA

Early in 1915 British troops attacked the Turks after a landing in the Persian Gulf. An advance was made to Kut but this was besieged by the Turks. A fierce battle was fought at Ctesiphon on November 22, 1915. The awful conditions of the sick and wounded is described in the following passage.

" THE BARGE SHE SAT IN LIKE A BURNISHT THRONE BURNT ON THE WATER . . ."

Dec. I was standing on the bridge in the evening when the *Medjidieh* arrived. She had two steel barges, without any protection against the rain, as far as I remember. As this ship, with two barges, came up to us I saw that she was absolutely packed, and the barges too, with men. The barges were slipped, and the *Medjidieh* was brought alongside the *Varela*. When she was about 300 or 400 yards off it looked as if she was festooned with ropes. The stench when she was close was quite definite, and I found that what I mistook for ropes were dried stalactites of human fæces. The patients were so huddled and crowded together on the ship that they could not perform the offices of nature clear of the edge of the ship, and the whole of the ship's side was covered with stalactites of human fæces. This is what I then saw. A certain number of men were standing and kneeling on the immediate perimeter of the ship. Then we found a mass of men huddled up anyhow—some with blankets and some without. They were lying in a pool of dysentery about 30 feet square. They were covered with dysentery and dejecta generally from head to foot. With regard to the first man I examined, I put my hand into his trousers, and I thought that he had a hæmorrhage. His trousers were full almost to his waist with something warm and slimy. I took my hand out, and thought it was blood clot. It was dysentery. The man had a fractured thigh, and his thigh was perforated in five or six places. He had apparently been writhing about the deck of the ship.

216

Many cases were almost as bad. There were a certain number of cases of terribly bad bedsores. In my report I describe mercilessly to the Government of India how I found men with their limbs splinted with wood strips from " Johnny Walker " whisky boxes, " Bhoosa " wire, and that sort of thing.

Major R. Markham Carter, in Mesopotamia Report.

THE RIGHT PLACE

AND then foreign travel, right on from the first bump and backward flinch of the ship from the baulks of a quay under the big reddish bluff that stands sentry to Havre—yes, you think you know Havre by that and the look of all the lines of railway sunk flush with the stone surface of the wharf. Perhaps you marched through haggard morning twilight, with powdery snow muting already the tramp of men, to entrain at a goods-yard cast away in a quarter such as goods-yards inhabit. You climbed from the ground level into closed trucks. Thirty men to a truck, every truck a complete wooden box, with a few bits of straw and dry snowflakes stirring uneasily over its much chipped and dinted floor. You sat or lay in darkness, closing every chink in the wheeled box lest more flakes of snow should join the little dry eddying dance of dust that tried to begin on any square foot of unoccupied floor. From far ahead a crescendo clanging of couplings came back till it jerked your truck into motion. Hour after hour that train would bump and rumble along, with pauses and checks without number. It swerved into grassy sidings where boughs brushed its sides, and waited there so long that it seemed to have retired wholly from the world, while more eager trains would overtake and outstrip it, like the Roman legions thundering past the dreaming East. You might open a chink and look out and see nothing but grey opaque air speckled, close to your eyes, with falling white spots. Or a little clearance might come and show you whether you were still among the Norman orchards or had reached the blown sand-dunes along the northern coast, or had struck inland among the low, rumpled Picardy hills.

If you had travelled at all in northern France before the War, these occasional glimpses, which seldom showed you the name of a station, amused and excited you curiously. Some biggish town would loom up in twilight, with several churches sticking up out of it. Was it Amiens? You searched for the slim toy spire of wood,

like a dart, glued on to a mighty stone plinth. No. Then Abbeville
perhaps ? Or St. Omer, sombre, enigmatical, Jesuit, with its three
mighty church towers thrust up at the sky, one dark and two spectrally
white, dominating the black mass of houses mediævally crowded
below ? or St. Riquier, perhaps, of the glorious façade ? Or Bethune,
with the great buttress tower ?

I remember a night of such travel, when snow had fallen all day
and then left a clear sky, full of stars burnished with frost. Everyone
else in the truck was curled up in sleep on the floor, but it seemed
waste to sleep while such things could be seen. Would life ever
bring them again ? I opened a shutter a couple of inches and saw
a wild shining white world all bejewelled with glints of light from a
sky inlaid with flashing brilliants. Heaven knows where we were.
I thought I saw osiers and watercress growing in linked chains of
lagoons near a river. That looked like the Somme. And then rows
of poplars, miles long, standing above a canal ; and that also looked
like the Somme. But then the ground crumpled itself into folds,
and high on one side a great road was marching along the crest of a
down, with all its roadside trees blown one way—all their lives,
probably—so that, even on this frozen windless night, they looked
like banners carried high in procession against a strong wind. Might
that be the famous highway from Arras through St. Pol and Hesdin,
the way that Spain's flooding power had rolled out westward from
Holland and then drawn back in ebb ? But soon the sky-line fell,
the roads, half masked with snow, grew twisty without any visible
reason ; they serpentined over dead flats sharply lined with the snow-
less black streaks of ditches, where the hedges would have been in
England. The way to Ypres ? Heaven knew. I searched for the
Great Bear and took the pointer to the Pole. Right over our engine
the Pole-Star was flashing. At times the train would yaw away to
the right. It seemed to have found the turning, the place whence to
go east and drop us into our unknown predestined slot—Arras, Loos,
Kemmel, Armentières, wherever our own fighting might have to be
done. And then it would bend north again, like a compass needle,
with random oscillations and yet with that wavering constancy to the
Pole.

It engendered a strange exaltation. Forces outside us and now
beyond our control, forces to which we had given ourselves in un-
reserved faith, had taken us up and were bearing us on as mothers

carry their infants. And now I was alone in that world : sleep had
for the moment dispeopled it. All the common look of the earth's
surface had turned to white blankness almost as featureless as mist-
filled air looked down upon from clear air above. With all these
starry gauges of infinite space filling the upper concave hemisphere of
the universe, and their reflected gleams lending a visionary lustre
almost as unearthlike to the mirroring surface of the earth, imagination
needed no forcing ; there came spontaneously the sensation of being
sped through interstellar space by some omnipotent force on some
inscrutable errand to some destination unimaginable as yet, oneself
knowing nothing, controlling nothing, only feeling an immeasurably deep repose of self-committal. Whatever might come was all
right ; wherever one went was the best place and the centre of the
world.

C. E. Montague.

THE SINKING OF THE *PERSIA*

On December 30 the " Persia," a passenger ship, not carrying muni-
tions, on her way to India, was torpedoed without warning by a German
submarine. Out of 501 persons on board, only 167 were saved. The
following is the narrative of an engineer.

I IMMEDIATELY got hold of a life-belt and started to make my way up
on deck. On my way I came across a lady I had met on the boat
who was standing dazed, doing nothing. I asked why she did not
get her belt on, and seeing that she was stupefied, I gave her mine and
went back to my cabin to get my own life-saving jacket ; she was not
amongst those who were saved. When I left my cabin the second
time, I noticed that women and children were lying about, some
evidently in a dead faint and others moaning and crying out. One
woman I remember particularly, a Frenchwoman, who was leaning
up against the rail in the corridor outside the cabins, was quite dazed.
Seeing she was not in a fit state to help herself, I pushed her along,
and that seemed to rouse her. I practically got her on to the deck,
where someone else took the life-belt from her, fastened it on her,
and pushed her overboard. She was saved.

When I got up to the boat-deck I found Knight and another man
in one end of the boat, and the carpenter and another sailor in the
other end. They were trying to get her away. The three pins had
been displaced and the fourth had stuck, as we had foreseen. Knight
said " An axe, Smith ; this is jammed." There were no axes in the
boat. I was then in the boat and looked around and picked up a
broken oar and handed it to him, and he gave the pin a whack with
it. The pin luckily gave way and the last lashing was free. By
this time the *Persia* was at a big angle, leaning over to the port side,
that is, on the side the torpedo had struck her, and so when we freed
the last lashing our boat swung out from the side of the vessel and

then bumped back again into her side. We all lost our feet in the boat, and one man was pitched over the side into the sea. Knight was pitched out of the boat, and I could only see his finger-tips above the side of the boat as he clung on. He managed to scramble on board our boat again.

By this time the stern of the *Persia* was settling down. While I was helping in our boat I saw a boat next to us, full of people, being lowered down. All of a sudden one of the davit ropes broke, and that end of the boat fell down and everyone and everything fell straight into the sea. The other davit rope then gave way, and the boat landed in the water right way up and quite dry, but no one was in her. People then, who, I supposed, had jumped off the *Persia* farther forward, began to climb into this empty boat until, I suppose, there were about twenty to thirty people in her. She had remained fast to the *Persia* by her painter or one of her davit ropes. I then saw another boat empty of people fall right on the top of the boat in the water, and it appeared to me that most of the people in her must have been crushed. I saw some of them pinned between the two boats. We had failed to get the davit ropes of our boat loose in time, and the stern of the *Persia* was now low in the water. We waited until our boat touched the water, and then, as the *Persia* sank, we unhooked the hooks of our davit ropes from the davits and thought we were free. Knight, however, cried out, " A knife, Smith ; the painter is fastened." He said the davit had caught our painter. I gave him my pocket-knife and he cut the painter with it and we were free. We then were sucked right across the stern of the sinking *Persia*. We were then in the boat six—three passengers and three crew, the latter all white.

We were fascinated by the sinking *Persia*, and also we were kept over the sinking boat by the suction. After she had sunk, we got out the oars and pulled out of the way of the wreckage. We immediately started to pull people in. There were a good many people in the water. All people we picked up had life-belts. After some time we got in, I suppose, nearly fifty people. Among them were five women. There was not room in the boats for all the people in the water. Five boats altogether, I believe, got away, but I only saw four—that is to say our own, No. 14, and No. 14a, which was next to ours on the *Persia* and must have floated off when the *Persia* sank. There was also No. 16 and the accident-boat, which was under the command of the chief officer. He took charge of all the boats, but we never had anyone who actually took charge in our boat. There were several seamen, besides the carpenter, but as there was no officer in the boat, the seamen were reluctant to obey in particular one of themselves, and if any one of the passengers offered a suggestion he was told to shut up. Some time after we had got clear I saw a small boat away on my side of the boat, and Knight saw one also on his side. I saw a boat, too, which I took to be a tramp, and as I watched her—this was about 4.30 p.m.—I saw an explosion take place forward of her foremast. She did not sink at once, as we watched her for an hour or more, but the next morning she was no longer there. Before nightfall the chief officer ordered us to make an anchor, which we let down, and the other boats were moored to us in a line.

After dark we saw the lights of a vessel, and we burnt our flares, but she took no notice of us. The next morning we saw a large Cunarder. Directly we saw her the chief officer instructed the second officer to set sail and head her off. This he did and got close to her, but directly she saw him she sheered off. This he told us afterwards. In the afternoon the chief officer, who had kept the best men in his boat—I think they were mostly passengers—said he was going to row in the direction of Port Said. This was about 3 p.m. After dark we saw the headlight of a vessel. We watched it anxiously and burnt our flares. Finally we also saw the starboard light, and then the port light, and we knew she was heading towards us. When she got fairly close to us all the people in our boat got up, and as no one controlled our boat, she was soon broadside on to the sea. I do not know why we did not capsize. Knight was shouting to everyone to sit down. Finally we got alongside. There was a bit of a sea running and they were only able to let down a rope ladder. We had some difficulty in getting the women up ; one of them stuck half-way up, and I thought she would get crushed the next time we rose on a wave, but Knight and I managed to push her up. Knight and I then scrambled on board. The ship was the *Mallow*, one of H.M. ships.

Asst.-Eng. W. E. Smith, quoted by Sir A. Hurd.

VOICES, 1915

I HAVE A RENDEZVOUS WITH DEATH

I HAVE a rendezvous with Death
At some disputed barricade,
When Spring comes back with rustling shade
And apple-blossoms fill the air—
I have a rendezvous with Death
When Spring brings back blue days and fair.

It may be he shall take my hand
And lead me into his dark land
And close my eyes and quench my breath—
It may be I shall pass him still.
I have a rendezvous with Death
On some scarred slope of battered hill,
When Spring comes round again this year
And the first meadow-flowers appear.

God knows 'twere better to be deep
Pillowed in silk and scented down,
Where Love throbs out in blissful sleep,
Pulse nigh to pulse, and breath to breath,
Where hushed awakenings are dear . . .
But I've a rendezvous with Death
At midnight in some flaming town,
When Spring trips north again this year,
And I to my pledged word am true,
I shall not fail that rendezvous.

Alan Seeger.

CHRISTMAS, 1915

For the first time, since I bore arms
  My soul's invaded by strange fears,
And melancholy's treacherous charms.

No craven I ; but my mind peers
  Towards the sunset, for my home,
And mine eyes brim with bitter tears.

To-day when joy and comfort come
  To all our race, I pine and grieve,
What shall it bring me, here ?   I roam

Far from my home and parents dear,—
  They too will feel this lonely hour ;
But soft ! They send their heart's love here,

Across the battle and the wild,
  Across the future, as the past :
And Hope and Love endure at last,
  Linked as the Mother to the Child.

Otto Braun.

DEATH AND THE SOLDIER

I saw a man this morning
  Who did not wish to die :
I ask, and cannot answer,
  If otherwise wish I.

Fair broke the day this morning
  Against the Dardanelles ;
The breeze blew soft, the morn's cheeks
  Were cold as cold sea-shells.

But other shells are waiting
  Across the Ægean Sea,
Shrapnel and high explosive,
  Shells and hells for me.

O hell of ships and cities,
  Hell of men like me,
Fatal second Helen,
  Why must I follow thee?

Achilles came to Troyland
  And I to Chersonese:
He turned from wrath to battle,
  And I from three days' peace.

Was it so hard, Achilles,
  So very hard to die?
Thou knowest and I know not—
  So much the happier I.

I will go back this morning
  From Imbros over the sea;
Stand in the trench, Achilles,
  Flame-capped, and shout for me.
        Lt.-Com. Patrick Shaw-Stewart, R.N.V.R.

NATURE AND MAN

31*st May*, 1915. . . . This morning I went for a walk to the farm Luxembourg. Only two or three tottering walls remain, and a pump in the cellar which still works and which feeds the battalion's cookers. A stream flows near by, bordered with enormous poplars. Eight of these giants, slashed by shells, lie pell-mell on top of one another across the stream. The approaches to the farm are pitted with shell-holes filled with stinking water. Further, here as often as in the front line, hangs the smell of death. It is ruin, devastation. It is perhaps the end of some rich farmers who set up here on the roadside in isolation because they knew they could be self-sufficient. I seem to see the ruin of their last hopes in the trampled-down, spotted red curtain which rots in a corner half under a heap of rubble. If they could see their home, I thought, how they would weep for all their lost trouble and pains. After the War, will they rebuild their broken nest? Yes, if they are young; but if they are old? . . . and I was afraid, afraid . . . when against the whiteness of a tiny bit of wall still standing, in the part of the farm facing the enemy, the east, I saw a picture form which gripped me. Yes ! in the first rays of the rising sun, they glittered brightly, and the last drops of dew shone like diamonds. They were roses.

By what miracle had these frail roses survived the machine-gun fire which has pulverized the walls, survived the flames which have blackened the beams and twisted the farm machines ? Yet there they were, happy to be alive and to be unfolding their petals. Their blood-red scarlet seemed to make the heap of plaster from which they sprang, still more pale. I thought I heard them say : " We are Nature : you, the scattered stones, the rubbish, you are Man, a proud vain being who destroys what he took such pains to build. Nature, whom you disdain so much, here takes her revenge and offers you a lesson. Nature is eternal and Man lasts but a day. So take as your end the eternity of Nature, struggle to reach it, or at least to approach it. Do not let yourself be defeated by a scourge which, terrible as it may be, is but a tiny event in the Eternity of Life. Link you one to another your ephemeral existences ; build a bridge from father to son and hand on the password, that you may all work in the same direction, that your fleeting part becomes continuity."

I looked at the ruins and the roses, strange flowers which preached peace in the midst of war, and which said, " Build," in the face of destruction. Nature is a good counsellor. If he will believe me, the farmer of Luxembourg will follow the example of his roses. He will rebuild his farm. Perhaps he will not have the time, the courage, the money ? Then let him hand on the password to his son or to whatever kinsman he likes. Let every farmer in the invaded region act in the same way, with the same thought of continuity : and in a short space, the north and the east will rise from their ashes. The invasion of 1914 will be no more than a memory ; the burden of horror will fall back to the place to which it belongs, to a common event, commonplace and human as death itself. For in general, death is nothing when life replaces it. The death of the father, nothing when he leaves behind him sons ready to carry on the task. So a series of existences, by themselves all fleeting, if they are bound by the same thought and directed to the same end, are on terms with eternity. It is exactly thus that France is eternal. She can be ravished, torn in pieces. Of their own accord, the frag-

ments will come together again ; of their own accord, the survivors,
linked by the idea of an eternal France, will raise once more their
ruins.   And after the long winter, the bright coloured spring will
come, the great renewal, the ruddy blossoms of roses in the midst
of the ruins.

So you see, dear Father, how for a handful of roses, this morning
I gave myself up to the same thoughts as yours in the matter of
my small cousin's birth.

L. Mairet (8ᵐ Régt. d'Infantrie).

1916

THE LAST DAY ON GALLIPOLI

The Dardanelles Campaign had proved a costly failure. On December 8, 1915 the British Government sent instructions to Sir C. Monro, who had succeeded Sir Ian Hamilton in the command, to effect the withdrawal of our troops. Suvla and Anzac were evacuated and by January 8 only the front-line trenches of Cape Helles were being held. The last detachments quitted these trenches at 11.45 p.m. without the Turks becoming aware of what was afoot.

8th Jan. All day long we have been looking at the weather in terror in case the wind should rise, but, thank the Lord, it is still only a gentle breeze. It takes one back to that other night, in April, when we waited on the ship and listened to the terrific bombardment at the landing—now it is just the opposite. I am waiting on shore and it is as quiet as the grave, except when the batteries from Asia send us an occasional shot. If they had any idea of what we are up to they would make hay of the beaches, and it's rather satisfactory to feel we are cheating them, and they will wake up in the morning and find us gone.

But, on the whole, it's nothing to be proud of for the British Army or the French either—nine months here, and pretty heavy losses, and now nothing for it but to clear out.

I and the French artillery commander (the only representative of his race now remaining), are passing the afternoon walking up and down with a great appearance of calm, looking at our watches, snuffing the air for the least suspicion of wind that might get up and be a nuisance, and from time to time lighting a new little bonfire and destroying a few more maps and papers (I have burnt a nice suit of khaki drill, a bowler-hat, and about twenty books, resolved not to leave the Turks even any intellectual pabulum). I really feel almost sorry to leave Seddul Bahr. . . .

The French general has put me down for the Legion of Honour, which is very sweet of him, and great fun. I am sorry to part with the French; it has been a very pleasant job as jobs go here, and I have not felt so hopelessly a square peg in a round hole as I have usually felt since the War began.

Lt.-Com. Patrick Shaw-Stewart.

ONE WAY OUT

Infantry Office, Hounslow. 15/1/1916.

SIR,

I regret to inform you that ——, 11th Battn. Middlesex Regt., G.S., is ill at 38th Field Ambulance, France, suffering from wounds and shock (mine explosion).

1st January, 1916.

DEAR MOTHER,

I am very sorry I did not write before now, but we were in the trenches on Christmas Day and we had a lot to do. Also I was sent to the hospital. I am feeling a little better, so don't get upset. Don't send any letters to the company, because I won't get them. Also you cannot send any letters to the hospital, as I won't get them. Dear Mother, do not worry, I will be all right. Hoping all of you are getting on well. I was only hurt in the back. I will try to send you letters every few days, to let you know how I am getting on. We get plenty of food in the hospital. Dear Mother, I know it will break your heart this, but don't get upset about it. I will be all right, but I would very much like to see you . . .

6th January, 1916.

. . . I have been in hospital nine days, lying in bed all the time, and now I have a sore heel . . . I had it cut and it is getting on better. . . .

20th January, 1916.

Dear Mother, I am quite well and I came out of hospital on Wednesday (19th).

24th January, 1916.

. . . Dear Mother, you don't know how I was longing for a letter from you ! I would like to know what the War Office said was the matter with me.

26th January, 1916.

. . . I am sending this photo of one of the officers who was killed. . . . He was very good to us. . . . Please frame it for a keepsake. . . .

23rd February, 1916.

Dear Mother, I have sent you a letter that I have received the parcel. I am well, hoping all of you are quite well.

Dear Mother, we were in the trenches and I was ill, so I went out and they took me to the prison, and I am in a bit of trouble now, and won't get any money for a long time. I will have to go in front of a Court. I will try my best to get out of it, so don't worry. But, dear Mother, try to send some money, not very much, but try your best. I will let you know in my next how I get on. Give my best love to Father, and Kate.

From your loving son,

ABY.

SIR,

I am directed to inform you that a report has been received from the War Office to the effect that No. ——, 11th Battn. Middlesex Regiment, G.S., was sentenced after trial by court martial to suffer death by being shot for desertion, and the sentence was duly executed on 20th March, 1916.

I am, Sir, your obedient servant,

P. G. HENDLEY, 2nd Lieut.,

for Colonel I.C. Infantry Records.

Hounslow, *8th April,* 1916.

Sylvia Pankhurst.

VERDUN

Verdun was the scene of fierce fighting between the French and the Germans throughout 1916.

THE MINCING MACHINE

WE were facing Vacherauville when in the middle of the night, I caught a glimpse of a dark line in a fold of the ground, from which human faces began to loom up. I at once informed the captain who rang up the battery of 75's supporting us, and, in a minute, we saw through our glasses gaps opened up by the French shells in the dark poorly camouflaged mass behind the line of earth. Yet in spite of the terrible execution of the French shrapnel, the Germans remained motionless. There was not a shout, not the slightest movement of disorder; everything bore witness to the calm reigning over the enemy's line. The battery ceased fire, and a silence even more disturbing fell. We felt a pressure at the heart. What was going to happen? These men, whom we saw clearly, steadily under the hail of fire and steel the guns were raining on them, what had they in store for us? Two, three minutes passed . . . not a move. The French guns opened again, dropped still more shells, and the silence persisted. After our first surprise, we could not guess what could possibly be happening in the dip which served as a rampart to the enemy, and we stood ready at our stand-to positions. When at last day appeared, we were able to perceive that our guns had been bombarding an enormous heap of German corpses.

E. Diatz-Retg.

SANNA-I-YAT

Sanna was one of the several bloody battles fought in the attempt to relieve Gen. Townshend's force in Kut.

APRIL 5th and 9th, 1916, stood out in our battalion annals. So I can safely say that the eve of the 9th saw us tramping down the corridor once more. This time to Sanna-i-yat, Falahiyah in the meantime having fallen into our hands. Once again the night was overcast. So thick was the gloom that the nearest objects were hidden from us. The path was fairly good and well trodden. At one point we seemed to run close to the Tigris bund, and it was here that we passed a stack of discarded rifles with bayonets attached. The platoon commander slipped from the ranks and took one from the stack. A stern reminder of coming events.

What other troops were making for the rendezvous and what already there I could not say. Of Sanna-i-yat defences we knew nothing. Eventually we found ourselves drawn up in line. In front was impenetrable darkness; no stir, no rap-tap-tap from a machine-gun; no crack from a sniper's rifle.

We were told to lie down. Of the distance between us and the Turkish trench we had no knowledge. The herbage was wet with dew, and while I lay there shivering I thought of Magersfontein, for I was as old as Brandreth, who lay by my side, when news of the Black Week came through from South Africa. And now we were up against troops adept in the use of small arms and trench defence, many of them veterans of the Balkan wars.

At last the agony of suspense was over. A rippling movement from the left and we were standing, a similar movement and we were moving forward. The silence was now broken by the swishing of many feet through the herbage, by the rustle of clothes, and the clicking of bayonet scabbards. We were uncomfortably crowded. Brandreth and I had decided to remain together if possible. The order came to incline to the left. The men on our right were soon in difficulties. Possibly some trench or nullah interfered with their formation. There was a tendency to run, and then to buckle. Shortly we had a phalanx instead of a line.

I was separated by the crush from Brandreth, and very soon lost view of the platoon commander. At all costs, I must regain touch, I thought, and was still worrying about my predicament when a flare curved over, showing up our front in a great white light. Then out of the dark came a hurricane of screaming lead and shot, so staggering that the men reeled under it in confusion. There was a rush forward on my left, instinctively I followed, and found myself against a bank or nullah, behind which I took cover along with the others.

I quickly realized that this was wrong, so turned from the nullah and ran forward. I found myself going over a white patch of ground, bare of grass, and already littered with the accoutrement of the wounded. I was alone. The machine-gun and rifle fire seemed to gather intensity. My sole thought on that short run was where the impact of the bullet would be. The irresistible impulse for self-preservation came uppermost again, and I flung myself on the ground, this time my cover being a discarded valise. I was now conscious of the dawn, and, peering forward, saw a trench. My first thought was, I am there !

This did not seem to worry me much, not near so much as the infernal screaming overhead; but when I became accustomed to the gloom I noticed that the faces in the trench were turned from me. Then came a hoarse voice calling, " Come on. mate ! " The firing was now less intense. I rushed forward and saw at once that the attack had failed. The Turks remained secure behind their wire.

All was quiet in front. The dim outline of the Turkish trench showed no breach. The scattered forms of the wounded and dead lay round about. On the left a few Turks came through the wire and began to bludgeon the wounded with the butt-ends of their rifles. They were soon driven back.

Nothing further could be done. So when the morning advanced we sought our depleted and scattered units, feeling subdued and shaken in spirit. The platoon had suffered severely. The commander was killed, also the sergeant and many others. Brandreth I never saw nor heard of again.

Soldiers have a nice sense of delicacy. They did not pry too closely into each other's movements on that fatal morning. They realize that success in war, as in other affairs of life, depends largely on circumstance. Neither did they blame their harassed leaders, though there was bitter comment because they felt they had not been given a fair chance.

Cpl. T. Clayton (8th Cheshire Regt.).

SPURLOS VERSENKT

As the war progressed Germany developed further her system for inculcating "frightfulness." Orders were issued to submarine commanders that neutral merchant shipping was to be sunk without a trace —"Spurlos versenkt."

THE steamer appeared to be close to us and looked colossal. I saw the captain walking on his bridge, a small whistle in his mouth. I saw the crew cleaning the deck forward, and I saw, with surprise and a slight shudder, long rows of wooden partitions right along all the decks, from which gleamed the shining black and brown backs of horses.

"Oh, heavens, horses! What a pity, those lovely beasts!"

"But it cannot be helped," I went on thinking. "War is war, and every horse the fewer on the Western front is a reduction of England's fighting power." I must acknowledge, however, that the thought of what must come was a most unpleasant one, and I will describe what happened as briefly as possible.

There were only a few more degrees to go before the steamer would be on the correct bearing. She would be there almost immediately; she was passing us at the proper distance, only a few hundred metres away.

"Stand-by for firing a torpedo!" I called down to the control-room.

That was a cautionary order to all hands on board. Everyone held his breath.

Now the bows of the steamer cut across the zero-line of my periscope—now the forecastle—the bridge—the foremast—funnel——

"FIRE!"

A slight tremor went through the boat—the torpedo had gone.

"Beware, when it is released!"

The death-bringing shot was a true one, and the torpedo ran towards the doomed ship at high speed. I could follow its course exactly by the light streak of bubbles which was left in its wake.

"Twenty seconds," counted the helmsman, who, watch in hand,

had to measure the exact interval of time between the departure of the torpedo and its arrival at its destination.

"Twenty-three seconds." Soon, soon this violent, terrifying thing would happen. I saw that the bubble-track of the torpedo had been discovered on the bridge of the steamer, as frightened arms pointed towards the water and the captain put his hands in front of his eyes and waited resignedly. Then a frightful explosion followed, and we were all thrown against one another by the concussion, and then, like Vulcan, huge and majestic, a column of water two hundred metres high and fifty metres broad, terrible in its beauty and power, shot up to the heavens.

"Hit abaft the second funnel," I shouted down to the control-room.

Then they fairly let themselves go down below. There was a real wave of enthusiasm, arising from hearts freed from suspense, a wave which rushed through the whole boat and whose joyous echoes reached me in the conning-tower. And over there? War is a hard task-master. A terrible drama was being enacted on board the ship, which was hard hit and in a sinking condition. She had a heavy and rapidly increasing list towards us.

All her decks lay visible to me. From all the hatchways a storming, despairing mass of men were fighting their way on deck, grimy stokers, officers, soldiers, grooms, cooks. They all rushed, ran, screamed for boats, tore and thrust one another from the ladders leading down to them, fought for the life-belts and jostled one another on the sloping deck. All amongst them, rearing, slipping horses were wedged. The starboard boats could not be lowered on account of the list; everyone therefore ran across to the port boats, which, in the hurry and panic, had been lowered with great stupidity either half-full or overcrowded. The men left behind were wringing their hands in despair and running to and fro along the decks; finally they threw themselves into the water so as to swim to the boats.

Then—a second explosion, followed by the escape of white hissing steam from all hatchways and scuttles. The white steam drove the horses mad. I saw a beautiful long-tailed dapple-grey horse take a mighty leap over the berthing rails and land into a fully laden boat. At that point I could not bear the sight any longer, and I lowered the periscope and dived deep.

Lt.-Com. Freiherr von Spiegel of Peckelsheim.

MESOPOTAMIA

THE " JULNAR "

A last attempt to throw supplies into Kut was made by sending up the river steamer, " Julnar." It failed. Kut surrendered on 29th April.

25th April. . . . Last night the *Julnar* left. I saw old Cowley, an old friend. He is to pilot her. He has been thirty-three years on this river. He is a proper Englishman. He laughed and chaffed with Philip Neville and me on the *Julnar* before starting. Firman was very glad to have got the job, and felt the responsibility. Everybody wanted to go. The sailors were moved. No cheers were allowed. They pushed off, almost stationary, into the river, that was a glory of light with the graceful mehailahs in an avenue on both sides of it, with masts and rigging a filigree against the gorgeous sunset. The faint bagpipes and the desert wind were the only music at their going. . . .

The *Julnar* has grounded above the Sinn position. Nothing is known of what happened to the crew. . . .

30th April. . . . He said that there had been two killed on the *Julnar*. He was afraid it was the two Captains. He was sorry. It made Beech and me very sad. I did hope they would have got through. Firman was a gallant man—he had had forty-eight hours' leave in four years—and old Cowley was a splendid old fellow. Well, if you are going to be killed, trying to relieve Townshend is not a bad way to end.

Hon. Aubrey Herbert.

EASTER WEEK

On Easter Monday, 1916, the Irish Republic was proclaimed in Dublin and all the principal buildings seized by the rebels, who counted on the active assistance of Germany. Terrible scenes were enacted before the volunteer stronghold surrendered.

"A TERRIBLE BEAUTY IS BORN"

24th April. At one o'clock I went to lunch. Passing the corner of Merrion Row I saw two small groups of people. These people were looking steadfastly in the direction of St. Stephen's Green park, and they spoke occasionally to one another with that detached confidence which proved they were mutually unknown. I also, but without approaching them, stared in the direction of the Green. I saw nothing but the narrow street which widened to the park. Some few people were standing in tentative attitudes, and all looking in the one direction. As I turned from them homewards I received an impression of silence and expectation and excitement.

On the way home I noticed that many silent people were standing in their doorways—an unusual thing in Dublin outside of the back streets. The glance of a Dublin man or woman conveys generally a criticism of one's personal appearance, and is a little hostile to the passer. The look of each person as I passed was steadfast, and contained an enquiry instead of a criticism. I felt faintly uneasy, but withdrew my mind to a meditation which I had covenanted with myself to perform daily, and passed to my house.

There I was told that there had been a great deal of rifle-firing all the morning, and we concluded that the Military recruits or Volunteer detachments were practising that arm. My return to business was by the way I had already come. At the corner of Merrion Row I found the same silent groups, who were still looking in the direction of the Green, and addressing each other occasionally with the detached confidence of strangers. Suddenly, and on the spur of the moment, I addressed one of these silent gazers.

"Has there been an accident?" said I. I indicated the people standing about. "What's all this for?"

He was a sleepy, rough-looking man about forty years of age, with a blunt red moustache, and the distant eyes which one sees in sailors. He looked at me, stared at me as at a person from a different country. He grew wakeful and vivid.

"Don't you know," said he. And then he saw that I did not know.

"The Sinn Feiners have seized the city this morning."

"Oh!" said I.

He continued with the savage earnestness of one who has amazement in his mouth:

"They seized the city at eleven o'clock this morning. The Green there is full of them. They have captured the castle. They have taken the post office."

"My God!" said I, staring at him, and instantly I turned and went running towards the Green.

In a few seconds I banished astonishment and began to walk. As I drew near the Green rifle fire began like sharply-cracking whips. It was from the farther side. I saw that the gates were closed and men were standing inside with guns on their shoulders. I passed a house, the windows of which were smashed in. As I went by a man in civilian clothes slipped through the park gates, which instantly closed behind him. He ran towards me, and I halted. He was carrying two small packets in his hand. He passed me hurriedly, and, placing his leg inside the broken window of the house behind me, he disappeared. Almost immediately another man in civilian clothes appeared from the broken window of another house. He also had something (I don't know what) in his hand. He ran urgently towards the gates, which opened, admitted him, and closed again.

In the centre of this side of the park a rough barricade of carts and motor-cars had been sketched. It was still full of gaps. Behind it was a halted tram, and along the vistas of the Green one saw other trams derelict, untenanted.

I came to the barricade. As I reached it and stood by the Shelbourne Hotel, which it faced, a loud cry came from the park. The gates opened and three men ran out. Two of them held rifles with fixed bayonets. The third gripped a heavy revolver in his fist. They ran towards a motor-car which had just turned the corner, and halted it. The men with bayonets took position instantly on either side of the car. The man with the revolver saluted, and I heard him begging the occupants to pardon him, and directing them to dismount. A man and woman got down. They were again saluted and requested to go to the sidewalk. They did so.

The man crossed and stood by me. He was very tall and thin, middle-aged, with a shaven, wasted face. " I want to get down to Armagh to-day," he said to no one in particular. The loose bluish skin under his eyes was twitching. The volunteers directed the chauffeur to drive to the barricade and lodge his car in a particular position there. He did it awkwardly, and after three attempts he succeeded in pleasing them. He was a big, brown-faced man, whose knees were rather high for the seat he was in, and they jerked with the speed and persistence of something moved with a powerful spring. His face was composed and fully under command, although his legs were not. He locked the car into the barricade, and then, being a man accustomed to be commanded, he awaited an order to descend. When the order came he walked directly to his master, still preserving all the solemnity of his features. These two men did not address a word to each other, but their drilled and expressionless eyes were loud with surprise and fear and rage. They went into the hotel.

I spoke to the man with the revolver. He was no more than a boy, not more certainly than twenty years of age, short in stature, with close curling red hair and blue eyes—a kindly-looking lad. The strap of his sombrero had torn loose on one side, and except while he held it in his teeth it flapped about his chin. His face was sunburnt and grimy with dust and sweat.

This young man did not appear to me to be acting from his reason. He was doing his work from a determination implanted previously, days, weeks perhaps, on his imagination. His mind was—where? It was not with his body. And continually his eyes went searching widely, looking for spaces, scanning hastily the clouds, the vistas of the streets, looking for something that did not hinder him, looking away for a moment from the immediacies and rigours which were impressed where his mind had been.

When I spoke he looked at me, and I know that for some seconds he did not see me. I said:

"What is the meaning of all this? What has happened?"

He replied collectedly enough in speech, but with that ramble and errancy clouding his eyes.

"We have taken the city. We are expecting an attack from the military at any moment, and those people," he indicated knots of men, women and children clustered towards the end of the Green, "won't go home for me. We have the post office, and the railways, and the castle. We have all the city. We have everything."

(Some men and two women drew behind me to listen.)

"This morning," said he, "the police rushed us. One ran at me to take my revolver. I fired but I missed him, and I hit a——"

"You have far too much talk," said a voice to the young man.

I turned a few steps away, and glancing back saw that he was staring after me, but I know that he did not see me—he was looking at turmoil, and blood, and at figures that ran towards him and ran away—a world in motion and he in the centre of it astonished.

The men with him did not utter a sound. They were both older. One, indeed, a short, sturdy man, had a heavy white moustache. He was quite collected, and took no notice of the skies, or the spaces. He saw a man in rubbers placing his hand on a motor bicycle in the barricade, and called to him instantly: "Let that alone."

The motorist did not at once remove his hand, whereupon the white-moustached man gripped his gun in both hands and ran violently towards him. He ran directly to him, body to body, and, as he was short and the motorist was very tall, stared fixedly up in his face. He roared up at his face in a mighty voice.

"Are you deaf? Are you deaf? Move back!"

The motorist moved away, pursued by an eye as steady and savage as the point of the bayonet that was level with it.

Another motor-car came round the Ely Place corner of the Green and wobbled at the sight of the barricade. The three men who had returned to the gates roared "Halt," but the driver made a tentative effort to turn his wheel. A great shout of many voices came then, and the three men ran to him.

"Drive to the barricade," came the order.

The driver turned his wheel a point farther towards escape, and instantly one of the men clapped a gun to the wheel and blew the tyre open. Some words were exchanged, and then a shout:

"Drive it on the rim, drive it."

The tone was very menacing, and the motorist turned his car slowly to the barricade and placed it in.

For an hour I tramped the city, seeing everywhere these knots of watchful strangers speaking together in low tones, and it sank into my mind that what I had heard was true, and that the city was in insurrection. It had been promised for so long, and had been threatened for so long. Now it was here. I had seen it in the Green, others had seen it in other parts—the same men clad in dark green and equipped with rifle, bayonet, and bandolier, the same silent activity. The police had disappeared from the streets. At that hour I did not see one policeman, nor did I see one for many days, and men said that several of them had been shot earlier in the morning; that an officer had been shot on Portobello Bridge, that many soldiers had been killed, and that a good many civilians were dead also.

Around me as I walked the rumour of war and death was in the air. Continually and from every direction rifles were crackling and rolling; sometimes there was only one shot, again it would be a roll of firing crested with single, short explosions, and sinking again to whip-like snaps and whip-like echoes; then for a moment silence, and then again the guns leaped in the air.

The rumour of positions, bridges, public places, railway stations, Government offices, having been seized was persistent, and was not denied by any voice.

I met some few people I knew. P.H., T.M., who said: "Well!" and thrust their eyes into me as though they were rummaging me for information.

But there were not very many people in the streets. The greater part of the population were away on Bank Holiday, and did not know anything of this business. Many of them would not know anything until they found they had to walk home from Kingstown, Dalkey, Howth, or wherever they were.

I returned to my office, decided that I would close it for the day. The men were very relieved when I came in, and were more relieved when I ordered the gong to be sounded. There were some few people in the place, and they were soon put out. The outer gates were locked, and the great door, but I kept the men on duty until the evening. We were the last public institution open; all the others had been closed for hours.

I went upstairs and sat down, but had barely reached the chair before I stood up again, and began to pace my room, to and fro, to and fro: amazed, expectant, inquiet; turning my ear to the shots, and my mind to speculations that began in the middle, and were chased from there by others before they had taken one thought forward. But then I took myself resolutely and sat me down, and I pencilled out exercises above the stave, and under the stave; and discovered suddenly that I was again marching the floor, to and fro, to and fro, with thoughts bursting about my head as though they were fired on me from concealed batteries.

At five o'clock I left. I met Miss P., all of whose rumours coincided with those I had gathered. She was in exceeding good spirits and interested. Leaving her I met Cy ——, and we turned together up to the Green. As we proceeded, the sound of firing grew more distinct, but when we reached the Green it died away again. We stood a little below the Shelbourne Hotel, looking at the barricade and into the park. We could see nothing. Not a volunteer was in sight. The Green seemed a desert. There were only the trees to be seen, and through them small green vistas of sward.

Just then a man stepped on the footpath and walked directly to the barricade. He stopped and gripped the shafts of a lorry lodged near the centre. At that instant the park exploded into life and sound; from nowhere armed men appeared at the railings, and they all shouted at the man.

"Put down that lorry. Let out and go away. Let out at once."

These were the cries. The man did not let out. He halted with the shafts in his hand, and looked towards the vociferous palings. Then, and very slowly, he began to draw the lorry out of the barricade. The shouts came to him again, very loud, very threatening, but he did not attend to them.

"He is the man that owns the lorry," said a voice beside me.

Dead silence fell on the people around while the man slowly drew his cart down by the footpath. Then three shots rang out in succession. At the distance he could not be missed, and it was obvious they were trying to frighten him.   He dropped the shafts, and instead of going away he walked over to the volunteers.

"He has a nerve," said another voice behind me.

The man walked directly towards the volunteers, who, to the number of about ten, were lining the railings.   He walked slowly, bent a little forward, with one hand raised and one finger up as though he were going to make a speech.   Ten guns were pointing at him, and a voice repeated many times :

"Go and put back that lorry or you are a dead man.   Go before I count four.   One, two, three, four——"

A rifle spat at him, and in two undulating movements the man sank on himself and sagged to the ground.

I ran to him with some others, while a woman screamed unmeaningly, all on one strident note.   The man was picked up and carried to a hospital beside the Arts Club.   There was a hole in the top of his head, and one does not know how ugly blood can look until it has been seen clotted in hair.   As the poor man was being carried in, a woman plumped to her knees in the road and began not to scream but to screech.

At that moment the volunteers were hated.   The men by whom I was and who were lifting the body, roared into the railings :

"We'll be coming back for you, damn you."

From the railings there came no reply, and in an instant the place was again deserted and silent, and the little green vistas were slumbering among the trees.

James Stephens.

THE BRITISH TROOPS

26th April.   At 4.40 p.m. the Brigadier sent for Lieut.-Colonel Oates and told him that the 2/7th had suffered terribly, that their C.O. and most of their officers were wounded and the Adjutant killed ; further that owing to the heavy casualties which they had suffered and the long period during which they had been under fire, they could not be expected to storm the Mount Street Schools. He was therefore ordered to bring his battalion up, pass through the 2/7th and "go on with job."   The exact orders given were : "Your battalion will storm the Mount Street Schools at all costs, *at all costs* mind, penetrate further if you can."

At 5.50 p.m. the O.C. 2/8th called for all officers and a few senior W.O.'s and N.C.O.'s, and gave the following orders. "Round the bend of the road, on the right, is the school and several houses strongly held. These must be taken to-night at all costs. "B" Company will lead, "A" will be in close support to press the attack home, "C" Company in Reserve. Start in 3 minutes—*once under fire move quickly*."

The schools which were just over 150 yards away were pointed out by the C.O., the Brigadier being present and listening to the orders given.

"B" Company moved off at 6 p.m. mostly down the left side of the street, losing very heavily from the start, and were checked just in front of the schools. "A" Company (less No. 2 platoon which had been detached to guard prisoners), gallantly led by Captain Quibell, at once moved up and realizing that the hottest fire was directed on the left side of the street, pressed forward on the right side of Northumberland Road, and got their attack home. The officer commanding the company climbed the railings in front of the school, and followed by his Coy. Sergt.-Major and the men of the leading platoon, speedily ousted the enemy from the building.

In the meantime Lieut. Daffen, who was commanding "B" Company led them down the left side of Northumberland Road in the endeavour to cross Mount Street Bridge, and capture Clanwilliam House, a strongly defended building which commanded the recently captured schools, and the approach to the bridge and schools. His gallantry cost him his life, as although 2nd Lieut. Browne and he succeeded in crossing the fire-swept bridge, they were both shot down just beyond its north-west corner, Lieut. Daffen being killed instantaneously and 2nd Lieut. Browne dying of his wounds two days later. These officers had been accompanied by Lieut. Hewitt and his scouts who were now reduced to two, and by Lieut. C. P. Elliott with what was left of his platoon. The latter also was severely wounded on the bridge, and Lieut. Hewitt taking cover at the south-west corner of the bridge, endeavoured, with the aid of his scouts to discount, by rapid fire on the windows of Clanwilliam House, the accuracy of the enemy's aim.

"B" Company as a fighting unit had practically ceased to exist, all its officers, its Sergt.-Major and all the Sergeants being either killed or wounded.

The Commanding Officer meanwhile had decided to bring up " C " (the Reserve Company) under Captain F. Cursham and despatched his Adjutant with the message. The latter, Captain A. B. Leslie-Melville, an old 4th Notts Officer, lost no time in doing this, and anxious to see some fighting went on with the company, only to fall very speedily severely wounded. His wound was very serious and necessitated 6 months' treatment in hospital. His loss was deeply deplored both by the battalion and the C.O., to whom he had been a loyal and efficient Adjutant for the past 18 months. Meanwhile Captain Quibell had been joined by Captain Cooper, Lieut. Foster and three or four men of the 2/7th near the schools, and these officers reinforced by Captains Cursham, Branston and 2nd Lieut. Curtis and " C " Company, worked their way up a narrow passage in rear of the school, and reached the canal bank slightly to the north-east of the bridge. Here they had the protection of the low canal wall, which directly faced Clanwilliam House, but their view of the house was masked by an advertisement boarding, raised above the wall. A few casualties occurred here owing to the fire from Clanwilliam House penetrating the boarding, and after a brief rest it was decided to try and rush the bridge and reach this fortified house. A certain amount of assistance was given by half a dozen men, who under the direction of the C.O. were firing from behind some steps at the six windows of Clanwilliam House, in an endeavour to assist the assaulting party.

Shouting to Lieut. Hewitt, who was crouching behind the bridge on the other side of the road, Captain Quibell gallantly led the charge across the bridge, closely followed by Lieut. Hewitt and Lieut. Foster of the 7th and a number of " C " Company under Captains Cursham and Branston. The Sergt.-Major of the company, Coy. Sergt.-Major Dixie, a very valuable N.C.O. was killed here and Captain Cursham and Lieut. Curtis wounded, but the charge swept on, and Clanwilliam House was reached only to find the doors barricaded. Captain Quibell, who had been slightly wounded, succeeded however in breaking a window and with Lieut. Foster entered the building.

Lieut. Hewitt realizing the necessity for bombs, very pluckily recrossed the bridge and succeeded in obtaining a bucketful, a supply of which our Brigadier had thoughtfully procured with great difficulty.

Returning with these to Clanwilliam House the lower rooms were bombed, and the staircase which was barricaded ascended with some difficulty. The remaining rebels were shot and in addition eight dead were counted.

The floors of the upper rooms were strewn with shavings and straw and caught fire, by what means is uncertain, and in an incredibly short time the whole house was burning fiercely, and had to be evacuated at 10.30 p.m.

No one who saw it will ever forget the spectacle—the blazing house in the background, with the spurts of fire coming from the rifles of the rebels concealed on the neighbouring housetops and behind the street windows, the answering shots from the troops, and grandest sight of all—four white-robed Red Cross Nurses calmly walking down the centre of the street between the combatants, their leader holding her right hand above her head, demanding that their errand of mercy should be undisturbed. Largely owing to the courage of these devoted women, assisted nobly by loyal inhabitants, the wounded were speedily dragged into the neighbouring houses and received whatever attention was possible on the spot.

It was obviously impossible to ascertain the position or state of these wounded for many days, as the battalion was fighting all next day, and left for the South of Ireland the day after, and greatly to his regret the Commanding Officer was unable to give relations of the wounded any information as to their condition, although the Irish Command did their utmost to help in the matter.

As signalling had been reported in Mount Street, Lieut. Hewitt with a small party was ordered to occupy an advanced post some 250 yards farther down Mount Street. Whilst acting under orders from the Irish Command to halt and consolidate on the line of the canal, the battalion set to work to render their position secure for the night.

"B" Company, commanded by Bandmaster Cooper, held the line of the canal from the bridge to Grand Canal Street, from which a hot enemy fire was coming, and strengthened the position by building a barricade composed of pieces of turf taken from a neighbouring stack.

A mixed picquet from "A" and "C" occupied the buildings in Percy Place, whilst the remainder of the battalion held the school buildings, and Battalion Head-quarters were situated at 23 Northumberland Road, a building used by the brigade for the same purpose when they moved forward from Ball's Bridge.

Lieut.-Col. W. C. Oates (2/8th Sherwood Foresters).

INSIDE THE G.P.O. P. H. PEARSE

26th April. All was dark within on the Wednesday evening that I had my last conversation with him. The fires glared in, distant volleys could be heard in the night, around lay men sleeping on the floor, others stood guard at the windows, peering through the sandbags at the strangest spectacle that men had ever seen in Dublin. I stood beside him as he sat upon a barrel, looking intently at the flames, very silent, his slightly-flushed face crowned by his turned-up hat. Suddenly he turned to me with the very last question that I ever expected to hear from him : " It was the right thing to do, was it not ? " he asked curiously. " Yes," I replied in astonishment. He gazed back at the leaping and fantastic blaze and turned towards me more intently. " And if we fail, it means the end of everything, volunteers, Ireland, all ? " " I suppose so," I replied. He spoke again. " When we are all wiped out, people will blame us for everything, condemn us. But for this protest, the War would have ended and nothing would have been done. After a few years they will see the meaning of what we tried to do." He rose, and we walked a few paces ahead. " Dublin's name will be glorious for ever," he said with deep feeling and passion. " Men will speak of her as one of the splendid cities, as they speak now of Paris. Dublin ! Paris ! Down along the quays there are hundreds of women helping us, carrying gelignite in spite of every danger."

Desmond Ryan.

AFTERMATH. THE TESTAMENT OF A PATRIOT

After various activities in Germany, including an attempt to raise a battalion among the Irish prisoners of war to fight against England, Roger Casement was smuggled over to Ireland in a German submarine, his intention being to organize the Easter rising. He was, however, captured soon after landing and was taken to London, to be tried for High Treason, June 29. After his conviction he made a speech from the dock in which the following passage occurs.

Then came the War. As Mr. Birrell said in his evidence recently laid before the Commission of Inquiry into the causes of the late rebellion in Ireland, " the War upset all our calculations." It upset mine no less than Mr. Birrell's, and put an end to my mission of peaceful effort in America. War between Great Britain and Germany meant, as I believed, ruin for all the hopes we had founded on the enrolment of the Irish Volunteers. A constitutional movement in Ireland is never very far from a breach of the constitution, as the Loyalists of Ulster had been so eager to show us. The cause is not far to seek. A constitution to be maintained intact must be the achievement and the pride of the people themselves; must rest on their own free will and on their own determination to sustain it, instead of being something resident in another land whose chief representative is an armed force—armed not to protect the population, but to hold it down. We had seen the working of the Irish constitution in the refusal of the army of occupation at the Curragh to obey the orders of the Crown. And now that we were told the first duty of an Irishman was to enter that army, in return for a promissory note, payable after death—a scrap of paper that might or might not be redeemed, I felt over there in America that my first duty was to keep Irishmen at home in the only army that could safeguard our national existence. If small nationalities were to be the pawns in this game of embattled giants, I saw no reason why Ireland should shed her blood in any cause but her own, and if that be treason beyond the seas I am not ashamed to avow it or to answer for it here with my life. And when we had the doctrine of Unionist loyalty at last—" Mausers and Kaisers and any King you like," and I have heard that at Hamburg, not far from Limburg on the Lahn —I felt I needed no other warrant than that these words conveyed —to go forth and do likewise. The difference between us was that the Unionist champions chose a path they felt would lead to the woolsack; while I went a road I knew must lead to the dock. And the event proves we were both right. The difference between us was that my " treason " was based on a ruthless sincerity that forced me to attempt in time and season to carry out in action what I said in word—whereas their treason lay in verbal incitements that they knew need never be made good in their bodies. And so, I am prouder to stand here to-day in the traitor's dock to answer this impeachment than to fill the place of my right honourable accusers.

We have been told, we have been asked to hope, that after this war Ireland will get Home Rule, as a reward for the life-blood shed

in a cause which whoever else its success may benefit can surely not
benefit Ireland. And what will Home Rule be in return for what
its vague promise has taken and still hopes to take away from Ireland ?
It is not necessary to climb the painful stairs of Irish history—that
treadmill of a nation whose labours are as vain for her own uplifting
as the convict's exertions are for his redemption—to review the long
list of British promises made only to be broken—of Irish hopes
raised only to be dashed to the ground. Home Rule when it comes,
if come it does, will find an Ireland drained of all that is vital to its
very existence—unless it be that unquenchable hope we build on the
graves of the dead. We are told that if Irishmen go by the thousand
to die, not for Ireland, but for Flanders, for Belgium, for a patch
of sand on the deserts of Mesopotamia, or a rocky trench on the
heights of Gallipoli, they are winning self-government for Ireland.
But if they dare to lay down their lives on their native soil, if they
dare to dream even that freedom can be won only at home by men
resolved to fight for it there, then they are traitors to their country,
and their dream and their deaths alike are phases of a dishonourable
phantasy. But history is not so recorded in other lands. In Ireland
alone in this twentieth century is loyalty held to be a crime. If
loyalty be something less than love and more than law, then we
have had enough of such loyalty for Ireland or Irishmen. If we are
to be indicted as criminals, to be shot as murderers, to be imprisoned
as convicts because our offence is that we love Ireland more than
we value our lives, then I know not what virtue resides in any offer
of self-government held out to brave men on such terms. Self-
government is our right, a thing born in us at birth ; a thing no
more to be doled out to us or withheld from us by another people
than the right to life itself—than the right to feel the sun or smell
the flowers, or to love our kind. It is only from the convict these
things are withheld for crime committed and proven—and Ireland
that has wronged no man, that has injured no land, that has sought no
dominion over others—Ireland is treated to-day among the nations
of the world as if she was a convicted criminal. If it be treason to
fight against such an unnatural fate as this, then I am proud to be
a rebel, and shall cling to my " rebellion " with the last drop of my
blood. If there be no right of rebellion against a state of things
that no savage tribe would endure without resistance, then I am sure
that it is better for men to fight and die without right than to live

in such a state of right as this. Where all your rights become only an accumulated wrong; where men must beg with bated breath for leave to subsist in their own land, to think their own thoughts, to sing their own songs, to garner the fruits of their own labours—and even while they beg, to see things inexorably withdrawn from them—then surely it is a braver, a saner and a truer thing, to be a rebel in act and deed against such circumstances as these than tamely to accept it as the natural lot of men.

Roger Casement.

MICHAEL COLLINS

On Easter Monday morning, Nineteen-Sixteen, small groups of Irish Volunteers gathered into a small drill hall on the Dublin quays opposite the Four Courts. From ten o'clock onwards a stream of grey-green uniformed men, of men in Sunday best, bent under the weight of rifles and harnessed in shoulder-straps, haversacks and water-bottles, of men in labouring garb armed with shot-guns and Martini rifles, of young lads in the kilts of the Fianna Eireann, passed through the narrow doorway in twos and threes.

Towards noon the door opened and Michael Collins swept out at the head of a small party, a rifle beneath his arm, his Cork accent vibrating. He and his men vanished into the network of lanes behind the hall. Tall and wiry, his jaw aggressively a-tilt, grey-blue eyes burning, Michael Collins vanished, the words floating back behind him:

> We died for England from Waterloo,
>   To Egypt and Dargai;
> And still there's enough for a corps or a crew,
>   Kelly and Burke and Shea.

Sometimes a burst of laughter came from the corner of the up-stairs room over Thomas O'Dea's, where Michael Collins and a party of young men were gathered. The songs stopped and Mick was called upon. He sat in his corner, looking in front of him lost in thought. He rose abruptly with his hands in his pockets, scanned the ceiling and the floor and recited " Kelly and Burke and Shea," shaking his head defiantly, and chanted until with the closing lines a passion and an assurance came into his voice :

> ' Oh, the fighting races don't die out,
>   If they seldom die in bed, .
>   For love is first in their hearts, no doubt,'
>   Said Burke ; then Kelly said :
> ' When Michael, the Irish Archangel, stands,
>   The angel with the sword,
>   And the battle dead from a hundred lands
>   Are ranged in one big horde,
>   Our line that for Gabriel's trumpet waits,
>   Will stretch three deep that day,
>   From Jehosophat to the Golden Gates—
>   Kelly and Burke and Shea.'
> ' Well here's thank God for the race and the sod ! '
>   Said Kelly and Burke and Shea.

Whereupon Michael Collins nodded to the company and sat down modestly before the echoes of his tense Cork accent had died away.

Desmond Ryan.

RETURN TO CIVILIZATION

Sir Ernest Shackleton sailed from England on August 1, 1914, in the " Endurance," intending to cross the Antarctic Continent by way of the South Pole. The " Endurance " was caught in the ice and crushed in October, 1915 ; after drifting on a flow for some months, and then crossing in open boats to Elephant Island, the 28 men eventually managed to reach South Georgia.

20*th May.* We were through the gap at 6 a.m. with anxious hearts as well as weary bodies. If the further slope had proved impassable, our situation would have been almost desperate ; but the worst was turning to the best for us. The twisted, wave-like rock formations of Husvik Harbour appeared right ahead in the opening of dawn. Without a word we shook hands with one another. . . .

At 6.30 a.m. I thought I heard the sound of a steam whistle. I dared not be certain, but I knew that the men at the whaling-station would be called from their beds about that time. Descending to the camp, I told the others, and in intense excitement we watched the chronometer for seven o'clock when the whalers would be summoned to work. Right to the minute the steam-whistle came to us, borne clearly on the wind across the intervening miles of rock and snow. Never had any one of us heard sweeter music. It was the first sound created by outside human agency that had come to our ears since we left Stromness Bay in December, 1914. . . .

At 1.30 p.m. we climbed round a final ridge and saw a little steamer, a whaling boat, entering the bay 2,500 feet below. A few moments later, as we hurried forward, the masts of a sailing ship lying at a wharf came into sight. Minute figures moving to and fro about the boats caught our gaze, and then we saw the sheds and factory of Stromness whaling station. . . .

Shivering with cold, yet with hearts light and happy, we set off towards the whaling station, not now more than a mile and a half distant. . . . We tried to straighten ourselves up a bit, for the thought that there might be women at the station made us painfully conscious of our uncivilized appearance. Our beards were long and our hair was matted. We were unwashed and the garments we had worn for nearly a year without a change were tattered and stained. . . . We reached the outskirts of the station and passed through the " digesting house," which was dark inside. Emerging at the other end, we met an old man who started as if he had seen the Devil himself and gave us no time to ask any question. He hurried away. This greeting was not friendly. Then we came to the wharf where the man in charge stuck to his station. I asked him if Mr. Sorlle, the manager, was in the house.

"Yes," he said as he stared at us.

"We would like to see him," said I.

"Who are you?" he asked.

"We have lost our ship and come over the island," I replied.

"You have come over the island," he said in a tone of entire disbelief. . . .

Mr. Sorlle came to the door and said, "Well?"

"Don't you know me?" I said.

"I know your voice," he replied doubtfully. "You're the mate of the *Daisy*."

"My name is Shackleton," I said.

Immediately he put out his hand and said, "Come in. Come in."

"Tell me, when was the War over?" I asked.

"The War is not over," he answered. "Millions are being killed. Europe is mad. The world is mad."

Sir Ernest Shackleton.

LES PASSAGÈRES

. . . I WENT a good deal to Ciro's. I saw a lot of a girl named Irene West. She had red hair, a pale face and a pert and pretty nose. She was like a petal—she was somehow less than a flower. Everything turned up and at the same angle—her nose, her upper lip and chin. She even had a way of looking at the top of your head when you talked to her. It always made me think my hair was mussed. She never smiled at any joke, but she laughed a lot. She was gay within. She laughed and danced and drank a great deal. She made life worth while—that particular life which belonged to that particular time.

I thought about her on parade. As I turned about and to the left and to the right, facing the barracks, the quartermaster's stores or the officers' ante-room, I pictured the evening that lay ahead.

I wonder what happened to girls like Irene after the War. They disappeared as completely as the men who were killed. They were a soldier's true companions. The excitement, the adventure, the risk of living involved them also. There existed a ready-made sympathy between the two.

Carroll Carstairs.

FRENCH MISSION

HE was a handsome Basque, whose favourite sport was bear-hunting in the Pyrenees, and many a tale could he tell of weeks spent in the high valleys, with a goat-skin of wine and a loaf the size of a tombstone, carried by his gillie. He smoked a pipe and drank whisky in the Mess, but I could never make out whether he shared those British tastes, or only thought he ought to. On the other hand, he certainly could and did write and publish poetry. Sport and good living were, however, his principal preoccupations. I enjoyed journeys made with him into France, which was our back area. He knew when and where to eat and drink as well as any man I ever met. His business method, however, was non-existent. Like de V., with military liaison at a standstill, he was supposed to represent French interests. I soon found out, however, that I could get much more quickly and surely to the hearts of those big, gaunt, Flemish-speaking farmers and officials by treating them as I might, under parallel circumstances, have treated the clerk of some Norfolk Parish Council, than by adopting his ways. I remember riding with him, for instance, to Houtkerque, to investigate the alleged theft and consumption by gunners of one of our brigades of a barrel of stout. We started early and splashed along the irretrievably ruined roads through a landscape of Hobbema, but Hobbema framed so as to form the back of a shower bath. We lost twenty minutes getting our horses past a light railway. Then a great humpty-shouldered church appeared above the elms, for all the world like Hingham, Norfolk, and we found the Mairie (over an estaminet, of course) and pushed through a crowd of villagers trying to get their sons exempted from conscription, and their places on the list of applicants for artificial manure unfairly promoted. In a tiny office, waist deep in official papers of all descriptions, sat an old man in a Dutch cap, smoking a clay pipe.

De G., glorious in strawberry and blue, shouted : " Monsieur le

Maire, nous sommes venus tirer au clair cette sombre histoire ! "
The old man looked puzzled. I insisted on seeing the broken door
or window through which the barrel had been removed. Then,
with the help of some English and some Flemish (the Maire spoke
rather less French than I did), we did " drag to light this sordid
story," while de G. ordered lunch. The barrel was there. You
could see it and test its emptiness. Nor was there much need. I
sympathized thoroughly with the gunners, and was able to recon-
struct the crime in which, alas, I had failed to participate. When the
Brigade, numbering, I suppose, five hundred men, even after months
of hammering, had watered and fed and set guards, they all made
for the place, demanding drink. The old man had started laboriously
filling glasses and mugs while those lasted, and then billycans, and
no doubt was soon stumped for change. Of course he got shoved
aside and the men simply filled every receptacle they had about them
until the barrel was empty. Some paid, he admitted, but the claim
was for the difference between the amount received and the value of
the contents of the barrel, and may have been two hundred francs.
After adjusting this valuation to reality, I settled the claim by the
present of a ton or so of manure. By that time de G. had procured
a chicken done to his liking, a salad, hare paté, jam and gingerbread,
and a bottle of label-less but excellent red wine, and honour and
everything else was satisfied.

R. H. Mottram.

PROMOTION COMETH NEITHER FROM THE EAST NOR FROM THE WEST

Towards the end of May, a dozen recruits joined the company, young reinforcements, boyish and slight. Early one morning the enemy began to shell the trench with whizz-bangs; it was a sudden angry storm, too fierce and too localized to last long. I had just passed the fire-bay in which Delivett was frying a rasher of bacon, with five of these lads watching him and waiting their turn to cook. I stopped in the next bay to reassure the others. Suddenly a pale and frightened youth came round the corner, halting indecisively when he saw me, turning again, but finally going back reluctantly to his fire-bay in despair of finding any escape from his trap. Between the crashes of the bursting shells a high-pitched sing-song soared up.

"You'll 'ev 'em all over," . . . Crash . . . "All the milky ones." . . . Crash . . . "All the milky coco-nuts . . ." " . . . You'll 'ev 'em all over . . . All the milky ones." . . . Crash . . . "Therree shies a penny . . . All the milky coco-nuts . . . You'll 'ev 'em all over." . . . Crash—and then silence, for the morning hate ended as suddenly as it began.

I walked to find Delivett still frying bacon, and the five youths smiling nervously, crouched below the firestep. I sent them away on some improvised errand and faced Delivett.

"That's a fine thing you did then, Delivett," I said. He looked up, mess-tin lid in his hand, saying nothing, but the lines round his mouth moved a little.

"You saved those lads from panic—they were frightened out of their wits," I added.

"Yes, sir, they was real scared," he replied.

"Delivett, you've spent a lot of time on Hampstead Heath."

"Yes sir . . . I ran a coco-nut shy there once . . ."

With these words a man and an environment fused into a unity, satisfying and complete in itself; here at last was a credible occupation for this quiet stranger.

"I'm going to tell the Colonel all about this," I said. Delivett thought hard for several seconds, and put his bacon back on the fire.

"Well, sir," he said diffidently, "if it's all the same to you, I'd much rather you made me Sanitary man."

"Do you mean that you'd really like to go round with a bucket of chloride of lime, picking up tins and . . ."

"Yes, sir, I'd like that job."

"You shall have it here and now. You are made Sanitary man for valour in the field, this very moment."

In half an hour Delivett was walking round with a bucket, his head a little higher in the air, spitting a little more deliberately than before, as his new dignity demanded. He had found a vocation.

Ll. Wyn Griffith (Royal Welch Fusiliers).

JUTLAND

Early on May 31 the German Fleet left its base and emerged into the North Sea. In the afternoon it was engaged by Beatty and later in the evening Jellicoe arrived on the scene with his battle fleet. The Battle of Jutland was the great naval battle of the War. There were heavy losses on both sides, though those of the British navy were the heavier. It was, however, a British victory in that the German Navy did not put to sea again for the rest of the War.

SINKING OF THE "INVINCIBLE"

31st May. At 7.40 p.m. enemy light cruisers and destroyers launched a torpedo attack against us. We therefore altered course to N.N.E., i.e. about six points to starboard.

The visibility was now so bad that it was difficult for us to distinguish the enemy ships. We were engaging light cruisers and destroyers. At 7.55 p.m. we turned on an easterly course, and at 8 p.m. the whole Battle-cruiser Squadron formed a line of bearing on a southerly course as the destroyers pressed home the attack. This brought us very effectively out of the line of the torpedoes that had been fired against us. At 8.12 p.m. we again altered course towards the enemy. During this time we had only fired intermittently with our heavy and secondary armament. At 8.15 p.m. we came under heavy fire. It flashed out on all sides. We could only make out the ships' hulls indistinctly, but as far as I was able to see the horizon, enemy ships were all around us. As I could not distinguish either the end or the beginning of the enemy line, I was unable to engage the " second ship from the right," but selected the one I could see best.

And now a terrific struggle began. Within a short time the din of the battle reached a climax. It was now perfectly clear to us that we were faced with the whole English Fleet. I could see from her gigantic hull that I had engaged a giant battleship. Between the two lines light cruiser and destroyer actions were still raging. All at once I saw through my periscope a German light cruiser passing us in flames. I recognized the *Wiesbaden*. She was almost hidden in smoke, with only the quarter-deck clear, and her after-gun firing incessantly at an English cruiser. Gallant *Wiesbaden* ! Gallant crew ! The only survivor was Chief Stoker Zenne, who was picked up by a Norwegian fishing-boat after drifting about for three days on a raft ; all the rest, including the poet, Gorch Fock, who loved the sea above all else, sealed their loyalty to their Kaiser and Empire by a sailor's death. The *Wiesbaden* was subjected to a heavy fire by an English light cruiser. Again and again her shells struck the poor *Wiesbaden*. Seized with fury, I abandoned my former target, had the English cruiser's range measured, gave the range and deflection, and " crash ! "—a salvo roared out at the *Wiesbaden's* tormentor. One more salvo and I had him. A column of smoke rose high in the air. Apparently a magazine had exploded. The cruiser turned away and hauled out at top speed, while I peppered her with two or three more salvoes.

At this moment Lieutenant-Commander Hausser, who had been engaging destroyers with his secondary armament, asked me : " Is this cruiser with four funnels German or English, sir ? " I examined the ship through the periscope. In the misty grey light the colours of the German and English ships were difficult to distinguish. The cruiser was not very far away from us. She had four funnels and two masts, like our *Rostock*. " She is certainly English," Lieutenant-Commander Hausser shouted. " May I fire ? "—" Yes, fire away." I was now certain she was a big English ship. The secondary armament was trained on the new target. Lieutenant-Commander Hausser gave the order : " 6,000 ! " Then, just as he was about to give the order : " Fire ! " something terrific happened : the English ship, which I had meanwhile identified as an old English armoured cruiser, broke in half with a tremendous explosion. Black smoke and debris shot into the air, a flame enveloped the whole ship, and then she sank before our eyes. There was nothing but a gigantic smoke cloud to mark the place where just before a proud ship had been fighting. I think she was destroyed by the fire of our next ahead, Admiral Hipper's flagship, the *Lützow*.

This all happened in a much shorter time than I have taken to tell it. The whole thing was over in a few seconds, and then we had already engaged new targets. The destroyed ship was the *Defence*, an old armoured cruiser of the same class as the *Black Prince*, which was sunk on the following night by the *Thuringen* and other ships of the line. She was a ship of 14,800 tons, armed with six 23·4-cm. and ten 15·2-cm. guns, and carrying a crew of 700 men. Not one of the whole ship's company was saved. She was blown to atoms and all the men were killed by the explosion. As we saw the ship at a comparatively short distance in good visibility, magnified fifteen times by the periscopes, we could see exactly what happened. The whole horror of this event is indelibly fixed on my mind.

I went on to engage other big ships, without any idea what kind of ships they were. At 8.22 p.m. we turned on a south-easterly course, but in the general confusion of the battle that was now raging I had lost all grasp of the tactical situation. Once the thought flashed across my mind : " Can we be firing at German ships ? " At that moment, however, the visibility, which changed from one minute to the next, but which on the whole was gradually growing worse, improved and revealed distinctly the typical English silhouette and dark grey colour. It is my opinion that our light grey colour was more favourable than the dark grey of the English ships. Our ships were much more quickly concealed by the thin films of mist which were now driving across the sea from east to west.

At 8.25 p.m. Lieutenant von der Decken, in the after-control, recorded : " *Lützow* heavily hit forward. Ship on fire. Much smoke." At 8.30 p.m. he wrote : " Three heavy hits on the *Derfflinger*." Of these one hit the 15-cm. battery on the port side, went clean through the centre gun and burst, killing or wounding the whole of the casemate crew. The explosion also knocked the first 15-cm. gun off its mounting and killed or wounded several men. The other hits were aft.

I now selected my target as far ahead as possible, the leading ship of the enemy line, for I saw that the *Lützow's* fire was now weak. At times the smoke from her burning forepart made fire-control on the *Lützow* impossible.

At 8.24 p.m. I began to engage large enemy battleships to the north-east. Even though the ranges were short, from 6,000 to 7,000 m., the ships often became invisible in the slowly advancing mists, mixed with the smoke from the guns and funnels. It was almost impossible to observe the splashes. All splashes that fell over could not be seen at all, and only those that fell very short could be distinguished clearly, which was not much help, for as soon as we got nearer the target again it became impossible to see where the shots fell. I was shooting by the measurements of the man in the fore-control, Leading-Seaman Hanel, who had been my loyal servant for five years. In view of the misty weather these measurements were very irregular and inexact but as no observation was possible I had no alternative. Meanwhile we were being subjected to a heavy, accurate and rapid fire from several ships at the same time. It was clear that the enemy could now see us much better than we could see them. This will be difficult to understand for anyone who does not know the sea, but it is a fact that in this sort of weather the differences in visibility are very great in different directions. A ship clear of the mist is much more clearly visible from a ship actually in the mist than vice versa. In determining visibility an important part is played by the position of the sun. In misty weather the ships with their shady side towards the enemy are much easier to see than those lit by the sun.

In this was a severe, unequal struggle developed. Several heavy shells pierced our ship with terrific force and exploded with a tremendous roar, which shook every seam and rivet. The Captain had again frequently to steer the ship out of the line in order to get out of the hail of fire. It was pretty heavy shooting.

This went on until 8.29 p.m.

At this moment the veil of mist in front of us split across like the curtain at a theatre. Clear and sharply silhouetted against the uncovered part of the horizon we saw a powerful battleship with two funnels between the masts and a third close against the forward tripod mast. She was steering an almost parellel course with ours at top speed. Her guns were trained on us and immediately another salvo crashed out, straddling us completely. " Range 9,000 ! " roared Leading-Seaman Hanel. " 9,000—Salvoes-fire ! " I ordered, and with feverish anxiety I waited for our splashes. " Over. Two hits ! " called out Lieutenant-Commander von Stosch. I gave the order : " 100 down. Good, Rapid ! " and thirty seconds after the first salvo the second left the guns. I observed two short splashes and two hits. Lieutenant-Commander von Stosch called : " Hits ! "

Every twenty seconds came the roar of another salvo. At 8.31 p.m. the *Derfflinger* fired her last salvo at this ship, and then for the third time we witnessed the dreadful spectacle that we had already seen in the case of the *Queen Mary* and the *Defence.*

As with the other ships there occurred a rapid succession of heavy explosions, masts collapsed, debris was hurled into the air, a gigantic column of black smoke rose towards the sky, and from the parting sections of the ship, coal dust spurted in all directions. Flames enveloped the ship, fresh explosions followed, and behind this murky shroud our enemy vanished from our sight. I shouted into the telephone : " Our enemy has blown up ! " and above the din of the battle a great cheer thundered through the ship and was transmitted to the fore-control by all the gunnery telephones and flashed from one gun-position to another. I sent up a short, fervent prayer of thanks to the Almighty, shouted to my servant : " Bravo, Hanel, jolly well measured ! " and then my order rang out : " Change target to the left. On the second battle-cruiser from the right ! " The battle continued. . . .

The *Derfflinger*, too, was now a pretty sorry sight. The masts and rigging had been badly damaged by countless shells, and the wireless aerials hung down in an inextricable tangle so that we could not transmit messages. A heavy shell had torn away two armour plates in the bows, leaving a huge gap quite 6 by 5 m., just above the water-line. With the pitching of the ship water streamed continually through this hole.

While we were steering west the Commander come on to the bridge and reported to the Captain : " The ship must stop at once. The after torpedo-net has been shot away and is hanging over the port screw. It must be cleared." The Captain gave the order : " All engines stop ! "

I surveyed the horizon through the periscope. There was nothing of the enemy to be seen at this moment. The *Seydlitz*, *Moltke* and *Von der Tann* were not in very close touch with us, but they now came up quickly and took their prescribed stations in the line. It was a very serious matter that we should have to stop like this in the immediate neighbourhood of the enemy, but if the torpedo-net were to foul the screw all would be up with us. How many times we had cursed in the ship at not having rid ourselves of these heavy steel torpedo-nets, weighing several hundred tons.

As we hardly ever anchored at sea they were useless and, in any case, they only protected part of the ship against torpedo fire. On the other hand, they were a serious source of danger, as they reduced the ship's speed considerably and were bound sooner or later to foul the screws, which meant the loss of the ship. For these reasons the English had scrapped their torpedo-nets shortly before the War—we did not do so until immediately after the battle of Skagerrak [1] and as a result of our present experience.

The boatswain and the turret-crews of the *Dora* and *Cæsar* turrets, under Lieutenant-Commander Boltenstern, worked like furies to lift the net, make it fast with chains and cut with axes the wire-hawsers and chains that were hanging loose. It was only a few minutes before the report came : " Engines can be started." We got under weigh at once.

The *Lützow* had now hauled out of the line and was steering a southerly course at low speed. The Captain wanted to signal to the other ships to follow the leader, but all the signal apparatus was out of action. The semaphores and heliographs had all been shot away and the flags all destroyed by fire. However, our stout ships followed without signal when the Captain turned on a northerly course and led the battle-cruisers to a position ahead of the main fleet.

Commander Georg von Hase (of the " Derfflinger ").

ATTACK OF 13TH DESTROYER FLOTILLA AND LOSS OF THE " NESTOR" AND THE " NOMAD "

Shortly after 4 p.m. the admiral signalled that the flotilla of destroyers ahead was to attack the enemy's battle-cruisers with torpedoes. . . .

I immediately hoisted the signal for full speed and ordered the destroyers to form a single line astern of me. Then shaping course a point and a half in towards the enemy, we ran full speed at 35 knots for half an hour, in order to reach an advantageous position on the enemy's bows, such as would enable me to launch the torpedo attack with the greatest possible prospect of success.

On drawing out to this position, we observed the enemy's fifteen destroyers coming out with the object of making a similar torpedo attack on our battle-cruisers.

[1] The German name for the Battle of Jutland.

At 4.40 p.m., having reached the desired position, I turned to north (approximately fourteen points to port), followed in succession by the rest of the destroyers. . . .

The German destroyers then immediately turned on a course parallel to ours, and the destroyer action thus commenced at a range of 10,000 yards. I promptly manœuvred to close this range.

At 4.45 the *Nomad*, my immediate follower, was hit in the boiler-room and hauled out of line disabled. We in the *Nestor* got the range very quickly, and pumped in three or four salvoes from our 4-in. guns. Two German destroyers disappeared beneath the surface, and though it is unreasonable definitely to claim the credit of sinking a given ship where many are concerned, my control officer is still prepared to affirm that the *Nestor's* guns accounted for one of them.

At 4.50 the enemy's destroyers turned tail and fled. Pursued by the British they divided themselves into two portions, one-half of which made for the head, while the other took cover under the tail, of the German battle-cruiser line. It must be remembered that although they were numerically superior to us, the enemy's destroyers were neither so large nor so heavily armed.

The British boats promptly turned to chase the enemy's fleeing T.B.D.'s, and while I proceeded with my division, now reduced to two boats (i.e. *Nestor* and *Nicator*), after those of the enemy's destroyers who were making for the head of the battle-cruiser line the other two divisions of the T.B.D.'s went after the remaining, and larger, portion of the German destroyers.

Just then the enemy's battle-cruisers altered course four points to port, that is, forty-five degrees to the left. Most probably this manœuvre was prompted by the warning splashes that marked the discharge of the British torpedoes, of which the *Nestor* had just fired her first two.

Thus I found myself with the solitary *Nicator* hot in the track of the fleeing destroyers and now rapidly approaching the head of the German battle-cruiser line, who were not slow in giving us an extremely warm welcome from their secondary armament. At a distance of 3,000 to 4,000 yards the *Nestor* fired her third torpedo and immediately afterwards at 4.58 turned away eight points to starboard, in order to get clear of the danger zone and to regain the line of the British battle-cruisers.

Suddenly from behind the head of the enemy's line there came a German light cruiser, who opened hot fire and straddled us. It was just about 5 o'clock when two boilers were put out of action by direct hits. From the bridge I saw at once that something of the kind had happened. A huge cloud of steam was rising from the boiler-room, completely enshrouding the whole ship, and it was painfully apparent that our speed was dropping every second. Our speed died away gradually, until at 5.30 p.m. we came to a dead stop.

Nothing daunted, the engine-room staff applied themselves with all the means in their power to the work of setting the engines in motion. But it was all without avail. The damage was of a nature which required, above all, time. Before anything could be done, the boilers had to be cooled off, and all pipes were in the overheated condition that results from a high-speed run.

The German light cruiser having crippled us, almost immediately turned back and rejoined her own battle-cruisers.

While lying helpless and broken down, we saw the opposing forces of battle-cruisers retracing their tracks to the N.W., fighting on parallel courses. The rival squadrons quickly disappeared behind the horizon, engaged furiously, and we were now left with the ocean to ourselves. But it was not to be for long. Fifteen minutes later my yeoman-of-signals reported: " German battleships on the horizon, shaping course in our direction." This was more than I had ever bargained for, and, using my own glasses, I was dumbfounded to see that it was in truth the main body of the German High Sea Fleet, steaming at top speed in a north-westerly direction and following the wake of their own battle-cruisers.

Their course necessarily led them first past the *Nomad*, and in another ten minutes the slaughter began. They literally smothered the destroyer with salvoes. Of my divisional mate nothing could be seen : great columns of spray and smoke alone gave an indication of her whereabouts. I shall never forget the sight, and mercifully it was a matter of a few minutes before the ship sank, at the time it seemed impossible that anyone on board could have survived.

Of what was in store for us there was now not the vestige of a doubt, and the problem was, how to keep all hands occupied for the few minutes that remained before the crash must come.

While the sub-lieutenant and myself were " ditching " all charts, confidential books, and documents, the first lieutenant and the men were executing my orders in providing biscuit and water for the boats ; lowering these to the water's edge ; hoisting out Carley floats ; and generally preparing for the moment when we should be obliged to leave the ship.

These orders were rapidly executed, and there was still time on our hands ; for nothing had as yet happened. By a brilliant inspiration, Bethell then suggested to me that the cables might be ranged on deck—ostensibly for use in case of a friendly tow, but in reality to keep the men busy to the last. This suggestion I readily accepted, and the hands were still thus employed when the end came.

From a distance of about five miles, the Germans commenced with their secondary armament, and very soon we were enveloped in a deluge of shell fire. Any reply from our own guns was absolutely out of the question at a range beyond the possibilities of our light shells ; to have answered any one of our numerous assailants would have been as effective as the use of a peashooter against a wall of steel. Just about this time we fired our last torpedo at the High Sea Fleet and it was seen to run well.

It was a matter of two or three minutes only before the *Nestor*, enwrapped in a cloud of smoke and spray, the centre of a whirlwind of shrieking shells, received not a few heavy and vital hits, and the ship began slowly to settle by the stern and then to take up a heavy list to starboard.

Her decks now showed the first signs of havoc amongst life and limb.

It was clear that the doomed *Nestor* was sinking rapidly, and at that moment I gave my last order as her commander, " Abandon ship."

The motor-boat and Carley floats were quickly filled ; and as the dinghy was badly broken up by shell-fire, there seemed to remain for me only the possibility of a place in the whaler.

Bethell was standing beside me, and I turned to him with the question, " Now where shall *we* go ? " His answer was only characteristic of that gallant spirit, " To Heaven, I trust, sir ! "

At that moment he turned aside to attend to a mortally wounded signalman and was seen no more amidst a cloud of fumes from a bursting shell.

I clambered into the whaler, where I found about eight others waiting, and we remained alongside until the last possible moment, hailing the partially submerged ship vigorously, in the unlikely event of any survivors being still on board. Finally we pushed off clear.

The whaler, however, had also been hit, probably at the same time as the dinghy, and before we had gone half a dozen strokes she filled and sank. We then struck out, I luckily having my " Miranda " life-saving waistcoat on, for the well-loaded motor-boat, lying some fifty yards ahead of the *Nestor,* where some of us were pulled in, the rest supporting themselves by holding on to the gunwale.

Looking now towards the *Nestor,* we saw the water lapping over the decks, and the forecastle high in the air, still the target of the German gun-layers, some of whose projectiles fell uncomfortably near us in the motor-boat and rafts.

In about three minutes, the destroyer suddenly raised herself into an absolutely perpendicular position, and thus slid down, stern first, to the bottom of the North Sea, leaving a quantity of oil and wreckage to mark the spot where she had last rested.

Hon. Barry Bingham.

H.M.S. " INDOMITABLE "

31*st May.* The first intimation that we had of any possibility of an action was at 2.23 p.m. when *Galatea* reported enemy ships in sight, and we intercepted her signal. At that time we were stationed ahead of the battle fleet, steering S. 50° E., and zigzagging, the speed of advance being 14 knots. The wireless office could hear Telefunken signals, strength 10, very loud and strong. At 3.57 p.m. we heard from the *Lion* that they were engaging the enemy, and shortly afterwards the sounds of heavy gunfire were plainly audible, and flashes were visible on the horizon.

The weather at this time was clear, but with patches of thin mist near the horizon, and visibility of approximately 16,000 yards ; the wind was south-west, force 2, and the sea smooth.

At 5.40 p.m. course was altered about 8 points to starboard, and at 5.50 p.m. *Invincible* opened fire on a three-funnelled light cruiser bearing 40° on the port bow, and was followed five minutes later by *Inflexible* and *Indomitable,* the squadron being in line ahead in that order. We could see, off the port bow, a light cruiser of the *Canterbury* class apparently stopped or moving very slowly, and heavily engaged with a squadron of four enemy light cruisers, which were advancing for torpedo attack. One of these was a four-funnelled cruiser, and seemed to be of the *Rostock* class.

Our opening range was 11,200 yards, closing by 6.0 p.m. to 8,900 yards. We had steamed between our own light cruiser and the enemy and had severely handled them, one of the Germans disappearing in a great cloud of steam and smoke which remained for a long time over one spot, so that I have no doubt at all that she sank ; and another, a three-funnelled cruiser, was badly on fire amidships, apparently stopped and settling down but I did not see her sink as we turned away to avoid torpedoes which were crossing the track. I could not see these torpedo tracks from the turret, of course, but was told afterwards that four had been sighted ; one passed under the ship, one passed ahead, one a few yards astern, and one was observed by the gunnery officer to be running slowly along the starboard side of the ship a few yards off and parallel to the ship, its distinctive red head being particularly noticeable. The enemy now made off, and were attacked at 6.9 p.m. by our destroyers, with what result the smoke and haze made it impossible to observe.

The noise of firing now became like the roll of continuous thunder, and the horizon to port was filled with whirling sheets of flame. Through the mist we could distinguish the Rosyth battle-cruisers hotly engaged with the enemy, whose number and class we could not make out. At 6.13 p.m. the *Invincible* stopped, and clouds of steam came from her exhaust pipes, but she appeared to be undamaged, and hoisting the " Disregard " signal shortly after went ahead at 20 knots with the signal to form single line ahead flying. It was the last time I saw her as a ship.

We were now (6.20 p.m.) heavily engaged with the enemy battle-cruisers and with, I think, the head of his battle line, the range being 8,200 yards, bearing 90 Green. Suddenly my left gun ceased firing. The thin metal bulkhead which had been built round the sighting position to render it, as far as possible, sound-proof prevented me from seeing what was wrong, and for a few moments I could get no reply to my enquiries from the loading officer. This was exasperating, and I began to fear that the turret had been hit although I had felt no concussion, when the welcome report came that it was only a cordite charge that had jammed and broken up.

It took but a short time to clear the jam, and two hands, with their arms full of cordite sticks, went up to the roof of the turret

and threw them over the side.   Both guns were in action again at
6.40 p.m., and we went into " Independent " at a range of 8,600
yards.   I think it was as well that my cabinet was sound-proof, as
my loading officer told me afterwards that the left gunlayer's language
was of the rare and fruity variety !

The enemy's shooting at this time was unpleasantly good, and
I observed several salvoes burst alongside, and could hear the whistle
of " overs."   There was a belief that the enemy used shrapnel for
a few rounds, but I cannot confirm that from personal observation.
Certainly the shell splinters found on board were very small, and
this may have given rise to the report.   An entry in my notebook
at this time reads, " Enemy salvoes bursting close."

At 6.35 p.m. we altered course slightly to port, reverting to controlled fire at a range of 10,700 yards.   Then upon the starboard bow
I saw the two ends of a ship standing perpendicularly above water,
the ship appearing to have broken in halves amidships, each half
resting on the bottom.   My gunlayer took her for a Hun, and the
crew cheered, but I could read the name *Invincible* on the stern and
so knew better.   Four or five survivors were clinging to floating
wreckage ; I have never seen anything more splendid than these few
cheering us as we raced by them.

The weather now got very much thicker, and at 6.42 p.m. fire
was checked, a few minutes after which the 1st B.C.S. came up, and
we turned round from ahead to take station astern of them, in the
order—*Lion, Princess Royal, Tiger, New Zealand, Indomitable,
Inflexible.*   As we turned we could see that the *Lion* had a small
fire just abaft the foremast, and we learned afterwards that our arrival
on the scene was most opportune, as it gave the crews of the 1st
B.C.S. a brief " stand easy," and enabled them to put out various
fires.   It was generally agreed that the period 6.20 to 6.42 p.m. was
the hottest part of the action, and observers in the *Princess Royal*
have said that they expected every moment to see us share the fate
of the *Invincible.*

We could now see the battle fleet coming up astern in three
columns, and at 7.12 p.m. they re-opened fire.   The spectacle was
truly magnificent, tongues of flame seeming to leap from end to end.
of the line, but owing to the dusk and smoke we could not see what
practice they were making.

At 7.20 p.m. we re-opened fire at the enemy battle-cruisers at a range of 14,000 yards, our squadron apparently making splendid practice. Time after time a dull orange glow would appear on board one or other of their ships, a glow which increased and brightened, then slowly dulled; yet, in spite of these hits, the enemy's volume of fire did not seem appreciably to diminish. One big ship turned out of her line to starboard, her after part enveloped in flame, and began slowly to drop astern. The remainder emitted dense volumes of smoke, which hung above the water like a pall, and through which, at 7.25 p.m., we could see about a dozen destroyers racing towards our line. Orders came through for the 4-inch guns' crews to close up, and, as the change of bearing was passed and the turret swung round, I could hear the staccato bark of these small guns joining in the general din. As the destroyers cleared the smoke screen, white pillars began to leap up amongst them like giant nine pins, to be knocked down and spring up again without ceasing as the big guns came into action. Almost half the distance had been covered by the attackers, when I saw two of these white towers of water rise simultaneously in front of the left-hand boat of the line, and as they sank no thrusting bow came through the spray, only a thinning streak of smoke. . . .

The 2nd Light Cruiser Squadron astern turned out to starboard and engaged the flotilla with 6-inch guns, and shortly afterwards the enemy swung round and sped back, but not before I had seen a second boat hit and destroyed.

The officer of X turret told me an amusing yarn of his turret during this attack. His gunlayer was a very smart man, but not above drawing the long bow, I'm afraid, and the trainer, though an excellent trainer, was rather slow-witted. The conversation between the two was something like this:

Gunlayer : " Train right—Train right—Little more."—Bang.

Trainer : " What were you firing at ? "

Gunlayer : " Destroyer."

Trainer : " I can't see it."

Gunlayer : " No. I've sunk her. Train right—Right—Right." Bang.

Trainer : " I didn't see it."

Gunlayer : " 'Nother destroyer. I've sunk her. Train right again—Too much—Left a little."—Bang.

Trainer (pathetically) : " I can't see anything."

After the action I believe the gunlayer was claiming eight boats to his own gun !

The enemy now increased his range, and fire was checked at 7.40 p.m., but astern of us the firing was continuous, although it was impossible to make out the ships engaged. This lull seemed a good opportunity for sending a few men away from the turret to get food for the remainder, which was accordingly done. Shortly afterwards we passed a small skiff, painted grey, of apparently German origin, containing the bodies of two men, and round about was a quantity of wreckage and oil, but, of course, we did not stop to enquire into what it was.

At 8.20 p.m. unexpectedly, the enemy battle-cruisers were again sighted closing towards us, and a few seconds later they opened fire. Most of my turret's crew had come up on top for a breath of fresh air and to hunt for splinters as souvenirs, so they tumbled back to their stations in a hurry, and by 8.26 p.m. we were hard at it again at a range of 8,800 yards. The German firing was fairly good, and we were straddled several times. Many of our squadron's salvoes hit, and large fires were observed on board several of their ships, and their speed seemed to decrease. By 8.42 p.m. they had had enough and drew off, so we ceased firing, although other ships in the squadron continued for a little time longer. At 8.44 p.m. a distinct shock and muffled explosion was felt and heard, but no damage could be discovered, nor could any definite cause be assigned to the occurrence.

At 9.0 p.m. heavy firing was heard astern, and 10 minutes later a solitary star shell was seen, followed by one heavy salvo. Firing then ceased. The south-westerly course was continued during the night, but, as far as we were concerned, nothing exciting happened during the night, apart from sighting many gun flashes from 11.45 to 12.30 a.m.

Should it be my good fortune to be engaged in another action, I shall take care that only one gramophone is taken into the turret. In my turret we had two, one in the gun-house and one in the working chamber, and during every lull in the action these two were started playing simultaneously, each with a different record. The result was one of the real horrors of the war.

Officer in fore-turret of H.M.S. " Indomitable," quoted by
Fawcett and Hooper.

SINKING OF THE " DEFENCE "

31*st May.* I think we only realized that we were at last in for a proper action when we heard the battle-cruisers firing ahead. We then began to get quite jubilant ; so much so, that when a German shell landed abreast us on the port side about 500 yards short there was a positive cheer from the *Malaya.* Then we heard the other ships of our own squadron open fire, one after the other ahead of us, each salvo helped on its way by a cheer. In our torpedo control tower we were so interested in what was going on, that when the *Malaya* herself opened fire the blast from X turret's guns, which were only a few feet away from us, sat us down with a " whump," and the range-taker came down from his seat with a crash.

From this time onwards my thoughts were really more like a nightmare than thoughts of a wide-awake human being. I don't think I felt fright, simply because what was going on around me was so unfamiliar that my brain was incapable of grasping it. Even now I can only think of the beginning of the action as through a dim gaze. I remember seeing the enemy line on the horizon with red specks coming out of them, which I tried to realize were the cause of projectiles landing around us, continually covering us with spray, but the fact refused to sink into my brain. We were all the time rather excited, and our enthusiasm knew no bounds when we passed a sunken ship with survivors swimming around her. We never dreamt that it was one of our own battle cruisers ; but it was the *Indefatigable,* and over a thousand dead men lay in her wreck. The same thing occurred when we passed the wreckage and survivors of the *Queen Mary.* Even when a man on some wreckage waved to us, we thought it must be a German wanting to be picked up. It is rather dreadful to think of now, especially as some men were not too keen on rescuing Germans after the *Lusitania* and similar atrocities, but I have often thought since how well it showed the confidence that we had in our own fleet that no one for a moment imagined that one of our own ships would be sunk so soon.

Before we turned to the north (at about 5 p.m.), we could see some of the German ships on fire, which cheered us very much. By this time we were under a very hot fire, and were zigzagging slightly to avoid it. I was very impressed by the absolute cloud of shells, which landed under the next-ahead's stern as she turned 16 points and I remember thinking what a mess her quarter-deck would have been in if she had been going a few knots slower.

After the turn I had no time for anything except to plot the enemy's deflection, as we were about to fire a torpedo. The foremost tube, however, jammed, and nothing could move the bar. The crew of the forward torpedo flat used some really artistic language when telling us that the starboard bar would not go out, either by power or by hand. We eventually fired from our starboard after-tube.

All this time I was gradually getting my thoughts out of their " dreamy " state, and was slowly beginning to realize that all these projectiles falling a few yards short and over were big ones, and that they were meant for us; and my thoughts, following their natural course, led me on to think of my life-saving waistcoat, which, like a fool, I had left in my sea-chest down below. There was no chance of getting it now.

All this time we were being thrown about by the blast of X turret, and we spent quite a portion of our time in ungraceful and rather painful positions on the deck, bumping against the range-finder, plotter, and other things with sharp corners.

The next thing of much interest that I remember was a very loud crash, followed by a sound like hail. After a short space of silent thought we disentangled ourselves, and I, being inexperienced, looked through the starboard sighting hole at X turret, the roof of which had become rather like a badly-made saucer, see-sawing on top of the turret. I caught a vision of the crew inside still going strong, but my interesting report of this was cut short by a salvo from that turret, which precipitated me backwards into the arms of an able seaman, and incidentally reduced me to a state of wandering wonder for several minutes. X turret had been hit by a shell on the roof, but was still in action.

Recovering from the shock of this, I was even nearer realizing what was happening around us—yet was still unaware of any desire to be elsewhere—when there came a sudden shudder and lurch through the ship, a frightful din of escaping steam, and the ship took an uncomfortable list to starboard. There followed tender enquiries from the torpedo flats, switch-board, and other stations below decks as to our welfare, whether we were still alive, and also whether there were still any Huns left. To both questions we replied in the affirmative.

At this period the battle-cruisers were well ahead, and the four ships of our squadron were getting the full hate of the German fleet, which was far from pleasant. About 6.15 p.m. the *Defence* appeared between us and the enemy, on our starboard quarter, and after firing several rounds was suddenly enveloped in smoke and flames, and when these lifted, there was only a small space of smooth water where two minutes before had been a ship and her crew of 900 men. Just before this I had been thinking of the four midshipmen of my term who were in her, so it is hardly surprising that the sight of her blowing up brought home to me just what we were taking part in ; what is more, it came with a distinct shock, and I had a fleeting glance of other ships having the same sudden end. I think I can truthfully say that it was at this stage of the action that I realized that the Germans were rather good shots, and also that there weren't many of us, but a deuce of a lot of them. In fact, to use another slang term, just about now I had " wind-up " ; but it was a comic feeling of being well scared and yet at the same time liking it, a feeling that I cannot quite describe in mere words. One thing I can express is the pleasure it was to see the *Agincourt* suddenly appear in sight ahead, looking more like a Brock's Benefit than a battleship, as she poured out salvoes from her broadside of fourteen 12-inch guns. After this we saw very little of the enemy, as it was very thick, and we were now the last ship in the battle line.

A midshipman in H.M.S. " Malaya," quoted by

Fawcett and Hooper.

S.M.S. " *LÜTZOW* "

31*st May*. When the enemy's big ships were signalled at 3 p.m. (G.M.T.) I could see battleships clearly, astern of the battle-cruisers. These latter were at least 26 kilometres from us—a proof of the remarkable visibility to the west at the start. As the battle-cruisers turned south, these ships proceeded calmly further to the north ; consequently they got ten miles astern of the battle-cruisers and could not at first take part in the action. In England critics have not failed to find fault with Admiral Beatty for his delay in making the 5th Battle Squadron join up at once.

Our rangefinders gave us good ranges commencing at 240 hm. [hectometres] and it seemed an eternity, actually it was twenty minutes, before we had reached our range of 190 hm. Even then we had to wait for the *Seydlitz* till the range was further reduced. Five points—57° is the enemy's bearing. Estimated speed 26 knots, course 110°. This made the rate of closing 4 hm. a minute. At a range of 167 hm. by our calculations the first turret salvo from A and B turrets was fired at 4.48 p.m. *Lützow* throughout the action fired alternate salvoes from her fore- and after-turrets, a system I cannot praise too highly. Both guns work as one, load simultaneously and are laid by one man. When loaded there is quiet in the turret. Gunlayers take turns at laying when necessary. The muzzle smoke is concentrated at one end of the ship ; one of the controls at least can observe even under the most unfavourable conditions. Once only I fired a full salvo from all turrets, the result did not encourage me to repeat it, the salvo fell short or mostly short and covered the whole target in an enormous column of water. . . . Time of flight 22 seconds. Fall 12/16 left ahead. " 12 right." " Salvo." " C and D fire." Fall ! Centre over ! " 8 back." " Salvo." Over ! " 8 back." " Salvo." Straddling ! A hit near the bridge. A sigh of relief and then on. It has taken two minutes for the battery to do this. What is the matter with the rangefinding ? It has gone down 16 hm. As to the enemy, it appeared as though he had commenced at 167 hm., been well over, and had spent an endless time in getting on. *Lion's* first straddling salvo after nine minutes was therefore quite a surprise. A slight hit well forward on the forecastle we do not notice, nor the fact that *Lion* and *Princess Mary*, the two leading enemy's ships, are concentrating on us. Our fire is now very accurate ; a sharp turn of 4 points by the enemy is noticed at once. At 4.52 we secure our third hit. Red flames shoot from the third turret and a great fragment, half the roof, goes up. After a considerable pause the turret suddenly flares up but the dying turret officer has had the magazine doors closed ; this saves *Lion* and the Admiral. Personally, I think that the surprising blowing up of the English ships was only due to powder catching fire and finally exploding. In our ships, powder catching fire always remained fire, devastating for the turret concerned, but not destructive to the ship. Various circumstances persuade me that it was not projectiles exploding which was the cause.

Seventeen minutes after fire was opened *Lion* turned sharply away, until we could see her from aft and *Princess Royal* pushed in front. I counted six hits in 31 salvoes. We have been hit three times, one of these exploded between A and B turrets and cleared out the forward action dressing station. All are dead there. Hit No. 3 seems to have hit the belt somewhere, a heavy shock but nothing put out of action. Although we clearly observed *Lion* leaving the line, the fact is not mentioned in our opponent's accounts and is only alluded to inaccurately as a turning away of the whole line. This is contradicted by the fact, established by photos in *The Fighting at Jutland*, that *Queen Mary* was second in the line when she blew up. It is certain that *Lion* later resumed the lead, but I cannot state when this happened.

At 5.8 we change target to *Princess Royal*. Our opponent keeps on altering course sharply and these changes are hard to see through the smoke and decreasing visibility. Range alters rapidly from 151 to 130, increases equally quickly to 190 and comes down to 150 again. On the engaged side a little ahead of the enemy there is now a destroyer emitting clouds of smoke and hiding the target. As the control top of our opponent is always visible over it, I suspected a stratagem on the part of the enemy using a fire director, but Admiral Beatty explains it as an anti-submarine screen and it impeded my opponent as much as it did me. In the meantime our opponent is not hitting us, while our fire remains good and hits can often be seen. After the *Queen Mary* blew up, which I could just see in my excellent periscope in the small field of sight (our target was the ship ahead), fierce destroyer actions develop between the lines; these give the second gunnery officer the longed-for opportunity of taking part, but practically entirely obscure my target. During this time *Lion* probably took the lead again and then we resumed firing at her as we always fired at the leading ship. . . .

The High Sea Fleet is right ahead. The enemy battle cruisers turn at once outwards on a reverse course. We follow five minutes later, also turning outwards. This opens the range considerably; the English battle-cruisers are four points ahead and withdraw to the limits of range, which is possible for them as at 6 p.m. we reduced to 18 knots. Fire is spasmodic as visibility gets much worse. It is not until Beatty knows that the Grand Fleet is quite near that he closes. At 5.41 we are heavily fired at by him and are hit four times. Two of these pierce the large 6-in. casemate from above, destroy both W/T sets and cause severe casualties. Another bursts amidships without seriously injuring the main armour deck; but the fastenings in the gunnery transmitting station, which were underneath, came adrift and smoke penetrated everywhere. The fire control was interrupted momentarily but was restarted shortly afterwards. Our own smoke becomes a nuisance; for a short time I had to let the after position carry on fire control.

The enemy has for the moment the upper hand and I cannot get rid of the idea that trouble is brewing. Then something unexpected happens. From right to left there appears in the field of the periscope, a ship, improbably large and close. At the first glance I recognize an old English armoured cruiser, and give the necessary orders. My arm is clutched, " Don't fire, that is *Rostock*." But I can see the turrets fore and aft. " Action." " Armoured cruiser." " Four funnels." " Bow left." " Left 30." " Range 76 hm." " Salvo." Five salvoes rapidly follow, of which three straddled ; then was repeated the now familiar sight of a ship blowing up, this time before the eyes of both fleets, for the English main fleet could see the *Defence* although we could not see them. Astern of her comes another ship of the same class, which we leave to the ship astern of us as the English battle-cruisers demand all our attention. They are astern of us to port about 130 hm. range and are scarcely visible, as we have turned to an easterly course.

And now there began a phase compared with which all that had hitherto happened was play. While our own smoke completely hid the target from me so that I had to hand over to the after control, a hail of hits descended on us from port aft and port ahead. There nothing can be seen but red flashes, not the shadow of a ship. Our turrets are trained right aft and are firing as well as they can at our old friends, Beatty's battle-cruisers. From this direction a shell pierces the upper deck abaft the fore-funnel, penetrates the casemate and bursts behind the under part of B turret, causes a serious fire and throws outwards both the armoured doors which lead from the casemate to the deck. The explosion occurred directly under the control position but did no damage to this and the two fore 6-in. single casemates which were quite close. A hit from forward hits the right gun of A turret, on the right-hand side just in front of the turret, tears a big bit out and goes slantwise upwards against the right side of B turret. The shell breaks up but the 10-in. plate is pierced and the piece broken out is hurled into the turret. There it destroys the breech gear of the right gun, kills the men standing there and sets alight the front and rear portions of a cartridge, which were ready in the upper lift. The officer of the turret is dead, the gunner unconscious, lights out, all the fuses of the power and light current fused, the pumps empty, the turret full of smoke and swimming with glycerine, but the left gun and its crew behind the splinter bulkhead are unharmed. The layer, C.P.O. Gunner Klopp, one of the best petty officers I ever knew, succeeds, with the help of artificer Arnold, in reporting, after half an hour's work, the turret's left gun ready. The pumps are filled with sea water from the fire-extinguishing apparatus. . . .

The fateful red flashes from port ahead come from the English 3rd Battle Cruiser Squadron, which, ahead of the enemy main fleet, steered for the sound of the guns and was able, itself unseen, to close us to the most effective range. Probably it inflicted on us at this moment the fatal damage, even if it was not till later that its full effects were felt. Every ship has weak spots ; our " Achilles heel " was the broadside torpedo flat, situated forward of turret A. Here, unfortunately for reasons of space, the torpedo bulkhead, that incomparable protection against hits below the water-line, which was such a marked advantage in German ships as compared with foreign ones, had been left out. So two heavy enemy shells succeeded in penetrating under the belt and burst so effectively that the whole of the ship forward of A turret filled practically at once. It caused a tremendous shock and our gunnery station would not stay still again. I hit the armour plating heavily with my head just as I was about to take out one of the slit covers and clear the water off the rangefinder.

From A turret comes news of the right gun being put out of action and the slow flooding of the magazines. Unfortunately the inner part of the barbette was connected with the torpedo flat by a small gap in the armour deck, an emergency exit, which must have been forced open by the explosion. When the cause of the inrush of water was guessed it was too late. The hole was deep under water in a small unget-at-able space.

Meanwhile we had turned south and suddenly there appeared plainly and comparatively near, an English battle-cruiser of the *Invincible* Class, four points aft. I cannot express the delight I felt at having one of these tormentors clearly in sight, and like lightning the orders are given. But already a dark object moves between my periscope and the enemy—the end of the Admiral's bridge—which uselessly limits by 10° the vision of the periscope. " Has the after-control the range ? " " Yes, 100 hm." " After control carry on." Lieut.-Commander Bode quickly and clearly takes over, and to the unspeakable delight of the whole ship, fifteen seconds later our turrets, except B, speak again. I hear through the telephone everything said by Bode at the gunnery centres and look again at the enemy. Over ! " 4 down." " Salvo." Astraddle ! " Salvo." As the sound of the fall-of-shot indicator squeaks, the red flame flashes up nicely and unmistakably from the water columns round the enemy. Signs of a hit like these make a very definite impression if one has seen them twice. And sure enough, only a few seconds pass before the red glow breaks out everywhere and this ship too blows up. It was the *Invincible*—the unconquerable conquered. *Derfflinger*, as well as ourselves had fired at her. For myself, I would not claim the credit from my highly-esteemed brother-in-arms, but to be just to Lieut.-Commander Bode, I must say that I have no doubts as to our being responsible. The squeaking sound and the straddling salvoes and the red flames, all were unmistakable, and it is as fresh in my memory as if it had just happened.

That, however, is the end of us as leader of the line. At 7.43 p.m. *Lützow* sheers out of the line to slacken speed ; the water is pouring in too fast at our bows. Four of our destroyers put up an enormous black veil of smoke between us and the enemy and at once we are out of the heavy fire. A rest from action ! After three and a half hours I leave my station for the first time. The Admiral with his staff is just leaving us ; charming and calm as ever, he takes leave of us standing near with hearty words of recognition. While he goes on board a destroyer which comes alongside, our battle-cruisers pass us to port. There is no time for careful examination, but with satis-faction I count four of them. *Derfflinger* and *Seydlitz* are a little lower in the water than usual, but otherwise all seems well. Then a hasty glance at our deck, which is scarcely recognizable. The chart-house has fallen as houses of cards are apt to do. Of the bow turrets, B is pointing hard to port and smoke is coming from all its openings. It should be trained fore and aft, so something is wrong there. I had not had any report as to this, but there comes from the central gunnery position the bad news, " B turret does not answer." Then the dance starts again. Red flashes to port out of the mist. "To the guns." In a moment I am in the control. Rangefinder 100 hm. "At the muzzle flashes." "Salvo." . . . Not a shot ! When the flash comes again, again "Salvo" . . . Not a shot ! It is impossible for the gunlayers to get on. If we only had "the director."

Two or three hits shake the ship further aft. One of these bursts in the lower deck, between C and D turrets, causing serious casualties in the after action dressing-station, among the wounded, surgeons and sick-bay attendants. At the same time it destroys part of the electric power leads to D turret, which here, for a short distance contrary to the usual practice, lie above the main armoured deck. Enemy shells find places like this with deadly accuracy; as a result D turret is reduced to training by hand which, in the case of a 12-in. turret, means practically complete inaction. This shell also tears up the main armoured deck, the only case of this happening, but does no damage to the powder magazines just underneath it.

Then we must have been lost to sight by the enemy, and, although the whole English line passed by us, we were not fired at and were able to devote all our energy to repairs. And there was plenty to do. First B turret. A number of dead, who had not been there before, were lying on the small strip of the upper deck near the turret, so some of the turret's crew were still alive. Then came the report from inside, "Left gun clear," and see, it swings round. The right gun of A turret has lost a semi-circular piece about one yard square on its upper side. The muzzle droops, as the elevating gear has been put out of action. I think to myself that I shall have four guns in a fit state for the night action. A survey of the secondary armament shows three guns left out of fourteen, only one of which is on the starboard side. Of our eight searchlights only one can be used, aft on the port side, but all its leads are broken. So we must use messengers from the gun crews available. The electricians must repair the cable to D turret. I report the state of the guns to the Commander who is cheerful and busy. Meanwhile the ship is well down by the head, the deck at the bows is on a level with the water. I hear that practically the whole fore part of the ship is water-logged, only one of the switch-rooms there is clear of water and there are a number of men down there below the level of the water on the upper platform deck. To help them was impossible. A turret now reports that the magazines had had to be abandoned after getting up all the ammunition that can be stowed; further, B turret's magazines are making water but it can be kept under.

Lützow was the first ship equipped with a grouped system of pumps, which provided one group of pumps forward, amidships and aft respectively. The bow section failed directly the main inrush of water took place, so that the bow could only be pumped out by letting the water run amidships. However, the apparatus for doing this, I think, was so quickly submerged while the ship was leading our line at a high speed, that it could not be operated. The reason for the ship sinking can be put down to these unfortunate circumstances. I breathe again when we go to night stations. It seemed that we could not help being attacked. When it was almost dark the spotting officer came down from the foremast. He had had the best view and a great deal to tell us. On his head he wore the band of his cap, a splinter had taken the top of it and the telephone ear pieces off, a fact he had quite forgotten. He asks me what the state of affairs is and I can only answer "I hope no destroyers find us to-night, and as to what will happen to-morrow, God knows." The speed of the ship has been reduced to seven knots on the earnest representations of the first officer, but with the corresponding revolutions she probably only developed about five. The very low forecastle—*Lützow* had no upper deck forward—was not under water. More sea had got up from the south-west and is breaking on the forecastle among the heaps of empty cartridge cases.

We were all dead beat, officers and men, and the night dragged endlessly on. What of the morning? We had seen the two fleets in action disappear to the south. At midnight searchlights and gunfire shone out in that direction. We did not doubt that the new day would herald a new action, it seemed impossible for touch to be lost. Could we be of any use? I should have liked to have asked the Commander if there was any chance of our keeping the water to its present limits, but he could not leave the control nor I the bridge. I always had hopes for the ship, but at midnight when the Captain called the senior officers to a conference, the Commander reported 7,500 tons of water on board and expressed his opinion that at the most we could keep afloat till 6 a.m. The news was a dreadful blow. The noble ship; but it had to be; the bows were now two metres under water, which was pouring through the open doors of the casemates into the battery and through the torn up plating on to the middle deck. The great oil-boiler rooms forward had had to be abandoned to save the men there. The draft forward was seventeen metres. The Captain, who up till now had steadily steered the ship in the direction in which the fleet had last been seen, sadly gave in, to prevent the useless sacrifice of human life which would have occurred if she had not been abandoned.

A final attempt to navigate her stern first failed because she could not be steered against wind and sea.

Shortly before 1 a.m. came the order " all aft," and the four destroyers which had stayed with us were ordered alongside, aft on the starboard side. I had not recollected them and was agreeably surprised at not having to swim. As long as there was time I went round the ship with other officers and trusted ratings looking for wounded and men who were asleep. Sure enough I found one gallant fellow fast asleep on the bench in the gunnery flat. The sight in the big 6-in. battery was indescribably desolate. Most of our casualties had been there. In B turret it was too dark to see anything, but from survivor's reports I heard with great satisfaction that the burning of a complete cartridge in two portions in the upper lift had had only a local effect. In the *Lützow* very careful precautions had been taken against the spread of a powder fire, with complete success. Unfortunately the officer of this turret, Lieut.-Commander Fischer, fell a victim to this fire, while others close to him were saved although badly burned and half suffocated. The final success was a triumph, the repair of the electrical connections of D turret.

The disembarkation of the crew was carried out perfectly, first the wounded, and then the rest without any trouble. As we cast off in the last boat I saw the ship in the grey light of morning ; A turret under water, B an island. Near the bridge the water was up to the superstructure. The stern was about two metres higher than usual. Then one of the destroyers fired a torpedo which hit amidships, whereupon the ship for a moment heeled over to starboard. It only needed a slight impact to hasten the sinking by one or two hours.

At 5.45 a.m. a detachment of one enemy cruiser and four destroyers reached the spot where she sank, they were thus cheated of an easy triumph. After our boats had had short sharp actions with this and another group of the enemy, we were picked up by the *Regensburg* before noon and landed at Wilhelmshaven in the evening.

Comm. Pascher (S.M.S. " Lützow ").

TORPEDO ATTACK

31st *May.* German destroyers were now observed ahead of the German battle-cruiser, *Lützow,* and soon afterwards they turned towards us to attack. Our secondary armament opened fire and scored a hit or two, but their attack was successfully made, and a number of torpedoes were fired, which gave us a few anxious minutes. We observed a great number of tracks of torpedoes, some as far away as 2½ miles. One torpedo crossed the line immediately under *Neptune's* stern, and directly afterwards another track was spotted which seemed to be coming straight for us. But apparently the officers on the bridge below had not seen it, and were in blissful ignorance of the danger that the ship was in. There was no time to explain, and a stentorian " hard-a-starboard " shouted down the voice pipe by the Gunnery Lieutenant was fortunately accepted without question and put on by the helmsman. The bridge then sighted the torpedo, and emergency full speed was ordered. We began to turn rapidly, but I vividly remember how the torpedo got closer and closer. From the fore-top we were craning our necks over the metal side, while the whole top was groaning and vibrating under the strain of the ship turning at full speed with full helm on. We looked down on the tops of the turrets and the decks below, and could see our shipmates working down there quite unconscious of the immediate peril. I personally had been torpedoed once before— in the *Formidable*—and had no delusions about the situation. The ship had turned a right angle, 8 points, and the torpedo was now dead astern following exactly in our course, but going faster than our fastest speed, and coming closer and closer, until our view in the fore-top was blanketed by the mainmast and after-platforms. We could do nothing, of course, but wait and wait, mouths open, like when one is expecting a gun to fire. Nothing happened. The time passed when it should have reached our stern and there should have been a big explosion, but still nothing happened. An enemy salvo splashed down close on our starboard bow, but nobody heeded it. Then somebody laughed, and breaking the spell, we knew that after all it was somehow all right. The miracle, for it really seemed miraculous, was accounted for in *Neptune's* report : " Torpedo was either deflected by the wash from *Neptune's* propellers or ran its range out. The latter is more likely."

About this time several other battleships besides the *Neptune* were hauling out of the line, dodging torpedoes, with the result that the line became considerably lengthened, and was irregular in places where ships were trying to regain their station. We had dropped astern, and for some seven minutes the *St. Vincent* was directly between us and the enemy and we were unable to fire. Just after we had successfully dodged the torpedo, we heard, or more exactly perhaps felt, a dull concussion, and saw the *Marlborough* haul out of the line to port listing heavily. She had been hit by a torpedo, but a few minutes later she regained her position in the line with now only a slight list, and we saw her firing again strongly.

A midshipman in H.M.S. " Neptune," quoted by

Fawcett and Hooper.

VERDUN

THE DEFENCE OF FORT VAUX

Fort Vaux lay east-north-east of Verdun, the next fort south of Fort Douaumont. It stood on the crest of a hill and was visible from the ridge behind, on which stood Fort Souville. Vaux had been dismantled but formed a strong point in the French line at the end of May. In this month French G.H.Q. asked for volunteers among officers who had been incapacitated, to take command of such positions. Commandant Raynal, 49 years of age, now recovering from his third wound, volunteered and was accepted. Hobbling along on his stick, he took over the command of the fort on the night 30/31 May. The garrison consisted chiefly of men of the 142ᵐᵉ Infanterie, with machine-gunners and other details, including 4 carrier pigeons and a cocker spaniel. The fort was victualled with preserved food, and there was a cistern of water. Unhappily the latter proved to contain far less than had been reported. On 31st May, after a 24-hour bombardment, the Germans assaulted, carried the outworks and made a lodgement on the roof. Thereafter for seven days, the French garrison made a heroic defence against all attacks, fighting in darkness in the passages. The attempts from outside to reinforce the defence failed, and Raynal received no messages, except a few brought by gallant men who ran the gauntlet of the enemy. At last, on 7th June, after 48 hours without water, he surrendered. The Germans recognized the gallantry of the defence, the Crown Prince personally returning Raynal his sword. The French also decorated him with the Legion of Honour. The following passages are from his own account of the last days, 4th–7th June.

So we came to 4th June, a day still more terrible. About 8.30 a.m., the Boches carried out two attacks in combination; one against the barricade of the observation-post, the other on the barricade of the left arches. Through the loopholes, they poured flame and gas, which gave off an intolerable smell and gripped our throats. Shouts of "gas-masks" came from both ends of the fort. In the left arches, the garrison, driven back by flame and smoke, fell back towards the central gallery. Here was posted brave Lieut. Girard. He dashed forward into the smoke to the machine-guns which his men had been forced to abandon. He had the luck to get there before the Boches, and at once opened fire on the sheet of gas which was pouring through the right-hand barricade. Inspired by his example, his men came back, stood to their guns and fired for an hour without stopping. After clearing the ground between the machine-guns and the barricade, Girard led forward the bombers who reoccupied their position and definitely drove the Boche off. In this bitter engagement, fought out in the midst of smoke and complete darkness (for the gas had put out all the lamps), Girard received several bits of bomb in his face and hands, fortunately slight wounds. He did not go back to the casemate of Bourges-Left until the position had been completely re-established. But on reaching it, he was seized with violent sickness from the gas he had swallowed, and fainted. Under the care that was taken of him, he revived and at once took over his sector.

At the same time in the right arches this attack was duplicated. Driven by flames and stifling smoke, our men fell back behind the rubble barricade.

While these fights were in progress and the danger of being swept away by sheer weight was doubled by the peril of being stifled, I took every disposition to avoid both and to thwart the enemy's calculations. The fans which carry the air into the bottom of the ditch, were first started. . . . All the windows of the large casemate were emptied of sand-bags and a huge current of air was thus created. The manœuvre was successful; in about three-quarters of an hour, the air was once more possible to breathe. Many of my men had been overcome and had fainted. I went down to the aid-post, and while M. Conte was giving me his report, I heard a wounded man, lying on a stretcher on the ground, exclaim in a rough voice : "You'll see a lot more, comrades. The Boche will show you some dirtier tricks still." Who was the man with this rough masculine way of encouraging his hearers? I looked and recognized Sous-Lieutenant de Roquette, very dangerously wounded in the thigh, and with one eye blinded by a bomb fragment. He was in very great pain, but his spirit did not waver, and he was to preserve this gallant attitude, in the midst of all trials, to the last moment. . . .

It was in the course of that afternoon that the sapper sergeant in charge of the stores came and asked to speak to me in private, and said in a hoarse voice : " Mon commandant, there is practically no water left in the cistern." I started, I made him repeat what he had said, I shook him.

" There has been dirty work here."

" No, sir, we have only served out the ration you laid down. It is the marks on the register which have been wrong."

Then our agony began. I gave orders to hold back the little that remained and to make no further allowance to-day. . . .

I sent off my two last carrier pigeons, making my reports more urgent. Yet I did not say to what extremity I was reduced as regards water. This method of communication is far from certain, and one of my carriers might fall into enemy hands. The precaution was not unavailing, for one of my messengers reached the loft at Verdun wounded and the message lost. Now that all my pigeons had been flown, how was I to communicate with the outer world ?

I had in the fort a small signal equipment, and when the engineers reported, they had told me that a similar equipment had been sent to Fort Souville to establish visual communication with Fort Vaux. Now, all the signals we had made to Souville yesterday and the day before had remained unanswered. I began once more and asked my questions not only to Souville, but also to all the points of the sky-line. The sky-line remained silent. I asked myself the reason. It was because to receive my messages, a post must be put in the open, on " the billiard-table " as the poilus say. And on the " billiard-table " was falling a thick murderous Boche barrage. . . .

(At this point, Raynal managed to slip two sappers out of the fort, and later again, aspirant-officer Buffet, to get into touch with the people behind. Thus he was able to send messages to Souville, but he received few in return, since Souville's messages would be picked up by the enemy. He did however receive certain information as to proposed counter-attacks through his very gallant messengers.)

Leaning over my instrument, by the loophole from which I could discern, or rather guess, the black mass of Souville, I called ! I called !

Nothing. No answer flickered in the night. The two men I

had sacrificed were perhaps by now lying on the road, and in the depth of my heart, I wept for these two heroes.

Before leaving the loophole, I made one last attempt; I sent one final call which would no doubt like the others be lost.

" Ah ! " In spite of myself a cry leapt to my lips. Over there, at Souville, a light sprang up which seemed to answer me. I tapped out : " Is that you ? " The light answered : " Souville ! "

I had my messages sent off; they were answered by the arranged signals. My first visual message was gone. I ended by asking again that something should be done to relieve us. . . .

5th June, the fifth day of Hell. Dawn broke, but in the arches and in the main gallery, deep darkness still hung. In the main gallery, I had to pay continual heed to keeping the lamps alight that passage should not be interrupted.

About 5 in the morning, the barricade of the covered way near the casemate Bourges-Left, went up in a terrific explosion which tumbled down part of the masonry, and in the breach thus made, the enemy appeared advancing behind flammenwerfer. Luckily, the huge draught which was created, prevented and turned to nothing the rush of the flames by blowing them back towards the nozzles of the apparatus. After a momentary surprise, our machine-gunners and bombers, led by Bazy and Girard, rushed back and counter-attacked with bombs. The enemy faltered. We re-established our barricade and picked up our dead and wounded, for this latest attack cost us further heavy losses. My two brave lieutenants, Bazy and Girard, were once more wounded, though not seriously, by bomb splinters. . . .

This 5th June, on which the Boches secured no more than a slight success in the right arches, a success for which they paid dearly, was for us a day of intense physical suffering. The short but violent fights of the morning had necessitated the employment of the whole garrison, and our men's strength had been drained away. I saw them gasping in the dust and the smoke. Yesterday I had already noted that they had scarcely touched their rations because of the lack of water. The preserved meat was salted, and could scarcely be forced down our dry throats. For my own part, I had eaten nothing yesterday, and to-day I felt little hunger—only thirst.

I could see my men broken with fatigue, silent and gloomy. If I had to call on them for still another effort, they would be incapable of carrying it out. So I decided to serve out the last drops of the corpse-smelling water which remained in the cistern. It represented scarcely a quart per man; it was nauseous, it was muddy, and yet we drank this horrible liquid with avidity. But there was too little and our thirst continued. . . .

(Shortly after this, Buffet succeeded in slipping back into the fort, bringing news that after a bombardment during this day and the next night, an attempt would be made to save the fort by a counter-attack from the west on the following morning. Raynal intended to co-operate, and Buffet again volunteered to make the dangerous journey to inform the troops behind of Raynal's intentions.)

The night passed in a fever of expectation of the great action which should deliver us. From 1.30 a.m. the sortie party was in position on the stairs which led to the doorway on to the ditch. Observers placed in the casemates of Bourges-Left and Right and at the windows of the main casemate, were to warn me of any movement they picked up.

At 2 a.m. our artillery lengthened range.

"Keep a sharp look-out, my lads."

No news came to me. Dawn began to break. On every side, we questioned the sky-line; invariably not a sign. About 3 a.m. there was still nothing, neither from the south, nor from the right. But from the casemate, Bourges-Left, they warned me that a small body of about the strength of a platoon were sheltering in shell-holes not far from the fort. And almost at once the same observers informed me that under a terrible fire, which had decimated them, this little body had thrown down its weapons and was being led off prisoners by the Germans. That was all that we saw of the counter-attack of 6th June. . . .

During this day, 6th June, the Boche became more active against our barricades. It was as if he guessed the drama which was being played out within, and in actual fact the sufferings of my men, above all of the wounded, increased terribly. Thirst, that horrible thirst raged.

I was in my command post with Sous-Lieutenant Roy, and my devoted sapper could find in his resourceful spirit no further remedy. Sounds of groans reached us. Mingled with the groans another noise struck our ear, that of a hesitant footstep and of hands rustling against the wall.

The door suddenly opened. There stood a terrifying apparition.

It was a wounded man, his naked chest swathed in bloody bandages. He leant with one hand against the door frame, and thrusting out a leg, went down on one knee. He held out to me his other hand in a supplicating gesture, and in a whisper, muttered : " Mon commandant, something to drink."

I went over to him and raised him up. " I have no water, my brave fellow. Do as I do—hope. They are coming to our rescue." Still groaning, my wounded man dragged himself back to the aid-post. I looked at Roy. Like my own, his eyes were clouded. . . .

It was the end. Unless a miracle happened, this would be the last night of our resistance. My men, who drank no more, ate no more, slept no longer, only held themselves upright by a prodigy of will.

I summoned my officers to my command post. Every one of these brave men now despaired. They saw no salvation for their men, who must be preserved for the sake of the country, except by immediate surrender. But suddenly the guns outside began to bark, and the barking grew to a tempest. They were French guns. The fort was not being touched, but the vicinity was being violently barraged. The flame of hope once more sprang up.

"Listen, comrades. That is the French artillery. It has never fired so strongly. It is the preparation for an attack. Go to your positions. To-morrow morning, if we have not been delivered, I promise to submit to cruel necessity."

Warmed by my words, the officers returned to their posts. About 11 p.m. our gun-fire abruptly ceased, and the night passed away in complete calm, more nerve-racking for me than the storm of battle. Not a sound, not a hint of movement. I thought of the promise I had made. Had I the right to prolong resistance beyond human strength and to compromise uselessly the life of these brave men who had done their duty so heroically ? I took a turn in the corridors. What I saw was frightening. Men were overcome with vomiting due to urine in the stomach, for so wretched were they that they had reached the point of drinking their own urine. Some lost consciousness. In the main gallery, a man was licking a little wet streak on the wall. . . .

7th June ! Day broke, and we scarcely noticed it. For us it was still night, a night in which all hope was extinguished. Aid from outside, if it came, would come too late. I sent off my last message, the last salute of the fort and its defenders to their country. Then I turned to my men :

"It is all over, my friends. You have done your duty, the whole of your duty. Thank you."

They understood, and together in one shout we repeated the last message which my instrument had just sent off : " *Vive la France !* "

In the minutes which followed a silence as of death fell upon the fort.

Commandant Raynal.

FATIGUE

I REMEMBER the commander of a trench-mortar battery, with bandaged head and respirator hung open to dry, counting in his men by the light of my sergeant's lantern. I could see him swaying as he stood, dizzy with gas and sleeplessness, and when he had seen his lot in, he turned uncertainly as if he did not know where he was. I took him by the elbow and guided him to the hut reserved for officers. He didn't speak, and so far as I know, may have been unconscious of my presence. His servant was setting out some food, but he simply seized the whisky, drank a gulp from the bottle, and fell down. I shoved something under his head, told his servant not to wake him in the morning, as I would take his parade. I knew so exactly how he felt, or, fortunately, did not feel.

R. H. Mottram.

THE PRISONERS FROM KUT

20th June. (Left Mosul *en route* for Ras al Ain). . . . We started off about 4.30 a.m. Early in the morning we passed a German machine-gun section, admirably turned out : all the section was mounted. . . . At about 9 a.m. we arrived on the banks of a stream, where the water was fairly good. We halted at the stream and a British soldier came and told us that there were about half a dozen of his comrades in a room at the post, two of whom were dangerously ill. We went in and found six British soldiers in a fearfully emaciated condition lying in a filthy stable. Of course, the Turks had done nothing for them. One of the men said : " We are like rats in a trap and they are just slowly killing us." They said that the German machine-gun section had been most kind to them. The officers had given them money ; the men had given them part of their rations. The General gave some gold to the senior of the party and Baines did what he could for the worst cases, two men who were very near death. We saw the senior Turkish official in charge of the post, a warrant officer. He was quite useless and could do nothing. . . .

21st June. . . . As soon as we arrived at Ras al Ain . . . the General asked to see the commandant . . . The commandant was a colonel. When we entered, he was reclining on a divan smoking a *hookah.* He at once got up, addressed us in good French and offered cigarettes and coffee. The General told me to tell him all we had seen on the way from Baghdad and to ask him to wire to Halil Pasha to have carts sent for our unfortunate men dying by the wayside. He refused, as he was not in Halil's command. The General then told him to wire to Aleppo. Another evasive reply. . . .

22nd June. We reached Aleppo (by train from Ras al Ain) about 9 a.m. After lunch we drove up to the barracks to interview the Turkish commander. . . . Presently Shefket Pasha entered. . . . The General then exposed the lamentable state of our men on the road and offered to pay for a telegram to Baghdad to ask them to send carts and pick up all the isolated parties. Shefket Pasha would not hear of this and wrote out a telegram himself and promised to send it. He also said he would do his utmost to better the condition of our men. . . .

23rd June. Arrived at Islahiya . . . a German warrant officer came and told me that there were a number of British troops suffering from dysentery in some Arab tents near by. The German had been to see them several times, but the Turks had warned him off and said that the men had cholera—a lie. He said that they were being starved to death. The General sent Baines to investigate this case, and Halim (Turkish interpreter with General Melliss's party) and self went to interview the commandant. The assistant surgeon came up from the prisoners and bore out what the German had told me. I then went with the General to the commandant to expose the case and ask him to have a telegram sent to Aleppo. He agreed to everything and said he would send a wire, but I doubt it. . . . The General sent me off to thank the German warrant officer; I found him in the rest house for German and Austro-Hungarian troops. He promised to do what he could for our men. . . .

24th June. We came to a spring and lying around it were three British soldiers. . . . All were horribly emaciated and in a dreadful state. They told us that they had been left behind by a column that had passed about two days ago, as they could not march. They had nothing to eat from the Turks, but a German wireless section, that we had met, had given them some food. We took these men on our carts to bring along with us.

On arriving at Hassan Begli I saw a German warrant officer talking to 24 British soldiers. He told me that they had been left here the night before by the party going out, as they were too ill to travel. He had seen the commandant several times and begged him to put them under shelter (they were lying by the road side) and to give them shelter and food; but each time the commandant gave an evasive reply and nothing was done. The General sent for the commandant and told him exactly what he thought of his behaviour. We now had 27 men on our hands. The commandant at once sent them into a large shed and sent down some rice and meat already cooked. The General sent me into the village to buy bread and eggs, which, thanks to the German, I got at very low prices. We brought these to the men and issued them out. The General told me to invite the German to breakfast. He was glad to come, as he had not met Europeans for so long. We had another interview with the commandant. The General told him that he must send on these 27 men by carts. He said he had no carts. The German said this was a lie. Finally, the commandant said our carts would go at 5 p.m. and at 6 p.m. the men should go with a convoy. But that did not suit the General, who said he would not stir till the men had been moved. The commandant then agreed to send them by carts and at about 5 p.m. we saw the men safely off. . . .

25*th June*. We arrived at . . . There we found the men we had sent on in the carts the night before sitting down enjoying hot coffee, the gift of some Austrian soldiers. One of our men told me that this was the first hot drink he had had since he had been a prisoner.

I went with the General to interview the German commandant (Major Schon). He was very amiable, sent for coffee for us and listened with great sympathy to my story of our suffering men. He told me that there were a large number of British and Indians here; at present they were under the Turks, but he hoped to take over soon for railway work; then their conditions would improve. . . .

Capt. A. J. Shakeshaft.

BEFORE THE SOMME

THE days slowly pass away. A few rare shells disturb the mustard and darnel blossoming along the parapet. The men rest during the afternoon. At stand-to, this summer evening almost conjures one to believe that war is a pleasant state. The sun has gone behind the ridge; but the sky is still flushed from his passage. Across the valley, the air is turning pearl grey, with here and there brown smudges where Fritz cooks his evening meal. Adinfer Wood has lost its sinister air and wild life must be waking among the trees to business no more cruel than our own. A lark bids a reluctant farewell to the day and drops down among the tussocks on the ridge. Faintly from far away comes the hum of an aeroplane. Now that pastoral music, the rumble of wheels, begins over the countryside, both east and west, the rumble of the ration limbers, English and German, creeping steadily towards the line. The air holds the sound, magnifies and disperses it, making of it a homely background, in front of which some familiar tune whistled by the man in the next bay as he rubs an oily rag over his rifle brings a fleeting nostalgia for an English lawn, shadowed by a walnut tree, dew, and a lamp behind a window pane. In the distance, a single gun, half afraid of the quiet, speaks once, and for a few seconds tears the evening into clanging echoes. The first flare rises from the trenches opposite, curves and sinks, a brilliant lily. Suddenly far away a wild murmur breaks out, rising and falling, a tuneless, tumbling *prestissimo* played by a muffled orchestra. Over my shoulder to the north I can see a cataract of lights rising and falling in all the shades of the prism; now and again, a flash as of a damp match quickly extinguished, bursting shrapnel. " Vimy Ridge again," murmurs Leader; " stand down." The darkness is blotting out the valley. " Stand down," repeats Sergeant Fake: " Corporal Lennox, is your wiring party ready? " The industrialism of war engulfs us again.

Guy Chapman (Royal Fusiliers).

A RAID

ENTERING the other dug-out I was slightly startled, for I had forgotten that the raiders were to have blacked faces (to avoid the danger of their mistaking one another for Germans). Exchanging boisterous jokes, they were putting the finishing touches to their make-up with bits of burnt cork. Showing the whites of their eyes and pretending not to recognize one another, those twenty-five shiny-faced nigger minstrels might almost have been getting ready for a concert. Everyone seemed to expect the entertainment to be a roaring success. But there were no looking-glasses or banjos, and they were brandishing knobkerries, stuffing Mills bombs into their pockets and hatchets into their belts, and " Who's for a Blighty one to-night ? " was the stock joke (if such a well-worn wish could be called a joke).

At 10.30 there was a sudden silence, and Barton told me to take the party up to Battalion Head-quarters. It surprises me when I remember that I set off without having had a drink, but I have always disliked the flavour of whisky, and in those days the helpfulness of alcohol in human affairs was a fact which had not yet been brought home to me. The raiders had been given only a small quantity, but it was enough to hearten them as they sploshed up the communication trench. None of us could know how insignificant we were in the so-called " Great Adventure " which was sending up its uneasy flares along the Western Front. No doubt we thought ourselves something very special. But what we thought never mattered ; nor does it matter what sort of an inflated fool I was when I blundered into Kinjack's Head-quarters at Maple Redoubt to report the presence of the raiders and ask whether I might go across with them. " Certainly not," said the Colonel, " your job is to stop in our trench and count the men as they come back." He spoke with emphasis and he was not a man who expected to have to say a thing twice. We stared at one another for a moment; some freak of my brain made me remember that in peace time he had been an enthusiastic rose grower—had won prizes with his roses, in fact; for he was a married man and had lived in a little house near the barracks.

My thought was nipped in the bud by his peremptory voice telling Major Robson, his second-in-command, to push off with the party. We were about 400 yards from the front line, and Robson now led us across the open to a point in the support trench, from which a red electric torch winked to guide us. Then up a trench to the starting-point, the men's feet clumping and drumming on the duck-boards. This noise, plus the clinking and drumming and creaking of weapons and equipment, suggested to my strained expectancy that the enemy would be well warned of our arrival. Mansfield and his two confederates now loomed squatly above us on the parapet; they had been laying a guiding line of lime across the craters. A gap had been cut in our wire, and it was believed that some sort of damage had been done to the German wire which had been " strafed " by trench mortars during the day.

The raiders were divided into four parties of five men; operation orders had optimistically assumed that the hostile trenches would be entered without difficulty; " A " party would go to the left, " B " party to the right, and so on and so forth. The object of the raid was to enter the enemy loop on the edge of the crater; to enter Kiel Trench at two points; to examine the portions of trench thus isolated, capture prisoners, bomb dug-outs, and kill Germans. An " evacuating party " (seven men carrying two ten-foot ladders and a red flash lamp) followed the others. The ladders were considered important, as the German front trench was believed to be deep and therefore difficult to get out of in a hurry. There were two mine-craters a few yards from our parapet; these craters were about fifty yards in diameter and about fifty feet deep; their sides were steep and composed of thin soft soil; there was water at the bottom of them. Our men crossed by a narrow bridge of earth be-tween the craters; the distance to the German wire was about sixty yards.

It was now midnight. The five parties had vanished into the darkness on all fours. It was raining quietly and persistently. I sat on the parapet waiting for something to happen. Except for two men at a sentry post near by (they were now only spectators) there seemed to be no one about. " They'll never keep that — inside the trench," muttered the sentry to his mate and even at that tense moment I valued the compliment. Major Robson and the stretcher-bearers had been called away by a message. There must be some trouble further along, I thought, wondering what it could be, for I hadn't heard a sound. Now and again I looked at my luminous watch. Five, ten, fifteen minutes passed in ominous silence. An occasional flare, never near our craters, revealed the streaming rain, blanched the tangles of wire that wound away into the gloom, and came to nothing, bringing down the night. Unable to remain inactive any longer, I crawled a little way out. As I went, a few shells began to drone across in their leisurely way. Our communication trench was being shelled. I joined the evacuating party; they were lying on the lip of the left-hand crater. A flare fizzed up, and I could see the rest of the men lying down, straight across the ridge, and was able to exchange a grimace with one of the black-faced ladder-carriers. Then some " whizz-bangs " rushed over to our front trench; one or two fell on the craters; this made the obstinate silence of Kiel Trench more menacing. Soon afterwards one of the bayonet men came crawling rapidly back. I followed him to our trench where he whispered his message. " They can't get through the second belt of wire; O'Brien says it's a wash-out; they're all going to throw a bomb and retire."

I suppose I ought to have tried to get the ladder-carriers in before the trouble started; but the idea didn't strike me as I waited with bumping heart; and almost immediately the explosions began. A bomb burst in the water of the left-hand crater, sending up a phosphorescent spume. Then a concentration of angry flashes, thudding bangs, and cracking shots broke itself up in hubbub and scurry, groans and curses, and stampeding confusion. Stumbling figures loomed up from below, scrambling clumsily over the parapet; black faces and whites of eyes showed grotesque in the antagonistic shining of alarmed flares. Dodging to and fro, I counted fourteen men in; they all blundered away down the trench. I went out, found Mansfield badly hit, and left him with two others who soon got him in. Other wounded men were crawling back. Among them was a grey-haired lance-corporal, who had one of his feet almost blown off; I half carried him in and when he was sitting on the fire-step he said, " Thank God Almighty for this; I've been waiting eighteen months for it and now I can go home." I told him we'd get him away on a stretcher soon, and then he muttered "Mick O'Brien's somewhere down in the craters."

All this had been quick work and not at all what I'd expected. Things were slowing down now. The excitement was finished, and O'Brien was somewhere down in the craters. The bombing and rifle-fire had slackened when I started out to look for him. I went mechanically, as though I were drowning myself in the darkness. This is no fun at all, was my only thought as I groped my way down the soft clogging side of the left-hand crater ; no fun at all, for they were still chucking an occasional bomb and firing circumspectly. I could hear the reloading click of rifle-bolts on the lip of the crater above me as I crawled along with mud-clogged fingers, or crouched and held my breath painfully. Bullets hit the water and little showers of earth pattered down from the banks. I knew that nothing in my previous experience of patrolling had ever been so grim as this, and I lay quite still for a bit, miserably wondering whether my number was up ; then I remembered that I was wearing my pre-War raincoat ; I could feel the pipe and tobacco-pouch in my pocket and somehow this made me less forlorn, though life seemed much farther away than the low mumble of voices in our trench. A flare would have helped my searchings, but they had stopped sending them up ; pawing the loose earth and dragging my legs after me, I worked my way round the crater. O'Brien wasn't there, so I got across into the other one, which was even more precipitous and squashy. Down there I discovered him. Another man was crouching beside him, wounded in one arm and patiently waiting for help. O'Brien moaned when I touched him ; he seemed to have been hit in several places. His companion whispered huskily, "Get a rope." As I clambered heavily up the bank I noticed that it had stopped raining. Robson was peering out of the trench ; he sent someone for a rope, urging him to be quick for already there was a faint beginning of daylight. With the rope, and a man to help, I got back to O'Brien, and we lifted him up the side of the crater.

It was heavy work, for he was tall and powerfully built, and the soft earth gave way under our feet as we lugged and hoisted the limp, shattered body. The Germans must have seen us in the half light, but they had stopped firing ; perhaps they felt sorry for us.

At last we lowered him over the parapet. A stretcher-bearer

bent over him and then straightened himself, taking off his helmet with a gesture that vaguely surprised me by its reverent simplicity. O'Brien had been one of the best men in our Company. I looked down at him and then turned away; the face was grotesquely terrible, smeared with last night's burnt cork, the forehead matted with a tangle of dark hair.

I had now accounted for everyone. Two killed and ten wounded was the only result of the raid. In the other Company sector the Germans had blown in one of our mine-galleries, and about thirty of the tunnelling company had been gassed or buried. Robson had been called there with the stretcher-bearers just as the raid began.

Nothing now remained for me to do except to see Kinjack on my way back. Entering his dug-out I looked at him with less diffidence than I'd ever done before. He was sitting on his plank bed, wearing a brown woollen cap with a tuft on the top. His blonde face was haggard; the last few hours had been no fun for him either. This was a Kinjack I'd never met before, and it was the first time I had ever shared any human equality with him. He spoke kindly to me in his rough way, and in doing so made me very thankful that I had done what I could to tidy up the mess in No Man's Land.

Larks were shrilling in the drizzling sky as I went down to 71 North. I felt a wild exultation. Behind me were the horror and the darkness. Kinjack had thanked me. It was splendid to be still alive, I thought, as I strode down the hill, skirting shell-holes and jumping over communication trenches, for I wasn't in a mood to bother about going along wet ditches. The landscape loomed around me, and the landscape was life, stretching away and away into freedom. Even the dreary little warren at 71 North seemed to await me with a welcome, and Flook was ready with some hot tea.

Siegfried Sassoon (Royal Welch Fusiliers).

CONSCIENTIOUS OBJECTOR

" IT was right at the beginning," he said, " that I learnt that the only people from whom I was to expect sympathy were the soldiers, and not the civilians. When I was waiting in that first guard-room, sitting down rather dazed on the floor, five men were bustled into the room, and the door was slammed on them. I made myself as inconspicuous as possible, hoping that they would not notice me. They were all in a towering rage. Their language was incredible. I gathered that they were all soldiers who, for some reason or other, either for breach of discipline or overstaying leave, were under arrest. They cursed and stormed for some time. Finally, they noticed me in my corner. They stopped swearing for a moment, and one of them walked up to me.

" ' What are you in here for, mate ? '

" I thought it best to be as simple as possible, so I said : ' Well, you see, I am a Quaker, and I refused to join the army, because I think that war is murder.'

" The man took a step backwards. A terrible light came into his eyes. He raised his arm, which had a wound stripe on it. I thought that he was going to spring at me. The room was very silent.

" ' Murder ? ' he whispered, ' murder ? It's *bloody* murder ! '

" And then we were friends. We had only a little while together, because the men were soon marched away, and I never saw them again. But as they went, they each came up to me, and shook me by the hand. ' Stick to it, matey ! Stick ! ' they said, one after another."

Told to Beverley Nichols, by Robert Mennell.

EAST AFRICA

From there, next day, with a native guide, we threaded our way along game paths, to find out at the various native villages whether there were Germans or Askari about. From the fact that the natives were quietly at their kraals I knew the Askari were gone, for whenever there are any about the local inhabitants take to flight. The Germans recruit their Askari from the savage tribes beyond the lakes, and they are much dreaded by the unwarlike people who live in this area. In the course of the morning I saw a lioness squatting on her haunches close to a millet field in which native women, their infants on their backs, were unconcernedly hoeing the ground, and they merely laughed when I pointed out the lioness to them, so little fear have they in the daytime of these brutes. For safety's sake, however, I fired a shot, and drove her away.

Next day we made for Chamballa, a series of water-holes among some hills. The place was crowded with troops, horses and wagons, that had come up, and van Deventer was there. He told me that General Smuts was also on the move. He had marched down the Pangani River, and was now striking south for the Central Railway on a course parallel to our own, some hundred and fifty miles to our left. His force and ours were ultimately to join hands, but in the meanwhile each was independently groping its way through unknown bush country.

As far as we were concerned, the Central Railway was still ninety miles away, and whereas in the past we had been hampered by too much water, we were now entering a region that looked as if no rain ever fell on it.

I was ordered next morning to take out a patrol and search for a pan of water, reported by local natives as lying some distance off the main road. It was an interesting ride. We were in game country once more, and herds of eland, wilde-beest and sassaby were grazing in all directions, and several times we saw giraffe. I never tired of looking at the strange and beautiful creatures of Africa, and I learned in these days the pity of killing them without need.

By midday our native guide brought us to the pan. As we approached we heard the trumpeting of elephant, and when we reached the water it was all muddy and churned where they had been drinking a few minutes before, but the animals themselves were crashing out of sight among the trees. I sent a man back to report the water, while we went on. We spent the night around big camp-fires, for the lions were again holding a concert, and next day we reached Hanetti, a desolate spot with a few muddy water-holes and a small native village. The natives told us that the German forces had passed through the previous day, and that a strong rear-guard was holding the next water at Chenene, twelve miles on, so we halted until our troops arrived.

Towards evening a weary horseman rode in from the left to say that the 1st and 3rd Mounted Regiments were held up at Tissu-Kwamedu, thirty miles east. They had made a flank march, and nearing there, after men and horses had gone for twenty-four hours without water, had found the place strongly occupied by the enemy. Our men were reported to be in a serious plight, as their animals were too exhausted to be ridden back to other water and the enemy were holding a fortified position before the wells. Van Deventer was requested to send reinforcements, but our troops that were arriving at Hanetti were too fatigued to undertake a forced march. He therefore ordered a patrol to ride hard for Tissu-Kwamedu, with a message that the two regiments were to take the wells at all costs.

We set out with a native guide, and trekked steadily all through the tropical night, seeing the dim forms of many animals silently moving in the dark. Soon after daybreak we heard the crackle of rifle-fire, and pushing forward, were just in time to see our mounted men gallop across a wide clearing at the far end of which lay the enemy around the wells. Desperate with thirst, they had anticipated van Deventer's instructions, and were riding full tilt upon the rifle-pits. The enemy had opened ragged fire, but as we hurried up we saw several hundred Askari rise to their feet, and make for the bush behind. Their German officers seemed to be trying to stop them, then they followed their men and the fight was over. It was now a pleasure to see horses and men drinking their fill from the cool, clear water, for these are famous wells, known for their excellent and abundant supply. They lie on the old caravan route to the coast, and I have read that for a thousand years and more the great slave convoys from the interior were halted there, before being driven to Dar-es-Salaam.

Three or four of our men were wounded, and there were about a dozen wounded Askari, and after a while a German officer came limping out of the bush to surrender.

Lieut.-Col. Deneys Reitz.

COUNTER-BATTERY

For over three months No. 3 Squadron had been occupied daily in ranging the heavy guns which night after night crept into their allotted positions in front of Albert. On 1st July, 1916, the Somme offensive opened with gas and smoke and a bombardment of unprecedented severity. To the pilots and observers in an artillery squadron the beginning of this battle brought a certain relief, for we were rather tired of flying up and down, being shot at continually by fairly accurate and remarkably well-hidden anti-aircraft batteries, while we registered endless guns on uninteresting points. On the German side of the trenches, before the battle, the country seemed almost peaceful and deserted. Anti-aircraft shells arrived and burst in large numbers, coming apparently from nowhere, for it was almost rare to see a flash on the German side; if one did, it was probably a dummy flash; and of movement, except for a few trains in the distance, there was none. Only an expert observer would know that the thin straight line was a light railway; that the white lines were paths made by the ration parties and reliefs following the dead ground when they came up at night; that the almost invisible line was a sunken pipe line for bringing water to the trenches, and that the shading which crept and thickened along the German reserve trenches showed that the German working parties were active at night if invisible in the day time. For the shading spelled barbed wire.

Only about half a dozen times during those three months did I have the luck to catch a German battery firing. When that happened one ceased the ranging work and called up something really heavy, for preference a nine-inch howitzer battery, which pulverized the Hun.

When the battle had started the counter-battery work became our main task. It was wonderfully exciting and interesting. Nothing can give a more solid feeling of satisfaction than when, after seeing the shells from the battery you are directing fall closer and closer to the target, you finally see a great explosion in a German gun-pit, and with a clear conscience can signal " O.K." During the battle we were much less worried by the anti-aircraft than we had been before. For some had been knocked out, some had retreated, and some had run out of ammunition, and in any case there were so many British planes to shoot at that they could not give to any one their undivided attention.

A. J. Evans (*R.F.C.*).

THE BATTLE OF THE SOMME

The official dates for the Battle of the Somme are from 1st July to 18th November, and the whole period is divided into twelve battles. Since most people do not even know the name by which their particular stunt is officially recognized, and refer simply to the sector in which they were occupied, often enough by the name of a trench or a shattered village, it has been thought better to treat the whole period as one. In spite of the many strange and terrible things which occurred in these months, the most striking is still that first day, a day of perfect summer weather, which witnessed the worst catastrophe to date to befall British soldiery since Hastings.

GOTT MIT UNS

You must know that I feel that every step in my plan has been taken with the Divine help—and I ask daily for aid, not merely in making the plan, but in carrying it out, and this I hope I shall continue to do until the end of all things which concern me on earth.

Sir Douglas Haig to Lady Haig on the eve of the battle.

BOMBARDMENT AT GOMMECOURT

1st July, Day " Z." The assault was to begin at " Zero time." All the programme of the day as regards bombardment, etc. had been arranged from zero time. Zero time was 7.30 a.m. At 6.20 the guns opened, and I made my way to O.P.T. with a telephonist. I passed through a ruined village on my way—not a soul to be seen—streets empty, billets cleared. At the O.P. I found H—— of D/241 who was also observing for counter-attacks.

The bombardment roar was terrific. The ear-splitting bark of the 18-pounders, the cough of the howitzers, the boom of the heavy guns, swelled into a jerky roar that was flung from horizon to horizon, as thunder is tossed from mountain to mountain. It was wonderful music—the mightiest I have ever heard. It seemed to throb, throb into our very veins, beating up and down and yet never quite reaching a climax, but always keeping one's nerves on the thrill. And then at last, ten minutes before zero, the guns opened their lungs. The climax had been reached. One felt inclined to laugh with the fierce exhilaration of it. After all, it was our voice, the voice of a whole Empire at war. At zero I looked out of the O.P. The din had quietened a little. What I saw made me cry out, so that the others, telephonists and all, ran up to me. It was smoke and gas. For a mile stretching away from me, the trench was belching forth dense columns of white, greenish, and orange smoke. It rose curling and twisting, blotting everything from view, and then swept, a solid rampart, over the German lines. For more than an hour this continued, and I could see nothing. Sometimes the smoke was streaked with a scarlet star as a shell burst among it, and sometimes a smoke candle would be hurled high into the air, spluttering and making a cloud of its own far above the rest. It seemed impossible that men could withstand this awful onslaught—even if it were only smoke. And yet a machine-gun played steadily all the time from the German front line. What fighters they are ! He swept the O.P., cutting twigs from above our heads, and splashing mud out of our sandbags. Somewhere on the right of that smoke the Infantry were advancing. I could see nothing. Reports and rumours came dancing down the wires.

" Our Infantry have taken the front line without resistance."

" Prisoners are coming in."

" Enemy giving themselves up in hundreds."

" Infantry have crossed the Serre Ridge."

" Beaumont Hamel is ours."

" More prisoners reported."

This continued until 11.30 when the smoke cleared, and I looked out upon the invisible battle ! Far as I could see not a soldier could be seen, not a movement of any sort. Could it be that we held those trenches. Had we captured Serre ? Once the village had been hidden by thick trees and hedges, now it stood bare and shattered, the trees leafless, as though a comb had been dragged through them.

The Germans were shelling their own trenches, that was all the sign of change I noticed.

I tried to observe while F—— ranged on hostile batteries, but the smoke was too confusing, and flying pieces and bullets made it a difficult matter. In the afternoon the Germans launched a counter-attack immediately opposite our O.P., but unfortunately invisible to us. Their shelling was heavy and accurate. Our O.P. swayed perilously, our wires were cut in four places within 100 yards of the O.P. ; a linesman of D/241 mended them, and I have mentioned him for distinction. We sat in the dug-out waiting and calculating.

The Captain from O.P.F. had a clear view of the counter-attack and switched the LX on it. In fact the LX and one other battery stopped the attack. Unfortunately I could see nothing, as I had to watch another point from which attacks had been expected.

The Infantry were cut to pieces, they came running back between the lines ; Germans stood on their parapets and shot them down. H—— and his men left soon after, but I stayed to register the guns on to —— Valley in case of a counter-attack in that direction. Then about 6.30 I came away.

Lieut. Adrian Consett Stephen, (R.F.A.).

GOMMECOURT

Next day they entered the trenches. Rain came. The attack was postponed. And again postponed. Twice Horden emptied his mind of fear, of all thought, and braced his body for the ordeal. Twice he had to relax, and become again the prey of tormenting incertitudes. There were no intervals of silence now in the trenches, when a man could deceive himself into thinking the War had stopped for a while. Day and night without cessation bombardment answered bombardment.

1st July. On the fourth morning at 7.30, dazed by the shelling which had begun at dawn, warm and sleepy with rum, Horden stumbled forward blindly across No Man's Land. It seemed to him that he was alone in a pelting storm of machine-gun bullets, shell fragments, and clods of earth. Alone, because the other men were like figures on a cinematograph screen—an old film that flickered violently—everybody in a desperate hurry—the air full of black rain. He could recognize some of the figures in an uninterested way. Some of them stopped and fell down slowly. The fact that they had been killed did not penetrate to his intelligence. He saw with mild surprise the figure that was Jewson disappear in a fountain of earth.   He saw with indifference the figure that was Bennison fall down and scramble up again.   They were unreal to him.   His mind was numbed by noise, the smoke, the dust—unable to apprehend anything but the necessity for hurrying frantically on—on, on—out of the storm.

When they reached the German barbed wire a measure of lucidity returned to him.   The entanglement had not been effectively destroyed by the bombardment.   He ran hither and hither with the others to find an opening ; tore madly through a partial gap, and fell into a flattened trench.   There was no one in the trench.   It had been abandoned.   They must go on.   On, on !   They dared not stop.   The earth spouted everywhere.   Hadn't the barrage lifted ?

He plunged along with bowed head as though in a snowstorm. He realized now that men were being killed, that his own turn might come at any moment.   He bent his head lower.   If he was hit, let it not be in his face.   It would hurt to be shot in the face. . . .   Blast the bloody wire ! . . .   He raised his head slightly.   Bennison was there on his right, a little in front.   There seemed queerly few other men.   He squinted to left and right.   " Don't bunch," they had been told.   They weren't bunching. . . .

Another trench.   Dead Germans in silly attitudes, their faces the colour of dirty bone.   Dribbles of blood. . . .   No stopping.   On, on, stupidly, drunkenly—the five-mile race at school. . . .   A man there, stopping, shaking his arm, flicking his hand off, softly collapsing. . . .   Benny gesticulating, urging him to hurry.   Bullets coming from behind now, from the left as well, right across their path. . . . Barbed wire leaping and scratching like wild cats. . . .   Benny running.   Himself sprinting, panting, all his equipment bumping on his body, belabouring him.   Jump !   Into a trench.   Doubled up— out of breath.

He stood up.   He was alone in a firebay which was the wrong way round.   It was a deep trench, intact at the point where he had entered it.   Was it occupied ?   Where was Benny ?   He gripped his rifle, and waited irresolutely, sitting on the firestep.   What now ? He took a bomb out of his pocket and put it beside him.   Why not stay where he was safe ?   No shells were falling here, and he was sheltered from the stream of machine-gun bullets flowing musically overhead.   " Yes, I'll stay here," he said aloud.   Then, instantly,

" No, you won't, you bloody little coward. You'll go on with the others."

He forced himself to his feet. A grey-uniformed figure lurched round the corner of the trench. He snatched up his bomb and flung it full in the German's face.

" Christ. That must have hurt," he said. " I forgot to pull the pin."

The German had fallen to his knees. Horden stood over him. Should he stick him with his bayonet, or shoot him ? The German lifted his face. The nose was smashed and bloody. Horden saw that the man's uniform was soaked with blood at his shoulder. He was already wounded. He had no weapons.

" I'm awfully——" Horden began, and realized with a rush the absurdity of the situation. About to apologize, was he ? " Bloody fool ! " he said to himself, and went quickly out of the firebay in the opposite direction. As he turned the corner he saw the light of a signal flare and the pale star of a rocket. The trench was broken down here. Bodies stretched across his path. English and German overlapping. He tried to avoid treading on them. Impossible. He turned another corner. Shelling began again. The air was thick with dust and things that sobbed and moaned and sang and whistled. Good God ! He was piddling in his trousers. A shell burst on the parapet. He jerked himself down. Loose earth rained upon him. He lay there, incapable of movement, paralysed. He had no feelings.

Bennison's face, dripping with sweat, approached him. Bennison was crawling towards him. He was shouting, " We can't stay here."

Horden knelt up. He possessed himself again.

" What's happening ? " he shouted.

" Don't know. Nobody's gone on. There's nobody left. We're wiped out."

Advancing slowly, ready to use their rifles at any minute, they crawled slowly along over the dead and wounded. The trench ended abruptly at a road swept by machine-gun bullets.

They crawled back.

" Stretcher-bearers ! " moaned the wounded.

Horden felt tears running down his face. " Poor Devils ! "

They came into the bay into which Horden had first jumped.

The wounded German lay motionless now. Horden dared not look at his face.

" O God ! make me callous," he prayed.

They found Larkin and Reeve crouching on their hands and knees in a latrine. The latrine had a roof ! Get under that roof, Horden urged himself, it's a shelter from the storm. Larkin and Reeve had their backs to him. They were quite still. Were they dead ? When he shouted to them they whipped round as though startled from sleep, and stared incredulously.

" Anybody else up this way ? " called Bennison.

Larkin seemed to be making an effort to speak, but no words came. Reeve jerked out " No," and returned to his crouching attitude. Larkin crawled slowly out of the latrine. He grinned gradually, feebly. Horden, looking at him, wondered if he were sane. He himself felt suddenly stronger.

" How goes it Larky ? " he shouted.

" Bloody," said Larkin. The sound of his own voice seemed to revive him. He crawled back into the latrine and seized Reeve's belt. " Pull yourself together, Reeve," he said. Reeve followed him into the trench.

The four men knelt there for a minute or two without speaking. Their bodies jerked and their eyes blinked at every explosion.

" Well ? " said Horden at length. He had wrestled for mastery of himself, and forced the word out like a stammerer who had won his way to speech after enormous effort.

" Best thing we can do," said Bennison briskly, as though a question had been asked once and repeated, " is to see where all the others are. Hordy and I have been up that way as far as a road. Nahpooh ! You two had better stay here and keep a look-out while we try the other way."

There were three more men alive and unwounded. Where were the rest ? Where were the officers ? What was to happen ? No one knew. The Germans had abandoned the trench. They might counter-attack. If they did, what hopes ? There was a machine-gun firing at the back of them. There must have been Germans hiding in that other trench. Impossible to go back. Impossible to go on. They had decided to give themselves up if they saw a chance.

" We shall be all right when the reinforcements come," said Horden. But he could not believe it. No reinforcements could reach them across the open. Farther along, the trench was completely filled for a distance of twenty yards across which no one dared to venture. The sound of rifle-firing was coming from beyond this gap, but whether from friend or enemy they could not tell.

Horden's mind refused to take in the full peril of their situation. He staved off the conviction that death or mutilation was inevitable. He lay there with Bennison watching an expanse of ground that was in motion like a stormy sea over which a light wavering mist was hanging. Startlingly near, a machine-gun opened fire, stopped, went on, stopped again like a man who had forgotten something learned by heart—then continued with growing rapidity. The bullets ploughed a furrow in the ground. The furrow changed its direction.

" Christ " said Horden. " I believe they're firing at us."

They drew themselves away from the gap, turned, and scuttled back into the friendly depth of the trench. They heard bullets smacking into the wall.

" No exit that way," said Bennison.

Daniel George (Queen's Westminster Rifles).

BELOW FRICOURT

1st July. It was the last hour of the bombardment—at least, I mean, before we went over the top—and as though there were some mysterious sympathy between the wonders of the ear and the eye, that bewildering tumult seemed to grow more insistent with the growing brilliance of the atmosphere and the intenser blue of the July sky. The sound was different, not only in magnitude but in quality, from anything known to me. It was not a succession of explosions or a continuous roar ; I, at least, never heard either a gun or a bursting shell. It was not a noise ; it was a symphony. And it did not move. It hung over us. It seemed as though the air were full of a vast and agonized passion, bursting now with groans and sighs, now into shrill screaming and pitiful whimpering, shuddering beneath terrible blows, torn by unearthly whips, vibrating with the solemn pulses of enormous wings. And the supernatural tumult did not pass in this direction or in that. It did not begin, intensify, decline, and end. It was poised in the air, a stationary panorama of sound, a condition of the atmosphere, not the creation of man. It seemed that one had only to lift one's eyes to be appalled by the writhing of the tormented element above one, that a hand raised ever so little above the level of the trench would be sucked away into a whirlpool revolving with cruel and incredible velocity over infinite depths. And this feeling, while it filled one with awe, filled one also with triumphant exultation, the exultation of struggling against a snowstorm in high mountains, or watching the current of a swift and destructive river. Yet all the time one was intent on practical details, wiping the trench dirt off the bolt of one's rifle, reminding the men of what each was to do, and when the message came round, " five minutes to go," seeing that all bayonets were fixed. At 7.30 we went up the ladders, doubled through the gaps in the wire, and lay down, waiting for the line to form up on each side of us. When it was ready, we went forward, not doubling, but at a walk. For we had 900 yards of rough ground to the trench which was our first objective, and about 1,500 yards to a further trench where we were to wait for orders. There was a bright light in the air, and the tufts of coarse grass were grey with dew.

I hadn't gone ten yards before I felt a load fall from me. There's a sentence at the end of *The Pilgrim's Progress*, which has always struck me as one of the most awful things invented by man : " Then I saw there was a way to Hell, even from the Gates of Heaven, as well as from the City of Destruction." To have gone so far and been rejected at last ! Yet undoubtedly man walks between precipices, and no one knows the rottenness in him till he cracks, and then it's too late. I had been worried by the thought : " Suppose one should lose one's head and get other men cut up ! Suppose one's legs should take fright and refuse to move ! " Now I knew it was all right. I shouldn't be frightened and I shouldn't lose my head. Just imagine the joy of that discovery ! I felt quite happy and self-possessed. It wasn't courage. That, I imagine, is the quality of facing danger which one knows to be danger, of making one's spirit triumph over the bestial desire to live in this body. But I knew that I was in no danger. I knew I shouldn't be hurt ; knew it positively, much more positively than most things I'm paid for knowing. I understood in a small way what St. Just meant when he told the soldiers who protested at his rashness that no bullet could touch the emissary of the Republic. And all the time, in spite of one's minor happiness, one was shouting the sort of thing that N.C.O.'s do shout and no one attends to : " Keep your extension." " Don't bunch." " Keep up on the left." I remember yelling the same things days after, in a dressing-station.

Well, we crossed three lines that had once been trenches, and tumbled into the fourth, our final objective. " If it's all like this, it's a cake walk," said a little man beside me, the kindest and bravest of friends, whom no weariness could discourage or danger disturb, the man whom I would choose of all others to have beside me at a pinch—but he's dead. While the men dug furiously to make a firestep I looked about me. On the parados lay a wounded man of another battalion, shot, to judge by the blood on his clothes, through the loins or stomach. I went to him and he grunted, as if to say, " I am in horrible pain, you must do something for me ; you must do something for me." I hate touching wounded men—moral cowardice, I suppose. One hurts them so much and there's so little to be done. I tried, without much success, to ease his equipment, and then thought of getting him into the trench. But it was crowded with men and there was no place to put him. So I left him. He grunted again angrily and looked at me with hatred as well as pain in his eyes. It was horrible. It was as though he cursed me for being alive and strong when he was in torture. I tried to forget him by taking a spade from one of the men and working fiercely on the parapet. But one's mind wasn't in it ; it was over " there," there where " they " were waiting for us. Far away, a thousand yards or so half-left, we could see tiny kilted figures running and leaping in front of a dazzling white Stonehenge, mannikins moving jerkily on a bright green cloth. " The Jocks bombing them out of Mametz," said someone. Then there was a sudden silence, and when I looked round, I saw the men staring stupidly, like calves smelling blood, at two figures. One was doubled up over his stomach hugging himself and frowning. The other was holding his hand out and looking at it with a puzzled expression. It was covered with blood—the fingers, I fancy, were blown off—and he seemed to be saying : " Well, this is a funny kind of thing to have for a hand." I'm thankful to say there was no question of what to do for them. It was time to advance again and we scrambled out of the trench.

I said it was time for us to advance towards our next objective. It was, perhaps, a little more than time. By my watch we were three minutes overdue, not altogether a trifle. For, as the artillery work by time, and were to lift from the next trench as soon as we went forward, the Germans had a chance of reoccupying it, supposing them to have withdrawn under the bombardment. Anyway, when we had topped a little "broo," we walked straight into a zone of machine-gun fire. The whole line dropped like one man, some dead and wounded, the rest taking instinctively to such cover as the ground offered. On my immediate right three men lay in a shell-hole. With their heads and feet just showing, they looked like fish in a basket.

In crossing No Man's Land we must have lost more men than I realized then. For the moment, the sight of the Germans drove everything else out of my head. Most men, I suppose, have a palæolithic savage somewhere in them, a beast that occasionally shouts to be given a chance of showing his joyful cunning in destruction. I have anyway, and from the age of catapults to that of shot-guns have always enjoyed aiming at anything that moved, though since manhood the pleasure has been sneaking and shamefaced. Now it was a duty to shoot, and there was a splendid target. For the Germans were brave men, idiotically brave. They actually knelt, even stood, on the top of their parapet, within less than 150 yards of us. It was insane. One couldn't miss them. Every man I fired at dropped except one. Him, the boldest of the lot, I missed repeatedly. I was puzzled and angry. Two hundred years ago I should have tried a silver bullet. Not that I wanted to hurt him or anyone else. It was missing I hated. That's the beastliest thing in war, the damnable frivolity. One's like a merry mischievous ape tearing up the image of God. When I read in the paper now about " the sporting spirit of the soldiers," it makes me almost sick. God forgive us all ! but there it was, as I say.

When the remaining Germans got back into their trench I stopped shooting and looked about me. Just in front of me lay a boy who had been my batman until I sacked him for slackness. I had cursed him the night before for being drunk. He lay quite flat, and might have been resting, except there was a big, ragged hole at the base of his skull where a bullet had come out. Next to me a man was trying with grimy hands to dap a field-dressing on the back of a lance-corporal who had been shot through the chest and sat up clutching his knees and rocking to and fro. My platoon officer lay on his back. His face and hands were as white as if they'd been marble. His lungs were labouring like a bellows worked by machinery. But his soul was gone. He was really dead already; in a minute or two he was what the doctors call " dead." " D'you think there's any chance for us, sergeant ? " a man whispered, and I said it would be all right, the ——s would be coming through us in an hour, and we would go forward with them. All the same it looked as if they wouldn't find much except corpses. The worst of it was the confusion; one didn't know how many of us were living, or where they were. I crawled along the line to see. A good many men were lying where they couldn't have hit anything except each other. They crawled up at once when spoken to, all except one who buried his head in the ground and didn't move. I think he was crying. I told him I would shoot him, and he came up like a lamb. Poor boy, he could have run from there to our billets before I'd have hurt him. I wriggled back, and told the only officer left that I'd seen about thirty men fit for anything, and our right flank in the air. Then I remembered that like a fool I'd forgotten to send anyone to see who was on our right, one of the very things for which I'd crawled down the line. So I told a man near me to go with a message. Like a brave fellow he at once left the comparative safety of his shell-hole; but I'd hardly turned my head when a man said: " He's hit." That hurt me. It was as if I'd condemned him to death. Anyway, I'd see to the left flank, where our A Company should have been, myself. The officer, a boy, protested, but finally he let me go. If A Company had made a muddle and stopped halfway, it was really important to get them to advance. In ten minutes, I thought, I shall be back, and with any luck we shall have another company on our left and be able to rush the trench. Of course, it was idiotic. If my company had lost two thirds of its strength, why should A Company have fared any better ? But there ! I suppose the idea of death in the mass takes a lot of hammering into one before one grasps it. Anyway, as I crawled back, first straight back, and then off to my right, everything seemed peaceful enough. One couldn't believe that the air a few feet above one's head was deadly. The weather was so fine and bright that the idea of death, if it had occurred to me, which it didn't, would have seemed absurd. Then I saw a lot of men lying down away to the right and waved to them " Reinforce." When they didn't move, I knelt up and waved again.

I don't know what most men feel like when they're wounded.

What I felt was that I had been hit by a tremendous iron hammer and then twisted with a sickening sort of wrench so that my back banged on the ground, and my feet struggled as though they didn't belong to me. For a second or two my breath wouldn't come. I thought, " This is death," and hoped it wouldn't take long. By and by, as nothing happened, I thought I couldn't be dying. I tried to turn on my side, but the pain stopped me dead. There was nothing to do but lie still on my back. After a few minutes two men in my platoon crawled past at a few yards distance. They saw me and seemed to be laughing, but they didn't stop. Probably they were wounded. I could have cried at their being so cruel. It's being cut off from human beings that's as bad as anything when one's wounded, and when a lad wriggled up to me and asked what was up, I loved him. I said, " Not dying, I think, but pretty bad," and he wriggled on. What else could he do ? Then I raised my knees to ease the pain in my stomach, and at once bullets came over ; so I put them down. Not that I much minded dying now. By a merciful arrangement when one's half dead, the extra plunge doesn't seem very terrible. One's lost part of one's interest in life. The roots are loosened, and seem ready to come away without any very agonizing wrench. Anyway though the rational part of me told me to lie flat, my stomach insisted on both my knees going up again in spite of the snipers, and it didn't bother me much when the Germans began shelling the trench about 80 to 100 yards behind me—with heavies. One heard them starting a long way off, and coming towards one with a glorious rush, like the swift rustling of enormous and incredibly powerful pinions. Then there was a thump, and I was covered with earth. After about the thirteenth thump, something hit me in the stomach and took my wind. I thought, " Thank Heaven, it's over this time," but it was only an extra heavy sod of earth. So the waiting began again. It was very hot. To save what was left of my water, I tried one of the acid drops issued the night before, the gift, I suppose, of some amiable lunatic in England. It was sweet and made me feel sick. I drank the rest of my water at a gulp. How I longed for the evening ! I'd lost my watch, so I tried to tell the time by the sun, cautiously shifting my tin hat off my eyes to have a peep. It stood straight overhead in an enormous arch of blue. After an age, I looked again. It still stood in the same place, as though performing a miracle for my special discomfort. Then I began to shout feebly for stretcher-bearers, calling out the name of my battalion and division, as though that would bring men running from all points of the compass. Of course, it was idiotic and cowardly. They couldn't hear, and, if they did, they oughtn't to have come. It was asking them to commit suicide. But I had lost my self-respect. I hoped I should faint, but I couldn't.

It was a lovely evening and a man stood beside me. I caught him by the ankle in terror lest he should vanish. In answer to his shouts—he was an R.A.M.C. corporal—a doctor came and looked at me. Then, promising to return in a minute, they went off to attend to someone else. That was the worst moment I had. I thought they were deceiving me—that they were leaving me for good. I did so want to be spoken kindly to, and I began to whimper, partly to myself, partly aloud. But they came back, and directly the doctor spoke to his orderly, I knew he was one of the best men I had ever met. He can't have been more than twenty-six or twenty-seven, but his face seemed to shine with love and comprehension, not of one's body only, but of one's soul, and with the joy of spending freely a wisdom and goodness drawn from inexhaustible sources. He listened like an angel when I told him a confused, nonsensical yarn about being hit in the back by the nose-cap of a shell. Then he said I'd been shot by a rifle bullet through the chest and abdomen, put a stiff bandage round me, and gave me morphia. There were no stretchers available, so it was out of the question to get me in that night. But after I had felt that divine compassion flow over me, I didn't care. I was like a dog kicked and bullied by everyone that has at last found a kind master, and in a grovelling kind of way, I worshipped him.

Our battalion attacked about 800 strong. It lost, I was told in hospital, about 450 the first day, and 290 or so the second. I suppose it was worth it.

N.C.O. (22nd Manchester Rifles).

ABOVE THIEPVAL

1st July. Suddenly the air is rent with deafening thunder ; never has such man-made noise been heard before ! The hour has struck ! 7.30 a.m. has arrived. The first wave goes over, " carrying the creeping barrage on its back." We wait. Instantly the enemy replies, putting down a counter-barrage which misses us by inches. Thanks to the steep slope of Speyside we are immune. That half-hour is the worst on record, for thoughts and forebodings; so we sing, but it is difficult to keep in tune or rhythm on account of the noise. At last our minute, our own minute arrives. I get up from the ground and whistle. The others rise. We move off, with steady pace. As we pass Gordon Castle we pick up coils of wire and iron posts. I feel sure in my innermost thoughts these things will never be carried all the way to the final objective; however, even if they get half-way it will be a help. Then I glance to the right through a gap in the trees. I see the 10th Rifles plodding on and then my eyes are riveted on a sight I shall never see again. It is the 32nd Division at its best. I see rows upon rows of British soldiers lying dead, dying or wounded, in No Man's Land. Here and there I see an officer urging on his followers. Occasionally I can see the hands thrown up and then a body flops to the ground. The bursting shells and smoke make visibility poor, but I see enough to convince me Thiepval village is still held, for it is now 8 a.m. and by 7.45 a.m. it should have fallen to allow of our passage forward on its flank. Bernard was right. My upper lip is stiff, my jaws are set. We proceed. Again I looked southward from a different angle and perceive heaped up masses of British corpses suspended on the German wire in front of the Thiepval stronghold, while live men rush forward in orderly procession to swell the weight of numbers in the spider's web. Will the last available and previously detailed man soon appear to do his futile duty unto death on the altar of sacrifice? We march on—I lose sight of the 10th Rifles and the human corn-stalks, falling before the Reaper. My pace unconsciously quickens, for I am less heavily burdened than the men behind me, and at last I see the light of day through the telescopic-like avenue which has been cut for our approach. We are nearing the fringe of the wood and the old fire trench. Shells burst at the rate of six a minute on this trench junction, for we have been marching above Elgin Avenue and alongside it. My adjutant, close behind me, tells me I am fifty yards in front of the head of the column. I slacken my pace and they close up to me. " Now for it," I say to Hine, " it's like sitting back for an enormous fence." My blood is up and I am literally seeing red. Still the shells burst at the head of Elgin, plomp, plomp—it is " good-bye," I think, as there is no way round. " This way to eternity,"

shouts a wag behind. Thirty yards ahead now, still a shell—plomp—
a splinter flies past my shoulder, and embeds itself in the leg of a
leading man behind. He falls and crawls out of the way, nothing
must stop the forward march of the column. " Lucky b——" says
one of his pals, " you're well out of it, Jimmy, good luck to you, give
'em our love, see you later," and so the banter continues. It's the
only way. The blood swells in my veins. God is merciful, and it
almost seems as though he chloroforms us on these occasions. I
cross the fire-trench. The next shell and I should have absolutely
synchronized. It does not arrive ! " What's up ? " I think. Still
once more too far ahead. I wait on the edge of the wood. They
close up once more. I double out to see what's up on the right.
Bernard, where is he ? Machine-guns open fire on us from Thiepval
village ; their range is wrong : " too high," I say to Hine. I survey
the situation still ; more machine-gun fire : they have lowered their
sights : pit, pit, the bullets hit the dry earth all round. The shelling
on to the wood edge has ceased. The men emerge. A miracle has
happened. " Now's the chance," I think to myself, " they must
quicken pace and get diagonally across to the sunken road, disengaging
from each other quickly, company by company." I stand still and
erect in the open, while each company passes. To each commander
I give the amended order. Men are falling here and there, but the
guns previously firing on the edge of the wood are quite silent.
First passes " A " with Montey at its head. His is the longest double
to the flank. George Gaffikin comes next waving an orange handkerchief. " Good-bye, sir, good luck," he shouts to me, *en passant*,
" tell them I died a teetotaller, put it on the stone if you find me."—
" Good luck, George," I say, " don't talk rot, anyhow you played the
game ! " He died that day after behaving with magnificent courage
and fortitude when stricken down. The baby captain of " C " comes
next. Never demonstrative, he thinks the more, and passes on to
play his part until he finds himself in a casualty clearing station with
Montey, later. " D " brings up the rear with Berry at its head.
Imagine a timed exposure with our camera. The button is pressed,
the shutters opens, another press and it again shuts. That is what
happened to us. The German shelling ceased for five minutes, we
hurried through the gap of mercy, and as Major Woods, bringing,
up the rear, was just clear of Elgin, the shelling started again. Most
of the men were spared for a further few hours of strenuous life that

day. Berry is badly wounded, and, with Gold, later finds himself in Germany. On the 3rd, I report him killed. Men have seen him lying dead. They are positive. Men in battle see fairies—and devils. He is found in Germany through the Geneva organization, much to my surprise. His people write me an indignant letter asking me what I meant by saying he is dead ! The War has made men's minds distorted. I send a post card back. " Why not count your blessings ? "

The battalion is now formed up lying down on the road. They are enfiladed from Thiepval village while field-guns open on them from the front. They can't stay here. Where is Colonel Bernard ? I walk over to find out. I find a few men of the 10th, and attach them to the right of my line. I blow shrill whistle calls and signal the advance. They go on their last journey. " Bunny," now a captain, comes up to me. He has lost his way. I set him on his path. Later he dies at the head of his company. And what of the dead and wounded ? This spirited dash across No Man's Land, carried out as if on parade, has cost us some fifty dead and seventy disabled. The dead no longer count. War has no use for dead men. With luck they will be buried later ; the wounded try to crawl back to our lines. Some are hit again in so doing, but the majority lie out all day, sun-baked, parched, uncared for, often delirious and at any rate in great pain. My immediate duty is to look after the situation and not bother about wounded men. I send a message to brigade and move to my battle head-quarters in the wood. It is a deep dug-out which has been allocated to me for my use. It needs to be deep to keep out heavy stuff. The telephone lines are all cut by shell-fire. Kelly, a burly six-feet-two-inches-high Irish National-alist, has been sent in a week before to look after emergency rations. He has endured the preliminary bombardment for a week already with the dead and dying, during which time he has had difficulty in going outside, even at night and then only between the shells. A wrong thing has been done. I find the place full of dead and wounded men. It has been used as a refuge. None of the wounded can walk. There are no stretchers. Most are in agony. They have seen no doctor. Some have been there for days. They have simply been pushed down the steep thirty-feet-deep entrance out of further harm's way and left—perhaps forgotten. As I enter the dug-out I am greeted with the most awful cries from these dreadfully wounded men. Their removal is a Herculean task, for it was never intended that the dying and the helpless should have to use the deep stairway. After a time, the last sufferer and the last corpse are removed. Meanwhile I mount the parapet to observe. The attack on the right has come to a standstill; the last detailed man has sacrificed himself on the German wire to the God of War. Thiepval village is masked with a wall of corpses.

The adjutant of the 10th tells me Colonel Bernard is no more. The colonel and half his men walked into the barrage of death during the advance. All died behind him as he resolutely faced the edge of the wood in an impossible effort to walk through a wall of raining iron and lead, which had lifted for us that brief five minutes.

All at once there is a shout. Someone seizes a Lewis gun. " The Germans are on us " goes round like wildfire. I see an advancing crowd of field grey. Fire is opened at six hundred yards' range. The men behind the guns have been with Bernard in the shambles. Their nerves are utterly unstrung. The enemy fell like grass before the scythe. " Damned . . ." shouts an officer, " give them hell." I look through my glasses. " Good heavens," I shout, " these men are prisoners surrendering, and some of our own wounded men are escorting them ! Cease fire, cease fire, for God's sake," I command. The fire ripples on for a time. The target is too good to lose. " After all they are only Germans," I hear a youngster say. But I get the upper hand at last—all is now quiet—for a few moments. The tedium of the battle continues.

I hear a rumour about Riflemen retiring on the left and go out to " stop the rot." At the corner of Elgin I wait to head them off. Meanwhile I see a German soldier, unarmed, sitting at a newly made shell-hole. I ask him if he speaks English. He does. He was once a waiter at Bude in Cornwall. He is fed up with the War, and glad to be where he is. I advise him to move away or he will not be there long as his countrymen shell that place badly. He thanks me. I offer him a cigarette. His eyes light up. He does not smoke although he takes it. I ask him why. He points to his throat. " Roach," I call out, " any water in your bottle ? If so, give this fellow some." He drinks the bottle dry and is profuse to Roach in his thanks. Might he stay with me he asks ! " You will be safer behind, old cock," I say. No, he would like to stay ! " Take him to the dug-out, Roach," I say, " give him some food and let him sleep—he tells me he hasn't slept for ten days on account of the shelling." The old sailor and the ex-German waiter walk along together, comparing notes and talking of England. Suddenly there is a cloud of smoke, a deafening roar—exit Roach and the unknown German soldier, killed by a German shell.

At that moment a strong rabble of tired, hungry and thirsty stragglers approach me from the east. I go out to meet them. " Where are you going ? " I ask. One says one thing, one another. They are marched to the water reserve, given a drink and hunted back to fight. Another more formidable party cuts across to the south. They mean business. They are damned if they are going to stay, it's all up. A young sprinting subaltern heads them off. They push by him. He draws his revolver and threatens them. They take no notice. He fires. Down drops a British soldier at his feet. The effect is instantaneous. They turn back to the assistance of their comrades in distress. It is now late afternoon. Most of my officers are dead and wounded. I send for twelve more who have been held in reserve, to swell the corpse roll. Other reinforcements arrive only to be thrown into the melting-pot for a similar result. The Germans launch an overwhelming counter-attack which proves successful. They win—to suffer later. At 10 p.m. the curtain rings down on hell. The cost ? Enormous. I have seventy men left, all told, out of seven hundred. George Gaffikin is dead ; Campbell too has passed on, and when I hear his name I remember his letter still in my pocket. " I must write a line with it," I remark to my adjutant. My dug-out door that night is like the entrance to a mad-house. One by one wounded officers and men are carried into the trench. McKee, a bright lad, is practically delirious, shot through the lung he still walks and talks. He has lain out in the broiling sun all day. I give him a brandy and soda for which he gives me abuse. We shove him off as soon as we can. Montgomery comes in torn, tattered, filthy and worn out, with wound on head and dent in helmet ; him too we push off after light refreshment. Robbins, a smart youngster, is carried in by two soldiers who are themselves badly wounded, his shrieks can be heard hundreds of yards away, for the firing has now ceased, both sides being exhausted. His leg is fractured below the knee, and he will probably lose it. I try to sleep, but the reaction is too great. I smoke instead, and meanwhile day dawns. The birds have gone, nature has been supplanted.

The wood itself has disappeared ; was ever there such a day ? Not in my recollection. The cavalry are busy all night bringing in the wounded from places which had not been reoccupied by the enemy, and I go out to No Man's Land, and the first German line, to see about the evacuation of the wounded. About seven hundred dead and wounded lie around in an area of perhaps a quarter of a mile square. Going to the left I am suddenly challenged by a German sentry. I pull out my revolver, fire and miss him ; but my orderly, who is behind me, sums up the situation and fires a Véry light pistol he is carrying, hitting the Boche in the head and blowing it off. There is another German behind who puts up his hands and shouts " Kamerad." The dark is lit up by the burning German whose uniform is on fire. We can take no chances, so I kill the other German with my second round. Then all is quiet and we steal away. We have been in a hornets' nest ! The dead can wait, they cannot be nursed back to fighting fitness. I am ordered, at midday, to organize a minor operation. This is a triumph, as I am the junior colonel of the brigade ! We lose more men while I gain in reputation ! By the morning of the third day I am permitted to withdraw to Martinsart, dazed, but automatic.

Brig.-Gen. F. P. Crozier (9th Royal Irish Rifles).

1ST JULY, 1916—CASUALTIES

	Killed or Died of Wounds.	Wounded.	Missing.	Prisoners of War.	Total.
Officers . .	993 . .	1,367 . .	96 . .	12 . .	2,438
Other Ranks .	18,247 . .	34,156 . .	2056 . .	573 . .	55,032

Total 57,470

TOUT VA BIEN

The news about 8 a.m. was not altogether good. We held Montauban in spite of a counter-attack delivered at dawn. This is good, but the enemy is still in Fricourt, La Boisselle, Thiepval. It was also said that we had two battalions cut off in the Schwaben Redoubt (on the hill north of Thiepval) and also that the VIII Corps (Hunter-Weston) had two battalions cut off at Serre.

At 9.30 a.m. I attended Church Service in a hut near Beauquesne. The Rev. Mr. Duncan preached an excellent sermon : " Ye are fellow-workers with God."

Sir D. Haig.

OVILLERS

7th July. A Company was the first wave starting from the British front line. We were badly shelled for about two hours before Zero by the guns that practically enfiladed the trench from the north (our left). We actually lost more men then, I think, than in getting across No Man's Land. Captain May, my company commander, got a shrapnel bullet through his tin hat about fifteen minutes before we went over ; although this was, I think, the wound which killed him, he kept on his feet and walked up and down the trench talking to the men till we attacked. He must have held out till Zero and then dropped.

In the actual attack we—my platoon, anyway—lost very few men. I had previously impressed on them that speed was the essence of the contract and that the German trench was the best place after we had left ours. I myself went across like a scalded cat, and when I got to the German front line I had to wait for a moment for our guns to lift.

As I was travelling light and the men were loaded with all sorts of junk, I got to the enemy line all alone. It was blown all to hell, but the dug-outs were obvious. There was not a soul in the trench and I realized I had got there before the Germans had come out of their burrows. I sat down facing the dug-out doors and got all the Germans as they came up. They had no idea I was there even, the ground was so blown up and I was in a hole ; they never knew what hit them. Broughall, a plucky little Canadian, was about the next of our people to arrive ; he was very excited at my bag, but, disgusted at their " hats " as they all had steel helmets or flat caps and he had promised himself the best spiked helmet (*pickelhaube*) in France.

This craving for a trophy was the cause of his getting to the fourth line, as related by Colonel Osborn. While we were cleaning up the front line we put up a big German wearing a very smart spiked helmet. Broughall, unaware that there were dozens of other helmets in the dug-outs, at once gave chase to the wearer. His platoon rallied to the cry of " Get that bloody hat " and followed him. The quarry ran up a communication trench and was finally pulled down in the German fourth line, where Broughall and his platoon settled him and held their own against repeated counter-attacks.

While we were rounding up the prisoners I came upon one of the Fusiliers being embraced round the knees by a trembling Hun who had a very nice wrist-watch. After hearing the man's plea for mercy the Fusilier said, " That's all right, mate, I accept your apology, but let's have that ticker."

We had cleaned up things in the first line by the time I saw the Commanding Officer again, and I showed him the best dug-out for Battalion H.Q. and left him examining German prisoners.

I started five men making a block on our left and told them to hold on there. While I was busy on our right the enemy attacked on our left, captured our block, killing the men I had left, and occupying the trench where the Battalion H.Q. dug-out (with Colonel Osborn inside it) was situated.

German stick-bombs were going off all over the place and things were a bit windy for a moment, but directly the men knew the Colonel was " in the ditch " they wanted no leading. We just went for the Germans, and they could not withstand the combination of Mills bombs and the 7th Battalion bereft of their Commanding Officer.

When we had cleared them well back and made good the line again, I hared to the top of the steps of the dug-out where the Colonel was ; there was someone lying dead at the bottom, and I thought for the moment it was the Colonel and shouted, " They have got the C.O." He heard me and, sticking his head round the corner said, " Oh, no, they haven't ! "

He then explained that the Germans had wounded his runner, who had been sitting on the steps, and had rushed on. He had been watching the different coloured legs go by in the trench as the scrap went on.

I then went into the dug-out myself and the Commanding Officer tied up my head. I did not take any further part in the show, as I found I was full of little bits of bomb. When it got dark I was told to get myself back if I could, and I started. I crawled and hobbled about for hours and twice ran into bits of trench which the Huns

z

held, but luckily heard them talking and lay low till I could sneak away again, until finally I found my way back to our old front line.

Capt. H. Sadler (9th Royal Sussex Regt.).

THE GERMANS IN MAMETZ WOOD

10*th July.* I looked through my glasses. I looked again, it was incredible. But there he was, an Englishman in khaki and steel helmet, standing bolt upright, regardless of cover as usual, near a long, bare tree-trunk. Looking more carefully, I saw others among the trees near by. They must have broken through and come past our left flank under cover of the trees in the bed of the valley, and that explained the sudden withdrawal of the 5th and 9th Companies. I ordered fire to be opened on the patrol at the wood edge, and the men moved away into the cover. It did not alter the fact, however, that Mametz Wood was now probably in British possession, threatening our line of retreat to Bazentin.

But the surprises of the day were not at an end. Whilst still searching with my glasses, there suddenly appeared in the big open clearing in Mametz Wood, across which was Wood Support Trench (Weissgraben), lines of skirmishers who advanced across the open directly against Wood Support. From that trench came no sound, it seemed that both the 5th and 9th Companies had vanished into space. Nevertheless, from our trench the advancing lines offered an excellent target, as we were in a position to enfilade them at a range of 600 yards. I scarcely needed to give the order. My men had already seen the target, and a rapid fire opened almost at once. Every rifle was at work, the officers picking up rifles and joining in, until soon all the rifle barrels were red hot. Not a single Englishman seemed to reach Wood Support trench, and a large number lay dead and wounded about the open clearing. From the firing in the wood it was evident that we had only held up the left flank guard of the main force advancing through the wood itself.

Our ammunition was getting short, and we scraped together all we could find in the trench and the dug-outs and from the dead and wounded. Shortly afterwards a line of skirmishers suddenly appeared from a fold in the ground near the line of tall trees in the valley and advanced against the left of our trench. We were only just in time to stop them, the first extended line being shot down within a few yards of us. Already the second line was moving forward, and this was dealt with in the same way.

Lieut. Kostlin (122nd R.I.R.).

LA BOISSELLE

July. As it was getting light I happened to be on the right, where Griffin's party was struggling with a huge traverse. A man beyond me said excitedly :

"There's someone coming along the trench. I can hear 'em talking."

"Hurrah," I thought, "this'll be the 17th." So I jumped on to the traverse and shouted "Hullo there ! Who the devil are you ? Are you the 17th ? "

Somebody along the trench stopped, and I heard whispering.

"Who are you ? " I shouted again, with less confidence.

There was a sound as of someone scuttling up the trench.

"Why, it must have been the jolly old Boches."

We had sent the A Company men back and organized our own men with sentries on the flanks and reserve platoon in the dug-out, and were feeling safe and happy, when again I heard something going on on the right.

"Stand to," there was a shout ; "they're coming ! "

My servant and another man who had been hanging about beyond the sentry-post came flying round the traverse.

"Allemans," they said ; "they're coming ! "

This was a very different matter from running about in noise and darkness. I suddenly thought of Prussian Guardsmen, burly and brutal, and bursting bombs, and hand-to-hand struggles with cold steel. My first impulse was to tell Bickersteth. It was his responsibility now.

"Thud ! " went a loud noise along the trench, and the air shook and whined with flying fragments.

I felt myself turning pale.

I found I was walking slowly away from the danger-point. "I must go and tell Bickersteth," I excused myself. I passed the word down the dug-out. Then I pulled myself together and got up to the front somehow. The men, too, were very panicky. Poor devils, they hadn't had a good sleep or a square meal for three days.

"Thud" went a bomb two bays away.

"Come along, let's get back to the bomb-stop," said I not very bravely. We were at a traverse two bays farther on where there was a sentry-post. Just then round the traverse from the dugout came Sergeant Adams, an old volunteer of many years' service in England. He was smoking a pipe and had a thin smile on his face.

"What's that, sir," he said pleasantly, "go back? No, sir, let's go forward," and he tucked his rifle under his arm and strolled along the trench alone—still smiling. A bomb burst in the bay beyond him. He climbed the traverse and took a snapshot with his rifle at some person beyond. A group of men stood wavering, and then I went and took my place beside him on the traverse.

Thirty or forty yards away I saw a hand and a grey sleeve come up out of the trench and throw a cylinder on the end of a wooden rod. It turned over and over in the air and seemed to take hours to approach. It fell just at the foot of the traverse where we stood, and burst with a shattering shock.

"The next one will get us," I thought.

Sergeant Adams pulled a bomb out of his pocket and threw it. I did the same, and immediately felt better. A young Lance-Corporal, Houghton, did the same. The next German bomb fell short. Then someone threw without remembering to pull the pin, and in a moment the bomb was caught up and thrown back at us by the enemy.

I snapped off my revolver once or twice at glimpses of the enemy. A little of last night's feeling was returning. Adams and Houghton had gone forward now, and I was just watching them over the traverse, when I had the impression that someone was throwing stones. Suddenly I saw lying in the middle of the trench a small black object, about the shape and size of a large duck's egg. There was a red band round it and a tube fixed in one end of it.

In a flash I guessed it must be some new sort of bomb.

It was lying less than a yard from my foot; I was right in the corner of the trench. What was I to do? In an instant of time I thought: Had I the nerve to pick it up and throw it away? Should I step over it and run? Or stay where I was? There was no room to lie down. But too late. The bomb burst with a roar at my feet. My eyes and nose were full of dust and pungent fumes. Not knowing if I was wounded or not, I found myself stumbling down the trench with a group of groaning men. One man, Allen, was swearing and shouting in a high-pitched voice and bleeding in the leg. All the nerve was blasted out of us.

I fetched up almost in tears, shaken out of my senses, at Bickersteth's feet. My clothes were a little torn and my hand was bleeding, but that was all.

Bickersteth was very cool. He was watching my fight through a periscope and organizing relays of bomb carriers.

" You must get these men together, Edmonds," he was saying, " and make a counter-attack."

" I'm damned if I will," said I ; " I'm done for," and I lay and panted.

He looked at me and saw I was useless. I hadn't an ounce of grit left in me.

It was Wells who collected the remnants and went up again to find my revolver, " shamefully cast away in the presence of the enemy," and Sergeant Adams still holding his own.

" Come along, Edmonds," said Bickersteth, and I came.

In a minute or two I felt better and went up. We got the Lewis-gun out and the whole party moved forward. Houghton was throwing well. We rushed a bay, and Houghton, who was leading, found himself face to face with a German unter-offizier, the length of the next bay between them. He threw a lucky bomb which burst right in the German's face. Their leader fallen, the heart went out of the enemy's attack. At the same moment there were two diversions. An 8-inch shell, one of those which had been falling occasionally on our right, suddenly landed right in the bay behind the German bomber, and his supporters fled. So ended their attack.

But as we moved forward a sniper fired almost from behind us. I felt the bullet crack in my ear, and Corporal Matthews, who was walking beside me, preoccupied and intent, fell dead in the twinkling of an eye. I was looking straight at him as the bullet struck him and was profoundly affected by the remembrance of his face, though at the time I hardly thought of it. He was alive, and then he was dead, and there was nothing human left in him. He fell with a neat round hole in his forehead and the back of his head blown out.

Other big shells followed the first, so we decided not to hold that part of the trench. We propped up the dead Boche as a warning to his friends against the furthest traverse, and set to work on a better bomb-stop behind, just where Corporal Matthews was hit.

Charles Edmonds (R. Warwickshire Regt.).

IN MAMETZ WOOD

There are times when fear drops below the threshold of the mind; never beyond recall, but far enough from the instant to become a background. Moments of great exaltation, of tremendous physical exertion, when activity can dominate over all rivals in the mind, the times of exhaustion that follow these great moments; these are, as I knew from the teachings of the months gone by, occasions of release from the governance of fear. As I hurried along the ride in this nightmare wood, stepping round the bodies clustered about the shell-holes, here and there helping a wounded man to clamber over a fallen tree-trunk, falling flat on my face when the whistle of an approaching shell grew into a shrieking " YOU," aimed at my ear, to paralyse before it killed, then stumbling on again through a cloud of bitter smoke, I learned that there was another way of making fear a thing of small account.

It was life rather than death that faded away into the distance, as I grew into a state of not-thinking, not-feeling, not-seeing. I moved past trees, past other things; men passed by me, carrying other men, some crying, some cursing, some silent. They were all shadows, and I was no greater than they. Living or dead, all were unreal. Balanced uneasily on the knife-edge between utter oblivion and this temporary not-knowing, it seemed a little matter whether I were destined to go forward to death or to come back to life. Past and future were equidistant and unattainable, throwing no bridge of desire across the gap that separated me both from my remembered self and from all that I had hoped to grasp. I walked as on a mountain in a mist, seeing neither sky above nor valley beneath, lost to all sense of far or near, up or down either in time or space. I saw no precipice, and so I feared none.

Thus it was that the passing seconds dealt a sequence of hammer-blows, at first so poignantly sharp that the mind recoiled in unbelief, but in their deadly repetition dulling the power of response and re-action into a blind acceptance of this tragedy, and in the merciful end, pounding all sensibility into an atrophy that refused to link sight to thought. A swirl of mist within me had thrown a curtain to conceal the chasm of fear, and I walked on unheeding and unexpectant.

I reached a cross-ride in the Wood where four lanes broadened into a confused patch of destruction. Fallen trees, shell-holes, a hurriedly dug trench beginning and ending in an uncertain manner, abandoned rifles, broken branches with their sagging leaves, an unopened box of ammunition, sandbags half-filled with bombs, a derelict machine-gun propping up the head of an immobile figure in uniform, with a belt of ammunition drooping from the breech into a pile of red-stained earth—this is the livery of war. Shells were falling, over and short, near and wide, to show that somewhere over the hill a gunner was playing the part of blind fate for all who walked past this well-marked spot. Here, in the struggle between bursting iron and growing timber, iron had triumphed and trampled over an uneven circle some forty yards in diameter. Against the surrounding wall of thick greenery, the earth showed red and fresh, lit by the clean sunlight, and the splintered tree-trunks shone with a damp whiteness, but the green curtains beyond could conceal nothing of greater horror than the disorder revealed in this clearing.

Even now, after all these years, this round ring of man-made hell bursts into my vision, elbowing into an infinity of distance the wall of my room, dwarfing into nothingness objects we call real. Blue sky above, a band of green trees, and a ploughed graveyard in which living men moved worm-like in and out of sight; three men digging a trench, thigh-deep in the red soil, digging their own graves, as it chanced, for a bursting shell turned their shelter into a tomb; two signallers crouched in a large shell hole, waiting for a summons to move, but bearing in their patient and tired inactivity the look of dead men ready to rise at the trump of a Last Judgment.

Other memories steal upon the screen of vision, growing imperceptibly from a dim remembrance of a part into a firmly-built unity of composition as the eye gains control over its focussing, but this image of war in its brutality flashes in an instant, sharp and clear in its uttermost detail. Then, at its first seeing, it was unreal, unrelated to my past, for the mist was within me, but now and for ever it must rise with every closing of my eyes into a stabbing reality that governs the future. So many things are seen more clearly now that the passing years have allowed the mud of action to settle at the bottom of the pool of life.

Near the edge of this ring I saw a group of officers. The Brigadier was talking to one of his battalion commanders, and Taylor, the Signals officer, was arguing with the Intelligence officer about the position on the map of two German machine-guns. The map itself was a sign of the shrinking of our world into a small compass : a sheet of foolscap paper bearing nothing but a large scale plan of Mametz Wood, with capital letters to identify its many corners, was chart enough for our adventure this day.

Ll. Wyn Griffith (R. Welch Fusiliers).

CAPTURE OF TRÔNES WOOD

14th *July.* . . . from 11 p.m. onwards kept busy for an attack on Trônes Wood, which has been taken (more or less) lost and re-taken, about three times or four. Finally, it had to be taken, and kept at all costs for certain military reasons, which are now in progress, and the Northants and my regiment, under myself, were ordered to do it. . . . My regiment was to lead, but had already been scattered by various orders, so when I reached the starting-point there were but two companies, so I had to put the Northamptons in front, and not wait for my people. We crossed just as dawn was breaking the half-mile of open to the wood, passing through a very thick enemy barrage of shell. . . . We got over wonderfully well, and only one or two parties were blown away. Men were very good and steady. On arrival at wood, my orders were for battalion to halt on edge and reform ; but the C.O. got muddled and didn't do this, and, consequently, hadn't a dog's chance of doing anything except be killed, just in the same way as other regiments had been for the same fault. Fortunately, I stopped mine inside and kept them in hand ; then waited for reports to come back from Northants. None came, nor could come, as they were soon lost and broken up into small bodies, playing just the game the G[ermans] like. . . .

Realizing after a time that it was another regiment gone for nothing, I had to beat round and get at the situation, and collect its remains, and with my own began to form a line clean across the wood, in the way I always meant to. To talk of a wood is to talk rot. It was the most dreadful tangle of dense trees and undergrowth imaginable, with deep yawning broken trenches criss-crossing about it; every tree broken off at top or bottom and branches cut away, so that the floor of the wood was almost an impenetrable tangle of timber, trenches, undergrowth, etc., blown to pieces by British and German heavy guns for a week.

Never was anything so perfectly dreadful to look at—at least I couldn't dream of anything worse—particularly with its dreadful addition of corpses and wounded men—many lying there for days and days. . . .

16th July. . . . I think I was telling you I organized a line or a drive, formed up scattered bodies of Northants and a nucleus of about one and a half companies of my own, under a job lot of about five very young officers, all the rest being *hors de combat*. After infinite difficulty, I got it shaped in the right direction, and then began the advance, very very slowly. Men nearly all much shaken by the clamour and din of shell-fire, and nervy and jumpy about advancing in such a tangle of debris and trenches, etc. I had meant only to organize and start the line, and then get back to my loathsome ditch, back near the edge of the wood where we had entered, so as to be in communication by runners with the Brigade and world outside. It is a fundamental principle that commanders of any sort should not play about, but keep in touch with the Higher Authorities behind. But though old enough soldier to realize this, and the wrath of my seniors for disregarding it, I immediately found that without my being there, the thing would collapse in a few minutes. Sounds vain, perhaps, but there is nothing of vanity about it really. So off I went with the line, *pulling* it on, keeping its direction, keeping it from the hopeless (and humanly natural) desire to get into a single file behind me, instead of a long line either side. Soon I made them advance with fixed bayonets, and ordered them by way of encouraging themselves, to fire ahead of them into the tangle all the way. This was a good move, and gave them confidence, and so we went on with constant halts to adjust the line. After slow progress in this way, my left came on a hornets' nest, and I halted the line and went for it with the left portion. A curtain may be drawn over this, and all that need be said was that many Germans ceased to live, and we took a machine-gun. Then on again, and then again, what I had hoped for. The Germans couldn't face a long line, offering no scattered groups to be killed, and they began to bolt, first back, then as the wood became narrow, they bolted out to the sides, and with rifle and automatic guns, we slew them. Right up to the very top this went on, and I could have had a much bigger bag, except that I did not want to show my people out of the wood, or too much out, for fear of letting the German artillery know how we had progressed, and so enable them to plaster the wood *pari passu* with our advance. So far they had only laid it on thick and strong and deadly in the belt we had left behind. However many we let go for this reason, we slew or picked up later.

And finally the job was done, and I was thankful for I thought we should never, never have got through with it.

Brig.-Gen. Frank Maxwell (12th Middlesex Regt.).

ATTACK

His mind reached back into the past day, groping among obscure and broken memories, for it seemed to him now that for the greater part of the time he had been stunned and blinded, and that what he had seen, he had seen in sudden, vivid flashes, instantaneously : he felt again the tension of waiting, that became impatience, and then the immense effort to move, and the momentary relief which came with movement, the sense of unreality and dread which descended on one, and some restoration of balance as one saw other men moving forward in a way that seemed commonplace, mechanical, as though at some moment of ordinary routine ; the restraint, and the haste that fought against it with every voice in one's being crying out to hurry. Hurry ? One cannot hurry, alone, into nowhere, into nothing. Every impulse created immediately its own violent contradiction. The confusion and tumult in his own mind was inseparable from the senseless fury about him, each reinforcing the other. He saw great chunks of the German line blown up, as the artillery blasted a way for them ; clouds of dust and smoke screened their advance, but the Hun searched for them scrupulously ; the air was alive with the rush and flutter of wings ; it was ripped by screaming shells, hissing like tons of molten metal plunging suddenly into water, there was the blast and concussion of their explosion, men smashed, obliterated in sudden eruptions of earth, rent and strewn in bloody fragments, shells that were like hell-cats humped and spitting, little sounds, unpleasantly close, like the plucking of tense

strings, and something tangling his feet, tearing at his trousers and
puttees as he stumbled over it, and then a face suddenly, an inconceivably distorted face, which raved and sobbed at him as he fell
with it into a shell-hole.   He saw with astonishment the bare back
of a Scotsman who had gone into action wearing only a kilt-apron ;
and then they righted themselves and looked at each other, bewildered
and humiliated.   There followed a moment of perfect lucidity, while
they took a breather ; and he found himself, though unwounded,
wondering with an insane prudence where the nearest dressing-station
was.   Other men came up ; two more Gordons joined them, and
then Mr. Halliday, who flung himself on top of them and, keeping
his head well down, called them a lot of bloody skulkers.   He had
a slight wound in the fore-arm.   They made a rush forward again,
the dust and smoke clearing a little, and they heard the elastic twang
of Mills bombs as they reached an empty trench, very narrow where
shelling had not wrecked or levelled it.   Mr. Halliday was hit again,
in the knee, before they reached the trench, and Bourne felt something pluck the front of his tunic at the same time.   They pulled
Mr. Halliday into the trench, and left him with one of the Gordons
who had also been hit.   Men were converging there, and he went
forward with some of his own company again.   From the moment
he had thrown himself into the shell-hole with the Scotsman something had changed in him ; the conflict and tumult of his mind had
gone, his mind itself seemed to have gone, to have contracted and
hardened within him ; fear remained, an implacable and restless
fear, but that, too, seemed to have been beaten and forged into a
point of exquisite sensibility and to have become indistinguishable
from hate.   Only the instincts of the beast survived in him, every
sense was alert and in that tension was some poignancy.   He neither
knew where he was, nor whither he was going, he could have no
plan because he could foresee nothing, everything happening was
inevitable and unexpected, he was an act in a whole chain of acts ;
and, though his movements had to conform to those of others, spontaneously, as part of some infinitely flexible plan, which he could not
comprehend very clearly even in regard to its immediate object, he
could rely on no one but himself.   They worked round a point still
held by machine-guns, through a rather intricate system of trenches
linking up shell-craters.   The trenches were little more than bolt-
holes through which the machine-gunners, after they had held up

the advancing infantry as long as possible, might hope to escape to some other appointed position farther back, and resume their work, thus gaining time for the troops behind to recover from the effect of the bombardment, and emerge from their hiding-places. They were singularly brave men, these Prussian machine-gunners, but the extreme of heroism, alike in foe or friend, is indistinguishable from despair. Bourne found himself playing again a game of his childhood, though not now among rocks from which reverberated heat quivered in wavy films, but in made fissures too chalky and unweathered for adequate concealment. One has not, perhaps, at thirty years the same zest in the game as one had at thirteen, but the sense of danger brought into play a latent experience which had become a kind of instinct with him, and he moved in those tortuous ways with the furtive cunning of a stoat or weasel. Stooping low at an angle in the trench he saw the next comparatively straight length empty, and when the man behind was close to him, ran forward still stooping. The advancing line, hung up at one point, inevitably tended to surround it, and it was suddenly abandoned by the few men holding it. Bourne, running, checked as a running Hun rounded the further angle precipitately, saw him stop, shrink back into a defensive posture, and fired without lifting the butt of his rifle quite level with his right breast. The man fell shot in the face, and someone screamed at Bourne to go on ; the body choked the narrow angle, and when he put his foot on it squirmed or moved, making him check again, fortunately, as a bomb exploded a couple of yards round the corner. He turned, dismayed, on the man behind him, but behind the bomber he saw the grim bulk of Captain Malet, and his strangely exultant face ; and Bourne, incapable of articulate speech, could only wave a hand to indicate the way he divined the Huns to have gone. Captain Malet swung himself above ground, and the men, following, overflowed the narrow channel of the trench ; but the two waves, which had swept round the machine-gun post, were now on the point of meeting ; men bunched together, and there were some casualties among them before they went to ground again. Captain Malet gave him a word in passing, and Bourne, looking at him with dull uncomprehending eyes, lagged a little to let others intervene between them. He had found himself immediately afterwards next to Company-Sergeant-Major Glasspool, who nodded to him swiftly and appreciatively ; and then Bourne understood. He was doing the right thing. In that last rush he had gone and got into the lead, somehow, for a brief moment; but he realized himself that he had only gone on because he had been unable to stand still. The sense of being one in a crowd did not give him the same confidence as at the start, the present stage seemed to call for a little more personal freedom. Presently, just because they were together, they would rush something in a hurry instead of stalking it. Two men of another regiment, who had presumably got lost, broke back momentarily demoralized, and Sergeant-Major Glasspool confronted them.

"Where the bloody hell do you reckon you're going?"

He rapped out the question with the staccato of a machine-gun; facing their hysterical disorder, he was the living embodiment of a threat.

"We were ordered back," one said, shamefaced and fearful.

"Yes. You take your —— orders from Fritz," Glasspool, white-lipped and with heaving chest, shot sneeringly at them. They came to heel quietly enough, but all the rage and hatred in their hearts found an object in him, now. He forgot them as soon as he found them in hand.

"You're all right, chum," whispered Bourne, to the one who had spoken. "Get among your own mob again as soon as there's a chance."

The man only looked at him stonily. In the next rush forward something struck Bourne's helmet, knocking it back over the nape of his neck so that the chin-strap tore his ears. For the moment he thought he had been knocked out, he had bitten his tongue, too, and his mouth was salt with blood. The blow had left a deep dent in the helmet, just fracturing the steel. He was still dazed and shaken when they reached some building ruins, which he seemed to remember. They were near the railway station.

F. Manning.

COMMENTARY ON THE ENGLISH

27th Aug., Hardecourt. My impressions of the English. Those I've seen (*a*) at Bray, a little incongruous. Some in caps, others in helmets. And the helmet, down to their noses. Horsemen who race. Otherwise, good material. (*b*) At Hardecourt. A major with ribbons, very polite. In general, calmness and indifference. Value of their artillery, one to three of ours. But they shoot " regardless." At Falfemont on the 24th, they broke down. Why? They said; stopped by machine-gun fire. The fact remains, they failed. Their faults : they look on war as a sport. Too much calmness which leads to a " go-to-hell " attitude. A gunner subaltern at Hardecourt came up to see where Combles lay ! No consistency in their work. They attack in and out of season, break down when they ought to go through; and with a certain spiritual strength, say : " Oh, well, failed to-day; it'll be all right to-morrow." Nevertheless, there are still so many shells wasted and so many men lost. To sum it up, they still lack savoir-faire.

Louis Mairet (12me *R. d'I.*).

AT HARDECOURT

28th/29th Aug. An incredible relief ! Marched off at midnight. Any number of halts. Got down into the communication trench because of the barrage. Blunder about on the ridge, shelled by guns of every calibre. At last down into the ravine. Halt in the shell-holes for the 105. Renewed blundering round the bushes. Guide loses his way. Everyone tired out. Shells fall right and left. P. wounded, R. with an arm broken. We stumble on to the railway line, then lose it again, and get stuck in chaos. They are hitting us from all sides. We stop, exhausted, resigned to death, lost among the trenches under the bombardment. At last we meet a relief who puts us on the right road. It is a hell at the foot of this hill strewn with bodies. A trench, That ! It is as wide as a shell-hole. It is in fact shell-holes which we begin to link up. The trench which was taken the other day and partially recaptured now belongs to neither side. Each sends out patrols, but that's all. We have not been able to consolidate because of the strafe, and because it is completely enfiladed. It's a pity, because there are still some dug-outs standing there, though full of bodies. But we'd have cleaned them up quick enough. There is a C.T. full of dead, which leads out of the trench, and comes in by us, allowing both sides to attack. It makes our position more insecure. The two ridges to left and right are occupied by the Boche. On the left, Falfemont

Farm, on the right the hillside. They have a machine-gun and a pom-pom. Terrible.

It is now 4 o'clock in the morning. The ration-party comes back, but there are some missing. P. killed, L. wounded, L. missing. Several sections have no rations. Ours has neither wine nor soup. Someone goes to look for P. He is in fragments, but the bread is found, all bloody. It is this bread I am eating. Soon afterwards two more are wounded by phosphorus shells. At last dawn, and we all go to ground.

Ibid.

THE RETURN

They moved off at once. Shells travelled overhead ; they heard one or two bump fairly close, but they saw nothing except the sides of the trench, whitish with chalk in places, and the steel helmet and lifting swaying shoulders of the man in front, or the frantic uplifted arms of shattered trees, and the sky with the clouds broken in places, through which opened the inaccessible peace of the stars. They seemed to hurry, as though the sense of escape filled them. The walls of the communication trench became gradually lower, the track sloping upward to the surface of the ground, and at last they emerged, the officer standing aside, to watch what was left of his men file out, and form up in two ranks before him. There was little light, but under the brims of the helmets one could see living eyes moving restlessly in blank faces. His face, too, was a blank from weariness, but he stood erect, an ash-stick under his arm, as the dun-coloured shadows shuffled into some sort of order. The words of command that came from him were no more than whispers, his voice was cracked and not quite under control, though there was still some harshness in it. Then they moved off in fours, away from the crest of the ridge, towards the place they called Happy Valley.

They had not far to go. As they were approaching the tents a crump dropped by the mule-lines, and that set them swaying a little, but not much. Captain Malet called them to attention a little later ; and from the tents, camp-details, cooks, snobs, and a few unfit men, gathered in groups to watch them, with a sympathy genuine enough, but tactfully aloof ; for there is a gulf between men just returned from action, and those who have not been in the show, as unbridgeable as that between the sober and the drunk. Captain Malet halted his men by the orderly-room tent. There was even a pretence to dress ranks. Then he looked at them, and they at him for a few seconds which seemed long. They were only shadows in the darkness.

"Dismiss!"

His voice was still pitched low, but they turned almost with the precision of troops on the square, each rifle was struck smartly, the officer saluting; and then the will which bound them together dissolved, the enervated muscles relaxed, and they lurched off to their tents as silent and as dispirited as beaten men. One of the tailors took his pipe out of his mouth and spat on the ground.

"They can say what they bloody well like," he said appreciatively, "but we're a —— fine mob."

F. Manning.

THE RELIEF

The moon is getting up. The men are going out in twos when silhouetted forms appear on top of the rise. It is the relieving company coming over all at once in extended order. Shots are fired and some of the shadowy forms drop. The next minute the trench is invaded, and our successors begin to "take over." While I am waiting in the mud-hole I overhear one of them talking to himself as he struggles to move down the trench. Every word is punctuated by the prodigious effort of drawing a leg out of the mud.

"Lloyd George," he growls, "said—this—was—a fight to the finish. The b—— had better—come out here—and finish it."

Rowley and I are the last to go. For the past two days, worried by our plight and the chits from head-quarters, he has been refusing food and relying on whisky; now he is as weak as a kitten, and when he falls is hardly persuaded to go on. We are sighted and shot at more than once, but the old luck holds. Struggling over the crest, we get out of direct range and sit for a long time by the side of a shell-hole which has a body lying in it. Then I persuade him to come along, and slowly we continue till we reach head-quarters' dug-out where the adjutant takes him down and gives him food and a hot drink.

Outside in the mud and the dark, I am talking to three of my volunteer stretcher-bearers when whizz-bangs come over, dropping among us. We disperse, but when the firing is over I can only find one of them and he is wounded.

Rowley returns. We pick up Hardy and together tramp the endless duck-boards. Posts have now been established, just off the duck-boards, where hot drinks are to be had, and but for these I question whether Rowley would have finished the journey to the rest-camp at Montauban.

Mark VII.

A RESCUE

Sept. Driver Wilkins (the rat-killer) came back to the Mess one night, an hour and a half after delivering the rations and leaving the battery with his empty cart. The face, that is, was the round, red face of Wilkins; the rest was mud—fresh, moist mud on mud that was lighter in colour, and dry. His request was that an officer should go with him to shoot his horse. . . .

Wilkins and his cart, it appeared, had been jostled by the traffic from the fairway of the road into a masterpiece of some working party of resting (and restive) Hussars from Bouzincourt. It was a " sump "—a device much in vogue at the time—an eight-foot cube cut out of the roadside and duly filled up again to road level by the sweeping and shovelling of mud by successive fatigues. Into this the stocky old roan had slowly subsided while Wilkins hacked the cook's cart free and out of it again.

No efforts of his, combined with those of the dozen interested volunteers he had collected from the more leisurely of the passers-by, could move the horse. It had fought, said Wilkins, like a lion; for Wilkins alone, of all the battery, believed anything but evil of his old roan.

He was right, however, in his estimate of its present condition; right, too (as Richards and Cartwright agreed after two or three soundings taken in the disk of torchlight with a shovel offered by a road party subaltern), in its surrender. . . .

But they had forgotten the ramifications of the power wielded by the Canadian : a lorry came trundling down from Pozières—the same lorry (now carrying only dozing men) that an hour before had tossed out two rolls of felt and a bag of nails by the tree-stump whereon Browne had sat, by appointment, waiting.

It pulled up, with inches to spare, at the side of the sump. Few words were spoken, or none, beyond something about "death or glory" from the Sergeant at the wheel and then something about a chain. In the light of volunteer torches Wilkins wrapped his coat, like a muffler, about the throat of his spent roan and around it fixed the chain with a great knot. Richards found a steel eye at the tail of the lorry for the hook at the other end of the chain.

"Hold tight, son!" said Wilkins to his roan as the lorry took the strain. It may be that that particular sergeant was the world's greatest artist in the matter of letting in a clutch; it may be that there are no two forces on earth whose antagonism can tear a horse's head asunder from its body.

The fact remains that the old roan came fantastically out of that mud and was hauled in the clinging shackles of mud like a pig in a sack, for a dozen feet till onlookers' shouts informed the Sergeant that his work was done.

He saw to it that his chain was duly shipped, and went his way.

Volunteers fell to work upon the roan. The mud was scraped and flung from his trembling flanks and heaving, colossally distended belly. Shovels and the lids of mess-tins; knives (table), pulled out of putties covering legs or out of sandbags covering putties; the smooth edges of helmets were set to shaving and scraping the sprawling champion. This was the unskilled contribution of casual enthusiasts. The expert Wilkins worked, sombrely as in the performance of a priestly rite, at the ears that some said were the bastard ears of a mule. Prodigious deflations rewarded the impressed workers. When the roan tottered to his feet they stood aside as men well satisfied. They faded away into the night along the ways they had been going—some "up," some "down."

Richard Blaker (11*th Div. Arty.*).

MEN'S TALK

"Chaps," said Weeper, suddenly, "for Christ's sake let's pray for rain!"

"What good would that do?" said Pacey, reasonably. "If they don't send us over the top here, they'll send us over somewhere else. It 'as got to be, an' if it 'as got to be, the sooner it's over an' done wi' the better. If we die, we die, an' it won't trouble nobody, leastways not for long it won't ; an' if we don't die now, we'd 'ave to die some other time."

"What d'you want to talk about dyin' for ? " said Martlow, resentfully. "I'd rather kill some other —— first. I want to have my fling before I die, I do."

"If you want to pray, you 'ad better pray for the war to stop," continued Pacey, "so as we can all go back to our own 'omes in peace. I'm a married man wi' two children, an' I don't say I'm any better'n the next man, but I've a bit o' religion in me still, an' I don't hold wi' sayin' such things in jest."

"Aye," said Madeley, bitterly ; "an' what good will all your prayin' do you ? If there were any truth in religion, would there be a war, would God let it go on ? "

"Some on us blame God for our own faults," said Pacey, coolly, "an' it were men what made the war. It's no manner o' use us sittin' 'ere pityin' ourselves, an' blamin' God for our own fault. I've got nowt to say again Mr. Rhys. 'E talks about liberty, an' fightin' for your country, an' posterity, an' so on ; but what I want to know is what all us'ns are fightin' for. . . ."

"We're fightin' for all we've bloody got," said Madeley, bluntly.

"An' that's sweet —— all," said Weeper Smart. "A tell thee, that all a want to do is to save me own bloody skin. An' the first thing a do, when a go into t' line, is to find out where t' bloody dressing-stations are ; an' if a can get a nice blighty, chaps, when once me face is turned towards home, I'm laughing. You won't see me bloody heels for dust. A'm not proud. A tell thee straight. Them as thinks different can 'ave all the bloody war they want, and me own share of it, too."

"Well, what the 'ell did you come out for ? " asked Madeley.

Weeper lifted up a large, spade-like hand with the solemnity of one making an affirmation.

"That's where th'ast got me beat, lad," he admitted. "When a saw all them as didn' know any better'n we did joinin' up, an' a went walkin' out wi' me girl on Sundays, as usual, a just felt ashamed. An' a put it away, an' a put it away, until in th'end it got me down. A knew what it'd be, but it got the better o' me, an' then, like a bloody fool, a went an' joined up too. A were ashamed to be seen walkin' in the streets, a were. But a tell thee, now, that if a were once out o' these togs an' in civvies again, a wouldn't mind all the shame in the world; no, not if I 'ad to slink through all the back streets, an' didn' dare put me nose in t'Old Vaults again. A've no pride left in me now, chaps, an' that's the plain truth a'm tellin'. Let them as made the war come an' fight it, that's what a say."

"That's what I say, too," said Glazier, a man of about Madeley's age, with an air of challenge. Short, stocky, and ruddy like Madeley, he was of coarser grain, with an air of brutality that the other lacked: the kind of man who, when he comes to grips, kills, and grunts with pleasure in killing. "Why should us'ns fight an' be killed for all them bloody slackers at 'ome? It ain't right. No matter what they say, it ain't right. We're doin' our duty, an' they ain't, an' they're coinin' money while we get ten bloody frong a week. They don't care a —— about us. Once we're in the army, they've got us by the short hairs. Talk about discipline! They don't try disciplinin' any o' them —— civvies, do they? We want to put some o' them bloody politicians in the front line, an' see 'em shelled to hell. That'd buck their ideas up."

"I'm not fightin' for a lot o' bloody civvies," said Madeley, reasonably. "I'm fightin' for myself an' me own folk. It's all bloody fine sayin' let them as made the war fight it. 'Twere Germany made the war."

"A tell thee," said Weeper, positively, "there are thousands o' poor beggars, over there in the German lines, as don' know, no more'n we do ourselves, what it's all about."

"Then what do the silly —— come an' fight for?" asked Madeley, indignantly. "Why didn' they stay 't 'ome? Tha'lt be sayin' next that the Frenchies sent 'em an invite."

"What a say is, that it weren't none o' our business. We'd no call to mix ourselves up wi' other folks' quarrels," replied Weeper.

"Well, I don't hold wi' that," said Glazier, judicially. "I'm not fightin' for them bloody slackers an' conchies at 'ome; but what I say is that the Fritzes 'ad to be stopped. If we 'adn't come in, an' they'd got the Frenchies beat, 'twould 'a' been our turn next."

"Too bloody true it would," said Madeley. "An' I'd rather come an' fight Fritz in France than 'ave 'im come over to Blighty an' start bashin' our 'ouses about, same as 'e's done 'ere."

" 'E'd never 'ave come to England. The Navy 'd 'ave seen to that," said Pacey.

" Don't you be too bloody sure about the Navy," said Corporal Hamley, entering into the discussion at last. " The Navy 'as got all it can bloody well do, as things are."

" Well, chaps," said Glazier, " maybe I'm right an' maybe I'm wrong, but that's neither here nor there ; only I've sometimes thought it would be a bloody good thing for us'ns, if the 'Un did land a few troops in England. Show 'em what war's like."

F. Manning.

A CORPORAL

Sept. " What is the life of man ! Is it not to shift from side to side ?—from sorrow to sorrow ?—to button up one cause of vexation—and unbutton another ? "

Side has lost his kit. A 5·9 dropped in his trench, while he was absent upon a business essential to health, and demolished the bay together with all Corporal Side's worldly effects in France. He is much aggrieved. I met him round the bend.

" I hear you've had a lucky escape," I remarked.

" The beggars 'a got all my kit," he replied lugubriously.

The good fortune of being alive seemed to have escaped his notice, perhaps because he has experienced it so often.

Side is a remarkable soldier. He looks less like a soldier than any man I have seen in France, and that is saying a good deal. He is short, cross-eyed, bandy-legged, and has a preference for boots and clothes sizes too big for him. In civil life I believe he is a rag-picker, and the character of his profession adheres, as it will, to the man. He joined the battalion two years ago as a stretcher-bearer, and on the 1st of July carried stretchers under fire continuously for twenty-four hours. Anyone who knows the weight of a loaded stretcher and remembers the heat, the condition of the ground, and what the firing was like upon that day, will agree with me that the Victoria Cross would have expressed rather less than Side's deserts. However, he for his bravery was promoted to full corporal in the fighting-ranks.

For parade purposes he really ought to be smuggled among the cooks : he would move any inspecting officer to fury. But in the trenches Side is a treasure. He is tireless and has the heart of a lion. The other day, when we were in the sap and shells were dropping uncomfortably near, some timid idiot set the rumour running that the Germans were coming over. I was standing close to Side when it reached him. "Coming over, are they?" he replied. "'Ere, gimme my rifle," and before one could say "knife" he was gone up the sap, apparently intending to put the Germans back in their places single-handed.

Yes, Side is not much to look at, but he has hold of what may be called the business end of the war.

Mark VII.

AT STUFF TRENCH

20–21*st Oct.* The clear autumn day was a mixed blessing for Harrison, who, in his determination to send over the companies to take Stuff Trench after as much "rest" as could be found in that Golgotha, had arranged that they should advance from the reserve trench direct to the assault. And by way of novelty the assault was ordered to be made a few minutes after noon; the men would therefore have to move forward in broad day and over a sufficiently long approach—liable to the air's jealous eyes. Watches were synchronized and reconsigned to the officers, the watch hands slipped round as they do at a dance or a prize distribution; then all the anxiety came to a height and piercing extreme, and the companies moving in "artillery formation"—groups presenting a kind of diamond diagram—passed by Harrison's head-quarters in foul Zollern Trench. I watched him as he stood on the mound roof of his dug-out, that simple and martial figure, calling out to those as they went in terms of faith and love. Lapworth, who had just joined us, went by at the head of his platoon, a youth with curling golden hair and drawing-room manners, sweetly swinging his most subalternish cane from its leather thong; and he was the last officer to go by.

Orders had been admirably obeyed; the waves extended, the artillery gave tongue at the exact moment. The barrage was heavy, but its uproar was diffused in this open region. Harrison had nothing to do but wait, and I with him, for I was acting as his right-hand man in this operation. News of the attack always seems to take

years in reaching head-quarters, and it almost always gets worse as
it is supplemented. At last some messages, wildly scribbled, as may
be imagined, but with a clearness of expression that may not be so
readily imagined, came to Zollern Trench. One was from Doogan :
Stuff Trench was taken, there were few men left, and he had
" established bombing blocks." G. Salter had sent back some forty
prisoners. A message was brought with some profanity by my old
friend C.S.M. Lee, whose ripped shirt was bloody, and who could
not frankly recommend Stuff Trench. The concrete emplacement
half-way thither, looking so dangerous on the maps, had not been
found dangerous, and the gunners' preparation there had been
adequate ; but, he said, we were being blown out of Stuff Trench.
Should we be able to hold it ? We-ll, we was 'olding it when I
got THIS ; and so departed Lee, tall, blasphemous, and brave. . . .

Another day arrived, and the men in Stuff Trench had to eat
their " iron rations," for we could not supply them. We had also
lost touch with our battalion doctor, who was somewhere towards
Thiepval, that slight protuberance on rising ground westward ; the
bearers of the wounded had to find another way out ; yet we were
in possession of Stuff Trench, and the Australians southward held
its continuation, Regina. That evening, gloomy and vast, lit up
with savage glares all round, a relieving battalion arrived, one disposed to quarrel with us as readily as with the Germans. " Take
the companies over to Stuff Trench," said Harrison to me, " and
see them settled in there." Cassells came with me. We were
lucky, the night being black, to find our way through that unholy
Schwaben Redoubt, but by this stage our polarity-sense was awakened
and we knew how little to expect of local identifications. At last,
after many doubts, we had passed (in the darkness) a fragment of
road metalling which assured me that all was right ; the grumbling
relief followed our slow steps, which we could not hasten, even
though one of many shells crashing into our neighbourhood caught
a section of the incomers and the moaning cries might have distracted more seasoned tacticians.

It was Geoffrey Salter speaking out firmly in the darkness. Stuff
Trench—this was Stuff Trench ; three feet deep, corpses underfoot,
corpses on the parapet. He told us, while still shell after shell slipped
in crescendo wailing into the vibrating ground, that his brother had
been killed, and he had buried him ; Doogan had been wounded,

gone downstairs into one of the dug-out shafts after hours of sweat, and a shell had come downstairs to finish him; "and," says he, "you can get a marvellous view of Grandcourt from this trench. We've been looking at it all day. Where's these men? Let me put 'em into the posts. No, you wait a bit, I'll see to it. That the sergeant-major?"

Moving along as he spoke with quick emotion and a new power (for hitherto his force of character had not appeared in the less exacting sort of war), he began to order the new-comers into sentry-groups; and stooping down to find what it was snuffing at my boots I found it was a dog. He was seemingly trying to keep me from treading on a body. I caught sight of him by some one's torch or flare; he was black and white; and I spoke to him, and at the end of a few moments he allowed me to carry him off. Cassells and myself had finished, and returned by ourselves by the shortest way; now the strain told, our feet weighed like lead, and our hope was out of action. I put down the dog, who came limpingly round the shadowy shell-holes, stopped, whined, came on again; what was the use? he perhaps thought; that way, too, there is this maniacal sport of high explosive, and the mud is evidently the same all over the world; I shall stay here. Warmly I wished to adopt this dog, but now I could scarcely stoop, and I reflected that the mud and shell zone extended a long way on; so there he stayed; feebly I passed along.

Edmund Blunden (11th *Royal Sussex Regt.*).

6TH GREEN HOWARDS AT STUFF REDOUBT

27th Oct. That day saw the end of those lusty and prodigious assaults that wring the so-called "heights" from an enemy that pressure could bend but no pressure seemed able to break.

And the "heights" were found, as yet, to be illusion. A man standing erect on a parapet of Stuff Redoubt could, perhaps, have seen over the dun wreckage and tumble of the immediate foreground; but a man projected cautiously upwards to the extent only of his cheek-bones above the dank bags—or even adding, precariously and inch by inch, the dozen or eighteen inches of the length of his cloaked and muffled periscope—was face to face with the foreground only. A corpse and a battered water-bottle; a helmet and a bent rifle;

crags sculptured in miniature, knolls and hummocks and canons, flat deserts and ranges of tiny mountains fashioned from the churning and ceaseless tossing of the drab, yielding mud ; shards of metal and jags of fractured timber. . . .

Conquest, as yet, had brought no breadth of vision ; and— around a twist of trench where men moved warily with lips sedately pursed and fingers alert near the safety-ring of a grenade—conquest abruptly ended. It ended in a sniper's shield built across the trench in a frame of sand-bags. A man leaned alone against the shield in the manner of a theatrical eavesdropper in some corridor scene. The men nearest to him, at the traverse, had bayonets fixed, and two grenades apiece on the parapet beside their rifles—as it were on the mantelpiece. The eavesdropper had a bomb-proof canopy above his head—timbers and boxes, expanded metal and a hump of bags.

The validity of its right to this title of " bomb-proof " Cartwright did not himself see tested.

He slunk forward to the plate and glanced, for some moments, through its eye. It looked into the similar eye of another plate— a dozen, or twenty, or eighty feet away. The space between them was a distorted drainful of entanglements. The bodies therein were flung in the expansive postures of death from shell-fire or bombs ; and huddled—" collected," as one would say of a horse's pose— where a bayonet-thrust had left them. Between them and about them were the bric-à-brac of stakes and tumbled knife-rests ; beds hacked out of the nearest dug-out ; a twist that might equally have been the relic of some ancient plough as the carriage of a flame-thrower ; and tangles of wire.

Carnage would have been inconspicuous in the mean squalor, the menace and wreckage that submerged that day into the gloom of evening. The cautious traversing of Cartwright's periscope was suddenly arrested once and struck still by the pale, impassive jowls of a German in the shadow of his low helmet. It was some seconds before Cartwright realized that his instrument was a magnificent telescope, that the face could not be five, but must be a hundred or two hundred yards away. Still, he wondered that no one saw that reckless, prying head, to drive it down to cover. He brought an infantry subaltern to the eyepiece of the periscope ; and someone thereafter did drive it down. The someone (a bony corporal) in due course slithered to the fire-step again with a neat hole in his throat and a frayed tear at the back of his neck; and Cartwright interfered no more in matters strictly concerning the Infantry. . . .

Everywhere the air was rain, and metal, and haggard expectancy. Information was scarce, save that which was arrived at by inference. From this it was clear, with persistent lucidity, that whatever else might have happened in quarters more distant, the situation at Regina Trench was still unchanged. Sammy prowled about with Black and without him, placing his guns, fidgeting and worrying. The Battalion Commander went round, scrubby-faced and dirty; assuring himself, in passing, that Cartwright's line to the battery was kept in order and repair. Alarms were given; black din hurtled up from behind Stuff Trench and Regina. Sammy's guns loosed off upon their appointed lines (and saw fit, immediately thereafter, to change their places). Fresh, answering din was added to the wretchedness of the garrison of Stuff; and—nothing happened.

Each time, whether the formation of the counter-attack was broken by the barrage, or whether, as some august and sardonic portent-readers had it, " he " could not be made to come over; whether, again, as Sammy's stalwarts had it, " he " did indeed begin to come until caught by Sammy's guns—the incredible fact remains that nothing happened.

The unobtrusively killed and wounded went their unobtrusive ways. Every man was damp where he was not wet; and dug-outs inhabited with such men sleeping were uninhabitable for dainty-stomached men awake.

Richard Blaker (R.F.A.)

THE GERMANS RETREAT

December. The door at the end of the hut was a patch of cold grey when it was opened by a gloved, fumbling hand. The enormously muffled figure—sentry or stable-picket—put down his lantern and immediately extinguished its pallid flame by thudding with his slime-muffled heel on the wooden floor beside it.

" Sir," he said; and then again—since " sir " was the only formality of collective and respectful address that he knew. " Sir—can I wake you up, sir ? "

He ᒪumped again on the floor.

Mugs shook on the rickety table; the lantern's handle tinkled against its slender ribs. " Sir . . ."

From the mumbled confusion of " Shut that door," " Get out," " Who the hell is it ? " and " What the devil's up now ? " he selected the last for his answer.

" A bit of news just come through, sir. A—it's Fritz, sir,—the ole Hun—he—he's gorn, sir . . ."

" For God's sake," mumbled someone ; "—that door ! You're freezing the place out, standing there. Shut it, and light something—on the table there. Here's a match ! "

A match-box shot along the floor.

" It's Gawd's truth, sir," said the man in the steam that leaped and curled from the turbaning of his head and face as he struck a match. " It's through to Brigade. Official. The message will be along to you in a minute. But I thought I'd just tell you—the brigade signaller told me the message on 'is way to the Adjutant and I give the tip to the sentry to tell the men ; and then I come along to you."

" Who the hell are you ? What message ? "

" D Battery stable-picket, sir. Fritz 'as gorn. 'Is front line's empty. Th' infantry's arfter 'im and 'e's burning up villages be'ind."

" D Battery stable picket " gave a vague, ridiculous pride that made the affair Cartwright's own.

" It's Tagney, isn't it ? " he asked. And then, " Where did this come from ? "

" Division or somewhere, sir," said the man. " The signaller 'ad it properly wrote out on a form for the Adjutant. . . . I *seen* the message, sir. . . . Wide front . . . all along . . . Fritz cleared out. . . ."

He finished in a hush of silence that is rare in audiences. His shadow splashed across the floor and curved up the sides of the hut, black and immensely shapeless. The four pairs of eyes peered at him ; and his own with a tiny candle-flame in them, between his muffler and his turban, shone back.

" Sir ! " he said, for that silence was impossible. " It's *truth*—so help me Gawd ! "

" Listen ! " said someone suddenly ; and he sat startled upright, holding up a hand and a finger, straining his ears beyond any near and trivial sounds towards the swamp and the roads and ragged heights beyond them.

Amazement was the only sensation that came in those moments, to those straining ears.

For there was not a sound.

Their lips at last breathed out softly . . . " God . . ." and again there was that silence.

Ibid.

MARCHING

We now marched in earnest.   Of all the treasured romances of the world, is there anything to make the blood sing itself along, to brighten the eye, to fill the ear with unheard melodies, like a marching battalion in which one's own body is going ?   From the pit, arise and shine, let the drum and trumpet mark the pride of your measure ; you have now learned that the light is sweet, that a day in peace is a jewel whose radiances vary and frolic innumerably as memory turns it in her hand, infinitude of mercy.   Here is this jewel ; kind Nature will shield it from the corrosions of yesterday ; yield yourself to this magical hour, a starling curving among tens of thousands above the blue mere, a star spinning in the bright magnetic pilgrimage of old God ; follow that God, and look you mock him not.

Edmund Blunden.

MATAHARI

October. The case of Margaret Gertrud Zeller, better known as Matahari (" Eye of the Morning "), has overshadowed all the other cases. Her father was a Dutchman who, while in the Dutch East Indies, married a Javanese woman. He brought her home to Holland, and there the daughter became known as an exponent of a form of voluptuous oriental dancing that was new to Europe at the time. She was tall and sinuous, with glowing black eyes and a dusky complexion, vivacious in manner, intelligent and quick in repartee. She was, besides, a linguist. When she was about twenty she married a Dutch naval officer of Scottish extraction named Macleod, who divorced her. She was well known in Paris, and until the outbreak of war she was believed to be earning considerable sums of money by her professional engagements. She had a reputation in Holland, where people were proud of her success, and, so cynics said, of her graceful carriage, which was rare in that country.

In July, 1915, she was fulfilling a dancing engagement in Madrid when information reached England that she was consorting with members of the German Secret Service, and might be expected before long to be on her way back to Germany via Holland. This actually happened early in 1916. The ship put into Falmouth, and she was brought ashore, together with her very large professional wardrobe, and escorted to London. I expected to see a lady who would bring the whole battery of her charms to bear upon the officers who were to question her. There walked into the room a severely practical person who was prepared to answer any question with a kind of reserved courtesy, who felt so sure of herself and of her innocence that all that remained in her was a desire to help her interrogators. The only thing graceful about her was her walk and the carriage of her head. She made no gestures and, to say truth, time had a little dimmed the charms of which we had heard so much, for at this time the lady must have been at least forty.

I have said she was openness itself. She was ready with an answer to every question, and of all the people that I examined during the course of the War she was the " quickest in the uptake." If I quoted to her the name of some person in Spain with whom it was compromising to be seen in conversation she was astounded. He a suspect ? Surely we must be mistaken.

" I see how it is," she said at last, " you suspect me. Can I speak to you alone ? " The room was cleared of all but one officer and myself. She looked at him interrogatively.

" I said ' Alone.' "

" Yes," I replied, " this gentleman and I may be regarded as one person."

" Very well," she said, " then I am going to make a confession to you. I am a spy, but not, as you think, for the Germans, but for one of your allies—the French."

I do not know to this moment whether she thought we would believe her, but she plunged then into a sea of reminiscence, telling us of the adventures she had undergone in pursuit of the objects of her employers. I wondered how many of them were true.

We had altogether two long interviews with Matahari, and I am sure that she thought she had had the best of it. We were convinced now that she was acting for the Germans, and that she was then on her way to Germany with information which she had committed to memory. On the other hand, she had no intention of landing on British soil or of committing any act of espionage in British jurisdiction, and with nothing to support our view we could not very well detain her in England ; so at the end of the second interview I said to her, " Madame " (she spoke no English), " we are going to send you back to Spain, and if you will take the advice of someone nearly twice your age, give up what you have been doing." She said, " Sir, I thank you from my heart. I shall not forget your advice. What I have been doing I will do no more. You may trust me implicitly," and within a month of her return to Spain she was at it again.

This time she was captured on the French side of the frontier and, as I heard at the time, with compromising documents upon her. I should have thought that so astute a lady would have avoided documents at all hazards. They carried her to Paris, put her on her trial, and on 25th July, 1916, condemned her to death, but there was, as there is usually in such cases, an interminable delay, and it was not until 15th October that she was taken from Saint Lazare Prison to Vincennes for execution. A French officer who was present described to me what happened. She was awakened at 5 o'clock in the morning, and she dressed herself in a dark dress trimmed with fur, with a large felt hat and lavender kid gloves. With an escort of two soldiers, her counsel and a padre, she was driven to Vincennes. When she came in sight of the troops she gently put aside the ministrations of the padre and waved a salute to the soldiers. She refused to be blindfolded, and she was in the act of smiling and greeting the firing-party when the volley sent her pagan spirit on its journey.

Sir Basil Thomson.

KOSTARINO

On December 6th the Bulgars, urged on and strengthened by Germans and Austrians, were attacking our sadly depleted ranks in earnest along the entire British line. It was maintained with no loss of vigour and with no definite success until the morning of the 7th, when an important peak standing alone on the right of the neck of the bottle fell into enemy hands after fierce fighting, and a struggle in which superiority in numbers, following a crushing artillery bombardment, was bound to tell.

This never-to-be-forgotten day had dawned grey, bleak and cold. The mist, which had scarcely lifted for 48 hours, enveloped us like a cloud of coal-dust, blotting out even the nearest objects and hiding what was happening in No Man's Land as effectually as darkness had done. The shrill rattle of musketry went on unceasingly and the enemy gunners were playing havoc on our trenches. Our own gunners played their part as well as mortal men could under the impossible conditions. Our machine-guns spat fire down into the ravine, which must soon have been crowded with enemy infantry, alive and dead. The unpenetrable mist hid everything, but our toll of the attackers must have been enormous. There can be no doubt of that.

My own platoon, in a shallow trench crossing the track leading into Kostarino Village, was wide awake, a report having come from the Dublins that the enemy were in the village in force. On the few occasions, however, when the mist lifted, to descend again with disconcerting suddenness, we could see no sign of them, but were rewarded for our inquisitiveness by a veritable hail of shrapnel and H.Es. While the mist played this dastardly game of lifting and lowering, we could now and again see long columns of enemy transport and reinforcements in the distance moving towards the enemy line along the Strumnitza road, but our guns had by this time become practically silent and they were allowed to continue the journey unmolested.

Evidently the enemy had given no thought to a failure of his plans. On our right, the attack was being pressed more vigorously than here. At 3 p.m., we had to realize that part of the line had gone, for we found ourselves in the uncomfortable position of being enfiladed.

"Hold on as long as you can and then retire on Three Tree Hill," came a yell from the back of us through a hail of bullets. A few minutes later, a messenger dashed breathlessly up to our trench with the comforting (!) news that the right of the line had gone. This was perfectly obvious. An hour later—the longest hour I have ever spent—our companies in the line were ordered to withdraw, and we left with the Bulgars swarming into the trenches. We suffered casualties as we crossed the open to Three Tree Hill. It was a slow process for we had our wounded with us. The mist, true to its previous performances in favour of the enemy, lifted and gave the Bulgar gunners and their infantry every chance of finishing us off. That we reached Three Tree Hill, where, in the shallow trench at the summit we received the most diabolical shelling; and later, withdrew to the Kajah Ravine on orders, will always remain a miracle to most of us. The enemy pounded us with their guns unmercifully, while, from our former positions, their infantry kept up a vigorous rifle and machine-gun fire on us as we withdrew.

Overhead, two Bosche planes swooped down to within a couple of hundred yards of us, directing the enemy guns and correcting their range, and at the same time adding to our discomfiture by the use of their machine-guns at short range.

Capt. A. Donovan Young.

WINTER SETS IN ON THE SOMME

12*th December.* The man who had sunk in up to his armpits had to be handed over as trench stores. Sgt. Dawson . . . went out into No Man's Land as soon as the relief was completed to have a look at the wire. He got some way into No Man's Land when he became hopelessly bogged and unable to move. He was found by a party of five Boches who proceeded to pull him out. He, of course, expected to be taken off to the Hun lines, but not a bit of it. They informed him that they were his prisoners and demanded to be taken across to our trenches. Sgt. Dawson had hopelessly lost his way and said so, but they said it was quite all right as they knew the way, and conducted him back to our advanced Bn. Hqs. On the way back they picked up another of our men, also bogged, and took him along with them. . . .

Col. C. J. Troyte-Bullock (7th Somerset Regt.).

AN ESCAPE

December. The next bit of excitement was the escape of Kicq and party. This happened when we had been in the fort about a month. Early on, Kicq had left Room 45 and gone into a French room, 41. One afternoon he asked me if I would help him to escape, which I agreed to do. His idea was to dress up as a German N.C.O., and with six Frenchmen and a Belgian named Callens to bluff themselves out of the main gate at about 6.30 in the evening. The scheme seemed to me almost impossible—but Kicq was enthusiastic about it, and persuaded me that it would probably come off, if only because it was so improbable that anyone would attempt such a thing. There were three sentries and three gates and a guardhouse to pass, and the real danger was that, if they passed the first sentry and gate and were stopped in front of the second, they would be caught in the outer courtyard at the tender mercy of two angry sentries, and in my opinion would stand an excellent chance of being stuck with a bayonet. However, Kicq realized that as well as I did ; and, as it is for every man to judge the risks he cares to take, I promised to do my part, which was quite simple.

About 6 p.m. I went into Room 41, and there they were all dressing up and painting their faces, etc., as if for private theatricals. Kicq was excellent as a German Unteroffizier. He had made a very passable pork-pie cap, of which the badge in front is very easy to imitate by painted paper. He had a dark overcoat on to which bright buttons, which would pass in the dark as German buttons, had been sewn, and he had a worn-out pair of German boots which had been given to one of the orderlies by a German. Some of the others had on the typical red trousers—but any sort of nondescript costume will do for a French orderly. They were timed to go as soon after 6.30 p.m. as the road was clear, and it was my job to give the signal. I was pleased to be able to report that I had never seen the sentry, who was on duty at the main gate, before, and it was most unlikely

367

that he knew any of their faces. I stood about opposite the packet-office, and Abel came along the passage and went in. Looking through the keyhole I saw that he was busy in there near the door and might come out at any moment. I reported this, and the whole party came and stood in the dark turning of the passage by the bath-room, from where they could watch me peering through the packet office keyhole. At last I saw Abel sit down at his table and begin writing, so I gave the signal. Immediately a whole troop of French orderlies, carrying mattresses, blankets, and bedding on their heads, came clattering down the passage, laughing and talking to one another in French. A German N.C.O. was among them, and as he went along he collided with a German-speaking Russian, a great friend of ours known as Charley, who naturally cursed his eyes out in German. Kicq took no notice, but going just ahead of his orderlies he cursed the sentry at the main gate for not opening the door more quickly for them, and stood aside counting them as they went out. One fellow came running down the passage a bit after the others—Kicq waited for him and then went out after them, and the door closed.

I waited most anxiously for any noise which would show that things had gone wrong. But after ten minutes it seemed certain that they had got clear away.

About half an hour of subdued rejoicing in the fort, for by that time the story had gone round, we suddenly heard an awful com-motion among the Huns. The guards were turning out at the double, clutching their rifles amid a regular pandemonium of shouts and orders, and the roar of the Commandant could be heard above the tumult. We turned out into the passages to see the fun. The C.O. was raving like a maniac. The minute he caught sight of us laughing at him he brandished his fists and shouted at us to go to our rooms. Oliphant and I started to argue that the bell had not gone and therefore we need not go to our rooms, but he told off a sentry, who drove us back at the point of the bayonet, Oliphant protesting in his worst German, " Sie durfen nicht so sprechen mit ein English Offizier."

We cheered like mad and sang the Marseillaise and " On les aura "—in fact, celebrated the occasion to the best of our ability.

What happened as soon as the party got outside the first door, Kicq told me afterwards. The second obstacle they had to pass was the gate which barred the roadway over the moat. This the sentry

opened for them without a word, whilst Kicq trod on his toes to
distract his attention. As they passed the guardhouse in the outer
court several men came out and shouted at them, but they were
unarmed, and Kicq and Co. paid no attention. The outer gate
consists of a double door which they knew would pull open without
being unlocked, once the bar was removed. They got the bar off
and tore open the gate, and found a sentry waiting for them with a
rifle and fixed bayonet outside. " Wer kommt dann hier ? " said
he. Kicq was out first, and holding up his hand, said, " Ruhig,
einer ist los ! " (Be quiet, a prisoner has got away), and rushed past
him into the darkness. Without giving the sentry time to recover
his wits, the rest pushed past, throwing their mattresses, etc., on the
ground at his feet, and disappeared. Kicq and Decugis went on
together for a bit, thinking that the rest must have been held up and
expecting to hear shots. Then they saw other figures moving near
them in the darkness and thought at first they were Germans searching,
but found they were the rest of the party. It was not for some
minutes afterwards that the alarm was given ; but the whole party,
after nearly running into a sentry on a neighbouring fort, managed
to get away from their pursuers. After a terribly hard eleven days'
march they were all caught near the frontier. It was in the middle
of winter, and they suffered most dreadfully from cold and bad feet.
All of them, with the exception of Kicq and Callens, had gone out
(according to English ideas of escaping) very badly prepared for such
a journey at that time of year. They had quite insufficient food
(though they had opportunities of carrying out any amount), insufficient socks, grease, and numerous other things. They also lost
their way rather badly the first two nights. Then Kicq took charge,
and the latter part of the journey they went by the same route which
Buckley and I afterwards followed. None of them had thought of
going into proper training, and to have reached the frontier under
such conditions was a wonderful feat of endurance. They were in
a terrible condition when they were caught. When within 70 kilometres of the frontier, just north of Stockach, they separated, the
Frenchmen going on together and making a forced march of 60
kilometres in one night, and the Belgians coming on in their own
time. Both parties were caught on the same day and about the
same time : the Frenchmen because they got into a country close
to the frontier where they could find no decent place to lie up, and,

as there was a light fall of snow, their tracks were traced. The Belgians were caught in a very unlucky manner. Their hiding-place was excellent, but on a Sunday the Germans usually go out shooting and a shooting party came on them. A dog came up and sniffed at them, and then an old German with a gun stared into the bush and said, " Es ist ein Fuchs " (It's a fox).

They soon found it was not a Fuchs, and Kicq and Callens were hauled out. The Würtembergers treated them very well indeed, and said they were almost sorry they had captured them, as they had made such a sporting effort, or words to that effect. They were escorted back to the fort by a very decent Würtemberg officer, who was furious with the Commandant when he laughed and jeered at them for being recaptured. " Well," said Kicq in excellent German to the Commandant, " if you leave all the gates open, how are prisoners to know that they are not allowed to go out that way ? " The Würtemberg officer remarked, as he said good-bye to them outside, that " the Prussians were brutes, but the Bavarians were swine." Which remark seems to me very much to the point. All the party, with the exception of a very young Frenchman called La Croix, had painful and swollen feet, and all without exception were ravenously hungry for a week or more after they had been returned to prison. One of them retired to hospital for several weeks, and I believe that there was a danger at one time that he would lose his feet owing to frost-bite. However, they healed in time.

A. J. Evans (R.F.C.).

SNOW

Snow on Western Russia! Somewhere above the forests lay the pivot of the storm. Round it, like the spokes and rim of a mighty crystal wheel, whirled legions of white flakes above the silent earth. The air was rent in pieces by the frenzied gusts. The storm swooped down, lashing and shrieking, upon tree-tops, hedges, and roofs— on all that stood up before it, and across the stretching plains that cowered beneath the blast. Myriads of flakes had begun to melt, but the cold laid hold upon them, and in a few hours the slush was covered with a solid and enduring robe of winter. The world was changing her face; it was becoming white, and black, and grey. The forests between Brest-Litovsk and Mervinsk were seething and howling with the storm. Flakes fell in the rivers and were drowned, but elsewhere they conquered. They swept over that vast land, falling thick and heavy among the tree-tops; the pine-needles were soon matted with their covering of snow, and in a few hours they would strain like sails beneath the storm. The stout sixty-year-old pines creaked in the wind like masts; they shuddered, bent, and swayed, but their roots held fast. The good months were over and the bad time had come again. . . . The beasts crouched in their lairs and hearkened to the onslaught of winter: badgers and hamsters, who are always careful to keep a well-filled larder; foxes, bold and fearless—the snow does not spoil their hunting; but the hares with quivering ears and the rabbits would come off badly in the next few weeks. Mother lynx with her now strong and healthy brood sniffed fearlessly at the icy wind; once again there would be chances of pulling down young deer whose long legs had got caught in the undergrowth. In the plantations, where the old trees had been cut down, the roe-deer lay huddled side by side, and the stag, his eyes mournful with presage of the lean months to come, raised his steaming nostrils to the sky, and laid back his branching antlers. Winter had come upon the world. The men out yonder in the interminable

371

trenches and dug-outs that war had made, watched drearily and grimly the beginning of yet another winter of war, drew gloves over their numbed fingers, piled wood into their stoves, and stamped savagely through the slush that squelched about their feet. " We shall be home for Christmas," said they, and they knew that they were lying ; while above their heads the spirit of the snow danced a wild dance over the desolate places and the forests, and strove with all his might to entangle the branches of the trees together, and strew the ground with heaps, drifts, and swathes of snow.

From Brest-Litovsk there stretched over the land a network of black lines in all directions : wires, flexible and coated with rubber, soaked in protective solution, and covered with twisted thread. Like thin black nerves, they coiled over the earth in shallow ditches, just beneath the surface, or traversed the air on tall poles. They accompanied the telegraph wires along all the railway lines ; they crossed the forests on straight paths decreed for them. The telephone wires of the army hung high above the earth in the forest tree-tops ; their course was marked on the map and the line was carefully secured wherever necessary. In the summer no one paid any attention to them, but in the winter they paid dearly for this neglect. The forests, where the wind-spirit waved his snowy hands, took little heed of these black rubber-coated wires. Suddenly the tree-tops and the branches would break under their great burden of snow, and bring the wire down with them. Sometimes it caught in the fork of a branch a little lower down, stretched taut like the string of a violin ; and a wire, that had been laid loosely across the trees, now had to stand a strain and the contraction of the cold. If only it were made of copper which is so tough and elastic ! But for a long time past steel wire had been used for all the army telephones, except for the Imperial Section between Mitau and the Palace at Berlin which was of pure copper; so the wire, in obedience to the laws of physics, broke. It stood the tension stubbornly for a while and then snapped ; one of the parted ends whistled through the air and curled round a branch like a lasso, tangled among the slender birch twigs ; the other sprang back, caught in the undergrowth, and lay there in loose folds ; in a few hours it was buried beneath half a yard of snow. At the edge of the forest, snowdrifts a yard high were heaped up before night-fall ; the wind was the master-mason of this wall. Roaring and exulting he laid his snow-bricks against trunks, undergrowth, and tree-tops; the swirling air, like a solid thing, served him both as trowel and as mortar. To the right or left of the railway lines, according to the direction of the wind, there rose silently or in tumult, slanting dunes of snow, which could engulf a man up to his chin. Twilight fell, and winter howled and laughed and moaned.

Throughout the land, in corrugated-iron hutments, the timber houses of the country, and cabins of tarred paste-board, were scattered the signallers, the telegraph-companies, repair-parties, and labour-companies. They knew there would be plenty for them to do next day, so they sat listening to the spirit of the snow as he clapped his hands and drummed and beat upon their walls, and they watched the cracks, which had let in so many draughts, getting gradually blocked up, so that a genial warmth began to spread about the room. There were some pleasant trips before them in the morning, but they would not think about that now. This evening they would play *skat* under the lamp or sleep in their bunks. It would do no harm to grease their boots again, oil the soles, and hold their puttees up against the light to see if there were any holes in them.

Arnold Zweig.

VOICES

AIRMAN'S LETTER HOME

25*th Aug.*

MY DEAREST MOTHER AND DAD,

Cheerio, dears. And, oh, the wind blows good out here. Do so hope it is the same with you.

Really, I am having too much luck for a boy. I will start straight away, and tell you all. On August 22nd I went up. Met twelve Huns.

No. 1 fight. I attacked and fired two drums, bringing the machine down just outside a village. All crashed up.

No. 2 fight. I attacked and got under machine, putting in two drums. Hun went down in flames.

No. 3 fight. I attacked and put in one drum. Machine went down and crashed on a housetop.

All these fights were seen and reported by other machines that saw them go down.

I only got hit eleven times in the planes, so I returned and got more ammunition. This time luck was not all on the spot. I was met by about 14 Huns, about 15 miles over their side. My windscreen was hit in four places, mirror broken, the spar of the left plane broken, also engine ran out of petrol. But I had good sport and good luck, but only just, for I was brought down about one mile over our side. I slept near the machine and had it repaired during the night.

This work was done while I was still in No. 11 Squadron. In the morning I flew over to No. 60 Squadron, and spent the 23rd and 24th in getting settled down. I had a short flight on the 24th but only chased one Hun.

The General came to me on the 24th and congratulated me. He said in fun, " I am putting your name on a big board in the trenches in order to frighten the Huns."

My C.O. rang up and told me that I am getting a flight C.O.'s job, so this means that I shall be a Captain. Oh, la la. Topping, isn't it? Well, this will come along in time; I think it a topping reward, don't you?

To-day is the 25th. And I have again been in for it. Three fights. Two machines I brought down, and one I crashed. Not so bad, four Huns in four days, is it? The Colonel came up to the aerodrome and congratulated me.

I have no more news of importance, and still less time to tell it, so I must now close.

Good night, dears. All my love.

Flight-Comm. Albert Ball, V.C.

GERMAN PRIVATE'S LETTER HOME

Slype, October 1st. Now that the horrible affair at Thiepval lies like a bad dream behind me, I will tell you in broad outline how I have been faring on the Somme. . . .

As we were passing through Cambrai we saw Hindenburg and greeted him with exultant cheers. The sight of him ran through our limbs like fire and filled us with boundless courage. We were going to feel the need of him too!

On the evening of September 11th we relieved the 5th Guards (Regulars) in the Thiepval position. The march up was awful. The nearer we got, the more intense became the gun-fire and the flatter the communication trenches, which at last disappeared altogether. Then we had to advance in spurts through the murderous shrapnel and shell-fire. Even there we had heavy casualties.

The next morning the English attack began and the guns were not silent for two hours during the day. At dawn I looked around me : what a ghastly picture ! Not a trace of a trench left ; nothing but shell-holes as far as the eye could reach—holes which had been filled by fresh explosions, blown up again and again filled. In them we lay as flat on the ground as if we were dead, for already flocks of enemy aeroplanes were humming over us. We were absolutely at their mercy, and with remorseless accuracy they directed the English heavy guns, shell after shell, into our line, and themselves fired with machine-guns at everybody who made the slightest movement below.

Hour after hour passed. The wounded lie helplessly groaning. The supply of water runs out. The day seems to stretch itself maliciously to twice its usual length. The fire increases to such bewildering intensity that it is no longer possible to distinguish between the crashes. Our mouths and ears are full of earth; three times buried and three times dug up again, we wait—wait for night or the enemy! Oh that waiting!—it scorches the brain and drives one frantic. And the bursting shells' dance-of-death becomes ever madder—one can see nothing for smoke, fire, and spurting earth. Feverishly one's eyes seek to penetrate the curtain of fire and detect the advancing enemy.

Suddenly the barrage lifts—the shells are falling behind us—and there, close in front, is the first wave of the enemy! Release at last! Everyone who is not wounded, everyone who can raise an arm, is up, and like a shower of hailstones our bombs pelt upon the attacking foe! The first wave lies prone in front of our holes, and already the second is upon us, and behind, the English are coming on in a dense mass. Anyone who reaches our line is at once polished off in a hand-to-hand bayonet fight, and now our bombs fly with redoubled force into the enemy's ranks. They do their gruesome work there, and like ripe ears of corn before the reaper the English attacking columns fall. Only a few escape in full flight back through the boyaux.

We sink down, dazed, upon the tortured earth, and tie up the wounded as well as we can, while awaiting the coming of a second attack or of the night. The machine-guns are buried in soil and smashed by shells; the stock of bombs is almost exhausted; the fire becomes more violent again; it makes one's head ache and one's lips burn. The issue lies now in the Hands of God. There is only one thought in every mind: "They shan't take us alive!" But the Tommies have had enough; they won't come back to-day. It gets darker and the fire becomes normal. I light a cigarette and try to think—to think of our dead and wounded; of the sufferings of humanity; to think back to—home! But away with such thoughts! The present demands its rights—it requires a real man, not a dreamer. Food arrives and drink—drink! The stretcher-bearers carry the wounded back as far as they can. Reinforcements arrive, things are cleared up and the dead buried, and a new day breaks, more horrible than the last!

Such is the battle of the Somme—Germany's bloody struggle for victory. This week represents the utmost limit of human endurance —it was hell !

Private Karl Gorzel.

BACK

They ask me where I've been,
And what I've done and seen.
But what can I reply
Who knows it wasn't I,
But someone just like me,
Who went across the sea
And with my head and hands
Killed men in foreign lands. . . .
Though I must bear the blame,
Because he bore my name.

Wilfrid Gibson.

PATRICK PEARSE'S LAST POEM

On the evening before the Easter Rising, his mother asked P. H. Pearse to write her a little poem " that I can recite later when you are no longer here." This is the poem which he wrote for her in his cell on the evening before his execution.

Dear Mary, thou didst see thy first-born son
Go forth to die amid the scorn of men
For whom He died.
Receive my first-born son into thy arms,
And keep him by thee till I come to him.
Dear Mary, I have shared thy sorrow,
And soon will share thy joy.

SOME REFLECTIONS OF A SOLDIER

It is very nice to be at home again. Yet am I at home ? One sometimes doubts it. There are occasions when I feel like a visitor among strangers whose intentions are kindly, but whose modes of

thought I neither altogether understand nor altogether approve.
find myself storing impressions, attempting hasty and unsatisfactory
summaries to appease the insatiable curiosity of the people with whom
I really am at home, the England that's not an island or an empire,
but a wet populous dyke stretching from Flanders to the Somme.
And then, just when my pencil is on the paper, I realize how hopeless
it is.   I used to sit at the feet of a philosopher, who thought he had
established a common intellectual medium between himself and an
Indian friend, till the latter elucidated his position by a hypothesis.
" Let us suppose," he said, " that God has chosen to assume the
form of an elephant."   With the concrete aloofness of that Oriental
imagery, my teacher strove in vain : the depth of the dividing chasm
was revealed by the bridge.

And somewhat the same difficulty troubles me.   As we exchange
views, one of you assumes as possible or probable something that
seems to us preposterous, or dismisses as too trivial for comment
what appears to us a fact of primary importance.   You speak lightly,
you assume that we shall speak lightly, of things, emotions, states
of mind, human relationships and affairs which are to us solemn or
terrible.   You seem ashamed, as if they were a kind of weakness,
of the ideas which sent us to France, and for which thousands of
sons and lovers have died.   You calculate the profits to be derived
from " War after the War," as though the unspeakable agonies
of the Somme were an item in a commercial proposition.   You make
us feel that the country to which we've returned is not the country
for which we went out to fight !   And your reticence as to the obvious
physical facts of war !   And your ignorance as to the sentiments
of your relations about it !

Yet I don't think I'm mad, for I find that other soldiers have
somewhat the same experience as myself.   Not that I profess to
speak for the Army !   I leave that to the officers who periodically
return to Parliament and tell it that the men at the front demand this,
or object to that.   I say " we," because I find it difficult to separate
opinions that I've formed myself from those formed for me by the
men with whom I lived, the chance conversations snatched during
a slack time in the trenches, of the comments of our mess when the
newspapers arrived with George's latest rhapsody about " cheerful
Tommies with the glint of battle in their eyes," or *The Times* military
expert's hundredth variation on the theme that the art of war consists

in killing more of the enemy than he kills of you, so that, whatever its losses—agreeable doctrine—the numerically preponderant side can always win, as it were, by one wicket. We used to blaspheme and laugh and say, " Oh, it's only the papers. People at home can't really be like that." But after some months in England I've come to the conclusion that your papers don't caricature you so mercilessly as we supposed. No, the fact is we've drifted apart. We have slaved for Rachel, but it looks as if we'd got to live with Leah.

We have drifted apart partly because we have changed and you have not ; partly, and that in the most important matters, because we have not changed and you have. Such a cleavage between the civilians who remain civilians and the civilians who become soldiers is, of course, no novelty. It occurred both in the American and in the English Civil Wars. It occurred most conspicuously in the French Armies of 1793 to 1809 or 1810, in which the Revolution survived as a spell that would charm men to death long after it had become an abomination or a curiosity in Paris. And always it seems to have brought something of the shock of an unexpected discovery to those who, not having borne the same life of corporate effort and endurance, forgot that the unquestioning obedience to which soldiers are trained is not obedience to popular opinions, and that the very absence of opportunities for discussion and self-expression tends, like solitude, to lend weight both to new impressions and to already formed mental habits. The contrast between the life which men have left and the unfamiliar duties imposed upon them creates a ferment, none the less powerful because often half-unconscious, in all but the least reflective minds. In particular, when, as has happened in the present war, men have taken up arms under the influence of some emotion or principle, they tend to be ruled by the idea which compelled them to enlist long after it has yielded, among civilians, to some more fashionable novelty. Less exposed than the civilian to new intellectual influences, the soldier is apt to retain firmly, or even to deepen, the impressions which made him, often reluctantly, a soldier in the first instance. He is like a piece of stone which, in spite of constant friction, preserves the form originally struck out in the fires of a volcanic upheaval. How often, fatigued beyond endurance or horrified by one's actions, does one not recur to those ideas for support and consolation ! " It is worth it, because——" " It is awful, but I need not loathe myself, because——" We see things which you can only imagine. We are strengthened by reflections which you have abandoned. Our minds differ from yours, both because they are more exposed to change, and because they are less changeable. While you seem—forgive me if I am rude—to have been surrendering your creeds with the nervous facility of a Tudor official, our foreground may be different, but our background is the same. It is that of August to November, 1914. We are your ghosts.

Anon. " The Nation," Oct. 21, 1916.

" 1916 "

The world bloodily-minded,
  The Church dead or polluted,
The blind leading the blinded,
  And the deaf dragging the muted.

Israel Zangwill.

1917

THE SOMME IN WINTER

Jany. Our rations came to Bull's Trench in bags of ten, per mules, and were carried thence by human mules. No water was brought, but the ice in the shell-holes was melted to obtain water. . . . An axe would soon be the means of filling the dixies with lumps of ice. We used it for tea several days until one chap noticed a pair of boots sticking out . . . and discovered they were attached to a body. . . . Many people here say it is the coldest winter they have ever experi- enced. I filled my water-bottle at Mametz at midday with boiling hot tea, and when I reached Bull's Trench at 5 p.m. it was frozen so hard that an ordinary knife made hardly any impression on it, and we broke it instead. Each man was supplied with two pairs of gloves —one worsted pair, and " trench " gloves lined with wool. . . . We generally managed to sleep warm by sleeping close together and sharing blankets—each man carried two. The cold, however, was far preferable to the mud. . . . We could move about.

Sergt. E. W. Simon (15th Australian Batt.).

THE FUTURE

PRIVATE ADOLF HITLER

THE first time I heard the name of Adolf Hitler was shortly after the end of the war, when a man named Franz Xavier Huber, a veteran who had had a leg shot away before Verdun in 1917, told me stories of a curious fellow who had been in his regiment at the front. . . .

The thing that had struck him most about " Private Hitler " was his grandiloquence. He was neither popular nor the reverse with his fellows ; they just smiled at him and his vague rambling speeches on everything in the world and out of it. He acquired very swiftly the reputation of being what in the British Army is called " an old soldier." That is, he showed distinct talent in avoiding disagreeable tasks, but he knew on which side his bread was buttered. He interested himself particularly in the important question of seeing the officers' washing done or doing it himself. This secured for him the good graces of the colonel who removed him from the more constant dangers of the trenches and appointed him runner between regimental head-quarters and the front line. . . .

Though he got the Iron Cross of the second class, no one in the regiment ever looked upon Hitler as any sort of a hero ; indeed they rather admired him for the skill with which he avoided hot corners. The regimental records contain not a line concerning an award of the Iron Cross of the first class to Hitler, though in latter years he has taken to wearing it prominently on his self-constructed uniform.

Anon. " New Statesman," 29th July, 1933.

ARRAS

2nd March. I have just returned from Arras. Oh, Lord ! what a spot ! For sheer desolation I have not seen anything to equal it, and I can't describe the feeling it gives to go into it. " B.V." ought to have lived to see it before he wrote *The City of Dreadful Night*, but as he didn't I expect I shall have to do it for him, when next I am inspired. It's far the biggest town I have seen, in fact I suppose it is the biggest on our front, and it is just in the state that makes the horror of it most impressive, like seeing a strong healthy man dying of some disgusting wasting disease, and his limbs dropping off with scurvy. We went through a sort of *Arc de Triomphe* straight into one of the main streets. The street was narrow, and all the houses on either side very tall. There are no inhabitants except for men living in the cellars, and every house shows hopeless dilapidations, but almost the worst part is that the outer walls are for the most part still standing, and through the unglazed windows and the holes from the shells, you saw the broken rafters, torn bits of wall paper, the debris of bricks and furniture at the bottom. And there was the long narrow ribbon of street utterly silent, and the walls, with nothing but ruin behind them, aslant and tottering, till it seemed a push with your hand would overset them : and indeed they do collapse frequently, for we saw many heaps of bricks, and there are large notices everywhere warning you to walk close into the walls and not in the middle of the streets. You can't conceive the effect of a really big town in that state, however you try ; it is far worse than seeing the place totally ruined, and in heaps of bricks and nothing more. It is those ghastly, sightless, purposeless walls that catch you, and the silence. For the life of me I could not have talked loud ; I think the echo would have sent me mad.

Capt. J. E. Crombie (Gordon Highlanders).

OLD STYLE AT LAJJ

5th March. The job of rounding up this convoy was assigned to the Thirteenth, and the Regiment drew ahead in the formation known as echelon of squadrons. We had not gone far when the whizz of bullets greeted our ears, and the order came to dismount for action— presumably owing to the impossibility, on account of the dust, of seeing what actually did lie in front of us. A lull in the dust-storm served to assure our leader that whatever opposition there was could be ridden down, and accordingly, after advancing a short distance dismounted, and snapping away with Hotchkiss gun and rifle, we were summarily recalled, ordered to mount, draw swords and finally charge. Shells by this time were bursting overhead, and the storm of bullets through which we rode gave the lie to the report that, with the exception of the convoy and its escort, all was clear ahead. We were quickly on top of a line of Turks who had abandoned their trench and were scurrying back to join their comrades in the rear lines. The horrible screeching told its own weird tale of the fate they met. In the onrush I got " winged " and was left, as I ultimately learned to my cost, a few yards from the Turkish main-line trench. As I stood there dazed amid the dust, I saw another squadron come galloping up. It was a sight I shall not readily forget. The leader to the fore with sword aloft, the line of panting horses, the grim eager faces of the men, the flashing swords—I thought of Lady Butler's painting " Floreat Etona," and marvelled at seeing the living parallel. Captain Eve was the leader, and as he approached " with a swiftness not to be conceived," I shook my right arm, which was hanging limply by my side, and shouted, " This thing's shattered." " Hard lines, old boy. Never mind," he called back, and was gone. The line had passed and disappeared in the dust.

When once again the dust had settled, the Turks, observing that the attack was for the moment over, sallied forth from their trenches to pay attention to the casualties. An Arab relieved me of my possessions and led me to an officer in the trench. This officer, on seeing me approach, forsook the machine-gun he had been manipulating and shook my uninjured member warmly—a thing which no good Mahomedan should have done, as such contact with the " infidel " is forbidden in terms of Koran regulations. Someone applied a tourniquet to my arm, which was still dripping, and I was taken to a bend in the trench where I came across Sergeants Gilbert and Spanton, and Trooper Morrison, the only other survivors amongst those who had fallen into Turkish hands. The horses of the two sergeants had been shot down, and Morrison was suffering from a wound in the forearm. We were led out of the trench and across the open country to the head-quarters of the Turkish forces (instead of rounding up a convoy the Thirteenth had ridden through a Division), and in the course of our journey to the rear had ample opportunity of realizing how much nastier is the effect of British shrapnel than that of the Turk. Arrived at head-quarters, we were separated and interrogated in a very polite manner by one who spoke English fluently. In this interrogation, to my surprise and the credit of the enemy, there was not the slightest suggestion of coercion to extract information. After a few hours' rest, Morrison and I, with some wounded Turkish soldiery, were given seats in a rickety waggon, and with Sergeants Gilbert and Spanton marching behind, we set out.

Lieut. E. F. Pinnington (XIIIth Hussars).

DECORATION

At our second billet on the way out of Ypres orders were issued that all men of the 4th Division who were to be decorated were to assemble at a certain village on a given Sunday. On this occasion I was the only " victim " in my battalion. Lieutenant Reg. Jones was detailed to parade me, and one Sunday morning we set out. After two solid hours of walking we had not reached the village. Jones cursed me, and I cursed the medal that was the cause of it all. When eventually we reached the parade, Jones duly obtained a receipt for me, told me I could go to hell now for all he cared, and went off home. After the church service, Birdie commenced handing out metals and crosses. When my name was called, he informed me that my medal had gone astray, and he would give me a piece of ribbon instead. Looking into my eyes and grasping my hand, he said : " Thank you ! Thank you for what you have done for us." I felt like a damned fool. He had a lovable personality, sincere and earnest, but he ruined much of the effect of it by ladling out what we called " bulsh " by the cartload. With it all, you could not help liking him. After this part of the show was over, I walked over to where a padre, who had just arrived from Australia, was standing. Some of his friends were mine also, and the thought of hearing about them thrilled me. But he was as cold as an iceberg, and his hand felt like a dead fish.

All this for a bit of ribbon. I went into the village to cheer myself up, and into the rowdiest *estaminet* I could find. Ordering four fried eggs, I sat back and watched the fun. Two rather nice-looking French girls were handing round drinks to a crowd of our fellows. The tables were close together, and one of the girls, in broken English, kept calling out : " Deeger, do not touch ze legs with ze hand," and occasionally making leaps and bounds like a young kangaroo. They were certainly a lot of rascals but a cheery crowd. By the time I was ready to leave, the girls were behind the counter and refused to come out. Their drapery must have been well tattooed by the Diggers' dirty beery fingers.

E. J. Rule (14th Batt., A.I.F.).

THE ARCH OF CTESIPHON

March. After the bonefield came a marvellous wood of willows, with catkins—a dancing piece of English spring. And then, they caught their breath as—over the desert, unbelievable as the first glimpse of Memnon and his brother statue, gazing from their immemorial thrones across the sands and seen by the traveller setting out at dawn from Luxor—rose the Arch of Ctesiphon. Here the desert glamour drew to a focus. Parthian dynasties had reigned here, Roman emperors had been slaves and captives. Julian had crossed the stream, and stormed the city of which this mighty mud wall was the only visible relic. Townshend had won his disastrous " victory " in its shadow ; let it be remembered to the praise of the English that their guns had not been ranged on it, however it may have served as an enemy observation post.

For a whole day, from the time when the first gold of morning shone through it and around it, till the time when dusk was filling its emptiness, the Arch loomed before Kenrick's eyes. Once you saw it, you could not take your eyes off it ; you marched upon it with your being rapt. They spent the night near it, on the slopes of the huge earthworks of millenniums ago. Abell dug into a barrow, and found a stone coffin, enclosing the skeleton of a child. The bones crumbled to dust in the air.

Edward Thompson.

BALLOON STRAFING

At this moment I was serenely sailing over the enemy trenches, keeping a sharp look-out for some sign of my own balloon. After flying five miles over the lines, I discovered it and circled around as a preliminary to diving down upon it. But just then I heard the rattle of machine-guns directly behind me and saw bullet-holes appear as if by magic in the wings of my machine. I pulled back as if to loop, sending the nose of my machine straight up into the air. As I did so the enemy scout shot by underneath me. I stood on my tail for a moment or two, then let the machine drop back, put her nose down, and dived after the Hun, opening fire straight behind him at very close range. He continued to dive away with increasing speed, and later was reported to have crashed just under where the combat had taken place. This victory I put down entirely to luck. The man flew directly in line with my gun and it would have been impossible to have missed him.

I proceeded now to dive for the balloon, but having had so much warning, it had been pulled down to the ground. I would have been justified in going home when I saw this, for our orders were not to go under 1,000 feet after the sausages. But I was just a bit peevish with this particular balloon, and to a certain extent my blood was up. So I decided to attack the ungainly monster in its " bed." I dived straight for it and when about 500 feet from the ground, opened fire. Nothing happened. So I continued to dive and fire rapid bursts until I was only 50 feet above the bag. Still there were no signs of it catching fire. I then turned my machine-gun on the balloon crew, who were working frantically on the ground. They scattered and ran all about the field. Meantime a " flaming onion " battery was attempting to pelt me with those unsavoury missiles, so I whirled upon them with a burst of twenty rounds or more. One of the onions had flared within a hundred yards of me.

This was all very exciting, but suddenly, with a feeling of faintness

I realized that my engine had failed. I thought that again, as during my first fight, the engine had oiled up from the steep diving I had done. It seemed but a moment before that I was coming down at a speed that must have been nearly 200 miles an hour. But I had lost it all in turning my machine upon the people on the ground.

There was no doubt in my mind this time as to just where I was, and there appeared no alternative but to land and give myself up. Underneath me was a large open field with a single tree in it. I glided down, intending to strike the tree with one wing just at the moment of landing, thus damaging the machine so it would be of little use to the Huns, without injuring myself.

I was within 15 feet of the ground, absolutely sick at heart with the uselessness of it all, my thoughts having turned to home, and the worry they would all feel when I was reported in the list of the missing, when, without warning, one of my nine cylinders gave a kick. Then a second one miraculously came to life, and in another moment the old engine—the best old engine in all the world—had picked up with a roar on all the nine cylinders. Once again the whole world changed for me. In less time than it takes to tell it, I was tearing away for home at a hundred miles an hour. My greatest safety from attack now lay in keeping close to the ground, and this I did. The " Archies ', cannot fire when you are so close to earth, and few pilots would have risked a dive at me at the altitude which I maintained. The machine-guns on the ground rattled rather spitefully several times, but worried me not at all. I had had my narrow squeak for this day, and nothing could stop me now. I even had time to glance back over my shoulder, and there, to my great joy, I saw a cloud of smoke and flames rising from my erstwhile *bête noir*—the sausage. We afterwards learned it was completely destroyed.

It was a strange thing to be skimming along just above the ground in enemy territory. From time to time I would come on groups of Huns who would attempt to fire on me with rifles and pistols, but I would dart at them and they would immediately scatter and run for cover. I flew so low that when I would come to a clump of trees I would have to pull my nose straight up toward the sky and " zoom " over them. Most of the Germans were so startled to see me right in their midst, as it were, they either forgot to fire or fired so badly as to insure my absolute safety. Crossing the three lines of German trenches was not so comfortable, but by zigzagging and quick dodging I negotiated them safely and climbed away to our aerodrome. There I found that no bullets had passed very close to me, although my wing-tips were fairly perforated.

Major W. A. Bishop, V.C.

GEMÜTLICHKEIT

Extract from a report by eight Spanish seamen who were captured from the steamship " Gravina " by a German submarine. The incident narrated occurred at Brandenburg Camp, apparently about the first week in March.

DEATH AT BRANDENBURG

March. Three days after arrival in camp we were awakened by the cries of the Russians who slept in the hut. We looked out of the door and saw prisoners running out of all the huts, the whole camp was afoot. Everybody was running maddeningly from one side to the other. The guard being quite unable to manage them. What had happened? There was one hut apart from the others which served as a dungeon where they shut up prisoners who were rebellious. That day six Russians, one Frenchman, and one Englishman were undergoing this punishment. Just against the hut there was a small workshop for repairs. Somebody had made a fire which had caught the timbers of the small prison. The prisoners noticed it, and called out naturally to be let out, but in vain. The sentry remained unmoved. No doubt he was waiting orders from his superiors. Those inside the dungeon were being choked. The Englishman broke the panes of a small window with the idea of freeing himself and his companions. The sentry seeing him leaning out of the window gave him a tremendous bayonet thrust in the chest. The wounded man fell like lead. A small but revolting struggle then took place. The prisoners attempted to get out, and the German soldier reddened his bayonet again and again with the blood of the men shut up, who saw with horror that the fire was increasing. The conflagration could not be extinguished by the other prisoners until it had done its work. The eight unhappy individuals who occupied the dungeon were corpses. For an hour afterwards nothing was heard but shouts of indignation. It looked as if a formidable outbreak would take place. The guards were immediately reinforced, and we were surrounded by a number of German soldiers. The commander of the camp issued an order stating that he was sorry for what had occurred, and that on the following day he would allow the funeral of the victims to take place with ceremony.

The Russians, who were skilful carpenters, made the coffins. When they were ready the cortège was organized to carry the bodies to the cemetery which was outside the camp, and where already four thousand prisoners lie buried. Fifty Russians led the procession carrying large wooden crosses. Following the six coffins of the Russians carried by the compatriots marched the remainder of the Russian prisoners. Then followed the coffin of the Frenchman escorted by those of his nationality and the eight Spaniards, and last of all the body of the Englishman and his fellow-countrymen. The chief officers of the camp formed part of the procession. Some ten thousand prisoners left the camp on the road to the cemetery about half a league away, proceeding along the road bordering with pine-trees and on the banks of a river. On arrival at the cemetery the three groups divided, and each one interred their dead comrades according to religious customs, pronouncing a short discourse afterwards. We returned to the camp as night was falling, each one carried an impression of the sad scenes which would not be blotted out. Some prayed and others cursed, and in the solitude of the night each one lying on his rough pallet thought with greater intensity of his destined home and his beloved ones.

Parliamentary Papers.

THE FIRST BATTLE OF GAZA

Ga{a was the scene of several battles between the British and the
Turks. It was eventually captured by Allenby on November 7, 1917.

27th March. The guns were crashing now among those immemorial
hills. The Imperial Mounted Division got their chance this day
some miles out on our flank, keeping off enemy reinforcements
attacking from Huj. The Yeomanry and the Imperial Camel Brigade
did their job. The 52nd Division (infantry) guarded us from Turks
expected from Khan Yunus way and across the wadi. But we
massed Australians and New Zealanders for hours were spectators of
the fight. It made our hearts bleed. Here we were gazing right
down into the city—and not allowed to enter it ! Our position was
unique, miles of the semi-circle battle was spread like a panorama
before us. This was the biggest battle the Desert Column had fought
in and yet we watched the main affray more plainly almost than a big
outpost fight. We could see the shells bursting over miles of country,
see the attacking battalions. With the most bewildered, utterly
indignant, with the saddest of feelings we watched the huge bulk of
Ali Muntar turning into a roaring volcano, its cactus crest obliterated
by the smoke and earth that vividly showed the crimson-black flame
of explosions. Toiling across the exposed country at its base, we
watched the little toy men of the 53rd Division plodding in waves
towards the grim fortress, roaring under its machine-gun fire.

And so, hours late, the first infantry attack developed, and right
then C Troops got orders to escort our prisoners away back to
divisional head-quarters. Away we went, the tired carriage ponies
stopping on crossing the ploughed fields, necessitating the officer
prisoners getting out and walking, which annoyed them. The
general in particular was quite cross. He strode behind the carriage,
frowning furiously, twirling his cane, twitching his moustache, snappy
to his subordinates.

Stan and I reined in and watched the attack on Ali Muntar through our glasses. The poor Welshmen coming up the open slopes towards the redoubts were utterly exposed to machine-gun and rifle-fire. Shrapnel had merged in a writhing white cloud over the advancing men. They plodded out of a haze of earth and smoke only to disappear into another barrage. It was pitifully sublime. When within close rifle range line after line lay down and fired while other lines ran past them to lie down and fire in turn. And thus they were slowly but so steadily advancing, under terrific fire. Every yard must have seemed death to them. We could see in between the smoke wreaths that when each line jumped up, it left big gaps. Some thousands of the poor chaps bled on Ali Muntar that day. And the pity of it was that they should have advanced in the fog and been saved that slaughter.

Stan and I cantered to catch up with the distant escort, now trekking among expectant bodies of New Zealanders and Yeomanry awaiting the order to go into action. The rough-looking Australians and En Zeds crowded around the toiling carriages. The nuggety little general was furious : I thought he would twirl his moustache off. He tried to hide back in his carriage but they poked their cameras in the door. He struck at some with his cane ; at which one sun-burned villain remonstrated : " Aw, be a sport, General ! "

The general wasn't—he launched a furious tirade at Chauvel against us chaps and haughtily demanded that Chauvel himself should escort him back to army head-quarters, as befitted the dignity of a Turkish general. Chauvel smiled. The Turkish general was mad when he had to go back with only an officer as escort.

It was late in the day when we handed the prisoners over. We learned there that Ali Muntar had been taken with the bayonet, but the Turks counter-charged and took it back again. As we rode smartly back we were in company with big bodies of horsemen pouring in from all the hills, closing in on what we confidently thought was the doomed city. Brigades were galloping—the air for miles was all floating clouds of dust and smoke. We watched battery after battery at full gallop from across the open plain, then drawing close to the hills, around the town wheel smartly on to their positions, unhook the teams and in a twinkling be firing in salvos. Then across the plain and on up the gentle slopes leading to the redoubts galloped a brigade of Light Horse of New Zealanders, I could not tell which, for dust and smoke. Squadron after squadron at a furious gallop with the flash in the puff of smoke above them. More furious and faster grew the flame bursts, the crash ! of the shells echoed over plain and hills ; there came back riderless horses whinnying as they galloped over the plain.

Squadrons of galloping Yeomanry followed into action—the declining sun flashing on the wheels of the guns—until the plain was a vast cloud of smoke and dust through which could be heard the galloping hoofs of thousands, the harsh rumbling of the gun-wheels, the faint shout of voices, the neigh of a maddened horse, the crash of bursting shells. It was grand, awe-inspiring, but it was terrible ! The section stood and listened—we could hardly watch—and the rolling roar of rifle and machine-gun fire rattled from the hills down on to the plain. It was a terrible sight of massed human courage. I wonder what other madnesses the human race will go through before the end of the world ? We know now that the Ali Muntar was taken and lost three times with the bayonet and then taken again. The section galloped into the haze to find the troop. We missed them but presently caught a glimpse of the regiment under heavy shell-fire riding out with bayonets all gleaming : we dug the spurs in and leaned over our horses' necks—a New Zealand brigade thundered by as we flew after the tail of the regiment—they were charging into a park of big trees that ran right up into the town. We galloped in among the trees—it was madly exciting. Rifles cracked viciously from cactus hedges, machine-guns snarled from a village on our right. Then we gaped as we galloped straight towards massive walls of cactus hedges ten feet high that ran as lanes right across the park. To our right was the only low hedge and Turkish infantry were enfilading us from there—Lieutenant Waite swerved his troop and the horses jumped the hedge down on to the Turks : we only got a glimpse of that scrap—the lieutenant firing with his revolver, his men from their saddles, until the lieutenant was hit in five places, but what Turks were not killed, ran, while we thundered on and I wondered what calamity might happen when we struck those giant walls of prickly pear. The colonel threw up his hand—we reined up our horses with their noses rearing from the pear—we jumped off—all along the hedge from tiny holes were squirting rifle-puffs, in other places the pear was spitting at us as the Turks standing behind simply fired through the juicy leaves. The horse-holders grabbed the horses while each man slashed with his bayonet to cut a hole through those cactus walls. The colonel was firing with his revolver at the juice spots bursting through the leaves—the New Zealanders had galloped by to the left of us, the 7th Light Horse were fighting on our right. Then came the fiercest individual excitement—man after man tore through the cactus to be met by the bayonets of the Turks, six to one. It was just berserk slaughter. A man sprang at the closest Turk and thrust and sprang aside and thrust again and again—some men howled as they rushed, others cursed to the shivery feeling of steel on steel—the grunting breaths, the gritting teeth and the staring eyes of the lunging Turk, the sobbing scream as the bayonet ripped home. The Turkish battalion simply melted away : it was all over in minutes. Men lay horribly bloody and dead ; others writhed on the stained grass, while all through the cactus lanes our men were chasing the demented Turks. Amateur soldiers we are supposed to be but, by heavens, I saw the finest soldiers of Turkey go down that day, in bayonet fighting in which only shock troops of regular armies are supposed to have any chance. How we thank now our own intense training.

The fighting was all in scattered groups ; we could only see a few yards around us for pear so I can tell what happened only to odd groups. Poor Sergeant Gahn met his death by treachery. He and Lieutenant Scott, Sergeant Hammond and Corporal Ogg rushed an officer with fifteen Turks who threw up their hands, but then seeing how few our men were snatched up their rifles, shot Gahn and bayoneted Ogg. Scott shot five quick and lively ; Hammond got one before the rest surrendered.

Lieutenant Graham emptied his revolver and had a lonesome bayonet duel with a huge Turk. Graham got the Turkish bayonet in his stomach. As the Turk lunged to finish the wounded man someone blew his brains out. The Turks only stood it for minutes, they became simply terrified and ran. No wonder ! It was they who were being killed, not us. While this was going on, Major Bolingbroke with a few men at Sheikh Redwan, crept up to an observation post that was directing some Turkish guns on our infantry, rushed them, and got away under machine-gun fire with all their range-finding instruments and telephones.

We rounded up the prisoners, sent them back, then carried on hacking our way through the hedges and simply killing or capturing any Turks who stood. If they wanted fight they got it; if they surrendered, well and good.

But A squadron luckily penetrated through the thinnest hedge of the cactus and eventually advanced with the New Zealanders right to the suburbs of the town, while the other two squadrons were still fighting up through the dense heart of the pear. The En Zed squadrons and troops were engaged in the always decisive hand-to-hand fighting too. Before our squadron linked up we heard a hair-raising war-cry and glimpsed the flash of steel among the trees as two En Zed troops plunged into a tiny lagoon towards a scarcely visible trench that was rattling with rifle-fire right until the En Zeds got into them. The Turks met steel with steel but the En Zeds bayoneted thirty-two of them—there were lots of those little trenches hidden all through the peaceful looking park. The comical thing though was after a squadron of the Wellington Mounted Rifles charged two Austrian guns that, entirely unsuspecting we were so close, were making the park reverberate as they fired over Ali Muntar at our infantry. The En Zeds rushed with an awful yell, the startled gunners and their supports snatched up weapons and fought with frantic terror. Bayonet-fighting is indescribable—a man's emotions race at feverish speed and afterwards words are incapable of describing feelings. In seconds only, it seemed, forty-two men were stretched dead around their guns ; the others kneeled or crouched or laid on the ground stretching up imploring arms. Everything was jolly lively here, we fired down the streets of the suburbs, the great mosque was quite close, the bulk of Ali Muntar was reverberating on our left right above us, bullets were ricochetting off the trees, machine-guns stuttering—our fellows were laughing and shouting what they would buy in the city shops.

Turks swarmed to counter-attack and take back the guns—confident big chaps they were. I thought how fine they looked as in massed formation they came roaring out of a street: "Allah ! Allah !" "Finish Australia !" with their waving rifles all steel-pointed. Things looked desperate for us little crowd around the guns when away to the right men burst through the prickly pear wearing the grimy felt hats of the 7th Light Horse—one man knelt down in the open, an officer levelled a Hotchkiss over the shoulder of the kneeling man and blazed away, taking the massed Turks in the flank : they fell in writhing masses sprayed by the

Hotchkiss bullets, and melted away under the crossfire of the New Zealanders.

Houses were full of lively snipers—one house only seventy yards away was furiously blazing with machine-guns. The En Zeds swung the captured guns around, a corporal swung open the breech-lock and pushed his face there instead of gazing down the barrel, the boys manhandled the wheels and to roars of laughter twisted the gun until the corporal could see a house through the barrel. They shoved in a shell, slammed home the block, fidgeted with the mechanism, until suddenly and unexpectedly bang ! crash ! up leapt the gun, its wheels spinning, men were flung among the dead gunners but the shell had gone clean through the house and out tumbled twenty-eight Turks with their hands up. We laughed delightedly, the boys grabbed the gun, manhandled it into position, the corporal sighted at another house, the boys held the wheels to keep the damned thing steady—bang ! crash ! through another house and out ran a lot more snipers coughing from the shell fumes. The boys warmed to their work, but the third time I don't know what they hit, for I sprang aside as the recoiling gun tried to climb a tree. A major came up bellowing that he didn't want any of his men killed by that " damned Krupp play-toy ! "

Turkish battalions were massing in the town, men were swarming down from the fortifications to counter-attack and there was a trench only two hundred yards away blazing into us, but the Turks had the wind up, their shooting was awfully poor. Major Cameron with about fifty A Squadron men under Major Bolingbroke and twenty-five New Zealanders rushed this trench with the bayonet, four machine-guns splaying the trench with lead as we charged. It was blood-boiling work but that charge was quickly over, the Turks would stand up to the steel now only for the first dreadful minute.

As the sun went down, a great shout came rippling faintly, then swelling from man to man right down the New Zealand line : " The Tommies have taken Ali Muntar ! Hurrah ! Hurrah ! Hurrah ! " We pressed forward to the town in a wild enthusiasm. Not twenty minutes later there came a staggering surprise—the order to retire ! Thousands of Turkish reinforcements were hurrying to the aid of the Gaza garrison and would cut the mounted men off—our infantry were retiring—we were to retire in all haste.

Never will I forget the utter amazement of all troops—we simply stood gazing down the streets of Gaza—officers shrieking for signallers to confirm the order lest it be the work of spies.   The sun was right down—repeated signal after signal came : " Retire ! Retire ! Retire ! "

Ion L. Idriess (5th Light Horse, A.I.F.).

THE BATTLE OF ARRAS

*The battle of Arras was one of the most important in the War.
The object of the Allies was to cross the River Scarpe, turn the newly-
constructed Hindenburg Line and advance on Cambrai. The attack
opened on April 9 and closed on May 5 without having achieved its
objective. British casualties numbered 132,000.*

ZERO HOUR FROM THE AIR

9th April. Dawn was due at 5.30 o'clock on Easter Monday, and that
was the exact hour set for the beginning of the Battle of Arras. We
were up and had our machines out of the hangars while it was still
night. The beautiful weather of a few hours before had vanished.
A strong, chill wind was blowing from the east and dark, menacing
clouds were scudding along low overhead.

We were detailed to fly at a low altitude over the advancing
infantry, firing into the enemy trenches, and dispersing any groups
of men or working troops we happened to see in the vicinity of the
lines. Some phases of this work are known as " contact patrols,"
the machines keeping track always of the infantry advance, watching
points where they may be held up, and returning from time to time
to report just how the battle is going. Working with the infantry in
a big attack is a most exciting experience. It means flying close to
the ground and constantly passing through our own shells as well as
those of the enemy.

The shell-fire this morning was simply indescribable. The
bombardment which had been going on all night gradually died down
about 5 o'clock, and the Germans must have felt that the British had
finished their nightly " strafing," were tired out and going to bed.
For a time almost complete silence reigned over the battlefields. All
along the German lines star-shells and rocket-lights were looping
through the darkness. The old Boche is always suspicious and likes

to have the country around him lighted up as much as possible so he can see what the enemy is about.

The wind kept growing stiffer and stiffer and there was a distinct feel of rain in the air. Precisely at the moment that all the British guns roared out their first salvo of the battle, the skies opened and the rain fell in torrents. Gunfire may or may not have anything to do with rainmaking, but there was a strange coincidence between the shock of battle and the commencement of the downpour this morning. It was beastly luck, and we felt it keenly. But we carried on.

The storm had delayed the coming of day by several minutes, but as soon as there was light enough to make our presence worth while we were in the air and braving the untoward elements just as the troops were below us. Lashed by the gale, the wind cut the face as we moved against the enemy. The ground seemed to be one mass of bursting shells. Farther back, where the guns were firing, the hot flames flashing from thousands of muzzles gave the impression of a long ribbon of incandescent light. The air seemed shaken and literally full of shells on their missions of death and destruction. Over and over again one felt a sudden jerk under a wing-tip, and the machine would heave quickly. This meant a shell had passed within a few feet of you. As the battle went on the work grew more terrifying, because reports came in that several of our machines had been hit by shells in flight and brought down. There was small wonder in this. The British barrage fire that morning was the most intense the war had ever known. There was a greater concentration of guns than at any time during the Somme. In fact, some of the German prisoners said afterwards that the Somme seemed a Paradise compared to the bombardment we carried out at Arras. While the British fire was at its height the Germans set up a counter-barrage. This was not so intense, but every shell added to the shrieking chorus that filled the stormy air made the lot of the flying man just so much more difficult. Yet the risk was one we could not avoid ; we had to endure it with the best spirit possible.

The waves of attacking infantry as they came out of their trenches and trudged forward behind the curtain of shells laid down by the artillery were an amazing sight. The men seemed to wander across No Man's Land, and into the enemy trenches, as if the battle was a great bore to them. From the air it looked as though they did not realize that they were at war and were taking it all entirely too quietly.

That is the way with clock-work warfare. These troops had been drilled to move forward at a given pace. They had been timed over and over again in marching a certain distance, and from this timing the " creeping " or rolling barrage which moved in front of them had been mathematically worked out. And the battle, so calmly entered into, was one of the tensest, bitterest of the entire world-war.

For days the battle continued, and it was hard work and no play for everybody concerned. The weather, instead of getting better, as spring weather should, gradually got worse. It was cold, windy, and wet. Every two or three hours sudden snow-storms would shut in, and flying in these squalls, which obliterated the landscape, was very ticklish business.

On the fourth day of the battle I happened to be flying about 500 feet above the trenches an hour after dawn. It had snowed during the night and the ground was covered with a new layer of white several inches thick. No marks of the battle of the day before were to be seen ; the only blemishes in the snow mantle were the marks of shells which had fallen during the last hour. No Man's Land itself, so often a filthy litter, was this morning quite clean and white.

Suddenly over the top of our parapets a thin line of infantry crawled up and commenced to stroll casually toward the enemy. To me it seemed that they must soon wake up and run ; that they were altogether too slow ; that they could not realize the great danger they were in. Here and there a shell would burst as the line advanced or halted for a moment. Three or four men near the burst would topple over like so many tin soldiers. Two or three other men would then come running up to the spot from the rear with a stretcher, pick up the wounded and the dying, and slowly walk back with them. I could not get the idea out of my head that it was just a game they were playing at ; it all seemed so unreal. Nor could I believe that the little brown figures moving about below me were really men— men going to the glory of victory or the glory of death. I could not make myself realize the full truth or meaning of it all. It seemed that I was in an entirely different world, looking down from another sphere on this strange, uncanny puppet-show.

Suddenly I heard that deadly rattle of a nest of machine-guns under me, and saw that the line of our troops at one place was growing very thin, with many figures sprawling on the ground. For three or four minutes I could not make out the concealed position of the German gunners. Our men had halted, and were lying on the ground evidently as much puzzled as I was. Then in a corner of a German trench I saw a group of about five men operating two machine-guns. They were slightly to the flank of our line, and evidently had been doing a great deal of damage. The sight of these men thoroughly woke me up to the reality of the whole scene beneath me. I dived vertically at them with a burst of rapid fire. The smoking bullets from my gun flashed into the ground, and it was an easy matter to get an accurate aim on the German automatics, one of which turned its muzzle toward me.

But in a fraction of a second I had reached a height of only 30 feet above the Huns, so low I could make out every detail of their frightened faces. With hate in my heart I fired every bullet I could into the group as I swept over it, then turned my machine away. A few minutes later I had the satisfaction of seeing our line again advancing, and before the time had come for me to return from my patrol, our men had occupied all the German positions they had set out to take. It was a wonderful sight and a wonderful experience.

Major W. A. Bishop, V.C.

FIRST BULLECOURT

10th April. Earlier in the night, as Jacka and Bradley (16th) were out in No Man's Land attending to their duty of laying the jumping-off tapes, they were surprised to see a couple of Huns approaching. Jacka and his partner sneaked round to the rear of them, and before the Huns knew what had happened Jacka was covering them with his revolver. One of the Huns started to squeal and kick up a fuss. Jacka walked up to him and, pushing the revolver into his face, soon quietened him. Jacka hit him over the head with it and the fellow calmed down and the pair of them were taken to our C.O. Here the Hun officer complained very bitterly of his treatment, but, when our colonel told him he was a b——y lucky man to be alive, he shut up. What information was gained from them, I don't know. Jacka made a thorough examination of the Hun line. I've heard that he crawled through the Hun wire and saw for himself the density of machine-guns and men in their trenches. I afterwards heard him say that he told all the heads that it was pure murder to attempt the operation, and Jacka's ideas about military affairs were well worth careful consideration. . . .

A little while after this—at 1 a.m. on the 11th—our mortars pelted gas-bombs into Bullecourt. As soon as they started, the Hun lit up the sky with Véry lights, and we could plainly see our gas-bombs bursting and giving off dense clouds of gas which were slowly drifting over the village, and it was so thick that it must have caught a few Huns. Strange to relate, no special retaliation came back, although odd shells were bursting here and there. Two 9-inch shells from the enemy batteries, that were rich in their results, arrived about this time. One landed on two trench-mortar crews and blotted them right out; between thirty and forty men were killed or wounded. . . .

At zero I saw the tanks waddle out and our boys follow them at a distance of about a hundred yards or so. The tank right in front of me got ditched almost as soon as they started, and the boys went on and left it. By what I saw of the tank crews afterwards, it was a question whether some of them had their hearts in this fight. Our guns opened at the same time, but not a shell was to be seen bursting on the Hun lines. Pretty soon the Hun opened with artillery and machine-guns, and the bullets flew around thickly. I ducked more than once as sparks of fire were flicked up in front of our trench. The Hun commenced to put up lights now, and during one lot that lit the place up like day I saw a sight that I'll never forget. Advancing along the side of the spur as if they were on parade, with their rifles held at the high port, was a line of our boys. I think that they were the third wave, and there were gaps here and there, and in one or two places big spaces. With such intense machine-gun fire, there was no need to enquire what was happening. When the lights died down, the scene vanished in the gloom.

I thought I was all on my own until I went for a bit of a walk under the bank, and there, in a dug-out, found a cold-footer of the 12th Brigade, who had funked it at the last minute. He had such a plausible tale that I did not tumble to him till afterwards. As daylight came, the first objects that we made out were the tanks— but, alas, they seemed to be in every place except where they were most needed, with one or two exceptions. One I saw, apparently over the Hun trenches on the outskirts of Riencourt and working along to the right. Even this one, after going a few hundred yards, headed back to the rear. A tank directly in front of me was stuck in a shell-hole, and its crew were tinkering around it. Later, another tank came to its assistance, but it seemed to me that it should have supported our troops instead of attending to other business in the back area. A third was between Bullecourt and Riencourt, and, as I watched it, it started to move towards the Hun wire. On reaching the wire it burst into flames—apparently no man escaped, for I saw none leave it. Another was retiring when a shell burst at its side. The crew jumped out, one at a time, and ran to shelter. Several others were burning fiercely, belching out dense clouds of black smoke, and they continued to burn for hours. What with one thing and another, not a tank escaped. . . .

When zero hour came, and the first wave went off, it had very soon overtaken the tanks, which were mostly floundering around close in front. Some of them even fired on our own men, but no one knows precisely how many they killed. As it was fatal to hesitate and wait for the tanks, the line advanced alone. As soon as it came in sight of the Huns the massacre commenced, the enemy lining his parapet and shooting our boys like rabbits. Lots of them reached the wire, but as it had not been cut, they had to run along it until they came to an opening. This turning to a flank caused them to bunch together and they fell in heaps on the wire and in front of it. The wonder is that any of them reached the trench. But reach it they did, and took the enemy's front line. . . .

The tanks which were to make things so easy had all failed, but, on account of them, the artillery was not being used. Fighting through the communication trenches, our men reached and took the second trench, and after a while it developed into a bomb-fight up and down the trenches and communicating trenches. As no one could get back to the rear for supplies without being fired on at close range, it cut off all hope of help, and it was just a case of whose bombs could hold out the longest. The Hun could bring up all the bombs he wanted, and it was not long before this inequality began to tell. Our boys used up all the Hun bombs they could find, and at last they were searching the dead to find them.

Captain Murray, V.C., of the 13th, was here, there, and everywhere, and, when at last he saw no other way to escape capture, he gave the order: "Everyone for himself." There were lots who never heard it, and fought on until surrounded by Huns who came in on them from the rear and the sides. Those who tried to break away were killed like flies, and it was only the foxy ones, who used their heads, that succeeded. Numbers leapt out and lay in shell-holes until darkness set in, but those who lay doggo too close to the German lines were collected by Hun patrols and sent back to Germany. . . .

At dusk on 11th April our battalion commenced to move out along the gully, and for safety's sake, some of us took a new path on the left-hand side. Just before this it had begun to sleet again, and it did not stop for hours. The tramp out that night was a heart-breaker. For a start we were robbed of almost every ounce of energy by the thick mud that we had to get over before reaching the road near Vaulx. Just outside Vaulx we came across a horse ambulance with its four horses laid out on the ground beside it. How many men were killed or wounded, we could not see, as they had been taken away, but it was a good haul for one shell. Once on the road we settled down to a steady tramp, but we fairly flew through Vaulx village—its reputation for shell-fire had us bluffed.

As we went along we overtook stragglers, some of them carrying about as much rum as they could hold. How they ever reached our camp I don't know, for the strongest of us had to struggle to get there. These drunks could obtain no shelter anywhere on the way, for the Hun had destroyed everything in the way of a bivouac or billet; and it was almost as much as your life was worth to lie down exposed to the weather. It seemed ages before the battalion came up to a man standing by the roadside, who directed us to the transport lines. Here we found Lieutenant Anderson, who was acting quartermaster; he had a lot of sandwiches and hot tea ready for us laid out on boxes. For those who wanted rum there was plenty—in the A.I.F. the rule was, no rum before a fight; the rum was given afterwards when the boys were dead beat. This feast looms up as one of the best I ever had. Standing out in the open (there was hardly a place where one could sit down), and with a couple of old lanterns to drive away a little of the blackness of the night, we fairly gorged ourselves like beasts. It was just on twenty-four hours since anyone had had a hot meal.

E. J. Rule (14th Batt., A.I.F.).

MONCHY-LE-PREUX

11*th April.* About this time of the morning, during a lull in the snowstorm, an excited shout was raised that our cavalry were coming up ! Sure enough, away behind us, moving quickly in extended order down the slope of Orange Hill, was line upon line of mounted men covering the whole extent of the hillside as far as we could see. . . . In their advance the lines of horsemen passed over us rapidly, although from our holes in the ground it was rather a "wormseye" view we got of the splendid spectacle of so many mounted men in action. It may have been a fine sight, but it was a wicked waste of men and horses, for the enemy immediately opened on them a hurricane of every kind of missile he had. If the cavalry advanced over us at the trot or canter, they came back at a gallop, including numbers of dismounted men and riderless horses, and— most fatal mistake of all, they bunched behind Monchy in a big mass, into which the Boche continued to put high-explosive shrapnel, whizz-bangs, and a hail of bullets, until the horsemen dispersed and finally melted away back over the hillside from where they came.

They left a number of dead and wounded men among us, however, but the horses seemed to have suffered most, and for a while after we put bullets into poor brutes that were aimlessly limping about on three legs, or else careering about madly in their agony ; like one I saw that had the whole of its muzzle blown away. With the dead and wounded horses lying about in the snow, the scene resembled an old-fashioned battle picture. . . .

While the snow was falling, and we could move about more freely without being observed by the Boche machine-gunners and snipers, some of us went out to give what help we could to the many wounded men lying about in the open. An extensive orchard belonging to the big château-farm on the north side of the village was full of dead and wounded men of our 45th Brigade. As I have already related, several units of that brigade in their first attack during the morning had swung round against the north side of Monchy, and in the snow beneath the masses of blossom on the fruit trees in that big orchard their dead and wounded were lying in heaps and rows. To add to the horror of it all, since the attack in the early morning in which these men had fallen, the Germans had heavily shelled the orchard and vicinity at the time the cavalry were retiring round that side of the village. As we moved through the orchard in the falling snow, wounded men on every side were shouting and blowing whistles to attract attention, but only too many of them lay like still hummocks of snow. I remember one of these hummocks heaved and cracked open on our approach, as a poor kilted Highlander turned over at the sound of our voices. His bare thigh was only a blackened stump, but he complacently and without a murmur accepted the cigarette we lit for him. He, and a great many others of the wounded, must have died that day from loss of blood and exposure. It was a pitiful sight; the sort of thing that made one rage at the utter futility of it all.

D. W. J. Cuddeford (12th *H.L.I.*).

GREENLAND HILL

28th *April.* The attack was to be launched at streak of dawn, 4.25; and at that moment a wild racket was once more loosed into the void. Once more the curtain of darkness was changed to a whirling screen in which flaming clusters, red, orange and gold, dropped and died; and dun smoke, illuminated by explosions, drifted away greyish white. Once more red and green rockets called frantically for aid. Once more eyes stared into this impenetrable cataract, vainly trying to pick out familiar outlines. The enemy's barrage joined the din. Black columns of smoke stormed up in the foreground. And through it all came wave on wave of the malicious chitter of machine-guns.

Slowly the darkness grew to grey, to opal, to gold; and the mist began to burn away. Shapes loomed up. Distances were deceptive in the haze. The round top of Greenland Hill came into outline. It was bare of life. A dark patch to the left became Square Wood. A contact plane hovering in the centre fired white Véry lights. Some red flares blossomed, like Chinese lanterns at a fête, on the edge of the Chemical Works.

As the day cleared, gunner officers and their linesmen began to come into the trench. Our shelling died down, but the enemy was shivering his old front line with vicious concentration. To the north, we could see men coming up and down the road from Gavrelle. Who they were no one could tell. We thought they were both English and German, but which was escorting which? . . .

Questioning the countryside, I caught in my glass a grey ant crawling over the edge of the railway cutting, followed by another, and then more. They hurried into a road behind a shallow bank and lay down. The sun polished their steel helmets into a row of little shining disks. More and more were now coming out of the cutting. I pinched the elbow of the gunner beside me.

" See that ? It's a counter-attack massing."

" Not on my line," he returned. " Besides, they're out of range of field-guns."

I tumbled impetuously down the stairs and called division. A quiet voice in the distance assured me that the heavies would deal with what I had seen. When I looked again, the assembled ants had moved. They came crawling over the top of Greenland Hill in three lines, about six hundred strong. They were just starting down the forward slope when something flashed in front of them. A column of bright terra-cotta smoke was flung upwards so high, that there shot into my memory the pictures of the djinns in an old copy of the *Arabian Nights*, and I half expected a leering hook-nosed face to look down from its summit. Another and another rose until an arcade of smoking pillars seemed to move across the hillside. " Six-inch Hows," shouted my neighbour excitedly, " firing one-o-six."

Already the grey ants had thinned. The first line was hardly there. It merged with the second and mechanically the whole inclined southwards to avoid the shells. But the guns followed the movement and another line of smoking columns fountained into the air. At last, reduced to one line, the minute figures turned and stumbled back over the crest of the hill.

Guy Chapman.

THE EVE OF ISTABULAT

20th April. All that has ever happened in time is photographed on the universe, and one day science will discover how to bring these pictures out, and develop them into the exact semblance of the sensitive life that was once theirs. We shall then not trouble to have our cinemas or any drama that has come out of a man's mind, since our theatres will be able to show us anything that has taken place, the burning of Cranmer or the victories of Napoleon. Men will be able to see the ten thousand coming up to the Median Wall ; or the British and Indian troops who couched in its shadow before they stormed Istabulat—so recently that their friends are still living and would be moved could they witness what we have not yet learned to show.

But Hart's vision was born of his imagination ; and it faded as the daylight went out. He lay awake, listening to the muffled and watchful low noises. His heart went out in a gush of such love and gratitude as he had never felt, to all the brave and gallant spirits that had lived until they had got beyond the need or desire to hear others praise them. Those men were the reality, the rest were ghosts that had walked in time and now had walked out of time for ever. He was neither lonely nor unhappy as he lay in the shelter of that enormous wall. This new mood that had come to him was so without all reason that he compelled himself to go over the last few months, in which he had felt so differently. He was not going to be fooled now, at the finish.

For the respite at Baghdad and in the pleasant groves beyond it had deepened his sickness of spirit. He had realized how worthless is any charm or richness of country, if the people are null. . . .

This land had drained the hopefulness out of every thinking man who had sojourned here. Julian dying had scorned as folly the philosophy by which he had lived. It was not so much that the Galilean had conquered, as that hope and valiancy had died. Xenophon had risen from sleep in those Sumaikchah wheatfields; the Athenian's eyes had brightened as they glanced over hyacinth and gladiolus and glowing emerald of massed corn-blades. But he was not condemned to stay here, he was the cavalryman earnestly thrusting ever northward, to where existence ceased to be sand and mirage, and became firm earth and unglimmering air. Yet what had been the use of it? Historians said his march was immensely important. It showed that Asia was weak, mere bulk without strength, and that Europe could smash it to pieces. It prepared the way for Alexander. Even so . . . was it worth the physical suffering of such multitudes of men and women, to establish simply the brute strength of Europe and the equally brute weakness of Asia? We knew that the one was hard—had it not all through the centuries been expressing itself in system, rule, discipline, law? The Attic hoplite, the Macedonian phalanx, Roman legionary and cohort, pike and arquebus and musket, maxim, machine-gun, naval gun—that was Europe. We knew the other was soft—even when an Arab from the desert fused it with the heats of religion, was it not still a luxurious relaxation into sex and sensuality, a continued dreaming on lust and loot and food? It was not the people's fault that there were long periods of starvation from these things which were all that they desired.

Alexander, the historians told us, had conquered because Xenophon's men had toiled through ambush and forest and ice-cold streams and deathly snows. But had man's spirit been in any way helped forward? Alexander's victories had ended in the Ptolemies and Seleucids, in teaching the Parthians to put a sharper edge of war upon their barbarism and the Indians to dragoon their own people into slavery. Was anything happening now because our own men had anguished through four months of incompetent leading a year ago, or were going on endlessly, from one battle to another? The agony represented by the aggregate of Shaiba and Ctesiphon and the countless combats in the twenty miles before Kut, was immense. But it was a drop in the agony of Europe, no one heeded it, it was right that no one should heed it, for it was of no importance. It did not matter how many thousand men died there, what battles were fought and won.

Edward Thompson.

THE FRENCH GROW WAR WEARY

THE STRONG HAND

30*th May*. General Franchet d'Esperey reports to the C.-in-C. that at the last moment, following on committee meetings of the soldiers, two regiments, 36th and 129th, had decided to " march on Paris." Precautions have been taken to disperse them. It is confirmed that at Dormans some men shouted : " Down with the War. Up the Revolution ! "

31*st May*. In the War Committee, Pétain read out two reports on the mutinies of the 36th and 129th Regiments. There has been no disrespect to the officers, but the men have decided among themselves to seize the trains, make for Paris and send a deputation to the Chamber to demand immediate peace. The rumour has spread among them that the Annamites stationed in Paris have fired on French troops. This baseless news rapidly swelled. Impossible to find out where it comes from. . . .

I put the question categorically to Pétain : " If there is an international socialist congress at Stockholm, and the French meet the Germans to discuss terms of peace, can you keep the army in hand ? Will you be in a position to make it go on fighting ? "

Pétain answered quite frankly : " No." The monosyllable, uttered in a strong voice, had a sharp effect on the Committee.

2*nd June*. Col. Herbillon brings me fresh news of mutinies, this time in the XXIst Corps. Some men have refused to go up to trenches.

3*rd June*. Further unpleasant incidents at the Front. Col. Fournier tells me that a division of the XXIst Corps has discussed whether it will go back to trenches and resume the offensive. It has decided to go up, but to remain on the defensive. Another division, this one in the VIIth Corps, has refused to relieve trenches.

Gen. Pétain is trying to discover the ringleaders whom he believes to be in touch with the C.G.T., and he will not continue in command unless steps are taken against pacifist propaganda.

4th June. Painlevé telephoned me during the night about the case of the two soldiers who have taken an active part in the recent mutinies. One, a schoolmaster in civil life, is a sergeant who was reduced to the ranks. I could not make out what Painlevé wanted, but from his agitation, I guessed he was asking for mercy for these soldiers. I answered that the time was not one for weakness. The army is being spoiled. The back-areas have little by little corrupted our magnificent soldiers, once so confident and heroic. Col. Herbillon reports still further incidents. One group marched along, shouting : " Down with Poincaré ! Down with Ribot ! " That is an unimportant detail. But to refuse to go up to trenches, to refuse obedience to orders when they are given, that alas ! is a good deal more serious. From another quarter I learn that some Annamite troops have just fired on a crowd at Saint-Ouen. . . .

5th June. Painlevé has seen Pétain about the two soldiers condemned to death after the first of the last few days' mutinies. . . . One of them is a schoolmaster, and he has set the socialist deputies to work. At the Cabinet meeting, Painlevé admits that in spite of their intervention, Pétain has insisted and the two men will be shot to-morrow.

26th June. According to Fournier, yet another regiment passing through Chalons shouted revolutionary slogans, calling out : " Up with the peace." The evil is not yet cured. Five more executions still have to be carried out alas ! following on the rejection of the appeal for mercy, on the insistence of Pétain and in accordance with the findings of the Ministers of War and Justice.

28th June. Before the Cabinet meeting, Ribot came up to me to tell me that a regiment, 298th of the Souilly group (Gen. Guillaumet) has given way to lamentable manifestations. In four companies, a large number of soldiers have sent round-robins to their company commanders in which they declare that they will not go back to trenches and demand the immediate conclusion of an honourable peace.

29th June. . . . Painlevé tells the Cabinet that eleven arrests have been made in the regiment which signed the petition for peace at Souilly, and that the regiment has been sent up to the Front. Up to the moment they have marched without protest ; but they have not yet come into the danger zone.

Raymond Poincaré.

PROMPT MEASURES MUST BE TAKEN

Two o'clock. We were on the Square in front of the Château, when a squad of M.P.'s burst from the guard-house, interrupted the traffic, ordered cars to draw to one side, and cleared the street. His curiosity aroused, Étienne whispered to me :

"They don't often do that. Stick around and we'll see . . ."

We stationed ourselves behind an unharnessed supply cart. And what I saw that day I shall never forget.

"Behind the tree, General Franchet . . ." murmured Étienne.

At the edge of the moat that separated the Château from the Square, stood the rusty trunk of a horse-chestnut tree, not yet in leaf. And behind the tree, a man, motionless, his hands behind his back : Franchet, the commanding general of the Group of Northern Armies. His heavy shoulders drooping, his face drawn from sleeplessness. A secretive face : that of a Mangin depressed, deadened, and softened. But the hard eyes looked out with a rough stare. The heavy chin overflowed its jaw-bones ; a paunch ; short legs, chopped off above and below by the coat and high boots.

He was alone. Not an officer beside him. Behind the trunk of this bare tree he crouched hidden.

At that moment, the road from Fontenoy disgorged what he had been looking for. A truck, followed by a second, and a third, and then more, and more . . . The trucks from Vingre, an armed M.P. beside the driver and another on the step. Inside, men in shirt-sleeves, bareheaded or wearing woollen caps ; thirty to a truck. It was the 217th, stripped of its arms and equipment, being shipped to the rear in a cloud of dust. Until the transport reached the Square the men sang in ringing tones, like harvesters returning from the fields. In front of the Château, they yelled, spat, and howled, at both the M.P.'s and the officers ; a few shook their fists in the air. As they started down the steep hill beyond the Square, the singing began again, broken by the jouncing of the trucks and mingled with the rattle of stones and iron. . . . Ah God, who shall be their judge ?

Behind the chestnut tree, a man was watching, listening, his brows drawn, his lips pressed together, riddled with despairing curses. On his face, neither anger, nor cruelty, nor contempt. Neither kindness nor grief. Nothing. An inert calmness, the face of a man asleep.

When the last truck had passed, and the dust fallen, he turned about abruptly. Slowly he crossed the lawn. At the steps an orderly saluted. Franchet lifted his head slightly and gazed into the orderly's eyes. Then he moved by, and on the empty terrace looked about him, as if searching for more eyes to meet, more eyes that he might force to drop beneath his gaze. . . .

Jacques Deval.

THE FUTURE

V. I. LENIN

AND just across the Neva, Lenin himself was speaking ! I saw him, on a raised platform, before the home of Kschensinska, a former *première ballerina* and favourite of the Tsar. A short, dumpy figure, with an enormous dome of a head, high cheek-bones giving a sinister contemptuousness to his Tartar eyes. The great Lenin ! But he was not " great " to any but a very few people then. He was just this undersized new agitator in an old double-breasted blue suit, his hands in his pockets, speaking with an entire absence of that hysterical arm-waving that so characterized all his fellow countrymen.

" Yes," he was saying, " it is the Capitalists and our diplomats who make the wars. Not the people. They get rich, we get killed. You left the soil and the factories to go to war, and when war is over—what ? You will go back to the soil and the factories to work under the Capitalist system again—those of you who are left alive. *What do you get from war ?* Wounds, suffering, and death."

Town workers, *moujiks*, soldiers and sailors looked up and listened, and then they looked at each other :

" *Da*, yes, he is right ! What do we get out of this war, but wounds and death and starvation. Back to the factories !—take them ! Take the land ! *Deloie boorjoie !* "

Negley Farson.

418

PRIMITIVE MAN

THOSE to whom life is bearable—and they are perforce a majority—are astonished when they examine the nature of the compensations that induce them to accept the inevitable. So with Skene. Just when it became impossible for him to feel any longer that it was his war, to be won by his own individual sacrifice, it became possible to feel that he need not sacrifice himself either immediately or continuously. Having so narrowly escaped death, he might now live a bit and not bother. To live was not so easy. Apart from getting bombed and shelled he had to find food, drink, housing and leave. Uncle was the finest possible tutor for a young man anxious to live. He taught the three arts of war, so much more necessary than musketry, field engineering or tactics. Or were they, perhaps, part of tactics? Wangling, Scrounging, and Winning.

Wangling was the art of obtaining one's just due by unfair means. For instance, every officer and man of the B.E.F. had his allotted daily rations, his camp or billet, his turn for leave. In practice, to get these necessities, it was well to know the man who provided them and do him some small service—a bottle of whisky, the loan of transport (if you had any) or of a fatigue party. Wangling extended to the lowest ranks. Men wangled from the N.C.O.s the better sorts of jam and extra turns off duty. The main stream of wangling flowed from the enormous and growing number of small units, like Uncle's, the apportionment of whose daily subsistence was at once a nuisance and an opportunity to the Supply Officers and the Railhead Panjandrums—for the bigger units, battalions, batteries, Head-quarters had to be and could be more easily provided for. But Wangling was by no means confined to troops in the field. As the War grew and grew—the contracts for supplying steel helmets to Americans, the command of smaller Allied Armies, the very sovereignty of nations all became subject to the Wangle, so remote had become the chances of justly obtaining bare justice.

To return to the unit in the field, when its Wangle was completed, behold it housed, fed and allowed some leave. But life was still very hard—almost insupportable; to bear it, men, those fathers of invention, evolved the art of Scrounging.

Scrounging could be defined as obtaining that to which one had not a shadow of a claim by unfair means. It was more insidious than the Wangle, but just as necessary—men scrounged the best dug-outs off one another, or off neighbouring sections. N.C.O.s scrounged rum by keeping a thumb in the dipper while doling it out. Officers scrounged the best horse-lines from other units. Colonials scrounged telephone wire to snare rabbits. Nations scrounged territory or trade. It was simply done. You walked about whistling, with your hands in your pockets and a cigarette in your mouth, until you saw what you wanted, and then took it. The main stream of Scrounging was for wood. The armies were provided with coal and coke and presumably intended to ignite it by holding a match to it. In result, millions of men during the five winters of the War, burnt a colossal cubage of wood. It was easy to obtain. Vast quantities were being cut by an entire Forestry Corps that had rights over several Picard and Norman forests and did nothing else but provide the timber required for dug-outs, railways, roads and gunpits. No great percentage ever reached its proper destination. A little was built into huts, horselines or billets. The bulk was burnt. From the timber dumps in the great cold of January, 1917, whole stacks disappeared. If any high authority went into the matter, a dumb, putty-faced sentry was produced who had heard nothing, seen nothing, knew nothing. But even the enormous quantity taken from dumps was not enough. Farms, houses, public buildings were ransacked. Shelving, forms, ladders, carts, partitions disappeared. In the Belgian hop-fields the British Army alone is said to have destroyed 1,000,000 hop-poles. Who shall blame them? Shall a soldier die of cold as well as of other things?

Wangling is known in peace-time. It is a necessity of civilization, where violence is difficult and costly. Scrounging was a necessity of war, for men must live. There was another Art that was more truly an Art than either of these. For it did not rest upon necessity, but was an ornament, a superfluity, a creative effort of the mind. This was the Art of Winning. It may be defined as

Stealing. More fully, it was the Art of obtaining that which one had no right to, for the sake of obtaining it, for the joy of possession.

Some say that it arose from taking millions of decent civilian people and planking them down upon battlefields from which the last sign of decency had disappeared, in a war so bloody and so endlessly long that the issue of it was beyond imagining. Some say it was simply the primeval joy of loot, ever present in man, and bursting out from time to time in Tudor or Elizabethan Filibuster, in Georgian Colonists, or Victorian Journalist .

As the War went on the contagion spread. Decent Flemish and Picard girls, with no particular tenderness for any one man, possessed glazed cases containing the badges of every unit in the B.E.F. Decent English boys conveyed or sent home every sort of appliance, equipment, projectile, arm—not one of which they had obtained by personal combat, but which they had found lying about and appropriated.

R. H. Mottram.

MORALE

June, 1917. All day, the Lord and I talked with no end of people of all sorts of rank, and always the same story. The fighting army (i.e. the younger men) are tired and depressed; the women are ditto; be careful.

I talked with Laguiche and his staff, with Boisveedy's staff, with infantry officers, with civilians—always the same story. Also Dun-cannon talking to everyone, finds the same.

Back to Wesserling to lunch with General Boyer. I had a long talk with him again, and with his Chief of Staff, and again got exactly the same impressions. Some success must be obtained to keep the French in.

Sir Henry Wilson.

All countries engaged in the war had periods of widespread mutiny, a fact which should be noticed and recorded, not hushed up. It took them all differently, according to their national characteristics. With Germany it was a continuous filtering-through of individuals or small parties who very logically concluded that they would be better off as prisoners in British hands than as combatants. In France, more spectacular defiance of orders paralysed initiative on two notable occasions. In Russia, the slow awakening of the peasant had the well-known results. In Italy it was a continuous corruption and lassitude that left the troops in the line provisioned with chestnut flour only. With the British, as might be expected, it occurred at the great base camp at Etaples, over some rumoured disagreement with the police. I never knew the truth, and perhaps no one does. For some days a great docile mob walked about the streets completely out of hand, relatively harmless, and eventually returning to camp to be fed. Shortly after, the miserable failure of an offensive was brought to a close. But the effect was permanent. From this time there developed a new spirit of taking care of one's self among the men, which ended, in late 1918, in few rifles being fired, and would, in a few more weeks, have meant the cessation of the War, by the front line not refusing but quietly omitting to do duty. The Armistice came just in time.

R. H. Mottram.

THE CRYSTAL BALL

May. It was a marvellously clear day. The visibility was perfect. We were flying east of Ypres and the Archie shells which burst around were not uncomfortably near. Looking round the sky I could see no other planes to worry about, and glanced downwards towards the ground. What I saw almost took my breath away.

Straight below—although we were three miles east of the trench-lines—lay the silver ruins of old Ypres, its stagnant moat and the stretching canals running ribbons across the country. Ahead was the coast of France and Belgium, with its yellow fringe of sandy foreshore. So close that it looked preposterous was Ostend, while farther inland lay Bruges. To the right front the yellow fringe ran north for miles to the islands off the Dutch and German coasts. To the left front was the real wonder. There England lay, with that comforting shallow of green sea mirroring between. Her white cliffs stood out in prominence and the land swept away from the cliffs to right and left. To the left, dimly seen, lay the Isle of Wight ; to the right the land ran out in a curving sweep around the Forelands before nestling back into the Thames estuary, where it was lost in the haze which extended from Gravesend Londonwards. In the Channel a convoy of ships moved over the sea, a tiny, black destroyer foaming ahead of them in wide curves.

The crack of a shell close behind us made me turn quickly. To the south the fighting line lay smeared across the fair face of France like the trail of a giant snail. Near Soissons the smoke of a continuous barrage mingled with the dark haze which lay below the sun-line and obscured the view beyond. Continuing the turn in a circle I swept the sky. There were no enemy aircraft to be seen. I checked our height. We were at ten thousand feet. We must have viewed the geometrical limit of vision, the distance at which a straight line makes tangent with the round earth. It struck me as curious how the more distant places—the islands of Borkum, Merkel and Vlissengen, the Isle of Wight and the North Foreland—appeared tilted up at an angle, while the shipping in the Channel looked as though it was sailing in the sky. We felt as though we were flying in the centre of a huge balloon with the sky and sea and earth painted on the outside of its transparent but all-enclosing sphere.

The patrol time was over and we were free to return to the aerodrome. Yet we lingered awhile, attracted by the splendour of the vision. Such a scene is the privilege of the airman alone. It is worth while having flown to have seen it. But unfortunately, such visibility is infrequent. Reluctantly I shut the engine off and glided slowly westward. Even Archie did not consider us worthy of further attention, or perhaps our solitary, silent glide escaped his notice. And as we glided west we saw the French coastline from Dunkerque to Le Havre, with Calais and Boulogne standing out unnaturally close.

Except for the destroyers and shipping moving in the Channel, the shell smoke drifting south near Soissons, and our idly turning propeller, the whole world was somnolent. Even Ypres was left alone, unshelled, a silent testimony to the inhumanity of war. Down, through thousands of feet, we glided towards the little aerodrome that lay just beyond the field of slowly-ripening corn. Down, to a second breakfast and a host of unbelievers who thought that we had dreamed, or that we romanced, about the length of visibility.

Captain Norman Macmillan (R.F.C.).

MESSINES

The battle of Messines, which won for the British the ill-omened Ypres Salient, began with the explosion of huge mines tunnelled beneath the enemy lines. The surprise and havoc caused by these explosions, accompanied by an intense bombardment, gave the British the Wytschaete-Messines Ridge with a minimum of losses.

7th June. The trench was newly dug somewhere on the hill and nowhere more than 4½ feet deep. We looked like getting a thrashing when the show commenced. The attack was to be preceded by the explosion of the mine. There in the bowels of the earth after many months of preparation, tunnelling, and counter-tunnelling by the enemy, an unprecedented amount of explosive had been buried and the effects of the detonation of such an immense charge were uncertain. We might all be involved. In any case our trenches might close in, and, to evade that possibility, we were ordered to lie out on top for the event.

The night was clear ; the guns were silent. Ever and anon an enemy Véry light went up from his line and spread a lurid glare over the scene. Those hours of waiting were hardly bearable. At last the first streaks of dawn showed in the sky, and whispered orders sent us to our positions a few yards in front of the trench. The last few minutes dragged with relentless slowness ; each second seemed an hour, each minute an eternity. The greyness of a new day now suffused the sky. I felt a tremor of fear run through my body ; the silence of the grave seemed to enfold the whole world. With a sharp report an enemy rocket began to mount towards the heavens. A voice behind cried " *Now !* " It was the hour, and that last enemy light never burst upon the day. The ground began to rock and I felt my body carried up and down as by the waves of the sea. In front the earth opened and a large black mass was carried to the sky on pillars of fire, and there seemed to remain suspended for some seconds while the awful red glare lit up the surrounding desolation.   No sound came.   I had been expecting a noise from the mine so tremendous as to be unbearable.   For a brief space all was silent, as though we had been too close to hear and the sound had leapt over us like some immense wave.   A line of men rose from the ground a few yards in front and advanced towards the upheaval, their helmets silhouetted and bayonets glinting in the redness of that unearthly dawn.   I saw no more.

We hurled ourselves back to the trench.   And then there was a tremendous roar and a tearing across the skies above us, as the barrage commenced with unerring accuracy.   It was as though a door had been suddenly flung open.   The skies behind our lines were lit by the flashes of many thousand guns, and above the booming din of the artillery came the rasping rattle of the Vickers guns pouring a continuous stream of lead over into the enemy's lines.   Never before, surely, had there been such a bombardment, and I shuddered for those unfortunates caught in that storm of death.

E. N. Gladden (11th *Northumberland Fusiliers*).

FIRST QUARTERMASTER-GENERAL

THE only touch of brightness in the lofty room was the pale blue of the walls, on which square patches, where pictures had hung, were not yet faded.

Major-General Schieffenzahn sat at work in a blue civilian jacket, and his front view was most impressive : a straight tall forehead over a pair of small grey eyes, the manifest nose of an autocrat, beneath it a moustache trimmed in the English manner, a shrewd, subtle mouth, the whole face set squarely upon a majestic double chin above the red collar of the General Staff. Broad-shouldered and tall, he sat enthroned at his writing-table, looking quickly through some newspapers, and marking them in blue and red pencil. But seen in profile, from near the great tiled stove, his appearance was far less imposing : the whole magnificent effect was strangely and sadly marred. He had the sagging cheeks of an old woman, his shoulders were too round, and from the oval outline of the weak, receding curves of chin and forehead the nose stood out sharply like the beak of a parrot, with two ominous wrinkles at the nostrils and the bridge deeply marked by the spectacles he wore for writing. And when he got up, as he did now—to put a sheet of paper covered with bluish writing on a pile of other such sheets—his appearance seemed to shrink. His legs in their black red-striped trousers were too short, and he had small hands and feet, so that although he could pass for a giant when seated, when standing he was revealed as no taller than a man of average height.

The public knew little of Albert Schieffenzahn but what was conveyed in phrases such as " our illustrious colleague . . ." or " our devoted comrade-in-arms . . ." followed by a certain famous name. It was, in fact, the truth that in that cropped skull was the directing brain of the whole area between the Baltic and the Carpathians. It was not, indeed, a mind that worked in darting flashes of inspiration ; it was far more like a brightly lit Central Exchange in which consciousness, judgment, and purpose were organized and controlled.   Behind that brow of his was a vast system of ordered knowledge.   Whether it had been decided to erect a new depot, or hospital, or lay out a new road or field-railway, he would make the scheme his own and ponder over it with loving care.   He had the constructive imagination of the artist in planning and carrying out great works.

His creative will was embodied and made manifest in that land. Not a single soldier's club or cinema was started, not a plank was laid for a munition depot, without his consent.   The railways in his area, their time-tables, their carrying capacity, their engines and rolling-stock, moved in his mind like the threads in the action of a play.   If any new task were laid upon him, he calmly called up such of the resources of his mighty brain as were needed to effect it.   In the first nine months of the War he had carried out the transport of troops, the organization of a complete system of civil government, though when he first took it in hand he knew nothing but the strength and position of the fortresses, Army Corps, Lines of Communication, and strategic railways.

Suddenly, with unimaginable comprehensiveness and speed, the whole country took shape in his mind : the forests and plains, the nature of the soil, the mineral resources, and the factories.   He summoned all manner of experts, who were ordered to lay before him statistics and plans from which he could deduce the possibilities of development in each area.   Then he perplexed these pundits with questions which showed that though he knew much less than they, he had a far deeper insight into all the districts and their several needs.   A new currency must be introduced ; he introduced it.   A system of savings-banks had to be established throughout the land according to the needs of urban or rural areas ; he established it. An entire system of education had to be set up, and it came into existence.   The sanitary administration of this war-stricken region was his especial work.   There rose up everywhere institutions for the " delousing " and disinfection of the population and their clothing, baths, isolation huts, and hospitals.   He enforced a system of travelling incinerators.   He introduced German book-shops in the towns, created field-libraries, and continually added to their stocks.   Newspapers in the seven languages of the country were needed, so paper factories had to be erected, and printing-presses soon were busy everywhere, printing in German, Russian, Lithuanian, Polish, Yiddish, Lettish, and Esthonian.

The distances in this part of the world were so great that he had already thought out and plotted on the map a scheme for the first regular aeroplane service of Europe, to supplement the communication between Libau and Brest-Litovsk ; then, with the machines he had to spare, he organized a systematic air-service, which was to ply in all weathers across his broad domain. The Operations Section of the Staff were indebted to him and his all-powerful imagination for the most illuminating hints on the minutest points ; but he took no less pains over the erection of mills on the faster rivers, for he wanted new water-power to provide the current for lighting his new constructions by electricity, and he controlled the close and far-flung meshes of the telephone-lines from the Front to his writing-table and thence right across Germany to Supreme Head-quarters.

The walls of his office were covered with huge tables, setting forth, as clearly as possible, the various nationalities of the occupied territory and the political parties of each one—indeed, he had extended his researches as far as Poland and even Russia proper. He had secret notes of the channels by which the various political groups might get into touch with the appropriate centres in Germany. By the agency of his Political Section he kept control over the intercourse between the population of the area and the civil authorities of the Empire, the Reichstag, the Government, and the political parties. Not a man of any importance could cross the frontier unless Albert Schieffenzahn had scrawled a " Yes " upon his application. Even the various religious bodies of the country, and their schools as well, felt his influence, in so far as he admitted, or (quite illegally) withheld, the money sent them from neutral countries for relief.

His colleagues worshipped him. In his husky, high-pitched voice, but always courteously, he gave his orders in the form of requests, or as if the suggestion had come from his subordinates and he was merely giving it expression. Numerous as was his Staff, he knew the trend of all their thoughts and the tastes and opinions of the " intellectuals " among them, while his eye rested unseen on the corrupt manœuvres of those who sought to enrich themselves, whether on a petty or a generous scale. He was remaking the country day by day, improving and modernizing it ; by ridding the land of weeds, testing suitable manures and seeds, by the encouragement of sheep-rearing and bee-keeping, by detailing parties of prisoners of war to provide extra labour, and by requisitioning boilers, machines, houses, and land.

The motive of his action may be stated in a word : he wanted this territory to be in a prosperous state when it came to be annexed to the German Empire after the War ; and he had already adapted the railway lines of his area to the German gauge. He was perfectly clear that the Germans were only just beginning to play their part in history : to his mind they were the nation chosen to rule and to create, and to fortify the breed of men. He had never spent a single hour in the west or in the south ; he therefore saw the people of those countries in the light of his reading, which was chosen, though quite unconsciously, to gratify his prejudices. At the present moment he was peacefully marking extracts from newspapers and from the reports of secret service agents which were circulated by the Foreign Office for the enlightenment of the uninitiated ; and he accepted as established fact reports that were solely designed to flatter the hopes of those who shared his views. For agents who dealt in unwelcome news soon fell into disfavour, and lost their employment ; they found themselves mysteriously recalled or transferred to the army.

In his work nothing troubled him so little as the wishes, views, and traditions of the population. He, Schieffenzahn, understood what was good for these gentry much better than they did themselves. They had to accept and carry out his edicts, even when they had no notion of their purpose. He looked on them as not yet of age, and in need of guidance, like the rank and file of the army, into whom he hammered his aims, his thoughts, and his political views, by means of his system of " patriotic instruction." It was for him to command ; and his was the responsibility. It was for them to obey, to follow and bow down. If they did not, they must be trodden underfoot. From a great height, as though from a captive balloon poised far above them, he looked down upon his realm, his towns, forests, fields, and scattered herds of men, and saw —nothing.

He said he had no need of honour, fame, or recognition ; power sufficed him. He enjoyed a cigar, good food, stories about Bismarck, his daily ride with only one or two companions, a drive in one of the Staff cars as far and as fast as possible, and cheerful and light conversation with his personal staff or his guests; and he enjoyed his measureless powers of work He hated opposition, independence of mind, laziness, the vast incompetence of human creatures; and remorselessly he hated disorder, sedition, the Western chatter about democracy, and the detestable Nihilistic revolution in the East.

Arnold Zweig.

MINERS

A WHISPERING wind sighed along the corridor by the sap-head—
the aching quiet before stand-to. Thousands of men in the Ypres
Magazine, the Prison, Asylum, Ramparts, and innumerable cellars,
were being detailed for their nightly labours. Soon the silent
road down to Potijze, past the château he could still dimly see
behind its mask of trunks, would echo with the clank of fatigue-
parties.

The ground rocked and stirred pleasantly like a gently disturbed
hammock. No sound of any explosion came to the little dug-out,
but the gallery had been blown. Bradshaw felt torn between a
savage desire to hear that dozens of Germans had been killed and a
hope that they'd discovered our intentions and cleared out of harm's
way. You never knew; Jerry might have had a mine right under
them at that moment.

White hurried along the gloomy trench; bent down to lift up
their dug-out flap.

"Ay, quick! There's two men in t' sap, deead!"

They rushed to the sap-head. Two miners lay at the foot of the
steps, one slightly moving. After a tremendous tussle they dragged
the nearer one up the narrow entrance and laid him along the communication trench duckboards.

"Try and get him round, Ernie."

Bradshaw raced down the steps again; found three more sappers
lying in their death sleep, facing the entrance they had been trying
to reach before being overcome by gases. He bent to lift the second
man; a dead, immovable weight. He felt helpless; groaned at the
weakness brought on by months of steady underfeeding. Several
small glass tubes containing oxygen tinkled in his iron ration pocket;
the M.O. had issued them at one of his lectures. He pulled them
out, looked despairingly for somewhere to crack them; then crushed
them in his palms, holding cupped hands to the insensible man's

432

nostrils. Up the stairs again, Bagnall, jubilation in his voice, cried :

" Ah've getten him breathin' agean, Dick ! "

" There's half a dozen more down there. . . . Where is everybody ? "

Only White there, who dare not leave his post. Company headquarters, usually busy with one or two officers, batmen, or signallers, was deserted. Bradshaw adjusted his respirator, and, remembering far back that the heaviest man could be carried by one of slighter build, descended light-headedly again : sinking, as if in water. Behind him followed Bagnall.

" Get back, Ernie . . . make sure of one."

Bradshaw strove ineffectually to lift the prostrate miner, but the bad air already in him made his efforts, in the confined space, feebler than ever. He flopped back dizzily on the bottom step, a warning instinct whispering caution. He turned and crawled gingerly up the endless steps, senses going.

One . . .

Two . . .

Three . . .

He'd never do it !

Four . . .

Five . . .

He collapsed limply against putteed legs.

Midnight in the château aid post. All that Bradshaw remembered of getting out of the sap was of Jem Fletcher, the M.O.'s big assistant, applying pressure with his huge palms to Bradshaw's stomach in an attempt to squeeze out the gases, and Bagnall standing by saying pathetically from a great distance :

" Dick ! Dick ! . . . He's aw reet, isn't he ? "

Now he lay back on a stretcher, when he should have been up in West Lane. An oil lamp and two candles flooded the room with yellow light. Two Jocks came in, gasping and coughing ; one a sergeant who cursed the other for whimpering. They'd been badly gassed ; Jerry was soaking their front with it. Gun-fire vibrated through the walls.

Bradshaw was so little in tune with the war that speculation on the outcome of the sap incident never entered his head. He learnt the next day that the blow, being unattended by any surface upheaval, had trapped all the " after damp," and the noxious gases, seeking an outlet, had filled the sap before the miners could reach the trench.

By the time the reviving oxygen apparatus arrived, all the men save the one Bagnall had saved were dead.   The M.O. told Bradshaw that box respirators were useless against " after damp."

W. V. Tilsley.

R.F.C. MESS

Not many weeks passed before that invitation came, and on the appointed day, at dusk, up rolled a sumptuous Crossley. Skene left his section and his conscience to " Uncle," and went spinning over the Route Nationale, to where, carefully placed far from church, windmill, railway or main road, the aerodrome was spread on un-cultivated clover, dotted with marquees, and striped with camouflage. His host explained : " We're such a small mess at the Section, I thought you'd rather come here ! " Waiting for the offensive, five squadrons and a balloon school were jammed together. The great hangars and workshops, the tenders, cars, cycles coming and going reminded Skene of a goods station. But no railway ever displayed such costly efficiency. He was taken to a marquee where a gramo-phone was being accompanied on the piano, and two smooth-faced schoolboys were playing diabolo. They all seemed schoolboys. Skene and the Doctor and the Quartermaster were the only men in the place over thirty. Yes, and the tragedy of that ! There was an atmosphere of waiting. An orderly fixed a blue-pencilled list to the tent-pole. And one by one, these pale, slim boys, with their blue-circled eyes, went up and looked at it. Curiously matter-of-fact and fatalistic that quiet procession ! Then those who were playing diabolo began again, those who were drinking drained their glasses, and ordered another; a new record was set on the gramophone. " List of patrols for to-morrow ! " said Skene's host, Carruthers of the balloon. They went in to dinner.

R. H. Mottram.

ARMENTIÈRES

THE English attacks in the summer of 1917 exasperated the German gunners who believed the town full of troops. . . . One July night, when the British were attacking at Ypres, several thousand gas-shells fell into Armentières. While the factories were still flaming in the shattered town, blinded women were dying, spitting blood. The motor ambulances have now carried off the last of the weavers, defeated, torn with wounds or scorched with gas.

The town is now deserted. The only noise in the houses is the clatter of the shutter which the wind shakes against the broken windows. The flutter of the last shreds of curtains adds a ripple of white bunting to the streets. Among the shell-smashed brickwork, in a heap of stained plaster, stands an iron skeleton. The iron frame of a staircase raises its arabesques over the crumbled relic of a burned-out house. The dwellings of the rich have been cast down on to those of the poor. The humility of suffering hangs over this broken town. The workers' dwellings, constructed in colonies, all built as alike as the slices of a loaf, are now varied. Those which have been pierced by shells display the deep rose of the brick, those which have been burned have wide shadows over the openings where the fire has passed. . . .

Notice boards in those districts still open to the troops read:

HAVE YOU GOT IT?
YOUR BOX RESPIRATOR
IN THE ALERT POSITION

for every soldier who passes through the town must wear his gas mask fixed on his chest like a baby's bib, so that he has only to lift it to cover his mouth.

The war has grown old on this country-side which has known it from its earliest days. The notices DRINKING WATER on metal signs are oxidized, scarcely legible.　Years of rust already eat them up.

Over the streets where so long the steps of workers have echoed, now hangs a vast silence broken by the reports of guns.　The gunner smashes the house, the wind and rain carry on the destruction.　The daily battle to stop up the holes in the walls has suddenly ceased. . . . This empty town is to-day handed over to shell-fire and bad weather ; and to stand deserted through a rainy winter will do it as much damage as a bombardment.

Pierre Hamp.

THE BULGAR

4th August. Our first impressions, formed in Serbia in 1915, were that the Bulgar was little better than an uncivilized savage, who lived for a lust of blood, and would delight in torturing his enemy for the pure joy of seeing him writhe. We heard terrible stories of the tortures inflicted on French soldiers who fell into their hands, and I have with my own eyes seen a Bulgar thrust his bayonet through an unarmed British soldier, who, cut off from his comrades, was offering to surrender.

The more we have seen of the Bulgar soldier, however, the more we have come into the way of thinking that he is not such a bad sort of fellow after all, and that he will play the game as long as his opponent plays the game too. Of the British he has no instinctive dislike. I am perfectly sure that, given the choice, individually, he would much prefer to fight with us than against us, especially after sampling the doubtful pleasures of German comradeship, during these many months of war. The Germans have done their best to instil a feeling of hatred for us in his mind, but apparently, with not quite so much success as they desire.

It is quite the Teutonic way to tell the less "kultured" Bulgar that horrible treatment awaits him at the hands of the British should he fall into our hands, either voluntarily or involuntarily. One deserter, who came in, assured us that he had been told he would be eaten alive.

" That is why you came across ? " questioned our Intelligence officer, cynically.

" I didn't believe it," replied the deserter.

In the struma fighting throughout the Bulgar has, up to the present, revealed a sporting quality with which few people, who do not know him, would credit him. The most striking instance of this was given at the Battle of Yenikoj after a fiercely delivered counter-attack had temporarily given the enemy a slight footing at the far end of the village. Both sides were engaged in the invigorating pastime of pouring "rapid" into each other at a distance of 100 yards or so, when three of our men, observing that three wounded comrades were lying in the open between the Bulgars and ourselves, dashed over the top in order to bring them in. The Bulgar fire on the particular part of the line where this very gallant deed was being performed, immediately ceased, though it continued in every other part, with the result that the three wounded men were safely brought in to our line, and their rescuers were untouched. It was an incident that revealed the Bulgar in a different light to that which many had previously considered him in. But this is by no means an isolated instance of the Bulgar's sporting qualities. I remember being on outpost duty at Topalova, in front of which a troop of Yeomanry were pursuing their task of keeping the Bulgar patrols in check. Several hundred yards in front lay Prosenik, a once flourishing town on the railway, which was then still in the enemy's possession. The troop of cavalry had dismounted when an unexpected Bulgar H.E. fell among the horses, and one frightened animal dashed away in a dead line for Prosenik. A trooper promptly jumped on to his horse and galloped after the runaway. So exciting went the chase that in a few seconds our infantry were following it from their parapets, standing up in full view of any wily Bulgar sniper who might be waiting for the opportunity of an exposed head. On dashed the runaway, the trooper still following it up, and then we realized that the Bulgar garrison of Prosenik had followed our example and was breathlessly following the race. It was a strange spectacle—Bulgar and British standing up in full view of each other, watching a runaway horse. At length the trooper headed the animal back towards our own lines, and returned with his captive without a single shot having been fired at him.

"The Bulgar is a humorous devil," is a remark one often hears passed, and it is certain that he possesses a deal greater sense of humour than his friend, the Bosche. There was rather a rage for some weeks on the part of ourselves, as well as the Bulgars, to post up (during expeditions into opposing territory) little messages for the edification of enterprising patrols on either side. I forget what the particular message was that I have in mind (they were legion), but on the day following its posting, pinned to the identical tree on which our message had been fixed, was the reply, and a P.S. which read, "For goodness' sake, Englishmen, write in English next time. Your French is awful." Needless to say, we rarely racked our mental French vocabulary after this in composing our letters to the enemy.

When told in one message from us that any Bulgar who would like to look us up would be welcomed and given plenty of bread (a subtle invitation in view of the enemy's reported shortage of bread), a reply was sent to the effect that any Britisher who thought of doing likewise would be warmly welcomed and that they had enough bread to feed all who came across, including the Commandant of —— (the officer who signed our original message). The Bulgars invariably commenced their message with the prefix "Noble English-men," and often reproached us for having invaded their "peaceful Macedonian soil." A subtle but amusing reference to Ireland was frequently included. But one day came a blood-curdling message to the effect that every loyal and true Bulgar's sole ambition was to plunge his bayonet deep in the breast of the hated British, and was so unlike our hitherto cordial exchange of letters that we unanimously ascribed it to a Teutonic hand. And I fancy we were not erring.

One day, a scratch football match was in progress behind our line, and well within view and range of the enemy guns, and it certainly was somewhat surprising that not a single shell came over to interrupt our game. It was in consequence of this forbearance on the part of our friends over the way that a conscientious O.C. Company, seeking an opportunity to fill up a sleepy hour by improving the bearing of his company by an hour's drill, paraded his company in as unexposed a spot as he could find and commenced arm drill. A shrapnel shell quickly dissipated the idea that this could be indulged in with impunity (to the delight of the whole company), and the following day a patrol discovered a message worded, as near as I can recollect—"We like to see you playing football, and we shall not shell you while you are playing football, and we are if we are going to watch you doing company drill."

One unfortunate (or fortunate) Bulgarian was brought in on one occasion with a broken leg, which our M.O. tended with the utmost care. The man merely shrugged his broad shoulders at each agonizing wrench, and uttered no complaint at the terrible pain he must have been suffering. Our interpreter was informed by the poor devil that the Bulgar doctor would have unhesitatingly cut the leg off above the knee instead of saving the leg. In gratitude he tore off a tunic button and pressed it on the M.O. as a souvenir.

It was just before Barakli Dzuma fell to the British that a deserter came in and greeted the officer, to whom he was conducted, with a swarthy smile, and the words, " English shelling at Barakli Dzuma very good, very nice. Me fed up."

While, on another occasion (though I cannot honestly vouch for the truth of this story), dawn revealed outside the barbed wire entanglements a Bulgar officer and his servant, the latter carrying the officer's kit and valise, being loth that his master should suffer any discomfort in his captivity.

One message I recollect—evidently of Hunnish origin—asked us why we persisted in declaring we were fighting for the liberties of small nations when we " made slaves of the Irish." This message, directed to our Irish Regiment, found its way to its destination, and as one might imagine, evoked considerable amusement among the sons of Erin who read it.

Whenever the Bulgar succeeded in taking any British in raids or patrol encounters, he invariably let us know how his prisoners were progressing. One over-bold British patrol one night walked into a Bulgar trap and none returned to tell the tale. On the following day we discovered in our neutral letter-box a long message which ran as follows : " Noble Englishmen—The Privates —— and —— are wounded and are being well treated. We buried at Ko Moroto (a village near Demir Hissar.—A.) the Privates —— and ——. Come to us and we will treat you the same ? The Bulgarians." Really rather a good example of unintentional humour. We sent back a reply thanking them for the information, adding, " Have you heard about the fall of Baghdad ? You should be fighting on our side." We never received the answer to this, for the next day our " relief " was due and we went back from the outpost line for a " rest." I could relate many more instances of Bulgar sportsmanship, but those I have already told you will suffice to show that the Bulgar, on the whole, is not a bad sort of fellow. He is a plucky fighter, but unsteady in a violent bombardment. He is seen at his best in open warfare and in a counter-attack, and at his worst in the defence of a position. Big and swarthy, and generally bearded, he is a decidedly unpleasant-looking person to see coming towards you at a run with the bayonet, but one's luck must be absolutely " out " to be hit by a Bulgar bullet (unless it comes from a machine-gun), for our swarthy foes are probably the worst shots among the nations at war to-day.

Capt. A. Donovan Young (I.A.)

ESCAPE FROM THE TURKS

September. Every minute on the beach was dangerous in daylight, but it was absolutely necessary, before we embarked, to ballast our boat with stones from the shore. Before this task could be completed, a soldier with a rifle appeared from a house to the west—which we had thought deserted—and began to ask questions. We lost no time in arguing, but disarmed him, and tied him to a tree, where he remained quite passively, consoled by the gift of a gold lira. We heard afterwards that he was the advance man of a patrol of ten coming from Aianjik, and that when he reported what had happened motor-boats armed with machine-guns were sent out from Ineboli, Samsun, and Sinope to look for us. Just after sunrise everything was ready, and we pushed off. There were fourteen of us on board—seven Circassians, two Georgians, one Anatolian Turk, one Armenian, and three Englishmen. All our friends were Turkish subjects, and the fact that they represented four different races bore testimony to the universal unpopularity of the Ottoman government.

While we had been embarking, another felucca, somewhat bigger than ours, had been creeping along the coast from the west, and we decided to anticipate any attempt she might make to stop us. Accordingly, all the weapons were hidden while we quietly pulled alongside, when our friends suddenly jumped up and levelled their rifles, in true pirate fashion, at the crew of five. They were unarmed (except the captain, who had a pistol) and surrendered at once. The boat was on her way to Samsun with a cargo of Rumanian kerosene, and as she belonged to the enemy we decided to take both her and her crew with us. Two of the *arqadash* [comrades], and in the evening two more were placed on board as prize crew, while the captain and one of his men were transferred to our boat. Being escaping prisoners ourselves, we enjoyed having prisoners of our own, but it is doubtful whether the captured crew saw the humorous side of their position.

Both vessels now hoisted sail, and as a five-knot breeze was blowing from the east we decided to make for the Crimea, not for Trebizond, although it was risky to attempt to cross the treacherous Black Sea in so small a boat. Within a few minutes we were out of rifle range of the beach, and within a couple of hours must have been out of sight. There was no indication of any pursuit, and we felt pretty safe from interference by the Turkish authorities, while the chance of meeting a German submarine seemed remote. On the other hand, we hoped with any luck to meet a vessel belonging to the Allies, and we did not learn till afterwards that ships proceeding to or from Batum or Trebizond did not usually cross the Black Sea, but crept round the coast, for fear of submarines. A German submarine actually passed athwart our course a few days later.

Our chief anxiety was for our own boat. She was very old and had to be baled out frequently; the boom was badly sprung, and repairs to the sail and rigging were much overdue. Nevertheless, everything held fast, and we made excellent progress during the morning. The sea was rather rough, and several of our friends lay at the bottom of the boat throughout the day, refusing to eat or drink and calling upon Allah to relieve their misery. In the afternoon the wind dropped and rowing became necessary—an office which we made our prisoners undertake. In the evening we again had a breeze, and before sunset the blue mountains of Anatolia disappeared from view. We were not sorry to see the last of them. Strabo mentions that these mountains and those of the Crimea can be seen simultaneously from the deck of a ship, but we ourselves were over fifty hours out of sight of land.

Our only modern map of the Black Sea, printed in Turkish, had been confiscated at Gerze, but I had managed to retain a tiny map, on the scale of 200 miles to an inch, taken from the Public Schools Classical Atlas sent to Kastamuni from London under the Prisoners of War Book Scheme. It showed the Greek colonies 500 years before Christ, and therefore did not mark Sevastopol, but it told us that the Crimea was slightly west of north from the point where we embarked. When, however, the captain of the captured crew, who volunteered to navigate us to Sevastopol, was placed at the helm we found that he steered north-east, and some of the *arqadash* who had nautical experience insisted that this was the right course. With our limited knowledge of Turkish we did not understand the reasons they gave, and at first did not venture to interfere.

Our compasses had also been taken from us at Gerze, and by day we had only the sun to steer by : no easy matter, though calculations with a watch were somewhat simplified by the fact that it was the equinox. When night fell we were astonished to find that neither our friends nor any of the other boat's crew, not even the captain, had any idea of steering by the stars. They did not even know which was the north star. Some of them had been at sea all their lives, but only in craft which hugged the coast; at night, out of sight of land, they were completely lost. We determined to take control. With our limited supply of food and water it was essential that we should hit the Crimean peninsula, and after estimating as well as we could the distance we had already come to the north-east, we resolved to steer north-north-west, as near as we could judge it. There were loud protests from our friends, who had got it into their heads that if we went west of north we should reach Rumania and be captured by the Germans, but after a great deal of argument Tipton succeeded in winning their obedience. Having had sailing experience in the Mersey he was put in command, and the three of us kept watches to ensure that the helmsman stuck to the course we had laid down. Whether north-north-west would bring us to the Crimea time would show. There were several unknown factors— the currents, the boat's leeway, and her position when we changed course. We could only hope that our luck would not desert us in the last lap.

About midnight the wind dropped, and we had to row for the remainder of the night. Next morning we were again making good progress under a breeze from the north-east when the other boat began to make signals of distress, and we at once lowered our sail and rowed to her assistance. As we drew alongside, our three prisoners aboard her were making as much hullabaloo as if she were sinking, but the trouble was only a broken rudder. Her captain did not consider it possible to make a new one or to steer her with an oar, and to save a long argument we decided to abandon one of the two vessels. The captured boat was much the better of the two, but as it was found impossible to fit our rudder in her stern-post we decided to take everybody along in our boat and to appropriate her boom. The change was duly carried out, and our old boom thrown overboard. Several bags of grain and flour and a keg containing about two gallons of fresh water were also transhipped, together with a pump, which saved us the labour of baling. The other boat, with her cargo of kerosene, was left to her fate, and there was little doubt that she would founder before long.

Our own boat now carried nineteen persons, and most of the ballast was thrown overboard. The wind again dropped, and our speed for the rest of the day did not exceed two knots. Throughout the second night there was practically no wind at all, and the boat was rowed the whole time, most of the work being done by our prisoners. Next day, the third of the voyage, there was no improvement in the weather, and the rowing continued. The Black Sea, so called by the Turks, was living up to its earlier Greek name only too successfully

Our bread had become mouldy, and in the evening some maize flour taken from the captured boat was boiled with sea-water into a sort of porridge, on a fire made with our own boat's floorboards, resting on what was left of the stone ballast. Salt water is all right, at a pinch, for boiling food in, and the concoction was much preferred to the bread, although it did not go very far towards removing the pangs of hunger. We were also able to distribute a few malted-milk tablets that we had reserved for the voyage, but they had agglomerated into a mass as hard as rock, and several teeth were broken in the effort to gnaw nourishment from it.

We had enough flour to ward off starvation for several days, but the water-supply gave anxiety. By the third evening the tin, the keg transferred from the other boat, two of the three water-bottles and the air-cushion were all empty. The cask which remained would only provide a pint and a quarter for each person, and we decided to introduce a strict ration system which would make the supply last for three days more.

Just as it was getting dark on this third day we sighted to the north-west what looked like a line of mountains, but we could not be absolutely certain they were not clouds, and night fell before we could get near enough to resolve our doubts. A good breeze sprang up at seven o'clock and we made excellent progress until 3 a.m., when the wind again dropped and rowing was resumed.

At dawn on the fourth day hope became certainty with the definite appearance of a line of hills on the north-west horizon. Our luck had held. The captured crew, who cherished an idea that they would be sent back to Turkey, and were quite as eager as any of us to land in Russia, redoubled their efforts at the oars, and everybody was given a good drink and the run—such as it was—of his teeth. The most excited people on board were the *arqadash*, who, although several hours must elapse before they could reach the shore, immediately began to don their bandoliers. We had some difficulty in convincing them that if we tried to land in Russia with too ostentatious a display of rifles and ammunition we might just possibly be mistaken for invaders.

Before long, houses were seen, and we steered for the nearest. At 12.30 p.m., after a voyage of three and a quarter days, and on the forty-ninth day after leaving Kastamuni, we grounded on the beach of a town which was evidently a watering-place, and which turned out to be Alupka, on the east coast of the Crimea, about thirty miles south-east of Sevastopol. It was virtually the nearest point in Russia to the place at which we had embarked, and our rough reckoning had not been far out. By the course we had followed our sea journey had covered about 250 miles. Apart from a few boats hugging the Anatolian or Crimean coast, we had seen no vessels of any sort. Quite possibly it was through steering north-east on the first day that we avoided the Turkish motor-boats sent out to look for us, just as by going east from Kastamuni we had eluded the pursuit on land.

Alupka is not a port, and there was no guard on the beach to question us, the arrival of a vessel being an unlooked-for event. In Kastamuni we had learned the Russian for " British prisoners," and we shouted out *Angliskie plennie* on approaching the shore, but as so often happens when an Englishman tries to speak the language of the country he is visiting, the reply came in perfect English, from a man bathing in the sea.

Opposite the point at which we disembarked were the municipal baths. Ever since leaving Kastamuni, what we had been looking forward to most eagerly was not good food or drink, linen sheets or European society, but a *hot bath*, and within half an hour of landing we were lying in the first we had known for seven weeks, and had discarded for ever our filthy rags and tattered boots.

E. H. Keeling.

BEAUTY IN DESOLATION: HERMIES

21st Aug. I wonder whether God has created this weather to show a more transcending mercy than heretofore, that a perfect day of sun can coincide with war and decide a beauty of its own. Last night and this morning !

After all, there rests some pleasure in life when two such harmonies of lovely colour and light float into vision and raise an enchanting face. The hollow road runs north and south, so that the rising sun measures off a gradation of gleam and shadow on the one side and the setting on the other. Two ladders of descending and ascending loveliness ! Below the sun-line a misty grey rounds off the edges of the corners, dwells in the hollows, and lingers on the road. The shed supports are bi-coloured—gold and pearl— and the stacks of boards, wire, iron, draw on the earthen wall a clearly outlined shadow, like an Assyrian picture. Then, above the line, what an overflow of dancing light ! Light in the earth shadow and the grass, light in the fields and broad sky so that the infinite seems to have descended to earth and embraced in a caress as infinite.

A khaki-clad officer comes down, half in shadow, half in sun. His feet move in a subdued twilight, while his head and shoulders are bathed in the gold. Cloverheads and thistles, in silhouette yet illuminated, hang drowsily their heads, uncertain of life and uncertain of light, mingling leaf and flower in a warm grey which gives a finer beauty to the dreamy azure overhead.

Then, last night, what a glory of haunting illumination was there ! The clouds had passed in a flurry of rose from the sky and left a subtle gradation of pure colour from zenith to horizon, hovering and smiling in a thousand shimmering lights. It passed from the loveliest purple to a warm orange, through lilac, pale turquoise, amethyst, rose, pearl-grey, lemon, and gold, like one of those evening

448

skies Stott paints to bathe an ordinary group of men or animals in a mysterious half-light, not dream and yet not reality.

Shadows slept in the road, blue as a sunlit sea and transparent as fine glass; above them the sun laid a long tapestry of orange, against which the grass tufts told startlingly. Men walking below had face and breast illuminated crudely, like figures in an impressionistic fresco—yellow features, outlined with dark-blue shadow. Yet with that, depth was in the air, a bottomless sea of beauty, where all thought of pain and yearning swam away in infinite peace, and the only reality of life was a sinking in it, a fortunate shipwreck, and the abiding truth came as vision, the chaste vision of an infinite harmony.

Hugh Quigley (12th Royal Scots).

THIRD YPRES

The third battle of Ypres was fought to secure the Armentières-Dixmude Ridge. It opened on June 7 and the first attack carried Messines. The second attack started on July 31 and the battle culminated in the capture of the Passchendaele Ridge on November 4.

WARNINGS

. . . As we could make no headway against Gough's determination to sink his Army in a bottomless bog, we took up the question with G.H.Q., but with no greater success. We pointed out that the surface soil was of small depth, that below it lay a bed of clay, that much of the ground we were to attack over had at one time or another been reclaimed from the sea, and that, bearing these points in mind, a bombardment would convert it into a bog. That this was likely was proved by the fact that in peace time the farmers were heavily fined if they did not keep their dikes and culverts clear. We pleaded eloquently enough, but we might just as well have appealed to a brick wall. . . .

. . . On the 7th (July) counter-battery work began, and on the 16th, the initial bombardment was opened. As ground was our supreme problem, Hotblack, determining to keep check on its destruction, arranged with the R.F.C. to have daily aeroplane photographs taken of the entire front over which tanks would eventually advance. From these, as the drainage system was more and more destroyed, he worked out the spread of the swamp areas. Then he transferred this information to a large-scale map, which we realistically called the " Swamp Map," and the Brigade Reconnaissance Officers also transferred it to plasticine models (raised maps) of the eventual battlefield. A copy of each day's " Swamp Map " was sent to G.H.Q., until we were instructed to discontinue sending them. Yet, strange to say, this in no way prevented these maps growing bluer and bluer, for blue was the colour used to denote the boggy areas.

Maj.-Gen. J. F. C. Fuller (Tank Corps).

FORECAST

July 30. Before this reaches you we shall have attacked again, the most important attack and, indeed, the only one that now matters for this year's fighting on this theatre. It is impossible to forecast the result. The only thing that is certain, is that most unfortunate of all things, a big casualty list. All the preparations are, I think, as good and as well advanced as those of our other two big attacks this year, and if we get as much success in this as in the others, great things will happen. My one fear is the weather. We have had most carefully prepared statistics of previous years—there are records of eighty years to refer to—and I do not think that we can hope for more than a fortnight, or at the best, three weeks of really fine weather. There has been a good deal of pretty hot discussion, almost controversy, as regards the time of attack.

We cannot hope for a surprise; our preparations must have been seen, and even if not, our bombardment must have warned the Germans, and no doubt they are already moving up troops towards our battle area. I had urged D.H. to attack on these grounds some days ago in spite of the fact that our preparations were not fully completed; it was a choice of evils. The Army Commanders wanted more time; the last conference was definitely heated. The Army Commanders pressed for delay; D.H. wanted the attack to go on at once, and in the end he accepted the Army Commanders' view. He could, indeed, do nothing else, for they have to carry out the job.

Brig.-Gen. John Charteris.

WARNINGS JUSTIFIED

I have been told that the gigantic clap of sound produced by the simultaneous discharge of two or three thousand guns at zero that morning was a phenomenon never to be forgotten by those who heard it. But I do not remember hearing it at all. Enclosed in a vibrating box of steel, the subdued throbbing of my engine drowned even this apocalyptic crash. And this effect of silence—for we were all so accustomed to the local noise of our machinery that it may be said we were unconscious of it—made yet more wonderful the really astounding display of pyrotechnics which in a second blazed up around the whole arc of the salient. At 3.49 a.m., when I looked at my clock for the last time, the night was dark and misty and very still. Heavier clouds had rolled up, and there was no sign of the dawn. Only the pistol lights still soared and died away about us. Precisely at 3.50 two or three thousand shells of every calibre burst virtually together in two great semicircles on or over the enemy's first and second lines—ten miles or so of sudden flame and horror. A few hundred yards in front of our leading tank the very earth seemed to erupt. It spouted fire and fragments like a volcano. The mist which hung over the trenches in the little valley was rent to tatters in a blaze of orange light, while hundreds of shrapnel-burst sparkled above, and the drums of thermit poured down their molten oil like burning rain. Far behind, where the 9·2 barrage fell along the crown of the ridge, great tongues of flame leapt and wavered in volumes of scarlet smoke. And from out of this instantaneous inferno arose strings of green and crimson rockets—the S.O.S. calls of the enemy. It was the apotheosis of the artillery barrage, although no one suspected it then : the greatest blast of gun-fire ever concentrated at once on any battlefield, and, so far at least as the British Army was concerned, the last of its kind. The next offensive battle, at Cambrai, was to inaugurate a new order of things.

From Hill Top, or Frascati, this great curve of spouting fire must have been a magnificent spectacle, and the sudden shattering noise of it appalling ; and I was so fascinated by the small part of it which I could see that I forgot entirely to start the tank. The whole of my crew was crowded forward behind the driver and myself, craning over our shoulders to watch through the flaps such a display of fireworks as they had never dreamed of. Realizing suddenly that the interval between G 46 and the tank in front was increasing I touched Johnstone on the arm ; and the roar of the engine deepened as, with a slight jerk, we also began to move. Already the glare of the bursting shells, still raining down upon the zero line, was dulled by a pall of smoke and dust. The spectacular glory of the barrage was at an end. Within a few seconds it was due to lift forward at a rate of a hundred yards every four minutes. But it still showed as a flickering haze of light across our front; and against this one could see the long line of tanks moving downward to Forward Cottage, about which point groups of dark figures were standing on the parapets or walking carelessly forward across Admiral's Road towards the German trenches.

It seemed a long time before G 46 reached these trenches. There were, in fact, continual stoppages as the tanks in front struggled to find a crossing in the narrow gap between Hampshire and Canadian farms. At length, after a particularly long halt, I swung out of the line to the right to make, if possible, a passage for myself. We were then somewhere in the middle of No Man's Land. Dawn had broken,—a miserable grey twilight behind heavy clouds; and the creeping barrage, with its following infantry, was already far up the ridge. It was when we drew up to the German front line that the cause of these irritating delays became painfully obvious. We had anticipated difficulties here, but the reality was worse than anything that I, for one, had imagined. The front line was not merely obliterated: it had been scorched and pulverized as if by an earthquake, stamped flat and heaved up again, caught as it fell and blown all ways; and when the four minutes' blast of destruction moved on, was left dissolved into its elements, heaped in fantastic mounds of mud, or excavated into crumbling pits already half-full of water. There cannot have been a live man left in it. At our point of crossing there was nothing to be seen which remotely resembled a trench: before us yawned a deep muddy gulf, out of whose slimy sides obtruded fragments of splintered timber, broken slabs of concrete, and several human legs clothed in German half-boots. Immediately beyond, a veritable lagoon, fringed by a few stripped and blackened willow-stumps, marked the site of Hampshire Farm. Infantry were strolling about here in a very casual manner, smoking, eating, and ferreting for souvenirs. The battle seemed a long way off. The morning was so dark, and the murk of mist and smoke so thick upon the ridge, that one could see only a few hundred yards in front. I was determined not to get ditched so early in the day if I could avoid it; and for five or ten minutes we hung over this black chasm, backing, swinging, nosing about in vain for a likely crossing. We were rather too much to the right of our proper track, but the ground everywhere was so broken and treacherous that there was little choice. We had made several tentative efforts, but had shied each time at the prospect of crumbling and slithery mud-heaps in front of us; and I was about to leave the tank to search for a crossing place myself when Kessel unexpectedly appeared outside. With his help we got over, at a point where some revetting-stakes and wire still survived, holding the soil together and providing a quasi-stable surface for the tracks to grip. . . . The great trouble at first was to find our right direction, for all our famous groups of trees were still invisible, and Kitchener's Wood was veiled completely by the smoke and dust of the barrage. The German trenches which we had studied on the map were blown to pieces and unrecognizable. One could see nothing anywhere, in fact, but a brown waste of mud blasted into ridges and hollows like a frozen sea, littered with debris, and melting on all hands into the prevailing haze. The gradient of the ridge was too slight to be a guide under the circumstances; my compass was chasing its tail and behaving generally as if it was drunk; and, after we had swung a dozen times to avoid the more dangerous craters that lay in our way, we might have been heading in almost any direction. It was therefore with some relief that Kessel and I detected presently, in the smoky distance, a familiar object that both of us, like Captain Reece's washerwoman, long had loved from afar. This was Lone Tree—a rotund bushy shrub near Kultur Farm, whose exceeding merit it was to look the same from every point of view. It was unmistakable; and now, happily preserved amid the universal ruin, it still stood, a little battered and entirely denuded of foliage, as a signpost on the way. Very shortly after, the ragged tree-tops of Kitchener's Wood came also into view.

Our own ultimate disaster was near at hand. There ran out of the salient the dismal remains of a thoroughfare known to us as Boundary Road, which, after crossing Admiral's Road in No Man's Land and then the German front line, zigzagged past the reserve trenches at Kempton Park and Gatwick Cottage to Hurst Park and Boche Castle itself, from where it hugged the north end of Kitchener's Wood before descending the reverse slope to a culvert over the Steenbeek. Up this latter part of it was laid a light railway, as disclosed by aeroplane photographs, and duly recorded on the map. Information from prisoners led to the belief that this road was mined; and Merchant and I had been warned time and again on no account to move along it. We were to cross it in the neighbourhood of Boche Castle, proceed parallel to it on the north, and recross it beyond the wood, thus reducing to a minimum the risk of striking one of the mines. The road itself, when I arrived at it, was indistinguishable from the surrounding mud; but the twisted metals of the light railway betrayed its site; and in accordance with my instructions, without thinking twice about it, I drove straight over it at a point midway between the wood and Boche Castle. I then swung to the right and moved forward parallel to it. As written down, this manœuvre sounds a simple one; but already another peculiarity of the salient was disturbingly manifest. Owing, as I suppose, to some arrangement of strata—the same phenomenon is to be found in parts of Dorsetshire, among other places—the water with which Flanders is too abundantly provided collects on top of the ridges as well as in the adjacent valleys. The boggy patch on the other side of Boche Castle before mentioned was a symptom of this eccentricity. And across the vanished road the conditions became at once appalling. The ground was one network of big shell-holes, and every one was full of water. There was no escaping it. On all hands lay these brimming pools, divided only by a sort of mesh of semi-liquid mud. I tried at once to get back to the road, preferring the possibility of mines to the certainty of being ignominiously engulfed, but in that amphibious world the engine was not powerful enough to induce the tank to reverse or swing. She would only plough her way slowly forward through the mud. The end was inevitable. We covered (and this in itself was something of a miracle) about two hundred yards of this quagmire, forcing our way through it rather than over it. . . . All this while we tried continually to swing back towards the road, a hundred yards away, but the tank was sunk in the mud to her belly, and would move only in the one direction. We arrived at length at a point abreast of the far edge of Kitchener's Wood: water lay everywhere about us; and immediately in front were two or three large shell-holes, full to the brim. It being impossible to avoid them, G 46, like a reluctant suicide, crawled straight into the first, which we could only hope was shallower than it appeared to be. The water rushed in through the tracks and sponson doors, covered the floor-boards, and flooded the sump: the flywheel thrashed through it for a second or two, sending showers about the interior; and then the tank, not having been constructed for submarine warfare, gave up the struggle. The engine raced with an increased but futile noise, for the wet clutch had ceased to grip, and we did not move.

Capt. D. G. Browne (Tank Corps).

THANK GOD, I HAVE DONE MY DUTY

August 4. All my fears about the weather have been realized. It has killed this attack. Every day's delay tells against us. We lose, hour by hour, the advantage of attack. The Germans can reorganize and reinforce. We can do nothing but wait. Even if the weather were to clear now, it will take days for the ground to harden, if indeed it ever can, before the winter frost. It is very difficult to keep from saying, "I told you so." But I am glad that I fought as hard as I did against that delay of three days in our attack. I went up to the front line this morning. Every brook is swollen and the ground is a quagmire. If it were not that all the records of previous years had given us fair warning, it would seem as if Providence had declared against us. It is terribly disappointing for us at G.H.Q., but it is much worse for the men.

Brig.-Gen. John Charteris.

NOT EVIDENCE AT G.H.Q.

August. I went to lunch with an old friend, Colonel Tandy of the Operations Branch of the General Staff. I was naturally plied with questions and I expressed my views with considerable candour and vigorous language. . . . I wound up by definitely stating that, in my opinion, the battle was "as dead as mutton," and had been so since the second day. . . .

I went with Tandy to his office. . . . While I sat there, an orderly came in and told me that Brigadier-General Davidson (at that time, Director of Operations, afterwards Major-General Sir John Davidson, K.C.B., D.S.O.) would like to see me before I left.

On entering Davidson's office, I found him seated at his table, his head in his hands.

"Sit down," he said. "I want to talk to you." I sat down and waited.

"I am very much upset by what you said at lunch, Baker," he began. "If it had been some junior officer, it wouldn't have mattered so much, but a man of your knowledge and experience has no right to speak like you did."

"You asked me how things really were, and I told you frankly."

"But what you say is impossible."

"It isn't. Nobody has any idea of the conditions."

"But they can't be as bad as you make out."

"Have you been there yourself?"

"No."

"Has anybody in O.A. been there?"

"No."

"Well then, if you don't believe me, it would be as well to send somebody up to find out. I'm sorry I've upset you, but you asked me what I thought, and I've told you."

Brig.-Gen. C. D. B. S. Baker-Carr.

THE OPTIMIST

August 21. D.H. has not only accepted *in toto* my report on fighting up to 16th, but has gone much farther. He has reported to W.O. that "time is fast approaching when Germany will be unable to maintain her armies at their present numerical strength." "In front of the XIVth Corps a large portion of their defending troops are reported both by our own men and by prisoners to have run away." "For all these reasons, although the struggle is likely to continue severe for some while yet, there is good reason to hope that very considerable results will then follow and with more rapidity than may seem likely at present." "If we are favoured with a fine autumn, therefore, I regard the prospects of clearing the coast before winter sets in as still very hopeful, notwithstanding the loss of time caused by the bad weather during the first half of August. At the least, I see no reason to doubt that we shall be able to gain positions from which subsequent operations to clear the coast will present a far easier problem than we had to cope with at the outset of this offensive, and in which the losses and hardships suffered round Ypres in previous winters will be much reduced. In these circumstances the right course to pursue, in my opinion, is undoubtedly to continue to press the enemy in Flanders without intermission and to the full extent of our powers, and if complete success is not gained before winter sets in, to renew the attack at the earliest possible moment next year. Success in clearing the coast may confidently be expected to have such strategical and political effects that they are likely to prove decisive."

Brig.-Gen. John Charteris.

CAMEL SCRAP

On the 10th of September I led five Camels of A. Flight on the north offensive patrol, which covered an area to the north of Ypres. We had not been long over the lines, and were flying at 14,000 feet, when I saw below us over Houthulst Forest a formation of enemy planes, made up of two D.F.W. two-seaters protected by five Albatros Scouts. I had previously arranged that, in the event of encountering escorted aeroplanes, I should attack with one Camel, while the deputy leader and the other Camels were to remain above to protect our tails from attack. On my left was a new pilot, 2nd Lieut. R. J. Brownell, M.M., a Tasmanian, who is now in the Royal Australian Air Force. I had told him that, until he got used to flying over the lines and rapidly spotting enemy craft as distinct from friendly, he must keep right alongside my plane and do whatever I did, maintaining formation station in all attitudes. Lieutenants Crossland, Moody and Smith made up the remainder of the Vee formation.

The enemy planes were flying south about a thousand feet below and ahead of us, well east of their lines, and probably climbing to gain height before crossing the trench-lines upon reconnaissance. I swung our formation round above them from the north-easterly course we followed and dived for the two-seaters. Brownell came down in station. He had seen nothing. He simply knew that I had dived and that he had to keep position. The remaining three Camels maintained their height.

Down I rushed through the crisp, cold air, watching my Hun through the sights, holding my control stick with both hands, thumbs resting on the double gun-triggers within the spade-shaped stick-top. The observer in my opponents' bus saw me and I saw him swing his gun to bear. I saw the double flash of his shots even as he grew to personality in my sights and I pressed the fateful triggers. At the very first burst he crumpled up and fell backwards into the cockpit. My streams of lead poured into the fuselage of the plane around the pilot's cockpit and the D.F.W. tipped up and over sideways and fell tumbling down to earth.

I looked round for Brownell and saw him close beside me on my level. Following me down in the dive without knowing why we dived, he suddenly found himself squarely on the tail of the second D.F.W. He pressed his triggers instinctively in a long burst. The Hun's tail rose upward. A curl of smoke came from his fuselage and he fell headlong, plunging like a flaming comet.

Above us the three Camels kept the five Albatros Scouts engaged, and, after seeing the two-seaters go down, Smith dived on the tail of one of the scouts and shot a hundred rounds into it, until it fell out of control.

Next day, in misty weather, with a patrol of seven, I saw a concentration of enemy planes, some twenty-one strong, flying below us east of Langemarck. There were three of the new Fokker triplanes, while the remainder were Albatros Scouts. They greatly outnumbered our strength. I could not determine whether they had observed us or not, but in any case I decided to attack. I dived on one of the triplanes, closed right in and as my burst went home I saw him falling down below his own formation. I knew that the Hun formation was so strong that it would be but to court disaster to follow him down. As I pulled forward from among the Huns for breathing space to review the situation I saw that one of my formation who had followed me closely had done just the thing I knew was wrong.

Engrossed on the shooting of an Albatros he had passed right through the Hun level. Instantly a Fokker pounced upon his tail. A burst of bullets caused the Camel pilot to look round and swerve away from the Albatros he followed. I saw the triplane close in upon the Camel's tail and I dived instantly upon it. As I dived I fired a short burst, before my sights were centred, because I knew that most Huns answered to the warning of bullets flying near. This fellow, however, was of a different breed. He looked round at me and, as I saw his begoggled face above his shoulder, he swerved slightly to one side, then followed on the Camel's tail.

I think the Camel pilot was wounded by the triplane's very first burst, because he did not use the Camel to manœuvre as he might.

I increased speed and pulled closer to the triplane. Then I

heard the splatter of Hun bullets rattling round my own ears. Glancing upward I saw two Albatros Scouts coming down upon me, but above them was another little Camel treating them the same.

I was almost dead upon the triplane's tail when the pilot looked around again. The range was so close that I could almost read the man's expression. I gave him another burst and saw the stream of tracer miss his head by inches as he swerved outward from my line of sight. The Camel was below him falling steeply in a gentle curve. When my burst ceased the German pilot looked again ahead.

Damn him! I thought. I'll get him next time. Each time I had fired a trifle earlier than I might have done, in the desire to shake him off the Camel's tail. And all the time we fell downward, losing height, fighting earthward from fourteen thousand feet along a pathway inclined at sixty degrees, rushing through the misty air towards the ground behind the German lines. From behind me came another burst of flying bullets.

Out of the corner of my eye I saw a solitary R.E. 8 heading towards us. I followed the swerving triplane and got squarely on his tail. Before I could fire he got out of my sights once more. Again I registered on him, dead. I pressed the triggers and saw my bullets flying home. His head did not look round this time. His angle of dive suddenly steepened. I increased my own to vertical, barely twenty feet behind him. Suddenly the R.E. 8 flashed in front of me between the German and my bus. I saw the wide-open mouth of the horror-struck observer. The wings passed across my vision as the pilot vainly strove to turn away.

For a fleeting instant of time I looked into the face of the observer and the cockpit in which he stood. He thought that I would hit him head on and wipe him from existence, torn to fragments with the whirring engine and propeller that I carried. So did I. For a fragment of time I hung in space, mentally, already dead. The observer and I saw each other as souls already hurled into the eternal cosmos.

There was but one thing to do.

" My God," I breathed in prayer, even as I did it. I yanked the Camel's stick hard into my stomach and flashed between the two-seater's wings and tail plane as my gallant little Camel answered to the pull. By a miracle we missed collision, by a miracle my Camel held together. I flat spun upside down on top of a loop and fell out sideways. I had lost height so rapidly in my downward rush from 14,000 feet that the pressure in my fuel-tank had not had time to stabilize to meet the higher atmospheric pressure, and my engine ceased to run. Not certain of the cause I tried her on the gravity tank and she picked up. I turned west and scanned the sky. High overhead I saw planes pass between the mist and sky like goldfish in a bowl held up against a curtained window. Around me and on my level there was nothing to be seen, no aeroplanes, enemy or friendly, except the R.E. 8 fast disappearing westward in the mist, westward towards the lines. The triplane and the Camel both had vanished. The ground below was free from shell-holes, but indistinct on account of mist. I climbed upward as I travelled west and found some Camels of the Squadron. Our patrol time was finished, and we returned to our aerodrome in formation. And as I went I cursed the damn-fool pilot of the British R.E. 8.

Norman Macmillan (R.F.C.).

SUDDEN DEATH

12*th Sept.* Yet my first experience of death was worse than this. Our battalion had entrained almost as far as Ypres, and we rested beside the railway for some time, with the engine standing stationary, sending a high pillar of smoke into the air. I expect the German observation balloons had seen it, for the enemy began to place shells on each side of the railway at regular intervals for about two hundred yards. Of course, we side-slipped until it stopped. Then we began to cross the railway : our two companies had just got over when I heard a scream of a shell. Instantly we got on our noses : I looked up cautiously, just in time to see it explode in a thick mass of the other companies on the railway. The scream of despair and agony was dreadful to hear, men shell-shocked out of reason and others dying of frightful wounds. That shell caused sixty casualties and shook the whole battalion for several days. Even when going through the market-square of Ypres, beneath the yellow flash of great howitzers and the roar of naval guns, we thought shells were bursting among us and looked fearfully at every corner, nerve-shaken and absolutely afraid. The sudden roar of a gun made us start guiltily, half-ashamed, and yet unable to control our agitation.

That cry of dying men will ring in my ears a long time after everything else will be forgotten.

Hugh Quigley (R. Scots).

" . . . BUT THAT I HAVE HAD BAD DREAMS"

Enduring a bombardment is the opportunity for that kind of nervous disease which made Dr. Johnson touch every post as he walked along Fleet Street. You think of absurd omens and fetishes to ward off the shell you hear coming. A strong inward feeling compels you to sit in a certain position, to touch a particular object, to whistle so many bars of a tune silently between your teeth. If you complete the charm in time you are safe—until the next one. This absurdity becomes a dark, overpowering fatalism. You contemplate with horror that you have made a slip in the self-imposed ritual, or that the augury sign of your own invention shows against you. You imagine that the shells are more deliberate and accurate than could be possible. They seem to have a volition of their own and to wander malevolently until they see a target on which to pounce ; they seem to hurl themselves with intention sounding in the fierce roar of their near approach ; they defy your mute relief when they fall far away, by sending slivers of jagged steel sighing and murmuring hundreds of yards towards you, long after the shock of the explosion is spent and gone.

Every gun and every kind of projectile had its own personality. Old soldiers always claimed that they knew the calibre of a shell by its sound and could always foretell which shells were going to fall dangerously close. Yet far more than they calculated depended on the range and the nature of the intervening ground. Sometimes a field-gun shell would leap jubilantly with the pop of a champagne cork from its muzzle, fly over with a steady buzzing crescendo, and burst with a fully expected bang ; sometimes a shell would be released from a distant battery of heavies to roll across a huge arc of sky, gathering speed and noise like an approaching express train, ponderous and certain. Shells flying over valleys and woods echoed strangely and defied anticipation ; shells falling in enclosed spaces simply arrived with a double bang and no warning at all. Some shells whistled, others shrieked, others wobbled through space gurgling like water poured from a decanter.

So all the day you listened, calculated, hoped or despaired, making imaginary bargains with fate, laying odds with yourself on the chances of these various horrors. One particular gun would seem to be firing more directly on you than the others. You would wait for its turn so intently as to forget other perhaps more real dangers. At last it comes. You hold frenziedly on to the conversation ; you talk a little too fast ; your nerves grow tense, and while you continue to look and talk like a man, your involuntary muscles get a little out of hand. Are your knees quivering a little ? Are you blinking ? Is your face contorted with fear ? You wonder and cannot know. Force yourself to do something, say something, think something, or you will lose control. Get yourself in hand with some voluntary action. Drum out a tune with your finger-tips upon your knee. Don't hurry—keep time—get it finished, and you will be safe this once. Here superstition and neurasthenia step in. Like the child who will not walk on the lines in the pavement and finds real safety in putting each foot on a square stone you feel that your ritual protects you. As the roar of an approaching shell rises nearer and louder you listen in inward frenzy to the shell, in outward calm to the conversation. Steady with those nervous drum-taps on your knee ; don't break time or the charm is broken and the augury vain. The shell roars near. What is Thorburn saying ?

" Oh, yes ! The rations came up at nine o'clock, enough for twice our numbers." (Explosion !)

Thank God, the tune was finished soon enough. But then comes an overwhelming rush of panic. The next shell will be the nearest, the climax of the day. What is the next shell when the air is never free from their sound ? The next that is at all near. But how near ? Which is near enough to break the tension ? Thorburn is saying, " We haven't issued the rum to-day. Best do it at dusk, don't you think ? " (Terrific explosion !) " God," you say with a gasp, dropping for an instant the mask of indifference. You eye the others guiltily and wonder if they are going through the same performance. At least you are keeping up appearances as well as they do ? What a comfort that Wolfe's augury is so optimistic.

Once in the afternoon I was on the point of breaking down. My luck turned ; the self-deluding charm failed ; omens were bad and a shell roared into the mud throwing clods and whining splinters on our heads. I swore and moved nervously and lost control of my features.

"Steady," said Thorburn, putting a hand on my arm.

That was my nadir. The shelling slackened and stopped, until between Wolfe's optimism and Thorburn's unconcern I revived my good spirits.

Charles Edmonds (R. Warwick Regt.).

NOW WAS SEEN WITH WHAT STRENGTH AND MAJESTY THE BRITISH SOLDIER FIGHTS

20 *Sept.* At ten minutes to six, hundreds, perhaps thousands, of guns behind us went off like one gun. All the inhabitants of hell seemed to have been let loose and to be screaming and raving in the sky overhead. The darkness just in front of us was rent and sundered. Blinding flashes in a long and accurate line blazed and vanished and blazed and vanished, while the guns bellowed and thumped and crashed in their own time. Their din was half-drowned by the variegated noises of the exploding shells. No maniac ever dreamed anything like it.

Matters didn't improve. The German was not asleep, and within a minute his own barrage had multiplied the inferno by two, while machine-guns broke out with the rattling of a thousand type-writers. I stood dazed by the din and didn't notice that our own barrage had lifted until somebody shouted, "Come on!"

I must say, without meaning to praise myself, that it was a good show. Nobody hesitated or looked back. I was simply a sheep and I went with the flock. We moved forward as if we were on the parade ground.

But it didn't last long. With shell-holes and impassable morasses we had to pick our way. It was no use looking for "dressing" to the section on the left or right, which was either in the same pre-dicament or had already been blotted out. Led by Edmonds my section made a detour, turning a little to the left and heading for some higher and drier ground. Unfortunately most of the battalion were compelled to do this.

I was in the rear of the section, and, through no fault of my own, kept ten yards behind the man in front of me. My burden of rifle-grenades pulled me lop-sided and I had to keep on hitching at my trousers. Edmonds kept on turning and waving me on, with the heroic gestures of a cavalry leader in the Napoleonic wars. I cursed him heartily, although he could not hear. Did the damned fool think I was funking it? No, my trousers were coming down.

My trousers seemed a positive curse to me, but I believe they were a blessing in disguise. They may have saved me from an extremity of terror. The human mind is not capable of concentrating on many things at once, and mine just then was principally concerned with my trousers. We fell into mud and writhed out again like wasps crawling out of plums, we passed a pill-box and came out on to a little plateau of about the size of a small suburban back garden. From there the ground sloped down to the bed of the Paddebeeke, but there was no stream left. It had been shelled into a bog. The Germans had left one long single plank bridge, and we should have known what was certain to happen if we attempted to cross it. But we went on to the edge of the plateau—and it was perhaps as well for us that we did—until Edmonds noticed that nobody else was standing up. Then he signalled to us to take cover. We flopped into a shell-hole, lying around the lip, for there was about six feet of water in the middle.

We had already seen what had happened to the first " ripple." They had all made for that spot of higher and drier ground, and the Germans, having retired over it, knew exactly what must happen, and the sky rained shells upon it. Shrapnel was bursting not much more than face high, and the liquid mud from ground shells was going up in clouds and coming down in rain.

The first " ripple " was blotted out. The dead and wounded were piled on each others' backs, and the second wave, coming up behind and being compelled to cluster like a flock of sheep, were knocked over in their tracks and lay in heaving mounds. The wounded tried to mark their places, so as to be found by stretcher-bearers, by sticking their bayonets into the ground, thus leaving their rifles upright with the butts pointing at the sky. There was a forest of rifles until they were uprooted by shell-bursts or knocked down by bullets like so many skittles.

The wounded who couldn't crawl into the dubious shelter of shell-holes were all doomed. They had to lie where they were until a stray bullet found them or they were blown to pieces. Their heartrending cries pierced the incessant din of explosions.

The stretcher-bearers, such as still survived, could do nothing as yet.

Well, I found myself in a shell-hole with the rest of the section, strangely intact. I had lost merely a bit of skin from the bridge of my nose. I had been stung by something a minute after we started to advance and, having applied the back of my hand, found blood on it. This was a close shave, but a miss was as good as a mile. But a tragedy worse than the precariousness of my trousers had befallen me. I had lost my rations.

While crossing the plateau it had seemed to me that somebody had given the pack on my back a good hard shove, and I had looked all round but there was nobody near. Then I was aware of things falling behind me. A piece of shell about the size of a dumb-bell had gone through my pack, and all my kit and food were dropping out. I didn't stop to pick anything up.

How my section had so far remained intact is a mystery which I shall never solve in this world. After a minute or two of stupor we discovered that we were all as thickly coated with mud from the shell-bursts as the icing on a Christmas cake. Our rifles were all clogged, and directly we tried to clean them more mud descended. If the Germans had counter-attacked we had nothing but our bayonets. In the whole battalion only one Lewis-gun was got into action, and I don't think that more than half a dozen men in the three attacking companies were able to use their rifles during the first few hours.

Ex-private X (63rd Div.).

AERIAL GUNNER

Pender did not swerve so quickly as the leader. He had not enough experience to make him act automatically. And, in the moment of thought before action, a bullet passed through the main petrol-tank between the cockpits and wounded him seriously in the back. He fainted before he had time to stop his engine; and, a second later, the bus was whirling madly round, spinning with the engine on.

Smith was quicker. He had his gun on the Hun like a flash. His aim was deadly. The range was too close to miss. And, although he was jerked from his feet when the bus dived and spun, he saw the Hun spinning down above them. Then he turned his attention to his own machine.

He knew instinctively what was wrong. And he knew how to right it. He had lain along the fuselage on the way home from previous jobs and handled the joystick. He knew all the gadgets. One of the pilots had explained them to him on the aerodrome.

His one thought was to get hold of the controls. He crawled along the four feet of thin plywood between the cockpits and tried. But Pender was a big man and his head and shoulders were in the way. He was unconscious and Smith could get no answer from him.

Smith knew the bus was none too strong to stand the strain of that mad, earthward whirl. He must act at once.

He climbed out of his cockpit four feet behind the pilot's, clinging to the strut in front. His mouth was blown open by the hurricane of wind. He could hardly breathe. The lower wing and fuselage were messed with the slither of oil that rotary engines continually threw out from the exhaust. He felt himself being thrown from his slippery hold of the spinning machine. Then, somehow, he got both feet out of the plane. He lunged forward with one hand for the strut in front, missed, and almost fell overboard. A cold sweat broke out all over his body. He tried again and succeeded. He hauled himself forward against the demon wind-rush and braced both legs against it. Hanging on like death, with one arm curled around the centre-section strut, he leant inside the pilot's cockpit. He turned a tap. . . . Nothing happened. He tried another, and the engine's roaring ceased. The wind-blast lessened, and he leant still farther inside the cockpit. The stick was wedged between the pilot's legs. He pulled Pender back and pushed the joystick forward; and was almost thrown again as the bus came out of the spinning nose-dive.

He shook Pender and shouted to him.

Field-gunners, with glasses to their eyes, watched the plane hurtle earthwards spinning, recover, and glide. They saw the figure of the observer out upon the wing; heard him shouting to the pilot.

"Wake up, Pender! For God's sake! wake up."

Pender stirred and opened his eyes drunkenly. He did not speak. He looked stupidly at Smith. And, with his right foot on the rudder bar, he was veering the bus round to Hunland.

" Turn left, sir. Turn left," Smith bawled.

Mechanically the pilot obeyed. They were going straight, due west, but losing height too rapidly. Smith turned back the tail wheel, and they flattened to a steady glide. . . . The wind pressure became less and Smith could manage fairly comfortably. He did not require to hang on by tooth and nail.

They glided towards a field of hops, straight for the midst of the poles. Smith called out to the pilot.

" Pull her up, sir. . . . Steady, sir, now back. . . . Pull her up, sir. . . . Land her."

Pender's hand followed the words, but Smith's inexperienced judgment was slightly out. They cleared the hop poles, and pancaked on the farther side. The machine crashed, but with very little damage.

Smith, standing out on the wing, was catapulted through the wires. He lay where he fell, unconscious. He opened his eyes to find a group of gunners round him. Someone was bending over him forcing brandy down his throat.

" How d'you feel now ? " asked the doctor.

" I'm all right," gasped Smith.

Norman Macmillan (R.F.C.).

EPITAPH ON A BELOVED SOLDIER

21st Sept.—Death of Brig.-Gen. Frank Maxwell, V.C., 27th Infantry Brigade

DEAR MADAM,

. . . A captain of the Scottish Rifles came along with us to his outpost. The General was showing him the land. I think the General wanted to have a machine-gun posted at this particular point. I was about five yards in front watching for any movement in shell-holes. I was lying flat with my rifle ready to shoot. The first bullet that was fired by the Huns went right into the ground by my left elbow. I shouted to the General to get down, as he was standing up at the time, and he did so. He sat for about two minutes, and then he got up again to show what he was saying to the captain, and was just opening his mouth to speak when he got shot. I caught him as he was falling, and jumped into a shell hole with him. I held his head against my breast till all was over. Madam, I cried till my heart was liking to burst. . . .

A. Laird, L/Cpl.

DIRECT HIT

4th Oct. There came one shattering clang. In the infinitesimal fraction of a second, I saw the pigeoneer, his hands fluttering, his face twisted like a martyr's in the fire, leap upward to the ceiling, and young Morgan, the runner, pitching forward on top of me. The candles shot up and died. I remember running trembling hands over my belly and legs, automatically searching for a wound. A complete silence fell. Then from the passage came one sigh, the simultaneous passing of life from the dozen wounded men lying there. Another silence, in which the pigeons began to coo and flutter ; and at that, there broke out from the aid-post a high shrilling. One of the orderlies had been half scythed in two by a piece of shell which had cleft him through the buttocks.

The candles were relit by our shaking hands. The shell had fallen directly on the bomb boxes by the door, exploding the contents, smashing the stone and burying a number of those standing by. For a space of time, we were all partially stunned and frozen by the shock. As we slowly recovered, one of the Rifle Brigade officers shot into the chamber and squatted down in front of Smith, shouting incoherently. His hair was grey-white, powdered with concrete, and stood on end. His face muscles leaped up and down as he gabbled. He was followed by a sergeant, who sank down beside him, and began shouting in his ear : " 'E's gone, poor old Mac's gone, 'e's buried under the blasted concrete. D'ye 'ear ? " repeating it again and again while tears trickled out of his eyes ; but the officer had been deafened by the explosion and took no notice. With eyes staring, he kept on chattering and waving his hands. We got them out at last and sent them back. Mackwood had given the poor aid-post boy a heavy dose of morphia, and the cries sank to groans and whimpers. He died half an hour later. The Rifle Brigade, without their bombs, went forward.

Somehow the pill-box was cleared and the night ended. A bright uncompassionate day came in.

Guy Chapman.

PASSCHENDAELE BATTLE SCENE

10th Oct. The slope . . . was littered with dead, both theirs and ours. I got to one pill-box to find it just a mass of dead, and so I passed on carefully to the one ahead. Here I found about fifty men alive, of the Manchesters. Never have I seen men so broken or demoralized. They were huddled up close behind the box in the last stages of exhaustion and fear. Fritz had been sniping them off all day, and had accounted for fifty-seven that day—the dead and dying lay in piles. The wounded were numerous—unattended and weak, they groaned and moaned all over the place . . . some had been there four days already. . . . Finally the company came up— the men done after a fearful struggle through the mud and shell-holes, not to speak of the barrage which the Hun put down and which caught numbers. The position was obscure—a dark night—no line—demoralized Tommies—and no sign of the enemy. So I pushed out my platoon, ready for anything, and ran into the foe some 80 yards ahead. He put in a few bursts of rapid fire and then fled. We could not pursue as we had to establish the line, which was accomplished about an hour later. I spent the rest of the night in a shell-hole, up to my knees in mud and with the rain teeming down. . . .

13th Oct. The next day we were ordered to retake the line, and then our units sank to the lowest pitch of which I have ever been cognisant. It looked hopeless—the men were so utterly done. However the attempt had to be made, and accordingly we moved up that night—a battalion 90 strong. I had A company with 23 men. We got up to our position somehow or other—and the fellows were dropping out unconscious along the road—they have guts, my word ! That's the way to express it. We found the line instead of being advanced, some thirty yards behind where we had left it—and the shell-stricken and trodden ground thick with dead and wounded— some of the Manchesters were there yet, seven days wounded and not looked to. But the men walked over them—no heed was paid to anything but the job. Our men gave all their food and water away, but that was all they could do.

That night my two runners were killed as they sat beside me, and casualties were numerous again. He blew me out of my shell-hole twice, so I shifted to an abandoned pill-box. There were twenty-four wounded men inside, two dead Huns on the floor and six outside, in various stages of decomposition. We got the wounded away at last as well as two wounded Huns. . . .

When day broke I looked over the position. Over forty dead lay within twenty yards of where I stood, and the whole valley was full of them.

Lieut. W. G. Fisher (42nd Batt. A.I.F.).

THE CLOTH HALL, YPRES

One episode still gives me a certain pleasure. One morning last week, two of us came down through the morning barrage into the square across the canal. Dead-beat, we asked a policeman where we would get a decent sleep for about three hours. He pointed out to us the old Cloth Hall, and there, beneath that massive tower, so dented and bruised that no more can be destroyed by shells, behind a wall of sand-bags, we fell asleep. About nine o'clock I woke up and explored a little : just inside the arch hung a delicately-wrought iron lamp, quite intact, with some fragments of glass still in it, and below, a pair of wooden wheels belonging to an old type of gun. Just beyond lay the ruins of the church, a mere blur of a building. The Cloth Hall seemed to have been so battered that not a single sculptured figure, or shadow of a figure, remained, except one gargoyle at the end, which leered down as jauntily as ever. When I come back, this incident will remain one of the treasured memories, something to recount time and again, as happening in a land of horror and dread whence few return, like that country Morris describes in the *Well at the World's End.*

Hugh Quigley (Royal Scots).

ZEPPELIN OVER ENGLAND

On the 19th October the final orders came and we left our shed [1] at half-past eleven. The journey over the sea was cold and misty. We barely sighted some of the other airships off the Frisian coast. There were at least twelve ships under orders to attack England, so I understood Kölle to tell the navigator, and from the radios that were taken on board I think they all must have started. We did not see them at all clearly, for it was the custom to fly independently while keeping a general direction. Once started the radio gave us little news. Once or twice we thought we saw another ship; L 54 we recognized by the setting of her cars; L 47 we distinguished through the glasses. Then I heard Kölle identify L 50, so it seemed to him, and he passed some disparaging remark about her commander, for he despised his skill as an airman no less than he suspected his determination. L 49 we thought we recognized, or so the navigator said, by her little flag that she flew from her forward car. But it was a dreary, windy crossing and owing to the cold and height many of us were feeling numbed and slack by the time we made the English coast at about 8 p.m. We could not be sure of our landfall as it was dark and our navigation was undoubtedly at fault. We should, so I believe, have crossed the Lincoln coast; but from an argument we had with the officers our navigating warrant officer, Hashagen, expressed grave doubts as to the landfall. I felt sure we were a long way south of that. Kölle, however, though looking anxious would not give way. I looked at my comrades in the car to see if I could read their thoughts, but only cold and anxiety were there. The wind must have freshened from the north for even then, like the lightning, some searchlights cut the air; all I could see by their warm beams was the leeway that we were making. Kölle swore and jumped at the ballast control cords. The ship rose rapidly. " 5,800 !"[i.e.

---

[1] L 45 was stationed at Tondern in Schleswig.

metres, 19,000 ft.] read Hashagen off the altimeter; the height and the cold made him look ghastly in the pale searchlight beam as he leant on the glass panels. I shall never forget his face. I felt, too, that I would get little sympathy from him, if I dropped out, for the height and anxiety were telling on him already. Guns opened on us too, but that did not trouble us.

For nearly two hours more we struggled to keep our westward course but the wind blew ever stronger and I could tell that our navigation was getting more and more uncertain. We dropped a few bombs at some faint lights but providence alone knows where they went. I scarcely believe that Lieutenant Schütz, our second-in-command even troubled to set the bombing sight.

By this time it was bitterly cold. Hashagen once read the thermometer aloud and gave over 30 degrees of frost [C. about 60° of frost F.]. I heard him mention Birmingham as our target, but he did not believe we had reached that locality. We climbed still higher as the weight of the bombs and petrol grew smaller and it grew still colder. Hahndorf, an engineer, now came in to report to Kölle that the men were feeling the cold. The sailmaker, in particular, who was attending to the valves of the gas-bags, complained of his feet. Well he might do so, for he could not wear his felt boots when climbing about the ship. He said he could not go on much longer. Two engineers, so Hahndorf said, were sleepy; while the petrol rating was grumbling and fumbling over his work.

Something must be done. The wind was rendering our progress westwards laborious. It was clear to us who had no say in the matter, that we ought to turn back, yet Kölle would not give in. The navigator and director began to express misgivings. Finally, Hahndorf re-appeared and gave it as his opinion that his engineers could not be trusted to go on much longer under such conditions. Reluctantly Kölle gave the order to turn; it was now about 11 o'clock. Hurriedly he gave his instructions for the return overland over Belgium. This was a bad sign, for it was not a step that our airship commanders would do unless the weather or other conditions were threatening. I could tell by the compass that we were now steering south-eastwards. The wind must have increased in violence and the cold was the worst I have ever experienced; I could scarcely continue, in spite of all felt boots and quilted clothing, it was terrible. It grew too cold to pull out the food to eat; the meat that one man pulled out was hard as stone.   Kölle clearly not knowing where he was let out more ballast ; we must have touched 6,500 metres or more.

At about 11.30 we began to see lights below and as the lights continued so it suddenly dawned upon us that it could only be the city of London that we were crossing in the air.   Even Kölle looked amazed at the dim lights as Schütz suddenly shouted " London ! " It was then that we first realized the fury of the savage tempest that had been driving us out of our course.   But Kölle clearly had but one thought—that was higher.   So he released more ballast and the bombs—first two sighting shots and then the rest.[1]   Over London ! We had achieved what no other German airship had done since Mathy had bombed that proud city over a year ago !   And his last trip across the city had proved his undoing.[2]   Fortunately for us we were unseen ; not a searchlight was unmasked ; not a shot was fired ; not an aeroplane was seen.   If the gale had driven us out of our course, it had also defeated the flying defences of the city !   It was misty or so it seemed, for we were above a thin veil of cloud.   The Thames we just dimly saw from the outline of the lights ; two great railway stations, I thought I saw, but the speed of the ship running almost before the gale was such that we could not distinguish much. We were half frozen, too, and the excitement was great.   It was all over in a flash.   The last big bomb was gone, and we were once more over the darkness and rushing onwards.

It was then that our misfortunes began.   Hahndorf reported to Kölle that the engine of the port wing car was scarcely working—he thought owing to the sooting of the plugs.   The plugs were cleaned by the engineers but alas ! their hands were so cold and they themselves so clumsy with lassitude and fatigue owing to the height that, by the time the plugs were cleaned and replaced, the engine had ceased to function—the cooling water had frozen ; the radiator had split and there was no means in our power to get the engine into action again.

From this moment our journey became one long story of misery and pain.   The cold grew intense and we all began to feel dejected at the consciousness that our real attack on England must have failed. The jubilation at having flown over the enemy's capital gave way to anxiety. At the helm of the ship we began to feel that the gale

[1] One of these fell near Piccadilly Circus.
[2] Mathy never crossed London on his last raid (1st October, 1916) ; he was brought down at Potter's Bar before flying over the Metropolis.

was driving us away, still further out of our course. We were so high that the earth was scarcely visible. Clouds were obviously being driven beneath us until we could not distinguish the sea. It was somewhere after midnight that Hahndorf came to report to the commander that the sailmaker could scarcely go on with his duties ; his feet were frostbitten and the poor fellow was now lying in his hammock unable to do more. The petrol rating was complaining of weariness and sickness, leaning up against his tanks. Two engineers were suffering from height : one of these had been relieved by the man from the port wing car. Kölle became visibly perturbed ! Even Schütz, usually so cheerful, looked pale and anxious. So we went on in gloomy silence.

For some two or three hours—we hardly knew how the time went by—we drove on, but, as events showed later, our course was now pure guess work. When and where we crossed the sea we could not tell. Hashagen argued we were now steering over Belgium, but somehow his voice lacked conviction. Kölle uttered not a word. We well knew that he was more than uneasy. The want of our port propeller told on the steering and I myself feared that this would endanger our safe return to Germany.

The hours dragged on. The petrol rating was now really ill. Both ratings from the port wing car were now relieving other sufferers. Hahndorf was growing anxious about his fuel supply and said so. Kölle stormed at him. But the man's worn, pale face and his frozen black moustache and beard deserved only pity. He was gallantly struggling against sickness.

At last dawn began to light up the sky. One, and then another, airship were barely distinguished against the eastern light. They could only be German, but we dared not use our radio, and that in itself was proof that we might be over the enemy's air defences. Kölle rapped out a bitter exclamation as this suspicion grew into certainty ; flashes on the ground showed hostile gun-fire to be at work ; whether shooting at us or not we could not tell. We saw no bursts. Still more, to our intense relief, we never sighted an aeroplane ! Schütz assumed a reassuring tone, but this was abruptly checked when we felt the forward engine behind us slowing down and finally stop ! Hahndorf came in ; he was almost breaking down. The petrol supply for the forward engine had given out and the radiator, as the engine ceased running, had frozen solid.

With this accident our hopes of reaching home decreased greatly. Yet somehow we could not realize it or else Kölle had succeeded in making us believe that things were better than they were. This failure of the engine, directly occasioned by the illness of the petrol rating, was the outcome of a bad leakage in a union of the feed pipe. It had occasioned the entire loss of two tanks of fuel before Hahndorf could discover the mishap. Worse still, the forward engine actuated the radio dynamo and this was now useless. The telegraphist had only a small accumulator to work with.

We tried to steer eastwards ; but, with two engines and two propellers gone, we began to make worse leeway. We could see the land below and it was becoming clear to me at least that this could not be Germany. The north wind was not abating and the struggle to fly eastwards became desperate. The telegraphist soon reported that his apparatus could no longer transmit. In the last attempt to fly eastward, Kölle determined to come down so as to avoid the tearing wind that was driving us more south than was safe for us. But there was little need to come down very far. In spite of the bombs, ballast and fuel that had gone, it seemed to me that we could scarcely have kept our extreme height, for we had lost much gas.

Shortly afterwards another misfortune overtook us : a third engine failed ! This time it was in the after car, where the men had been refilling one of the radiators that had all been steaming heavily owing to the height of our flight. The water-inlet cover had been clumsily replaced, the water had been jolted out or steamed away until the engine grew so hot that the exhaust side was red. In vain they struggled to rectify the damage—it was all to no purpose, and the pistons seized before it could be remedied.

It was, if I remember, at this same time while at a height of some 4,000 metres or rather less that we flew over a large town [1] in the early morning. What it was I do not know. A voice in the car exclaimed " Dijon ! " That caused me to think. If that indeed was Dijon then we must fly over Switzerland to reach our own country. We still struggled on, but it was now obvious to me that we should never bring the ship home to our country. Before nine o'clock Hahndorf came to report that the petrol supply was failing and that his men were nearly exhausted.

Kölle turned to his charts once more, but could find none to help

[1] This was Lyons.

him, for they did not extend so far south. So he brought the ship down nearer the ground to look where he might be.

By this time we thought we were over Switzerland and it appeared as if internment in a neutral country would be the only method of putting an end to our sufferings and of avoiding a total wreck of the ship with evil consequences to ourselves. Kölle was doing the right thing, so I felt. Two of the others, as we were coming down, exclaimed " Switzerland ! See the snow mountains ! " People could now be seen streaming out of their houses to look at the ship, which was now only 1,500 metres up. That fact alone made us feel sure that we had not reached Germany, for at home the population would never be seen rushing out to look at a Zeppelin airship like this. Before we could land we were to have further unpleasant experiences.

Between 8 a.m. and 9 a.m. we sighted a curious little town in a gorge, such as might be expected in central Switzerland. But the country was growing rocky and Kölle turned north again to look for level ground for a landing. The valley here grew broad and level— a good place for an emergency descent and we might still save the ship—who could tell ? But we were to have a rude shock. Suddenly we saw a large tract of ground all cultivated with vegetables. On this there were working some gangs of coloured men—so we could see from their heads and bare arms—all dressed in blue.

" Black men ! French soldiers ! " rang out a cry. Kölle stamped his foot and hurriedly ordered full speed on an eastward course again. But Hahndorf came in and talked rapidly. His men were exhausted ; and the petrol supply was nearly running out : he could not go on with only two engines out of five and two propellers out of four in action. It was risky and he pointed to the mountains eastwards. A forced landing would be the only means of saving the crew.

Kölle bowed to the inevitable and manœuvred as though descending at Ahlhorn in Germany itself. He calmly ordered the emergency land flags to be flown and manœuvred the valves for the landing. We could not but admire our commander in this moment for his conduct was well worthy of what a German naval officer's should be. But ill-luck was to pursue him to the bitter end. In this mountainous valley [1] where we now found ourselves, the north wind was no longer blowing as it had done high overhead, but sharp

---

[1] This was the valley of the River Bueche, near Laragne, in the Department of the Hautes Alpes.

little squalls were felt at times. As we were touching the ground, one of these eddies came swirling across the water to our ship. She heeled over to port and the wing car was torn off as it scraped the ground. Two men from the car jumped clear to land. Then lightened of this weight the whole ship seemed to pivot on her nose and was again caught by the wind. Swaying and jolting, we were tossed across the stream until the whole craft came hard against the eastern side of the valley where she stuck fast entangled in the bushes and wedged among the stones. It was almost with a sense of gratitude that we clambered or jumped out of the cars. The long ordeal was over, but at what cost ! No sooner were we on the ground than Kölle ordered us to fall into line by the ship. All the ship's charts and papers, all our private papers, he and Schütz collected from us. They were stacked into the forward car. The tools were distributed to us and with them we proceeded to break all the instruments and batter the forward car. Hahndorf drew out the emergency pistol, and fired a blazing charge into the central gas-bags, which were still more than partly inflated. With beating hearts we watched the fire take hold of our fine airship. Some of us who were not too exhausted felt as though our last link with the Fatherland was snapped and that the future mattered nothing. We were brought to our senses as the last few tanks of petrol exploded and we had to run from the blazing gas and spirit. Some were almost too exhausted to move and were helped away to safety. Kölle was splendid in this trying moment. We then gave a last salute to the ship and the ensign as it was vanishing in the flames. But with a hoarse shout as though in pain Kölle made us fall in and marched us up a narrow track out of the valley. The sailmaker had to be carried for his feet were frozen stiff, while two others were almost too ill to walk. So our little party of thirteen struggled on to the neighbouring farm where we found a German sergeant in charge of a party of prisoners ! What a strange meeting in the enemy's country. This man called his party to him and they helped us to the farm where we surrendered, weak, exhausted and dejected, but still proud of our ship, our commander, and the great flight that we had just completed. Few men could boast as we might do, that they had accomplished such a journey and thrown bombs at the enemy's great capital ! But we were too exhausted to do more or go further.

Helmsman of the L 45, writing in the Journal of
Royal United Service Institute.

SOLDIER'S LETTER

TEKRIT

5th Nov. I must have the luck of the devil, as my horse got a flesh-wound—bullet—in the leg, but is practically all right again now.

We've got six honours in the Regt., my squadron leader and a Lieutenant in B—M.C's, a sergt. in my troop D.C.M., 2 M.M's in other sqdns., and—hold your breath—they've given me one— Military Medal. So I suppose you'll have to put that in *The Times* now—eh ! what ! It seemed to be nothing to me when I was in it. We charged about 300 Infantry on the road and in the trenches, with machine-guns and artillery behind 'em. We caught 'em weak—just about 100 of us—2 weak sqdns.—in the mist of dusk—and, my God ! it seemed as if we were riding into Hades. Funny thing tho', I didn't have wind up then, was feeling rather elated cos we'd waited, and moved about, practically all day, for a real rut at them, and been bombed from aeroplanes, shelled and sniped, till we were just itching to get at 'em. Well, they got pukka wind up when we got in amongst 'em, and started firing wildly, some trying to use bayonets, others holding up their mitts and shouting " Kamerad." Then we got order to rally as we weren't strong enough for pursuit. Starting to come back, I spotted a youngster badly wounded in the foot and horse shot, so I dismounted and put him up on my steed, which was too bobbery to carry the two of us. He got back O.K. Then my fun started. I had my revolver and about 14 rounds and began to think about getting back somehow myself, when I spotted a chum of mine lying about 60 yards from the trenches. Well, two of us tried to get him out of it, but he would not have it—thigh shattered, blood in spurts, mad with pain. J. Turk, seeing us retiring, heartened up again and potted at us like blazes, shrapnel, machine-guns and every bally thing. At the finish I had to leave him, to my sorrow, altho' we got him away afterwards. Still he suffered a hell of a lot from exposure, as the devils came out and stripped him—he'd be unconscious by then—in the dark. I hear that he's very bad in hospital, but likely to recover.

I haven't got the gong yet, owing, I suppose, to Gen. Maude's death, but they've made as much fuss over it as if we were—millions of V.C.'s. I've shaken hands with two Generals, and been in about half a dozen parades till I'm fairly fed up, and nearly said, " Keep the old gong and let's have a bit of peace."

Well, I'll think about drying up now. Am in the pink and quite fit ; hope you are all the same, and that you, dear mother, are carrying on.

Trooper Hugh H. Mortimer (XIIIth Hussars).

WAR AIMS

THE RUMP SHOWS ITS TEETH

6th November, 1917. *House of Commons.*

MR. RICHARD LAMBERT : Some people no doubt would be glad to find a Peace Conference at the present time rendered impossible. But peace has got to come some time or other, and remember this : That every day that passes every hour that elapses, means so many of our own gallant men killed or mutilated or injured in some way or other. I do say, most seriously and most earnestly, that this House ought to lose no opportunity and take every chance that offers to try, if it can, to do something to bring this horrible War to a close. Let me revert for a moment to the question of Alsace-Lorraine. I dare say I shall be told that the problem of Alsace-Lorraine is really an economic one. I know perfectly well that 80 per cent. of Germany's iron comes from Western Lorraine. I know there are great economic difficulties in giving up Western Lorraine to France, but I believe that if we can adopt the policy of the Open Door, if we can establish something in the nature of a League of Nations, we shall get over nine-tenths, if not all, of the difficulties which at the present time seem so insurmountable. But we must remember it is of no use attempting to approach this question of peace unless you are prepared to deal fairly and justly and impartially by all parties to the bargain. A League of Nations can be no success—it cannot even be begun, it can hardly be thought of—unless you are going to have all the nations of Europe parties to it. If Germany were excluded, or if Germany were not welcomed into it with open arms—(Hon. Members : " Oh oh ! " and " Never ! ") Yes, I say, with open arms—(An Hon. Member : " Remember the *Lusitania* ! ")—if you are going to have a League of Nations you must make up your minds that Germany as well as ourselves—(Hon. Members : " Never ! ")— must be welcomed.

Mr. G. Faber : Would you shake her bloody hand ?

Mr. Lambert : Because, unless you do, you are merely perpetuating the old trouble of two great armed camps in Europe. You will have that trouble all over again. The whole basis of the League of Nations, the absolute foundation of it, must be that all nations are party to it. I do most earnestly ask the House not to be carried away by the raw passions, which I know are natural. Do not let us be carried away by our passions at the present time and take a view which I think is more likely to militate against the future peace of the world, and which most certainly cannot possibly assist towards ending this terrible War.

Parliamentary Debates.

REVOLT IN THE FRONT LINE

I CRAWLED into the hot entrails of the armoured car, followed by Albizzi. He shouted to the driver, " Back to Kalush ! "

The smell of overheated oil and powder fumes was sickening enough, but when the car started rolling and pitching on the bumps of the road I felt irresistibly sick. Albizzi was putting a new belt into the machine-gun. Through the port-hole in front I could see the sun-burned neck of the driver and a pair of sergeant's shoulder-straps. A fine blond moustache protruded out of a hollow, martial cheek.

" He's all right ! " Albizzi shouted over the din.

The car must have reached the streets of the town, for it rattled on cobblestones. Smoke was filtering in through the narrow embrasures of the armour. I could not stand it any more, and pushed the trap open. The wide street, lined with two- and three-story houses, with their blue and green shutters, presented a grotesque sight : there was a kind of snowstorm raging in spite of the heat.

It was the down from the heaps of feather-beds lying on the pave-ments, ripped open by the mutineers. Several drunken figures were sprawling on the grey heaps. Down the street a house was burning, with soldiers running in and out of it, carrying petticoats, kitchen utensils, pillows. The body of an old Jew was hanging out of one of the windows, his arms nailed to the window-sill. At that moment I felt that moral nausea can be much worse than its physical name-sake . . . The mutineers had thrown their rifles away in order to loot unhampered, and all they could do was to shake their fists at us as we rumbled along towards the square ahead. The agonizing shriek of a woman rang somewhere in a house.

I yelled to Albizzi, " Tell him to stop here ! Let's get out ! "

Ghighi's teeth were sunk in his lower lip, and he shook his head, pointing forward, towards the square. He rotated the machine-gun, to make sure it would swing easily. An Austrian shrapnel shell burst overhead, and a bullet thumped against the armour plate of the car. The driver shot forward between two smouldering houses, to avoid the possibility of flying embers setting fire to our petrol-tank. We dived out of a cloud of thick smoke with reddish glows throbbing in it. The first thing I saw in the square was a soldier, reeling on his feet, urinating on the body of a prostrate comrade.

A muddy stream of alcohol was running in the gutter. Dozens of men were lying on their bellies, drinking the liquid, vomiting into the gutter, and pushing their faces into the stream again. One of the men was dead, his head bashed in.

I felt an actual physical pain in the eyes as they registered the horrible scene in the square. A thin curtain of smoke was drifting across it, like the gauze which is lowered on the stage when a scene must be not seen but only imagined by the spectator. The lighting was reddish, flaring up and dimming as the billows of smoke drifted in front of the sun.

A few feet from our car a man was lying, stripped to the waist. There was a pair of bright-red epaulettes on his naked white shoulders the mutineers had cut out strips of skin to simulate the insignia of an officer. The face was partly blown off by a point-blank shot.

The houses around the square were throbbing with the looting and destruction which were going on inside. Things were being thrown out of the windows, smashing themselves on the roadway.

The square was like an ant-hill : groups of alcohol-crazed soldiers with bloodshot eyes, collars ripped open, beltless, many barefooted, were running around aimlessly, shooting, fighting over measly bits of booty, stopping to drink out of bottles they had in their pockets, and dropping to the ground, stupefied.

A soldier, dressed in the white surplice of a Catholic priest, galloped across the square, riding a little shaggy white horse bareback. He was waving a bottle in the air and was shouting hoarsely.

The mutineers did not seem to notice our car : I doubt whether many among them were actually able to see.

A house belched out a group of about fifty men. They were apparently dragging somebody with them. A head covered with a kerchief drifted among them like a white wood-shaving in a muddy stream. The men huddled together in a ring, and seemed to watch something which was going on on the ground.

A beautiful vision obliterated the scene for a second : I was galloping into the square at the head of my squadron, sweeping it clear of these monsters, cutting, stabbing, lashing . . . avenging !

Crash-crash-crash-crash ! A salvo of shrapnel burst over the square. The ring of soldiers around the mysterious object scattered, ducking the flying bullets. A woman was lying on the road, her skirt thrown over her head. The legs, clad in striped stockings, were flung apart. The huge pregnant belly protruded like an abscess.

One of the mutineers staggered back to the body, raised his rifle, and thrust the bayonet into the belly, nailing it to the ground.

Our driver let go a terrific oath and shouted into the port-hole :

" For God's sake, let 'em have it, your Honour ! I can't . . . I can't . . ."

It seemed that somebody had picked up the whole car and was pounding it on a sheet of metal. A hot gust of air rushed past my cheek : Albizzi was sweeping the square with his machine-gun.

It is hard to believe that the sight of writhing, falling, crawling human bodies, torn by bullets, can give such an intense, painful pleasure. Enraptured, my breath choking me, I was watching the shambles which Ghighi was conjuring up with his masterful fire.

The stupefied men did not know where to run. They darted back and forth, pounded on closed doors, scratched the cobble-stones, trying to dig in. The belt came to an end, and the machine-gun was silent. Paradoxically, it felt as if a sound-proof door had burst open, letting the frenzied clamour escape again. Once more the machine-gun went into action and drowned everything out. The scene itself became silent again and, because of that, more grotesque.

Albizzi swung the gun to the right, dousing a cluster of soldiers who were trying to crash the closed gate of a yard. They slid down the red boards as flies drop off a wall when sprayed with insecticide.

There was now hardly a man standing on his feet in the square.

" I've used up the last belt ! . . . Let's go back ! " Albizzi shouted through the embrasure of the turret.

My ears were dinning, and a terrible thirst was burning me. I ducked inside, and immediately was sick on a heap of oily rags. Ghighi snapped the breech of the machine-gun and threw the end of the empty belt on the floor.

" Well, we mopped them up all right, didn't we ? "

The car backed and turned round. I felt it speeding up for a dash between the two burning houses. There was a shock, as if it had hit a body, and the wheels rolled over something soft. The driver half turned back.

" I got one of them, too, sir ! "

I cupped my hands and yelled to Albizzi, " I was supposed to find out if somebody is holding the line beyond Kalush."

He crawled to me on his knees, holding on to the swaying walls of the car.

" I went out there before : the shock battalions of that division are occupying the trenches . . . all volunteers. They'll hold the enemy for a while."

Sergei Kournakoff.

CAPORETTO

On October 24 the Austrians opened a heavy bombardment on the Tolmino-Caporetto front. They attacked and met with such success that on the 27th the Italians began to retire, continuing the retreat until they were able to re-form beyond the Piave.

27th Oct. When the Major came back, he called all the men together and said " I am not going to conceal anything from you. The situation is serious. The Italians have had a bad reverse up north. But there is no need for anyone to get panicky. We shall pull out and go back to-night. That is all I know at present. When I know more, I will tell you more. One gun will remain in action till the last. No. 2 is the easiest to get out, so I have chosen her for the post of honour." As the men scattered, I heard several saying, " Good old No. 2 ! "

The Major told me that the Austrians were almost in Cividale, staggering news. Tractors and lorries were to come and take away our guns and stores in the evening. But the number of tractors was very limited and Raven was doubtful if enough would come in time. The whole Third Army was retreating, and three British batteries, ourselves, the battery in Pec village and the battery at Rupa, would be the last three batteries of medium or heavy calibre left on this part of the front.

All through the afternoon and evening Italian Infantry and Artillery were retreating through Pec. Some looked stolid, others depressed, others merely puzzled. But a little later a battalion came along the road the other way, going up to be sacrificed on Nad Logem. They halted to rest by the roadside, full of gaiety and courage. They cheered our men on No. 2 gun who were pumping out shells as fast as they could. " Bravi inglesi ! " cried the Italians, and some of our men replied, " Good luck, Johnny ! " Unknown Italians were always " Johnny."

As the dark came on, ammunition dumps began to go up everywhere; the Italians were deliberately exploding them, and great flashes of light, brighter than even an Italian noonday, lit up the whole sky for minutes at a time. Romano's battery next door to us threw the remains of their ammunition into the river, and pulled out and away about 6.30. They were horse-drawn and did not need to wait for tractors. We wished each other good-bye, and hoped we might meet again some better day. We too got orders to destroy all ammunition we could not fire, as there would be no transport to take it away. So we gave No. 2 a generous ration and heaved the rest into the waters of the Vippacco.

No. 2 went on firing ceaselessly. So did one gun of the battery in the village, and one gun at Rupa. That battery, being the farthest forward, was in the greatest danger of the three. About 7 o'clock our first tractor arrived and took away No. 1 gun with Winterton and Manzoni. Enemy bombing planes came over frequently. One came right over us and then turned down the Vallone, and there was a series of heavy explosions, and great clouds of brownish smoke leapt up beneath her track.

Why, I kept asking myself, didn't the fools shell Pec village, where a crowd of men and guns were waiting for transport? Why didn't they put over gas-shell? Why didn't they bomb us? Evidently there were no Germans here! About a quarter to nine No. 2 finished her ammunition, and we pulled her out. The other three guns had gone now and the other two British batteries were clear, all but two lorries. Just after nine o'clock our last tractor came along and took off No. 2 with Darrell in charge of her. How the Italians had managed to get all these lorries and tractors for us, I don't know for, in the Third Army as a whole, they were terribly short of transport. Many made the criticism that we should have kept out in Italy our own transport. But the Italians certainly did us very handsomely, at the cost of losing some bigger guns of their own.

After the last British gun had ceased to fire there was for about five minutes an eerie stillness, as though all our Artillery had gone and theirs was holding its fire. And then an Italian Field Battery opened again on the right of Pec. For over an hour now I had been expecting minute by minute, to see the enemy infantry come swarming along the Nad Logem in the dusk, cutting off our retreat, for I knew we had nothing but rear-guards left up there. But they did not come! . . .

28*th Oct.* We had slept for less than an hour, when we were hurriedly awakened. The Italians had orders to set fire to the house. . . . . We marched off again through pouring rain, our path lit up by the flames, which in places thrust their long tongues right across the road. The wind blew clouds of smoke in our faces. The air was full of the roaring of fires, the crackle of blazing woodwork, the crash of houses falling in, the loud explosions of ammunition dumps and petrol stores which now and again for a few seconds lighted up the whole sky for miles around with a terrific glare, and then died down again. Far as the eye could reach the night was studded with red and golden fires. . . .

29*th Oct.* Enemy planes now began to appear in the sky, some scouting only, others dropping bombs. They did more damage to the wretched refugees than to the military. What chances they missed that day ! Once or twice, when we were stationary, I gave the order to scatter in the fields to left and right of the road. But they never came near to hitting us. They flew very high and their marksmanship was atrocious.

Atrocious also was our tractor. Finally when it broke down and we had no fresh accumulator, we had to unlimber the front gun, attach ropes to the tractor, haul vigorously on the ropes until the engine started up, then back the tractor and front limber back to the guns, limber up, cast off the ropes, and go ahead again. We did this three or four times in the course of an hour, and enjoyed the sense of triumphing over obstacles. But it was very laborious, and the intervals between the successive breakdowns grew shorter and shorter. And the last time the trick didn't work, though we had all heaved and heaved till we were very near exhaustion. We were fairly stuck now, half blocking the road. Great excitement, as was only natural, developed among those behind. . . .

I saw, a little distance in front, an Italian Artillery Colonel in a state of wild excitement. He was rushing about with an unopened bottle of red wine in his hand, waving it ferociously at the heads of refugees, and driving them and their carts off the road down a side track. A queer pathetic freight some of these carts carried, marble clocks and blankets, big wine flasks and canaries in cages. The Colonel had driven off the road also a certain Captain Medola, of whom I shall have more to say in a moment, and who was sitting sulkily on his horse among the civilian carts. The Colonel's object, it appeared, was to get a number of field batteries through. He had cleared a gap in the blocked traffic and his field-guns were now streaming past at a sharp trot. But he was an extraordinary spectacle and made me want to laugh. Treading very delicately, I approached this infuriated man, and explained the helpless position of our guns, pointing out that we were also unwillingly impeding the movements of his own. I asked if he could order any transport to be provided for us. He waved his bottle at me, showed no sign of either civility or comprehension, only screaming at the top of his voice, " Va via, va via ! "

I gave him up as hopeless, and went back to my guns, intending to wait till he had disappeared and things had quieted down again, and then to look for help elsewhere. But the Latin mind also follows a thread of order through what an Anglo-Saxon is apt to mistake for a mere hurricane of confused commotion. Within five minutes Captain Medola came up to me and said that the Colonel had ordered him to drag our tractor and guns. Medola was in command of a battery of long guns, and had one of these attached to a powerful tractor on the road in front.of us. To this long gun, therefore, we now attached our tractor, useless as a tractor but containing valuable gun stores, and our three guns. It was a tremendous strain for one tractor, however strong, to pull, and we decided a little later to abandon our tractor and most of its contents.

Medola, having handed his horse over to an orderly, who was to ride on ahead and arrange for a fresh supply of petrol for his tractors, of which there were three, mounted the front of the leading tractor and I got up beside him. . . .

We saw another battery of Italian heavy guns going along the road heavier than either ours or Medola's. They were an ancient type, which we had seen sometimes on the Carso, and not of very high military value. But the gunners took a regimental and affectionate pride in those old guns. They had neither tractors nor horses, but they had dragged their beloved pieces for thirty miles from the rocky heights of the Carso, along good roads and bad, up and down hills, through impossible traffic blocks, down on to the plains as far as Palmanova, with nothing but long ropes and their own strong arms. They had forty men hauling on each gun. At Palmanova new hauling parties had been put on, who dragged the guns another thirty miles to the far side of the Tagliamento at Latisana.

And as they hauled, they sang, until they were too tired to go on singing, and could only raise, from time to time, their rhythmical periodic cry of " Sforza ! . . . Sforza ! " . . .

As we passed through Muzzano, the town and road were heavily bombed. The bell in the campanile jangled wildly and weeping women crowded into the church, as though thinking to find sanctuary there. Others stood gazing helplessly up into the sky. Here I saw some Italian infantry, mostly young, who were delighted to be retreating. " Forward, you militarists," they cried to us as we passed. " This is your punishment ! How much longer do you think the war is going to last ? What about Trieste now ? " . . .

At nightfall we were still eight or nine kilometres from Latisana. The traffic block grew worse and worse, and there were too few carabinieri to exercise proper control. We stuck for hours at a time, with nothing moving for miles, three motionless lines of traffic abreast on the road, all pointing in the same direction. Tired men slept and wakeful men waited and watched and cursed at the delay. Behind us, far off, we could hear the booming of the guns, which seemed from hour to hour to come a little nearer, and flashes of distant gun-fire flickered in the night sky. . . .

And behind and around us burning villages were still flaming in the dark, and throwing up the sharp black outlines of trees. . . .

30th Oct. At last we turned the last corner and came in sight of the Tagliamento. The bridge was still intact. Italian generals were rushing to and fro, gesticulating, giving orders. General Pettiti sent a special orderly to ask if mine were the last guns. I told him yes. Our tractor broke down three times on the bridge itself. But at last we were over. One of our party had an Italian flag and waved it and cried " Viva l'Italia ! " Not along after, the bridge went up, with an explosion that could be heard for miles around.

Hugh Dalton (R.G.A.).

THE BATTLE OF CAMBRAI

In the autumn of 1917 *preparations were being made for a surprise tank attack on the Cambrai section of the Western front.   General Byng was in command, and six divisions, with* 381 *tanks, went over the top on November* 20.   *In spite of our initial success in penetrating the German lines—a success that aroused such enthusiasm that for the first and only time during the war the bells of London were rung to acclaim a " victory " —the attack was a failure ; but the German counter-attack which followed a few days later was not.*

THE TANKS ADVANCE

BEFORE midnight that evening, from Havrincourt Wood and Dessart Wood, from Gouzeaucourt and Villers-Guislain, scores of tanks had uncamouflaged and moved out and were already on their way.   It was such a gathering of these singular machines as never had been seen before, and was to be seen only once again—on 8th August of the following year.   Section after section, company after company (twenty-seven companies were there, as against two on the Somme a year earlier), they crawled forward in long columns that split up after a while into smaller ones, and then again into twos and threes, until towards five o'clock the whole were deploying into a single lines six miles long—a threatening, silent, curving line that faced and corresponded to the larger salients and re-entrants of the Hindenburg trenches.

So silently had this approach been carried out that many of the infantry, assembling behind the gaps in our own wire, heard no tanks at all, and inquired with some anxiety if they had arrived.   A few had broken down, and were replaced at once from the mechanical reserve.   Upwards of 350 were in position.   The night was very dark, with a dense ground mist, but so complete were all arrangements that this caused no inconvenience, while it helped to screen the massing of this unparalleled armada.   A sudden burst of shelling and trench-mortar fire from the German lines about 4.30 startled everyone and provoked suspicions of a premature discovery, but it died away in half an hour. From five o'clock until zero the whole front was quiet. At ten minutes past six tanks and infantry began to move; and at 6.20, with the sky lightening rapidly above the mist, the barrage exploded with a shattering crash of sound along the German outpost line, some 250 yards in front of the " advance-guard " machines. In the centre of the six-mile line, in a tank called the " Hilda " of H Battalion, General Elles was leading into the most revolutionary battle of the war the corps which had made it possible, and which he had controlled almost from its infancy. It was not the ordinary post for the commander of a large organization, but this was not an ordinary occasion. It was the consummation of two years of struggle and disappointment. There can have been little doubt in his mind, or in that of any other man in the 350 tanks, as to what the result would be now that the adventure was fairly launched.

The immediate onset of the tanks inevitably was overwhelming. The German outposts, dazed or annihilated by the sudden deluge of shells, were overrun in an instant. The triple belts of wire were crossed as if they had been beds of nettles, and 350 pathways were sheared through them for the infantry. The defenders of the front trench, scrambling out of dug-outs and shelters to meet the crash and flame of the barrage, saw the leading tanks almost upon them, their appearance made the more grotesque and terrifying by the huge black bundles they carried on their cabs. As these tanks swung left-handed and fired down into the trench, others also surmounted by these appalling objects, appeared in multitudes behind them out of the mist. It is small wonder that the front Hindenburg Line, that fabulous excavation which was to be the bulwark of Germany, gave little trouble. The great fascines were loosed and rolled over the parapet to the trench floor; and down the whole line tanks were dipping and rearing up and clawing their way across into the almost unravaged country beyond. The defenders of the line were running panic-stricken, casting away arms and equipment.

The Hindenburg Reserve, with its own massive entanglements, went the way of the first trenches; and so far our following infantry had found little to do beyond firing on the fugitives and rounding up gangs of half-stupefied prisoners. It was now broad day, the mist was thinning, and everywhere from Havrincourt to Banteux on the canal was rout and consternation. The Grand Ravin, a gully with an unarmed mob streaming eastward. The garrison of Havrincourt had put up a fight, but tanks closed on it from the north, and it was cleared by the 62nd Division.[1]

La Vacquerie had gone in the first onset; and now Ribecourt was carried, and tanks and infantry were approaching the vital canal bridges at Marcoing and Masnieres. Over the whole southern half of the battlefield, the triangle I have described, the defence had collapsed; and this area was virtually cleared by midday.

D. G. Browne (Tank Corps).

THE CAVALRY

20th Nov. But where were the Cavalry? It was nearly eleven o'clock. All the tanks and Infantry had reached their objective in our part of the line. Marcoing had been captured. The Germans were in flight. When would the Cavalry arrive to exploit the success? I began to feel seriously alarmed. Bryce and I climbed up the hill towards Premy Chapel, from which point we could look back to our old front line; but no Cavalry were in sight. A signal tank was not far off; I sent back a message to Tank Corps Head-quarters giving an outline of the situation, so favourable for immediate exploitation. Another hour passed; still no sign of any Cavalry. The precious moments were slipping by and giving the Germans time to rally in front of Cambrai. I grew desperate. We still had some pigeons; I used three of them to send off a " Priority " message to be repeated to Corps Head-quarters and G.H.Q. It would be dark at five;

---

[1] M'Elroy, of 19 Company, won the D.S.O. at Havrincourt in remarkable circumstances. The leading tanks and infantry had passed through the village, which was believed to be cleared of the enemy. M'Elroy's machine, following behind, caught fire just as about 100 Germans appeared round it from various hiding-places. Two of the crew, jumping out of one door to escape the flames, were killed instantly. The remainder, except the tank commander, scrambled out of the other door into a shell-hole. The Germans bombed them and killed one man, and then came and looked down into the shell-hole, where the survivors pretended also to be dead. M'Elroy, in the meantime, had remained in the tank and extinguished the fire. He then drove off the Germans with machine-gun fire and kept them at bay for nearly an hour until some infantry arrived. All this time other tank crews, a few hundred yards away, were walking about outside their machines, unconscious of the little battle going on behind them.

unless the Cavalry arrived very soon there would be no chance of effecting anything that day.

But I had to go ; Courage had said that I was to be back at our Brigade Head-quarters by 3 p.m., and I must start at once. Cazalet and I began our homeward trek ; and after walking for nearly an hour we met the vanguard of the Cavalry. It was at the village of Ribecourt, a place that had been in our hands since seven o'clock that morning. And what was the Cavalry doing ? Why, carrying out the regular tactics for advancing by stages into an enemy's country !— troop halted in sunken road behind the village, two scouts sent forward to reconnoitre, one of them returns to report to the officer. No wonder they were late ! I was furious with that young Cavalry officer. It was really too absurd. Ribecourt had been captured at 7 a.m., the R.E. were loading up material from a German dump just outside the village at 9 a.m., and now, four hours later, the Cavalry were advancing as cautiously as if Germans might be expected round every corner. Half an hour later I met Courage and told him what I had seen ; as an old Cavalryman himself (15th Hussars) he was explosive in his wrath. But it was no good ; it was all too late. The Cavalry squadrons were only just crossing No Man's Land and it was nearly 2 p.m., just six hours after the barbed wire entanglements had been cleared for them by special tanks detailed for that purpose. We heard afterwards that the head of the Cavalry column did not start until noon from Fins, which was four miles behind our original front line !

Stephen Foot (Tank Corps).

WARNING FROM THE INFANTRY

20th Nov. Captain le Hardy who was commanding A Company could see quite clearly from his new head-quarters the villages of Banteux and Bantouzelle in the valley of the St. Quentin Canal. He noticed with some surprise that although the houses appeared intact there was no sign of life in them. He accordingly detailed an officer's patrol under Lieutenant R. M. Howe to reconnoitre. This patrol had a curious experience. It penetrated into Banteux, crossed the canal by the bridge leading into Bantouzelle, walked right through that village (and some way up the hill beyond) without meeting or seeing a solitary German. In his initial panic the enemy had abandoned both villages, as well as the two covering trench lines (Pelican and Bitch Trenches) on the slope running down from the Cambrai Road.

This information was reported to the Adjutant, who passed it on to the Brigade, but since the villages were out of our area nothing further could be done by us. We heard nothing more of the matter. The Higher Command here missed a golden opportunity of occupying unopposed what undoubtedly was the key to the canal-crossing on our front, the importance of which was evidently not unknown to them, for the following had appeared in Divisional Orders : " In order to render the flank more secure it is proposed to destroy the bridges at Les Rues des Vignes and Banteux and drive the enemy with tanks from the Western Bank," while the Divisional History states : " The weakness of the position was the inability to command the lower portions of the Canal Valley, either by fire or observation." These statements render the inertia displayed even more inexplicable. No orders were given to the Royal Engineers as to demolitions, which the infantry could not have carried out without expert assistance. There can be no doubt that even if the question of occupying these important positions was ever thoroughly considered it had been entirely shelved, in spite of the fact that the buildings of the villages and the small woods and folds in the ground provided the enemy with admirable cover for hidden concentration.

It was not until the 23rd that General Pulteney, our Corps Commander, awoke to the importance of occupying Pelican Trench and thus of obtaining observation over the canal. It was now too late.

Owen Rutter.

BOURLON WOOD

27th Nov. I am standing with my observers on high ground near the entrance to the dug-out. I am thrilled. The sound of battle is in the air—a light cannonade on both sides and a great rattle of machine-gun fire coming from the German lines. A shell bursting near us comes, so to speak, to punctuate the excitement I felt. I am safe. One of too many for mishap to single out.

But our eyes cannot pierce the mist that hangs over the battlefield. For purpose of observation our position is useless. Soon I receive orders to proceed to the foot of the village and, obtaining touch with the Companies, to relay messages back to Battalion Head-quarters. I start out with six observers, cutting across the field behind Nos. 1 and 2 Companies. We pass Sergeant Rhodes, V.C., D.C.M., mortally wounded, being carried back on a stretcher. He was a fine big man, but lying deep in the stretcher and covered with a blanket, seems immeasurably to have shrunk. Only his head, immense and white, like an indomitable will appears to keep life in him. But soon he will be a corpse, all his great strength and courage are ebbing fast.

I question him, but although conscious, he can say little. Poor man, I am thinking, poor man! It was only a few months ago that he captured an enemy pill-box single-handed. Among his prisoners was an artillery forward observing officer.

The full orchestra of battle is on. The air seems alive with invisible wires being twanged, while the earth is thumped and beaten.

The bullets zip, whiz, whistle, spin, sing and sigh according to their proximity and their point of flight. They constitute in reality the spray off the wave of lead being poured into Nos. 1 and 2 Companies, although I scarcely realize this at the time.

We have reached the foot of the village without a casualty. I am standing on ground newly won. To my left and right stretch deserted enemy entrenchments. Near me lie two wounded Grenadiers. One is in a ditch full of water. They are remarkably quiet. I must get them back somehow, but there are no stretcher-bearers about.

Out of the house next to which I am standing appear three Germans. They are holding up their hands. One has his foot in a bandage and is being helped along by the others. They look frightened and miserable. While they are chattering in German, a wounded Grenadier turns up quite off his head.

"That's all right, sir," he addresses me. "I'll kill them."

"I wouldn't do that," I remonstrate.

"Oh, that's quite all right. You just leave them to me." He threatens them with his rifle. The wounded German starts to whimper and shuffles off.

The Grenadier follows, herding his little party together. He uses his rifle like a shepherd's staff. Could he have been a shepherd in civilian life? They disappear in the direction of an out-house.

Whatever happened to them? They were not heading strictly for the British lines.

Another small party of prisoners appears with a wounded Grenadier as escort. He is dazed and shaking with fright.

" Take a door off this house and have these prisoners carry back this wounded man." But he doesn't understand.

The prisoners stand nervously about wishing to be gone. I show them what I want done and they comply with alacrity. Soon they are off, carrying the wounded Grenadier. It must be a heavy load. I could not help fearing they would drop him half-way in their eagerness to get out of danger. But if they had any thought of doing so it was intercepted by a German shell which burst in their midst after they had gone two hundred yards.

More prisoners turning up, remove another door from a house, on which they place the man lying in the ditch of water.

Suddenly a large group of Germans approaches. Their leader is a big man and the rest follow with a martial tread that contrasts oddly with their upraised hands and white handkerchiefs, energetically waved by some. One or two dodge into houses, but the rest march on until they have reached us. The big man addresses me and I feel like a traffic policeman as I point to the British lines and watch them hurry off.

Messages arrive from Nos. 3 and 4 Companies. They have captured their objectives, they are held up by heavy German machine-gun fire, they have suffered considerably and are in need of reinforcements. No word from either Nos. 1 or 2 Companies—a bad sign.

The Commanding Officer turns up. I salute as though on parade.

He looks anxious.

" We must go up and see what is happening."

Together we proceed up the main street of Fontaine-Notre-Dame, down which machine-gun bullets are pouring with the volume of water from a fire-hose. We hug the houses to minimize the danger of being hit.

We reach the cross-roads and I marvel that a man can get so far and remain alive. We are in the van of the battle. It seems a miracle has happened to me.

Knollys greets us. His Company Commander has been wounded. IIe is holding his position with about forty men and one machine-gun. It is almost all that is left of the battalion. Nos. 1 and 2 Companies have disappeared into the blue. They were, as a matter of fact, wiped out. All officers (including both Company Commanders killed) both Sergeant-Majors, and all Sergeants were casualties, and two-thirds of the men. Knollys is not certain but he thinks No. 4 Company is somewhere up on the left.

On the extreme left of Knollys's position the road turns sharp to the right. Up this I am sent to reconnoitre, and never did a road seem more empty nor I more solitary.

I find Carrington with about thirty men, all that is left of No. 4 Company. He looks exhausted. He is standing beside a German field-gun. We should have put it out of commission.

Our consultation is interrupted by the appearance of a tank. It stops, and out of it an officer descends.

" Do you want me any more ? "

" No." I feel as though I were dismissing a taxi.

He climbs back into the tank and down the street it waddles away.

We occupy a difficult position. The road to our rear joins with the left flank of No. 3 Company. We stand at the junction of the two other roads, one of which leads to the station and the other in the direction of Bourlon Wood. The 1st Coldstreams are somewhere on our left. A wide gap divides us, a gap impossible to bridge.

Suddenly to our right we see the enemy attacking down the main road that leads to the centre of No. 3 Company's position. We are well placed to enfilade, which we do with a will. We watch Germans being beaten back, holding up their arms before their faces as though warding off blows from sticks and stones.

With that attack driven back we think of No. 3 Company as secure. The men are posted to overlook the roads. We have no thought of our rear. I have sent a runner with a message giving our position.

I have whisky in my water bottle and some milk chocolate in my pockets. Some twenty yards below the junction of roads is a house. On the side facing No. 3 Company's position runs a wall enclosing a small yard. Carrington and I enter the house. A house recently evacuated ; chairs and table and everything just as they were left. We eat some chocolate and take a pull at my water-bottle. We say little—one or two irrelevant remarks. Our situation is awkward, to say the least.   Sixty men with both flanks in the air cannot hold a village against a strong and inevitable counter-attack.

I catch sight of my face in a mirror.   It is pink and normal. I haven't taken in the seriousness of our position.   I am still in a kind of a dream.   A mental smoke-screen obscures my vision.

Even the Sergeant's astonishing announcement reaches me dimly. " Germans are coming up be'ind ! "

By no selective reasoning do I find myself, with revolver drawn, behind the wall, while the others stand in the entrance of the yard. And to be suddenly shooting at grey uniformed Germans is accompanied by no thrill.   How big they are !   Is it because he is aiming straight at my head that this German appears so big ?   The motion of his rifle coming up to his shoulder increases his stature.   My revolver loses power to hurt, for after I have fired the Germans remain in the same position.   And yet they are so near it would seem impossible to miss them.   It does not seem as though I am missing but rather as though my bullets, turning into pellets, are bounding harmlessly off,   Nor does the German's rifle seem to function. There is no smoke, no flash, and I hear no bullet whistle uncomfortably close to my head.   The whole thing takes on the unreality of a " movie " until one of the Germans drops.   It seems the signal for which his fellows have been waiting, for with one accord they spin round and run away.   I have never seen people run so fast. Look at that man as he turns the corner, the play of his big grey legs from hip to knee.   He is gone.

I gaze at Carrington and he at me.   It is from our rear that we have been attacked.   Where is No. 3 Company ?

It is the Sergeant who shows presence of mind.

" We must follow."

Someone shouts.   " Collect the rest of the men."

We break into a run ; following in the wake of the Germans.   We pass the wounded German.   He has raised himself on his elbow and, stretching out a hand, says something.   A plea for mercy, for help ? The bullet had hit the bone below the eye, leaving a bloody gash.

We have reached the bend in the road.   This had been the left of No. 3 Company's position.   Only a dead Grenadier remains. Do we expect to meet the enemy as we stop stockstill at the corner ? I expect nothing.   I have ceased to think.   It is as though our legs have outstripped thought.   Time itself has stopped.   The surprise attack, the brief duel, the pursuit following in swift succession, all seem to belong to the same moment. Only now is time passing. An eternity, while one stands irresolute, wondering what to do.

" We must cut in be'ind these 'ouses, otherwise we're lost." It is the Sergeant again who is speaking.

It is true enough. We can soon expect an attack in force, and from several directions. The rest of the Company has joined us. Some thirty Britishers in the village of Fontaine.

The apparently deserted houses seem haunted. The windows take on the semblance of glassy eyes. Soon we shall be the victims of a dangerous game of hide and seek. How many of the enemy are near at hand, lurking around corners, organizing an attack? What resistance can we make? Already the reconnoitring party we had met must have reported our presence. Soon the enemy will be upon us in force. These fears, not voiced, scarcely appre-hended, race like shadows across the mind. The men are on the move, quietly and in good order. Once through the first house, I wait to see the last man over the wall into the next garden, terrified now that my back is turned to the enemy : a slow-motion picture could not express my own sensation of movement as we climb from one garden to another.

We are clear of the village. We stand opposite Nos. 3 and 4 Companies' old positions. A hostile barrage is coming down with some power, but we pass through it with a feeling of comparative safety, now that we are quit of the village itself.

We find the remnant of No. 3 Company reinforced by a company of the 4th Grenadiers. " Cocky " Hoare of the 4th Battalion is much exc·ted. I am surprised at his agitation. He anticipates a big counter-attack on our very heels. I stay with him until it occurs to me that the Commanding Officer would like to know what has happened to No. 4 Company.

Experience, at first stimulating, ends by draining the system. Through the high storm of enemy shelling I pass, with any capacity for registering further emotion at last microscopically diminished. I feel no fear because I can feel nothing more.

Slithering down the steep and muddy flight of stairs into the dim interior of Battalion Head-quarters' dug-out is a purely mechanical performance, and its shadowy occupants unreal. Its gloom and earthen smell remind my subconscious self of former rest and security which acts soporifically upon me and, at the end of my narrative, I fall forward on to the table into a sleep more profound and dreamless than any I have ever known.

I wake into a strange world. The events of the preceding hours rush kaleidoscopically upon me, leaving me to fit myself, like a piece in a picture puzzle, into my immediate surroundings.

The Battalion is soon to move. Billy is sitting with his head in his hands saying, " Oh, my head ! Oh, my head ! "

In the midst of the most acute anxiety, disappointment and distress, the Commanding Officer has patience to repeat for the *n*th time, " Poor Billy ! "

The Adjutant and the Padre return from a final futile hunt for the bodies of " Nibs " and " Mary." " Missing, believed killed " they will remain until the end of time, with the rest of a generation missing.

A miserable and stricken little family, the survivors of the 3rd Battalion leave the " line."

Carroll Carstairs (3rd Grenadier Guards).

CATASTROPHE

On the morning of the 30th a sense of coming danger aroused me about 4 a.m. ; ordinarily I slept till much later. I don't know whether it was premonition or whether the explanation was simply mechanical ; the lull before a big attack may be as disturbing to a sleeper as the stopping of the engines on an ocean liner ; awake and restless, I dressed and went outside a good hour before dawn.

All was quiet, almost too quiet ; my presentiment of a big attack was strong. The Germans could not surely be quite such fools as to fail to take advantage of the absurd weakness of our position when our only line of retreat was so exposed. For my own convenience I had converted my Advance Dressing Station into my main head-quarters, and I knew I would be blamed for any consequent disaster to my unit. I walked down the hill to a house where the Sergeant-Major slept. He looked at me reproachfully when I woke him. I told him to get up and turn out all the men of the motor-transport section and get the engines running. . . .

The rest of my directions were drowned in a long harsh screech and then a loud explosion. An armour-piercing shell from a German naval gun had skimmed close over our heads and, passing clean through the far wall of the roofless building we had turned into a dressing-station, had burst amongst our howitzer batteries just across the road.

" You needn't bother about waking the officers, Eldridge. That'll wake 'em."

The unmistakable dull ground-shaking rumble of drum fire had begun away on the right—to the east. The early morning sky on that side was already tinged with smoke. The German attack had begun, and it developed and enveloped us with the most astonishing speed. In a moment or two salvoes of high explosive shells were beginning to fall into the yard below us from which I had just cleared out the motor-transport belonging to the three Divisional Field Ambulances. There were the usual " hurricane " effects of heavy shelling and the whistling of flying splinters of shell casing. Eastward, over the crest about eleven hundred yards away, I thought I could see groups of men with bayonets. I looked at them through my glasses ; our infantry were surely retiring rather soon ! A moment or two later I looked again. There was something unfamiliar about their movements ; they were running down the hill and towards us in line. Suddenly I realized they were Germans coming over, and in very good order too ! That looked as if they must have walked right through our 20th and 29th Divisions !

I could hardly believe my eyes. We must leg it even sooner than I expected. The cars had been rapidly loaded and were now chock-full. I ran across the road to tell the driver of the train of Decauville trucks to get off at top speed and save his engine and train whatever happened. He went off with stragglers and lightly wounded men clambering on to every footboard, some even on the roofs of his trucks. As the narrow gauge train like a long snake steamed away down the hill towards Fins, a group of enemy shells tore up the track just behind it. We seemed to be in a circle of heavy fire, disorganization was rapid, from every direction artillerymen came running past. Our N.C.O. shouted that a group of our howitzer batteries had been abandoned. Though unwounded, some of these men tried to climb into one of my motor ambulances, already overfull, that was just leaving.

. . . As I tried to disconnect the receiver and collect my own secret papers, B.A.B. trench-codes, and other things, and stuff them into my pockets, two German aeroplanes swept down to within fifty or sixty feet of the ground, raking the road and the little enclosure I was standing in with machine-guns. They missed me by inches. I could see that some, though only a few, of the German infantry had nearly reached the bottom of the street where our motors had been parked. Men of many units were now running through the main street of Gouzeaucourt towards Fins, some without rifles. The din had become terrific. Two of the motor ambulances had already left, crammed with wounded and personnel. Shouting to everyone to get into any sort of vehicle and make for Fins, I jumped on to the front of one of them.

As we started I heard someone shouting—it was E., Lord R's eldest son, a Staff Captain of one of our brigades—running breathless and dusty behind us. We slowed down for a moment as he jumped in alongside me and the driver.

" Your brigade ! " I shouted. " What's happened ? "

" Mostly gone ! I was damn near captured myself. I have been knocked over three times in the last two hundred yards by shells bursting all along the road from Villers. I'm afraid the division have lost nearly everything—including all the divisional artillery."

As our car dashed out of Gouzeaucourt we narrowly missed a shell which burst on the side of the road between the second and third ambulance. Going as fast as the shell-pitted road would allow us, we made for main Divisional Head-quarters some miles down the main road towards Fins. On either side of us men of all sorts and conditions, some half dressed, were bolting down the road. Strings of excited pioneers were running back to the road from the fields on either side, some throwing away their spades, also Artillerymen, men of the 29th Division Transport, Canadians, and Royal Engineers—it was becoming a real panic. A good many must have been wounded as they ran, for the first mile or so of the road between Gouzeaucourt and Fins was not only treeless but open on all sides, and it was being peppered with German shell. One man at full gallop was struck by a shell which carried away the hinder half of his horse and part of his hips. For a moment, a yard or two, this white-faced phantom seemed to cling to the still moving half of his horse. Then, as we sped by, both dead things crashed forward together on the *pavé*. . . .

About eight hundred yards farther on I ordered the ambulance I was in to run into the yard outside the Divisional Head-quarters. Jumping off, I went in to where they were all comfortably at breakfast. They stared at me in surprise. What had I come in for so early? Had I left my Advanced Dressing Station at Gouzeaucourt?

"Well, the Germans are there now. We had to skedaddle."

"The Germans . . . !"

"Yes, I suppose they are coming down the main Fins-Gouzeaucourt road!"

They stared incredulously; then they looked at E. who had followed me in—a Staff Captain, capless, his knuckles bleeding, unshaven, dusty. Even then I think they might have suspected we were merely a couple of panic-stricken lunatics had not a well-aimed and timely German shell exploded fairly near their mess kitchen. Then all the possibilities must have flashed through their minds— the strong south-westerly wind, cut telephone wires, and the unlikelihood of our both being demented. Then another shell arrived. I had not time to watch the effect of the second on the Brass Hats, but was told that this pleasant breakfast party also broke up a little hurriedly.

E. had pluck. It was a miracle he got through, for the road from Villers Plouich was being well hammered. The information he brought back must have been invaluable at such a moment.

Arriving at my own head-quarters about a quarter of a mile farther back, there was some satisfaction in seeing the lines of horses and wagons I had sent down the night before and the motor-transport of several of the Field Ambulances intact. The personnel of my own unit, and the greater part of the other units that were working under my orders, had for the most part been also saved.

Within twenty minutes our bearer sections were equipped again, and we were all marching back along the road towards Gouzeaucourt behind a motley collection hastily scraped together of scratch riflemen, cooks, officers' servants, and odd men from the neighbouring parks and dumps who were being hastily thrown into the gap to save what might have been an almost complete break-through by the Germans and one of the most serious disasters of the War. In three-quarters of an hour we had opened a new Advanced Dressing Station near the crater at Trescault cross-roads.

Lt.-Col. Arthur Osburn (R.A.M.C.).

BASE HOSPITAL

"Never in my life have I been so absolutely filthy as I get on duty here," I wrote to my mother on December 5th in answer to her request for a description of my work.

"Sister A. has six wards and there is no V.A.D. in the next-door one, only an orderly, so neither she nor he spend very much time in here. Consequently I am Sister, V.A.D. and orderly all in one (somebody said the other day that no one less than God Almighty could give a correct definition of the job of a V.A.D. !) and after, quite apart from the nursing, I have stoked the stove all night, done two or three rounds of bed-pans and kept the kettles going and prepared feeds on exceedingly black Beatrice oil-stoves and refilled them from the steam-kettles, literally wallowing in paraffin all the time, I feel as if I had been dragged through the gutter ! Possibly acute surgical is the heaviest kind of work there is, but acute medical is, I think, more wearing than anything else on earth. You are kept on the go the whole time and in the end there seems nothing definite to show for it—except that one or two people are still alive who might otherwise have been dead."

The rest of my letter referred to the effect, upon ourselves, of the new offensive at Cambrai.

"The hospital is very heavy now—as heavy as when I came ; the fighting is continuing very long this year, and the convoys keep coming down, two or three a night . . . Sometimes in the middle of the night we have to turn people out of bed and make them sleep on the floor to make room for more seriously ill ones that have come down from the line. We have heaps of gassed cases at present who came in a day or two ago ; there are 10 in this ward alone. I wish those people who write so glibly about this being a holy war, and the orators who talk so much about going on no matter how long the War lasts and what it may mean, could see a case— to say nothing of 10 cases—of mustard gas in its early stages—

could see the poor things burnt and blistered all over with great mustard-coloured suppurating blisters, with blind eyes—sometimes temporally [*sic*], sometimes permanently—all sticky and stuck to-gether, and always fighting for breath, with voices a mere whisper, saying that their throats are closing and they know they will choke. The only thing one can say is that such severe cases don't last long ; either they die soon or else improve—usually the former ; they certainly never reach England in the state we have them here, and yet people persist in saying that God made the War, when there are such inventions of the Devil about . . .

" Morning work—i.e. beds, T.P.Rs (temperatures, pulses, respira-tions), washings, medicines, etc., which in Malta I started at 6.0, start here at 3.30 ! The other morning there were no less than 17 people to wash ! . . . Cold is terrific ; the windows of the ward are all covered with icicles and the taps outside frozen. I am going about the ward in a jersey and long coat."

Vera Brittain.

PATROL

As intelligence officer, I, too, was many times out in No Man's Land here. It may be well to say more. The wirers were out already, clanking and whispering with what seemed a desperate energy. The men lying at each listening-post were freezing stiff, and would take half an hour's buffeting and rubbing on return to avoid becoming casualties. Moonlight, steely and steady, flooded the flat space between us and the Germans. I sent my name along, " Patrol going out," and, followed by my batman, blundered over the parapet and through our meagre but mazy wire. Come, once again.

The snow is hardened and crunches with a sort of music. Only me, Worley. He lays a gloved hand on my sleeve, puts his head close, and says, " God bless you, sir—don't stay out too long." Then we stoop along his wire to a row of willows crop-headed, nine in a row, pointing to the German line. We go along these. At the third we stop. This may have been a farm track—a wagon way. But, the question for us is, what about that German ambush, or waiting patrol? Somewhere, just about here, officers were taken prisoner, or killed, a fortnight ago. There is no sound as we kneel. A German flare rises, but the moonlight will not be much enkindled. I have counted our steps from the first pollard. We come to the last. There are black, crouching forms, if our eyes do not lie, not far ahead ; but, patience at last exhausted, we move on again. The forms are harmless shapes of earth or timber, though we still think someone beside ourselves has moved. I am looking for two saps, which the aeroplane photographs disclose boldly enough, and one of which is held at times. And here is one. Hold hard.

That one is vague and shallow. We enter, and creep along, but it does not promise well ; then we step up, and cross over to the other. At the extremity is a small brushwood shelter, and this may mean—it does, but not now : yet this mess-tin and this unfrosty overcoat are not so derelict. We cannot avoid the feeling that we are being stalked, and we are equally amazed that in this moonlight we are not riddled with bullets. The enemy's parapet is scarcely out of bombing range. Far off we hear German wheels; but the trenches are silent. Probably we are being studied as a typical patrol. I do not like this telegraph wire here, which is not so continuously buried in snow as it ought to be. I have put my foot to it gently, and it is a wire. It leads to a stick bomb ready to be exploded. We move again, with our trophies. I still keep count of our paces.

Spike-like tree-trunks here stand surrounding an oval moat, which in turn encloses a curious mount. We must carry in some idea of this, and we coast it, but nothing happens, and so far as the difficult moonlight shows it is desolate and harmless as its two lean elm-trees. And now turning home, we see that our wirers have packed up, and we are amazed that we have been out over two hours. It is not so easy (once we have slipped over our parapet again) to leave the front line for battalion head-quarters; it has magnetized the mind; and for a moment one feels that to " break the horrid silence " would be an act of creation.

Edmund Blunden (11th *R. Sussex Reg.*).

THE KEYS OF JERUSALEM

9th Dec. Towards noon the resistance of the Turks collapsed. They fled east and north, and the advanced troops of the British force on the road from Jaffa pressed forward with an eagerness which was noteworthy. It may have been due to expectation. We had come far, and now the goal was close at hand. The Syrian monk at Enab had told us that El Kubeibeh—the valley where war's intrusion seemed an outrage, so peaceful was the aspect of its sycamores and cypresses and the broad sheet of precious water among those barren hills—once had been called Emmaus, and we knew it was only three-score furlongs distant from the City, a Sunday morning's walk.

After crossing the bottom of a deep ravine, the road skirted its southern edge and climbed in zigzags to a rocky plateau. The word passed round that this was the last stage ; yet even when that long ascent had been accomplished, no city could be seen, and already the short winter day was drawing in. At a bend, where the ravine turned north and the road ran in an easterly direction, were two houses ; one was in ruins. Beyond them the ground sloped downwards to another valley into which we could not see. To our right, in the south, a storm was brewing : the mountain-tops were blotted out by leaden clouds beneath which the landscape seemed convulsed, and from that seething cauldron white mists crept along the hidden valley, while wisps of fleecy vapour bore down on the plateau where we stood like riders of the sky.

One mountain, rising straight ahead, the storm had not yet reached. We had noted it many times before that day, the two towers on its summit, and a grove of trees surrounding a church with many domes in an enclosure on its side.

"How far off is the top of that hill ? " asked a General.

"Just over five thousand yards to the left-hand tower," was the answer.

The hill in question was the Mount of Olives, the enclosure

the Garden of Gethsemane, below which the still invisible city lay, not more than one mile off.

"Remember that no one is to go inside the walls. The Bull [1] will be furious if anything of that kind happens." This last injunction given, the General went back in his car to announce to Head-quarters and the world that Jerusalem had fallen.

Meanwhile, a small crowd had assembled in and around the ruined house ; it consisted of signallers establishing telephonic communication, a German doctor, two Americans, and three Turks. One of the Turks was the Mayor of the Holy City, and he had brought with him the keys as a token of surrender. They were large keys and quite ordinary, except that they were very clean and shone like silver. There were several ; no doubt "the keys of all the creeds" were in that bunch. They had been offered to two private soldiers, who had refused to have anything to do with them ; their duties as cooks were far too pressing and began only when camp was reached. Dalliance on the road for such as these would have been criminal ; others might traffic with key-bearing Mayors ; their business was to serve hungry, exacting comrades and shout out at the earliest moment possible the glad tidings "Dinners Up ! "

An Artillery Major had also been approached, but with the same result. He was a solicitor in private life, and the effect of artillery training on his legal mind had been to increase its cautiousness. Those keys were not for him, he felt that instinctively ; his ambition was a D.S.O. ; whereas the keys of Jerusalem were for people who might aspire to a K.C.B. or even higher. But when he thought of the local Press at home, in Yorkshire, of a whole column devoted to his doughty deeds, headed "A Tyke takes Temple," with a photograph of himself and three heathen Turks inset (one of the Americans had brought a camera), he was sorely tempted.

The keys were still undisposed of when the senior General called up on the telephone. He wanted further details before sending off a telegram ; but on being told of what had transpired since he left, his voice became eager, anxious, and imperative.

"The Mayor with the keys ? Has he still got them ? . . . Keep him till I come ; on no account let him go away or give them to anybody else. I will receive them ! "

[1] General Allenby.

Preparations for the ceremony were made at once : a few women and children had by this time assembled, bringing flowers, and a camera was got into position.

If Robert the Bruce had achieved his heart's desire and been able to fulfil his vow, he might have ridden by that road after lying overnight at Enab.   But he would not have stopped one moment by the wayside in his impatience ; the keys would have been received by Douglas, the faithful servant of his King.   Godfrey of Bouillon, too —" a quiet, pious, hard-fighting knight, who was chosen to rule in Jerusalem because he had no dangerous qualities and no obvious defects "—would have left either to Bohemund or Baldwin what to him would have seemed an empty show.   But he, of course, was not successful, only the hero of a legend and some songs.   The man who actually received the keys was neither King nor Pilgrim, though in some ways a Crusader ; his satisfaction was unbounded as he stood, the observed of all observers (and there were at least a dozen present,) by the roadside with the ruin as a background. Ruins and conquerors go well together.

Click, went the camera, and the General smiled approval ; at least there was a record of this historical event with himself the central figure.

In regard to publicity the Solicitor and the General had much in common ; but naturally the latter's outlook on affairs was wider. No local Press for him ; he aimed at nothing less than the front page of a Sunday illustrated paper—some weekly compendium of sport, vulgarity, follies, crimes, and lies, with an occasional contribution from a Cabinet Minister.   This is an age of doubt ; people believe little of what they read but still retain a touching faith in photographs.   His niche in the temple of fame and limelight would be secure if a million so-called Sunday readers knew him by sight. And how opportune it was !   With any luck the negative would be in London by Christmas week.   Thus, suddenly, is a garish glory gained.

A whole series of photographs had in fact been taken, his was the last.   The first was of two British Tommies, in shorts, conferring with a Turkish Mayor and two City Councillors, accepting cigarettes and flowers, smiling their gratitude for these gifts.   The second was of their backs as they plodded stolidly eastwards, keyless and careless, while three disconsolate City Fathers stared after them, baffled and charmed by their simplicity. The third showed a big, strong man seated squarely on a horse; and looking up at him, appealingly, a frail old Turk holding a bunch of keys. The horseman's face was twitching under the stress of inner conflicts between caution and desire. He was neither buying nor selling, but, metaphorically, was looking a gift horse in the mouth. A strange position for a Yorkshireman. " Château qui parle; femme qui écoute." The proverb is incomplete. In all probability, if he, who had neither spoken nor listened to Jerusalem's first Magistrate, had looked at those keys a moment longer he would have yielded. But caution triumphed. The fourth photograph showed a wistful figure, standing apart, watching; the solicitor had lingered, held by some instinct, until the General's car arrived. If to suffer in silence were a military virtue, that solitary spectator earned a D.S.O. during the next five minutes. A Major, of course, should always give way to a General; but this man was only one-third Major; he had two other sides which did not wear khaki. Another man, because he was a General, was getting what he, a Yorkshire solicitor, might have got, for nothing. It was enough to make anyone a Bolshevik. He wondered if the smiling recipient of those keys was Irish—quite a quarter of the Generals in the British Army were of that fighting race—and shuddered at the thought.

A few hundred yards farther on were the first houses of the western suburb. Neither pomp nor circumstances attended our arrival; we were not entering the walled city, only surrounding it, and marched through squalid streets from a corner near the Jaffa Gate to the main road leading to Damascus. While we passed the storm broke; an icy wind swept up the valley of the Kedron, rain fell in torrents and drenched the tired troops.

Brig.-Gen. C. B. Thomson.

TRADE RISKS

On the morning of December 18th we were proceeding on the surface and hoped to make port that evening in time for dinner. About 9 a.m. we sighted a convoy to the westward and dived. The convoy passed right over us and we distinctly heard the throb of the propellers. I was on watch and I waited fully ten minutes from the time the sounds had died away and then gave the order to rise to thirty feet.

The sea was still choppy. As I raised the periscope and looked in the direction of the receding vessels we broke surface accidentally. The convoy was at least two miles away and it was unlikely that they had seen us, so I turned the periscope around to make sure that all was clear elsewhere. I was horrified to see a destroyer not more than five hundred yards away and a little on our port quarter.

The men at the hydroplanes got the boat under control and she was soon completely submerged. I hoped we had escaped detection, but I was soon disillusioned. Watching through the periscope, I saw the destroyer—an American one—turn and head right for us. As I looked I saw the black smoke belch from her funnels as she increased speed, and a white puff centred with a streak of flame came from her forward guns. There was nothing we could do but wait. There was no time to come to the surface and fire the recognition signals. Our fate lay in the hands of the gods.

My mind naturally flew to the forthcoming depth-charge attack and I decided to remain as near the surface as possible because I knew that the depth charges were set to explode at between eighty and one hundred feet. My reason told me that we were safer near the surface than deeper down, because the explosion would be farther away and the pressure less.

In an unbelievably short time the destroyer passed over us, so close that we actually felt her keel scrape our jumping wires. She had tried to ram us and failed. But as she passed over the spot where we had disappeared she laid her infernal eggs.

B-O-O-M !

The concussion shook the boat to the core. The stern rose up and the bows went down at a sickening angle. We went into a terrific nose-dive. Many lights went out. Some of the electric fuses in the switchboard blew out. My gaze centred on the depth gauge. 60-70-80-90-100 feet, the indicator hand quickly flew. 120-130-150-160-180-200 feet, and still we went downward.

" Blow the main tanks ! "—Coltart had taken charge and issued the order.

I saw the electric hydroplane control was out of action—but there was no need to issue orders ; the coxswain who happened to be on duty was putting them into hand-gear. The angle the boat was diving at was easily forty-five degrees. The low-pressure depth indicator only registered to two hundred feet. The depth gauge showed three hundred feet. That was as far as it would register.

The coxswain, with great presence of mind, had now the hydroplane controls into hand gear. His mate, who had been thrown from his stool when the boat took her perpendicular dive, scrambled back to his station. They whirled the wheels hard to rise. The hull was creaking and groaning under the terrific outside pressure of the water. Then she started to rise.

" Check the main tanks ! " Coltart ordered.

I felt the boat straighten herself under the influence of the horizontal rudders and the added buoyancy.

" Shut off the air ! "

Could we prevent her breaking surface again ? That was the question which flashed through my mind. If not we would be easy victims of the destroyer's guns.

B-o-o-m ! B-o-o-m ! Crash ! went two more depth charges, but they were farther away and did no more than jar us.

" Steady her at eighty feet ! " The coxswain and his assistant at the hydroplane adjusted the horizontal rudders to check the boat from rushing to the surface. Still she rose, and water was ordered into No. 2 and No. 3 tanks. We arrested her upward rush at forty feet, and after a little juggling got complete control at sixty feet.

All I have recounted happened in less than two minutes, and a great deal of credit must go to the men who had charge of the motors. Notwithstanding the fact that the explosion of the depth charge blew in the packing of the port shaft and allowed salt water to reach the motor, which went off with a flash of blue flame and smoke that filled the after-compartments, they stuck to their posts calmly and continued to work the starboard motor as instructed from the control room. It was fortunate that the explosion affected only the port motor, which was already useless owing to the cracked shaft. Otherwise this story would never have been told.

After anxiously waiting for upward of half an hour to see if the destroyer intended to renew its attack, we rose as cautiously as possible to the surface and took a look-see. The destroyer was evidently quite satisfied that she had done a good job, because she was hull down, headed straight for Plymouth.

Since all was clear, we came to the surface, hoisted our mast and flag—also our wireless to show we were innocent of any wrongful intentions—and headed after her. But all the world was against us that day. Although we had our flag flying and masts up, a fool of a trawler took a couple of shots at us before we could convince her that we were giving her the right challenge for the day. When she was convinced she kindly turned and escorted us into port.

After we were securely moored we made arrangements for the comfort of our crew, and then Coltart, Pryor, and I headed for the officers' quarters at Devonport Barracks. Coated with brine and black with oil fumes, we looked like three stokers, but there was one thing we needed more than anything else, and that was a good stiff whisky-and-soda so we entered the smoke-room just as we were to order the drinks.

The room was crowded with officers waiting for dinner to be announced, and in the centre of an interested group were three American officers telling of their good fortune in sinking an enemy submarine that morning.

" There was no question about it," the commander was saying. " She broke surface right under our bows. We fired a couple of shots that seemed to strike home ; then we rammed her and, to make sure, dropped three depth charges right over the spot where she disappeared."

Coltart edged his way into the group.

" Sorry to disillusion you, old chap," he drawled, " but it was my boat you tried to scupper. If a whisky-and-soda or a cocktail will make up for the D.S.O. you won't get, you are welcome to have one on me, and here's wishing you better luck next time."

William Guy Carr.

A WATCHER QUESTIONS THE SKY

AT the moment of midnight, December 31, 1917, I stood with some acquaintances in a camp finely overlooking the whole Ypres battle-field. It was bitterly cold, and the deep snow all round lay frozen. We drank healths, and stared out across the snowy miles to the line of casual flares, still rising and floating and dropping. Their writing on the night was as the earliest scribbling of children, meaningless; they answered none of the questions with which a watcher's eyes were painfully wide. Midnight; successions of coloured lights from one point, of white ones from another, bullying salutes of guns in brief bombardment, crackling of machine-guns small on the tingling air; but the sole answer to unspoken but importunate questions was the line of lights in the same relation to Flanders as at midnight a year before.

Edmund Blunden.

VOICES—1917–18

LOOK WELL AT DEATH!

10*th March*, 1917.   Death !   That word which booms like the echo
of sea caverns, striking and re-striking in dark and unseen depths.
Between this war and the last, we did not die : we ended.   Neatly,
in the shelter of a room, in the warmth of a bed.   Now, we die.   It
is the wet death, the muddy death, death dripping with blood, death
by drowning, death by sucking under, death in the slaughter house.
The bodies lie frozen in the earth which gradually sucks them in.
The luckiest depart, wrapped in canvas from a tent, to sleep in the
nearest cemetery.

L. Mairet (*killed in action April*, 1917).

THE POET RETURNS TO THE WAR

31*st Dec.*   And so I have come to the true measure of man.   I
am not dissatisfied [with] my years.   Everything has been done in
bouts : bouts of awful labour at Shrewsbury and Bordeaux ; bouts
of amazing pleasure in the Pyrenees, and play at Craiglockhart ;
bouts of religion at Dunsden ; bouts of horrible danger on the
Somme ; bouts of poetry always ; of your affection always ; of
sympathy for the oppressed always.   I go out of this year a poet,
my dear mother, as which I did not enter it.   I am held peer by
the Georgians ; I am a poet's poet.   I am started.   The tugs have
left me ; I feel the great swelling of the open sea taking my galleon.
Last year, at this time (it is just midnight, and now is the intolerable
instant of the Change), last year I lay awake in a windy tent in the
middle of a vast, dreadful encampment.   It seemed neither France
nor England, but a kind of paddock where the beasts are kept a few
days before the shambles.   I heard the revelling of the Scotch troops,
who are now dead, and who knew they would be dead.   I thought

519

of this present night, and whether I should indeed—whether we should indeed—whether you would indeed—but I thought neither long nor deeply, for I am master of elision. But chiefly I thought of the very strange look on all faces in that camp ; an incomprehensible look, which a man will never see in England, though wars should be in England ; nor can it be seen in any battle. But only in Étaples. It was not despair, or terror, it was more terrible than terror, for it was a blindfold look, and without expression, like a dead rabbit's. It will never be painted, and no actor will ever seize it. And to describe it, I think I must go back and be with them. We are sending seven officers straight out to-morrow. I have not said what I am thinking this night, but next December I will surely do so.

Wilfred Owen (killed in action, Nov. 1918).

IT IS TIME TO GO

22 *July*, 1917. The time of waiting is over. I received my marching orders to-day and am off to-morrow. How different this departure is from the last ! and how different, again, from the first in December, 1914 ! Things have become more and more serious, and, in spite of all our victories, the burden presses more and more heavily upon our country. And that impatient longing to fight, the wild joy at the idea of being on the spot when the enemy got his *coup de grâce*, that cannot be expected from anybody who knows what life in the trenches is like and who has experienced in his own body the full gravity of the situation. I am delighted when I see such feelings exhibited by our boys, and I should think it an outrage to try and quench them by cold-blooded sarcasm ; but we, who have seen the dark side, must substitute for that enthusiasm a deep-seated determination to stand by the Fatherland whatever happens as long as it has need of us. We know that death is not the worst thing that we have to face. Thoroughly to realize everything and yet to go back, not under compulsion but willingly, is not easy. To try and deceive oneself by working oneself up into a state of excitement is, I hold, unworthy. Only genuine self-command is any use to me.

I know that I have been permitted by a benign fate to drink deeply of the clear spring of the German nation's courageous attitude towards life in itself. On wonderful journeys my eyes have been gladdened with the sight of Germany's beauty, and I have a home that I can truly love. This shows me where I belong when it is a case of defending that land. That was how I felt when I went to the Front for the first time, and it is just the same now.

A new chapter of life is beginning, and I must learn afresh to face the end with calm. One must not omit to examine oneself as to one's merits and deserts in the past. We do not practise auricular confession, but one must honourably clear these things up in one's own mind. One thing I must say to you, anyhow : I shall most certainly be fully conscious of all the kindness and comfort and friendly sympathy which I have met with even where I did not deserve it. For your large share in this I thank you from the bottom of my heart. Don't grieve because I have to go out again. My place is at the Front. That you must recognize.

Johannes Philippsen (*killed in action*, 20*th Sept.*, 1917).

BREAK OF DAY IN THE TRENCHES

The darkness crumbles away—
It is the same old druid Time as ever.
Only a live thing leaps my hand—
A queer sardonic rat—
As I pull the parapet's poppy
To stick behind my ear.
Droll rat, they would shoot you if they knew
Your cosmopolitan sympathies
(And God knows what antipathies).
Now you have touched this English hand
You will do the same to a German—
Soon, no doubt, if it be your pleasure
To cross the sleeping green between
It seems you inwardly grin as you pass
Strong limbs, fine eyes, haughty athletes
Less chanced than you for life,
Bonds to the whims of murder,
Sprawled in the bowels of the earth,
The torn fields of France.
What do you see in our eyes
At the striking of iron and flame,

Hurled through still heavens ?
What quaver—what heart aghast ?
Poppies whose roots are in man's veins
Drop, and are ever dropping ;
But mine in my ear is safe,
Just a little white with the dust.

Isaac Rosenberg (killed in action, March, 1918).

MY FRIEND, MY BROTHER

11th April, 1918. *In the Field.* I received definite news that
Kurt Gerschel has fallen. Thus are they all torn away, those that
were any good, that were young, courageous and full of hope in
the future. He was such a frank, fresh, clean fellow, honest and
straight as but few are, such a lovable being ! A real lesson to Anti-
Semites, brave and proud and true. May he rest in peace !

Otto Braun (Killed in action, May, 1918).

EXPOSURE

Our brains ache, in the merciless iced east winds that knive us . . .
Wearied we keep awake because the night is silent . . .
Low, drooping flares confuse our memory of the salient . . .
Worried by silence, sentries whisper, curious, nervous,
    But nothing happens.

Watching, we hear the mad gusts tugging on the wire,
Like twitching agonies of men among its brambles.
Northward, incessantly, the flickering gunnery rumbles,
Far off, like a dull rumour of some other war.
    What are we doing here ?

The poignant misery of dawn begins to grow . . .
We only know war lasts, rain soaks, and clouds sag stormy.
Dawn massing in the east her melancholy army
Attacks once more in ranks on shivering ranks of grey
    But nothing happens.

Sudden successive flights of bullets streak the silence.
Less deadly than the air that shudders black with snow,
With sidelong flowing flakes that flock, pause, and renew,
We watch them wandering up and down the wind's nonchalance,
    But nothing happens.

Pale flakes with fingering stealth come feeling for our faces—
We cringe in holes, back on forgotten dreams, and stare, snow-dazed,
Deep into grassier ditches. So we drowse, sun-dozed,
Littered with blossoms trickling where the blackbird fusses.
    Is it that we are dying?

Slowly our ghosts drag home : glimpsing the sunk fires, glozed
With crusted dark-red jewels ; crickets jingle there ;
For hours the innocent mice rejoice : the house is theirs ;
Shutters and doors, all closed : on us the doors are closed,—
    We turn back to our dying.

Since we believe not otherwise can kind fires burn ;
Nor ever suns smile true on child, or field, or fruit.
For God's invincible spring our love is made afraid ;
Therefore, not loath, we lie out here ; therefore were born,
    For love of God seems dying.

To-night, His frost will fasten on this mud and us,
Shrivelling many hands, puckering foreheads crisp.
The burying-party, picks and shovels in their shaking grasp,
Pause over half-known faces. All their eyes are ice,
    But nothing happens.

                        Wilfred Owen.

1918

MUST NOT OCCUR AGAIN

FRONT LINE, LEMPIRE

January 10, 1918. A few minutes before four o'clock this morning the enemy tried to raid one of my Lewis-gun posts which is placed, necessarily in an isolated position, well out in No Man's Land, about 150 yards off the fire-trench, in a sunken road which crosses both lines of trenches. The raiders came across the snow in the dark, camouflaged in white overalls.

In parenthesis, I may explain that while I have been away there have been two unfortunate cases of sentries mistaking wiring parties of the Divisional pioneer battalion for the enemy—whether owing to the failure of the wiring parties to report properly before going out, or to over-eagerness on the part of the sentries, I do not profess to know. No one was hurt on either occasion, but a good deal of fuss was made about it, our new Brigadier blaming the men who did the shooting—his own men—and saying so pretty forcibly.

When I first heard of this I thought that a mistake had been made—if for no other reason than there would for a time at any rate be a disinclination on the part of sentries to shoot promptly, which might prove dangerous—and that is what happened this morning.

The double sentries on duty in the sunken road heard, but in the darkness did not see, a movement in front of them. Hesitating to shoot, they challenged. The immediate reply was a volley of hand-grenades. Private Mayne, who had charge of the Lewis-gun, was hit " all over," in many parts, including the stomach. His left arm was reduced to pulp. Nevertheless, he struggled up, and leaning against the parapet, with his uninjured hand discharged a full magazine (forty-seven rounds) into the enemy, who broke, not a man reaching our trench. Then he collapsed and fell insensible across his gun.

The second sentry's foot was so badly shattered that it had to be amputated in the trench. The doctor has just told me that he performed this operation without chloroform, which was unnecessary owing to the man's numbed condition, and that while he did it the man himself looked on, smoking a cigarette, and with true Irish courtesy thanked him for his kindness when it was over.

Words cannot express my feelings of admiration for Private Mayne's magnificent act of gallantry, which I consider well worthy of the V.C. It is, however, improbable that he will live to enjoy any decoration that may be conferred upon him.

Lieut.-Col. Rowland Feilding (6th Connaught Rangers).

VILLERS FAUCON

January 12, 1918. The incident of the morning before last had so filled me with pride of the battalion that I confess I have been aghast at receiving—instead of any acknowledgment of the successful and heroic repulse of the German raiders by Private Mayne and his companion—the following memorandum, which has been circulated in the Division. I quote from memory:

"Another instance has occurred of an enemy patrol reaching within bombing distance of our line. This must not occur again. Our patrols must meet the enemy patrols boldly in No Man's Land," etc., etc., etc.

How simple and how grand it sounds! I think I can see the writer, with his scarlet tabs, seated in his nice office 7 or 8 miles behind the line, penning this pompous admonition.

So Private Mayne, it seems, will go unrecognized and unrewarded. In the meantime he has died, and I can only say, "God rest his soul!"

Ibid.

BERLIN BLOCKADED

Soon after the outbreak of the war the food shortage began. In the end we could hardly buy a pea without a ration card. No fat, no milk, no eggs, and Fritz and I needed them so urgently. Our growing bones were bare of flesh and only covered with a greyish skin. " Stork leg, stork leg ! " called the children in the street as soon as they saw us, hateful creatures, none of them fatter than ourselves.

Day after day we had to queue up for the barest necessities of life. When I came to London a few years ago and saw the waiting crowds outside the theatres, my mind was haunted by a bitter memory. Innumerable winter afternoons. Thawed snow covering the pavement with wet mud. Drumming rain. Or a biting wind. And freezing cold. Along the houses, in front of every sixth shop, long rows of women and children, four abreast, pressed against each other and the walls. For hours before the shop was opened, the colourless crowd stood waiting, bent down by weather and misery, distortions of mankind. Yet a single policeman was enough to keep hundreds of them in their places.

Under-nourished and thinly dressed, too tall for my ten years, I stood among them to get a piece of meat or a pound of bones. My numb hand was scarcely able to hold the money and the ration card. Anxiously I thought of my mother. She was as thin as a lost goat and looked old and ugly with her sunken cheeks and the blue rims around her eyes. She never ate her full rations but went without in order to feed Fritz and me a little better than our own tiny share would have allowed her. Now she was queuing up at the grocer's round the corner for ounces of sugar and flour more precious than caviare. Would she get it? Or would the supply be sold out again before it was her turn? Sugar was absolutely necessary to make *Ersatz-Kaffee*—dish water, as we called it—at all drinkable. To dream of a drop of milk with it was simply ridiculous in its extravagance. For days we nourished ourselves on a sweet, greenish pulp : indigestible ruins of frozen potatoes. Or was it only a bad imitation of them, as all the rest of our food was only imitating real stuff ? To overcome the foul taste we poured *Ersatz-Sauce* over them, but the only similarity with gravy was its dark brown colour. As for its other attributes—it seemed to be made of nothing else but pebbles, ground to grit. We consoled ourselves, saying, " It cleans the stomach, anyhow." The same raw material was used for the manufacture of soap, which was advertised with the slogan : " Avoids the superfluous lather ! " Sand was also the essential ingredient of a certain soup and of a " sand "—wich paste. The difference was only caused by the amount of water that factories or kitchens added. Sand I heard scratch under the spoon on my plate, sand I saw in tiny clods on my potatoes, sand I felt between my teeth and sand I rubbed between my meagre hands. If I should shake my body long enough it would begin to trickle out of my open pores.

I was getting tired of standing in the crowd. I thought of Fritz, who at the same time was queueing up somewhere for turnips. They were useful in many ways. Not only could they be eaten simply as a vegetable—and they were delicious cooked with bones or a slice of horsemeat, of which I was especially fond—but they could be turned into almost anything from salad to marmalade. Fritz was a fool, he was so timid that he always got pushed behind by the robuster crowd. To-day he might even feel weaker than usual. The day before, whilst my mother was out to see a friend, Fritz and I felt hungry, and after a mutual " council of war " we went to invade the larder. It was nearly empty. Only a few potatoes, a crust of bread, a last remnant of treacle, some spices, a bottle of vinegar, and the weekly butter portion—one and a half ounces for the three of us—which my mother had just fetched before she left. The dry bread and the potatoes tempted neither of us. We shared fraternally in the treacle. Then I dipped my finger into the soft butter. Fritz did the same. Suddenly a furious desire seized upon me, which after a moment's hesitation I did no longer try to resist : I grasped the lump, squeezed it into my mouth and licked the plate. My chin and palms were shining with grease. I felt sick and spat the last bit on the floor.

Fritz looked at me with longing eyes. There was nothing left

for him.   Wistfully he put his foot on the mixture of fat and spittle
and spread it over the tiles.

"Why don't you drink the vinegar?   You like vinegar, don't
you?"

"But I can't drink vinegar?"

"Who says so?   Of course you can.   Try it, just for fun."

So he lifted the bottle to his lips and drank, encouraged not to
stop, until his face grew green.   When my mother came home
afterwards we had just emptied our stomachs into the sink and looked
like ghosts, sitting in front of the open larder—too weak to shut the
door.   At the first look my mother saw the empty plate.   Then
she looked at us and immediately understood.   Yet she could not
believe it.

"Where has the butter gone?   Have you eaten it?   Who has
eaten it?"

"I have.   I was hungry."

"But this was all our butter for the whole week.   Good heavens,
what am I going to do.   No butter.   Go away, go out of the kitchen
you two, let me alone, I don't want to see you any more."

Hastily we got up from our chairs and slunk off towards the
door.   But Fritz came only as far as the sink, where he vomited
again.   Startled, my mother followed us and put us both to bed.
She did not speak a word, but tears kept running down her cheeks.
She was tired of fighting in the void, too tired for anything.   Life
was not worth the trouble.   To lie down and die—what a temptation.
But she could not leave us children, she had to carry on.   I was
older than my age, I knew what she felt.   My own heart was hopeless,
too, and full of useless remorse.   Oh, in future I would try all I
could to help my mother.   I would eat less and would run from one
shop to the other to get food.   Nobody should dare to push me
back.   Oh, I knew how to use my tongue and was not to be frightened
by a rain of abuse from the neighbouring women.

Shivering with cold and weariness, I stared into the dim light
of the half-lit lanterns.   I began to imagine long conversations
with the women around me, full of insults and swear words.   Everybody was laughing at my ready wit and admiring my superiority.
No doubt I had grown up in East Berlin and I was not to be intimidated.

But it was so horribly cold and I had already waited for two hours.

Lilo Linke.

ESCAPE FROM SCHWEIDNITZ

WE dressed in Loder's room about an hour before roll-call on the evening of the 1st of March and got all our things ready. We divided up our money in case one or other of us should be taken, and we carried our sets of papers apart, so that there might be no confusion. As far as Hanover we were, we decided, to be Aachen men, and from there on were to state that we lived at Schweidnitz.

We got into civilians and, pulling our khaki slacks over our black trousers, appeared on parade in greatcoats. By the time roll-call was over it was dark, and the lights were turned on, but we thought ourselves safe in removing our khaki trousers, for there were many civilians in the camp and we felt that our military great-coats would prevent any suspicion being aroused. We then filled our pockets with the food we were taking; Loder took his spectacles and some soap, I my brush and a razor, and we were prepared !

The accomplices were already in position as we walked out, and though we spoke no word to them they knew precisely how to act. We were to walk to the other side of the camp and then back, by which time both sentries were to be on the far side of the hut. The orderly would, it had been arranged, go into the building to fetch another sandwich while the sentry waited, and the officer was of opinion that he would be able to engage his man for about two minutes—and no longer, for his stock of German words was very limited. Should the sentry on the stand see us we were done, but of this we had to take the risk and think ourselves lucky that it was no worse.

As we walked on our return journey towards the wall I felt myself almost choking with excitement. We pretended to be talking and laughed as we passed groups of prisoners, but I think there was little real mirth left in either of us at that moment. If we failed— if we *failed* ! We mustn't dream of it ; the thing was unthinkable —we were going Home !

We had passed the end of the hut, and had now turned the corner. We walked on about ten yards and then Loder suddenly flung off his coat and started to climb the wire fence, while I looked anxiously from left to right. Not a sentry was in sight with the exception of the man on the stand, but the wall looked positively white in the blaze of the arc-lamps, and I cursed those lamps, fearing they would prove our downfall yet. A window behind me opened, and the Canadian threw out our coats on to the ground. I leapt to pick them up, and in an instant had flung them clear over the wall and was tearing off the one I wore. I thrust the collar of it through the bars and my friend dragged it through, and Loder's after it.

"Good luck!" he whispered.

"Good-bye and good luck," said I, and then quoting from a song we were both very fond of: "I'm going way back home to have a wonderful time!"

I heard him laugh as he closed the window with a click, and then, turning, I found that Loder had reached the top of the wall and was endeavouring to swing his legs across before dropping on the other side. I had crossed the wire and the instant his hands disappeared I gripped a branch of the little tree and started to climb. I felt it lean from the wall as I mounted, for Loder's weight had torn away the fastenings, and during one dreadful moment I feared that it would crash with me to the ground. But it was growing wood and tough, and it held long enough to enable me to grip the stone coping. A heave—and my elbows were up; another—and I was kneeling on the cushion while the glass crackled under me, and below me Loder whispered: "Drop—drop, you're all right."

It seemed to me as though I spent minutes in getting my legs clear of the glass, but at last I hung by one hand, reached for the cushion with the other, and then let go. I felt as though I should never hit the ground, but when I landed it was upon a heap of leaf manure, and I was not even jolted. Loder had collected the coats and, keeping close within the shadow of the wall, we crept away.

We were, we knew, in the grounds of a military hospital, and descending a steep hill were not surprised to find our exit barred by a high wire fence and a locked gate. Beyond the fence was a narrow strip of ground, and then came the canal, but we thought we should be able to walk along here until we reached the bridge. We were obliged to wait some time, for there were many couples passing along the canal bank, but at last our opportunity came and we climbed the fence. In doing so I knocked my hat off against the branch of a tree, and found to my horror, on searching for it in the grass, that it had fallen into the water and sunk. Loder had joined me and I said :

" I've done it, old boy ; my hat's gone."

There was a short pause in which we stood there thinking, and then he said :

" Well, take mine, and go and buy another in the town. I'll wait here for you."

I took it, and he lay down in the long grass where he could not be easily seen, and then, hating though I did to leave him there with no hat, and no means of accounting for himself should he be challenged, I set off along the canal bank for the town.

I had walked for half an hour and had lost all sense of direction by the time I reached the shopping district, and here I stopped an old woman and asked her if she could direct me to the nearest hat shop. She told me that there was one in the next street, and so delighted was I that I presented her with a cake of soap and then hurried away without even waiting for her thanks. I was afraid that I might be asked for a permit, it being forbidden in many parts of Germany to sell anything made of cloth except against a *Bezugschein*, but nothing of the sort was demanded and I bought a very smart Homburg for eight marks. It was now a quarter to nine, and it became apparent to me that we should miss the train, which would mean waiting until after eleven. I had the greatest difficulty in finding my way back, and was at last obliged to ask a man whether he could direct me to the prisoners' camp, adding that I was the new inter- preter. He showed me the way, and once I saw the lights of the lager ahead of me I knew where I was, and succeeded in reaching the canal bank. Along here I ran at full speed, and Loder, hearing me coming, and seeing in the moonlight that I carried a paper bag, knew that my mission had been successful, and rose, beaming from the grass. He put on his hat, fixed his spectacles to his satisfaction, and we then set off for the station.

(*The prisoners travelled without serious difficulty through Dresden, Leipzig, Cologne, to Aachen, where they alighted.*)

The sight of the enormous crowd at the barrier there assured me that we had nothing to fear in the way of supervision of papers, and we found ourselves before long in the darkened streets. It was now midnight and we had a certain five hours of darkness in which to cover the few miles which lay between us and the frontier. I made Loder a little bow and said :

"There's my part done. The rest is up to you, and I'm only a passenger."

"That's all you need to be," he answered. "This is my show."

He appeared indeed to know the way well, and, though it was over a year since he had been in Aachen, he remembered the smallest details and was able to tell me exactly what turnings we should pass and which bridges we had to cross. A tram passed going in the direction of Richtericht and we boarded it, and thus saved ourselves two miles of tramping. Getting off just before reaching the last-named place, we walked back a short distance in the direction from which we had come, and then suddenly leaving the road started to cross through rough and broken country. I had no idea where we were going, but followed Loder blindly, for I had the most perfect confidence in his word that he could, and would, fulfil his part of the contract.

We reached a railway cutting which Loder believed to be patrolled and we descended into it with the greatest caution, crossed the lines, and then, having climbed the other bank, ran for some distance. We were circling all the time to the right in an effort to strike a road of which Loder knew, and which would give him his direction, and this road we at last found after some time of anxious wandering. From then we pushed on steadily, keeping the road always in sight, and the fact that every hedge was wired showed us that we were very near our goal. We saw several sentries and had constantly to crawl for long distances, and the state of our clothes can be well imagined, for it had been raining. We eventually found ourselves plodding wearily through heavy plough-land, and often we would seize each other by the arm at the sight of a sentry, who turned out more than once to be merely the stump of a tree. We were both very, very tired, and at last, seeing a small group of houses ahead of us, decided to approach them in the hope of finding something which might tell us where we were.

Every window was dark and not so much as the bark of a dog was to be heard as we tiptoed through that tiny village of white-washed houses, and we were almost abreast of the last building, when we heard behind us the clatter of heavy boots on the hard road, and a voice cried :

" Halt ! "

" Don't run ! don't run ! " Loder whispered, and we turned to find two soldiers unslinging their rifles.   In the dark it was impossible to see their uniforms and we walked slowly towards them, determined if they were Germans to put them off their guard and then attack them.   I say this in no boastful spirit, but we were desperate, and after all, I thought, Loder was a match for any two !

Speaking in German, I called out :

" Look here, we are Dutch, and we have crossed into Germany by accident—can you show us our way back ? "

There was a pause, and then one of them replied in broken German :

" I don't understand."

Scarcely able to believe our ears, scarcely able to breathe for the hammering of our hearts, we approached still nearer, and suddenly Loder shouted at the top of his voice :

" By God ! They're Dutchmen ! "

" Dutchmen ? " I said stupidly.   " But, if that's so, we must be in Holland."

" We are, old thing," said he.

And then, in the slowest and most precise German, I started to tell them that we were two escaped British officers, and I asked them whether we were far over the frontier.   They were all smiles now and told us that we were fifty yards over the border, and, pointing to a light about a hundred yards away, explained that the house from which it shone stood on German soil.   Loder was dancing in the road like a crazy creature, and I—well, I just stood there and tried to realize it.

Capt. J. L. Hardy.

THE MARCH RETREAT

In the early months of 1918 *it was known that the Germans were going to make an attack on some section of the British line. Information obtained from prisoners and aerial observation indicated where this was likely to be but when, in the early hours of the foggy morning of March* 21, *after one of the most terrific bombardments in the whole of the war, the Germans advanced against that portion of the line held by the Fifth Army, they broke through and after fierce fighting pushed the British back until the old Somme battlefield was again in German hands. South of Amiens and Soissons they penetrated many miles beyond the line on which they had been held during the years of trench warfare.*

THE OPENING. BEHIND VENDEUIL

20*th March.* That night our dinner guest was the former captain of our 4·5 howitzer battery, now in command of a heavy battery that had come into action within a quarter of a mile of our H.Q. The " MAN BATTLE POSITIONS," the order succeeding " PREPARE FOR ATTACK " in the defence programme, was not expected that night, and we gossiped and talked war and new gunnery devices much as usual. No story goes so well at mess as the account of some fatuous muddle brought about by the administrative bewilderments that are apparently inevitable in the monster armies of to-day. This was one told with quiet relish by our guest that night :

" You remember the Cambrai show ? " he said. " A lot of stores were, of course, lost in the scramble ; and, soon after I joined my present battery, I had to sit on an enquiry into the mysterious loss of six wagons belonging to a 60-pounder battery. Two courts of enquiry had already sat on the matter and failed to trace the where-abouts of the wagons, which had been reported in all sorts of places. At the third enquiry a witness stated that the last place the wagons were seen at before getting lost was such and such a place. A member of the court asked casually whether anyone had since visited the spot ;

and as it was near lunch-time someone else suggested that the court adjourn while an officer motor-cycled over and made enquiries. And I'm hanged," concluded the teller of the story, " if the officer didn't come back and report that the wagons were still there, had been there all the time, and were in good condition and under a guard. Piles of official correspondence had been written over the matter, and the investigation had drifted through all sorts of channels."

21st March. Midnight: I had sent out the night-firing order to our four batteries, checked watches over the telephone, and put in a twenty minutes' wrestle with the brain-racking Army Form B.213. The doctor and signalling officer had slipped away to bed, and the colonel was writing his nightly letter home. I smoked a final cigarette and turned in at 12.30 a.m.

3.30 a.m.: The telephone-bell above my head was tinkling. It was the brigade-major's voice that spoke. " Will you put your batteries on some extra bursts of fire between 3.45 and 4.10—at places where the enemy, if they are going to attack, are likely to be forming up ? Right !—that gives you a quarter of an hour to arrange with the batteries. Good night ! "

My marked map with registered targets for the various batteries was by the bedside, and I was able, without getting up, to carry out the brigade-major's instructions. One battery was slow in answering and as time began to press I complained with some force, when the captain—his battery commander was away on a course—at last got on the telephone. Poor Hodgson. He was very apologetic. I never spoke to him again. He was a dead man within nine hours.

I suppose I had been asleep again about twenty minutes when a rolling boom, the scream of approaching shells and regular cracking bursts to right and left woke me up. Now and again one heard the swish and the " plop " of gas-shells. A hostile bombardment, without a doubt. I looked at my watch—4.33 a.m.

It was hours afterwards before I realized that this was the opening bombardment of perhaps the mightiest, most overpowering assault in military history. Had not the " PREPARE FOR ATTACK " warning come in I should have been in pyjamas, and might possibly have lain in bed for two or three minutes, listening quietly and comfortably while estimating the extent and intensity of the barrage. But this occasion was different, and I was up and about a couple of minutes after waking. Opening my door, I encountered the not

unpleasant smell of lachrymatory gas.   The Infantry Battalion head-
quarters' staff were already moving out of the quarry to their forward
station. . . .

. . . 4 p.m. : I telephoned to the regimental sergeant-major and
told him to come up with the mess cart and the G.S. wagon for
remaining kit, and ordered the servants to pack up.   Twenty minutes
later Currie returned, dusty and dispirited.

" Well, Currie, what news ? " enquired the colonel quickly.

" I couldn't get to the battery, sir—the enemy are round it,
between it and our infantry," began Currie in cut-up tones.

" The nearest I got was in a trench held by the 7th Buffs.   An
officer told me that an advanced party of the enemy came over the
crest about 12.30.   They fired Véry lights in response to a Hun
contact plane that flew towards the switch-trench leading N.E.
towards the battery.   By 2 o'clock more enemy infantry were coming
from the south, apparently to join up with the advanced party who
had sat tight.   Both A and B Batteries fired on this new body, and
they seemed to be dispersed.   But by half-past three, while I was
there, Germans in small parties were crawling through the wire in
front of A Battery, and getting into our trenches."

He paused and wiped his streaming face with his handkerchief.

" What were our infantry doing ? " the colonel interrogated.

" There were only small parties of them, sir, and very scattered,"
went on Currie.   " The officer and myself, with a dozen men, got
along a trench to within thirty yards of some Huns and fired on them.
But another party, from almost behind us, came along and bombed
us back.   We had two killed and brought one wounded man back
with us.   Another lot came up on our left and we had to move
farther back."

" Was the battery still firing when you came away ? " demanded
the colonel.

" Yes, sir, firing well, but mostly on fresh parties of Boche eight
hundred yards away."

A knock at the door, and the entrance of a quick-eyed, dapper
bombardier from the very battery talked of prevented Currie
continuing.

" From Major Dennes, sir," he said, saluting.

Just a slip from an Army Book 136, in Dennes's neat cramped
handwriting.   And the message itself was formal enough : a plain,

bald statement of a situation that contained heroism, drama, a fight against odds—despair, probably, were the truth known; but despair crowned with the halo of glory and self-sacrifice. The message ran—

"I have fired 2,200 rounds, and have only 200 rounds left. My S.A.A. for Lewis-guns and rifles is also running short. Can more ammunition be sent up immediately, please?

"The enemy has got through the wire in front of the battery, and is now on two sides of us. If the infantry can assist we can hold out until dark, when I will retire to rear position."

The note was timed 3.40 p.m. It was now 4.30 p.m.

The colonel was never more collected or more rapid in acting than at this moment. In two minutes he had spoken to the Infantry brigadier, and asked whether immediate assistance could not be sent. Then he wrote this note to Major Dennes—

"Your message timed 3.40 p.m. received at 4.30 p.m.

"Hold on: you are doing splendidly, and counter-attacks are being organized.

"Teams with limbers to withdraw your guns to rear position by 8 p.m. are being sent for."

"I hope the counter-attack is in time," he said to me with a certain sad thoughtfulness before handing the note to the bombardier. "Do you think you can get back to the battery, bombardier?" he added. "I'm afraid you'll find more Boches there now."

"I'll try, sir," replied the bombardier stoutly.

"Off you go, then, but be careful!"

In the period of waiting that followed we seemed to have forgotten that three hours ago we were expecting every minute to have to turn out and face the Boche with rifle and revolver. Save for the colonel and two or three of the signallers and a couple of servants, none of us were experienced soldiers; all our previous experience had been in attack; it was something new, this feeling that a powerful, energetic, determined foe was beating down our opposition and getting nearer and nearer. Yet, whatever they may have felt, not one of our little band showed signs of depression or nervous excitement. The signalling-sergeant was cursing the sanitary orderly for not having cleared up a particular litter of tins and empty cigarette packets; the officers' cook was peeling potatoes for dinner, and I heard the old wheeler singing softly to himself some stupid, old-time, music-hall ditty.

In the mess no one spoke a word, but each of us knew that our one thought was whether A battery would be able to hold out.

5.30 p.m. The answer, a grim and saddening one. A sergeant came hurrying in.

" They've captured the battery, sir," he said bluntly, " and Major Dennes is killed. I came to report, sir. I was the only one to get away."

I think sometimes of famous cases of tragedy and passion I have heard unfolded at the Old Bailey and the Law Courts, and the intense, almost theatrical atmosphere surrounding them, and compare it to the simple setting of this story, told in matter-of-fact tones by a sergeant standing to attention. " We finished all our ammunition, sir," he began, addressing the colonel, " and took our rifles. Major Dennes was shot by a machine-gun while he was detailing us to defend the two gun-pits farthest from the place where the enemy had got past our wire. He fell into my gun-pit, sir, shot in the head. Mr. Jones, who took command, said we would keep on with rifles, and Bombardier Clidstone was doing fine work with his Lewis-gun. The Huns didn't seem inclined to come close, and after a conference in my gun-pit with Mr. Dawnay, Mr. Jones asked for a volunteer to try and find the nearest infantry, and to tell them we'd hold on if they could engage the enemy and prevent him rushing us. I said I would try, and crawled on my belly, sir, through the grass to an empty trench. The battery fired several fine volleys ; I heard them for a long time. It was slow work crawling away without being seen, and when I had got 600 yards and was trying to get my bearing—I don't know what time it was.

" Then I noticed that no firing came from the battery. There was no sound at all for over ten minutes. Then about a hundred Germans rushed forward and started bombing the gun-pits, and some of our men came up. I saw about a dozen of them marched off as prisoners."

" You are quite sure Major Dennes was killed ? " asked the colonel quietly.

" Yes, sir ; he fell right in my gun-pit."

" *Quex* " (*Captain G. H. F. Nichols, 18th Div. Art.*).

1st *ROYAL SCOTS FUSILIERS AT THE COJEUL RIVER*

20/21st Mar. It was the calm before the storm. Towards evening, I walked to the Cojeul Valley to see the guns, and on my return took out a fatigue party to Wancourt Tower ; for our Brigadier, General Tanner, looked in on his way down the line and suggested that as I was best acquainted with the locality, I should point out the dead bodies still lying there from previous fighting, and have them buried.

I supervised this ghoulish work for some hours, and when I considered that the men had done enough, I dismissed them, and retired to our pill-box dug-out for the night.

At exactly 4.30 a.m. next morning a tremendous roll of fire brought us to our feet, and even in the depths of the shaft we could distinguish the thunder of gas projectors being fired in enormous quantities.

I hurried up the staircase to see what was happening, and immediately ran into a cloud of gas that sent me choking and gasping below for my box-respirator.

At first only projectors were being fired, and we still thought that it might merely betoken a big-scale raid. Then our uncertainty was dispelled by the instantaneous crash, the like of which was never heard before on sea or land, from thousands upon thousands of guns roaring on a front of thirty miles, and we knew that the hurricane had broken on us at last. The noise transcended anything I had ever conceived, but it would be hopeless to attempt a description of the monstrous din. Hastily throwing on our equipment, Col. Gordon and I climbed the stairs, and made for Battalion Head-quarters a hundred yards up the trench, in order to get in touch with our companies and platoons.

As we ran, we were stunned by the concussion of literally thousands of bursting shells, and although the light was uncertain, for there hung a mist, we could see that all our front stood wrapped in a sea of smoke and flame, and the earth heaved and twisted under our feet. Amid this pandemonium we heard the guns booming for many miles along the line, to tell us that the great battle was joined. We reached Head-quarters dug-out in safety to find that already all the telephone lines had been smashed by the bombardment.

We ordered up three signallers with an electric flashlamp to communicate with Brigade Head-quarters in the rear, but they were blown to pieces within ten minutes, and for the rest of the time we held the front we were isolated, except for some runners that got through. . . .

When the attack opened, the 2nd Royal Scots were in the forward line, we were in the second trench two hundred yards back, and the Shrops. were behind us. To our left lay the 79th and 9th Infantry Brigades of the 3rd Division and to our right were other units of the 3rd Army, with General Gough's 5th Army hinging on us.

We had a good field of fire over the heads of the Royal Scots but visibility was poor, and when at nine o'clock the German troops advanced, we caught but dim glimpses of their oncoming waves. We were nevertheless able to bring a heavy rifle and Lewis-gun fire to bear on them to swell that of the Royal Scots, and the Shrops. in turn were able to fire into the enemy from the rear and in no single instance did a German soldier get nearer than bombing-distance from our front line, in spite of all their courage.

All through March 21st and 22nd repeated attacks were made and every one of them broke down. We were drenched with gas for thirty hours on end, and they pounded and battered our trenches until we hardly recognized them, but the men who were left clung doggedly to their shattered ramparts and fought on. With the trench in ruins, it was wonderful that anyone survived at all, and our casualties were heavy. The Royal Scots, who bore the brunt of the attack, had fewer men killed than we, and we had less than the Shrops. behind us, for the German bombardment was more intense the farther it worked to the rear, and was lightest on the front line, for fear of hitting their own men. I was twice gassed, for it was impossible to wear one's respirator continuously. The Blue Cross mixture that the Germans were putting over caused eyes and throat to smart and burn, and made me violently sick, but did not otherwise incapacitate me. . . .

At midday on the 22nd a runner got through to us with a report that I still have :

Secret to 1st R.S.F.

2nd R. Scots,

7th K.S.L.I.

"IIIrd Division, G.B. 50 begins. Germans have broken into right Corps sector. We still hold front line of 3rd (purple) system roughly from right Corps boundary to St. Leger wood, thence along Factory Avenue to Swift Support.

"IIIrd Division will readjust its line along Croisilles Switch to Sensée River, thence to Brown Line. Aeroplane has dropped message to say infantry visible on wide front long way through British positions from Croisilles southwards."

This was disastrous news. It meant that the 5th Army on our right had given way, and it meant that we were outflanked and in grave danger of being surrounded. Col. Gordon decided to form a defensive flank along 1st Avenue, a communication trench running back from the front line, and preparations were made to move into it after dark.

We spent an anxious afternoon under heavy fire, knowing that only about fifteen hundred yards away the enemy were well in behind us on the slopes of Hénin Hill, and we could see for ourselves that to our left they had taken Monchy.

In the evening, Capt. Gosling, our Brigade Major, and another young staff officer, managed to reach us through the barrage. They carried instructions that the entire front zone was to be evacuated, and that we were to withdraw to Hénin, three miles back, before daylight. He told us that the Germans were in possession of the hill looking down on Hénin, practically at our rear.

Supplies were to be destroyed, excepting shovels, which were to be brought along to dig a fresh defensive line ; and the withdrawal was to be completed before sunrise.

It was a sore blow to surrender what the men had held so bravely. We burnt all papers and maps, and dumped our stock of Mills grenades down a disused shaft. The question of removing our reserve of small-arms ammunition had been solved long before, for the whole lot had been set alight by a shell, and the boxes of cartridges were blazing and crackling fiercely in the concrete pill-box in which they had been stored.

Col. Gordon ordered me to lead a party of runners to Hénin to reconnoitre the new ground we were to take up between Boiry-Bequerelle and Boyelles. I sprinted down to the remains of our sleeping dug-out to see that nothing had been overlooked. When I got there I found my servant, McColl, setting a match to letters and papers, having come on his own initiative to see to this. I noticed that the German concrete redoubt that had stood over the entrance had been completely blown away since Col. Gordon and I had left the place on the morning of the opening attack.

On my return I assembled my runners and we set off down Foster Avenue to the rear. Foster Avenue was considered to be the finest communication trench in France. It had a double track of duckboards, and was revetted through its length. Bissett used to say he would undertake to ride a motor-cycle up it, and there was a standing rule that any incoming battalion was to maintain the trench in the same good order as received, so we had taken especial care of its upkeep.

But now, as we picked our way along, I could scarcely recognize it, after the two days' bombardment, for our favourite C.T. had been reduced to a series of shell craters, with fragments of duckboard and wire entangling our feet.

It was full moon, so we were able to make fair speed over the tumbled surface, and we wasted no time, for the shell-fire, though slackened, was still heavy, and great projectiles crashed around us as we went.

Soon we reached the exit, where Foster Avenue abutted on the Cojeul Valley, which we had to cross to reach the plank road leading to Hénin. The shelling in the valley, too, was considerably lessened, but the valley lay under a haze of gas, through which we made our way past broken guns, wrecked gunpits, and dead gunners, all looking weird and ghostly through the goggles of our masks. When we reached the plank road outside the ruins of Héninel, we found the gas so thin that we could remove our respirators, and rest awhile beside the Cojeul, here more like a water-furrow than a river.

The plank road, though badly knocked about, and full of loose beam-ends and shell craters, was still practicable, and it was crowded with horse teams that had come up to fetch away the guns before dawn.

On the bank near by were stretched long rows of wounded for transport to the rear, and already, off the road, came the muffled tramp of men, and we could make out columns of infantry withdrawing to the next line of resistance.

After a short rest I went on with my little party, following the left bank of the Cojeul. As we walked, we passed four men of the 2nd Royal Scots carrying a dead officer on an improvised bier, made from a length of duckboarding. The moon shone full on the dead man's face, and I saw that it was Capt. Newlands, whom I knew very well. He looked calm and restful, and he might have been asleep, so little was there of death in his countenance. I asked the men where they were carrying the body to, and one of them said they weren't going to allow no bl——dy Boche to bury the Skipper, so the worthy fellows had taken upon themselves the self-imposed task of carrying their company commander back to the next line of defence, to ensure him against alien burial.

At length we reached the crossroad at Hénin, and I set about making arrangements for the laying-out of a fresh position. It was still night, but away to our right the countryside was lit by columns of fire pouring from the shafts of the Hindenburg Tunnel. The great gallery was alight, and huge pillars of flame were shooting upward, for the heavily timbered interior had become like a blast furnace. The conflagration lent an added note of desolation to the scene.

Lt.-Col. Deneys Reitz.

C BATTERY, H.A.C. (293 A.F.A. BRIGADE) NEAR VÉLU

21/22nd Mar. At 11 p.m. we started forward, but I cannot say that I was very hopeful, for it seemed most likely that by now the guns would have been captured, since when we left them in the afternoon, they were already in front of our infantry. We pushed on to Vélu . . . Through the village there was only one way . . . but all was quiet. Not far from the level crossing some sappers were clearing the line for a locomotive, and they did so with success, for during the night, this withdrew the long-range howitzer from Vélu Wood. Beyond this the way was inevitably difficult, for there were many new trenches and a good deal of barbed wire. But a more serious and unexpected difficulty was the mist which now settled down again, very thick and white, so that one could only see two or three yards, and for a mile and a half I had great trouble in maintaining direction through it, whilst finding a way in and out of trench lines which made several complicated detours necessary. But, checking myself by compass every now and then, and aided by the reconnaissance of the afternoon, I made only one mistake and fortunately realized this before I had lost my way. . . . We moved slowly forward, the teams keeping well closed up, each one close behind the other, and so at last we passed through the gap which had been left in the main trench and thus we arrived in good shape at the battery position. There stood the three guns just as we had left them, looking very lonely and forgotten, each faintly seen in the hazy light which pierced the mist from the low lying moon. Now was the most anxious time. The trench 200 yards in rear of the guns was manned with scattered infantry. This was good, but it showed that this trench had definitely become our front line and that the guns were now in No Man's Land. In the evening, when we had withdrawn, the enemy had been only a thousand yards away in front and on the left flank, and it seemed to me certain that by now they must be quite close up, and all ready to prevent us from saving the guns. I had given strict order as to silence, and from now on all instructions were given in whispers and every effort was made to keep the horses and limbers clear of anything that might make a noise. In silence I led three teams forward to the three right guns. The drivers did their work beautifully, and in almost complete quiet we limbered them up and then moved back about fifty yards. There I had to leave them, whilst Ogilvie and I took teams to the other two guns 400 yards away from the main position over the hill to the left. I dared not send back the three guns now limbered up, for I was sure that in the darkness and the mist they could not possibly find the way, and that once lost, I could never find them again ; and I also felt sure that I should need Ogilvie's help to recover the other two guns. Yet I hated to leave them where they were, for every moment I expected a burst of machine-gun fire or shelling, and to either of these they would be entirely exposed. But during the hour we were in the position everything remained wrapped in complete silence, which was made even more intense by the deadening effect of the heavy mist ; no gun-fire ; no rifle-fire ; all was as peaceful as a night on Salisbury Plain, and it was in very strange contrast to the tremendous noises of the day just past.

Major Ronald Ogier Ward, R.F.A.

6TH CONNAUGHT RANGERS AT TINCOURT

22nd Mar. The night and early morning passed quietly.

Throughout the day that followed, owing to our heavy losses in guns the previous day, we were practically without artillery support.

At 3.30 a.m. all stood to, but in spite of a thick fog which seemed entirely to favour the enemy, daylight arrived without any sign of further activity on his part.

It was beginning to look as if we might be going to have a restful day, when, at about six o'clock, three German prisoners (an officer and two other ranks) were passed back from the fire-trench. They spoke English fluently, and upon being questioned as to whether it was intended to renew the attack during the morning, replied that it was.

One of these prisoners—a vapid-looking youth with spectacles—was inclined to be talkative. Explaining his capture he said : " To tell you the truth, sir, I lost my way " : but, from the smile on his face, I judged that he was not sorry to be out of it.

The information we had extracted was at once sent back to Brigade, and in less than half an hour, its accuracy was confirmed by the sudden outburst of the enemy's barrage on a similar scale to that of the previous day. This was followed in due course by the German infantry, who swept forward, wave after wave, in overwhelming hordes.

The story of this day is well known—how our troops, having endured twenty-six hours of the most terrible punishment ; largely reduced in numbers ; the Lewis-guns or their teams (which is the same thing) knocked out, were overcome or surrounded after a stubborn resistance.

In the case of my own Companies, which, as I have described, had already suffered so severely, and had lost three Captains and two seconds in command out of four during the counter-attack of the preceding afternoon, not an officer escaped.

There being no communication trench, the firing line was, from the moment the attack started, cut off from all behind it, and though two of the battalion signallers made a gallant attempt to cross the exposed strip of ground that separated Head-quarters from the Companies, they succeeded in delivering their message only at the cost of one of their lives, the other being wounded.

The Germans continued to shell furiously throughout the morning, and, as our forward areas passed into the hands of their out-numbering infantry, they gradually lifted their guns, and by midday the bombardment of Villers Faucon and the ridges around had become intense.

In the afternoon a general retirement was ordered to a prepared line (the Green line), in front of Tincourt, some miles behind the original front line. We reached it at the cost of a few casualties from shell-fire. I must say I had hoped to find some fresh troops there, but there were none. Indeed, the trench was practically empty.

The battalion was now reduced to the Head-quarters Company and thirty-four stragglers.

At dusk I was ordered to line the Tincourt-Templeux La Fosse road (my left on Tincourt Wood), with the 1st Munsters on my left and the 2nd Leinsters on my right ; the latter (reduced to the strength of about a Company) having been temporarily placed under my command. My instructions were to cover the retreat of the remnant of the 49th Brigade, which was in front, should it become necessary to withdraw from the Green line, allowing them to pass through my ranks ; then to follow after them, and to take up a position on the Doingt-Bois des Flacques line, in front of Peronne.

I made my Head-quarters for the night in an exceedingly comfortable three-roomed hut in Tincourt Wood, formerly the abode of an officer of the Divisional Staff, whose Head-quarters had been here until the proximity of the enemy during the last two days had driven them further back.

Having in my mind the heroic exhortations which had of late been coming so unsparingly, addressed to us in the front line from this wood, I confess I was not prepared for the aspect of sudden abandonment which the hut presented.

Its appearance suggested that some sudden and deadly cataclysm had overcome the occupant while he was having his breakfast, the remains of which, together with one or two half-finished cups of tea, still littered the table. The walls were hung with book-shelves and maps (of which latter I have annexed a useful specimen) : the floor had a carpet : expensive oil lamps, crockery, and a profusion of knick-knacks lay about : but there was no sign of any effort having been made to save these treasures, so rapid, apparently, had been the owner's exit. Lastly, and to our great satisfaction, there were two camp-beds and a mattress of the softest down.

Think of the exhausting hours through which we had passed, and you will understand that I shall not easily forget that night's rest, the only pity being that we did not get enough of it, and that the few hours we did have were spasmodic and disturbed.

Lieut.-Col. Rowland Feilding.

2ND GREEN HOWARDS AT ROUPY.

22nd Mar. Again the morning was thickly misty. Our own artillery fire was desultory and useless. Under cover of the mist, the enemy massed in battle formation, and the third attack commenced about 7 a.m. We only heard a babel in the mist. Now our artillery was firing short among our men in the redoubt. About ten o'clock the enemy penetrated our left flank, presumably in the gap between us and the battalion on our left, which was still in position. Machine-gun fire began to harass us from that direction, somewhere in the ruins of the village. We never heard from the battalion on our right, and a runner I sent there did not return. I think they must have withdrawn about ten o'clock.

This new attack petered out. I fancy it was only half-hearted on the part of the enemy—probably only a demonstration to see if we intended to make a determined resistance, or to fight only a rearguard action. Finding the resistance determined enough, they evidently retired to prepare the real thing.

This fourth attack was delivered about midday. The mist still persisted thinly. One could perhaps see objects fifty yards away. I don't know what resistance the platoon-keeps offered. They were in a hopeless position, and would easily have been swamped in a mass attack.

Shortly after midday, the enemy came in direct contact with the inner ring of the redoubt.

We fired like maniacs. Every round of ammunition had been distributed. The Lewis-guns jammed; rifle-bolts grew stiff and unworkable with the expansion of heat.

In the lull before noon, the colonel and I had left the dug-out, in which we were beginning to feel like rats in a trap, and had found an old gun-pit about two hundred and fifty yards farther back, and here we established our head-quarters. An extraordinary thing happened. The gun-pit was dug out of the bank on the roadside. About two o'clock one of our guns, evidently assuming that Roupy had been evacuated, began to pound the road between Roupy and Fluquières. One of these shells landed clean on the road edge of our pit. We were all hurled to the ground by the explosion, but, on recovering ourselves, found only one casualty : the colonel had received a nasty gash in the forearm. We then went two hundred to three hundred yards across the open, away from the road, and found a smaller over-grown pit. The colonel refused to regard his wound as serious ; but he soon began to feel dizzy, and was compelled to go back to the dressing-station. I was then left in charge of the battalion.

It was now about 2.30. The attack still persisted in a guerilla fashion. But the enemy was massing troops in the trenches already taken. At 4 p.m. the intensity of the attack deepened suddenly. A new intention had come into the enemy's mind ; he was directing his attack on the flanks of our position in an effort to close round us like pincers. On the left he made use of cover offered by the ruined village, and eventually brought machine-guns to bear against us from our left rear. On the right he made use of the trenches evacuated by the Inniskillings.

In the height of this attack, while my heart was heavy with anxiety, I received a message from the brigade. Surely reinforcements were coming to our aid ? Or was I at length given permission to with-draw ? Neither : it was a rhetorical appeal to hold on to the last man. I rather bitterly resolved to obey the command.

Another hour passed. The enemy pressed on relentlessly with a determined, insidious energy, reckless of cost. Our position was now appallingly precarious. I therefore resolved to act independently, and do as perhaps I should have done hours earlier. I ordered B. to organize a withdrawal. This message despatched, I lay on my belly in the grass and watched through my field-glasses every minute trickling of the enemy's progress. Gradually they made way round the rim of the redoubt, bombing along the traverses. And now we only held it as lips might touch the rim of a saucer. I could see the heads of my men, very dense and in a little space. And on either side, incredibly active, gathered the grey helmets of the Boches. It was like a long bowstring along the horizon, and our diminished forces the arrow to be shot into a void. A great many hostile machine-guns had now been brought up, and the plain was sprayed with hissing bullets. They impinged and spluttered about the little pit in which I crouched.

I waited anxiously for B. to take the open. I saw men crawl out of the trenches, and lie flat on the parados, still firing at the enemy. Then, after a little while, the arrow was launched. I saw a piteous band of men rise from the ground, and run rapidly towards me. A great shout went up from the Germans : a cry of mingled triumph and horror. " Halt Eenglisch ! " they cried, and for a moment were too amazed to fire ; as though aghast at the folly of men who could plunge into such a storm of death.   But the first silent gasp of horror expended, then broke the crackling storm.   I don't remember in the whole war an intenser taste of hell.   My men came along spreading rapidly to a line of some two hundred yards length, but bunched here and there.   On the left, by the main road, the enemy rushed out to cut them off.   Bayonets clashed there.   Along the line men were falling swiftly as the bullets hit them.   Each second they fell, now one crumpling up, now two or three at once.   I saw men stop to pick up their wounded mates, and as they carried them along, themselves get hit and fall with their inert burdens.   Now they were near me, so I rushed out of my pit and ran with them to the line of trenches some three hundred yards behind.

It seemed to take a long time to race across those few hundred yards.   My heart beat nervously, and I felt infinitely weary.   The bullets hissed about me, and I thought : then this is the moment of death.   But I had no emotions.   I remembered having read how in battle men are hit, and never feel the hurt till later, and I wondered if I had yet been hit.   Then I reached the line.   I stood petrified, enormously aghast.   *The trench had not been dug, and no reinforcements occupied it.*   It was as we had passed it on the morning of the 21st, the sods dug off the surface, leaving an immaculately patterned " mock " trench.   A hundred yards on the right a machine-gun corps had taken up a position, and was already covering our retreat. I looked about me wildly, running along the line and signalling to the men to drop as they reached the slender parapet of sods.   But the whole basis of my previous tactics had been destroyed.   I should never have ordered my men to cross that plain of death, but for the expectation that we were falling back to reinforce a new line.   We found an empty mockery, and I was in despair.   But I must steady the line.   On the actual plain the men obeyed my signals, and crouched in the shallow trench.   But even as they crouched, the bullets struck them.   On the road, the straight white road leading to the western safety, there was something like a stampede.   S. and the sergeant-major went and held it with pointed revolvers.   But it was all useless— hopeless.   On the right, I saw the enemy creeping round.   They would soon enfilade us, and then our shallow defence would be a death-trap.   I accordingly gave the signal to withdraw, bidding the

two Lewis-guns to cover us as long as possible.   Once more we rose
and scattered in retreat.   It would be about seven hundred yards to
the next trenches—the village line round Fluquières, and this we
covered fairly well, sections occasionally halting to give covering
fire.   The enemy had not yet ventured from the redoubt, and our
distance apart was now great enough to make his fire of little effect.
And I think as we moved up the slope towards the village we must
have been in " dead " ground, so far as the enemy advancing on the
right was concerned.

We reached Fluquières, which lay on the top of the slope, and
found there some deep trenches on each side of the road at the entrance
of the village.   Further to the left, I found certain London troops
commanded by a major.   One of my Lewis-guns still remained
intact, and this I placed to fire down the straight road to Roupy.   The
enemy had now left the redoubt and were advancing in line formation.

We were at Fluquières about an hour.   The enemy evidently
did not intend to rest content with his capture of the redoubt.   It
was just beginning to get dusk.   Earlier we had noticed sporadic
contact lights go up.   But now they shot into the sky from all along
the plain.   Low-flying aeroplanes hovered over the advancing line,
and their wireless messages soon put the German guns on to us.
Big black high-explosive shells began to fall on our position, making
our tired flesh shudder.   I now began to be amazed at the advancing
contact lights.   They did not merely stretch in a line *in front of us :
they encircled us like a horse-shoe, the points of which seemed* (and
actually were) *miles behind us.*   On the right the enemy was enfilading
us with machine-gun fire.

I searched for the major commanding the troops on my left, but
could not find him.   By this time I was determined to act, and therefore gave the order to withdraw.   The men filed through the village
gathering fresh ammunition from a dump at the cross-roads.   From
the village the road went up a slope leading to Aubigny.   The
enemy's fire soon followed us, and we proceeded along the ditches
on each side of the road.

Three-quarters of the way up the slope I observed a trench running
at right angles to the road on each side of it.   I ordered the London
men to go to the left, my own to the right, there to reorganise into
companies.   The twilight was now fairly deep, and I thought that
with evening the enemy's advance would stay.   The major I had

seen in Fluquières now appeared again, and cursed me for giving the order to retire. I was too tired to argue, and even then a gust of machine-gun fire swept above our heads. They were going to attack again. We could hear them moving in the semi-darkness. Something else we could hear too—the throb of a motor-cycle behind us. It was a despatch rider, and when he drew level to us, he stopped his machine and came towards me with a message. I opened it. It ordered all troops east of the Aubigny defences to retire through Ham.

Herbert Read.

90TH BRIGADE R.G.A. BEHIND MORY

23rd March. " Wake up ! Wake up ! "

I stirred drowsily.

The Colonel shook me. " Wake up ! " he said abruptly.

Still half asleep, I sat up rubbing my eyes. It was quite dark ; the atmosphere of the room was thick : the Doctor and the Signal Officer were snoring softly on the floor beside me. Outside, but far away, I could hear the galloping noise of heavy gun-fire.

" What's up, sir ? " I asked, closing my eyes again and nodding.

" Read this ! " The Colonel thrust a message form into my hand and switched on his electric lamp.

Something in his tone aroused me. I looked at the paper and read with a shock of dismay :

" The enemy has broken through at Mory. We have no troops left to put in the line. Sixth Corps."

That was all ; I remember the utter despair I felt. We had done our best. . . . Was this the end ? . . .

The Colonel was lacing his boots. " Wake up the others and tell them to dress," he said bitterly. " Tell an officer of each battery to stand by the 'phone. I'm going up to Corps Heavies to see what they are going to do."

" Did the message come through them, sir ? "

" Yes ! " The Colonel took up his lamp and went out.

Good lord, it couldn't be true ! And yet, with that infernal gun-fire in the middle of the night anything might be happening. . . . Oh, damn the Sixth Corps !

I woke the others and told them the news; we dressed silently and I think we half expected the Boche to be upon us that very minute.

I stood by the doorway watching and listening; away to the north-east the sky was flickering incessantly. How the guns were pounding away! Around Grévillers everything was still. Suddenly a great flash lit up the night. Bang! Bang! Bang! Bang!—a sixty-pounder battery at the end of the village had opened fire. The shells tore through the cold night air with a hollow blasting roar; the ruins echoed and re-echoed; a flock of startled birds rose from the church and wheeled and wheeled over my head. A six-inch howitzer battery just in front opened up. What were they shooting at? What was happening?

Then I saw the light of the Colonel's lamp coming back down the duckboard path.

"It's only an S.O.S.!" he cried scornfully. "Corps Heavies trying to find out who sent that message—someone ought to be shot. We've just spoken to Sixth Corps. The Guards Division is in the line at Mory: it's only an S.O.S. Are those officers on the 'phone?" The Colonel took up the receiver. "Yes—who's that? Officer, Toc 4? S.O.S. on the Corps on our left; take down this target. Mory. M-o-r-y. Damn it, M-O-R-Y! Yes, Sheet 57c. Beer twenty-one. Yes, anywhere in Mory. Get them off quick as you can. Come on, exchange, give me Toc 3 now!"

Capt. Arthur F. Behrend (R.G.A.).

63RD DIVISION AT YTRES

23rd March. That night we were marched back to the old huts in Havrincourt Wood, where we got a little sleep; and in the morning we had actually paraded to do a working party, when there was another panic.

"Battle order immediately. Don't waste a second. They're right on top of us."

We didn't waste many seconds. In a few minutes we were marching down the road towards Ytres—the same road which I had taken to go home on leave only three weeks since. Eighteen-pounders, blazing away as quickly as they could be charged, were strung out in the open spaces of the field on our left. I don't know what became of the guns or the men who served them, for I saw none of them pass through our lines.

There was a prepared line of trenches in front of Ytres which we manned and we had not been in them many minutes when the first Germans showed themselves on the outskirts of the wood. Rifles spat and Lewis-guns chattered, the battery out in front poured point-blank fire on to the edge of the wood, and then within a minute or two all was quiet again. . . .

Late in the afternoon some of the 47th Division attached themselves to us, bringing the disquieting news that the Germans had come through on our right, and once more we were " in the air." They said that they had killed thousands of Jerries earlier in the day, but how true this was I never found out. Towards dusk we began to be shelled from our right flank, and slightly from the rear. . . .

All the while I could hear what I took to be guns firing from the middle of Ytres behind us, and was comforted to think that we were not left without the cover of artillery. I should have been rather hot and bothered if I had known the truth. The R.E.'s had set fire to the station and sidings on which were many truckloads of shells, and what we actually heard was these shells exploding.

Still no direct attack came, but even the least intelligent of us knew that we were holding on much too long to an untenable position. Our gallant colonel, having already lost communication with Brigade, had received no orders to retire, and it was not until midnight that he did so on his own initiative—and probably only then under pressure of the company commanders. Then, of course, it was too late. We came to a sudden halt in the streets of Ytres. We were already surrounded.

C Company was on the north of the village, and they were bayoneted almost to a man without the rest of us knowing at the time what was going on. We heard the " hoy ! hoy ! hoy ! " of Germans shouting quite close to us, but that was all.

The position actually was that Brigade had retired to Barrastre, and the Germans were already in Bus on our direct line of retreat. A very brave lance-corporal named Talland-Brown, who could speak German, volunteered to take another man with him and get through the enemy line to Barrastre to let Brigade know where we were and ask for instructions. Outside Bus he was challenged by a German sentry, and he replied in good colloquial German something to the effect of : " Shut your bloody mouth ! Do you want to get us all shot ? " So the sentry said, " Pass, friend." . . .

An hour or two before dawn—when Talland-Brown and his companion had got safely back with orders—we were led out of Ytres two or three hundred yards on our line of retreat, and told to dig ourselves in with our entrenching tools. This should have been done before. Indeed, I don't know why we weren't taken straight on to Barrastre. The German cordon around us could not have been a strong one, and we could have burst through it with fixed bayonets under cover of darkness and met practically no opposition.

One of my fellow stretcher-bearers, named Jones, was badly wounded and unable to move. A Company had no stretcher now— I can't pretend to remember what had become of it if I even knew— and I offered to try to take him out on my back. He replied that he'd damned sight sooner be taken prisoner, and in the light of subsequent events I am very glad that he declined the offer. I know I should have had to dump him, and the memory of that would have worried me to this day.

We dug in with showers of bullets whizzing harmlessly overhead. In good ground it is extraordinary how quickly one can dig with an entrenching tool a hole big enough to shelter oneself. In a very few minutes I was as snug as a bird in a nest and sound asleep.

Ex-private X.

CASUALTY CLEARING STATION NEAR PÉRONNE

23rd Mar. The night before last, after writing to you on my way to bed, things looked a bit hot, so I lay down in my clothes for a few hours rather than not go to bed at all, as history was making itself so rapidly, and the map was altering every hour for the worse. As you know by now, ours was the place where they broke through and came on with their guns at a great pace. We found the General of the 24th Division, one of the Divisions that took the brunt of the first onslaught here, sitting on the road-side outside our Orderly Room Tent with a few of his Staff, and the Divisional Flag stuck up in the field, using our telephone as his Divisional H.Q. His Division was practically napoo for the moment—they did wonders afterwards— masses of his transport were spread out opposite and a steady stream of everything flowed past us all day the wrong way, like Mons. The

Germans came straight through one of the other Divisions, the 16th, and another was the one you had for a year at Colchester—the 66th : it stuck it well. A Black Watch man on a stretcher was asked where the 9th Division were. " They're in Germany now," he said. They are all Scotch and South Africans. I've met them all through the War.

All the hot busy morning wind-up increased and faces looked graver every hour. The guns came nearer, and soon Field Ambulances were behind us and Archies cracking the sky with their noise. We stopped taking in because no Field Ambulances were working, and we stopped operating because it was obvious we must evacuate everybody living or dying, or all be made prisoners if anybody survived the shelling that was approaching. Telephone communication with the D.M.S. was more off than on, and roads were getting blocked for many miles, and the railway also. We had about 1,000 patients, all wounded except 130 gassed and 150 walking sick who were in before the battle, until a train came at 9 a.m. and took 300. Every ward was full and there were two lines of stretchers down the central duck-walk in the sun ; we dressed them, fed them, propped them up, picked out the dying at intervals as the day went on, and waited for orders, trains, cars or lorries or anything that might turn up. At 10 a.m. the Colonel wanted me to get all my 40 Sisters away on the Ambulance train, but as we had these hundreds of badly wounded, we decided to stay and take our chance till definite orders came for us to run.

At mid-day the Matron-in-Chief turned up in her car from Abbeville. It was a stroke of genius on her part to pick out the one shaky place remaining on the whole front where Sisters were left and come to look out for her 80 Sisters—40 with me and 40 at the other C.C.S. It was decided that Sisters must leave and transport be found for them. The Divisional General (24th) offered lorries if he could find them, but they were away in the blue, looking for rations. The O.C. of the Motor Ambulance near by offered a despatch rider to get some of his cars from somewhere else. A made-up temporary train for wounded was expected, and we were to go on whichever Transport turned up first and scrap all our kit except hand-baggage. Miss McCarthy lunched with us, and saw the Sister-in-Charge of the other C.C.S. and the two refugee Sisters-in-Charge from farther up who were with us. She said nice things to us, and took two Sisters away in her car. They all behaved with the calmness of a garden party, and were all prepared to carry on with shelling, or Germans, or whatever might come ; packing was done in reliefs from running the wounded, who were as quiet and uncomplaining and marvellous as ever. The Officers' Ward was a brave but unhappy place. The Resuscitation Ward was of course indescribable and the ward of penetrating-chests was packed and dreadful. Some of the others died peacefully in the sun and were taken away and buried immediately.

At about 5 p.m. the Railway Transport Officer of the ruined village produced a train with 50 trucks of the 8 *chevaux* or 40 *hommes* pattern, and ran it alongside the Camp ; not enough of course for the wounded of both Hospitals but enough to make some impression. Never was a dirty old empty truck-train given a more eager welcome or greeted with more profound relief. The 150 walking-cases (all the rest were stretchers) were got into open trucks, and the stretchers were quickly handed into the others, with an Orderly, a pail of water, feeders and other necessaries in each. One truck was for us and our kit, so I got a supply of morphia and hypodermics to use at the stoppages all down the train. Then orders came from the D.M.S. that Ambulance Cars were coming for us. So the Medical Officers (one from us and one from the other) took the morphia and most of our kit to God knows where with the wounded, and we mustered on the roadside for the cars. There were 300 stretcher cases left, but another train was coming in for them. The Sister-in-Charge of the other C.C.S. told me Rothenstein was helping in the Wards like an orderly.

The Boche was 4 miles this side of Ham, just into Péronne, and 3 miles from us—13 miles nearer in 2 days. We were trying to hold them at the Somme at St. Christ, the little place we walked to the other day, 3 miles away, with the blue lake where the Yankee sappers were building a bridge. I am glad I've seen Péronne. The 8th Warwicks marched in on March 19th, 1917. The Germans will take down our notice board on March 23rd, 1918, and put up theirs.

We had a great send off and got in 4 Ambulance Cars escorted by three Motor Ambulance Convoy Officers, one on a motor-cycle and two in a Staff car. They had to take us some way round through Chaulnes, over battlefields with pill-boxes in them, and ghastly wrecked woods and villages, as he was shelling the usual road heavily

between us and our destination, Amiens. We took five hours getting
there, owing to the blocked state of the roads, with Divisions retreating
and Divisions reinforcing, French refugees, and big guns being
trundled into safety and other little affairs of that kind. He chose
that evening to bomb Amiens for four hours, and we saw this going
on, and waited under the trees a few miles out until he'd finished.
He has been over bombing again twice this morning and is doing it
this minute. . . .

24th Mar. On Abbeville Station (that vast place one comes to
in the night on the way to Switzerland) was a seething mass of British
soldiers and French refugees, some coming in from the invaded area
and some leaving for safer regions still. There I found our Colonel
at my elbow telling me all our kit was got away but he didn't know
where to. He had brought the last 300 stretcher cases down the
evening before in open trucks with all the M.O.'s and personnel.
Our wounded were lying in rows along the platform with our
Orderlies ; they had been in the trucks all night and all day and only
one Ambulance Car was found to take them to the Hospital in return
journeys. One I saw was jerking with tetanus. Some had died,
and were in a closed van lower down, but all were got away. The
Padre was burying the others in the field with a sort of running funeral,
up to the time they left. They were taken straight to their graves as
they died.

K. E. Luard, R.R.C.

RESTORING THE INFANTRY'S CONFIDENCE

24th Mar. We were crouching down in the narrow trench
talking casually of when we had had a square meal last, and what was
more important, the chances of getting one in the near future, when
a jingling sound made us look round. We stared incredulously as
a crowd of horsemen emerged from the trees. They took no notice
of our heads, bobbing up from the ground, and manœuvred their
mounts into some kind of order. They were Colonials, and their
uniforms were spick and span. The horses snorted and their coats
shone. The men were big fellows and their bronze faces were keen
and oddly intent. They were very splendid compared to us. . . .

We ducked in alarm as the squadron spurred their horse into a
gallop and came straight at us. With a thunderous drumming of

hoofs they took our trench in their stride.   From the bottom, as I cowered down, I had a momentary glimpse of a horse's belly and powerful haunches as they were over and away like the wind, sword in hand.

They spread out as they went into two lines and were half-way across the open when there came a sudden pulsating blast of fire, and gaps appeared in the double line.   Bullets came hissing about our heads.   A man a couple of yards away from me slithered down to his knees, and then sprawled full length on the floor of the trench. Realizing our danger we ducked.   Looking down I saw blood gushing from a wound in his throat. . . .

Then uncontrollable excitement possessed me and, defying the bullets, I raised my head and looked at the cavalry.   Their ranks were much thinner now.   Just as the foremost of them reached the trees they hesitated, turned and came racing back, lying low in the saddle.

The machine-guns barked triumphantly at their victory over mere flesh and blood.   Only a handful of the once proud squadron put their blowing horses at the trench and lunged across to the shelter of the wood behind.   Others tailed away on either side and in a moment were hidden from view among the friendly trees.

The whole thing from when we saw them first had only occupied a bare five minutes.   We stared at each other in amazement.   The fire died down.   Looking over the top we saw that the ground in front, which before had been bare, was dotted here and there with shapeless mounds.

The screams of horses in agony pierced our ears with shrill intensity.   As we looked animals struggled convulsively to their feet and galloped off at a tangent.   Some of them swayed drunkenly and fell back, with their legs in the air.   Smaller, more feeble movements showed that some of the troopers were still alive.

Single rifle-shots sounded, whether from our side or not, I didn't know, and by and by the horses were mercifully silent, but men moved at intervals—crawling behind the horses for cover, perhaps.[1]

Herbert Hill.

---

[1] The charge near Villescle was made by 150 of the Fort Garry Horse, of whom 73 were casualties.   The Official History states : " And the confidence of the infantry was restored."

THE RETREAT GOES ON

25th Mar. The traffic was now moving with a swing; after I had waited half an hour big gaps began to appear and occasional Field Batteries went past at the trot. How long was " as long as possible " I began to wonder anxiously, and started up the motor-cycle to make sure it would go all right when the time came.

The traffic was getting less and less ; at last I noticed that people were apprehensively looking behind them as though expecting the Boche. Five minutes later I could stick it no longer ; I got on the motor-cycle and rode into Bucquoy.

Events were exciting indeed ; Military Policemen with drawn revolvers were directing the traffic which was now moving at a gallop. Horse transport was being sent by one road, motor transport by another. A smart, clean looking battalion of infantry had just arrived ; the soldiers were filing into the houses and gardens at the eastern end of the village. Machine-gunners were testing their machine-guns and Lewis-gunners and riflemen were making loop-holes in the walls. It was obvious that the Boche was not far away.

I felt I ought to hang on a minute or two longer so I waited beside the Military Policemen. Suddenly I saw the most welcome sight of all—the Brigade car ! Thompson was driving furiously ; the Colonel, wearing his tin hat, yelled as he swept past, " They've all got away ; come on ! "

I afterwards heard that Thompson had distinguished himself by taking a wrong turning thereby driving the car through a hot Boche barrage. The road was blocked so he had to turn round and drive back through the barrage !

I followed the car ; before I had gone very far I heard behind me a sudden crackle of musketry from Bucquoy—the Boche had arrived.

For the next couple of miles we all moved along at nearly twenty miles an hour, but when we had passed Puisieux the pace slowed down considerably and half a mile farther on I caught up the Brigade lorries. I saw one of the despatch riders sitting on the tail-board so I shouted to him to hop off and take over the motor-cycle. I climbed up on the front seat beside the Artillery Clerk and promptly dozed off.

I woke up several times during the journey ; I remember hearing someone shout, " Halt ! Action left ! " to a Field Battery which left the road just in front of us ; I remember seeing a battalion of infantry bivouacking in the open ; I remember seeing another cleaning out an overgrown trench—disused since 1916—with their entrenching tools ; I remember passing a notice board which announced " THIS IS SERRE " and only those who have seen can visualize the dreadful utterness of the desolation.

I remember entering Mailly-Maillet which gave me great pleasure for it contained the first complete houses I had seen for weeks. Wondering women and children stood at the gates of their cottages and watched us driving past ; they did not seem to realise what had happened.

The scenery was so different and was changing so quickly that we seemed to be in another world ; it was more like going on leave than fleeing from the Boche. I remember the windmill at Colincamps and the windmill at Bertrancourt ; whenever I see a windmill to-day I think of dust and lorries and flight.

I remember rattling through Bertrancourt ; last time we had passed through Bertrancourt we were on our way to Gézaincourt for a fortnight's rest. I remember passing the railhead on the Bertrancourt-Acheux road which, though we would never have believed it then, was destined to be our future ammunition dump. I remember passing the big chimney on the outskirts of Acheux which the Colonel —and no one else—afterwards wanted to use as a reserve O.P.

At last we pulled up beside the Y.M.C.A. in Acheux Square. The Y.M.C.A. were giving their stock away ; our men rushed in for tea and biscuits. After the sack of the Bapaume Canteen, mere giving away seemed very flat. The shops around the square were frenziedly selling off at bargain prices.

A few minutes later the Brigade car arrived ; we followed it into the château grounds, scattering right and left fat ducks and angry geese. The Colonel hurried into the château to report to the General. Half an hour later we were off again but only, thank goodness, to park our lorries and howitzers on the Acheux-Forceville road and billet in Forceville for the night.

The Colonel stood in the middle of Forceville marshalling the traffic like a Military Policeman ; as soon as the howitzers, four-wheel-drives and lorries were all neatly parked in the line along the road he sent me back to the château to report that all our batteries had arrived safely except Toc 1, which was missing. Nothing was known of them except that they had been very short of petrol.

The General and the Brigade-Major were sitting in a large and beautiful furnished *salon*. I told them the news and was turning to go when an orderly hurried in. As I was shutting the door the General shouted, " Come back ! "

" How long will it take you to get to your Colonel ? " he asked quickly.

" About four minutes, sir."

" Then get off as quickly as you can and tell him to continue the retreat AT ONCE. The Germans captured Albert half an hour ago. Make for Doullens ; either the Brigade-Major or I will be at the Town Hall there to give you fresh orders. Hurry up—Forceville is only six miles from Albert ! "

I ran to my motor-cycle. Heavens, Doullens was another twelve damned miles away—some retreat, this ; would it ever stop ? I tore along the Acheux-Forceville road like the wind ; people rushed out of the way and turned round to stare at me as if I were mad.

The Colonel was still standing complacently in the middle of Forceville surveying the neatly stretched-out Brigade with a proud and fatherly eye. The lorry drivers were cleaning down their lorries ; the gunners were cleaning up their guns. Billets had already been found for half the Brigade, the other half had already found its way into the estaminets.

Within twelve minutes we were all on the move again and with real dismay in our hearts.

Again I fell into a doze ; the journey seemed endless. It soon grew dark ; the road was flanked by great trees which loomed up and faded away in endless succession ; the roar of our lorry became a lullaby ; the broad road seemed to go on and on for ever like a great white ribbon. Dust and petrol vapour was everywhere ; it, filled ears and eyes, nose and mouth. Kilometre stone after kilometre stone went past ; it was impossible to grasp the fact that we were in flight . . . it seemed like some great game in which distance and villages and woods all meant nothing. In the days that followed I journeyed many a dozen times to and fro along the Acheux-Doullens road but never again did it seem so endless and we so small. Once we stopped ; I woke up to find that some big gun in front of us had fallen off the road ; our lorries could only just creep round.

We hurried on through Louvencourt and Vauchelles and Marieux and Sarton; between Sarton and Orville a despatch rider overtook us.

"Nine-O Brigade?" he shouted.

"Yes!"

"Here's a letter from Corps Heavies!"

The Colonel read it; we were to park for the night in Orville where the men were to be given billets; at 9 a.m. in the morning the Colonel was to report for orders at the Town Hall, Doullens.

Capt. Arthur F. Behrend, R.G.A.

THE LEADERS AGREE AND FIND THEIR SCAPEGOAT

26th March. Left with Milner at 8 a.m. and went to Dury. Gough just established his head-quarters there, but as our meeting had been changed to Doullens we pushed on through Amiens, which was fairly quiet and not being shelled. A certain amount of natives on the move. Doullens at midday.

Poincaré, Clemenceau, Loucheur, Foch, Pétain, Milner, Haig, self (and Plumer, Byng, Horne in attendance). Milner, Haig, and I had a preliminary talk, and Haig agreed to my proposal for Foch to co-ordinate. Then meeting of Poincaré, Clemenceau, Foch, Pétain, Milner, Haig and self. After discussion, in which I fell out with Pétain . . .

F.-M. Sir Henry Wilson.

It is evident, General Pétain added, that everything possible must be done to defend Amiens. At the mention of this name, Foch inter-jected: "We must fight in front of Amiens, we must fight where we are now. As we have not been able to stop the Germans on the Somme, we must not now retire a single inch." On this outburst Field-Marshal Haig was heard to say: "If General Foch will consent to give me his advice, I will gladly follow it." All present felt the decisive moment had arrived.

The " Loucheur Memorandum."

Milner put up the proposition for Foch to co-ordinate, and, all agreeing, Clemenceau and Milner signed the document.

Then I discussed the removal of Gough, and told Haig he could have Rawly and Rawly's old Fourth Army Staff from Versailles, to replace Gough. Haig agreed to this. . . .

F.-M. Sir H. Wilson.

WAS FÜR PLÜNDERN

28*th Mar.* To-day the advance of our infantry suddenly stopped near Albert. Nobody could understand why. Our airmen had reported no enemy between Albert and Amiens. The enemy's guns were only firing now and again on the very edge of affairs. Our way seemed entirely clear. I jumped into a car with orders to find out what was causing the stoppage in front. Our division was right in front of the advance, and could not possibly be tired out. It was quite fresh. When I asked the Brigade Commander on the far side of Meaux why there was no movement forward he shrugged his shoulders and said he did not know either; for some reason the divisions which had been pushed on through Albert on our right flank were not advancing, and he supposed that this was what had caused the check. I turned round at once and took a sharp turn with the car into Albert.

As soon as I got near the town I began to see curious sights. Strange figures, which looked very little like soldiers, and certainly showed no sign of advancing, were making their way back out of the town. There were men driving cows before them on a line; others who carried a hen under one arm and a box of notepaper under the other. Men carrying a bottle of wine under their arm and another one open in their hand. Men who had torn a silk drawing-room curtain from off its rod and were dragging it to the rear as a useful bit of loot. More men with writing-paper and coloured notebooks. Evidently they had found it desirable to sack a stationer's shop. Men dressed up in comic disguise. Men with top-hats on their heads. Men staggering. Men who could hardly walk.

They were mostly troops from one of the Marine divisions. When I got into the town the streets were running with wine. Out of a cellar came a lieutenant of the Second Marine Division, helpless and in despair. I asked him, " What is going to happen ? " It was essential for them to get forward immediately. He replied, solemnly and emphatically, " I cannot get my men out of this cellar without bloodshed." When I insisted, assuming from my white dragoon facings that I belonged to the same division as himself, he invited me to try my hand ; but it was no business of mine, and I saw, too, that I could have done no more than he.

Rudolf Binding.

CANADIAN CAVALRY BRIGADE NEAR MOREUIL

30*th Mar.* Then, with my aide-de-camp, an orderly with a little red pennant and my signal troop, I galloped down the hill, across the bridge over the Luce, through a field of young wheat and over a road to our front line. A few bullets flew about, but not many, for we were in dead ground, except to the enemy at the point of the wood.

As I rode through our front line, who were lying down and firing, I said to a young captain : " We are going to retake the ridge. Fire on both sides of us, as close as you can, while the rest of us go up." He knelt up and shouted : " Good luck to you, sir." Our infantry opened a glorious fire on both sides of us as we galloped on. Five out of about twelve of my signal troop were shot by the enemy, but the remaining seven reached the wood, jumped off and opened fire. My orderly jammed the red flag into the ground at the point of the wood, and I looked back, to see my gallant brigade galloping forward by the way I had come. . . .

Soon the brigade arrived. It is curious how galloping horses seem to magnify in power and number ; it looked like a great host sweeping forward over the open country. I galloped up to Flower-dew, who commanded the leading squadron of Strathcona's, and as we rode along together I told him that his was the most adventurous task of all, but that I was confident he would succeed. With his gentle smile he turned to me and said : " I know, sir, I know, it is a splendid moment. I will try not to fail you."

The Dragoons just ahead of us had suffered heavily and had failed to reach the north-east corner. But they had turned into the wood and engaged the enemy. The air was alive with bullets, but nobody minded a bit. It was strange to see the horses roll over like rabbits, and the men, when unwounded, jump up and run forward, sometimes catching the stirrups of their still mounted comrades.

I went with Flowerdew to where we could see round the corner of the wood. He had lost comparatively few men up till then. He wheeled his four troops into line, and with a wild shout, a hundred yards in front of his men, charged down on the long thin column of Germans, marching into the wood. . . .

A short time later, when I arrived on the eastern face with the supporting squadron I found the survivors of this desperate charge securely ensconced in a little ditch, which bordered the wood, in twos and threes, each with a German machine-gun and with three or four Germans lying dead by their side. It was recorded that seventy Germans were killed by sword thrust alone outside the wood. I saw perhaps another two or three hundred lying there, who had been killed by machine-gun fire. In those brief moments we lost over eight hundred horses, but only three hundred men killed and wounded. The fanatical valour of my men on this strange day was equalled by the Bavarian defenders now surrounded in the wood. Hundreds of them were shot while they ran to their left to join their comrades still holding on to the south-east corner. Hundreds more stood their ground and were shot at point-blank range or were killed with the bayonet. Not one single man surrendered. As I rode through the wood on Warrior with the dismounted squadrons of Strathcona's I saw a handsome young Bavarian twenty yards in front of me miss an approaching Strathcona, and, as a consequence, receive a bayonet thrust right through the neck. He sank down with his back against a tree, the blood pouring from his throat. As I came close up to him I shouted out in German, " Lie still, a stretcher-bearer will look after you." His eyes in his ashen-grey face seemed to blaze fire as he snatched up his rifle and fired his last shot at me, saying loudly : " Nein, nein. Ich will ungefangen sterben." Then he collapsed in a heap.

After seeing the position at the eastern face of the wood I galloped back to my head-quarters, which Connolly had moved up to about a third of the way along the northern front.

Maj.-Gen. Seely (Lord Mottistone).

VISIONS AND A RAID

There was little chance to get to know patients who arrived in the morning and left before the evening, and in the daily rush of dressings and convoys I had not much time for talking, but once or twice I became aware of strange discussions being carried on by the

men. On one occasion I stopped to listen, and was impelled to
remain ; I wrote down the conversation a few weeks afterwards, and
though it cannot have been verbally exact, I reproduced it as it appeared
in my 1918 " novel " of nursing in France :

" 'Ave yer come down from Albert way ? " enquired a sergeant
of a corporal in the next bed, who, like himself, wore a 1914 ribbon.

" Yus," was the reply, " I have. There's some mighty queer
things happenin' on the Somme just now, ain't there, mate ? "

" That there be," said the sergeant. " I can tell yer of one rum
thing that 'appened to me, meself."

" Git on then, chum, let's hear it."

" Well, when the old regiment first came out in '16, we had a
Captain with us—O.C. of our company, 'e was—a mighty fine chap.
One day at the beginning of the Somme battle some of the boys
got into a tight place—a bit foolish-like, maybe, some of them was
—and 'e comes along and pulls 'em out of it. One or two of 'em
had got the wind up a bit, and 'e tells 'em then not to lose 'eart if they
gets into difficulties, for 'e sorter knows, 'e says, when the boys 'as
need of 'im, and wherever 'e is, 'e says, 'e'll do 'is best to be there.
Well, 'e was killed, 'elpin' the boys as usual, at the end of the fightin'
on the Somme, and we mourned for 'im like a brother, as you might
say. . . . 'E were a tall fine chap, no mistakin' 'im, there wasn't.
Well, the other day, just before the Boches got into Albert, we was
in a bit of a fix, and I was doin' all I knew how to get us out. Suddenly
I turns round, and there I sees 'im with 'is bright eyes and 'is old smile,
bringin' up the rear.

" ' Well, Willis, it's been a narrow shave this time,' 'e says. " But
I think we've pulled it off.'

" An' forgettin' 'ow it was, I makes as if to answer 'im, and all
of a sudden 'e ain't there at all. Struck me all of a heap for a bit,
like. What do you make of it, mate ? "

" It's more nor I can tell," answered the corporal. " 'Cos another
very queer thing happened to some chaps in our company. In the
old days on the Somme we had a tophole party of stretcher-bearers,
and one day a coal-box comes and wipes out the lot. But last week
some of our chaps sees 'em again, carrying the wounded down the
communication trench. And I met a chum in the train who swears
he was carried out by two of 'em."

A Lancashire boy from an opposite bed leaned forward eagerly.

" I can tell yer summat that'll beat that," he said. " T'other day when we was gettin' clear of Péronne, I found a chap beside me lookin' very white and done-up, like, as if 'e could scarcely walk; fair clemmed, 'e seemed to me. I found I'd got one or two of them 'ard biscuits in me pocket, an' I pulls one out and hands it to 'im. ' 'Ave a biscuit, mate,' sez I.

" ' Thank you, chum,' 'e sez, ' I don't mind if I do.'

" And 'e takes the biscuit and gives it a bite. As 'e puts out 'is 'and for it I sees 'e's got one o' them swanky identity-disks on 'is wrist, and I reads 'is number as plain as anythink. Then 'e gets mixed up wi' t'others, and I don't see 'im no more. And it's not till I gets back to billets that I remembers.

" ' Lawks,' I sez to meself, ' if that ain't the chap I 'elped Jim to bury more'n a week agone, my name ain't Bill Bennett.'

" An' sure enough, mates, I remember takin' the silver identity-disk off 'is wrist, an' readin' the number on it as plain as plain. An' it were the number of the man I gave the biscuit."

There was an awed silence in the ward, and I turned from the dressing I was doing to ask breathlessly :

" Do you really mean that in the middle of the battle you met those men again whom you'd thought were dead ? "

The sergeant's reply was insistent.

" Aye, Sister, they're dead right enough. They're our mates as was knocked out on the Somme in '16. And it's our belief they're fightin' with us still."

Certainly no Angels of Mons were watching over Étaples, or they would not have allowed mutilated men and exhausted women to be further oppressed by the series of nocturnal air-raids which for over a month supplied the camps beside the railway with periodic intimations of the less pleasing characteristics of a front-line trench. The offensive seemed to have lasted since the beginning of creation, but must actually have been on for less than a fortnight, when the lights suddenly went out one evening as the day-staff was finishing its belated supper. Instead of the usual interval of silence followed by the return of the lights, an almost immediate series of crashes showed this alarm to be real.

After days of continuous heavy duty and scamped, inadequate meals, our nerves were none too reliable, and I don't suppose I was the only member of the staff whose teeth chattered with sheer terror as we groped our way to our individual huts in response to the order to scatter. Hope Milroy and I, thinking that we might as well be killed together, sat glassy-eyed in her small, pitch-black room. Suddenly, intermittent flashes half blinded us, and we listened frantically in the deafening din for the bugle-call which we knew would summon us to join the night-staff in the wards if bombs began to fall on the hospital.

One young Sister, who had previously been shelled at a Casualty Clearing Station, lost her nerve and rushed screaming through the Mess; two others seized her and forcibly put her to bed, holding her down while the raid lasted to prevent her from causing a panic. I knew that I was more frightened than I had ever been in my life, yet all the time a tense, triumphant pride that I was not revealing my fear to the others held me to the semblance of self-control.

When a momentary lull came in the booms and the flashes, Hope, who had also been under fire at a C.C.S., gave way to the sudden bravado of rushing into the open to see whether the raiders had gone; she was still wearing her white cap, and a dozen trembling hands instantly pulled her indoors again, a dozen shakily shrill voices scolded her indiscretion. Gradually, after another brief burst of firing, the camp became quiet, though the lights were not turned on again that night. Next day we were told that most of the bombs had fallen on the village; the bridge over the Canche, it was reported, had been smashed, and the train service had to be suspended while the engineers performed the exciting feat of mending it for twelve hours.

Vera Brittain.

GROUND STRAFING

April. On the next day, Saturday the sixth of April, rain spread over northern Europe in the early morning, and in places continued all day. In London those with relatives in the R.A.F. hoped that this would be a real day's rest for them, and bore with patience the damping addition to the horrors of week-end shopping; but in Picardy it cleared up in the afternoon and there was plenty of flying, for the enemy was making yet another assault on the defences of Amiens, and there seemed very little reason why they should not carry them, unless it might be their own exhaustion. The British reply to the attack was to bomb from the air more intensely than ever. The clouds lifted to some three thousand feet, so that machines of all descriptions could be used. When C. flight arrived at the scene of action soon after three o'clock the air was crowded with machines coming and going, and it was quite difficult to avoid back-wash. An instinct made Tom aware that there were Huns about too, waiting to pounce; but none was visible at the moment.

Beal wasted no time, but went right down to a hundred feet. He had thought out a new idea, by which he and Tom would work close together in front, and Miller with the other two would follow a little after, or attack from another angle. He hoped by this to deliver a concentrated attack without their all getting in each other's way. Tom was nearly upset by a shell bursting right underneath his tail, and he lurched as though a giant had given him a push. He hung desperately on to Beal, dropping bombs where he did, not at all sure where. Then he followed him as he went nosing along communication trenches for troops going up. Tom slewed about as much as he could, but Beal seemed entirely unconcerned about bullets; he was after prey. But suddenly Tom saw something that made him go alongside Beal and waggle his wings. There was a bunch of Huns, possibly a dozen, coming down on them. Beal saw them and turned just as they opened fire. He went down in a spin, hit either from the air or from the ground. Tom completed his turn amid an appalling pop-pop-pop-pop-pop-pop of machine-guns, and zigzagged westwards. The Huns had dived and pulled out and he was still alive. His Aldis was smashed. He was aware of a group of holes in his left bottom plane. They apparently weren't going to attack again. But there was a crack-crack-crack-crack in a different key. Splinters from a centre-section strut flew in his face. A landing wire broke and the ends rattled about. Something tore a leg of his sidcot. He must be flying straight over a machine-gun nest at about fifty feet. His engine spluttered and his hand switched over to gravity automatically. There was a terrible din going on now his engine wasn't roaring. He was not particularly afraid. His body was functioning as an automaton and his mind was anæsthetized to everything but surprise or curiosity. What was happening, was going to happen? There were bullet-holes everywhere. It was preposterous that he wasn't hit. He was going down. He would probably be dead in a second or two. It was impossible to live through this. Then the engine picked up, and he thought he was across the lines, but the cracking still continued. There could be nothing shooting at him, but the noise went on, and fear returned. What was this unaccountable machine-gun-like row? He couldn't make it out. Was the aeroplane breaking up? Should he land somewhere at once? He throttled down and glided in panic towards the shattered ground. Then he saw a strip of torn canvas that was flapping in the wind on the fuselage just behind him.

He opened out again and climbed away. He was shot to blazes, and it was a miracle that he was alive. There was a smell of petrol. Perhaps it would be better to land as soon as possible. He crept along cautiously on half throttle, and tried to collect his thoughts. What had happened? There had been a dash into Hunland, right on the floor, and here he was, dazed but alive. Beal had gone. They had been shot at from the air and ground at the same time. Beal was dead. What a rattle of guns there had been; that damned staccato chatter. He really didn't remember details.

Some one came alongside him. It was Miller, followed by Smith and Dubois. He waved and joined them, but would not fly faster than eighty miles an hour and they soon left him behind. They came back and had a look at him and amused themselves by fooling about round him. He wouldn't throw a stunt for the world. And there was a damnable smell of petrol. He might burst into flames. Beal, his admirable enemy, had gone and he remained. These twin facts swung round in his head like a planet and moon. Fate manifestly hadn't the interest of the Allies in view. Those Huns had done a good day's work. Where the devil had they appeared from so suddenly? It was weird the way things appeared from and vanished into nowhere upstairs. You had to be as watchful as a goshawk. Then what had happened? The Huns had left him alone and some of their pals on the ground had taken advantage of his preoccupation with them to finish him off, nevertheless their bullets had hit everything but him, and here he was floating insecurely home. He would like to get his bus home. It would break all records. Never had anyone been so shot up and got home. It would be amusing and dramatic if the wing collapsed when he landed, that landing wire being broken. He hoped it would. The rattling and cracking were alarming though they seemed to arise from harmless causes.

He was glad to see home at length; not so profoundly relieved as he expected to be after his unsafe journey; he seemed to have lost some of his capacity for feeling.

His escort let him land first, which he did without losing any time. He made a good landing and watched his damaged wing as he touched earth. It dropped, and scraped its tip along the ground; but this was because the whole aeroplane was tilted, not because it had collapsed. Tom switched off and swung round the pivot of his dropped wing to a standstill.

He climbed out to see what had happened. The tyre of one of the landing-wheels was flat, punctured in the air. It struck him as extremely funny to get a puncture in the air. He laughed and laughed and leaned over the bottom plane and laughed till he ached, with his face over a group of six bullets that represented a bit of good shooting by one of those Fokkers.

Two mechanics with a spare wheel and tools were the first to arrive. Then Williamson and Hudson. Then Baker and Reeve, very new comers to the squadron, who gazed with reverential horror at the gaping wounds.

" Good God, man! " exclaimed Hudson, " what the bloody hell have you been up to ? Even your sidcot is shot through. Aren't you hurt ? "

" I'm all right. I've only been following Beal. He won't be back."

There was a scorched tear in his right thigh, and a brown mark as though someone had laid a hot poker lightly on his left arm, which meant that a bullet had grazed. A piece was smashed out of a centre-section strut within a few inches of his face; he remembered feeling the splinters blow against him. Several bracing wires were broken, and the petrol tank holed near the top. There were two holes in the floor of the cockpit. The total number of bullet-holes was over sixty. It must be one of the most remarkable escapes ever made. He certainly had a reliable guardian angel.

V. M. Yeates.

GEORGETTE—DISTANT VIEW

Georgette was the name given by the German General Staff to the northern offensive between Givenchy and Armentières. It was originally called St. George but owing to the lack of troops available, the scale of the attack was cut down and the code-name changed as above.

9th April. From our huts on the slope above Bouvigny this new battlefield lay visible in its entirety. It was twelve miles away, but from our elevated site it was easy with good binoculars to follow the course of the advance. The country north of the La Bassée Canal is utterly flat, drained by innumerable small streams and ditches, and covered with orchards and villages, then full of prosperous people hardly touched by war. It had been a quiet front since Neuve Chapelle. Even Armentières, two miles behind the line, was an inhabited town, with shops and cafés open, until the Germans began to shell it in earnest shortly before 21st March. And now, evening after evening, we used to gather with our maps and field-glasses behind our row of huts and watch the great wedge of burning villages pushing farther and farther westward behind Béthune. Those evenings were exceptionally clear, so that far across the smoking plain the church tower of Bailleul was visible against the grey background of Mont Rouge. Bailleul was a charming little town, with a wonderful red-brick belfry to its Hotel de Ville, and one of the best officers' clubs in France. Within a fortnight it was in ruins.

Capt. D. G. Browne.

CONVERSATION PIECE

ROUND the corner, I could hear the batmen in husky argument.

"'E's not a bad little chap," said a voice.

"Little, all right," replied my own batman, Johns; "why 'e don't come even as high as my Tich even." (I mutely thanked him for the comparison.)

The voice of the mess cook took up the discourse.

"That there young Knappett, y'know, 'e's too regimental, making us all come up for the rum every night. Now young Brench-ley, 'e knows 'ow to treat us. The other night, when the Sar'nt wants us all one by one, 'e says—didn't 'e, Johns?—'All right, sar'nt,' 'e says; 'I can trust the servants.' See. Trusts us, 'e does. 'Member when we was on the Menin Road, old Nobby an' me was lyin' in a shell-'ole. 'E comes over the top. ' 'Ow are yer gettin' on,' 'e says; 'would yer like a drop of rum?' Would we like a drop of rum! And 'e brings it over' isself. Oh, 'e's my ideel of an orficer, 'e is."

Guy Chapman.

THE PLEASURES OF THE CHASE

12th April. When Cairns continued to fly towards and underneath the approaching machines, I naturally assumed they were comrades, but the Triplane puzzled me, and as I couldn't recognize the type of the others, I became more and more anxious. I remembered Mick's advice about fighting Triplanes. Through my mind flashed the thoughts—Are they Huns? No! Yes! No! Yes! I couldn't make up my mind, but as we were fast approaching, the black Maltese crosses on their wings soon settled the question. For a moment I was fascinated by those little black crosses. It was months since I had seen any. How pretty they looked! And what pretty machines! They were all colours of the rainbow! Black and red, bright blue and dark blue, grey and yellow, etc. It never struck me that they were aeroplanes flown by men—possibly by the crack pilots of the German Air Force. Men whom I knew as Huns. Death-dealing gentlemen, possibly smothered with Iron Crosses and Orders *Pour le Mérite.* I looked on them for a moment as rather a pretty flock of birds. But I was soon rudely awakened from my reverie.

Cairns, as soon as he had seen the black crosses, turned sharply left to get away and improve his tactical position, as they were diving to the attack. Skeddon and Jones could easily turn tightly with him, and Begbie and Giles, by crossing over positions, could turn fairly quickly. But I, being so far behind, was left standing, so to speak. The enemy leader soon took advantage of the gap between me and my flight, and brought his formation into it, ignoring the remainder of the flight, and soon he was on my tail, firing sweet bullets of welcome to No. 74 Squadron. Wisely I kept my head, and immediately put my machine into a vertical bank, held the stick tight into my stomach, kept my throttle wide open and prayed hard! According to Mick's advice.

It did not take me long to realize that the gentleman who was doing his best to kill me was an old hand at the game. A sure sign of an old hand is that he reserves his ammunition and only fires in short bursts ; if he is aiming straight he knows that a burst of twenty is as good as a burst of 200 and much more economical. Having only about 1,000 bullets in all, it is foolish for a pilot to use them up when he knows that his aim is not good, on the off-chance that an odd bullet may hit his opponent. Once he has used up his ammunition, he then becomes defenceless himself. Mick had warned us that we had to be careful of a Hun who fired in short bursts ; on the other hand, if the Hun is firing long bursts at you, he said, you can be sure that he is frightened and probably a beginner. " Fight him like hell, he should be easy meat." This Hun on my tail was so close that I could easily discern his features. His machine was painted black with a white band round his fuselage just behind his cockpit, and he was flying it superbly. It seemed to slither round after me. Round and round we waltzed, in what was no doubt, to my opponents, a waltz of death, but this morbid aspect of the situation fortunately never occurred to me. Of course, I could see the big idea. The leader was to shoot me down while his eight companions prevented anyone coming to my assistance, or myself from getting back to my lines. Some of them kept above and on the north side (the side that Cairns and his flight were climbing), and the remainder kept on the west side of me at various heights, so that I would have to run their gauntlet of fire if I chose to quit. As we waltzed around, I kept on repeating to myself, " Keep cool, Van Ira, he can't hit you. His bullets are going behind." I could see the track of his bullets as he was using tracers, and this fact encouraged me to keep cool. I had no desire to have a burning bullet roasting my intestines, especially before breakfast ! So keep cool I did.

Occasionally I shouted at the top of my voice at him, telling him to do his damnedest. I also used most indecent language. Of course, he could not hear me, but it gave me satisfaction and temporarily acted as a stimulant to my sorely tested courage. While he flew close to my tail but did not fire, I did not mind very much, but whenever I heard the Kak-Kak-Kak of his Spandaus and saw the spurting sheets of flame close behind me, I felt a little anxious of a stray bullet hitting me. Every now and then my attacker would zoom up and a couple of his comrades would make a dive-and-zoom attack hoping that I would get out of my vertical bank—but I wasn't having any, as I knew of this old trick from past experience. Once they got me out of the vertical bank, the gent on my tail (he may have been Richthofen, Udet, or any of the other Hun star-turns as far as I know) would no doubt have soon put paid to my account. After a while I feared that unless I got out of the mess I was in quickly, the fickle jade Fate might step in and stop my engine, or worse still put a stray tracer bullet through my petrol tank, and send me down to Hunland in a blaze of glory—a glorious death for an airman, but not one that I wanted on my first patrol. I wanted to kill a couple of Huns myself first. As we waltzed around one another, sparring for an opening, I kept my eye on the big green mass of trees about five miles away—the Forest of Nieppe. I knew that those trees were in our territory, anyway. It was a consoling thought. But I could not make up my mind when to make my dash, the Triplane kept on nagging me with his bullets—so did his companions, and the longer I stayed as their guest, the more attention they paid me. Occasionally two or three would have a crack simultaneously. I would sometimes fire for moral effect only.

The seconds passed like years, and the minutes like eternity. The tension grew as the minutes rolled by, until eventually in desperation I decided to make a bid for home as soon as the Triplane did his next zoom. I watched my opponent carefully, as he was then only about 25 yards behind and he seemed to be grinning as I looked at him over my left shoulder ; as soon as I saw him commence to zoom up to change his position I obeyed Mick's instructions and " put on full bottom rudder " and my machine did a turn of a spin. When I came out of it, I found I was facing east instead of west, so another spot of bottom rudder to turn her round westward was quickly applied, and there in front, a few miles away, was my landmark—the Forest of Nieppe. Between me and my objective were half a dozen Huns, hungry and angry Huns, just waiting for me to come their way. So their way I went, accepting their challenge like a mad bull charging a toreador. I knew this was my only chance. It was now or never. So, barging through the middle of them— neither looking to left nor right, as I had often done before through a rugger scrum when cornered, I went for home like Hell, kicking my rudder from side to side to make the shooting more difficult for the enemy—and praying hard. It was a grand thrill, that run for the lines—I knew by the incessant angry barking of the enemy's guns that there were hundreds, if not thousands, of death-dealing bullets chasing my little machine. Occasionally during my mad careering, I looked over my shoulder to see whether I was gaining on my enemies ; to my joy I could see I was—but the bullets, I realized, were still faster, and it was not until I was well clear of the enemy—half a mile away, that I knew I was safe. It was a joy to see my little S.E.5 gaining ground on the Triplane and the Pfalz, and to listen to the fading rattle of the staccato barking of the enemy's guns as my machine gradually outstripped her opponents. I crossed our lines just to the north of the forest, right down close to the ground and fortunately my enemies feared to follow me owing to the approaching of Cairns from a higher altitude. Cairns then chased them miles over their lines.

James Van Ira (74th Squadron, R.F.C.), quoted by Ira Jones.

THE VITAL SPARK

April 22nd. Just before we left we were standing with the French Colonel looking at the end of the sunset behind our line, and suddenly all his guns, in a shadowy place under the sunset, broke out into a line of little twinkling sparks, starting a barrage to pass over our heads and fall a few hundred yards beyond, protecting us all. He pointed to them and said to me, " Regardez, mon Capitaine ! La guerre elle-même a sa poésie "—not a bit in a hackneyed or conventional way, but with boyish ardour—really wonderful elasticity in anyone who has had long to bear the responsibility of front-line commands in this war and has done the work with all his might. The French are wonderful in their reserves of fortitude—what a wild, stupid saying it was of that person who called them " delirious with suffering " !   One can never admire too much their firmness and shining brightness of spirit, and if we can equal them we shall do finely.

C. E. Montague.

THE *VINDICTIVE* AT ZEEBRUGGE

A naval attempt to curb the German submarine menace was made on April 22, 1918, when the cruiser " Vindictive " and a number of smaller boats stormed the Mole at Zeebrugge and scuttled two blocking ships in the harbour. Operations of a similar nature were carried out at Ostend. The whole enterprise was a brilliant piece of work and the occasion of much gallantry, nine V.C.s being awarded.

23rd April. At this moment from behind us and far away out to sea there came a dull thud ! thud ! It was the great monitors waking Zeebrugge with their enormous shells. The attack had begun. It was tremendously hearty and encouraging to hear our own big guns opening the dance, and to think that we were getting all the help in our adventure that could be given us. Still a minute or two ticked away, and nothing happened ; still there might have been nothing but open sea ahead of us ; but in fact the guns of Zeebrugge must be less than a mile away. It was incredible that nothing should be happening. Had they no patrols or searchlights at all ? Fortune was favouring us beyond our dreams. This was the critical time ; every second almost that passed now without our being observed much increased our chance of getting alongside. I stepped up to the projecting embrasure of the gun to have a look round. The foggy air was streaky with some thicker fumes than fog, and behind me I could just descry in the darkness a line of faint, grey plumes ; it was the motor craft pouring out smoke in order to screen us.

Then far, far away on our left the brilliant light of a German star-shell appeared suddenly in the sky, then another nearer at hand, and then one right overhead, which, to our seeming, lit the whole ship and the surrounding sea with an illumination so brilliant that we must be visible for a hundred miles. One could see each individual face in the crowd on deck staring angrily up at the star in hard black shadows and white lights. But still the Germans did not open fire, and looking out from the embrasure I could guess the reason. The sky was now thick with a perfect rain of shell-stars; but clearly as they showed us to ourselves it did not follow that they showed us to the Germans. As each star fell into the smoke screen that now covered the sea, unless it was within a very few hundred yards of us, it was eclipsed as a star and became a large, vague nebula. Although then there was plenty of light about, a few hundred yards from the ship everything was blotted out in wreaths, eddies, and whirls of glowing vapour. The German gunners, I imagine, were peering into the vapour, unable to perceive any definite object in the shifting, dazzling glow, and wondering what in the name of goodness was going to come out of it. So we steamed on until we were some four hundred yards from the Mole, and we had just begun to turn to starboard in order to run alongside when the storm broke. This was the beginning of the bad three minutes that we had expected.[1] A searchlight shone out from the end of the Mole, swung to left and right, and settled on the ship. At once the guns on the Mole opened fire. From our dark bay we could see their quick flashes on our port bow, and there was a faint popping in the sea all round the ship. More accustomed to the crash which a shell makes when it bursts ashore, I did not realize at the time that this was the noise of shells that had missed us and were bursting in the sea. At the next instant they began to hit. " When is the top going to begin ? " I thought. " Will it never begin ? "

During the next few minutes we had by far the greater part of our heavy casualties. They were swift, shaking detonations close by, and one blinding flash of blue light right in our eyes. It was at this moment that Captain Halahan and Colonel Elliot were killed on the landing-deck a few feet away; but at the time my attention was so wholly fixed in listening impatiently for the first shot from the top, in order that the 6-inch guns might begin too, that I hardly noticed what was going on. It was afterwards that I remembered the eruptions of sparks where the shells struck, the crash of splintering steel, the cries, and that smell which must haunt the memory of any-one who has been in a sea-fight—the smell of blood and burning.

Casting a glance out through the embrasure I saw a fine sight. The wind during the last few minutes had dropped, the smoke-screen

[1] In fact, I believe, the bigger guns ashore had already been firing at random into the smoke for nearly twenty minutes, but I was quite unaware of that at the time.

was no longer drifting ahead of us, and the sea and everything on it was lit up continuously by leaping flashes, so that we were plainly visible to the gunners on the Mole. Quick as thought one of the motor-craft grasped the situation and dashed forward, leaping—almost flying—across the waves with furious haste, pouring out smoke as she came. She swung across our bows, right between us and the batteries and under the very muzzles of their guns, and vanished into her own smoke unharmed. It was a gallant act, and glorious to see.

For a time it was the last thing that I saw. Something went ponk ! just behind me. A Titan blacksmith whirled a heavy sledge-hammer and hit me with all his might a blow on the right arm that sent me spinning down the narrow entry, to fall in the middle of a group of marines who were crouching on the battery deck.

" Why, whatever's the matter with you ? " said one in a surprised voice, and stirred me tentatively with his foot.

The universe became a black star which had its radiant point just below my right shoulder.

When things became reasonable again I found that I was in need of help, but that I could crawl. I remembered that there was a dressing-station at the foot of a ladder near by. The crash and flame of striking shells was still making an inferno of the upper deck. It was no good lying about where I was. I might as well do something, so I crawled to the hatch amongst bodies and wreckage, and climbed down the ladder. While I was climbing down a shell burst a little farther forward in the same space, and the concussion knocked me off the ladder, but I was not hit. The space below was crowded with ammunition-parties and wounded men. The whole floor of the next compartment, which was being used as a dressing-station, was already covered with white bandaged figures of the dead and wounded, amongst whom the dressers were busy. There was hardly a clear inch of space, but someone gave me a stool on which to sit and to wait, and presently a dresser came and bandaged me. He was a stout fellow, as busy, quiet, and collected in that dreadful place as if he had been in a hospital ward. I was very sick, and a minute or two after that I found myself recovered.

When I got up on deck again the *Vindictive* was alongside the Mole, and sheltered for the time from the fire of the Mole batteries, but she was still being hit occasionally by shots from the batteries ashore. There were sudden eruptions of din alternating with dead silence. The wet, jade-green curve of the wall was dimly visible sweeping up out of the dark, and back into it again. The last of the landing-parties was going over the brows, and there was an intermittent crackling and flashing of rifle and machine-gun fire up and down the Mole. From our top came bursts of the deafening uproar of the pom-poms, the most ear-splitting noise in the world. Every now and then there was a loud roar and a bright flash aft on the quarter-deck. I thought for a time that big shells were hitting us there, but it was our 11-inch howitzer which Brooks and his marines kept firing away steadily all the time in spite of every distraction. Looking out on to the forecastle, I saw the dim bulk of the *Daffodil* nosing into our starboard bow, and kicking the water out behind her as hard as she could. It was her business to hold us into the side of the Mole. Ferguson and some of the crew were busy there making fast a wire hawser in order to help her to keep her difficult position. Rifle bullets from the Mole made little splashes of fire on the deck about them as they worked.

I had to find out how far my guns' crews had got in the procedure that we had so often rehearsed, and I climbed up to our forward hook in search of them. The davit was turned out, but the hook was gone. I went aft along the landing-deck to the second hook, and I found the crews working at it under the lee of the house of the flame-thrower. A lot of things seemed to be hitting the far side of the house ; I suppose that it was rifle-fire from down the Mole. The davit was turned out, but it did not reach to the Mole, and the hook was dangling useless between the Mole and the ship. We tried again and again to get it into place, but we did not succeed. Rosoman came along and tried too, but ultimately he told us to leave it ; the Captain was going to keep the *Daffodil* shoving against our bows, and we must trust to her to hold us in. I went up one of the brows on to the Mole in order to see how they were resting. The swell, which had been very bad at first, was diminishing, and such of the brows as survived seemed to be resting comfortably enough. There was a lull in the firing close at hand just then, and a glance up and down the Mole showed nothing but a few rifle flashes, but I could hear in the comparative silence the steady thud ! thud ! of the guns ashore and of the monitors out at sea. That noise went on all the time as the background of the prevailing din ; one heard them thumping, and then one of our pom-poms in the top, or some Lewis-gunners or bombers near at hand, would break in and drown everything else with their uproar.

I went back on board to rejoin the guns' crews at the prescribed meeting-place in the starboard battery. Whilst making my way thither across the dark and littered deck I stumbled over somebody at the foot of one of the wooden ramps that led to the landing-deck. As well as I could see in the dark, there was a platoon of marines still waiting there crouched on the deck. A marine officer looked down from the landing platform.

" Aren't these folks going over ? " I asked.

" These are all gone," he said.

I was sitting down for a minute on a mushroom head in the battery, when shells began to strike our upper works and the funnels and cowls which stuck up above the sheltering Mole. The German destroyers had seen them from inside the harbour, and were shooting at them from a few hundred yards away. When a shell struck a cowl or a funnel a spray of splinters from the thin steel structure dashed down into the battery and caused many casualties there. Our top also stuck up above the Mole just ahead of the funnels, and it was, no doubt, the uproar of its automatic guns that attracted the attention of the destroyers. But the fire thus directed on them at point-blank range did not affect the resolution of Rigby and his stout crew of six marine artillerymen in the top. While the destroyers' shells were striking our upper works close beside them I heard the guns there still bursting out at regular intervals into their mad barking. But soon there came a crash and a shower of sparks, and silence followed it. They are all gone, I said to myself ; but in a minute or two a single gun in the top broke out again, and barked and barked. Then there was another crash, and the silence of the top became unbroken. Words cannot tell with what a glow of pride and exultation one heard that last gun speak. It seemed impossible that there should be anyone left alive in the top after the first shell struck it, and when the gun spoke again it seemed as if the very dead could not be driven from their duty. We learned afterwards that the first shell killed Rigby and all his crew except the sergeant. The sergeant was severely wounded, but he managed to get a gun back into action before the second shell struck, wounding him again, and putting his gun out of action. Would that Rigby had lived to know how faithfully his trust was discharged by the last member of his crew !

We could not see from the deck what was going on above us on the Mole, but whenever for a moment the *Vindictive* was silent we listened to the firing ashore and tried to guess what was happening there. I more than half expected a few survivors of our parties to come tumbling down the brows, followed by a rush of Germans to board the ship. But the Germans never made any attempt at a counter-attack of any sort or kind. When the *Vindictive* jumped at the Mole, as it must have seemed to them, out of the smoke, with her batteries of big guns and little guns, mortars and machine-guns, crashing and vomiting fire all together, they cleared away from the place at which she ran alongside, and contented themselves with holding strong points farther up and down the Mole. The marines established themselves some two hundred yards towards the beach and engaged the strong points ahead of them. Bryan Adams led all that was left of the seamen's landing-parties in a gallant attack on the batteries at the lighthouse end of the Mole. Those were the batteries that had to be silenced in order to help the blockships to get in. Nearly half of the seamen's parties were casualties before the ship got alongside, and owing to the heavy swell the reinforcing parties from the *Iris* and *Daffodil* could not get ashore. With numbers that were all too few to start with, and that dwindled rapidly, under the fire of the numerous machine-guns opposed to him, Adams led rush after rush along the Mole, trying to get to the batteries and to destroy the guns. Harrison, who was in command of this party, was severely wounded during the approach. When his wounds had been bound he joined Adams and his men on the Mole, and was killed leading one of the rushes, a most glorious victor over pain and death. The attack of this gallant band died away for sheer lack of men to carry it on ; but it achieved its purpose. When the blockships passed they encountered a severe fire from the guns on the extension of the Mole, but the most dangerous battery, the big battery at the end of the Mole itself, was silent. I think that it is probable that all the gunners had left the battery in order to resist Harrison's and Adam's attack.

One reason, no doubt, for the absence of any attempt at a counter-attack by the enemy was the complete success of one of the old sub-marines—that in command of Sandford—in blowing up the viaduct at the landward end of the Mole. A big gap was made in the viaduct which cut the Mole off from the shore, so that the enemy could send out no reinforcements to help the defenders of the Mole. Those who saw the explosion say that it was the biggest ever seen ; but I was busy at the moment with the *Iris*, and never even noticed it.

The *Iris* had appeared out of the dark and come alongside us at our starboard waist. Owing to the heavy swell she had found it impossible to carry out her intention of landing her men on the Mole ahead of us. The scaling ladders could not be made fast, and Bradford and Hawkins, the leaders of her landing-parties of seamen, who had climbed on to the Mole in order to try to secure the ladders, had both been killed in the attempt. Bradford climbed up a davit and jumped ashore ; Hawkins, his second-in-command, climbed up by a line. The Mole at that point was swept by machine-gun and rifle-fire, and was incessantly illuminated by star-shells and rockets. They must have known well that their undertaking was all but hopeless ; there could not have been a more gallant act.

Now the *Iris* was going to try to land her parties over the *Vindictive*, which, thanks to the continual thrust of the *Daffodil* against her bow, was keeping her position fairly comfortably alongside. But beside the *Vindictive* the *Iris* still danced in the swell like a cork, and it was some time before we could get a hawser on board from her or secure it when we had got it. Twice the hawser carried away, but at last it was done, and the men in the *Iris*, watching their opportunity, began to jump into the *Vindictive*. But meanwhile time had fled. We seemed to have been alongside a few minutes only ; we had been there an hour, and it was almost time to go. The order came that no more men were to land, that the *Iris* and the *Daffodil* were to blow their sirens (our own had been shot away) in order to recall the landing-parties, and that then the *Iris* was to go.

The sirens bellowed, we cast off the *Iris's* hawser, and backing away from our side she turned and steamed out to sea on a course that took her right across the front of the Mole batteries at four or five hundred yards' distance. I watched her with a sinking heart, knowing how we had suffered on the same course coming in. She had not gone five hundred yards before the batteries began to crash and bang. It was a terrible thing to watch. At that short range the light fabric of the little ship was hulled through and through, flames and smoke spurting from her far side as the shells struck her.

She disappeared from sight in the darkness enveloped in a thick cloud of smoke. I thought at the time that she had been sunk ; in fact she survived, after suffering terribly heavy casualties.

Recalled by the bellowing sirens, the landing-parties poured back on board of us over the two remaining brows and streamed down below. For good or ill our part was done. The blockships were either past or sunk, we did not know which, and if we were to get away at all we must go now, or we should not be out of range of the enemy's big guns before dawn. The *Daffodil* gave a snort, expressive of relief at being released from her long, hard shove, and of satisfaction at its complete success, and backed away, giving our bow a pull out as she did so. Helped by the set of the tide, our bow began to swing away from the Mole, and in a minute we were clear, and our propellers were throbbing.

As soon as our guns were no longer masked by the Mole we were to be ready to engage the Mole batteries, and I established myself once more by my voice-pipe at the forward port 6-inch gun. Mr. Cobby, our gunner (now lieutenant), came and helped me, and by shoving and hustling in the darkness managed to get everything ready at the gun, and to collect the emergency hands who were needed to replace casualties in the crew, so that I had plenty of time in which to think things over. My first thoughts were, " What luck we have had so far ! We are actually leaving the Mole. A bit more luck, and really and truly we may pull through." Then I thought, " What has happened on the Mole ? What has happened to the blockships ? I wish that I knew ! " And then I remembered what I had seen when the *Iris* passed the batteries, and I thought, " In two minutes that will be happening to us." My thoughts travelled no farther, and I waited for what was coming.

We stole on in deep silence. The din of firing had wholly ceased ; all but the guns' crews were below, the decks were empty, and there was nothing to hear now but the wash of the waves alongside. The ship seemed to be waiting with her guns ready and her attention strained for the crash of a striking shell. But the minutes were passing. When was it going to begin ?

Thick black fumes were eddying about the decks from our smoke apparatus. Once again, as on the approach, there came a faint popping from the sea. Each moment we expected the crash and the flame ; but the moments passed, and still the silence of the ship's progress was unbroken. The moments passed, and astonishment crept into my mind. How much longer than I expected it was taking before the bad time began ! " I wish we could hurry up," I thought, " and get it over, one way or another." And then I noticed that the popping in the sea had stopped. " Whatever can be the matter with them ? " I wondered ; and then I realized with a flash that while I had been waiting and wondering a good ten minutes had passed, and that we must be past the front of the Mole batteries and leaving them fast behind.

I could hardly trust myself to believe it. Had we perhaps been making a detour inshore, and were the batteries yet to pass ? Cobby was standing by the embrasure and could see out.

" What are we doing ? " I called to him.

" We are well away," he said. " Here come our destroyers."

So by the biggest wonder of that night of wonders we repassed the batteries not only unsunk but unhit. Confused by our smoke-screen, and flurried, no doubt, by what had been happening on the Mole, the Germans dropped behind us every shot that they fired, in a furious and perfectly harmless bombardment of our wake.

We had pulled through, but we still had a race against time before us—to get out of range of the big guns ashore before we were revealed to them by the dawn that was about to break. With flames pouring from her battered funnels and burdened with triumph, death, and pain, the *Vindictive* sped away from Zeebrugge into the North Sea.

Lt.-Com. E. Hilton Young (Lord Kennet).

ACROSS JORDAN

1st May. When it was too dusk for enemy observation, the battalion fell in. They marched swiftly to the river, and crossed. Here, again, were worlds conducting their existence in entire disconnection. The river, a fiercely purposeful thing, was sweeping up mighty armfuls of dark water and flinging them downward, to disappear into swirling masses beneath the bridge. Again, and infinitely again, the process was repeated, a magnificence of effort which came out of omnipotence and would pass eternally into it. Over all this effort, that was proceeding so far else whither from them, moved the lines of men, their tread sounding dully on the swaying bridge, their equipment sending out a metallic clank. Of these men, how small was the purview and limit within which each was vivid and real ! His own mind, inside of which his own being and experience were a flame ; the minds of those few, his close companions, where it was a faint and occasional shadow. The battalion outside, where he was a number and presently might be an identity disk, to be sent home when time and other jobs permitted. . . .

It had been a jumpy business, this crossing in semi-darkness. Spasms of machine-gun fire, though their source had been pushed into pockets of the transjordanic hills that no longer commanded the river, sent strays splashing the lead with a sudden spurt of silver. A few bullets sang over the bridge ; several men were hit, and one killed. There was intermittent shelling, due to grow fiercer when night deepened ; Martin was glad that the Claphams were after the Brentfords, and not the other way round. Once a shell, aimed at that teasing random which is so hard to endure—it is a tugging at the nerves, when you see shells bursting far apart, and know that your foe is firing without observation, but for that very reason is going to try all possible targets—burst in the river, so little above the bridge that it was almost under it. Jacko had the range all right ! It was only luck that he had not caught them. That plane

591

which had spotted them this morning had reported that there would be night crossings; every yard of the road beyond the river would be plastered! Each man felt his heart sink sickeningly as out of night came that swoop and descent. We have lost our fathers' dread of demons; but you who have known a quiet road at night without warning pass into an inferno of shelling know also what Guthlac abroad in a shrieking winter darkness imagined. All the eyes are with your foe; he sees, and strikes out of the blackness. He lets you go forward a while, for no reason but malignant pleasure in your terror, and then he has you. A mighty geyser shot up, the bridge was blinded with spray, a huge muscular beast of water with points of brightness like so many eyes swung over it, serpentine, irresistible. The bridge rocked like a bamboo suspension in a Himalayan storm, the men nearest the shell-burst were tossed against the rail. Two missed it, and when the beast had ebbed again, they had gone with it. Scylla had pounced and taken her prey. . . .

The stealthy flowing forward in night had ended, and in a bleak morning, not yet fissured with grey, the Brentfords took up their positions of attack. At 4 a.m., when a white eyelid opened in a low gap of the hills, the attack was launched. The racket of the guns as yet neither helped nor hindered. Presently, out of the grey emerged the features of the world. The oleanders of the Wadi Shunet Nimrin became a watchful blackness, such a covert as might conceal the conscious stream's presiding divinity; they changed to sullen red, to laughing crimson. The Brentfords saw they were still in an avenue of thorns and gleaming-appled poison-bush; and about them, and above them, hung the immeasurable heights they were to storm, a conglomerate of fanged and shelving stone. Throughout that day they raged, as might have raged some valiant child of men, confronted by a foe out of legend, who was cloaked with invisibility and with armour from celestial smithies.

A blood-stained advance brought them to the road where it narrowed, mounting fast. They thrust forward, in single file and by such rushes as the slope and their weariness permitted. Windings that exposed them had to be taken, under cover of their own small-arms fire flung at almost random, in an uncharted, sightless waste. Always above and around were the menacing rocks, naked of visible foe but alive with capricious and terrifying activity. The white sweet broom was in blossom ; red and creamy cistus made a glorious heath ; from cliff faces hung the trailing caper, the hyssop that springeth out of the wall, looking out of blue-veined, hairy eyes.

With knowledge of their task's impossibility, despair came early. If it had been the bursting of one lock it might have been done—at that lock's price. It was the bursting of a succession of locks, clamped tight in these narrow doors. For their own numerous dead and wounded no return could be exacted. Nevertheless, the London men, fighting a battle without hope, endured, trusting that elsewhere their useless valour might bring in gain ; the Anzacs were engaged to north of them.

One thing was burnt into Martin Chapman's mind (and into hundreds of other minds), and became the setting of the nightmare which was all he carried hence. This was the rows of seeming endless red towering hollyhocks through which they moved. For many of them they were the lurid candles on their lykewalk to the Brig of Death. . . .

Snipers appeared above the cliff. They could do little harm, firing into such a confusion of stone and scrub ; but they added a fresh reason for jumpiness, and for keeping your head down. Worse, they could signal and observe. A heavy barrage was tossed down, and for twenty minutes the air round the Brentfords was an infernal thing, a whirl of bushes, stumps, fragments of rock. Fifty miles above the earth, some say, such a wind speeds ever, carrying in its course meteorites and star-dust. You who have known modern shell-fire laugh at the catapults of the ancients, slinging their useless stones ! Laugh, that is, if you have not read of the siege of Jerusalem, and learned that there was terror before the Somme was fought. The grotesque and ghastly mingled when a chunk of rock the size of a child's head came spinning over and left a man stunned or with face smashed in. You could not dig real trenches in that limestone, and men felt more exposed than they actually were. But with every movement of position came exposure of the most naked kind.

A belt of machine-gun fire drew closer in. In its wake a hand-to-hand assault developed ; out of the innumerable tiny valleys men came swarming, with the terrifying precipitancy of a troll-army springing from its burrows. When they were repulsed, it was to hang in nearer than they were ; and the Londoners had many dead and wounded. The telephone wire, which had been cut, was repaired at the cost of a life. Martin had known so little that it was from Battalion Head-quarters that he got word that his company commander was killed. Warren Remfry was next in succession, since two senior subalterns were casualties.

The Anzacs' attack to north of them had gone badly, the enemy had forced a wedge between them and the London Division and threatened to isolate the latter. He captured a raised promontory between the Richmonds and the Brentfords, from which he enfiladed men who gave better targets than they could themselves find. He grew insolent, with prospects of such another capture as he had made at the second battle of Gaza. The wires went wrong again ; and Martin, wondering from minute to minute when his handful would be overwhelmed by a wave out of the tumbled, featureless world which shut them in with ignorance and blindness, was grateful when a runner—if the name can be given to a man who has had to squirm his way through a hundred yards of scrub and limestone—brought him Warren's order to withdraw to a point fifty yards to the rear. This was merely to a momentary halting-place ; a general retirement was in process, and the step was in anticipation of the new assault expected.

Warren's company fell back in sections, under cover of their own furious small-arms fire. The battle-front, curving inward and round a mountain, had removed them from artillery support. The random character of their defence was not lost on the enemy, who followed up boldly, and put down a barrage on the new line. Martin prayed for speedy repetition of the order to retreat. Where each man took hasty cover behind any rock that lifted above its fellows, and there was no connecting regularity of trenches, a fresh risk appeared. The line was disintegrating, the platoons were breaking up into individuals. . . .

That evening, and from the first breaking up of dusk next day, the Brentfords slipped through the hills. It was baneful shepherding. There were countless episodes of the sort our ready writers term Homeric, knowing neither Homer nor modern war. There were hasty snatchings of cover and loosings off of machine-gun and rifle-fire ; the foe was both too wary to come within close range and too fortunate to require to. When the mountain road curved outward into pinnacled eminence and naked exposure, a gust of bullets might lay a human swathe low ; or a shell burst and dash half a dozen men against the rocks. The wounded had to be gathered, had to be helped forward. There was a place (whose outlines are bitten, as with acid, into minds that yet move among men) where a thick brush of oleanders swept up out of the brook and across the winding of the way. It was dimming when the last of the Brentfords passed this point ; and Remfry, hard pressed, left a handful to hold it. He knew Martin's thought, its anguish and shame and horror, and it was in his charge that he gave the ambush. It was magnificently successful, for the enemy, thinking the night had drawn his prey into the deeper darkness of the Valley thrust forward and almost into the Lewis-guns and the rifles. Not Achilles flinging Trojan lives as a sacrifice to his wounded friendship felt a sterner relief of vengeance than came to Martin. There was a slaughter sufficient to ensure that the foe thereafter crept careful-footed again and at distance.

But the episode, though it brought rest when rest or destruction must have come, came only at the end of long wretchedness. Not till the Division had withdrawn into the Valley could their own guns render effectual assistance. Not until night fell was there any respite. Through the long dusk they moved borne despairingly downward and backward, through the riot of white and crimson cistus and creamy broom and beneath cliffs where the blue, spider-eyed hyssop seemed to watch them. Always in never-ending avenue, towered the red hollyhocks, a nightmare of mocking brightness.

Edward Thompson.

MASTER PILOT

MAJOR EDWARD MANNOCK, V.C., D.S.O., M.C., AT WORK

May 21st. In his first fight, which commenced at 12,000 feet, there were six Pfalz scouts flying east from Kemmel Hill direction. One he shot to pieces after firing a long burst from directly behind and above; another he crashed; it spun into the ground after it had been hit by a deflection shot; the other, a silver bird, he had a fine set-to with, while his patrol watched the Master at work. It was a wonderful sight. First, they waltzed around one another like a couple of turkey-cocks, Mick being tight on his adversary's tail. Then the Pfalz half-rolled and fell a few hundred feet beneath him. Mick followed, firing as soon as he got in position. The Hun then looped —Mick looped too, coming out behind and above his opponent and firing short bursts. The Pfalz then spun Mick spun also, firing as he spun. This shooting appeared to me a waste of ammunition. The Hun eventually pulled out; Mick was fast on his tail—they were now down to 4,000 feet. The Pfalz now started twisting and turning, which was a sure sign of " wind-up." After a sharp burst close up, Mick administered the *coup de grâce*, and the poor old fellow went down headlong and crashed.

This was a really remarkable exhibition of cruel, cool, calculating Hun-straffing. A marvellous show. I felt sorry for the poor Hun, for he put up a wonderful show of defensive fighting. His effort reminded me of mine on April 12th. The only difference was, that he was miles over his own lines and had a slower machine. Had he only kept spinning down to the ground, I think he would have got away with it.

I asked Mick after we landed why he fired during the spin. He replied : " Just to intensify his wind-up." And a very good answer, too ! This was the first occasion that I have seen a machine loop during a fight. It was obvious to us watching that to loop under such circumstances is foolish. Mick managed, however, to keep behind him, though, and did not lose contact with him although it was obvious by his manœuvres after he came out of the loop that the Pfalz pilot was all at sea, for he twisted and turned his machine in a series of erratic jerks just as if he was a dog stung on his tail ! Mick says he only looped as well for a bit of fun, as he felt his opponent was " cold meat." He says what he should have done instead of looping was to have made a zooming climbing turn as the Pfalz looped, then half-rolled and come back on his tail as he came out of the loop. By this means he would have been able to keep the Hun in sight all the time, while he would not have lost control of his machine as the Hun did while coming out of the loop.

Mick's other Hun was a Hannoveranner two-seater, which he shot down after a burst at right angles. The old boy crashed into a tree near La Couronne, south of Vieux.

Four in one day ! What is the secret ? Undoubtedly the gift of accurate shooting, combined with determination to get to close quarters before firing.

It's an amazing gift, for no pilot in France goes nearer to a Hun before firing than the C.O., but he only gets one down here and there, in spite of the fact that his tracer bullets appear to be going through his opponent's body ! Mick on the other hand takes an angle shot and—Hun in flames.

James Van Ira (74th Squadron, R.F.C.), quoted by Ira Jones.

ERSATZ

SOME began to come barefooted to school, in normal times a revolutionary attack on the dignity of the institute. The head master seized the opportunity of a Monday morning sermon to express the hope that it would not become a habit, that those who had decent shoes were still expected to wear them, but that the others need not feel ashamed or be afraid that they had done something wrong, in fact that it was brave of them to face the necessity in a cheerful spirit. I was able to avoid this humiliation of walking like an elementary schoolgirl, but at the beginning of the winter my only pair of leather shoes had lost their soles and heels and were beyond all possibility of repair. My mother bought me new ones made of paper cloth with wooden soles. They were heavy and clumsy, the snow which fell in abundance stuck to them in thick layers. I walked as if on clump feet. Every morning, standing in the house door, I cried because of the shoes and the cold and the misery of this wretched life. I was deprived not only of comfort and luxury, but of the barest necessities of existence.

Lilo Linke.

PRISONERS AT GOLPA

" The State may utilize the labour of prisoners of war, other than officers, according to their rank and aptitude. Their tasks shall not be excessive. . . . The Government into whose hands prisoners of war have fallen is bound to maintain them. . . ." Lord Birkenhead, *" International Law."*

THE coal-mine at Golpa was a surface mine; that is, open to the sky, although the workings were some distance beneath the ground level. . . .

Prisoners were employed in various ways at Golpa, but most of them worked in gangs on the cliff edge, where the continual scraping of coal made it necessary to move back the railway metals.

Our third day's work in the mine found us with a gang of a hundred or so Russians, and with them we spent the day moving rails, or " ricking," as it was termed.

Each man was given an iron crowbar, and placed at intervals along a section of the line—at the back of us stood the " Director " —a prisoner who chanted the signals for each man to place his bar beneath the rail, and pull in unison.

That day we pulled and pulled, to the sound of a quaint chanty : Ho ! brrrr—Ho ! brrrr—describes how it sounded ; the brrr effect being obtained by causing the tongue to oscillate in the mouth.

By afternoon we were heartily tired of this task, yet no relief was allowed for our weary backs.

Once a section was completed, we passed on, and started to lever again without any pause. The work went on without interruption : with continuous shouting, the director of the proceeding soon became voiceless, and was replaced by others. Johnson and Jack Smith pulled on either side of me, and, though the latter had been used to hard work, his hands like mine, soon became a mass of blisters.

About three o'clock Johnson explained to us that he had discovered the secret of working without exertion.

"You must understand," he said, "that it is not necessary to put all one's energies into the pulling, but go through the motion with apparent effort, and they won't see that you aren't really straining hard."

This method, I believe, was adopted by the Russians, but they were so crafty that the Germans were easily baffled.

Johnson was soon spotted, heartily cursed by the foreman of the gang, and called a swine Englishman: his temporary lapse resulted in a more vigorous speeding up of the work.

At 6 p.m., tired and weary, and almost incapable of even talking, we left for barracks, thankful to rest and try to forget the day's work, that had seemed to us a month in duration.

On our return we received a little parcel of food from the Englishmen in the adjoining barracks, and a half-dozen biscuits each from the Frenchmen in the compound.

We did not resume the rail-shifting next day, as the distance we had to walk to our midday meal was more than we could manage in the time allotted us. Instead, we were put to a task in the lowest depths of the mine that was nearer to our barracks.

We worked there until after the Armistice, doing alternate weeks of day and night shift, loading trucks of coal with civilians. . . .

The work was not only laborious, but extremely dirty. As the coal was merely dust, it sifted into one's clothes and boots, and came down in showers from the top of the cliffs, almost choking and blinding those below.

When the truck was filled, the prisoners took it off to the endless chain, that carried the wagons up to the factory.

It required a little nicety of turning to run it from the side lines to the main track, and as there were no proper turntables, there were many wagons upset at these junctions.

The righting of the truck was a very heavy task, and one that called for more energy than any of us could easily put forth.

One factor alone saved us from being absolutely worked to death; this being the lack of proper lubricating oil, that was the cause of the frequent failure of the engine which propelled the endless chain.

When this happened, the empty trucks could not be brought up, or the full wagons sent off, so that we had many rests whilst waiting for the machinery to recommence.

Machinery there, as elsewhere in Germany, was failing for the lack of oil : even the wagon-wheels were greased with a mixture of tar compounds.

Later in the year, we began to see that lack of oil and grease was also responsible to a large degree for the breakdown of the physical condition of the German race. . . .

Coffee was brought in at five-thirty each morning, but was a wretched drink, and most unlike the real thing.

The bread was very poor in quality, of a dark brown colour, and sometimes almost like clay in composition. At other times it was dry and brittle, with fragments of straw and hard pieces of potatoes buried in it ; and at all times it had a sour flavour, and gave us severe heartburn ; yet, had we been able to get it, we could each have eaten a whole loaf per day.

When hunger became more and more intense, we took it in turns to eat the fragments that fell to the table on the dividing of the loaf.

Each evening, the knowledge that we had that slice of bread really worried us, and self-control could scarcely be exercised.

I often found myself going to look at my ration, and cutting off what I imagined was an uneven piece, only to cut it crookedly, and begin the levelling up process again and again, until it had all disappeared.

When I did save my bread until next day, I used to cut off tiny fragments with a knife, in order to make it last longer, and so flatter myself I had eaten a square meal.

On these meagre rations we found work was becoming more and more laborious, and instead of feeling lighter in the stomach, we walked as if carrying a continual weight in that part.

Soon our legs lost power, and a wretched numbed feeling seemed to load them down. If our work had not consisted very largely in pushing the trucks along, we could not have carried on, because the moving truck largely assisted our walking.

Day by day we gradually became a little weaker, yet we struggled on, hoping that by a miracle our parcels might reach us by July.

Many times we told the civilians of our hunger, but they either did not believe us or had no sympathy.

One day I took a sample of the toadstool soup to the German

with whom I was working, but he refused to believe that we were eating such rubbish, and regarded my story as an imaginary grumble.

Men who went on night shift were on Sunday evenings given a bowl of soup in the factory cook-house.

When we first began on Sunday, we went up to the building where soup was served, and waited with a crowd of hungry Russians. The four of us were the only English present !—all other English were getting parcels, and could be independent of that extra bowl of soup—but we felt that the other unfortunates regarded us as more than greedy.

A second helping was often served, but to get this, one had to gulp down the hot liquid as speedily as possible, and line up at the end of the queue.

The first occasion on which we attended this distribution we did not realize what had to be done to get more, but after a few visits, we used to tack ourselves on to the rear of the waiting queue, and drink as we walked along. It seems very amusing now to remember how desperate we were for that little extra, but at the time I know it was a very serious affair.

I think it also amused the Germans to see Englishmen fighting to get such common soup, and the guard who was there to keep order, with the help of a wolfhound, wore a very cynical smile. . . .

Sometimes we sat at the chain-head waiting for wagons, and often fell asleep on the instant, only to wake again and feel incapable of fighting the insistent drowsiness. Some of the older prisoners warned us against this continual snatching of a few moments' sleep, for they told us that in this way so many men had died without giving warning, when in a weak condition.

E. C. Pattison.

THE AISNE

The relative failure of their great attacks of March and April forced the German General Staff to realize that the only means of keeping the initiative in their hands was to launch another blow elsewhere. At 1 a.m. in the night of May 26–27 a bombardment began along the front between the Ailette, the Aisne and the Chemin-des-Dames. It took the British and French completely by surprise; at 4.40 the Germans came over the top and began their advance. A desperate resistance was put up to stem the attack but they got to within 40 miles of Paris before the Allies were able to hold them.

THE WORST BOMBARDMENT OF THE WAR

NEXT day I spent a long time at my observation post, and watched the disturbing spectacle of enemy linesmen laying out new telephone wires. I was therefore not surprised to learn on returning to Brigade Head-quarters that a telegram had just come stating that deserters taken by the French XIth Corps had predicted a general attack on our front at 1 a.m. of the following morning (the 27th).

At a minute to one next morning our signal officer called up all our battalions in order to test the lines. At one o'clock precisely a terrific drum-fire with a large proportion of gas-shells crashed like an avalanche all over our area, and when a minute later the signal officer tested the lines again there was no reply—every cable had already been cut by direct hits into the trenches. As the shelling went on steadily hour after hour communication could never be restored, and all information had to be by messenger. I spent several hours at an artillery observation post, but could see nothing as there was a fog till about 8 a.m., and merely swallowed a quantity of gas. The enemy attack probably developed between 3 and 4 a.m., but as our isolated companies east of the treacherous canal were annihilated we never knew exactly. Throughout the morning our

603

battalions fought hard in the area between the Cauroy-Cormicy road and the canal; the area east of the canal, and the near bank of the canal itself, were certainly lost by 7 a.m.

D. V. Kelly (110*th Inf. Bde.*).

PUSHED BACK

27th/28th May. 4 a.m. Last night we were paraded and marched quickly up a steep road into a wood. Jerry began a big bumping as we went up the road, and we had to go by the ditch. All night the ground over the deep dug-out we are in has been hammered with the shells. . . .

6 a.m. A sergeant has shouted down, " Fall in." I must get this pad in my haversack. We have no overcoats or packs, only battle order. There is a machine-gun firing, but it is a long way off. It is a German—slow and deliberate—rat-a-tat—stop—rat-a-tat. Somebody says, " Come in, mind the step," and we all laugh, a bit.

What a lot has happened in a few days. I have all day to write. I have slept for twenty-four hours, and something has changed inside me.

We filed from the dug-out, up the steep road to the top of the hill. The road at the top was camouflaged all along the side, and over the top, with long strips of stuff like dried seaweed. But Jerry caught us right away with his shells. They screamed upwards from an immense plain up on to the ridgetop. We took to the ditch, and then wound down the hillside, and Jerry tried to hit us all the way. We could hear the gun bang as the shell shrieked towards us. Ben said they were firing point-blank. Our necks shorten and we want to stop, but the officer shouts, " Keep moving, there." There are fountains of earth and stones rising and dropping on us.

All the plain below was drifting smoke, just as if it were mist, but it was shells. We could see the yellow flame. We went down to some trenches they said were called the " Labyrinth ", shallow trenches, with thick, low shrubbery, back and front. Shells were whistling and yelling from all angles. It was no use ducking or dropping. Every second the nose caps hit the earth—drdrdrdrdrdr —thus. A small shell hit the ground near my foot, and slithered along. I did not hear it coming in the row. It was a dud.

The officer and the corporal with two men went through the

shrubbery. Looking through it I could see a big *route nationale*. There were hundreds of our fellows running along it, like a football crowd running for the trams. Jerry's machine-guns were going and they were dropping, a score at a time and lying in heaps, khaki heaps.

The officer came back and the two men were carrying the corporal. His face and body and legs were all covered with blood, and he was all grey and yellow. They were carrying him back. We said, "Good luck, corporal." He whispered, "It's you as wants the good luck. I'm out of it." I liked the corporal. He liked me, and he always smiled as he passed.

From the "Labyrinth" we fell back down a woody lane. A captain of artillery was sitting by the roadside, holding the bridle of a chestnut horse. The colonel, who was with us, said, "Where is your battery?" The officer pointed to his horse, "Here it is, sir."

There was shelling at all points. We could see Jerries now, coming over the fields, through the wire and camouflage. They looked like harvesters or men mowing. We fired at them for a short time, and then fell back. Their shells covered the fields in front of them, and fell always a bit nearer to us.

We defiled through a wood, crossed an open space, and lined the edge of another wood. Jerry came out of the wood we had left in ones and twos, but dodged back when we fired at him. The range was 500 yards. There was now no sign of any movement in the wood.

Suddenly a machine-gun opens out behind us, and we lie flat in the shrubbery. Our team crawl away from the sound, then round towards it, from the rear. Ben is leading with the gun, then Number Two, then myself and the carriers behind. Lying flat and looking through the undergrowth and tree trunks we can see a bit of bluish uniform. Ben gets the legs of the Lewis-gun well planted. He looks along it. The patch of uniform is ten yards off. Pop-pop-pop—pop-popop-pop. We pass up ammunition and Number Two claps it on like lightning. The Jerry gun has stopped. Ben says, "Wait here." He crawls off to the right and disappears. We wait and watch the place where the gun was firing closely, and never take our rifles from it. Ben comes crawling back. He says, "Four of them, and their gun's riddled too." . . .

Later that day we fell back again, not very far. It was hard to see any Jerries, but we could hear their machine-guns all over in the woods. Towards dusk we came to a small French strong point. It was surrounded with rusty wire, about a foot high, for fifty yards all round, back and front.

We had a grand officer with us, just our platoon. We had not seen any of the Company since afternoon. There were twenty-five of us, with one Lewis-gun. He had guided us all the afternoon and evening with his map out. Neither he nor us knew our way. He is tall and rather ugly, and always quite undisturbed, yet thinking and " all there." . . .

In the strong point the riflemen gave us all their ammunition, keeping only ten rounds, and we refilled the drums.

When we had done this the officer walked out in front, with only his walking-stick and revolver. He suddenly wheeled round and shouted in a big voice, " Beat it, lads, for the wood." We struggled through the wire behind the post. Jerry had a machine-gun on us, and the bullets whistled it seemed under one's arms and between one's legs. We could hear their deep shouts. When we lay in the copse the officer said, " They were lying in a dip, a half-company with umpteen machine-guns."

At dusk from the copse we could see files of Germans passing at 100 yards' range on each side of us. They were dim in the mist, and they looked enormous, and the machine guns they were carrying stuck up like chimneys. They must have seen us and took us for Jerries. Just before the sky turned quite black, the officer led us across an open space from the copse into a deep forest. A straight narrow lane ran right through it. The officer left Ben and Number Two at the end of that lane, with nearly all our ammunition, to do their best with Jerry till it was all spent.

We fell back, and we heard the gun begin its short bursts. He had some fine targets, for files of Germans were moving forward all over the fields towards the forest. Back a long way we went and now we could not hear Ben's gun, but all was silent, and the German lights rose in the wood all around. They sailed in the air, hung, and dropped quickly. They threw a yellow and black trellis-work of the trees over the road. There was no moon.

On a hill in the middle of the forest there was the rest of the battalion. They were lining a breastwork, and peering into the dark, and shouted gladly when they saw us. From here we could see over the black waste of tree-tops, and from them rose the yellow globes of light in a dead straight line for many miles, as though drawn with a ruler.

An hour before dawn Ben came back. He came through the trees, with his long, stooping stride, with his machine-gun on his shoulder and Number Two behind. We rushed round him and asked him questions, but he was very tired and was trying to hide his relief at finding us. As I lay near him in the night I heard him crying.

When light came we were out of the forest. We could never have held that place in the woods. Since the morning before there had been no artillery fire on either side, except only two British field-guns that banged away, though now they were in front of us and a long way off. When they were nearer they sounded like an anvil when it is beaten ; now they were far off, they were like the taps of a drum.

We were on a main road, at the end of a village, called Sapicourt. The French were with us, and we were about a hundred yards behind them. The villagers were hurrying off down the road with hand-carts full of mattresses and bundles. . . .

The French were in front in a little thin wood, about 50 yards long. We could hear the Germans rat-tatting, and the French guns spitting back at them. They had very light machine-guns, with a crescent-shaped magazine. Many of these French were oldish men. Some were stout, and had long black beards, but they ran like children ; from one end of the wood to the other, carrying their machine-guns, putting them down in the trees, firing away, and then moving behind the wood to the other end, and going through the performance again.

In the afternoon the Germans had a balloon up over the wood. It seemed so near we could see every detail. Then a gun began to drop shells near the road. It was only a small gun, but the shells dropped nearer every time. The whistle of the shell seemed to cleave one's brain. We sheltered in the ditch, but one chap had a nasty cut on the arm from a flying stone. It cut a big piece of flesh away. He was in pain. The officer joked him a lot about Blighty, and he cheered up.

The French, towards evening, were firing all their machine-guns for hours without a stop. Then they fell back through us. When their firing stopped, we could hear a storm of British machine-guns on the right and left. The officer said we ten were the front line now ; and we had to wait here till the South Staffs and the D.L.I. should be drawn in from the right and left, where they had been forming defensive flanks. Soon Jerry's lights were going up in the wood the French had left, though it was not yet quite dark.

It seemed a long time till the Staffs filed past from the left, about eighty of them. Then after a long time came the Durhams. They were very few, and when we asked how they had gone on they said, " Abeggarahail !   Ould   Jerry's   swarming.   Thousands of the bastards."

We fell back about six kilos that night. In the dark we lined a trench very near a long, black wood. There was no moon. A 'plane came grunting over and dropped four bombs in the field behind us. None of us knew we were being bombed until it was over. When we heard the shriek of the bombs we thought it was shells. The officer said, " Heavy ones. He won't be carrying many more." The concussion when they hit the ground swayed the road from side to side. . . .

We sat in a breast-high trench in the first part of the night and nobody spoke. Suddenly in the wood in front there began a shouting and screaming, high screams of warning and fear and hate, and the crack of bombs, and the clashing of steel, the most horrible sound that there is to hear. The officer drew us out of the trench and we lay nearer the wood with our rifles towards it. The clashing of steel and the screaming continued. From the dark of the trees there came French stretcher-bearers carrying men all wringing wet with blood. It dripped through the stretchers on the bearers, oldish men who were trembling but grinned when they saw, we were English. One man was groaning and crying and muttering words in a deep voice of agony. He was like a large piece of raw meat, so covered with blood.

It grew quiet in the wood, and the German lights began to surge up. We went back to the trench.

At dawn we left the trench in file. Five Germans came out of a copse twenty yards away. We turned quickly towards them and threw ourselves into the long grass. A sergeant only a foot in front of me, gurgled and turned on his back. His eyes turned up—and there was a look in them as if he were trying to understand something. He was dead. A lance-corporal, one pace behind me in the file, was on his back and rattling in his throat. He was dead.

I realized I had got the group of Germans in a line as I fell in the grass. I fired a round towards them, low, near the ground. I heard a terrible scream, as though the bullet had passed right down the length of someone's body.

We crawled along through the grass to a cross-roads. There was a fat French sentry in a box, a very old man. I said, " Allemand tout près." He loped across a field towards a wood on a rise about a mile away. When he was half-way we saw him turn off to the left, still trotting, and we could hear a hellish machine-gun strafe had started in the wood, and we could see the tiny blue figures dodging about all over it, in the trees and on the stone wall around it.

We moved on into a stone quarry, and here we got a bit of our own back on Jerry. A 'plane came over very low and flew round and round the quarry. We could not spare the machine-gun ammunition, so four of us began to fire at it, casually, and dully, with rifles. Suddenly it somersaulted, and shot down and hit the field nose first near last night's wood, 600 yards off. Some Germans ran out to it, and one of our fellows fired at them and they ran back. So far we had seen no British 'plane all this time and only one French.

Just now I cannot remember all that happened in this day. The Germans were close to us, behind, in front, at the sides, always with machine-guns, and were hard to see. But we got some of their transport with our Lewis-gun, at 1,500 yards, two lorries which ran wild on a steep road right in front of us, and then turned over and over on their sides. And we got a big target of Jerries on a road, 600 yards. In the afternoon we saw plenty of them singly, but we could not fire at them—only at groups—as we'd hardly a shot left. . . .

We came to some marshes covered with thin reeds much higher than a man. We put the machine-gun down, pointing towards where we thought Jerry would be. But soon we could hear his deep voice talking and shouting behind us. Ben carried the gun a bit away to the flank. I was the last in the file, and turning round there was a Jerry behind me with his rifle at the port. He was a little chap, with a drooping black moustache. I fired at him, and dodged into the reeds.

It was terribly hot and we had no water. We came out of the

reeds in file, following the captain of "A" Company, and there was all the battalion together now. . . . The captain of "A" Company said, "Unfix." We followed him in file up a steep hill, heavy with trees, and across a field of long grass. Then the hill dropped hugely and miles of plain appeared far below. We lay out along the top of the crest. There was a line of blue-coats with us. They were of the French Colonial Infantry.

It grew darker. Far below there was a town at the foot of this immense ridge. Shells were bursting all over it like small balls of grey wool. Somewhere from our left rear there was a German machine-gunner who swept the ridge with a long burst of fire at intervals. I asked a French soldier the name of the town and he said, "Rheims."

In the late twilight there came a rush of Jerries on the left. A Lewis-gun rattled just a few bursts, and it stopped. But six of the French next to me were already well on their way down the hill. A little second-lieutenant with an overcoat down to his heels chased them, rounded them up with his revolver and they lay down again on the crest.

There was a "second loot" with us now, an ex-ranker with the M.M. He had been sitting mournfully with his knees up, chewing a blade of grass. Now he said, "Ask him what the bloody hell it's all about." I asked the French officer if his men had run away. He said in French, "Yes, but they are now returned." He is a grand little chap, but smothered with his overcoat. Our "second-loot" says, as though talking to himself, "Eighty kilometres to Paris —twenty kilometres a day—Paris in four days."

Night came. We were withdrawn down the hill to make a defensive flank facing the north. The French are still at the top of the hill, with some of our men of "A" Company. The "second-loot" and our machine-gun team are on the roadside at the foot of the ridge. Some French fellows passed with a little Jerry prisoner. They're grinning and joking and seem delighted with him. He looks about sixteen, and has a little round, cropped, fair head. The "second-loot" says, "Ask him what the bloody hell it's all about." The little Jerry said, "Prusienne compagnie—na hinten—nein Englische prisonnier." He was very aggressive, and self-important and excited. I told the officer, "I think he is trying to say that there's a Prussian company over the hill and that they say they'll take no English prisoners." He said, " That sounds bloody cheery, anyway."

We were taken away from the ridge in the thick black of the night. We had formed in fours on the road, waiting for the different battalions to come in, and French troops were passing us in fours on our left. They cursed us and said things of which I could only catch the drift, all about the English—" Sacré's " and " Merde's" and deep spitting, bitter things. I hoped they'd find Jerry in the same mood as we'd left him.

There were 80 Huntshires. We waited and there came a few Durhams, then 19 Northumberlands and some oddments of other lots. There were 119 all told. There were none of one battalion of Huntshires. The division moved off.

Behind us, on each side, in the fields, the machine-guns seemed very close, and for miles in a dead straight line the Véry lights soared, hung yellow, and fell in fields or behind the tree-tops.

R. H. Kiernan (8th Leicestershire Regt.).

NIGHT BOMBER

It is a quarter to eight. Eight thousand feet above the coast near Dunkerque we move. My pilot is a senior officer, and I have never flown with him before, so I sit quietly and do not talk, as I watch carefully the dials of my petrol instruments, and also keep a careful eye on the country below. The pilot looks at the engines with a satisfied glance, and the machine swings round and points east.

Soon the dim pattern of the Dixmude floods lie below, reflecting the gleam of a quivering star-shell. In the sky above Thorout appears a dazzling Véry light which drifts and dies—German machines are abroad in the darkness also. Far below now lies Thorout, and for a minute or two its pale beam waves vainly and impotent in the moonlit sky, its strength so dissipated that it is useless. Soon south of Ghent we move, and see to our right the landing lights of the huge Gotha aerodrome of Gontrode.

I stand up and look across the pilot, and count the lights.

" Eight on each side—two red at the west ! " I say.

" I make it more," he comments. " Count again ! "

I make sure of my accuracy, and draw in my notebook a detailed sketch of the landing arrangements.

" Look ! " suddenly cried the pilot. " We've been heard ! "

I peer down once more and see only the two red lights glowing on the ground. The two lines of white electric lamps have been switched off, for the drone of our engines has been heard high above the aerodrome.

Suddenly I realize that we will be heard through the whole of our long journey. The absence of searchlights and shell fire in these undefended regions makes one forget that from town to town, from village to village, the report of our progress is sent to a thousand military centres in a vast radius. Already our passage into virgin territory (for not for years has country east of Ghent been bombed at night) must be causing a sensation. Brussels must be apprehensive : Aix-la-Chapelle is feeling anxiety : Cologne is uneasy. . . .

Far ahead I can see a light flashing and flashing in a regular code. I presume it to be near Brussels, and point it out to the pilot. In a few minutes through the slight haze of the distance appears a great number of twinkling lights, and soon to our left I see a vast sea of glittering, shimmering gems, with lines of lights radiating outwards from it like the tentacles of an octopus. I suddenly realize that it is Brussels, and with a cry of utter delight stand up to look down more clearly at it. It is a wonderful spectacle. There, in one wide sweep before my eyes, lies the whole city, triumphantly blazing out into the night. I can see the long lines of the boulevards stretching through the mass of lights, on the outskirts of which glitter little villages, from which also radiate the lines of street lamps, as though illuminated starfish lay here and there across the country. . . .

Brussels passes. Road and forest and village flow beneath us in a regular and expected stream. Slowly the minutes go by. Ten minutes to ten says the watch. For over two hours we have been in the air, and our engines show no signs of wavering. On them alone now depend our chances of return. Soon I see far ahead of me the silver ribbon of the Meuse shining in the haze of the horizon, and then the lights of Namur, cold and sparkling, appear by the side of the river. I examine every tiny landmark on the ground below, and check it with my map. There is no doubt. There lie the lights of the town—there lies the forest on its outskirts—there lie the two bridges, from one of which the thin black line of the railway trails off into the distance.

"Namur" ! I say to the pilot.

He looks down and flies round in a wide circle in order to examine every point, and to ensure for himself that no doubt whatever exists as to the identity of the place. He is quite satisfied, and turns the machine towards the south-east. We cross the river south of the town as I explain to him my intentions. I want him to turn north-west, against wind, and to throttle the engines. We will glide down parallel to the railway line, which will help me to get a good line. We will reach the bridge at a low altitude, and I will drop my bombs. We will turn quickly down wind to escape.

Before I crawl into the back I point out to him some very bright lights in the direction of the Namur Zeppelin sheds, which seem to confirm my supposition of the activity of German airships to-night. Then, with a final word of explanation, I stoop through the door behind my seat and lie on the floor of the machine. I slide open the little trap-door beneath the pilot's seat, and see a small square picture of moonlit country. Ahead there is just visible the curve of the river, and the black line of the bridge across it. Beneath me runs the railway track which is to be my guide. To my joy I can see, at one place upon this thin dark line, the intermittent red glowing of an engine's fire-box. In a swift moment I realize the actuality of the country below. For a second it ceases to be a map and becomes peopled with busy human beings. Oh, Namur (think I), ablaze with lights, you enjoy this moonlight night of late September, far, far from the turmoil of war, little conscious that overhead this very moment lies a fur-clad airman peering down at you, preparing to drop his terrific missiles, packed with fierce explosive ! Laugh on in your cafés, you exquisitely-clad German embusqués ! For me this moment is rich and ecstatic. Then the difficulty of the task absorbs my mind. The noise of the engines has ceased. Through the machine sounds the faint rush of wind hissing and sighing round the tight-strung wires and planes as we sink lower and lower. My bomb-sight draws nearer and nearer to the bridge. Pressing the buttons of the direction indicator I steer the machine to right and left, as green or red glow the lights before the eyes of the pilot. The direction bar touches the bridge and drifts off to the left. I swing the machine round quickly, again the bar crosses the bridge, again it drifts off. We are flying slightly side to wind, and I can scarce keep the head of the machine on a straight course. The pale-glowing range-bars draw nearer and nearer, with a slow progression, to the black edge of the silver river. Again I press the right button ; again a green light glows ; again the machine swings towards the bridge. The range-bars cross the base of it. I press over the bomb handle quickly . . . and again. Clatter-click-clatter-click-click-clatter sound the opening and closing bomb doors behind me as bomb after bomb slides out into the moonlight depths below. For a moment I see the fat yellow shapes, clear-lit in the pale light beneath me, go tumbling down and down towards the dim face of the country.

I hurry back to my seat besides the pilot.

" Half dropped, sir. 'Fraid they will not get it. Oh ! I am sorry, sir ! I am sorry ! We drifted ! "

One, two, three red flashes leap up in the water of the river some hundred yards to the south of the bridge. One, two more flashes, more rapid and brilliant, leap up on the moonlight embankment, leaving large white clouds of smoke.

" Jolly good ! You didn't miss by much ! " he says encouragingly.

Boom-boom-Boom-boom-BOOM ! sound the five explosions as we turn. It is strange to look at Namur—still sparkling beautifully with a wealth of light under the stars—still unchanged, though we know that the thundering clamour of these five unexpected explosions must have stirred up the placid life of the little tranquil town till it is seething like an ant-hill upset by the wayside. In the squares and streets must run the alarmed population, rushing to and fro aimlessly, utterly terrified. In the military head-quarters the telephones and telegraphs must have burst into a sudden activity. The vibrant roar of the explosions must have been heard for a great distance. Even in remote Aix-la-Chapelle the strolling Germans must have wondered at the far-away sound drifting to them under the stars.

Again we fly to the south : again we turn and start on our second " run " over the target : again I crawl into the back, steeled this time by a great anxiety and a great determination, for I realize the enormous responsibility which is mine. With this sense of responsibility weighing heavily on me I lie down, peering through the little square hold. My face is wet with the perspiration of anxiety in spite of the intense cold of the biting wind : my hands shake with excitement. I decide to take the machine to the river along the railway line, and slightly to the east of it, and then to judge the wind drift so that the machine is turned by it to the left, when I will press the starboard signal button and swing the machine at an angle across the bridge, and then drop my bombs. It is a great risk, and unless I judge exactly I will not succeed.

In a fever of apprehension, and with my whole being concentrated on the relation of the fine wires and bars of my bomb-sight with the black thread of the railway far below me, I lie on the varnished strips of wood on the floor of the machine, my legs flung wide apart behind me, my bare hands and face frozen with the icy blast of wind, my uncovered eyes running with water. Nearer and nearer to the bridge draw the two range-bars. Gently and rarely do I touch the starboard signal button, to swing the machine again and again to the right as the wind drifts it to the left. We are near the bridge—we are almost over it. I press the starboard button determinedly, and I see the glow of green light illuminate the dashboard. To the right swings the machine. White glows a light as I press the central button. I look below quivering with anxiety. The machine ceases its leftward drift and swings to the right, and the two luminous range-bars are in line with the bridge. I grasp the bomb-handle and once, twice, press it over. I look behind—the bombs are all gone. It is all over! The irrevocable deed has been done! The failure or success of the long raid is sealed. I climb clumsily to my feet and look through the door beside the pilot.

"All gone, sir, I . . . Oh! look, *look!*"

Upon the thin black line of the bridge leap out two great flashes leaving a cloud of moonlit smoke which entirely obscures one end, of it.

"Oh—damn good—damn good!" yells out the pilot excitedly. "Hit it! *Hit it!* You've hit it! Oh—priceless—priceless!"

"Good—oh, sir! I am glad. It is hit, isn't it, sir? Two of them. I *am* bucked!"

Almost crying with joy we shake hands, and he thumps me cheerfully on the back.

"Something for you for this when we get back!" he says. "Oh! damn good—damn good, Paul. Priceless—priceless!"

I look round, and in the back of the machine I see a sight which left the clearest image of this raid in my mind. There stands the moonlit figure of the tall good-humoured gunlayer, and with a characteristic gesture I see him put out his arms with the thumbs pointing upwards—the most sincere expression of congratulation he can deliver. My heart goes out in gratitude to this solitary man who already, for nearly three hours, has stood alone on a thin platform in the back of the machine, watching and eager, knowing that he has no control over his destiny, that his life lies in the hands of the little figure whose black head he can see so far away from him in the nose of the machine.

Now we turn at once and start on our long homeward trail. . . Charleroi sparkles on our left. Near it at La Louvière flashes an aerial lighthouse, whose presence I record on my notebook. Having found our way to Namur by map, we seem to return by a curious kind of homing instinct. We know where we are as if by second nature. Indeed so little do I trouble that I mistake Courtrai for Roulers, but it makes but little difference. Such confidence have I in our safety, so lively is the moon-drenched night, so friendly are the undefended skies, that we fly on and on as in a stupor of utter bliss. We know that if we return we are famous, and we know that we will return. Song and laughter, and rich thoughts of far-distant London and its proffered glories when next comes leave, fill my drowsy brain. I hug the pilot's arm affectionately. At twelve o'clock he was at Dover, now scarcely eleven hours after he is coming back from Namur. How wonderful it is—how wonderful he is !

Ypres flickers to the left with its ever uneasy artillery fire. In our ease we do not even trouble to cross the lines as soon as possible, but fly on parallel to them, some five miles on the German side. At last we turn and cross slowly over the white blossoms of the ever-rising, ever-drooping star-shells.

Paul Bewsher.

IF HE WANTS FRIGHTFULNESS

BELLEAU WOOD

6th June. Those were before the days of lavish maps, to which the American afterwards attained. There was one map to each company. exclusive property of the captain. Platoon commanders had a look at it.—" You're here. The objective is a square patch of woods a kilometre and a half north-east, about. See ?—this. Form your platoons in four waves—the guide will be right. Third battalion is advancing their flank to conform. French on the left. . . ." Platoons were formed in four waves, the attack formation taught by the French, a formation proved in trench warfare, where there was a short way to go, and you calculated on losing the first three waves and getting the fourth one to the objective. The Marines never used it again. It was a formation unadapted for open warfare, and incredibly vulnerable. It didn't take long to learn better, but there was a price to pay for the learning.

The platoons came out of the woods as dawn was getting grey. The light was strong when they advanced into the open wheat, now all starred with dewy poppies, red as blood. To the east the sun appeared, immensely red and round, a handbreadth above the horizon ; a German shell burst black across the face of it, just to the left of the line. Men turned their heads to see, and many there looked no more upon the sun forever. " Boys, it's a fine, clear mornin' ! Guess we get chow after we get done molestin' these here Heinies, hey ? "— One old non-com—was it Jerry Finnegan of the 49th ?—had out a can of salmon, hoarded somehow against hard times. He haggled it open with his bayonet, and went forward so, eating chunks of goldfish from the point of that wicked knife. " Finnegan "—his platoon commander, a young gentleman inclined to peevishness before he'd had his morning coffee, was annoyed—" when you are quite through with your refreshments, you can—damn well fix that bayonet and get on with the war ! "—" Aye, aye, sir ! " Finnegan was an old Haitian soldier, and had a breezy manner with young lieutenants— " Th' lootenant want some ? "—Two hours later Sergeant Jerry Finnegan lay dead across a Maxim-gun with his bayonet in the body of the gunner. . . .

It was a beautiful deployment, lines all dressed and guiding true. Such matters were of deep concern to this outfit. The day was without a cloud, promising heat later, but now it was pleasant in the wheat, and the woods around looked blue and cool. Pretty country, those rolling wheat-lands north-west of Château-Thierry, with copses of trees and little tidy forests where French sportsmen maintained hunting lodge and game preserves. Since the first Marne there had been no war here. The files found it very different from the mangled red terrain around Verdun, and much nicer to look at. " Those poppies now. Right pretty, ain't they ? "—a tall corporal picked one and stuck it in his helmet buckle, where it blazed against his leathery cheek. There was some shelling—not much, for few of the German guns had caught up, the French had lost all theirs, and the American artillery was still arriving.

Across this wheat-field there were more woods, and in the edge of these woods the old Boche, lots of him, infantry and machine-guns. Surely he had seen the platoons forming a few hundred yards away— it is possible that he did not believe his eyes. He let them come close before he opened fire. The American fighting man has his failings. He is prone to many regrettable errors. But the sagacious enemy will never let him get close enough to see whom he is attacking. When he has seen the enemy, the American regular will come on in. To stop him you must kill him. And when he is properly trained and has somebody to say " Come on ! " to him, he will stand as much killing as anybody on earth.

The platoons, assailed now by a fury of small-arms fire, narrowed their eyes and inclined their bodies forward, like men in heavy rain, and went on. Second waves reinforced the first, fourth waves the third, as prescribed. Officers yelled " Battlesight ! fire at will "— and the leaders, making out green-grey, clumsy uniforms and round pot-helmets in the gloom of the woods, took it up with Springfields, aimed shots. Automatic riflemen brought their chaut-chauts into action from the hip—a chaut-chaut is as accurate from the hip as it ever is—and wrangled furiously with their ammunition-carriers—

" Come on, kid—bag o'clips ! "—" Aw—I lent it to Ed to carry, last night—didn't think——"—" Yeh, and Ed lent it to a fence-post when he got tired—get me some off a casualty, before I——" A very respectable volume of fire came from the advancing platoons. There was yelling and swearing in the wheat, and the lines, much thinned, got into the woods. Some grenades went off; there was screaming and a tumult, and the " taka-taka-taka-taka " of the Maxim-guns died down. " Hi ! Sergeant !—hold on ! Major said he wanted some prisoners——"—" Well, sir, they looked like they was gonna start somethin'——"—" All right ! All right ! but you catch some alive the next place, you hear ?——"—" Quickly, now—get some kind of a line——"—" Can't make four waves——"—" Well, make two—an' put the chaut-chauts in the second—no use gettin' 'em bumped off before we can use 'em——" The attack went on, platoons much smaller, sergeants and corporals commanding many of them.

A spray of fugitive Boche went before the attack, holding where the ground offered cover, working his light machine-guns with devilish skill, retiring, on the whole, commendably. He had not expected to fight a defensive battle here, and was not heavily entrenched, but the place was stiff with his troops, and he was in good quality, as Marine casualty lists were presently to show. There was more wheat, and more woods, and obscure savage fighting among individuals in a brushy ravine. The attack, especially the inboard platoons of the 49th and 67 Companies, burst from the trees upon a gentle slope of wheat that mounted to a crest of orderly pines, black against the sky. A three-cornered coppice this side of the pines commanded the slope ; now it blazed with machine-guns and rifles ; the air was populous with wicked keening noises. Most of the front waves went down ; all hands, very sensibly, flung themselves prone. " Can't walk up to these babies——"—" No—won't be enough of us left to get on with the war——"—" Pass the word : crawl forward, keepin' touch with the man on your right ! Fire where you can——" That officer, a big man, who has picked up a German light machine-gun somewhere, with a vague idea of using it in a pinch, or, in any case, keeping it for a souvenir, received the attention of a heavy Maxim and went down with a dozen bullets through his chest.

Men crawled forward ; the wheat was agitated, and the Boche, directing his fire by observers in tree-tops, browned the slope industriously. Men were wounded, wounded again as the lines of fire swept back and forth, and finally killed. It helped some to bag the feldwebels in the trees ; there were men in that line who could hit at 750 yards, three times out of five. Sweating, hot, and angry with a bleak, cold anger, the Marines worked forward. They were there, and the Germans, and there was nothing else in the clanging world. An officer, risking his head above the wheat, observed progress, and detached a corporal with his squad to get forward by the flank. " Get far enough past that flank gun, now, close as you can, and rush it—we'll keep it busy." . . . Nothing sounds as mad as rifle-fire, staccato, furious—— The corporal judged that he was far enough, and rose with a yell, his squad leaping with him. He was not past the flank ; two guns swung that way, and cut the squad down like a grass-hook levels a clump of weeds. . . . They lay there for days, eight Marines in a dozen yards, face down on their rifles. But they had done their job. The men in the wheat were close enough to use the split-second interval in the firing. They got in, cursing and stabbing. Meanwhile, to the left a little group of men lay in the wheat under the very muzzle of a gun that clipped the stalks around their ears and riddled their combat packs—firing high by a matter of inches and the mercy of God. A man can stand just so much of that. Life presently ceases to be desirable ; the only desirable thing is to kill that gunner, kill him with your hands ! One of them, a corporal named, Geer, said : " By God, let's get him ! " And they got him. One fellow seized the spitting muzzle and up-ended it on the gunner ; he lost a hand in the matter. Bayonets flashed in, and a rifle-butt rose and fell. The battle tore through the coppice. The machine-gunners were brave men, and many of the Prussian infantry were brave men, and they died. A few streamed back through the brush, and hunters and hunted burst in a frantic medley on the open at the crest of the hill. Impartial machine-guns, down the hill to the left, took toll of both. Presently the remnants of the assault companies were panting in the trees on the edge of the hill. It was the objective of the attack, but distance had ceased to have any meaning, time was not, and the country was full of square patches of woods. In the valley below were more Germans, and on the next hill. Most of the officers were down, and all hands went on.

They went down the brushy slope, across a little run, across a road where two heavy Maxims were caught sitting, and mopped up and up the next long, smooth slope. Some Marines branched off down that road and went into the town of Torcy. There was fighting in Torcy, and a French avion reported Americans in it, but they never came out again . . . a handful of impudent fellows against a battalion of Sturm-Truppen. . . . Then the men who mounted the slope found themselves in a cleared area, full of orderly French wood-piles, and apparently there was a machine-gun to every wood-pile. Jerry Finnegan died here, sprawled across one of them. Lieutenant Somers died here. One lieutenant found himself behind a wood-pile, with a big auto-rifleman. Just across from them, very near, a machine-gun behind another wood-pile was searching for them. The lieutenant, all his world narrowed to that little place, peered vainly for a loophole; the sticks were jumping and shaking as the Maxim flailed them; bullets rang under his helmet. " Here, Morgan," he said, " I'll poke my tin hat around this side, and you watch and see if you can get the chaut-chaut on them——" He stuck the helmet on his bayonet, and thrust it out. Something struck it violently from the point, and the rifle made his fingers tingle. The chaut-chaut went off, once. In the same breath there was an odd noise above him . . . the machine-gun . . . he looked up. Morgan's body was slumping down to its knees; it leaned forward against the wood, the chaut-chaut, still grasped in a clenched hand, coming to the ground butt first. The man's head was gone from the eyes up; his helmet slid stickily back over his combat pack and lay on the ground . . . " My mother," reflected the lieutenant " will never find my grave in this place ! " He picked up the chaut-chaut, and examined it professionally, noting a spatter of little thick red drops on the breech, and the fact that the clip showed one round expended. The charging handle was back. He got to his feet with deliberation, laid the gun across the wood-pile, and sighted . . . three Boche with very red faces; their eyes looked pale under their deep helmets. . . . He gave them the whole clip, and they appeared to wilt. Then he came away from there. Later he was in the little run at the foot of the hill with three men, all wounded. He never knew how he got there. It just happened.

Capt. John W. Thomason (5th U.S. Marines).

U-BOAT ADVENTURE

WHEN our newly-commissioned UB 88 had repeatedly carried out the prescribed diving and manœuvring tests, she was ordered to put to sea on June 13th, 1918. To the Commander's disgust, a little company of wives and sweethearts turned up from Kiel and the surrounding district, and the cables were cast off to the accompaniment of many waving handkerchiefs.

UB 88 set out at full speed on a northerly course. Night was falling.

I was at the wheel, and thus able to enjoy the lovely June evening as I kept a look-out for the buoy that marked our route, letting my eyes wander now and then towards the evening horizon and the Schleswig coast. It grew gradually darker; I was already steering by compass, and was glad to note that we were not making for the Kaiser Wilhelm Canal, but northward to the Little Sound. . . . The passage from the Canal to the German Gulf and the North Sea was not very popular in the Imperial Navy : Tommy had snapped up too many of our U-Boats in those waters.

As I was enjoying the stillness of the evening I heard behind me a sudden movement of alarm. The officer of the watch was staring into the distance through his binoculars; suddenly he shouted down the speaking-tube : " Report to Commander lighted waterspout to port ! " This sounded interesting. Being at the wheel, I had no binoculars and had to search for this singular natural phenomenon with the naked eye. I could see nothing, and Heim, the aft look-out man, refused to let me have a look through his glasses. The Commander threw aside the Navigating Officer's maps and hurried up on deck, but could at first distinguish nothing. In a minute or two, however, the set expression on the officer's face darkened into gloom, as the Commander suddenly smiled genially and remarked :

" That's not a lighted waterspout ; that's the moon ! "

Far away on the horizon a bright streak of light was visible ; it increased with every second, and finally emerged from the waves in the form of a slender crescent. The young officer had received his baptism of fire at the very beginning of the voyage. It was no doubt to dispel the delighted expressions on the faces of the crew that he offered a new dollar to the man who first sighted a ship in the blockade zone.

Our boat was making its way through the relatively narrow passage between Germany, or, rather, what was then still Germany, and Denmark. Some distance away we could see a broad expanse of light on the Danish coast ; it was the large town of Esbjerg blazing into the night. Why not ? She had nothing to fear from air or sea. To the right of us, the coast was shrouded in darkness. We knew, of course, that there, too, life went on, but only under cover of the night. On our boat, too, the lights were turned off or lowered ; for we had entered the war area.

Our thudding engines drove us onwards through the North Sea. It was now daylight, and we were confronted with an unpleasant-looking mine-barrier : some of them were rocking on the surface, plainly visible ; others, we knew, were anchored out of sight. But we made our way safely through them and drew in towards England. Not a single vessel had been sighted as we turned northwards, a few miles off the English coast, when suddenly Lieutenant Schmitz's promised dollar looked like being won.

" Smoke-cloud four points on starboard bow."

This brought the Commander on deck, and no sooner had he got into the conning-tower than we were promptly ordered below :

" Diving-stations ! Flood tanks ! Periscope-depth ! "

All this happened so quickly that it could not be precisely decided to whom the promised dollar should fall. The crew swung themselves down the conning-tower to the control-room and hurried to their posts ; a fusillade of orders followed.

I had to abandon my peaceful consumption of a plate of beans and bacon, and in an instant was at my action-station at the wheel. The main periscope dynamo began its rhythmical hum, as the periscope was dipped and raised to make sure that only the tip of it showed above the surface. The Navigating Officer appeared in the conning-tower with his bearings apparatus, and the boat was at last moving steadily at the required depth of $10\frac{1}{2}$ metres, when the following order rang out :

" Clear first and third tubes."

" First and third tubes clear."

" Torpedo depth—$4\frac{1}{2}$ metres."

" . . . $4\frac{1}{2}$ metres it is."

" Twenty degrees more to port."

All this and much more I had to repeat ; and I had to keep a very accurate course, for the man at the wheel really aims the torpedo-tube, which is a fixed part of the vessel, and the whole operation is dependent on his skill.

" Five men ready to dress the boat ! '

These five men are our movable ballast. The Chief Engineer cannot get his pumps to work as quickly as these smart fellows can dash from the control-station into the bows and thus compensate for the lost weight of the fired torpedo. Otherwise the bow would tip out of the water at a most inopportune moment.

" Ten degrees more to port ; Warrant Officer, note—s.s. *Farewell*, 2,000 tons, two funnels, deep in cargo.'

(" Good God," thought I ; " we must be pretty near if he can read the ship's name.")

" Lower periscope, dive full speed to 20 metres ; every man forward." . . . " Hard a-port ; both engines full speed ahead."

A destroyer, perhaps ? It looked as if we had nearly collided with something. And, indeed, the periscope was not lowered in time ; a grinding sound was heard, which meant the end of that too inquisitive periscope.

What had happened was that our victim had made an unexpected turn which we could not follow, and we had had to dive under her. The only thing was to keep quiet and see whether the enemy had noticed us. The rhythmic beat of the steamer's engines and pro-pellers suddenly stopped, so we ventured up again to have another look at our friend through the spare periscope. All this seemed to happen in a flash.

" Clear first tube . . . Fire ! "

. . . Hit !

" Every man forward . . . Dive to 40 metres . . . to the bottom . . . Silence in the boat . . ."

When the depth-gauge recorded 38 metres the boat bumped very audibly on a sandy bottom ; we were on the sea-floor and there we lay. Engines, pumps, compass-dynamo—all were turned off so that not a sound should betray the position of the boat. But, although we lay in utter silence, there was plenty of noise in our immediate neighbourhood. Enemy patrol-boats were already dashing about above us and persistently dropping their noisy visiting-cards. Dozens of depth-charges set for 30 metres exploded with every variety of detonation over our heads.

After half an hour or so the patrols decided that they·had better give up, and the bombardment ceased. Since the order " Silence in the boat," none of us had left our action-stations ; I was still standing at the wheel in the conning-tower, entering up the steering-book, in which all changes of course—depth, engine speed, with the times at which they were made, and, last but not least, complete details of all torpedo actions—have to be recorded. In such encounters the man at the wheel needs a ready pen.

As I stood writing, I heard a faint tacking sound ; I put the listening microphones to my ears and heard the same sound, much intensified. At first I did not pay much attention ; then an unpleasant suspicion crept into my mind. I mentioned it to the Commander, who was still in the conning-tower, and he shouted down to the engine-room : " Both engines half speed ahead." The boat moved forward jerkily, then stopped. " Both engines half speed astern." More jerks, and a sudden stop. After the silence, the noise of the engines was quite exhilarating. Every moment I expected to hear the crash of a depth-charge, or the scraping of a grapnel across the hull.

" I believe the steamer is on top of us," I said to the Commander.

" Looks like it," he answered, and shouted down to the control-station. " Ask the Chief to come up, please."

When the Chief Engineer appeared, the Commander said in low tone :

" That steamer seems to have sunk on top of us ; don't let the crew know yet. We'll wait a bit and then see if we can get up to the surface by using compressed air as well as the engines. If not, we must try to get out of the boat somehow."

The crew were now told they could leave their diving-stations. With the exception of the men at the compass and in the engine-room they all went to their bunks, some to make up for lost sleep, others to play cards or read a book from the *Reclam* library.

All was peace, except for me. It was agonizing to realize that the masts or keel of a steamer were lying across our hull, and our chances of escape were very small ; and the Commander must have felt no less. I had once caught sight of his family in Kiel, a charming wife and two pretty children, and I could well imagine that he, too, would rather be in Kiel than at the bottom of the sea. However, the afternoon wore slowly to an end, until it was thought that the patrol-boats had almost certainly given up the search.

It was half-past seven in the evening when we were ordered to diving-stations, and the compressed air was slowly injected into the tanks. In the interval, the tide had turned ; it was now just high tide, and the depth-gauge showed 42 metres. The boat rose very gradually to $40\frac{1}{2}$ metres and then stopped. More compressed air was let in, but she would not move. We were clearly caught in the steamer's rigging. Both engines were run at full speed ahead for a time, until the lamps grew redder and redder. The electric accumulator battery was now running down. Just as we were growing desperate, Neptune himself, perhaps, came to our rescue, and shifted the rope that had caught us ; the boat moved upwards. Our struggles were over, and we rose at half speed to periscope-depth. The coast must have been clear, as the boat was ordered to the surface : the Diesel engines were started, and the look-outs went up on to the conning-tower.

We gasped with relief to find ourselves alive.

" Both engines full speed ahead ; recharge motors."

But the coast was not yet altogether clear. One patrol-boat which was still cruising in the neighbourhood dashed towards us with thick bursts of smoke, and wished us good evening with its 5-inch gun. In our condition, with empty accumulators, we could not be drawn into a fight with her and the destroyer flotilla that she must already have summoned. So we had to try to disappear as quickly as we could in the gathering twilight ; we set a rapid zigzag course and soon escaped.

Thus, under difficulties, we sank our first steamer. When night fell we made our way northwards, round England and Ireland, and out into the Bay of Biscay, where we set ourselves to sinking American munition ships and transports.

Leading Seaman Karl Stolz, quoted by K. Neureuther.

THE GUIDES OVER THE PAMIRS

THE pass that we were on seemed to be well over 15,000 feet, possibly 16,000, and we had climbed well over 4,000 feet up to it. The rough descent led down into a straight, narrow valley with steep, straightly sloping hillsides still dotted with pines. At about midday we came to a hut with as many fields around it as would total up in area to a suburban back-yard. There were no men here, only two women and three small children. They were of the little-known tribe of Pokhpu, who are supposed to be aborgines of pre-Uighur times, and to speak an unknown and lost language. . . . We had no time for scientific investigations, however, and asked them our questions in plain Turki, so that the solving of the mystery of the Pokhpu language did not receive any aid from us.

The tiny stream in the bottom of this valley was now dry, but a slightly brackish spring afforded a little water.

We made our midday halt here, and hastened on down along the steep, straight, pine-dotted slopes of the V-shaped valley. We soon came to the sizable Pokhpu flowing down a large valley at right angles to our course ; that is to say, it ran north and south roughly. There was a tiny habitation here, and it seemed as though we should go downstream to the northwards. However, no vestige of a trail could be found on the river-banks, and the sides of the valley lower down seemed to close in to form an impassable cañon, so we were, by fear of getting into a cul-de-sac, forced to follow the track across the main valley and up a steep, dry watercourse of yellow sandstone on the east side. . . .

As soon as we had crossed we found ourselves again following a steep trail up to yet another pass, the third that day. However, there was nothing for it, so we toiled desperately upwards to the summit. This pass is the Sakrigu, which means Deaf (or Soundless), and when one stood on the crest in the awful solitude the name seemed well chosen.

The height of this appeared little short of 16,000 feet, and we were very weary by the time we had finished the climb and commenced the heart-breaking descent into another bare, deep gully of loess.

Soon the herbage disappeared from the slopes and the gully became a gorge. This became deeper and still deeper, and after a time we found ourselves toiling over huge smooth boulders where there was not the vestige of a track, along the narrow bottom of an abyss between walls of cliff that towered up to the very stars. The windings of this dreadful chasm seemed in the dark night to have no end, and we could well have believed that we were treading some path of Tartarus, or Inferno pictured by Doré. Weary to the very bone and crushed, as it seemed, by those titanic and ghostly cliffs, suddenly we came upon a giant excrescence of rock jutting out some hundreds of feet above, and, lit up by a single moonbeam, it showed like a perfectly formed ace of spades.

This we took for a good omen, and soon after, following a sudden turn, at midnight we came out upon the stony desolate valley of the Ka-listhan River (this signifies " the place where a robber was hanged "). . . .

After the nightmare of this fourth pass we were numb and dizzy with fatigue, and it was in a sorry plight that at four in the morning we threw ourselves down in a deserted, but in a sandy, waterless valley called Jibrail (the Archangel Gabriel).

During that appalling single march I estimated that we climbed upwards, and toiled downwards, something like 30,000 feet, between seven of one morning and four o'clock of the next. . . .

We were still behind in the chase ; we had lost ground in spite of that last immense march, so we were off again at midnight, after five hours' sleep. We marched by compass north-eastwards over the low range of sandy hills that divides the Kökyar Valley from the Tiznaf. I hoped to cut back obliquely on to the trail we had lost ; by the time the sun was well up, with good luck and careful steering we dropped down into the village of Arpat Bulung. Still no trace of the pursued. I told off one of the men to investigate a trail that led to the westwards. A reliable villager was sent into Karghalik town, three marches to the north, to make certain unostentatious arrangements there, and the main body pushed on again. All that afternoon and night and next morning, fighting against sleep, we marched across the sand-dunes of the desert, dotted by a few infrequent hamlets, sprung from the attempts at irrigation made by some energetic mandarin, towards Khan Langar, a big village of plains. Here we struck the trail again, halted for a very few hours' sleep, pushed on again at night, dodging about amongst the many channels and intricate irrigation ditches of the great Raskam River in its maturity. . . .

At midnight, in a labyrinth of water-cuts, I told the Haji to find an inhabitant who could show us the way without delay. Coming to a house, we hammered at the big locked courtyard gate with rifle-butts. Soon a harsh, croaking voice within told us to keep away. The Haji demanded admittance in the name of the " Chinese Republic," whereupon the awful voice said that we might kill the inmates before they would allow our ingress. This seemed most suspicious ; in a moment the gates were forced, and we rushed in to find a weird emptiness where we had expected a struggle with armed men. An N.C.O. ran up a ladder to the flat roof and there found a dreadful handful of lepers in the last stages of their mutilating disease. It was in silence that we marched on through the night. Posgam, a stage east of Yarkand, was reached in the early hours, and by the time the sun was well up the detachment had cantered the remaining dozen miles to the Chini Bagh, a walled garden, a few hundred yards outside the ramparts of ancient Yarkand. One of the men went in, disguised, to fetch out an acquaintance of 1914, who, as we hoped, was able to tell us that a party of suspicious strangers had come into the city some eighteen hours before, and was now probably in the Sarai of Badakshan. Before the sleepy inhabitants of the narrow alleys of the depraved city knew what was happening, we had cantered inside the walls and thrown open the great iron-studded gates of the Badakshi Sarai.

Its hundred or so ruffianly Afghan denizens sprang to their feet, but their hands went up above their heads in a flash when they saw behind the bayonets gleaming in the morning sun the sixteen gaunt, wolfish faces of Pathan and Punjabi, Kanjuti, and Hazara.

Capt. L. V. S. Blacker (The Guides).

INTERNMENT CAMP

THE FORTRESS OF ILE D'YEU

When a man has lost everything, and his life hangs by no more than a hair, he watches over it with an aching anxiety that he never had for the riches of his former life. I had nothing left but the empty, beastly inaction of my fourth year in imprisonment—the mattress in the casemate, the daily turnips, the ever-dwindling bread ration—yet I clung to it with a wild, instinctive stubbornness, watched over it restlessly that my consciousness should not slip from it, for if it once left that fragment nothing else could follow but an endless, dark wandering in madness.

On the morning after that night, and every morning after it, I got up glad only to hear the bugle, glad of the thin coffee and the watery, tasteless vegetables, glad to see the soldiers' bayonets, and if in those heavily passing hours and days I felt consciousness again trying to leave me I ran out into the yard, trod out the counted steps of my walk, shut my eyes, ears, spirit to the vertigo of temptation, and blind and deaf and thoughtless ran and ran till I had left the haunting behind me and nothing was left but the life of a prisoner. I could not read any more, for I was afraid of memories and dreamings. It was always a dangerous bridge on which the imagination slipped across to frightening paths. There only remained the cold water, the walks, the talk and the cards and the chess and the meals and sometimes the beastly unconsciousness of drink. And even then it often happened that I would spring up in the middle of cards or talking and have to run out into the yard because I thought I was going mad . . . The number of serious nerve cases increased in that fourth winter. Two Germans went raving mad. They were taken to a French lunatic asylum, and there they died. The other cases were only wrecks, but apparently there was enough life in them to prevent them being sent home.

Tutschek was long past all nervousness and restlessness. He had never come to himself again, nor ever did. If he heard his own name he used to say he had known someone of that name, but that was a long time ago. Sometimes there came black-bordered letters from his wife. He never opened them, but collected them in a pile. He said he would one day give them to the man to whom they were addressed. He still did nothing but kneel and pray. He had so lost the habit of walking that he could not take a couple of steps without his knees giving under him.

An oldish Austrian house-painter, called Heipel, turned just so quietly mad. He lived in No. 54. He used to collect every rag and rubbish possible on his mattress and in his trunk. He had arrived in imprisonment with hair and moustache still dyed black, but now the dye had thinned and his shaggy hair and moustache had grown and turned an awe-inspiring shade of green. He used to spend all day painting pictures of the Citadel which he would sell for a couple of sous to the soldiers and the other men. Later, when he ran out of customers and paper, he painted his prison-pictures on bits of rag, on the benches in the casemates, on the wall, on the paving-stones, everywhere, and it seemed no space was enough for him to realize his gloomy vision. The green-haired old painter never washed and did not change his linen for months on end, with the result that he was ridden with lice and gave off an intolerable stench. To this had to be added the awful smell of the filthy rags and rotting objects collected on his mattress, on his shelf and in his trunk, making the air unbearable for a yard or two around him. Since no one could persuade him to keep clean and he would on no account be separated from his noisome possessions, he was at last reported to the Administrator. Then the poor old man was forcibly bathed, struggling and whimpering like a child, put into a fresh shirt and pants from the Red Cross stores, and then his collection of rags and his trunk were dumped out in the yard for him to choose out anything that was still usable. He stood weeping beside his outcast treasures. He stayed there for hours, holding one or two things in his hand. The choice was difficult, almost impossible. He simply could not tear himself away from anything ; all that stinking jumble had become as much a part of his life as of others a house, a car and comfortable furniture. In the end we persuaded him with great difficulty to come away at least for a little. We told him we would make an inventory of everything, pack it all up carefully and store the whole thing with the Administration till the day of his release. . . .

But a still more astonishing form of madness appeared in a certain big-bearded, very proper-looking German called Klopfer. This gentleman had enjoyed the greatest respect among the other men for four years. His name was never pronounced without the prefatory " Herr." Herr Klopfer might have become a member of the Committee, his bearing almost marking him out for it, but he never accepted any such worthless distinction. He lived among us like an exiled monarch. He walked always alone, his hands behind his back, with large and dignified strides. His curly, chestnut-brown beard, which Wachsmann used to singe with a quite especial lovingness, spread out over his carefully brushed overcoat like a strange fur bib ; he wore a bowler hat and eyeglasses hanging on a golden chain. No one knew exactly who he was, but everyone respected him highly. Then suddenly in the last months of 1917 his behaviour changed. The bearded authority began to honour his fellow-prisoners with his addresses. He would beckon a man aside with an important, elegant gesture, and when they were alone he would offer some strange, lewd object for sale, a perfectly simple article which one had to hold between the thumb and first finger when an obscene object resulted. At first everyone received the offer in blank amazement, but later they grew accustomed to what it meant if Herr Klopfer called you aside. The elegant, bearded gentleman had a great number of pornographic papers as well, which he also sold. His big trunk was an inexhaustible store of erotically conceived wares. In the end we were driven to conclude that Herr Klopfer was no amateur collector of such things but had lived from their sale in peace-time. Some men even thought they remembered him from the night-traffic of the Boulevard des Italiens. Perhaps he had begun as an erotic cicerone, a top-hatted, living, street-corner advertisement indicating with a statuesque arm some suspicious-looking establishment in a side-street. Then he had risen to be a gentleman, Herr Klopfer, and perhaps had meant in imprisonment to put on a new life and a new countenance. And in the end the long confinement and lack of money had thrown him back and down again to where he had begun life.

Herr Klopfer was only one of several, an exaggerated instance

of us all.   I only realized this when my own nervous fears appeared.
Then I understood that everyone of us was a little undermined.   The
first man with whom I talked about it was Schneider, the pale-faced
baker from Pozsony.   He told me the fear of madness had first come
to him when he was bugling.   He had suddenly forgotten the call
he had played scores and scores of times.   The bugle choked in a
queer, unmeaning squeak.   Those who had heard it had laughed
at him ; but the Pozsony baker had gone even paler.   Afterwards
I learnt from him that Kilar, his partner in the coffee-stall business,
was just such a cold-water curist as Neubert or Neuhaus.   I talked
to Nagel and Daumling about those terrifying failures of memory,
and discovered that the two Germans had been doing memory
exercises regularly for the last year.

They warned me against drink.   It only gave momentary for-
getfulness, and then the worn nerves the more easily fell prey to
crazy fantasies.   We had a ghastly example of it in Varvey, the one-
time Bordeaux teacher : now he could not give his English lessons
even in the mornings : he talked nonsense, his brain was permanently
fuddled and he could never remember what he was talking about.
By the afternoon he was quite drunk.   With his dwindled income
he could only afford rum, and on that he got drunk in a few minutes.
Every day towards dusk he was to be seen in front of one of the ways
up to the rampart, sitting on the ground, his eyes bulging and bloodshot, his mouth open and the saliva dribbling from it.   Sometimes
he would be holding a little medallion in his hand with the photograph of his daughter in it.   He would look at it, and then without
cause he would begin to laugh, a horrible, bestial laugh.   Drunken
squabbles and fights were now everyday affairs.   The guard no
longer bothered with prisoners who came staggering out of the
canteen ; only if a drunk fell against one of the soldiers, then they
kicked him.   Once several men, their faces all bloody, were lying
in front of the entrance gateway, flat on the ground, for several
hours. . . .

After that I even less often touched wine ; I had no liking for it,
anyway.   Dudas drank considerably.   He was no alcoholist, but he
already behaved consistently when he was drunk, being assailed
always by the same fixed ideas.   It might eventually have become
dangerous for him if he had not struggled with all his strength against
the temptation.   One of his constant drunken imaginations was that

his young German friends had stolen the plans of his aeroplanes. When he was drunk he would talk about this for hours on end, and it was quite impossible to persuade him that he was talking nonsense. He had some stories, too, about Dr. Herz and others which he generally only told when he was under the influence of alcohol. He would spend the evening telling these at length to everyone, and then the next day he would spend the morning talking to those with whom he had quarrelled when he was drunk and apologizing and making up for everything. His struggle was pathetic. He still had fight in him, though by that time he had had many troubles. His money had run out, he was receiving nothing but bad news from home and he kept himself simply by selling the things out of his trunk. Nearly everything was bought by the Administrator. One morning Biesenbach and von der Hohe took up the " coffin " itself to the Administration. There was indeed a lot buried in it : Dudas's one-time prosperity, luxury, carelessness and in all probability his youth as well, for ever.

Aladar Kuncz.

LOOT IN ARRAS

As we march, houses appear more numerous. Soon they line the road. Still no sign of life in any of them. It seems as though a pestilence had swept over this part of the country. We do not see any signs of fighting, not even a solitary shell-hole.

Soon we are in cobble-paved streets. We see shops.

No shopkeepers. We look at the signs over the entrances of the stores.

We are in the city of Arras.

It is a large city for northern France. There are hotels, churches, stores, wine-shops. It is broad daylight now, but there is not a single soul in sight other than the marching troops. Our heavy footsteps echo down the empty streets.

There is an old-world quaintness about the buildings. We pass a soft brown Gothic cathedral, and in a few minutes are marching past the enormous rococo Hotel de Ville. We look at the signs at the street corners. We read : Grande Place. The square is flanked by Flemish houses which are built with their upper stories projecting over the footways and supported by columns so as to form an arcade. Not a civilian soul can be seen.

We halt. We are in one of the main streets. On both sides of the street are stores—grocery stores, tobacco shops, clothing stores, wine-shops. In the windows we see displays of food and cigarettes temptingly displayed—tins of lobster, glass jars of caviare, tinsel-capped magnums of champagne. I look through a glass window and read : *Veuve Cliquot*—the bottle looks important and inviting. In another window I read : " Smoke De Reszke cigarettes."

We ask our captain—a fidgety, middle-aged man by the name of Penny—why the town is deserted. He explains that the Germans dropped a few long-range shells into the city a few days ago, and the inhabitants, thinking that Heinie was about to enter, fled leaving the city as we now see it.

We rest on the kerb of the street, looking hungrily at the food and cigarettes behind the thin glass partitions. Little knots of soldiers gather and talk among themselves.

As I stand talking to Broadbent a man in the company ahead of us idly kicks a cobble-stone loose from its bed. He picks it up and crashes it through a wide, gleaming shop window. The crash and the sound of the splintering, falling glass stills the hum of conversation. The soldier steps through the window and comes out with a basketful of cigarettes. He tosses packages to his comrades.

Another crash !

More men stream through the gaping windows.

Officers run here and there trying to pacify the men.

As far as I can see, men are hurling stones through windows and clambering in for supplies.

The street is a mass of scurrying soldiers.

Discipline has disappeared.

I step through an open, splintered window and soon come out laden with tins of peas, lobster, caviare, bottles of wine. Broadbent and I visit many shops. In each are crowds of soldiers ransacking shelves, cupboards, cellars. Some of them are chewing food as they pillage.

When we have filled our bags with food, drink and cigarettes, we make off to look for a place to rest.

We climb through a window of a pretentious-looking dwelling. It is deserted. We prowl through the house. In the dining-room the table is set for the next meal. There is no sign of disorder— the inhabitants must have fled without preparation of any sort.

We dump our sacks down in the centre of the room and begin to prepare the food. In a little while we are tackling lobster salad, small French peas, bread and butter, and washing it down with great gulps of Sauterne. We do not speak, but simply devour the food with wolfish greed.

At last we are sated. We search in the sacks and find tins of choice Turkish cigarettes. We light up, putting our dirty feet on the table and smoke in luxury.

We hunt through the house and find the owner's room. Water is boiled and soon we are shaved and powdered with the late owner's razor and talcum. We throw ourselves on the valanced beds and fall asleep.

We are wakened by the sound of crashing noises downstairs. We descend. A party is going on in the drawing-room. Some of our men have found the house. They are drunk. Some sprawl on the old-fashioned brocaded gilt furniture. Some dance with each other.

More men arrive.

One of the recruits, a machine-gunner, draws his revolver from his holster and takes pot-shots at a row of china plates which line a shelf over the mantelpiece.

His companions upbraid him :

" Hey, cut out that bloody shooting ; you're filling the damned room with smoke."

The conversation is boastful and rowdy.

" Some of the men bust into the church and took all the gold and silver ornaments. . . ."

" . . . There's wine-cellars in this town as big as a house. They'll never get the outfit out of here. . . ."

" They'll send for the M.P's . . ."

" We'll give 'em what-for when they come, don't worry. . . ."

Broadbent and I go out into the street. It is nearly dark. Men stagger about burdened with bags of loot. They are tipsy. The officers are nowhere to be seen. Up towards the line the sky is beginning to be lit with the early evening's gun flashes.

Over to the south side of the town a red glow colours the sky. Some of our men must have set fire to some houses. As we look we see flames and a shower of sparks leap into the air.

We look at each other in amazement.

" Do you know that this is looting a town ? " Broadbent says.

" Of course it is."

" There will be merry hell to pay for this."

We turn into the Grande Place. Men lie drunk in the gutters. Others run down the street howling, blind drunk.

There is nothing to do, so we walk into a wineshop. We find a bottle of cognac and drink it between us. We go out again.

The streets are bedlams.

From the houses come sounds of pianos as though they were being played by madmen. Men laugh, sing, brawl.

We find an officer and ask where we are to report. He is a little drunk, too. He does not know and staggers on.

The flames of the fire to the south leap higher and higher.

Overhead we hear the whirr of motors. Planes are reporting that the city is occupied. Shells begin to scream into the city. The detonations sound louder in the echoing streets.

Falling masonry and bricks make it dangerous to stay out of doors.

The shells come faster and faster.

Bodies begin to litter the streets.

The explosions swell into the steady roar of a bombardment.

The streets are lit with the flashes of the shell-bursts.

Buildings take fire.

Men run to shelter. The revelry turns into nightmare.

Broadbent and I find a deep cellar. Over our heads the rafters shiver with the force of the shell-bursts.

Other men come streaming down the stairs. The bombardment has sobered them.

Sacks of food and drink are piled into the corners of the cellar. After a while we fall asleep. . . .

In the morning we awake with champagne hang-overs. We feel groggy and thirsty. We go out into the streets. Soldiers are scurrying about carrying sacks of looted provisions.

By noon most of the men are drunk again. Men stagger through the streets waving empty wine bottles. Some of them have found a French quartermaster storehouse where some French officer uniforms were stored. They cut ludicrous figures in the ill-fitting blue tunics.

News of the looting has spread to Army Head-quarters.

A detachment of mounted English Military Police approach the town.

The police are our traditional enemies.

We organize a volunteer defence corps.

We post ourselves on the roofs of houses which overlook the road which leads into the city. We are armed with rifles, machine-guns, hand-grenades.

As the police canter close to the town they are met with a burst of rifle-fire.

Two horses are hit and rear madly into the air. The M.P's draw rein and about face.

This is our first victory over the police. The retreat is greeted with cheers.

We celebrate the event by going back into the main streets and drinking more wine.

Comrades meet and relate incidents of the day.

" . . . the officers are as drunk as we are. . . ."

" . . . two guys got into a cellar that had one of those big vats . . . they turned on the faucet and started to drink out of their mess-tins . . . got so drunk that they forgot to turn it off after a while . . . when we looked through the trap-door this morning they were floating in about five feet of wine . . ."

" . . . God, who would've thought that plain gravel-crushers like us would ever get rich pickin's like this . . ."

" . . . the soldier's dream come true, all right, all right . . ."

" . . . hey, the frogs is supposed to be our allies. . . ."

" What, with *vin rouge* at five francs a bottle ? "

" Well, why the hell didn't they bring the grub up . . ."

Charles Yale Harrison.

GOURAUD'S MANŒUVRE

General Pétain had some difficulty in persuading General Gouraud to thin out his front line prior to the German attack, in order that the enemy should waste his strength before coming to the main line of resistance. He eventually succeeded by telling him that the world would ring with the fame of " Gouraud's manœuvre."

16th July. I have lived through the most disheartening day of the whole War, though it was by no means the most dangerous. This wilderness of chalk is not very big, but it seems endless when one gets held up in it, and we are held up. Under a merciless sun, which set the air quivering in a dance of heat, and sent wave after hot wave up from the grilling soil, the treeless, waterless chalk downs lay devoid of all colour, like stones at white-heat. No shade, no paths, not even roads ; just crumbling white streaks on a flat plate. Across this wind rusty snakes of barbed wire. Into this the French deliberately lured us. They put up no resistance in front ; they had neither infantry nor artillery in this forward battle-zone, the full use and value of which they had learned from Ludendorff. Our guns bombarded empty trenches ; our gas-shells gassed empty artillery positions ; only in little hidden folds of the ground, sparsely distributed, lay machine-gun posts, like lice in the seams and folds of a garment, to give the attacking force a warm reception. The barrage, which was to have preceded and protected it, went right on somewhere over the enemy's rear positions, while in front the first real line of resistance was not yet carried.

After uninterrupted fighting from five o'clock in the morning until the night, smothered all the time with carefully directed fire, we only succeeded in advancing about three kilometres in the direction of the high-lying Roman road, which traverses the whole fighting front like a cross-beam. . . .

Meanwhile in the whole area in which we were kept confined

by the enemy's fire and our own helplessness neither man nor beast had had anything to eat or drink. When at the end of the day I tried to find my own division again, I found myself leading my horse by the bridle with my eyes on the ground, dead-beat and half-asleep.

The achievements of all the other divisions in this sector were on the same scale. We did not see a single dead Frenchman, let alone a captured gun or machine-gun, and we had suffered heavy losses. On one of the chalk-hills I saw an artillery ammunition-column which had all its horses killed. What it was doing up there nobody knows, for not even the guns had got so far. The drivers hadn't had the sense to turn round when they found they had come too far. They just stood there in view of the enemy, as if they were bewitched or spell-bound, until the damage was done.

Everything seemed to go wrong. My own work was useless. None of my reports had reached the G.S.O.1 of the division. I found our H.Q. again in the evening, thanks to a marvellous instinct for direction combined with pure chance. I walked beside my horse, wondering whether there was any remedy for human folly, and came to the conclusion that there would be none so long as the human race lasted.

Rudolf Binding.

18*th July.* Since our experiences of July 16th I know that we are finished. My thoughts oppress me. How are we to recover ourselves? Kultur, as it will be known after the War, will be of no use ; mankind itself will probably be of still less use.

Ibid.

THE BEGINNING OF THE END

July. He had hardly spoken a word when the quiet was loudly disturbed by hostile shelling. They all got into the bottom of the trench. Several shells ripped over and burst behind. They heard others crack in front. Blaven looked over. Lisle's men were all low in their trench. More shells came ; it was clear now that the gunners over the way were suspicious. Shells began falling regularly within definite limits. Blaven was glad to see that, for it was an old method of the enemy ; he kept pounding some spot, as if he was sure that there he was on a good target. Some more wandering shells burst in other places, nothing to grumble about in itself, but it showed alertness. There was five minutes still to go ; then guns and infantry would attack together.

Blaven kept watching the trench below. Every now and then Lisle looked over ; here and there a man raised himself to change his position. Most of the men were crouching on their heels. Dawn was beginning to master the moonlight. It was possible to count the nearest tree-stumps in the marsh, the others receded more and more faintly into the mist hanging over the river. The steep slope beyond the morass was wholly hidden.

Blaven heard an order pass along the trench, and the snap of bayonets being fixed. There were three minutes to go. These men, stooping over their rifles, pushing home their sharp blades, were so close to him, so intimate and familiar ; a London street, a Channel steamer, any part of the whole world then known to him would have seemed strange without brown uniformed soldiers. Yet just beyond this last line of them there were none—something else, not men, not individuals, not parts of any known world—but yet figures of men, like them, but things no one could go near, fatal, ready to kill. It was impossible to think of them as creatures having friendly feeling for each other. Blaven could only think of them as creatures seeing straight in front of them, unaware of anything to left or right, aware only of launching death straight in front.

Then the English barrage opened. It seemed as if myriads of intelligent birds had suddenly been uncaged, and knew exactly where they wanted to go, and flew thither with incredible speed, hurrying through the air in coveys, in twos and great single ones, some like eagles, high above the others, soaring and dropping to far destinations known only to themselves. Under this woof of sound, the fine strands making and breaking, Lisle and his men waited. Down and across, cutting cleanly through the domed surface of flight, came the sough and hiss of hostile shells. By the river, the quick smoke of shrapnel and the blacker clouds of high explosives thickened the mist. Here and there a pure white cloud was born instantaneously, and dragged out into a streamer, or puffed up a perfect smoke ring. Here and there a yellow smoke ghost wriggled along the ground, and dissipated into a pale cloud. Here and there a pyramid of fragments shot vertically from the earth, the falling pieces shot through by the living white smoke of air-bursts. The centre of this wall of mist and smoke and explosive hung over the river. It was almost time. . . .

The men were all standing up now, and had spread along the trench, leaving an interval between each man and his neighbour. Lisle was standing almost opposite the entrance to the communication trench, only a few yards from Blaven. His presence, so near, distressed Blaven. He felt sure Lisle would turn and see him. . . .

Blaven went forward ; a few steps took him to Lisle's side. He was not sure if he were aware of his coming. Lisle was twining and untwining his revolver lanyard round his hand, as if wondering what to do with it. Then Blaven saw that this was play ; he was really looking at his wrist-watch.

" Two minutes to go ! "

Had he said it aloud ? He thought Lisle nodded. Lisle's right foot was raised and punched into a hole, two feet above the bottom of the trench. Every man was ready. The curtain of mist and smoke still hung by the river, added to continually by shrapnel smoke and shell-bursts. The air was still singing with big shells, and it was impossible to tell now which came and which went.

Then, as if the enemy knew, the hostile machine-guns from up and down the line opened fire. Low, almost level with their heads, the lead hissed, and cracked like explosive bullets as it passed. Everyone cowered with bent heads, and stood close in to the parapet. And these men were going to leave him, going to clamber out of the cramping trench into the open. Of course they were. This was only a waiting place. In a moment the whole world would be moving forward, every man of it who made it a living world. No men were of any importance except these men, no officer except Lisle. To be left behind by Lisle was to be left out of the world, but to go with Lisle ? The bullets still fled over, hissing and cracking. Over the marsh something gleamed. The barrage had passed the river, the mist over the water was thinning. Stealthily, as if he were afraid of starting an avalanche, Blaven undid the flap of his revolver case. The leather came off the brass pin with a little flick. He pulled out the piece of oily rag he kept squeezed between the barrel and the side. Lisle had stopped playing with his lanyard. The sudden fire of the hostile machine-guns had made no difference . . . no difference . . . that was part of the life above, in the open . . . absolutely . . . couldn't expect . . . a walk over . . .

One minute to go.

" Get ready ! " Lisle called out. His hand eased his revolver in its holder, then both hands went forward and clutched the top of the parapet.

" Onee, and twoee, and threeee, and fouree " . . . he was count-ing out loud, counting seconds in a way of his own . . . " and sevenee, and eightee."

Blaven's hands went out in front of him ; his right foot felt for a hold ; he swung his leg and dug out a toe-hole . . . " twenty-onee, and twoee, and three." . . . What a way to count seconds ! He would mess himself up frightfully, wriggling over the edge. What a nuisance the gas-bag was ; he folded over the open flap ; yes, they all had theirs snicked, that was the correct thing to do . . . " forty and onee and twoee and threeee." . . . What a long time twenty seconds lasted ! It gave time easily to think about all sorts of things, the battery . . . the battery and Saxon . . . Damn Saxon . . . Good-bye, B. Battery . . .

" Fifty and onee and twoee and threeee."

Suddenly a new sound was added to the others, a vibration rather than a sound, penetrating every interstice of a man's attention, filling every corner of space, speeding close along the ground ; the rap and swish of a new group of hostile machine guns opposite. The bullets buzzed like a razor-edged scimitar spun horizontally at a terrible speed, covering, it seemed, every yard of the flat space immediately above the trench. Sometimes the mouth spitting this deadly poison was turned directly towards him, sometimes deviated, reaching out into another quarter, back again, away again, back again, lashing the air.

" Fivee and sixee."

What power on earth was going to push these men up and out into that current of death ? It was nearer . . . they'd go. He cowered lower, bullets ripped the edge of the parapet . . . hurry, hurry . . . thousands of bullets . . . naked, fine, sizzling . . . touching nothing . . . going on, where ? Men moving below, men with clothes on . . . rifles . . . pointed sharp bayonets . . . that gun wasn't traversing . . . on one line, streaming on, on, obstinate. Ah, it had swept off . . . back again . . . one shell . . . another nearer . . . this time this time.

" Sevenee and eigthee and——"

Blaven's hand went up to his chin . . . his own . . . mud on it . . . the stubble . . . the soft skin below. Bang ! A stone buzzed down . . . up, up a stinger richochetted . . . wollupy, wollupy winding spirals of sound . . . thousands flew low, straight . . . cutting along low.

" Time ! "

Lisle shouted to his men and heaved himself out of the trench. He looked immense, aloft between the parapet and the sky. Then he was gone, all the others too ; the whole trench was empty.

Blaven's hands trembled. He tried to still them, gripped his revolver case, remembered the flap was open, and with difficulty pinned it up. A shell burst on the parapet, and he crouched down for shelter from the flying pieces of metal, then he turned and went back to his signallers. Hodges had taken the 'phone, and the bombardier was looking out from between the sandbags . . . On and on the bullets . . . why now ? . . .

" Let me come there, Bombardier."

The man saw he was trembling. " Near one that last, sir."

" He thinks that's why I'm shaking." Blaven looked through the opening. A ragged line of men was disappearing into the bank of smoke, some tumbling and picking themselves up, disappearing into holes, and getting out again. Two lay still. One was crawling back on all-fours. The barrage still roared, and machine-guns rattled.

Patrick Miller (R.F.A.)

IN SECRECY AND HASTE

28th July. We had just issued instructions for a repeat order of our 500-man working party, when the chill voice of the " Beer Emma " over the wheezy 'phone advised of the working party being cancelled. " You will move by train to-morrow, where I know not, when I know not."

The evening was spent in preparation, anticipation and manufacture of rumours. First, it was south we were bound, then rearward, then north and, finally, to Russia. About 10 p.m. we were informed that our destination was Arneke, and that we were to be moved by strategic train. Well, what was to become of us ? What is a strategic train, and how can a train show strategy ?

29th July. The G.O.C. Division and G.O.C. Brigade were there to wish us *bon voyage.* The remainder of our brigade stayed behind ; in fact, so far as we knew, the Canadian Corps and the whole of the dependable military world.

No, there is no brigade operation order attached. We moved on pink signal forms and faith. No one knew to whom we belonged, but no doubt some kind staff officer would claim us at our destination.

The train did better than most troop trains in France. We travelled *via* St. Pol, Aire and St. Omer, and reached Arneke at about midnight. The R.T.O.—a very meek, pious, dyspeptic-looking spectacled youth—detrained us with the assistance of a still more promising one-" pipped " Town Major. We were told we were in the X Corps and that we would be billetted.

30th July. A very promising map, in two colours, a list of billets as long as your arm, and the freedom of the area were presented to the Commanding Officer. We were to move in the morning and the Town Major knew of a good field and a kind farmer, so we carried on—to the field. We found a really hospitable farmer who got out of bed, turned over his barn for the officers and tucked every one away splendidly.

From a Canadian Battalion's War Diary.

647

THE ADVANCE

On July 18 *the Allies began to advance in the Marne Salient. The main Allied offensive was opened on August* 8, *and thenceforward the War hastened to its conclusion, with the retreat of the Germans the whole length of their line.*

BEFORE THE DAWN BREAKS

7/8*th Aug.*   Night came on cloudless and windless and braced with autumn's first astringent tang of coolness.   Above, as I lay on my back in the meadow, the whole dome had a stir of life in its shimmering fresco, stars winking with that eager air of having great things to impart—they have it on frosty nights in the Alps, over a high bivouac. We were all worked up, you see.   Could it be coming at last, I thought as I went to sleep—the battle unlike other battles?   How many I had seen outlive their little youth of groundless hope, from the approach along darkened roads through summer nights, the eastern sky pulsating with its crimson flush, the wild glow always leaping up and always drawing in, and the waiting cavalry's lances upright, black and multitudinous in roadside fields, impaling the blenching sky just above the horizon ; and then, in the bald dawn, the backward trickles of wastage swelling into great streams or rather endless friezes seen in silhouette across the fields, the trailing processions of wounded, English and German, on foot and on stretchers, dripping so much blood that some of the tracks were flamboyantly marked for miles across country ; and then the evening's reports with their anxious efforts to show that we had gained something worth having.   Was it to be only Loos and the Somme and Arras and Flanders and Cambrai, all over again ?

Thought must have passed into dream when I was awakened by some bird that may have had a dream too and had fallen right off its perch in a bush near my head, with a disconcerted squeak and a scuffling sound among dry leaves. Opening my eyes, I found that a thickish veil was drawn over the stars. When I sat up, the veil was gone; my eyes were above it; a quilt of white mist, about a foot thick, had spread itself over the meadow. Good! Let it thicken away and be shoes of silence and armour of darkness at dawn for our men. Soon night's habitual sounds brought on sleep again. An owl in the wood by the little chalk stream would hoot, patiently wait for the answering call that should come, and then hoot again, and listen again. The low, dry, continuous buzz of an aeroplane engine, more evenly humming than any of ours, droned itself into hearing and softly ascended the scale of audibility; overhead, as the enemy passed, was slowly drawn across the sky from east to west a line of momentarily obscured stars, each coming back into sight as the next one was deleted. In the east, the low, slow grumbling sound of a few guns from fifty miles of front seemed, in its approach to quietude, like the audible breath of a sleeper. The war was taking its rest. . . .

C. E. Montague.

THE BLACK DAY OF THE GERMAN ARMY

In the morning mist the tanks broke through the enemy defences and were lumbering into the fields and billets behind their lines before the Germans were aware that an attack had taken place. The fear caused by the tanks and the subsequent cavalry advance so seriously affected the morale of the Germans that Ludendorff described August 8 as " the black day in the history of the German Army."

8th Aug. We were roused at 3 a.m., and ate a hot meal at the cookers by the light of flickering candles. Cigarettes glowed in a few brief puffs before the whistle went for fall-in. We paraded upon the flat ground above the top of the bank, platoons were checked, and we stood under our equipment waiting for the battle to begin. A heavy ground mist hung low. Low-flying planes droned heavily in the distance; they were purposely disguising the noise made by the tanks getting into position at the front line. Darkness and ground-mist were hiding the movement into attack positions of an array of 100,000 infantry, and the gun-crews around the battery positions, with guns loaded and run out, and ranges checked, waited for their watches to crawl round to the fatal hour 4.20 a.m.

At zero hour the bombardment fell in one mighty blast. The rush of the shells through the air sounded like express trains passing. The mist was stabbed with flashes. The earth appeared to tremble with the concussion, and when the order to move was given the officers and N.C.O's had to roar at the top of their voices. Company after company, platoon after platoon, moved forward into the bank of mist. Up in front the barrage sounded like strokes on a mighty drum. We knew that at the first descent of this curtain of shells the men of the 2nd and 3rd Australian Divisions, the Tommies on our left, and the Canadians on our right would, in their battle formations, advance behind that moving wall of death, to assault the front line of German trenches. The rat-tat-tat of machine-guns firing continuously, belt after belt, told us that the fight was on.

Day broke as we started on the ascent near the town. Now we saw the batteries working as though their crews were driven by the devil. The blasts from the guns made our steel helmets jump on our heads; the acrid smell of cordite burnt our nostrils. . . .

The sun broke through the pall of mist and smoke. The sun of Austerlitz had been an omen of victory to Napoleon; I thought of it this day.

H. R. Williams.

THE BRIGHT DAY

8th Aug. . . . And then the mist lifted. It rolled right up into the sky in one piece, like a theatre curtain, almost suddenly taking its white quilted thickness away from between our eyes and the vision so much longed for during four years. Beyond the river a miracle— *the* miracle—had begun. It was going on fast. . . . Across the level Santerre, which the sun was beginning to fill with a mist-filtered lustre, two endless columns of British guns, wagons, and troops were marching steadily east, unshelled, over ground that the Germans had held until dawn. . . . Far off, six thousand yards off, in the shining south-east, tanks and cavalry were at work, shifting and gleaming and looking huge on the sky-line of some little rumpled fold of the Santerre plateau. Nearer, the glass could make out an enemy battery, captured complete, caught with the leather caps still on the muzzles of guns. The British dead on the plain, horses and men, lay scattered thinly over wide spaces; scarcely a foundered tank could be seen;

the ground had turf on it still ; it was only speckled with shell-holes, not disembowelled or flayed. . . . For a moment, the object of all dream and desire seemed to have come ; the flaming sword was gone, and the gate of the garden open.

C. E. Montague.

AT BUCQUOY

21st Aug. . . . A mist began to rise soon after and thickened so fast that all fear of our being seen was at an end. Before morning it was a veritable fog, which, lasting until ten o'clock, was to hamper seriously the first phase of the attack. I spent an hour on an errand to C Company later on, and as I was returning saw the Mark V.'s of the 10th Battalion drawn up in the valley our tanks had just left. The mist was very dense when I rejoined the Major at the 111th Brigade Head-quarters in a dug-out in Top Trench, the support line. I remember getting some sleep here. Shortly before zero runners came in from all three sections to report the tanks lined up in No Man's Land. We climbed up into the trench, to find we could not see a hundred yards in front of us ; and a few minutes later the massed batteries behind broke the silence with an appalling crash of sound, a torrent of shells whined overhead, and the attack had begun.

For all we could see, we might have remained in the dug-out. The fiendish uproar of the guns seemed to increase, if that were possible—a modern barrage is one continuous throbbing blast of noise beyond description—but, looking back, there was not even a flicker of light to be seen from all those smoking muzzles. Dawn had broken, and we could see one another, but that was all. Even Misty Trench (appropriately named), only two or three hundred yards in front, was invisible. I cannot recall anything outside a London fog as dense as that capricious mist which covered the whole battle-field during the early morning of the 21st. The road in which Wright's tanks had been concealed cut through Top Trench close to where we were standing, and presently the last section of C Company, detailed for the second objective, came rolling along it out of the gloom. It was now full day, and we could see perhaps a quarter of a mile at the most. Bucquoy was still entirely hidden. A brigade staff of the 63rd Naval Division, which was to pass through the 37th to attack the railway, had come up to the neighbourhood of Top

Trench, and its members were standing about flapping maps, sending and receiving telephone messages, and cursing the fog. Runners and despatch-riders were coming and going busily in our vague radius of vision. There was a constant bustle about the mouth of the dugout, where the 111th Brigade was receiving reports every minute by telephone from the head-quarters of its battalions; and enquiries here confirmed the impression that the first objectives had been carried with ease, in spite of the mist. The latter was at last thinning as the sun rose, and at length the trees of Bucquoy, 1,000 yards away, became faintly visible, like ghostly and tattered scarecrows. It was now, I suppose, about seven o'clock, and the Major and I began to make our way toward Ablainzevelle. A few walking wounded were straggling rearwards, and the endless torrent of shells was wailing overhead; but there was nothing else to be seen or heard of the battle. The northern end of Bucquoy, through which we passed, reeked of gases and corruption, but the one or two dead bodies visible had only too palpably been lying there for days. The Ayette road was more forlorn than ever, and littered with a new layer of bricks and branches. The appearance behind us of some cavalry, who rode into the village with a great clatter and parade, indicated that the attack so far had progressed satisfactorily. A little way up the Ablainzevelle road we met the first tank returning, followed by several more. As I had suspected would be the case, there had been little or no fighting in the village. The fog had caused far more trouble than the Germans, of whom hardly any had been seen. One machine-gun had kept firing from a ruined house until a tank drove over it, one or two others had loosed a few bursts before their crews fled, and then proceedings had degenerated into a hunt for souvenirs. There were plenty of these, for the attack had come as a complete surprise.

Capt. D. G. Browne (Tank Corps).

FAVREUIL

24th Aug. At 6.15 a despatch-rider summoned the company commanders to Captain von Weyhe.

" I have to make the serious announcement that we are to attack. After half an hour's artillery preparation the battalion will advance at 7 (!) from the western edge of Favreuil and storm the enemy lines. You are to march on the church tower of Sapignies."

After brief coming and going and a hearty hand-shake we rushed back to our companies, as the artillery fire began in ten minutes and we had still a good way to march.

"By sections in single file at twenty metres interval. Direction, half-left, tree-tops at Favreuil."

A good sign of the spirit that was in the men now as ever was that I had to detail one man to stay behind to tell the cookers where to go. No one would volunteer.

I walked far ahead of the company with my company staff and Sergeant-Major Reinecke. The shots of our guns were bursting out from behind hedges and ruins. Their fire sounded more like a furious yapping than a wave of destruction. Behind me I saw my sections advancing in perfect order. Close to them like dust flew the clouds of shots from aeroplanes; the shrapnel, bullets, empty shells, and driving bands drove with a hellish whirr between the files of the thin human fire. On the right Beugnâtre lay under heavy shell-fire, and jagged fragments of iron hurtled heavily overhead and drove with a sudden jab into the clayey ground.

Our advance was still more unpleasant behind the Beugnâtre-Bapaume road. A salvo of H.E. went up madly behind and before and among us. We scattered and threw ourselves into shell-holes. The smoke of shell after shell hung in clouds over the edge of Favreuil, and through it rose and fell again brown fountains of earth, one rapidly succeeding another. I went forward alone, as far as the first ruined houses, to find the way, and then gave the signal with my cane to follow.

It was already seven. Looking from between fragments of houses and stumps of trees, I saw an attacking party advance across the open in two waves under moderate rifle-fire. It must be the 5th.

I drew up my men in the sunken road and gave the order to advance in two waves. "At a hundred metres interval. I myself will be between the first and second waves."

It was our last storm. How often in years gone by we had stepped out into the western sun in a mood the same as now! Les Eparges, Guillemont, St. Pierre Vaast, Langemarck, Passchendaele, Mœuvres, Vraucourt, Mory! Again the carnival of carnage beckoned.

We left the sunken road quite according to programme, only "I myself," as the formula of command finely puts it, suddenly found myself near Lieutenant Schrader far in front of the first wave.

Isolated rifle-shots rang out in front of us. My cane in my right hand and revolver in the left, I stumped ahead and, without observing it, left the advancing lines of the 5th Company partly behind us and partly on our right.

The ground began to fall. Indistinct figures were seen in motion against a background of brown earth. A machine-gun spat out its bullets at us. A sense of aimlessness took hold of me. Nevertheless, we began to charge at the double. In mid-jump over a piece of trench a piercing shock through the chest took away my breath. I spun head over heels with a loud cry and fell stunned to the ground.

I woke with a sense of great misfortune. I was pinned between narrow walls of earth, and along a row of crouching figures the cry was taken up : " Stretcher-bearers ! The company commander is wounded."

An elderly man of another company was leaning over me with a kindly expression, loosening my belt and opening my tunic. Two blood-red circular marks shone out on the middle of my right breast and on my back. I was crippled and chained to earth, and the close air of the narrow trench bathed me in sweat. My good Samaritan revived me by fanning me with my map-case. My hope as I struggled for breath was for darkness to come soon, so that I could be carried back.

Of a sudden a hurricane of fire broke on us from Sapignies. It was clear that this unbroken roll, this even and regular roaring and stamping, betokened more than a defensive measure against so poorly staged an attack as ours. Above me I could see beneath his helmet Schrader's strong face, as like a machine he loaded and fired, loaded and fired.

Above rose a cry of horror and ran from mouth to mouth : " They're through on the left ! We're surrounded ! "

This gave me back my old strength again. I fastened upon a hole that a mole had bored in the trench wall and pulled myself to my feet, while the blood poured from my mouth. With bare head and open coat I stared, revolver in hand, into the fight.

Through whitish swathes of smoke a row of men with packs came on in a straight line. Some fell and lay there, others turned head over heels like shot hares. A hundred metres in front of us the last were sucked down in the shell-pocked earth. They must have been young troops, still unacquainted with the effects of the modern rifle, for they came on with all the hardihood of ignorance.

As though drawn by strings, four tanks crept over the crest of a rise. In a few minutes our artillery had trodden them into the ground. One broke across like a tin engine. On my right the brave Mohrmann collapsed with a cry of death.

It did not seem that all was lost. I whispered to Fähnrich Wilsky to creep to the left and enfilade the gap in our line. He came back almost at once and announced that twenty metres from us the show was up and all were surrendering. It was part of the 99th Regiment there (Zabern). I turned round and saw a strange sight. From the rear there were men coming forward with their hands up. The enemy must already have taken the village from which we went to attack. . . .

The scene became more and more lively. We were surrounded by a circle of Germans and English and called upon to throw down our weapons. I urged those nearest to me in a weak voice to fight it out to the death. Friend and foe were fired on alike. Some who surrounded our little band were shouting, some were dumb. On the left two gigantic Englishmen were using their bayonets in a length of trench from which hands were held up imploring mercy.

Among us, too, there was heard a tumult of voices. " It's all up ! Throw away your rifle ! Don't shoot, Kameraden ! "

I looked at the two officers who were with me in the trench. They smiled back and with a shrug let their belts fall to the ground.

There was left only the choice of being taken or being shot. And now the moment had come to show whether all that I had often said to the men when on rest about the fighting spirit was more than empty phrases. I crawled out of the trench and staggered off in the direction of Favreuil. Two Englishmen who were taking a haul of prisoners of the 99th Regiment to their own lines barred my way. I shot the nearest one in the middle of the body with my revolver. He collapsed like a dummy figure. The other blazed his rifle at me and missed. These quick movements caused the blood to be driven clear of the lung in deep pulsations. I could breathe more freely, and set off at a run over the open beside the trench. Lieutenant Schläger was crouching behind a traverse with a section who were still firing. They joined forces with me. Some English who were going over the open stopped to get a Lewis-gun in position and began shooting at us. Except for me, Schläger, and two others, not one escaped. Schläger, who had lost his pince-nez, told me afterward that he saw nothing but my map-case flying up and down. The continuous loss of blood gave me the lightness and airiness of intoxication. One thing only bothered me—that I might collapse too soon. . . .

At last we reached a half-moon-shaped earthwork to the right of Favreuil whence half a dozen heavy machine-guns were pumping lead on friend and foe without distinction. Enemy shots were splittering against the parapet ; men danced to and fro in the greatest excitement. A N.C.O. of the Medical Corps attached to the 6th Company tore off my tunic and advised me to lie down at once, as otherwise I might bleed to death in a very few minutes.

I was rolled in a ground-sheet and carried past the outskirts of Favreuil.

Ernst Jünger (73rd Hanoverian Fusiliers).

REVENGE.

And on that penultimate day they took off from the dusty aerodrome at 11.15 o'clock and flew unhurryingly to the lines, a journey of thirty miles now. In front of Albert he saw a formation of strange machines above them. Snipes, by God. They were having a look at the lines, and very soon would be taking part in the war. And Mac was coming, and the Fokkers would be driven out of the air. He went alongside Bill, pointed upwards, and waved his fist in an orbit of cheering. Bill nodded and did a thumbs-up in reply. Tom dropped back into place.

They split up before Péronne and went to look for targets individually. Tom, as usual, kept near Bill. Only three more jobs at the most after this one. The war was going splendidly. The Huns were on the run, and it was hardly possible they would ever be able to stand against all the tanks that were crawling after them. For a moment his heart was lighter, but then they went down.

Williamson had taken a good look round before crossing the line between Bapaume and St. Pierre-Vaast Wood, and there seemed to be no Fokkers about. A patrol of SE's was protecting low fliers. They went east beyond Sailly-Saillisel and zigzagged southwards behind St. Pierre-Vaast Wood. Files and straggles of Huns were retreating out of the wood. A wonderful target. They let their bombs go. Most of the Huns vanished at once, but the bombs must have done damage. Bill was diving and firing. Tom followed him. He supposed he'd better loose off a few rounds, and wished he wasn't shaking so much. Bill did a roll. He did not come out. A double roll. What the devil. He was spinning. Christ, oh Christ. " Come out, Bill ! " he shouted. It couldn't be happening to Bill. He followed him down. Oh God, Bill was hit, he would never get out.

" Bill, Bill, for Christ's sake, Bill," he screamed. The camel spun on. Full engine. It crashed behind the wood. It hit the ground and burst to fragments. It was like a shell exploding. A cloud of dust and smoke flew up. It did not burn, but Bill was smashed to bits.

He flew right down on the crash. Bullets were holing his planes. He saw flashes of machine-guns. There were two in an open pit. They had killed Bill. Damn and blast them. God, he would get them. He was grinding his teeth and drawing back his lips with rage and hatred. God, he'd get them.

He climbed and sideslipped away, watching. They were firing at him. He must be cunning. It would be no use diving straight at a pair of machine-guns ; he would give them a sitting shot, and they would probably get him first ; get him as well as Bill. There seemed to be three men in the pit. He circled about sideslipping and wondering what to do. He dived away from them and fired a short burst at nothing in particular to warm his guns and to make them think he had not seen them.

He could dive vertically on them ; they would be unable to reply effectively, but he could not go right down on them vertically. No, he must attack them at an angle that would let him dive right into the pit so that they wouldn't have a chance. He would shoot them from a dozen feet.

What cover had they ? There seemed to be a darker patch on the north side that might be a scoop or shallow dugout. He must attack from the south so as to fire into it in case they ran in.

He got in position just in time. One of the guns was not firing. They were doing something to it. It would be out of action some seconds at least. He would take a chance of outshooting one gun with his two.

He dived steeply, pressing his trigger, and eased slowly out, bringing his sights on to his target with his guns already firing. The Huns should not have the advantage of getting in the first burst.

The pit came into the centre of the Aldis. He held it there expertly. Tracers flashed inches away. Chips flew from struts. The engine was hit.

Then it was over. He pulled up out of the pit. There were two dead men in it. He must have riddled them. One man seemed to have got away.

Rage was gone. There was no feeling left in him. He was shaking. Bill was killed. He had avenged him: what was the good? Bill was gone. He did not even know for certain that it was his killers he had killed.

He made for home, engine missing. He was being shot at. They would not get him. He crossed the lines, and flew dazedly westwards, homing by instinct. He landed and walked to the office.

V. M. Yeates (R.F.C.)

TAFAS

The Arabs told us that the Turkish column—Jemal Pasha's lancer regiment—was already entering Tafas. When we got within sight we found they had taken the village (from which sounded an occasional shot) and were halted about it. Small pyres of smoke were going up from between the houses. On the rising ground to this side, knee deep in the thistles, stood a remnant of old men, women and children, telling terrible stories of what had happened when the Turks rushed in an hour before.

We lay on watch, and saw the enemy force march away from their assembly ground behind the houses. They headed in good order towards Miskin, the lancers in front and rear, composite formations of infantry disposed in column with machine-gun support as flank guards, guns and a mass of transport in the centre. We opened fire on the head of their line when it showed itself beyond the houses. They turned two field-guns upon us, for reply. The shrapnel was as usual over-fused, and passed safely above our heads.

Nuri came with Pisani. Before their ranks rode Auda abu Tayi, expectant, and Tallal, nearly frantic with the tales his people poured out of the sufferings of the village. The last Turks were now quitting it. We slipped down behind them to end Tallal's suspense, while our infantry took position and fired strongly with the Hotchkiss; Pisani advanced his half battery among them; so that the French high-explosive threw the rear-guard into confusion.

The village lay stilly under its slow wreaths of white smoke, as we rode near, on our guard. Some grey heaps seemed to hide in the long grass, embracing the ground in the close way of corpses. We looked away from these, knowing they were dead; but from one a little figure tottered off, as if to escape us. It was a child, three or four years old, whose dirty smock was stained red over one shoulder and side, with blood from a large half-fibrous wound, perhaps a lance thrust, just where neck and body joined.

The child ran a few steps, then stood and cried to us in a tone of astonishing strength (all else being very silent), " Don't hit me, Baba." Abd el Aziz, choking out something—this was his village, and she might be of his family—flung himself off his camel, and stumbled, kneeling, in the grass beside the child. His suddenness frightened her, for she threw up her arms and tried to scream ; but, instead, dropped in a little heap, while the blood rushed out again over her clothes ; then, I think, she died.

We rode past the other bodies of men and women and four more dead babies, looking very soiled in the daylight, towards the village ; whose loneliness we now knew meant death and horror. By the outskirts were low mud walls, sheepfolds, and on one something red and white. I looked close and saw the body of a woman folded across it, bottom upwards, nailed there by a saw bayonet whose haft stuck hideously into the air from between her naked legs. About her lay others, perhaps twenty in all, variously killed.

The Zaagi burst into wild peals of laughter, the more desolate for the warm sunshine and clear air of this upland afternoon. I said, " The best of you brings me the most Turkish dead," and we turned after the fading enemy, on our way shooting down those who had fallen out by the roadside and came imploring our pity. One wounded Turk, half-naked, not able to stand, sat and wept to us. Abdulla turned away his camel's head, but the Zaagi, with curses, crossed his track and whipped three bullets from his automatic through the man's bare chest. The blood came out with his heartbeats, throb, throb, throb, slower and slower.

Tallal had seen what we had seen. He gave one moan like a hurt animal ; then rode to the upper ground and sat there a while on his mare, shivering and looking fixedly after the Turks. I moved near to speak to him, but Auda caught my rein and stayed me. Very slowly Tallal drew his headcloth about his face ; and then he seemed suddenly to take hold of himself, for he dashed his stirrups into the mare's flanks and galloped headlong, bending low and swaying in the saddle, right at the main body of the enemy.

It was a long ride down a gentle slope and across a hollow. We sat there like stone while he rushed forward, the drumming of his hoofs unnaturally loud in our ears, for we had stopped shooting, and the Turks had stopped. Both armies waited for him ; and he rocked on in the hushed evening till only a few lengths from the enemy.

Then he sat up in the saddle and cried his war cry, ' Tallal, Tallal,' twice in a tremendous shout. Instantly their rifles and machine-guns crashed out, and he and his mare, riddled through and through with bullets, fell dead among the lance points.

Auda looked very cold and grim. " God give him mercy ; we will take his price." He shook his rein and moved slowly after the enemy. We called up the peasants, now drunk with fear and blood, and sent them from this side and that against the retreating column. The old lion of battle waked in Auda's heart, and made him again our natural, inevitable leader. By a skilful turn he drove the Turks into bad ground and split their formation into three parts.

The third part, the smallest, was mostly made up of German and Austrian machine-gunners grouped round three motor-cars and a handful of mounted officers or troopers. They fought magnificently and repulsed us time and again despite our hardiness. The Arabs were fighting like devils, the sweat blurring their eyes, dust parching their throats ; while the flame of cruelty and revenge which was burning in their bodies so twisted them that their hands could hardly shoot. By my order we took no prisoners, for the only time in our war.

At last we left this stern section behind, and pursued the faster two. They were in panic ; and by sunset we had destroyed all but the smallest pieces of them, gaining as and by what they lost. Parties of peasants flowed in on our advance. At first there were five or six to a weapon : then one would win a bayonet, another a sword, a third a pistol. An hour later those who had been on foot would be on donkeys. Afterwards every man had a rifle and a captured horse. By nightfall the horses were laden, and the rich plain was scattered over with dead men and animals. In a madness born of the horror of Tafas we killed and killed, even blowing in the heads of the fallen and of the animals ; as though their death and running blood could slake our agony.

However, what with wounds and aches and weariness I could not rest from thinking of Tallal, the splendid leader, the fine horseman, the courteous and strong companion of the road ; and after a while I had my other camel brought, and with one of my bodyguard rode out into the night to join our men hunting the greater Deraa column.

It was very dark, with a wind beating in great gusts from the south and east ; and only by the noise of shots it tossed across to us and by occasional gun flashes, did we at length come to the fighting. Every field and valley had its Turks stumbling blindly northward. Our men were clinging on. The fall of night had made them bolder, and they were now closing with the enemy. Each village, as the fight rolled to it, took up the work; and the black, icy wind was wild with rifle-fire, shoutings, volleys from the Turks, and the rush of gallops, as small parties of either side crashed frantically together.

The enemy had tried to halt and camp at sunset, but Khalid had shaken them again into movement. Some marched, some stayed. Many dropped asleep in their tracks with fatigue. They had lost order and coherence, and were drifting through the blast in lorn packets, ready to shoot and run at every contact with us or with each other; and the Arabs were as scattered, and nearly as uncertain.

Exceptions were the German detachments; and here, for the first time, I grew proud of the enemy who had killed my brothers. They were two thousand miles from home, without hope and without guides, in conditions mad enough to break the bravest nerves. Yet their sections held together in firm rank, sheering through the wrack of Turk and Arab like armoured ships, high-faced and silent. When attacked they halted, took position, fired to order. There was no haste, no crying, no hesitation. They were glorious.

T. E. Lawrence.

BOOBY TRAPS

He went into the farm-house. The door opened directly upon the living-room. Taine and Maybright were sitting at the table ; they both rose when they saw who it was.

" Don't move." Blaven put his hand on Taine's shoulder and pressed him back into the chair. Maybright pulled out another for him. But Blaven had his things to take off. He looked for a nail. It was a long brown room, almost naked. The chairs and table looked makeshift. On the wall opposite the two casement windows a brightly coloured print of the Madonna was fixed over a bracket holding a silver-framed In Memoriam card. Nothing else on the walls. There was an open fire at the far end, and close together, at one side of it, an old man and an old woman were sitting. The mess cook was crouched beside them blowing up a flame round his kettle. The burning wood gave off a smell of decay.

The old man sat bent forward, his wrists nipped between his knees, with his hands hanging loose, their grooved, thinly veined backs to the flame. He wore a big peakless cap, the frayed edge almost touching his grey shaggy eyebrows. The woman, plain-looking and white-haired, seemed far more present than her husband. When Blaven came forward she touched the man's arm. He looked up at her first, then at Blaven, and, in answer to his greeting, raised his hand a few inches and let it flop again between his knees. Blaven thought of the old toppling chimney and the unsteady thatch.

" They're both deaf, sir," said Taine.

" Tea . . . tea . . . tea ! " said Blaven. The kettle began singing.

Starkie came in. Blaven felt he hardly knew him yet by sight ; a tall, healthy, rather fat young man, ambitious to grow a moustache, and the beginnings of it were red. He was very excited.

" There's quite a tunnel under the house," he announced. " Make a ripping funk-hole." He wanted them all to come and look.

"Let's have tea first," said Taine. "Can't we, sir?"

"Yes, get tea going," said Blaven, and went alone with Starkie. In the corner of the dairy, steps had been cut out on the soft red rock on which the house stood. They were rounded with use, and slimy. Blaven went down carefully, shining his light. Two passages radiated from the foot. They had been tunnelled through the rock, and were unsupported.

"Look, sir, the old folk sleep here," said Starkie.

"Just as well. Can't have been pleasant when we were strafing the village."

A palliasse and blankets lay on the ground in the first tunnel. They stepped over them.

"Just about room beyond for us," said Starkie.

This tunnel came to an end, and they turned and went back.

"Have you had a look at the other one?" Blaven asked.

"Not yet, sir. I didn't care to; the roof doesn't look too strong."

Blaven shone his flash-lamp down the passage. The beam lit up some wooden props.

"Looks as if they had been doubtful of it themselves." Blaven went along the tunnel. It widened to a bottle-shaped end. Rough timbers had been placed between floor and ceiling, and at first glance they appeared to strengthen the roof. Wedges had been driven under the foot of each to tighten the prop against the arches of the tunnel. Between the head of the prop and the rock a block had been inserted. Blaven held up his lamp close to one of them, then put up his hand to feel it. The block was not of wood: it had a greasy feeling, like a long bar of washing soap. Blaven felt all round it and found what he sought.

"Quick! There's a plug with a wire in each of them. It's a mine! Be quick! Hold your lamp." He ran round and pulled a long copper plug out of each of the blocks. The long prop in the middle held a block of explosive too high for them to reach. They kicked out the wedge and the gelatine fell with a thud. Blaven tugged out the fuse.

"See where the wires lead to."

Starkie pulled at it, and the dirt under their feet came up where the wire had lain buried. They went back, ripping it up from the passage floor as they went. At the meeting of the two passages it climbed the wall and then disappeared into the rock. Blaven put his ear to the wall.

" Don't move."

Far away there was the sound of a big detonation. The house trembled. Blaven did not stir.

" Was that a mine going off ? " cried Starkie.

" Hush ! "

" Been the hell of a blow up in the village ! " Maybright called down the stair.

" Will you shut up ? " Blaven cried.

" Sorry sir, I thought you might——"

Starkie went to the stair and signalled. There was silence. Blaven heard the regular, muffled tick of a clock somewhere within the rock.

When the subalterns had gone to assist with the digging (for the mine-firing mechanism had not yet been found) Blaven spoke slow French loudly into madam's ear. Didn't the Germans, he wanted to know, tell them to clear out of the farm ? The woman understood and spoke to the man ; she did not speak loudly, but rapidly. He looked up at Blaven ; he raised one shoulder and one hand ; he looked more helpless in action than in repose, and together the pair bleated : " Oui . . . oui . . . mais. . .? " His hand fell again. His shoulders sank, his head turned towards the fire.

" Send for a pickaxe . . . and who is orderly officer ? "

" I am, sir," Starkie answered.

" Get Sergeant Porter and turn the men out."

" It's pouring again, sir."

" Every man out of that barn . . ."

" Where to ? "

" Anywhere, clear of this, up to the guns . . . and the rest of you get a move on and search. The sooner we know there's no more of this about the sooner the men get back and down to it."

They traced one more wire and found another piece of gelatine. It had been hidden under some hay in the barn. Bombardier Short had been sitting on it, repeating :

" This 'ere cawn't be kep' up . . . cawn't be done. What now ? Turn out, again ? God blimey ! call 'im a battery commander ! . . . Wind-up ! . . ." They had to kick him out into the rain.

Patrick Miller (*R.F.A.*)

THE BATTLE OF DOIRAN

20th Sept. The Battle of Doiran is now a forgotten episode of the Great War, overshadowed by the doings of Haig in France and of Allenby in Palestine. There was no full contemporary account of the battle in any English newspaper. Sir George Milne's dispatch was not published and did not appear in *The Times* until January 23rd, 1919, and then only in a truncated form. The very name of the battle is unknown to most Englishmen. And yet, in singularity of horror and in tragedy of defeated heroism, it is unique among the records of British arms.

The real work of the assault was entrusted to the men of the 22nd and 26th Divisions, who were to attack the Doiran hills, co-operating with a Greek division and a regiment of unreliable Zouaves.

In the early light of an almost unclouded morning the British and Greek forces advanced in order of battle. The noise of our guns had abruptly ceased before daybreak, and there came that awful pause in which defenders and attackers are braced up to face the ordeal, with fear or desperation, with cool courage or with blazing ardour.

Slowly the pale grey smoke lifted in layers of thin film above the ridges, blue shadows deep in every fold or hollow and a dim golden glow on scrub and rock and heather. No one could tell what had been the effect of our gun-fire upon those fortified hills. The infantry soldier relies upon the guns behind him, trusting in their power to smash a way for his advance by killing or demoralizing the enemy and by cutting up his defences. In this case, if he had any hopes or illusions, the infantry soldier was quickly undeceived.

Our attack on the Pip Ridge was led by the 12th Cheshire. The battle opened with a crash of machine-gun fire, and a cloud of dusty smoke began to blur the outline of the hills.

Almost immediately the advancing battalion was overwhelmed in a deadly stream of bullets which came whipping and whistling down the open slopes. Those who survived were followed by a battalion of Lancashire men, and a remnant of this undaunted infantry fought its way over the first and second lines of trenches—if, indeed, the term " line " can be applied to a highly complicated and irregular system of defence, taking full advantage of every fold or contortion of the ground. In its turn, a Shropshire battalion ascended the fatal ridge.

By this time the battle of the " Pips " was a mere confusion of massacre, noise, and futile bravery. Nearly all the men of the first two battalions were lying dead or wounded on the hillside. Colonel Clegg and Colonel Bishop were killed ; the few surviving troops were toiling and fighting in the face of what appeared to be inevitable and immediate death. The attack was ending in a bloody disaster. No orders could reach the isolated cluster of men who were still trying to advance on the Ridge. Contact aeroplanes came roaring down through the yellow haze of dust and vapour, hardly able to see what was going on, and even flying below the levels of the Ridge and the Grand Couronné.

There was only one possible ending to the assault. Our troops, in the military phrase of their Commander, " fell back to their original positions." Of this falling back I will say nothing. There are times when even desperate heroism has to acknowledge defeat.

While the 66th Brigade was thus repulsed on the Ridge, a Greek regiment was thrown into disorder by a counter-attack on the right. At the same time the Welsh Brigade was advancing towards the Grand Couronné.

No feat of arms can ever surpass the glorious bravery of those Welshmen. There was lingering gas in the Jumeaux Ravine (probably our own gas) and some of the men had to fight in respirators.

Imagine, if you can, what it means to fight up a hillside under a deadly fire, wearing a hot mask over your face, dimly staring through a pair of clouded goggles, and sucking the end of a rubber nozzle in your mouth. At the same time, heat is pouring down upon you from a brazen sky. In this plight you are called on to endure the blast of machine-gun fire, the pointed steel or bursting shell of the enemy. Nor are you called on to endure alone ; you must vigorously fire back, and vigorously assail with your own bayonet. It is as much like hell as anything you can think of.

Welch Fusiliers got as far as the Hilt, only half a mile below the central fortress, and were driven back by a fierce Bulgarian charge. Every officer was killed or wounded.

Following these came the 11th Welsh, who were also compelled to retire fighting. For a time, however, a few of the enemy's trenches, full of dead or dying men, remained in our possession.

A third Welsh battalion was offered up, to perish, on that awful day. The 7th South Wales Borderers nobly stormed up through the haze of battle until they had come near the hills of the Tassel and the Knot. Then, all at once, the haze lifted, and they were left exposed in the open to a sweeping and overwhelming fire. Melting away as they charged, a party of Welshmen ran up to the slopes of the Grand Couronné itself and fell dead among the broken rocks. Of the whole battalion, only one officer and some eighteen men were alive at the end of the day. All night, unheard in the tumult of a new bombardment, wounded men were crying on the hillsides or down in the long ravines.

Whatever Sir George Milne now thought of his own plans, he must have been gratified by the behaviour of his troops. Those troops had been flung against positions which no infantry in the world could ever have taken by a frontal attack, and they had proved themselves to be good soldiers. Two entire Brigades had been practically annihilated. . . .

A fresh and equally futile massacre on the Doiran hills was arranged for the following day, in spite of the total breakdown of the general scheme.

It was now the turn of the Scotsmen. Fusiliers, Rifles and Highlanders of the 77th Brigade, undismayed by dreadful evidence of havoc, ran forward among the Welsh and Bulgarian dead. Artillery demoralized the regiment of Zouaves on their left. A storm of machine-gun fire blew away the Greeks on their right in panic, or at least in uncontrollable disorder.

Fighting on into a maze of enemy entanglements, the Scotsmen were being gradually annihilated, their flanks withering under a terrible enfilade. A fine battalion of the East Lancashire attempted to move up in support. The 65th Brigade launched another forlorn attack on the Pip Ridge. The broken remains of the two Brigades were presently in retreat, leaving behind more than half their number, killed, wounded or missing.

We had now sustained 3,871 casualties in the Doiran Battle. Our

troops were incapable of any further effort. A terribly high proportion had been lost or disabled. We had gained only the unimportant ruins of Doiran Town and a cluster of hills immediately
above it, never of any value to the enemy or strongly defended. The
fortress of the Grand Couronné was unshaken, with crumpled bodies
of men and a litter of awful wreckage below it.

Anon, in Fusilier Bluff.

A FOOTNOTE TO DOIRAN

25th Sept. Only a few days ago a Captain of the 11th Welsh
died in this hospital. He was mortally wounded in the Battle of
Doiran. He is buried near the hospital. Our chaplain decided to
hold a short funeral service over the grave ; but everyone is busy,
and I am only able to collect a few sanitary men and runners. The
Captain's name has been neatly painted in good English letters on a
white cross. I'm afraid our ceremony is not very impressive. The
chaplain is a dear, serious little man, but he does not look well in
khaki. The men are dingy and apathetic, and are probably thinking
(if they are thinking at all) about something else. Nobody has a
prayer book. Nobody knows what the poor Captain looked like
when he was alive, and so the ordinary invocation of sentiment or
memory is impossible. We only know that he was desperately
wounded in the fighting of the 18th, and that he was taken away by
the Bulgars to die in their hospital. He was among the " missing."
It is quite certain that he was one of those who were cut down near
the Grand Couronné. Behind us, people are going about their duties
in the camp, hardly glancing at our little group, which has the appearance of something perfunctory and uninspired. I don't believe the
officers are really so busy as they pretend to be, and I think it would
have been decent if some of them had come to attend the service.

Ibid.

THE ADVANCE

Two obstacles lay along the greater part of the Allied front in the North—the Canal du Nord and the formidable wire defences of the Hindenburg Line. On 26 September the French and Americans opened the attack against them; at 5.20 a.m. on the 27th, after a terrific bombardment along the whole of the British front, an advance was made on a sector of thirteen miles from Gouzeaucourt northwards. By that evening over 10,000 prisoners and 200 guns had been taken, and the Canal du Nord crossed; in two days' time the Hindenburg line was in Allied hands.

TANK ATTACK

27th Sept. It was now six o'clock, and the horizon ahead, just visible in the still faint morning light, suddenly became a golden red sheet of flame, accompanied by a terrific noise like the sound of a thousand thunders. The air appeared to vibrate with the reverberations, and the ground even seemed to tremble, whilst this deathly fusillade sent a quiver through our bodies. " That's our barrage," said an officer near by, scanning the horizon, glowing in continual fire, with a combined look of wonder and awe. The battle had commenced on this Sunday morning, heralded by a thousand iron throats, constituting one of those barrages for which the last four months of the year were famous. All being ready, I lit a cigarette and went round to the opposite side for a quiet smoke. I had not been there long before I heard our officer making enquiries for me. Putting the remaining half of my cigarette into the case with my right hand, which I little thought then was never to touch again, I reported myself to him. " Get started up and take your seat," he said. This done, a few minutes later we had started for the battle-field where hell was already let loose, and which to me was to prove almost fatal. Half a mile out a collision was narrowly avoided. A driver changing gear on a slope, which is not permissible with a tank, took a charge backwards, and was stopped just in time. A little later our path lay across a sunken road ; one tank was already ditched and another in lesser difficulties. Our officer and crew were outside. I was alone in the driver's seat. Noting the troubles of those two who preceded us I almost despaired of getting across safely. Selecting a suitable spot, I drove forward, when, notwithstanding the utmost care, the tank slid down the slippery side with a crash upon the bottom, our fascine grating and grinding like a ship's revolving capstan. To our great relief we crossed all intact, proceeding up the rough surface of a hill and nearing a bend in the road. Suddenly I heard a tremendous clatter of chains overhead above the noise made by the engine and internal gears. Casting my eyes upward through the still open ports, I saw our fascine slipping forward. Striking the revolving tracks it was pitched on the left side with a terrible thud ; the fellows walking on that side jumped away just in time to prevent being crushed by our derelict fascine. The retaining bolt had broken in two by sheer strain, one half still remaining in the hole. Another mile and we were amongst Scotch, Australian and American infantry, following up in reserve. On either side were lines of cavalry—a composite mass, horse soldiers, foot soldiers, and tanks, the former waging war with different weapons, but by the same means as it has been waged for ages, the latter representing the changed conditions of warfare. It was the latest addition to our fighting methods, illustrative of the mechanical ingenuity of the age. Above us flew the aeroplanes of both combatants, while here and there batteries of artillery spoke in tongues of fire. Leaving the cavalry behind, we still passed troops of infantry, some resting by the way upon the low banks either side, others toiling laboriously along the muddy road. Here the first batches of wounded were met, some walking, others borne upon stretchers, some carried by our own men, and some by recently taken German prisoners pressed into service. This area became very dangerous by the amount of shrapnel flying about ; then the enemy used gas shells, gas masks having to be worn. This was a very trying ordeal inside the tank, the heat given off by the engine being intense, and the petrol fumes produced a semi-suffocating feeling, much relieved after passing this gas-shelled territory by the removal of the mask. Coming out upon a hillside and being observed by the enemy, who must have had it under close observation, we got a bunch of high-explosive shells all around which fortunately left us unhurt, although splinters, earth, and stones fell in showers. At the foot of this hill we turned to the right across a flat burrowed with trenches and large bomb-holes. Into one of these old trenches we slid, its wet decayed sides giving way beneath our weight. Successful in getting out, we negotiated another maze of pitfalls, finally striking the hard road once more. But our troubles were not yet ended. After another quarter-mile we entered the densest smoke barrage I have ever seen, in fact it was impossible to proceed. Here we stopped for twenty minutes, and took the opportunity to unload the bridge sections we carried. The cloud lifting slightly, we recommenced our journey, half-suffocated by the phosphorus smoke. Even now I could not see more than two yards ahead, one of the crew being obliged to walk as a guide just in front, following our officer, who himself followed the preceding tank. Emerging from this smoke envelope, we soon entered a wrecked village crowded with troops, some preparing to go on with us in the advance, others consolidating the ground already taken. Having parted from the rest of our Company farther back, only two other tanks beside ourselves were here lined up in single file in the village street, protected from shell-fire by the ruins on either side. Against these ruins crouched hundreds of infantrymen seeking shelter from German machine-gun fire which swept over the village. Opening the man-hole cover overhead (which could be done now that we had lost our fascine, a circumstance I never regretted) I looked out for a little fresh air. No sooner was my head above the cabin roof than an enemy aeroplane flying low, covered by the smoke which still hung like a pall over the village, emptied his machine-gun amongst the troops below, who rushed madly about seeking shelter from the rain of bullets that ricochetted on the stones. Our tanks being stationary, some cowered underneath the bottoms in perfect safety. The three tanks, moving a little further clear of the village, stopped to empty the thirty gallons of petrol reserve carried in tins, into the petrol reservoir. We were obliged to perform this operation with shells bursting all around and bullets whirring past us. I had just emptied the second tin when our officer ordered us to close down covers and get inside, saying, "It's too hot here." Then we moved off in different directions, seeing the others no more. Having driven the greater part of the journey, I was now relieved by the second driver, who, having been outside a great deal previously to this, was comparatively fresh. I was tired, hungry, and exhausted by heat and fumes. The driving of a Mark V tank is laborious work ; the steering-levers, counteracted by strong springs, require much effort to move, whilst the clutch-lever and left-foot brake also require considerable energy to operate properly. Each man was now at his gun, three of which were already sending forth a deadly hail. Enemy machine-gun bullets could be heard tapping against our sponsons like hailstones upon glass roofs, whilst notwithstanding the new splinter-proof protectors which had been specially fixed for this action, our faces got marked with fine hot splinters, producing a sensation similar to pinpricks. This induced me to wear the splinter mask with which we were provided ; this is a steel mask padded in leather, the eyes protected by small flat steel bars one-sixteenth of an inch apart, and a steel chain about six inches by three hangs over the mouth and chin, very similar to the face armour worn by knights in the Middle Ages. After ten minutes' going— the enemy in full flight—I heard groaning. Looking across the tank I saw one of the gunners lying full length on the floor with blood running fast from his nose. Satisfied that he was not wounded, I returned to my gun. Five minutes later the tank stopped. Looking forward, I found the officer was beckoning me to come up into the driver's seat again. I obeyed, and went forward once more. Turning hastily around, I saw the driver who had just vacated the position I held sitting on the gear-box cover and vomiting as a consequence of the poisonous fumes he had inhaled. It was now a veritable hell inside ; machine-gun bullets beat like hail upon the outside, from which hot splinters pricked the gunners' faces, whilst shells could be heard bursting in close proximity. Inside, above the noise of the engine, was heard the sharp cracking of our own machine-guns, mingled with the groaning and whining of the gunner who lay stretched along the blood and oil-saturated floor ; this, with the vomiting of our second driver, intense heat, exhaust petrol fumes, and nauseous vapour from the guns made an inferno that no outside observer would have thought possible to exist within those steel plates. We still went forward across country traversed by trenches, pitted with shell-holes, with here and there a road. The whinings of the sick man increased like the howling of a dog by night ; his groans were piteous, his nerves seemed to have become entirely unstrung, and it was beginning to affect the morale of the others. The crisis came; he appeared either to be dying or going insane. Then the officer ordered two men to put him outside. The tank was stopped, and he was laid upon the grass in "No Man's Land." We continued across some trenches just vacated by the enemy, climbed to the top of a hill, and passed over a small sunken road, meeting another trench. Just in front, about three hundred yards distant, lay a village facing us; here the enemy forces were concentrated. Machine-guns swept the hillside upon which we stood; the Australian and American infantry, who came up behind us, crouched in the trenches and sunken road for safety with intent to make a circuit. Our commander now bade me go back in reverse, so, altering gear and changing the reversing lever, we went back, at the same time pulling the right-hand epicyclic brake, in order to turn the nose to the left. Under cover of the trees that surrounded this village the Germans had a concealed battery who awaited our approach, undisturbed by our own artillery, which had long since ceased fire. The hesitancy displayed by our officer in determining his direction thus allowed us to stand in one place for some three or four minutes, enabled these German gunners to lay accurately point-blank at our cabin in front, and instantaneous would have been the death of us both had it not been for the right-hand brake which, as Fortune willed, turned its head just in time to receive that terrible high explosive-shell upon the right track at the end of the cabin, twelve inches from my head, severing the steel plate as though it were matchwood. I well remember the terrific explosion near my head and the sickening smell of the explosive gases, then nothing more until some minutes later, when consciousness returned, I found myself leaning forward against the front. It was a little time before I recollected what had happened, then the blood dripping from the severed artery of my right arm upon the steel plates reminded me of my injuries, for as yet I felt no pain whatever, nothing but a numbness produced by the concussion. When sufficiently recovered I looked around; everything was now still inside, the tank was deserted, the engine silent. I was alone and nearly helpless; my right arm was powerless; there was a big gaping wound on the first finger of my left hand, blood leaked from my chin from wounds the whereabouts of which I did not then know; my trousers were torn in several places where steel fragments had entered. With an extreme effort I pulled myself up with my only, half-disabled hand, and with great difficulty succeeded in getting outside. Lying exhausted and alone upon the grass, the pain commenced, and for the next two hours it was agony, increased by the indescribable feelings produced by fumes upon an empty stomach.

I really thought I was dying, and gave up hopes of ever seeing home again. I looked despairingly around for someone to give me a drink from my water-bottle, which I was too weak to get, but there was no one about. I could feel my strength fast ebbing with the blood still flowing freely as I writhed in agony upon that sunken grass-covered road. After half an hour our Australian infantry observer returned and bound up my wounds with the dressings, of which we had an abundant supply in the medical bag carried by every tank. Following my instructions, he brought from the officer's locker a bottle of champagne and one of rum; this revived me much, but my thirst was insatiable. Then the sunken road became full of Americans and Australians seeking shelter from the withering fusillade that swept across it. At this juncture the rest of our crew came back with the man who had been put outside and who had by this time recovered. Our officer never returned, and I saw him no more. Soon the infantry retired, and then the crew left with promises to send help. I was now alone with an Australian and an American, both badly hit by machine-gun bullets. We lay under cover of the tank for the next five hours, during which the tank was repeatedly shelled by the Germans in the hope of totally destroying it, these shells falling all around, sometimes spraying us with earth and small stones. We were momentarily in expectation of one dropping amongst us, making a finish once and for all.

Hour after hour we watched for the promised assistance, but in vain; not a man saw we during that interminable afternoon. We were in "No Man's Land"; the ceaseless click, click of German machine-guns from the village was plainly heard; overhead aeroplane combatants could be seen fighting with their guns, but our fighting was done. There we lay, like many thousands of other poor soldiers stricken on the field, hoping against hope for the help which never came.

Arthur Jenkin (Tank Corps).

" WE HAVE NOT BEEN BEATEN "

7th Oct. We are all for peace. We, the few, have been warning and imploring, but no Government of ours would bring itself to look facts in the face.

Now they have let themselves be stampeded without due reflection and with the time not yet ripe.

When the army is in retreat, that is no time to begin negotiations ; you must first steady the front line.

The army should have been made to see that the new spirit in state and people can strengthen the hands and the will of the fighting line. Then Wilson should have been asked what he meant by some of the most specious of his Fourteen Points, in particular with regard to Alsace-Lorraine, Poland and Reparation for the Western territories. This premature request for an armistice was a mistake.

Our country is unviolated, its resources are not exhausted, its people is unwearied. We have gone back, but we have not been beaten. . . .

The people must be prepared to rise in the defence of the nation ; a Ministry of Defence must be erected. These plans are only to be put into force if bitter necessity compels it, if we meet with a rebuff ; but not a day can be lost.

Such a Ministry should not be attached to any existing department : it should consist of citizens and soldiers together and have far-reaching powers.

Its task would be threefold :

First of all it is to appeal to the people in the ungarnished language of truth. Let everyone offer himself who feels himself called to such a task ; there will be enough elderly men to be found who are yet sound, full of a passionate patriotism, and ready to help their tired brothers at the front with all their powers of body and soul.

Secondly, all the " Field-greys," who are to-day to be met with in our towns, at the stations and on the railways, must go back to the front, however hard it may be for many of them to have their well-earned leave cut short.

Lastly, the men capable of bearing arms must be combed out at the offices, the guard-rooms and the depôts, in East and West, at the bases and at home. What use have we to-day for Armies of Occupation and Russian Expeditions? Yet at this moment we have hardly half of the total available troops upon the Western Front.

Our front is worn out; when our front has been restored, we shall be offered different conditions.

It is not war we desire but peace; and yet not a peace of abject submission.

Walter Rathenau, quoted by Prince Max of Baden.

AT LEAST, NOT IF WE CAN GET AN
ARMISTICE

GENERAL LUDENDORFF had arrived on 9th October. I saw him shortly before the meeting. He did not give the impression of being shaken in health.

I thought it necessary to remind him of the way in which the armistice offer had originated—I who was already being called the "Pacifist Prince," and being made responsible for the armistice request. I told the General that, to avoid disclosing our weakness still more, I was not in a position to lay bare the true state of affairs before the public—that I was now obliged to cover the armistice offer with my name. The General replied : "I thank Your Grand Ducal Highness in the name of the Supreme Command and in the name of the Army."

In the course of the meeting General Ludendorff gave a verbal answer to the questions which had been sent him on 8th October :

Prince Max : How long is the present critical situation expected to last ? Will the crisis be past when the enemy is compelled to give up attacks *en masse*, and when will this probably take place ?

Ludendorff : Yes, only attacks *en masse* are dangerous.

Prince Max : After the crisis has been past, can we count on being able to consolidate our front, and by what means can such consolidation be assured ?

Ludendorff : If the attacks are given up, the danger is past.

Prince Max : What are the conditions as to reserves and supplies ?

Ludendorff : Our reserves are short by 70,000 men a month. There is a sufficiency of supplies.

Prince Max : Does the Supreme Command expect that an adequate reinforcement would be afforded by the *levée en masse*, as recommended by Walter Rathenau in the *Vossische Zeitung ?*

Ludendorff : No. In spite of our lack of men I have no belief in the *levée en masse.* What we always wanted was an increase of working efficiency. I am not able to judge whether shirkers could be got hold of by this method. In the view of the Supreme Command the Garrison Service classification should be given up ; on the present system the man once passed for Garrison Service will fight no more. Through a more rigorous combing out at home we could get more men. The *levée en masse* would cause more disturbance than we can stand.

Prince Max : If the present peace action should fail, could the war be carried on by us alone till the spring, in spite of the desertion of one of the two allies that remain to us ?

I received the answer : We need a breathing-space ; after that we can re-form.

In other words, I asked : Can we hold out if we do *not* obtain a breathing-space ? and received the answer : Yes, if we obtain a breathing-space, we can hold out.

Our situation was therefore dark and difficult indeed.

General Ludendorff did not contradict Colonel Heye as he said : " For the Supreme Command not to hasten on the peace negotiations would be playing a mere game of chance. . . . Yesterday the penetration of our line came within a hairbreadth of succeeding."

Prince Max of Baden.

VACILLATION

6th Nov. About midday, as had been arranged, the Social Democratic Party Leaders and Trades Union officials arrived at the Chancellery for their conversation with General Groener. Scheidemann, Bauer, Legien, Robert Schmidt, David, Suedekum and Ebert had put in an appearance—and Haeften, too, was present at the meeting. At the very first moment, I was told, the old feelings of confidence were renewed. They seemed to say, We, Labour Leaders and General, have already proved that we can work together in loyal partnership for the welfare of the country. We have now come to renew this partnership. Groener is our last hope. Should he fail, the State is doomed. . . .

Ebert was the first to speak : The present was not a time, he said, to allot the blame for the general collapse. Popular opinion blamed the Kaiser ; whether rightly or wrongly was a matter of indifference. The main thing was that the people wanted to see the men it considered were to blame removed from their high places. Thus if the masses were to be prevented from going over into the revolutionary camp, the Kaiser's abdication was indispensable. He proposed that the Kaiser should announce his abdication next day at the latest, and name one of his sons, Oskar or Eitel Friedrich, as his deputy. The Crown Prince was so well-hated by the masses as to be now impossible.

Groener's reply was short and sharp : Abdication was out of the question ; at a moment when the army was engaged in a fierce struggle with the enemy, it was impossible to deprive it of its Supreme War Lord. The interests of the Army must be put before all others. Thus he must refuse in the most categorical terms to take any step whatever on the abdication question or to make any representations to the Kaiser in this sense.

David and Suedekum pleaded : That they had no objection to the Monarchy itself, and that this step would by no means involve the abolition of the Monarchy in Germany ; large sections of the Social Democrats would be perfectly content to have a Monarchy with social-reformist leanings and governing on a Parliamentary basis.

In the course of David's rather academic disquisitions Scheidemann returned. He was white with excitement.

" Further discussion of the abdication is pointless, the Revolution is in full swing. In Hamburg and Hanover sailors from Kiel have seized the helm of State. Gentlemen, the present is no time for discussion ; now it is time to act. We cannot be sure that to-morrow we shall still be sitting in these chairs."

Ebert preserved an unshakable calm : " Nothing decisive has happened yet. Unlike the other gentlemen I am a convinced Republican—not only in theory—but I, too, would put up with a Monarchy on a Parliamentary basis and with a social-reformist tinge. Once more, General, I strongly advise you to seize your last opportunity of saving the Monarchy and take immediate steps to have one of the Imperial Princes entrusted with the Regency."

Ebert was supported by Suedekum ; with tears in his eyes he appealed to the General to accept Ebert's proposal, otherwise a fearful catastrophe with consequences that none could foresee would overtake us. Legien too addressed himself imploringly to Groener.

The General stood firm : the proposal was for him quite out of the question he said. He was authorized to announce that all the Princes had unanimously made a Declaration to the effect that were their father to abdicate against his will, they would all refuse to take over the Regency.

Thereupon Ebert said : " Under the circumstances any further discussion is superfluous. Events must take their course."

Then turning to Groener : " We are grateful to you, Your Excellency, for this frank exchange of views, and shall always have pleasant recollections of our work with you during the war. We have reached the parting of the ways ; who knows whether we shall ever see one another again."

Prince Max of Baden.

THE ADVANCE

THE LAST ATTACK

TEN days before the end, the battery was in action before Le Quesnoy. Merredew had left to command a battery in the north. The guns were in a little field, sloping down to a stream on the other side of which was a large mill. The only road to the front ran over the bridge past the mill. All day long the columns of men, guns, and transport passed over this bridge, and all day long the enemy shelled it with a high-velocity gun. In the afternoon when the gunners had ceased firing they lay back on the grass and speculated which of the endless teams of horses and mules, limbers and guns would get safely across the bridge. The sappers were working hard at repairs under this steady shell-fire. A gallant party of military police and others were clearing away the dead horses and men that littered the road both sides of the stream. A gun team would come trotting down the hill towards the bridge and a hundred yards from it, break into a gallop. "Hooray! they are safely across. Here come the next lot! Bang! That's got them. No, it hasn't——!" as horses and men, less one driver, emerge from the smoke, and gallop up the road into safety the other side. At dusk the enemy ceased fire, and the mill being the only available billet, the men moved into its vast, underground store-room, whilst Shadbolt and the officers occupied an upstairs room, where there were some beds. Soon after midnight that accursed gun began again. Whee-oo! Whoosh! Bang! The shells sailed over the mill-house and crashed on to the road beyond. An argument began between Queenie and the Cherub as to whether a retirement to the cellar would not be sound policy. CRASH! and Shadbolt woke up, soaked to the skin, his bedclothes in ribbons—unhurt! The shell had come through the roof and burst in the attic above, upsetting a bucket of water and ripping a great hole in the ceiling. At this critical moment Mr. Prout appeared, dignified and urbane even at that hour. " Excuse me, sir, but before retiring to rest I deemed it advisable to put the officers' kit in the cellar. I have laid out your valise and placed your flannel trousers and a clean shirt under the pillow."

The next day they moved forward again and supported the New Zealanders in the assault on Le Quesnoy. The brigade car was the first to enter the town, where the Colonel, to his intense embarrassment, was soundly kissed by a grateful old woman. He was so unnerved that on his return to head-quarters he poured himself out a tumblerful of neat gin and started to drink, thinking it was water. His staff watched him with amusement. Expressions of astonishment, anger, defiance, and gratification chased each other in succession across his face as without a word, he emptied the tumbler.

Alone 2XX went forward into the Forest of Mormal. It was here, on the 8th of November, that news was received that Merredew had been killed four days earlier at Moen on the Scheldt.

Very early on the last morning Shadbolt was watching the men dragging the heavy howitzers into a little clearing in the wood. The day was grey and overcast and the raindrops from a recent shower were dripping sadly off the trees. Above them a few pigeons, disturbed by the movements and cries of the men, circled and wheeled. A despatch rider rode up and handed him a message form. " Hostilities will cease at 11 a.m. to-day. A.A.A. No firing will take place after this hour." He sat down on the stump of a tree. In any case, the order did not affect them. The enemy was already out of range, and they could move no further.

This then, was the end. Visions of the early days, their hopes and ambitions, swam before his eyes. He saw again his pre-historic howitzer in the orchard at Festubert, and Alington's long legs moved towards him through the trees. He was back with the Australians in their dug-out below Pozieres. He saw the long slope of the hill at Heninel, covered with guns, ammunition dumps, tents and dugouts. Ypres, the Salient, Trois Tours, St. Julien—the names made unforgettable pictures in his mind. Happy days at Beugny and Beaussart, they were gone and the bad ones with them. Hugh was gone, and Tyler and little Rawson ; Sergeant Powell, that brave old man ; Elliot and James and Johnson—the names of his dead gunners strung themselves before him. This was the very end. What good had it all been? To serve what purpose had they all died? For the moment he could find no answer. His brain was too numb with memories.

"Mr. Straker."

"Sir."

"You can fall the men out for breakfast. The war is over."

"Very good, sir."

Overhead the pigeons circled and wheeled.

Lt.-Col. F. Lushington.

THE RETREAT FROM BELGIUM

Next morning we moved off. It had grown cold, but the sun shone. The wide road ran straight through a flat landscape that looked cheerful. But as the day went on it became unfriendly. The trees looked grey to me, and the place we marched into looked inhospitable. Against the walls of a dismal church leaned a number of machine-guns. Artillery of all descriptions was standing in the churchyard.

One of our machine-gun companies had halted before it and were flinging their guns inside. These were weapons which had to be surrendered to the enemy after the armistice. They would let them stand in the rain, and soon they would all be old iron.

We marched for fully two weeks through the Flemish part of Belgium and came at last to the French-speaking part. As permanent rearguard we marched always a day's march ahead of the pursuing enemy. Before the houses stood civilians who looked at us with hatred and cursed.

Again we were to have received flour and sugar, and again the troops in front of us had sold the whole of it to the natives for a song. The feeling against the revolutionaries grew bitterer than ever, and Höhle and Lance-Corporal Mann kept stirring it up, while Hermann, the social democrat, tried to soothe it down. This Hermann with his perpetual surly expression had the soul of a petty official and was against any decisive step.

In the neighbourhood of Liége we were given a day's rest. Mehling went into Liége with some of the other men. I took a walk to a fortress near by and had a look at the deep fosse and the broken concrete defences.

In front of a big farm several men from our regiment were arguing with a Belgian.

" Sergeant "—one of them turned to me—" we have a requisition form for straw from our quartermaster, but this man here won't part with any."

" And why won't he ? "

" He says he won't have enough left for himself. But he has a whole barn full."

" Then you must go to an officer about it. If I say anything to the farmer it'll have no effect."

Mehling did not come back from Liége until late ; he related that the whole town was beflagged. French, English and Belgian soldiers were there already. They sat in the cafés. They were playing the " Marseillaise " and shouting hurrah. Mehling was still full of happiness and elation from having seen it. But I felt sad. The damned old Fatherland was still dear to me !

Next morning we went over the Maas by a long bridge ; the river here is really a majestic sight. Then we wound hour after hour up the heights on the other side.

When it was growing dark we marched into a little village with a church and lying in a valley. It was cold. We halted on a bridge under which a stream babbled. The billeting officers came.

" How is it here ? "

" Good quarters," they cried.

We scattered. I suddenly noticed that I had a pain in my right foot, where my wound had been. It was not like the pain from a blister, but a sort of dull internal pain.

We went across a steep grassy slope with fruit trees and came to a wooden house standing by itself. The wooden stair inside shone as if it were polished, and the landing on the first floor was panelled in plain dark wood without embellishment. A few chests, a few wooden stools and a tall clock stood against the walls.

Out of a door came a young man with his wife and invited us with a friendly look into a big room, where mattresses and blankets were lying on the floor.

I pulled off my boot at once and felt my foot. The scar on the ball of my foot was sensitive. We had been marching now for three weeks. I went to the kitchen and asked for warm water.

" Blessé ? " asked the man, pointing to my foot.

" Oui, Monsieur."

He got up at once. His wife brought a bucket and a chair, so that I might sit with them and put my foot in the water at once. There I sat on my chair with them before the hearth. Outside the moon shone coldly on the sloping meadow. Perhaps it was freezing again. The man and his wife looked healthy. They sat in contented silence. Why should one trouble, anyway, to put into words what the other knew ?

I was happy in that house.

While we fell in next morning Ssymank and Hanfstengel were cursing the awful people who stayed in this village. They had been billeted on the priest, and he had refused them water to wash in and anything else that he could. When they took him to task for this, he had spoken of barbarians and " Boches," who should be beaten to death. Ssymank had become so furious that he had wanted to lay hands on the priest. But Hanfstengel had held him back.

Thereupon Ssymank had turned to the priest in a fury, shouted, " You're a swine ! " and marched out.

We marched gaily throughout the day, which was overcast. My foot was all right again. To-day we should cross the German frontier.

Early in the afternoon began a series of halts. We kept pushing our way up a valley a few steps at a time towards a village in front.

The men were in good spirits.

" Another little yard and another little yard and a—yupp ! " they shouted in chorus. Then some of them began to sing :

> " For this 'ere *cam*paign
> Ain't no express train.
> So take some sandpaper
> And wipe your tears away."

In two or three hours we reached the village and a crossroads. From the left came the marching column of a division we did not know, and our column issuing from the valley had to take the same road. Our regimental commander pulled up his horse and tried to get his regiment forward. There was a General with the other division. He stood near his car, which was drawn up in the square before a café. Men from all ranks of the service were standing there, or sitting on chairs or on the kerb blowing on coffee, which

in their tin mugs had to cool first before they could put their lips
to it.

Others were tossing down tots of brandy. Mehling had already
pushed his way through the crowd into the café. I knew it was
more than six miles to the frontier, and we should certainly have to
march a good bit beyond that. I sat down by the kerb to rest my
foot.

It was not until dusk that our column got going again. We
were tired with hanging about. When after an hour and a half the
column began to stick again, there was a fresh roar of " Another
little yard, and another little yard, and a—yupp ! " Then they
sang :

> " In Hamburg I've been often seen,
> In silks and satins like a queen ;
> But don't you ask my name, sonny,
> For I'm a girl that's out for money."

They sang it in a sentimental yearning drawl into the night.
Some had sat down in the road. A corporal of artillery came riding
along. " Make way ! " They scrambled up cursing.

A motor-car slid past with the General.

" He can leg it like us ones ! "

The march got going again.

Another car overtook us. " Make way ! " There were four
airmen in it, with cocked bonnets.

" What are they swanking for in a car ? "

" Footpads ! " cried one of the men in the car jeeringly.

" Turn them out, they're swine from the base ! "

Several men made a rush at the car, but it accelerated recklessly
right into the middle of the men in front of us. They jumped to the
side. " Heave 'em out ! " cried one man, but no longer playfully.
The car vanished.

We were continually blocked. The cry " Heave 'em out ! "
grew more and more frequent.

We were approaching a rumbling noise of heavy lorries.

" That's the frontier road we're coming to," said Hanfstengel.

" How far off is it, sir ? "

" I make it another hour and a half, if we can keep moving."

" I'm not able to do it, sir," grumbled a corporal.

" We can do without you," laughed Mehling. " Just make

yourself comfortable in the ditch. Meanwhile we'll look for a better hole."

Somebody laughed. The corporal muttered away to himself.

The rumbling noise was now quite near. I could discern the road, which came at right angles towards ours. From the right, two parallel lines of heavy guns were rolling past.

We got very slowly on to the road. "Lieutenant!" cried someone, who could not be identified in the darkness and the hubbub of men, horses and lorries, "the Major says the companies are to play follow-my-leader along the ditch!"

Now we had to go in single file, sometimes at a crawl, sometimes half running, along the uneven surface of the ditch. My foot began to ache. I tried to set it down firmly with an even balance, but that only wearied my ankle.

About eleven o'clock, while the lorries and gun carriages were still rumbling along on our right, the dark outlines of some factories rose to the left of the road. We halted.

"Why can't we go on? We want our billets!"

Lieutenant Schubring stood there as stiff as a poker, watching the clattering lorries roll by.

"We can get along well enough without any officers!"

"Shut your mouths!" cried Höhle. "The Lieutenant can't conjure the billeting officers here! Have you any notion of where to go?"

We had to go on waiting. Even Hanfstengel, who was so popular, was abused by his men.

Mehling said to me privately, "If you'll take my rifle I'll go and look for the billeting officers. They're sure to be somewhere on the road, and all I need to do is to yell for them every few paces."

I went over to my platoon and told them Mehling was on the hunt.

"What a bloody mess!"

"The war might have taught you where to find a billeting officer, surely."

"When are we going to be demobilized, sergeant?" asked a reedy voice.

"That I can't tell you," said I.

"You won't be demobbed at all. This bloody mess is going on for ever. We'll have to leg it ourselves!"

It grew pretty cold.

At long last, after an hour and a half, Schubring had found the billeting officers. He had abused them, and they had yelled at him. " If you will muck your men about like that ! "

Mehling was missing.

We marched in the moonlight down a by-road, which we had to ourselves. The fields on either side looked black. To be marching on a firm surface again did me good. But my foot was aching a lot.

After midnight we reached a small village. An enormous building towered there ; its door opened, letting out a reddish light. A man was standing in the door.

" Where do we bunk ? " asked one man in a surly voice.

All at once Mehling appeared. " Behave yourselves decently. The miller here has had coffee made, and we're to have a warm room."

" Just come in," said the man in a friendly way. " Up the stairs ! I can't do it so quickly as you."

Upstairs in the room there lay sacks of straw. The miller went round asking if we had enough water, and : " There is the closet, just outside to the right."

" Let's play Squat ! " suggested a young lad.

" You've gone dotty ! I've had enough and to spare from the march."

Our field-kitchens and the other lorries did not arrive until noon. They took the covers off at once and handed out coffee.

" Going strong, aren't you ? " said Höhle.

" Well, at least we're not like the rabble in the other lorries, that never have been at the front and are blowing now all over the place ! "

" Are they giving themselves airs ? "

" Not half," said the other cook. " And they've no business to poke in their noses at all ; a crowd of half-men, half-blind or half-dead or groggy in the heart. Not that I believe a word of it. They only didn't want to be sent to the front."

" They're all swine ! " said the driver, leading his heavy horses into the stable.

" If they get too cocky," said Höhle, " just you tell us. We'll lead them a fine dance ! "

" Don't you bother," laughed the smaller of the two cooks.

"I could take them all on myself. And as for Max here, he was the pet of the athletic club in Dessau!"

In the afternoon we marched off and reached Aix-la-Chapelle at dusk. All the houses were beflagged. Our band played up for a while in front of us, and the drums echoed from the houses, from which people were gazing out. A crowd accompanied us as we marched.

We were the last German troops in front of the advancing French and Belgians.

Next day we moved to the station and waited in pouring rain for our train. It was well on in the night before it arrived. There were only cattle-trucks with sliding doors. We did not know where we were going to, except that it was not yet straight to our homes.

Ludwig Renn.

THE GERMANS DEPART

Early the next morning they left. But the general retreat was in full swing along the military road, and they had to wait for hours before the line broke so that they could join it. In the night white notices had been plastered on all the walls. They were signed by Hindenburg, and they called on the troops not to lose their heads, to form soldiers' councils and to obey their decisions. Schlump could feel what this decision must have cost the white-haired old commander, who had not abandoned his troops; and later on he understood what service the old general had rendered his people by this command and how much suffering he had prevented by it. A spirit of responsibility came over the soldiers; they went into council with their officers, and thus a horrible danger was averted: the danger of chaos.

At last Schlump and his comrades were able to break the line, and now they were part of that interminable stream which went un-rolling slowly through Belgium, towards the homeland. They marched along the banks of the Maas, past wonderful castles which were reflected in the green waters of the proud wide river. But on both sides of the road lay the first victims of the retreat: dead men, abandoned cars, dying horses, which kicked out blindly with their hind legs as if to unseat their new rider—Death. Belgian peasants lined the roads at certain spots, each one with his neat little basket on his arm. They offered the soldiers butter, for which the fanciest prices were paid. At Huy they left the beautiful valley and the magnificent stream and wheeled to the left. Then the road began to ascend steeply, leading up to the plateau. The heavy wagons, the dismantled artillery and the big motor-cars continued by the lower road in the direction of Liége, which they had conquered four years before. Huy is an old Belgian nest clinging to the rocks, which here descend sheer to the Maas. From the top the view was marvellous ; the sun shone, and in the distance the blue woods beckoned. Jolles rode at the head of the group on his bicycle ; the captain had found a walking-stick and marched side by side with the horses ; behind him were two orderlies. Schlump sat on the wagon and sang cheerfully. But behind him marched the philosopher, Sack, his pack on his back, his rifle on his shoulder. He was scowling, and he muttered all the time to himself. They went through quiet woods in which the autumn had kindled points of gold. The sky had retained all the colours of the autumn, and a cool sweet wind blew on them, and Schlump stopped singing and fell into a dream. He thought of that evening before the outbreak of war, that warm summer evening when he kissed Johanna. He thought of the ghastly winter in the trenches, of poor Michel, of the nightingale which had captivated him, and of that long strange dream. It seemed to him that now he would continue that dream ; that Michel was now walking invisibly by his side, together with his wife, pointing to the blue hills which he was approaching. He believed, with a pure honest belief, that in the end everything would be well ; he thought of the saintly Johanna in the church at Bohain—she who was the same as the Johanna at home whom he would perhaps soon be holding in his embrace. He saw the world and its future in a thousand glorious colours. He would work, just like happy Michel, he would surely get somewhere with his work, for soon it would be peace. Peace ! Soon ! Peace and decency ! Oh, how lovely life must be then ! What a golden time that was ! Suddenly, out of pure joy, he began to laugh, so that the driver looked round at him in amazement. Schlump was all cheerful again now, and began once more to sing joyfully. Then his eyes fell on the dark philosopher, who marched along behind him.

"Man ! What's the matter with you ? " asked Schlump, laughing. " Have you got a pain somewhere ? "

The dark philosopher rolled his eyes and looked at him wildly :
" I ate my last bread the day before yesterday."

" But man alive ! Isn't there plenty of bread here, and meat,
and everything you could wish for ? "

The philosopher raised his voice till the woods re-echoed with
it. " Do you think," he thundered, " that I am a thief, a robber,
a plunderer ? All that you offer me has been stolen. Aren't you
ashamed of yourself ? "

Schlump stared at him in boundless astonishment and made no
answer. They had now advanced far into the hills of Belgium, the
road wound from one height to the next, they descended into a small
valley and went up the steep road on the other side. Before them
and behind them they saw that long long train moving forward
slowly. It was as though the road had become alive and went along
with them eastward, homeward.

The evening came. They found shelter for the horses and for
themselves. Early in the morning they continued. The captain
complained that he had had to sleep on straw. Whereupon the
soldiers laughed, and Jolles said, " You ought to be glad, captain,
that you weren't in the war, because sometimes we had to sleep in
sh——" They rode through Stavelot and came to Malmedy. Here
they learned that the revolution had really broken out in Berlin and
in other big towns. They halted for a long time near the railway
station.

There was a rumour that a train was standing ready to draw out.
Jolles said : " We haven't got much more food left. The best
thing would be for every man to try to get home as soon as he can."
Thereupon the men made up their packs and divided out the bread
and the canned meat. The captain stood among a group of officers.
The philosopher undertook to stand guard over the captain's
share.

On the other side of the railway station a terrible sight greeted
them. A trainload of flour had been derailed and the flour lay between
the tracks, so that they sank knee-deep into it. There actually was
a train in the station, ready to pull out, and the soldiers ran backwards
and forwards along the track looking for a place. But the train
was packed. Every section was jammed with men ; the windows
had been smashed as if there had been a terrific fight for every place.
Suddenly there was a whistle from Jolles. He had managed to find

the brakeman's van : the two of them clambered in ; the others—
the cook and the orderlies—had disappeared.

And still more soldiers continued to climb on to the train ; Russian
prisoners in their clay-coloured uniforms perched on the buffers and
on the roofs of the cars. A large detachment of recruits, young
boys most of them, kept running up and down the platform. They
clambered up on the steps of the carriages and of the brakemen's
van. Schlump put his head out of the window : " Boys," he
said, " hold on fast when the train starts."

And suddenly the dark philosopher, Sack, turned up, with his
pack and his arms. He went up and down the length of the train,
searching, until he found Schlump. He looked like a wild man ;
he had not shaved for several days, his eyes were deep sunk, and his
voice had a funereal ring.

" Schlump," he said, " I call upon you not to forget the oath of
allegiance which you took when you joined the army : I call upon
you to return to your captain." He said this so loud that half the
train heard him. They stared at him from all the windows, and
a shout of laughter greeted his words. One man yelled at him, in
a shrill, mocking voice : " Hey, you, don't be a damned fool. The
Kaiser himself hooked it." The philosopher shrank when he heard
the name of the Kaiser mentioned. He rolled his eyes—then he
drew out a service pistol which he had managed to pick up somewhere and shot himself in the breast. He cast one last glance at
Schlump and collapsed.

The pack slipped over his head as he fell, the straps were loose,
and huge sheaves of paper covered with close writing slid out over
his face.

At that instant the locomotive began to pull, and the train moved
out.

They pulled slowly into the hills. In the night the train came
to a halt. Jolles got out. He wanted to go on foot as far as Aix-
la-Chapelle, where he had a sister. It was ice-cold. The poor men
who had been clinging to the steps of the cars had disappeared ; so
had the Russian soldiers who had climbed on to the roof. Only
two of them remained : they were frozen stiff. Jolles disappeared
into the darkness. The parting was brief, and they never saw each
other again. At Fingerrath the train stopped again, this time for
good. Schlump went down into the waiting-room to try and warm

himself. He was alone. A couple of soldiers were fast asleep. After an hour or two he went out again. There on the track he saw a tremendous column of soldiers. They had fallen in, twenty to a row, and waited there, silent and motionless. There were probably more than a thousand of them. They were waiting for the express from Strasburg, which would take them to Cologne. And Schlump knew that there would be a terrific struggle for places. He was right. A drumming was heard on the rails. The column of soldiers waited, tense, rigid, like some huge monster ready to spring. Two white lights came out of the night. The monster stirred—and then suddenly the storm broke. Schlump ran along with the rest. A fearful struggle took place round each window. They crawled into the engine, into the tender; the night rang with wild voices and with the splintering of glass. And then it was silent. The lights drew out into the night.

Schlump returned to the waiting-room. He was hungry. He took out food from his pack and ate in peace. He heard another train drawing in outside. He went on eating. A couple of hours later he went out again. An enormously long local train stood on the tracks. He went up to one of the cars; it was dark. Then he heard voices.

"Any room in there?" asked Schlump.

No one answered. Someone laughed. He knew then that it was hopeless. He went forward towards the engine. There he saw a faint shimmer of light: it came out of the baggage car. Schlump took the fifty-mark note out of his pocket and waited. At last some-one came out—a postal official. Schlump went up to him, thrust the fifty-mark note into his hand, and said, " Good morning, comrade. Do you think you can find room for me?" The man took out a pocket-lamp, examined the fifty-mark note, and answered, " You come along." He led the happy Schlump into the warm baggage car. It was cosy in there. A couple of truck drivers and Q.M.C. men sat playing cards. "You got any cigarettes?" they asked. "We'll give you whiskey." Schlump had a couple of boxes in his coat pocket. They came from the officer's restaurant in Charleroi.

The train pulled out and Schlump fell asleep, stretched out com-fortably on the soft bales.

In Cologne they got down from the train. On the platform stood a detachment of sailors, their arms shouldered, barrels downwards. The tunnel below the tracks was filled with arms piled as high as the roof. The officers wore no shoulder-pieces.

Finally Schlump got on to a slow train for Cassel, and there he found another train marked Halle. There was still some room. But they had to wait in the unheated cars from noon till six in the evening. At four o'clock a locomotive came puffing up, coughing and wheezing—but the train would not budge : it just shuddered faintly. At six o'clock a second locomotive came along. The journey to Halle lasted twelve hours. There Schlump got immediate connections—and he was astounded that things were still running smoothly. He travelled another twelve hours. And when he stepped out of the station of his own town the conductor asked him for his ticket. Schlump looked at him, dazed. " Comrade," he said, " they didn't give us time to get tickets."

He stepped out into the station a simple soldier, just as on the day when he had left.

Schlump.

THE ARMISTICE NEGOTIATIONS

THE NARRATIVES OF ADMIRAL LORD WESTER WEMYSS AND HERR MAX ERZBERGER

WESTER WEMYSS. *Thursday, 7th Nov.* I joined the Marshal's train at 5 p.m. Hope, Marriott and Bagot accompany me. We immediately steamed away and the train was taken into a siding in the Forest of Compiegne. The train containing the German delegates is expected during the night, and will stand in a siding close to ours.

The Frenchmen are all naturally very elated, but dignified and calm, the Marshal quiet and confident. He told me he proposed to do as little talking as possible, to let the Germans do it all and then hand them the terms of the Armistice. If they accept the principles, he may discuss details.

Friday, 8th Nov. The train containing the Germans arrived at 7 a.m. I saw the Marshal early and found him rather nervous, but dignified. A message was sent over that we would receive them at 9 a.m. The plenipotentiaries are Erzberger, Count von Oberndorff, General von Winterfeldt and Captain Vanselow. The mission walked over at 9 a.m. and were shown into the saloon by General Weygand.

ERZBERGER : In the saloon stood a wide table with four places on either side. We entered the saloon first and took the places allotted to us. In a few minutes Marshal Foch appeared, a little man with hard energetic features which at first glance betrayed the habit of command. He was accompanied by his Chief-of-Staff and three English naval officers. He greeted us with soldierly curtness and bowed. In German I introduced my companions and handed over our authority which Marshal Foch accepted. He thereupon presented his companions, the English First Sea Lord, Sir (Wester) Wemyss, his Chief of Staff, Weygand, the English Admiral Hope, with the interpreters, for the French, Laperche, and for the English, Bagot. Thus there appeared neither Americans, Italians, nor Belgians at the armistice negotiations, but only the Supreme Command of the Allies.

WESTER WEMYSS : Their credentials . . . they handed to the Marshal, and he and I left the saloon to examine them. They were quite in order, were signed by Prince Max of Baden, but gave no power to sign any armistice.

ERZBERGER : Marshal Foch returned, and asked in French : " What brings these gentlemen here ? What do you want of me ? " I replied that I expected proposals which might lead to the conclusion of an armistice on sea, on land, and in the air, and on all fronts. Upon this Marshal Foch replied in a deliberate voice : " I have no proposals to make."

WESTER WEMYSS : General Winterfeldt, reading from a scrap of paper, then asked on behalf of the German High Command that hostilities might cease immediately. He said that such an action might save many lives. Foch replied that cessation of hostilities would only take place after the Armistice had been signed. Germany then formally asked for a copy of the terms, which were given them, and a short discussion took place as to the manner of transmitting them to Berlin. They have come without cyphers. The meeting then was closed and the answer has to be given by 11 a.m. on Monday.

All the Germans are very much distressed—naturally so. Erzberger showing most nervousness—but Winterfeldt and Vanselow looked the most distressed. The General in his little speech asking for cessation of hostilities used the word " déroute " in connection with the German Armies. The naval and military terms did not seem to affect them so much as the civil and financial ones. Bourbon-Busset, who was in charge of them, said he thought they were all very down.

An extra 24 hours was asked for, but this was refused. The time has been calculated and is sufficient.

Erzberger is a common-looking man, a typical German bourgeois.

ERZBERGER : During the reading, the English Admiral, Sir (Wester) Wemyss made a display of great indifference and lack of interest, but his ceaseless fidgeting with his eyeglass and great horn-rimmed spectacle betrayed his secret excitement. Marshal Foch sat at the table with stony calm, but sometimes he pulled vigorously at his moustache. During the whole recital no comment was made.

WESTER WEMYSS : It is a curious scene in the middle of the forest—raining and leaves falling, and yet there is nothing sad—at any rate for us. The two trains 200 yards off each other. Stray sentries in blue-grey can be seen amongst the trees. Nothing else in sight. We are in telephonic communication with Paris and the world.

Apparently the German Army is getting demoralized. Meanwhile papers have arrived and the whole story of the Naval mutiny is out. How will it affect the Naval terms ? It will be difficult for them to comply.

The Marshal told me, were the Armistice not to be signed, he would have the capitulation of the whole lot in three weeks. He also said that yesterday a whole regiment of Boches had laid down their arms and came in crying that now there was peace. Bourbon-Busset told me that the Germans were throwing away their arms and to-day a telegram came to say that they are actually leaving their field-kitchens behind. The Mission said nothing about Bolshevism.

No further regular meeting.

Hope saw Vanselow, who merely asked questions relative to the terms. He is afraid of the blockade and seems actually to think that we shall keep it up for the purpose of starving their country during the Armistice ! Such is their mentality, so I suppose that is what they would have done had the cases been reversed. Vanselow also asked if we should sink any submarines during the Armistice ! Really it is unbelievable. He said that Bolshevism had appeared in their Army during the months of April and May. The fact is that that was the time of their enormous losses and to speak of the decline of morale as Bolshevism is ridiculous. I am told that all day Friday the state of the delegates was deplorable but that they bucked up a little during dinner.

Friday evening I had a long conversation with Foch. In reply to my questions he told me that the hardest terms in the Armistice was the time that the 9th Army had to retire in. If carried out, it meant that they must leave everything behind. He is determined that the German Army shall be thoroughly beaten. Foch is very ignorant about all matters Naval. I gave him certain information which interested him, and tried to explain to him what the Navy was doing and had done. I think he began to grasp the subject a little. He explained to me the difficulties the enemy would encounter in withdrawing from Belgium, from which I began to understand why Vanselow had spoken about using German ships in Antwerp for evacuating their troops. Foch won't have this at any price. Also we must have all the German ships in the pool for revictualling all countries.

Sunday, 10th Nov. Yesterday morning we motored to Soissons. Truly a dreadful sight—not one single house is habitable. The Cathedral is literally torn in two. Going through the streets gave one the impression of visiting Pompeii. We were shown some of the outlying houses which with great ingenuity and without any change in their external appearance had been made into regular fortresses. The news which reached us during Saturday was tremendous and varied. The abdication of the Emperor—at first it was thought that Max of Baden remained as Chancellor. Then a manifesto to the German people and world, saying that a Socialist Democratic Government had been formed and that the functions of Chancellor had been taken over by Ebert. In the meantime a republic seems to have been proclaimed in Bavaria. All seems to be confusion. It would appear that the plenipotentiaries have no longer any powers and one would think that Erzberger at any rate has no longer any standing.

Last night I telegraphed to the Prime Minister telling him that the Mission feared that the continuance of the blockade would mean the starving of the country and that I proposed to tell them that we should consider the revictualling of the country.

Von Oberndorff yesterday saw Weygand and pointed out certain clauses which they think should be altered.

On the Sunday afternoon I took a long walk with G. Hope—there was nothing doing. A German courier had left at noon on Friday ; in spite of all preparations being made, it was found he could not get through the lines because of the German fire—the first intimation that the German fire discipline was getting bad. The courier was finally despatched by aeroplane.

On Sunday evening I had been talking to the Marshal for a long time after dinner and was just going to bed when an A.D.C. came and told me with the Marshal's compliments that he thought that the

German Envoys had received instructions and would probably want to see us to-night and would I therefore be ready. Consequently I did not go to bed but lay down until midnight, when I was told that the Envoys had asked to be received immediately. They came into the train and we resumed our seats as we did on Friday morning. There was but slight inclination on the part of any of the Germans to any protest. In one or two small matters, such as number of locomotives or aeroplanes to be delivered, they assured us that it was impossible to accede to the demands since we had over-estimated their strength and the Marshal showed reasonableness and to all intents and purposes the Military terms of the Armistice were signed. In the case of the German forces in East Africa the word capitulated which appeared in the original text of the Armistice was allowed to be altered.

When it came to discussing the Naval terms, Vanselow showed a captiousness which was tiresome and quite unavailing. He made the remark, was it admissible that their fleet should be interned seeing that they had not been beaten ?—the reply to this was obvious and it gave me a certain amount of pleasure to observe that they only had to come out !

On discussing the submarine situation, he told me, somewhat to my surprise, that there were not nearly a hundred and sixty to be had— this gave me the chance of getting what I had always wanted, viz. *all* the submarines. I may say here that the question of the Naval terms of Armistice had caused a good deal of discussion. I had originally asked for the " surrender " of eleven battleships, six battle-cruisers, eight light cruisers fifty destroyers and all the submarines. The politicians, however, were frightened and considered these terms as too heavy and desired to make them lighter, because they feared that there was a point beyond which the Germans would not go and they (very rightly) considered, so far as Great Britain was concerned, the present was the best psychological moment for obtaining a peace. I had many arguments with the Prime Minister on the subject and was quite aware that the French for the same reason wanted the general terms eased, and that this should be done at the expense of the French Army. During some of the discussions on this subject Foch had said : " Do you expect my men to go on fighting for the sake of ships that do not come out ? " thereby displaying his entire ignorance of the general situation and of the part which the Navy had played in the war. Lloyd George had endeavoured to whittle down these terms and had suggested every sort and kind of compromise—a reduction of the ships to be delivered, etc., and had eventually agreed to the internment of the surface vessels as a compromise. This I had accepted as the best to be got, and with an undertaking from him that these ships should never be returned to Germany but surrendered at the peace. It was the same with the question of the submarines ; Lloyd George had objected to the word " *all.*" By fixing a number which I felt sure would give us what they had got I had hoped to achieve my end—which I did. It was therefore a pleasure and a satisfaction to me to get the opportunity of inserting the word *all* in the terms.

ERZBERGER : The liveliest debate arose over Article 26, centering on the continuation of the blockade. For over an hour we argued the point. I specifically stated that during a substantial part of the World War England had pursued a policy of starvation by which German women and children had suffered to the limit. Count Oberndorff and I insisted that it was " not fair," a remark which the English admiral countered irritably with : " Not fair ? You sank our ships without picking and choosing." The English would not go further than agree to transmit our plea for the raising of the blockade to their government. One important improvement was secured in the promise that the Entente would supply Germany with food during the Armistice. The discussion of the articles lasted until 5.12 a.m. On the suggestion of Marshal Foch, it was agreed that the time should be taken as 5 a.m. and that the Armistice should come into force six hours later, at 11 a.m. French time.

The negotiations were now broken off and I at once informed General Head-quarters by telephone of the conclusion of the Armistice. . . . The signing of the terms began at 5.20. Two copies were prepared. First Marshal Foch and Admiral Wemyss signed, then the German delegates. Our two gallant officers, General von Winterfeldt and Capt. Vanselow had tears in their eyes as with considerable emotion they signed their names. I then made a further declaration of assurance that we would loyally endeavour to fulfil the stipulations. I once again referred to our counter-proposals to the terms, and pointed out that many details might prove impossible to carry out. I ended my speech with the words : " A people of 70 millions suffers, but does not die." to which Marshal Foch replied : " *Très bien.*" At 5.30 a.m., the two delegations parted from each other by rising from their chairs. We did not shake hands.

WESTER WEMYSS : The Germans then went back to their train, and we dispersed. Having to start for Paris at 7.30 a.m., I felt it was too late to go to bed, and so Hope and I went for a walk in the forest, and it was a queer feeling that I had that the war was at last over and that bloodshed would cease at 11 o'clock.

Admiral Lord Wester Wemyss.
Max Erzberger.

AS IT WAS IN THE BEGINNING . . .

IN the early days of November, 1918, the Allied Forces had for some days been advancing in pursuit of the retreating German Army. The advance was being carried out according to a schedule. Each Division was given a line to which it must attain before nightfall ; and this meant that each battalion in a division had to reach a certain point by a certain time. The schedule was in general being well adhered to, but the opposition encountered varied considerably at different points.

On November 10th, a certain English battalion had been continuously harassed by machine-gun fire, and late in the afternoon was still far from its objective. Advancing under cover, it reached the edge of a plantation from which stretched a wide open space of cultivated land, with a village in front about 500 yards away. The officer in charge of the scouts was sent ahead with a corporal and two men to reconnoitre, and this little party reached the outskirts of the village without observing any signs of occupation. At the entrance of the village, propped against a tree, they found a German officer, wounded severely in the thigh. He was quite conscious and looked up calmly as Lieut. S—— approached him. He spoke English, and when questioned, intimated that the village had been evacuated by the Germans two hours ago.

Thereupon Lieut. S—— signalled back to the battalion, who then advanced along the road in marching formation. It was nearly dusk when they reached the small *place* in front of the church, and there they were halted. Immediately from several points, but chiefly from the tower of the church, a number of machine-guns opened fire on the massed men. A wild cry went up, and the men fled in rage and terror to the shelter of the houses, leaving a hundred of their companions and five officers dead or dying on the pavement. In the houses and the church they routed out the ambushed Germans and mercilessly bayoneted them.

The corporal who had been with Lieut. S—— ran to the entrance of the village, to settle with the wounded officer who had betrayed them. The German seemed to be expecting him ; his face did not flinch as the bayonet descended.

When the wounded had been attended to, and the dead gathered together, the remaining men retired to the schoolhouse to rest for the night. The officers then went to the château of the village, and there in a gardener's cottage, searching for fuel, the corporal already mentioned found the naked body of a young girl. Both legs were severed, and one severed arm was found in another room. The body itself was covered with bayonet wounds. When the discovery was reported to Lieut. S——, he went to verify the strange crime, but there was nothing to be done : he was, moreover, sick and tired. He found a bed in another cottage near the château, where some old peasants were still cowering behind a screen. He fell into a deep sleep, and did not wake until the next morning, the 11th of November, 1918.

Herbert Read.

ARMISTICE DAY

10th Nov. I looked at my watch—it was 11 p.m.—and I remember noticing my crest and reading the motto, " *Gloria Finis*," inscribed on the back. Somehow I felt that this was a good omen. How ridiculous and superstitious ! Still, I only happened to have this particular watch, because the one I usually carried had been broken. Yes, it was a good omen, and I could not get the idea out of my head. I then fell asleep.

On the morning of the 11th of November there were rumours of an Armistice, but we did not attach much importance to them. At about 10.45 a.m. we were in action against the Germans, east of Mons, and one of our troops had just charged some German machine-guns. A private soldier came galloping towards us ; he was much excited, had lost his cap, and could not stop his horse. As he passed us he shouted : " The war's over ! The war's over ! " We thought, undoubtedly, the poor fellow was suffering from shell-shock. Soon after an official message came, saying that operations would cease at 11 a.m., and that we were to establish ourselves on the ground we held at that hour. It sounded like the end of peace manœuvres when the customary three balloons used to be sent up. Messengers were immediately dispatched at full gallop to stop any further fighting.

It was a strange coincidence that, after more than four years of war, we should finish fighting within less than a mile of the place where we had first come into action against the Germans, while with us was the same Horse Battery that came into action with us at the same place in August, 1914. This battery must have fired about the first shell of the war, and now, on the same ground, it was going to fire the last.

At two seconds before 11 a.m., I ordered them to fire a last salvo. One of these empty shell-cases, which was kindly presented to me, is the only souvenir of the war that I possess. It was exactly 11 a.m., as I put my watch away, I looked at the motto on the back, and thought

to myself : He was right in more ways than one.   The news had
circulated everywhere by 11 a.m.   Out came the inevitable cigarette,
but there was no cheering, or wild exuberance of feelings.
  " Random Reminiscences of an Ordinary Soldier in the Great
                              War " in " Army Quarterly."

Starting from Hampstead to go by omnibus to Chancery Lane
that morning, I noticed how everything appeared to be proceeding
as " for the duration " of the war, till we were near Mornington Square
Tube Station.   Suddenly maroons went off, a startling explosion just
above us.   An air-raid, another air-raid !   A woman ran out of a
house and gazed anxiously at the sky.   But before one could recollect
that it might mean the Armistice, people were pouring out of buildings, streaming into the streets.   The war was ended.   Tools must
have been downed in no time.   Crowds grew bigger every minute.

There was great liveliness, calls, cries, whistles and hooters
sounding, noise and crowds grew as we proceeded.   Chancery Lane
was very lively.   Going out for lunch about one o'clock, great
excitement prevailed ; happy, daylight mafficking produced most
unusual sights.   Every vehicle going along the Strand was being
boarded by people, most of whom waved flags.   Boys and girls
flung themselves on anywhere and clung as best they might.   One
scene was more unusual than others.   At the corner of Chancery
Lane a stout policeman on point duty was surrounded by girls all
clamouring to dance with him.   The London bobby rose to the
occasion—without a word he took on one after another for a turn
round on the narrow pavement as they stood, whilst his countenance
remained absolutely impassive.   Custom and convention melted
away as if a new world had indeed dawned.   Officers and privates
mixed in equal comradeship.   Privates drilled officers, munitionettes
commanded platoons made up of both.   The spirit of militarism
was turned into comedy.

Never in history perhaps have such great multitudes experienced
such restoration of joyousness in the twinkling of an eye.

This great spontaneous joy of relief helps us to fathom the long
endured, agonizing strain, rarely acknowledged, usually hidden away
and overlaid with wartime's preoccupations, exactions and hazardous
undertakings.   We were freed, the burden was rolled away.   The
demon of ardour no longer drove us.

The transition from war to peace conditions began forthwith. Recruiting was stopped, call-up notices were cancelled. Bells might be rung and public clocks might chime again at night. The light in the tower of the Houses of Parliament and other lights reappeared on the first evening. Just as hearts had sunk when the extinction of lights brought home the incredible certainty that Britain was at war, so now, seeing the lights shine out, men dared believe that the great war was indeed over.

There was every right to be thankful, and to join in the shouting on the great day, November 11, 1918. Thousands went into the churches, the Baltic Exchange sang the Doxology, and the Stock Exchange the hymn, *O God, our help in ages past.*

People flocked through the doors of St. Paul's until the building was filled from end to end. It was manifest that hearts overflowed with gratitude. " In the Abbey the crowd seemed swept away as on a vast stream of thankfulness." The hearts of civilians and soldiers overflowed with gratitude and joy during the brief but most memorable service.

Caroline E. Playne.

On 11th November we marched back fifteen miles to Bethencourt. A blanket of fog covered the countryside. At eleven o'clock we slung on our packs and tramped on along the muddy *pavé*. The band played, but there was very little singing. " Before a man comes to be wise, he is half dead with catarrhes and aches, with sore eyes, and a worn-out body." We were very old, very tired, and now very wise. We took over our billets and listlessly devoured a meal. In an effort to cure our apathy, the little American doctor from Vermont who had joined us a fortnight earlier broke his invincible teetotalism, drank half a bottle of whisky, and danced a cachucha. We looked at his antics with dull eyes and at last put him to bed.

Guy Chapman.

. . . November 11th found us in rather a depressed mood. We were on very short rations as our parcels had diminished very much in the past three weeks.

That week was night shift for us, and we were having German soup and boiled potatoes at a quarter-past five at night, preparatory to starting out for work.

About a quarter to six, one of the Frenchmen returning from his day's work came in and told us that the Armistice had been signed that morning. It may appear strange to say that we received the news with no display of enthusiasm—not one of the English passed any comment.

Food was the greatest interest to us, although we knew all that it meant to us, for we had been told that release of prisoners was one of the first conditions.

Before we left the barracks that evening, another Frenchman brought in the Armistice terms, and the numbers of wagons and railway stock that had to be surrendered.

Even this failed to arouse any excitement, though I suspect that in every one's heart there was a sense of thankfulness that our days in the mine were numbered.

E. C. Pattison.

THE OTHER SIDE OF THE PICTURE

The day was cold and damp and grey. I was wedged hotly and uncomfortably among the crowd. The buzz of excitement re-echoed from the houses, as we waited, listening and chattering, shivering with the cold and damp.

All at once the soldiers appeared. We scarcely heard them, but there was a sudden movement among the crowd. A few shouts were heard, which no one took up and which soon died down again. A woman wept, her shoulders heaving, sobbing quietly, her hands clenched.

The police spread out their arms and tried to keep back the crowd. They were swallowed up as the wall of people pressed forward.

There they were ! There they were : grey figures, a forest of rifles over the round flat helmets.

" Why is there no music ? " somebody whispered hoarsely, breathlessly. " Why hasn't the mayor arranged any music ? " Indignant whispers ; then a deathly silence. Then a voice shouted " Hurrah . . . " from somewhere at the back. Then again silence.

The soldiers marched quickly, in close formation. They had stony, expressionless faces. They looked neither to right nor left, but straight ahead, fixedly, as though magnetized by some terrible goal, as though they were gazing from dug-outs and trenches over a wounded world. Not a word was spoken by those haggard-faced men. Just once, when someone sprang forward and almost imploringly offered a little box to the soldiers, the lieutenant waved him aside impatiently, saying : " For goodness' sake don't do that. A whole division is following on."

One platoon passed, the ranks close, a second, a third. Then a space. More space. Could this be a whole company ? Three platoons ? God ! how terrible these men looked !—gaunt, immobile faces under shrapnel helmets, wasted limbs, ragged, dusty uniforms. . . . Did they still carry terrible visions of battle in their minds, as they carried the dust of the mangled earth on their garments ? The strain was almost unbearable. They marched as though they were envoys of the deadliest loneliest, iciest cold. Yet they had come home ; here was warmth and happiness ; why were they so silent ? Why did they not shout and cheer ; why did they not laugh ?

The next company advanced. The crowd thronged forward again. But the soldiers trudged on rapidly, doggedly, blindly, untouched by the thousand wishes, hopes, greetings which hovered round them. And the crowd was silent.

Very few of the soldiers were wearing flowers. The little bunches which hung on their gun-barrels were faded. Most of the girls in the crowd were carrying flowers, but they stood trembling, uncertain, diffident, their faces pale and twitching, as they looked at the soldiers with anxious eyes. The march went on. An officer was carrying a laurel wreath negligently, dangling it in his hand, hunching his shoulders.

The crowd pulled itself together. A few hoarse shouts were heard, as though from rusty throats. Here and there a handkerchief was waved. One man murmured, convulsed : " Our heroes, our heroes ! " They passed on, unmoved, shoulders thrust forward, their steel helmets almost hidden by bulky packs, dragging their feet, company after company, little knots of men with wide spaces between. Sweat ran from their helmets down their worn grey cheeks, their noses stood out sharply from their faces.

Not a flag, not a sign of victory. The baggage wagons were already coming in sight. So this was a whole regiment !

Ernst von Salomon.

VOICES—1918-19

BACCHANAL

(*November*, 1918)

Into the twilight of Trafalgar Square
They pour from every quarter, banging drums
And tootling penny trumpets—to a blare
Of tin mouth-organs, while a sailor strums
A solitary banjo, lads and girls
Locked in embraces in a wild dishevel
Of flags and streaming hair, with curdling skirls
Surge in a frenzied reeling panic revel.

Lads who so long have stared death in the face,
Girls who so long have tended death's machines,
Released from the numb terror shriek and prance—
And, watching them, I see the outrageous dance,
The frantic torches and the tambourines
Tumultuous on the midnight hills of Thrace.

Wilfrid Gibson.

HIGH WOOD

Ladies and gentlemen, this is High Wood,
Called by the French, Bois des Fourneaux,
The famous spot which in Nineteen-Sixteen,
July, August and September was the scene
Of long and bitterly contested strife,
By reason of its High commanding site.
Observe the effect of shell-fire in the trees
Standing and fallen ; here is wire ; this trench

710

For months inhabited, twelve times changed hands;
(They soon fall in), used later as a grave.
It has been said on good authority
That in the fighting for this patch of wood
Were killed somewhere above eight thousand men,
Of whom the greater part were buried here,
This mound on which you stand being . . .
                              Madam, please,
You are requested kindly not to touch
Or take away the Company's property
As souvenirs; you'll find we have on sale
A large variety, all guaranteed.
As I was saying, all is as it was,
This is an unknown British officer,
The tunic having lately rotted off.
Please follow me—this way . . . the *path*, sir, *please*,
The ground which was secured at great expense
The company keeps absolutely untouched,
And in that dug-out (genuine) we provide
Refreshments at a reasonable rate.
You are requested not to leave about
Paper, or ginger-beer bottles, or orange-peel,
There are waste-paper-baskets at the gate.
                              Philip Johnstone.

THE LAMENT OF THE DEMOBILIZED

" Four years," some say consolingly. " Oh, well,
What's that? You're young. And then it must have been
A very fine experience for you ! "
And they forget
How others stayed behind and just got on—
Got on the better since we were away.
And we came home and found
They had achieved, and men revered their names,
But never mentioned ours;
And no one talked heroics now, and we
Must just go back and start again once more.

"You threw four years into the melting-pot—
Did you, indeed!" these other cry. "Oh, well,
The more fool you!"
And we're beginning to agree with them.

Vera Brittain.

STRANGE MEETING

It seemed that out of battle I escaped
Down some profound dull tunnel, long since scooped
Through granites which titanic wars had groined.
Yet also there encumbered sleepers groaned,
Too fast in thought or death to be bestirred.
Then, as I probed them, one sprang up, and stared
With piteous recognition in fixed eyes,
Lifting distressful hands as if to bless.
And by his smile, I knew that sullen hall,
By his dead smile I knew we stood in Hell.
With a thousand pains that vision's face was grained;
Yet no blood reached there from the upper ground,
And no guns thumped, or down the flues made moan.
"Strange friend," I said, "here is no cause to mourn."
"None," said the other, "save the undone years,
The hopelessness. Whatever hope is yours,
Was my life also; I went hunting wild
After the wildest beauty in the world,
Which lies not calm in eyes, or braided hair,
But mocks the steady running of the hour,
And if it grieves, grieves richlier than here.
For by my glee might many men have laughed,
And of my weeping something had been left,
Which must die now. I mean the truth untold,
The pity of war, the pity war distilled.
Now men will go content with what we spoiled.
Or, discontent, boil bloody, and be spilled.
They will be swift with swiftness of the tigress,
None will break ranks, though nations trek from progress.
Courage was mine, and I had mastery;
To miss the march of this retreating world

Into vain citadels that are not walled.
Then, when much blood had clogged their chariot-wheels
I would go up and wash them from sweet wells,
Even with truths that lie too deep for taint.
I would have poured my spirit without stint
But not through wounds; not on the cess of war.
Foreheads of men have bled where no wounds were.
I am the enemy you killed, my friend.
I knew you in this dark; for so you frowned
Yesterday through me as you jabbed and killed.
I parried; but my hands were loath and cold.
Let us sleep now . . ."

Wilfred Owen.

Epilogue

WAR AIMS

SIR ERIC GEDDES, FIRST LORD OF THE ADMIRALTY,
AT THE DRILL HALL, CAMBRIDGE

9th Dec. If I am returned, Germany is going to pay restitution, reparation and indemnity, and I have personally no doubt we will get everything out of her that you can squeeze out of a lemon and a bit more, but there are some things I would not take from Germany because that would hurt our industries. I propose that every bit of German property, movable and immovable, in Allied and neutral countries, whether State property or the private property of Germans should be surrendered to the Allies, and that Germany should pay her precious citizens in her precious paper money. No German should be allowed to own anything in this country. If Germany has got anything to buy with, she can pay that in indemnities. I propose that not only all the gold Germany has got, but all the silver and jewels she has got shall be handed over. All her pictures and libraries and everything of that kind should be sold to the neutral and Allied world, and the proceeds given to paying the indemnity. I would strip Germany as she has stripped Belgium.

As reported in " The Times " (10th *Dec.,* 1918).

IN OCCUPATION

ONE night before Christmas I thought I heard voices outside my quarters long after curfew, and went to look out from my balcony high up in the Domhof into the moon-flooded expanse of the Cathedral square below. By rights there should have been no figures there at that hour, German or British. But there were three ; two tipsy Highlanders—" Women from Hell," as German soldiers used to call the demonic stabbers in kilts—gravely dispensing the consolations of chivalry to a stout burgher of Cologne. " Och, dinna tak' it to hairrt, mon. I tell ye that your lads were grond." It was like a last leap of the flame that had burnt clear and high four years before.

For the day of the fighting man, him and his chivalric hobbies, was over. The guns had hardly ceased to fire before from the rear, from the bases, from London, there came flooding up the braves who for all those four years had been squealing threats and abuse, some of them begging off service in arms on the plea that squealing was indispensable national work. We had not been long in Cologne when there arrived in hot haste a young pressman from London, one of the first of a swarm. He looked a fine strong man. He seemed to be one of the male Vestals who have it for their trade of feeding the eternal flame of hatred between nations, instead of clearing out stables or doing some other work fit for a male. His train had fortunately brought him just in time for luncheon. This he ate and drank with goodwill, complaining only that the wine, which seemed to me good, was not better. He then slept on his bed until tea-time. Reanimated with tea, he said genially, " Well, I must be getting on with my mission of hate," and retired to his room to write a vivacious account of the wealth and luxury of Cologne, the guzzling in all cafés and restaurants, the fair round bellies of all the working class, the sleek and rosy children of the poor. I read it, two days after, in his paper. Our men who had helped to fight Germany down were going short of food at the time, through feeding the children in houses where they were billeted. " Proper Zoo there is in this place," one of them told me. " Proper lions and tigers. Me and my friend are taking the kids from our billet soon's we've got them fatted up a bit. If you'll believe me, sir, them kiddies ain't safe in a Zoo. They could walk in through the bars and get patting the lions." I had just seen some of the major carnivora in their cages close to the Rhine, each a rectangular lamine of fur and bone like the tottering cats I had seen pass through incredible slits of space in Amiens a month after the people had fled from the city that spring. But little it mattered in London what he or I saw. The nimble scamps had the ear of the world ; what the soldier said was not evidence. . . .

Sir Douglas Haig came to Cologne when we had been there a few days. On the grandiose bridge over the Rhine he made a short speech to a few of us. Most of it sounded as if the thing were a job he had got to get through with, and did not much care for. Perhaps the speech, like those of other great men who wisely hate making speeches, had been written for him by somebody else. But once he looked up from the paper and put in some words which I felt sure were his own ; " I only hope that, now we have won, we shall not lose our heads, as the Germans did after 1870. It has brought them to this." He looked at the gigantic mounted statue of the Kaiser overhead, a thing crying out in its pride for fire from heaven to fall and consume it, and at the homely, squat British sentry moving below on his post. I think the speech was reported. But none of our foremen at home took any notice of it at all. They knew a trick worth two of Haig's. They were as moonstruck as any victorious Prussian.

C. E. Montague.

THE PRESIDENT AND THE PRIME MINISTER

THE first impression of Mr. Wilson at close quarters was to impair some but not all of these illusions. His head and features were finely cut and exactly like his photographs, and the muscles of his neck and the carriage of his head were distinguished. But, like Odysseus, the President looked wiser when he was seated; and his hands, though capable and fairly strong, were wanting in sensitiveness and finesse. The first glance at the President suggested not only that, whatever else he might be, his temperament was not primarily that of the student or the scholar, but that he had not much even of that culture of the world which marks M. Clemenceau and Mr. Balfour as exquisitely cultivated gentlemen of their class and generation. But more serious than this, he was not only insensitive to his surroundings in the external sense, he was not sensitive to his environment at all. What chance could such a man have against Mr. Lloyd George's unerring, almost medium-like, sensibility to everyone immediately round him? To see the British Prime Minister watching the company, with six or seven senses not available to ordinary men, judging character, motive, and sub-conscious impulse, perceiving what each was thinking and even what each was going to say next, and compounding with telepathic instinct the argument or appeal best suited to the vanity, weakness, or self-interest of his immediate auditor, was to realize that the poor President would be playing blind man's buff in that party. Never could a man have stepped into the parlour a more perfect and predestined victim to the finished accomplishments of the Prime Minister. The old World was tough in wickedness anyhow; the old World's heart of stone might blunt the sharpest blade of the bravest knight-errant. But this blind and deaf Don Quixote was entering a cavern where the swift and glittering blade was in the hands of the adversary.

J. M. Keynes.

THE TIGER

CLEMENCEAU was by far the most eminent member of the Council of Four, and he had taken the measure of his colleagues. He alone both had an idea and had considered it in all its consequences. His age, his character, his wit, and his appearance joined to give him objectivity and a defined outline in an environment of confusion. One could not despise Clemenceau or dislike him, but only take a different view as to the nature of civilized man, or indulge, at least, a different hope.

The figure and bearing of Clemenceau are universally familiar. At the Council of Four he wore a square-tailed coat of very good, thick black broad-cloth, and on his hands, which were never un-covered, grey suede gloves; his boots were of thick black leather, very good, but of a country style, and sometimes fastened in front curiously, by a buckle instead of laces. His seat in the room in the President's house, where the regular meetings of the Council of Four were held (as distinguished from their private and unattended conferences in a smaller chamber below), was on a square brocaded chair in the middle of the semicircle facing the fire-place, with Signor Orlando on his left, the President next by the fire-place, and the Prime Minister opposite on the other side of the fire-place on his right. He carried no papers and no portfolio, and was unattended by any personal secretary, though several French ministers and officials appropriate to the particular matter in hand would be present round him. His walk, his hand, and his voice were not lacking in vigour, but he bore nevertheless, especially after the attempt upon him, the aspect of a very old man conserving his strength for im-portant occasions. He spoke seldom, leaving the initial statement of the French case to his ministers or officials; he closed his eyes often and sat back in his chair with an impassive face of parchment, his grey gloved hands clasped in front of him.. A short sentence, decisive or cynical, was generally sufficient, a question, an unqualified abandonment of his ministers, whose face would not be saved, or a display of obstinacy reinforced by a few words in a piquantly delivered English.[1] But speech and passion were not lacking when they were wanted, and the sudden outburst of words, often followed by a fit of deep coughing from the chest, produced their impression rather by force and surprise than by persuasion.

Not infrequently Mr. Lloyd George, after delivering a speech in English, would, during the period of its interpretation into French, cross the hearthrug to the President to reinforce his case by some *ad hominem* argument in private conversation, or to sound the ground for a compromise—and this would sometimes be the signal for a general upheaval and disorder. The President's advisers would press round him, a moment later the British experts would dribble across to learn the result or see that all was well, and next the French would be there, a little suspicious lest the others were arranging something behind them, until all the room were on their feet and conversation was general in both languages. My last and most vivid impression is of such a scene—the President and the Prime Minister as the centre of a surging mob and a babel of sound, a welter of eager, impromptu compromises and counter-compromises, all sound and fury and signifying nothing, on what was an unreal question anyhow, the great issues of the morning's meeting forgotten and neglected; and Clemenceau, silent and aloof on the outskirts—for nothing which touched the security of France was forward—throned, in his grey gloves, on the brocade chair, dry in soul and empty of hope, very old and tired, but surveying the scene with a cynical and almost impish air; and when at last silence was restored and the company had returned to their places, it was to discover that he had disappeared.

He felt about France what Pericles felt of Athens—unique value in her, nothing else mattering; but his theory of politics was Bismarck's. He had one illusion—France; and one disillusion— mankind, including Frenchmen, and his colleagues not least. His principles for the Peace can be expressed simply. In the first place he was a foremost believer in the view of German psychology that the

---

[1] He alone amongst the Four could speak and understand both languages, Orlando knowing only French and the Prime Minister and President only English; and it is of historical importance that Orlando and the President had no direct means of communication.

German understands and can understand nothing but intimidation, that he is without generosity or remorse in negotiation, that there is no advantage he will not take of you, and no extent to which he will not demean himself for profit, that he is without honour, pride, or mercy. Therefore you must never negotiate with a German or conciliate him ; you must dictate to him. On no other terms will he respect you, or will you prevent him from cheating you. But it is doubtful how far he thought these characteristics peculiar to Germany, or whether his candid view of some other nations was fundamentally different. His philosophy had, therefore, no place for " sentimentality " in international relations. Nations are real things, of whom you love one and feel for the rest indifference—or hatred. The glory of the nation you love is a desirable end—but generally to be obtained at your neighbour's expense. The politics of power are inevitable, and there is nothing very new to learn about this war or the end it was fought for ; England had destroyed, as in each preceding century, a trade rival ; a mighty chapter had been closed in the secular struggle between the glories of Germany and of France. Prudence required some measure of lip service to the " ideals " of foolish Americans and hypocritical Englishmen ; but it would be stupid to believe that there is much room in the world, as it really is, for such affairs as the League of Nations, or any sense in the principle of self-determination except as an ingenious formula for rearranging the balance of power in one's own interests.

J. M. Keynes.

YOUTH IN BERLIN

ONLY those who knew the conditions under which this student was living could realize what a depth of gratitude this gift of two precious eggs meant.

This nearness to despair was known to too many students, and too often became real despair.

One day I was sitting stamping the student cards in one of the dining centres when a student came up to me, put out his hand, and said, " Good-bye. To-morrow I shall be dead."

I looked up for a brief moment, with, " Cheer up, Herr F. I hope it's not as bad as that," dismissing him and what I thought was an attempt at the dramatic from my too Anglo-Saxon mind : but the next day he was dead, for he had shot himself not long after leaving me.

This was the beginning of many suicides and they had their influence on our club and on our students.

One day I noticed a girl coming out of the dining-room in a great hurry. She had no time to say more than " Mahlzeit " as she passed out, but as she turned politely towards me I saw her face, and there was a look so strangely sad upon it that I felt impelled to run after and speak to her. I asked her if she were not well.

" Thank you, yes. I am quite well, only a little tired, as are all people," and she admitted me no further. I turned to go back to my seat, but felt that I could not, that I must not allow this girl to escape me in this way, so I followed her. It was not a comfortable feeling, and I was hot and embarrassed lest she should turn round and find me following her, but I kept on until we turned in, after some long distance, at the doorway of a high block of poor flats. At the top landing she closed a door just as I began to climb the staircase, but I guessed the door from the sound—there were only two doors, but no name-plates were there, for brass and copper were precious, and the name-plates had either been sold or more probably stolen.

I stood some moments wondering what to do, then summoned up my courage and knocked. The door was opened by Marie herself, who met me with an indignant politeness.

I did not know what to say, so said nothing, and I do not know now whether I was asked into the room or whether I walked in, but I found myself face to face with Frau S., the mother of Marie. I murmured something about thinking that Marie looked ill, but I felt that the woman was not listening to me at all, looking at me as if I came from another world with no possibility of any human relationship. I cannot describe this look : it was not that of a mad woman, but of someone who has seen so far that it is impossible to focus on things that are visible at any distance measurable to us. I could not help thinking that so Lazarus must have looked when he was questioned.

Marie spoke. " It is kind of you to come to us, but it is no good now. We have no future. We have thought of all that is before us. My mother's pension is so small that it provides nothing. We have no friends or relations to whom we can go for help, for they are all poor too. I get the Quaker Speisung, but there is nothing to look forward to, and without hope it is better to die. We have no heat and no food. Faith and courage we had, but they have left us now too." And then she added with complete calmness, " To-night we have decided to kill ourselves." Then the woman said, but not to me :

" It is better, far better so," and there was something so inevitable and unalterable in this decision that I could find no word of protest. I could not intrude. I stood there with them in a long, deep silence, then I left them.

What should I do ? Tell the neighbours ? Ring up the police ? I could not. It seemed to me that I had forced myself into their intimate lives and must respect their privacy, but I felt greatly troubled.

I ran back to the office, collected a parcel of food, bought some briquettes and some milk and rushed back with them, but I did not wish to be seen again and placed the supplies outside the door, knocked and disappeared. I waited a few minutes below, but no one opened the door, yet I could not find the will—I do not think it was lack of courage, but something positive that prevented me—to force admittance again, so I came away.

I lay awake most of the night, wondering whether I had not made one of the gravest errors of judgment of my life, and as soon as it was possible I went back to the flat; the parcels were not to be seen, but a fear crossed my mind that in any case they would have been stolen by this time. I did knock, however, this time, and waited with a horribly beating heart, and Frau S. herself appeared trembling and swollen-eyed, and I learned that the critical moment the knowledge that one person had come, as it were miraculously, to them had made it impossible for her to kill herself, and both were alive.

Later we were able to help Frau S. She became one of the women who mended those of the clothes sent out to us for distribution that were in too untidy a condition to be given away immediately, and this enabled her to gain sufficient money for light and food. Afterwards her pension was stabilized, and Marie became a teacher, but it was three years before they ever invited me again into their home. At first I did not understand this, but I realized that to many of the students I brought back too vividly the times of their greatest misery and humiliations, and I learned to wait until these experiences had been accepted and absorbed, and never from that day to this has this incident been referred to in any way.

May I never see despair like this again ! So passionless an acceptance of death in life is a terrible thing.

Winifred Wilkinson.

LA BELLE JOURNÉE ! EN ÊTES VOUS SUR ?

28*th June, Saturday.* La journée de Versailles. Lunch early and leave the Majestic in a car with Headlam Morley. He is a historian, yet he dislikes historical occasions. Apart from that he is a sensitive person and does not rejoice in seeing great nations humbled. I, having none of such acquirements or decencies, am just excited.

There is no crowd at all until we reach Ville d'Avray. But there are poilus at every cross-road waving red flags and stopping all other traffic. When we reach Versailles the crowd thickens. The avenue up to the château is lined with cavalry in steel-blue helmets. The pennants of their lances flutter red and white in the sun. In the Cour d'Honneur, from which the captured German cannon have tactfully been removed, are further troops. There are Generals, Pétain, Gouraud, Mangin. There are St. Cyriens. Very military and orderly. Headlam Morley and I creep out of our car hurriedly. Feeling civilian and grubby. And wholly unimportant. We hurry through the door.

Magnificent upon the staircase stand the Gardes Républicains— two caryatids on every step—their sabres at the salute. This is a great ordeal, but there are other people climbing the stairs with us. Headlam and I have an eye-meet. His thin cigaretted fingers make a gesture of dismissal. He is not a militarist.

We enter the two anterooms, our feet softening on to the thickest of *savonnerie* carpets. They have ransacked the garde-meubles for their finest pieces. Never, since the Grand Siècle, has Versailles been more ostentatious or more embossed. " I hate Versailles," I whisper to Headlam. " You hate what ? " he answers, being only a trifle deaf. " Versailles," I answer. " Oh," he says, " you mean the Treaty."—" What Treaty ? say—thinking of 1871." I do not know why I record this conversation, but I am doing this section of the diary very carefully. It will amuse Ben and Nigel, " This Treaty," he answers. " Oh," I say, " I see what you mean—the German

Treaty." And of course it will be called not the Treaty of Paris, but the Treaty of Versailles. "A toutes les gloires de la France."

We enter the Galerie des Glaces. It is divided into three sections. At the far end are the Press already thickly installed. In the middle there is a horse-shoe table for the plenipotentiaries. In front of that, like a guillotine, is the table for the signatures. It is supposed to be raised on a dais but, if so, the dais can be but a few inches high. In the nearer distance are rows and rows of tabourets for the distinguished guests, the deputies, the senators and the members of the delegations. There must be seats for over a thousand persons. This robs the ceremony of all privilege and therefore of all dignity. It is like the Aeolian Hall.

Clemenceau is already seated under the heavy ceiling as we arrive. "Le roi," runs the scroll above him, "gouverne par lui-même." He looks small and yellow. A crunched homunculus.

Conversation clatters out among the mixed groups around us. It is, as always on such occasions, like water running into a tin bath. I have never been able to get other people to recognize that similarity. There was a tin bath in my house at Wellington : one turned it on when one had finished and ran upstairs shouting " Baath ready " to one's successor : " Right-ho," he would answer : and then would come the sound of water pouring into the tin bath below, while he hurried into his dressing-gown. It is exactly the sound of people talking in undertones in a closed room. But it is not an analogy which I can get others to accept.

People step over the Aubusson benches and *escabeaux* to talk to friends. Meanwhile the delegates arrive in little bunches and push up the central aisle slowly. Wilson and Lloyd George are among the last. They take their seats at the central table. The table is at last full. Clemenceau glances to right and left. People sit down upon their *escabeaux* but continue chattering. Clemenceau makes a sign to the ushers. They say " Ssh ! Ssh ! Ssh ! " People cease chattering and there is only the sound of occasional coughing and the dry rustle of programmes. The officials of the Protocol of the Foreign Office move up the aisle and say, " Ssh ! Ssh ! " again. There is then an absolute hush, followed by a sharp military order. The Gardes Republicains at the doorway flash their swords into their scabbards with a loud click. " Faites entrer les Allemands," says Clemenceau in the ensuing silence. His voice is distant but harshly penetrating. A hush follows.

Through the door at the end appear two *huissiers* with silver chains. They march in single file. After them come four officers of France, Great Britain, America and Italy. And then, isolated and pitiable, come the two German delegates. Dr. Müller, Dr. Bell. The silence is terrifying. Their feet upon a strip of parquet between the *savonnerie* carpets echo hollow and duplicate. They keep their eyes fixed away from those two thousand staring eyes, fixed upon the ceiling. They are deathly pale. They do not appear as representatives of a brutal militarism. The one is thin and pink-eyelidded : the second fiddle in a Brunswick orchestra. The other is moon-faced and suffering : a *Privatdozent*. It is all most painful.

They are conducted to their chairs. Clemenceau at once breaks the silence. " Messieurs," he rasps, " la séance est ouverte." He adds a few ill-chosen words. " We are here to sign a Treaty of Peace." The Germans leap up anxiously when he has finished, since they know that they are the first to sign. William Martin, as if a theatre manager, motions them petulantly to sit down again. Mantoux translates Clemenceau's words into English. Then St. Quentin advances towards the Germans and with the utmost dignity leads them to the little table on which the Treaty is expanded. There is a general relaxation. Conversation hums again in an undertone. The delegates stand up one by one and pass onwards to the queue which waits by the signature table. Meanwhile people buzz round the main table getting autographs. The single file of plenipotentiaries waiting to approach the table gets thicker. It goes quickly. The officials of the Quai d'Orsay stand round, indicating places to sign, indicating procedure, blotting with neat little pads.

Suddenly from outside comes the crash of guns thundering a salute. It announces to Paris that the second Treaty of Versailles has been signed by Dr. Müller and Dr. Bell. Through the few open windows comes the sound of distant crowds cheering hoarsely. And still the signature goes on.

We had been warned it might last three hours. Yet almost at once it seemed that the queue was getting thin. Only three, then two, and then one delegate remained to sign. His name had hardly been blotted before the *huissiers* began again their " Ssh ! Ssh ! " cutting suddenly short the wide murmur which had again begun.

There was a final hush. " La séance est levée," rasped Clemenceau. Not a word more or less.

We kept our seats while the Germans were conducted like prisoners from the dock, their eyes still fixed upon some distant point of the horizon.

We still kept our seats to allow the big five to pass down the aisle. Wilson, Lloyd George, the Dominions, others. Finally, Clemenceau, with his rolling satirical gait. Painlevé, who was sitting one off me, rose to greet him. He stretched out both his hands and grasped Clemenceau's right glove. He congratulated him. " Oui," says Clemenceau, " c'est une belle journée." There were tears in his bleary eyes.

Marie Murat was near me and had overheard. " En êtes-vous sure ? " I ask her. " Pas du tout," she answers, being a woman of intelligence.

Slowly the crowd in the room clears, the Press through the Rotonde, and the rest through the Salle d'Honneur. I walk across the room, pushing past empty tabourets, to a wide-open window which gives out upon the terrace and the famous Versailles view. The fountains spurt vociferously. I look out over the *tapis vert* towards a tranquil sweep of open country. The clouds, white on blue, race across the sky and a squadron of aeroplanes races after them. Clemenceau emerges through the door below me. He is joined by Wilson and Lloyd George. The crowds upon the terrace burst through the cordon of troops. The top-hats of the Big Four and the uniforms of the accompanying Generals are lost in a sea of gesticulation. Fortunately it was only a privileged crowd. A platoon arrives at the double and rescues the big four. I find Headlam Morley standing miserably in the littered immensity of the Galerie des Glaces. We say nothing to each other. It has all been horrible.

And so through crowds cheering " Vive l'Angleterre " (for our car carries the Union Jack) and back to the comparative refinement of the Majestic.

In the car I told Headlam Morley of a day, years ago, when Tom Spring Rice had dined with the Prime Minister. He was young at the time, myopic and shy. The other guests were very prosperous politicians. When the women had gone upstairs they all took their glasses of port and bunched around the Prime Minister. Tom was left out. Opposite him was Eddie Marsh, also at a tail-end. Eddie took his glass round to Tom's side of the table and sat beside him. " Success," he said, " is beastly, isn't it ? "

Headlam Morley agreed that success, when emphasized, was very beastly indeed.

Celebrations in the hotel afterwards. We are given free champagne. Go out on to the boulevards afterwards.

To bed, sick of life.

Hon. Harold Nicolson.

MIRAUMONT

THE village was flooded when last I was here; the Germans had gone the night previously, and no guns were firing, for the enemy had walked out of range.

I remember the Bengal Lancers filing through the ruins: bearded, turban'd, dark-skinned soldiers, with the pennons on their upheld lances scarcely fluttering in the windless air. A battalion of the Yorkshire Regiment was " on fatigue," laying balks of timber over the liquid mud of the broken road. As I passed on my horse I saw a pallid hand sticking out between two balks, and a sodden grey uniform cuff; a young soldier laughingly put the handle of a broken spade between the stiff fingers, saying, " Now then, Jerry, get on wi' it; no bluudy skrimshankin' 'ere."

I entered an *estaminet* near the station and asked for bread and cheese and wine. It was an untidy place like the village, a place of shapeless shacks and sheds made of rusty sheets of wartime corrugated sheet-iron among buildings partly rebuilt. There were several young men in the room watching two men playing a game of billiards. An idiot child was running about the room, and seeing me, but without human recognition, it came up and took my stick out of my hand. Its father, a man of about thirty-five years of age, in slovenly clothes, shouted something as he raised himself from a leaning position over the billiard table, and then resumed his preparation for a stroke. A female voice replied shrilly and rapidly from the unseen kitchen, and a moment later a woman ran out, seized the child by its wrist, wrenched the stick out of its fingers, returned it to me without a glance, and dragged the child through a door into the kitchen.

I waited five minutes, ten minutes, but no one took any notice of me; the game continued with much jabbering of voices, which is another way of saying that I understood only one word in fifty of the language of the country in which I was a foreigner.

732

At the end of a quarter of an hour madame came back, less untidy and less worried, and agreed to cook me an omelette.

I ate in silence when it arrived ; and I had just finished it when the game ended and the patron (I am ignorant of the right word ; my authority for this term is a hazy boyish memory of the international works of the late Mr. William Le Queux) came to speak with me. I told him in my weak French that I was a returned soldier ; I gave him a laboured account of the village as it had appeared in the winter of 1916–17. He said that his wife had been there until November, 1916, when the English advanced up the valley from Beaumont Hamel ; le pauvre petit—he indicated the idiot child—had been a baby of two years then, and had been struck in the head by a piece of English shell—c'est la guerre. . . . The other men stopped talking, and listened ; I explained that I was meditating a novel, or novels, of the War, the story of an insignificant and obscure family which had helped, in its small way, to prepare and make the Great War. I would of course, have to draw on some of my own experiences, as Henri Barbusse had in *Le Feu*.

Their eyes lit up ; they exclaimed with enthusiasm at that name. That was reality, la verité ! Only the week before a German soldier, looking for the grave of his brother, had come to the village, and it so chanced that he had read Barbusse, and had declared that it was true for the German soldier as well as for the French ! He was a comrade, that Boche . . . no, Boche was a bad word, part of the old world : pas vrai ! He was a man like themselves, but in the War his uniform happened to be a different colour. He was a brother !

It was amazing, the animation on the faces of those men. Their eyes were lit by inner fire ; they smiled eagerly, their gestures and attitudes were vital and happy. What had brought this miracle— to use a term of the old world ? A stranger had come, a German ; a stranger had come, an Englishman ; after the mention of a name there was no reserve, no suspicion, no distrust ; all shared a common humanity. Something not supernatural, but supernational.

" Bonne chance, camarade ! Bonne chance ! "

I settled the very small bill, adding a few francs extra, and left gaily in the rain, and turned to see them watching me from the doorway. All of us waved together.

Henry Williamson.

A NATION'S GRATITUDE

THURINGIAN Field Artillery Regt. No. . . .
2nd Battery   In the Field, 16th June, 1915.
To :
Staff Medical Officer Dr. A.,
Infantry Regt. No. . . .
In the Field.
DEAR DR. A.,
The battery regrets to have to inform you that your son, Volunteer N.C.O. Kurt A., died a hero's death for the Fatherland on the morning of June 13th. He fell defending the gun entrusted to his care. With you the battery mourns the death of this exemplary and courageous comrade. May God help you to bear this pain and give you comfort.
With deepest respect,

. . . .
Captain Commanding Battery.

Baden Infantry Regt. No. . . .
Regimental Staff.   In the Field, 23rd Sept., 1917.
To :
Staff Medical Officer Dr. A.,
Infantry Regt. No. . . .
In the Field.
DEAR DR. A.,
With the deepest regret I have the honour to inform you that our comrade, your son, Lieutenant of Reserve Walter A., did not return on the morning of 22nd September from a patrol for which he volunteered. He was shot in the chest by a rifle bullet, and died at once. I regret that it has not yet been possible to recover the body of your son ; I am making efforts to do so and will at once inform you when the regiment has succeeded in what it considers a duty of honour.

The regiment which had the honour of numbering your son among its officers sincerely mourns his death. As the commander of his regiment I beg you, sir, to rest assured that I was at all times proud of your son, who on all occasions proved a dauntless officer, respected by his comrades and his subordinates. He will himself have told you that the Iron Cross, First Class, was conferred on him ten days ago.

In sincere sorrow,

. . . .

Lieut.-Col. Commanding Regiment.

2nd Res. Batt. Infantry Regt. . . .

5th November, 1917.

The N.C.O. Hans A. 3/11, transferred from the field to reserve battalion, is promoted to junior medical officer. He is to be employed in a military hospital and, as the last surviving son of a family, is not to be sent into the field.

. . . .

Lieut. and Adjutant.

Admission Committee for the
Medical District of . . .
Health Insurance.   *1st June,* 1933.

To :
Dr. Hans A.

DEAR SIR,

I have to inform you that as a non-Aryan without the qualification of service at the front you have been removed from panel practice.

You are to refrain from all participation in panel practice. Your accounts will no longer be settled. Your attention is expressly drawn to the inevitable consequences of failure to adhere strictly to these instructions.

Heil Hitler !

. . . .

Chairman of Admission Committee.

Admission Committee for the
Medical District of . . .
Health Insurance.   10*th August,* 1933.

To :
Dr. Hans A.
DEAR SIR,
    Your application for re-admission to panel practice cannot be
complied with.   The regulations in this respect are quite unequivocal.
The fact that your two brothers were killed in the war and that your
father served at the front cannot be taken into account.   It would
be different if your father had fallen in the field.
                              Heil Hitler !
                              . . . .
                        Chairman of Admission Committee.

Medical Councillor Dr. Max A.
Specialist in internal diseases.   5*th September,* 1933.

To :
The Admission Committee for the
Medical District of . . .
Health Insurance.
GENTLEMEN,
    I hereby apply for re-admission to panel practice.   As may be
seen from the enclosed documents I was at the front from 3rd September, 1914, to 16th March, 1918, at first as medical officer and
later as Staff Medical Officer and Regimental Medical Officer.   I was
wounded twice and am the possessor of the Iron Cross, First and
Second Class.
    For reasons of health I resigned from my panel practice in favour
of my son in the summer of 1924, but he has since been deprived of
it as non-ex-front fighter and non-Aryan.   Since my other sons fell
in the war, and since I lost all I possessed in the inflation and a private
practice for my son in our industrial town is beyond possibility, I
find myself compelled to apply for re-admission despite my age.

Admission Committee for the
Medical District of . . .
Health Insurance. *5th September*, 1934.

To :
Medical Councillor Dr. Max A.

DEAR SIR,

We have been informed by colleagues in the profession that, owing to your age and to ill health resulting from your war wounds, you are not in a position to carry on your practice and have always been represented by your son, Dr. Hans A., who as a non-ex-front fighter and non-Aryan cannot be admitted to panel practice.

In view of the regulations this is inadmissible. As you knew this, the Medical Union cancelled your admission to panel practice on 31st August, 1934.

Heil Hitler !

. . . .

Chairman of Admission Committee.

General-Anzeiger of 10th October, 1934 : " . . . 9th October, 1934. The city fire brigade received a call yesterday. In a house in the Bahnhofstrasse, Medical Councillor Dr. Max A. was found dead from gas poisoning. The motive appears to have been financial worry."

" The Yellow Spot."

THIS NOT THE SONG THEY WISH TO HEAR

I

REACH back to years I spent, to men I knew,
to days I drank each minute dry,
give tongue to want: I must not die
mere wisdom-bound because the hurt
grew great and this my loss is loss of men.

Reach hand to touch rough-coated arm,
let none dismiss with pity grief
this company of ghosts about my heart
they were my youth, the sorrow mine.

I bought this peace but paid no price
so great as theirs.
                    Sing to them now,
they sang and I.
                    What if I find
but little solace at the end?
                    The song is theirs.
Trace out their destiny to dust
through hope through fear
and if a voice can reach,
bring answer to this newer time
what world-laid-waste the land looked then.
                    Sing to them now
the young the brave who cast their coin.
Sing truth: no answer else.
A bitter tune made sharp by joy
small joy beneath a bitter tune.
Sing twenty years' remembering.
                    Sing to them now?

II

Brothers . . . I would be young again, unfearing.

There is a flame will drive this knowledge
hell-begot, this shrinking into fear so far
beyond the plain of age :
Bring me a torch to touch your eyes
rekindle mine walk grandly wearing happiness
a mantle for my pride :
Bring Autumn in a golden blush
where Severn lies in silver under trees.
The layered years' decay is rust
and I must strip my soul while yet I may.

If this be youth,
to know a joy in skill of limb,
let me be proud again
unprison me.

No greying eyes, pain-racked faces pale,
still as sorrow in the night.
None of these.
Let them stay caverned in the dark years,
they were reward we knew not ours.
Turn back the pages hurriedly, read them not.
Forget the end.

Birch throwing gold and silver coin
across the lane, ochred leaves jewels
in the hedge, a russet carpet
underneath the beech, sky royal
arrogant in blue,
sun captive in bracken.
All this I know and you waiting
close-ranked upon the green.
Make room for me, I am of your kin.
I held my weapon and perfected skill
strutted in pride made play of work,

each mile of greenwalled lane a song.
Let trumpets sound
for I was glad in arms.

Is there no joy in trust of men?

They have grown old with me, these memories.
To what far end
this fervour toil unspared
this hardwon art?
So little worth to fashion men
into the mould of war, to mint
a coin soon to be trodden into mire
forever lost from currency of race.
Give praise to God
He will not lift the veil?

Destroy this pomp this pleasure
tear the robes and show
the gaping stark mad idiocy
of lust within the outward-smiling
lecherous shape of war:
an act of faith.
These days turned vain made spendthrift waste
and youthful pride a bubble bayonet-pricked,
this house of skill a ruin
nettle-strewn and void:
an act of faith.
Stand true to later seeing
lead no generation but my own
where death lies ambushed
death with no eyes for age.
An act of faith.

III

Grey is the sky, the rain
grey in the dawn declined from dark
sodden weary benumbed. No life
but in this round of rain and wind

no tree and all is strange
the world halted an instant here.
      There is a drum beats in the East
and Drummer Death is strong
Not Yet his drum-beats say Not Yet
I drink not wine of youth unbittered
with herb of pain Not Yet
I have a cellar in the East
will hold your days till they be ripe.
O rest sink deep your feet in mire
till you be customwise to earthy touch
of your unnumbered kin.
      So Death.
The column moves, the bugles flaunt the rain.

Each day a testament of dying years
a wreath of mist upon the trees
tall unregarding in the dusk and still,
so far removed from all . . .
      If this be life, to count falling hours
in youth, hoard minutes,
ape the mood of age
before a line be scribed by wisdom
on this vellum of the brow
      If this be life . . .
No stars pinking the mantled grey
no moon no stir of wind waking
along the road a file of men
and through the hundred hearts a shrinking boldness
in-and-out, longing and fear, an eager dread.

This lightning East this thunder sunk to earth
this pulse of what new devilment
now loud now soft what rhythm this?
A screech uprising hell-governed in its course
through wild long octaves of alarm
until the noise puts end to noise
and all is emptiness and thirst
what rhythm this?

" There is a fear of Fear
hath greater skill to halt the blood
and break the man within
than aught in armoury of war."

Quick summon pride
to master shrinking flesh to man the walls
in my defence.
         Were there not men
withstood this press before their lives
sank into tales of bravery?

But there are eyes regard me, search me.
I am no man but in their faith
that I am more than they . . .
so little worth their trust,
sent to-and-fro by doubt and pride . . .
so little worth.
This fear I conquered now
hath it not heirs unnumbered
waiting my fall?
These tongue-dried moments . . .

    I have a salve saith Time
release from fear from stabbing awe
this anodyne

         Count all my coin
there is no price I would not pay

    Turn to thy task
this gold unstamped with pain is dross.
Hark to the Drummer . . .
He is thy foe stand to thy weapon now
seek not so soon this balm
there are elder brethren wait.

East to the prison-wall of trench.
The tenant of this plain beyond forbids

my gaze upon his husbandry.
This clotted waste breast-high
into the far rim of hedge
a splintered tree a mass of spears
against what fate what unconcern?

Grey imprint on the bird-bare field
pockmarked and foul
slimed with the trail of folly blind-distraught:
a land remote, soilbordered scars.
Soiled I this land with hate?

I have no hate but of this ugliness
no fear but that I sink below
the grey disaster spread to hide
cool pricking green and May
a gift to other eyes in other lands
colour on cloud above the hills.

This servitude of mud
this sly recumbency beneath a threat
lurking in rat-disputed dyke
this endless struggle with a mastery
of seeping water, husbandry of filth
and rank decay, this toil to build a grave
where once the plough made furrow . . .
Gave I my freedom thus to spend?

But I have men who wait with me,
stars pricking a song upon the sheet of sky.
I knew not men till now,
I knew not succour in a laughing word,
affection in a curse,
blood-brethren now, Cain-marked or free.

Eyes slow to warn the limbs
void where was richness and warm blood
no path through flesh cold-weary
deaf to my bidding, rebel to my will.

All is afar, haze-hidden,
a petty thought revolves an endless trill of haste
O bring me sleep silent and smooth
cool coverlet of sleep,
and in the end release.

Too swift a word, too kind,
respite is all free-given now
but gift enough.

Savour of living air,
hard crust of stone against the feet
boughs patterncurved against the stars
quiet shuttered house, reprieve of voice :
eyes born in the dark to sweep
borders of the seen-unseen
Limbs free to move unshrinkingly
ears sharp to laughter and O
this unremembered beauty of the dusk
when all is still to greet the moon :
slow patient cattle in the grass.
Long catalogue of smallness bursting great
upon a starved heart, day turned long life
to spend recklessly gladly
in joy in gratitude
But there is a morrow
and this I know a scene upon a stage
mere trick of art to cozen me
I am kin with man.

Believe it not . . . hark to the drums.

I have played at in-and-out with danger
a thousand times, grown old in craft,
plumbed hidden fear beneath the heart.
I am known to Death. His iron hand
to right and left moves quickly . . .
Hath it an end, this pilgrimage ?

Bring dark bring day
scatter the stars to bridge the sky
drive cloud to hold the moon,
no liberty of flesh, the burden falls not.
My metal thins to a thread will snap
and I turned worshipper of little gods
who scatter chance to man.

This giant impotence shadows me
blinds me.

IV

INTERLUDE

No wilderness but there is beauty waiting
and life moves not from its hidden course
though all our strivings fill the days
with noise of purpose and paraded aim,
plot and pursuit enmesh the mind
but there are older hungers . . .
   A voice unstilled and with it Love
threading an ancient way within,
eyes yielding not, strong in their tenderness,
child-tender, beckoning me across the pit.
   No other trust than this, no burning bush :
beacon enough to lead me out of dark
if I be true, throw all upon the turn of love.

This cannot be . . . to touch lips,
waking to find I dream not.
There is wizardry here and I the child of maze.
Some devilment concealed.

Green bravery upon the mountainside
rising falling with the rounded slopes,
a fleece of trees thrust o'er the shoulder of a hill
and all is beauty, silence

           Let not that lamb cry out again
I have heard men in their pain
this world-old cry. There is no answer.
And all is beauty, silence.

Drink deep to love : I am but half-aware of sorrow.
This birch waving her tresses in the wind,
moonsilver bark in shower of feathered green
a fairy caught in earth's mortality
and named a tree.
Noon is a silence dusk a candlelight,
on rough walls slanting.
Heap wood upon the fire : no evil in this flame.

Would I were done with all but love
and in the morning grey smoke curling
above the chimney and a voice singing.
Farewell, my love . . . live with thy hope
Look not on Time . . . farewell my love.
Brief song long silence and a new desire

Farewell, my love.

V

A knave in borrowed clothes this Spring across the sea,
trust it not . . . look there is murder here
grey behind a thorn, snare in the willow's curve
and rusty barb in the ragwort's yellow ranks.

My flesh is quick to-night : I had forgotten fear.
Love stripped me naked.

Hark to the drumbeats . . . this Drummer
hath he report I fled his parade ?
Make room for me, this odour calls me
sharp to kill all fragrance
      I have said Farewell my love

This man, is he dead ?
I had forgotten death cold hunger fury
torment and toil leaden drag of limb
fumes of the pit, grey lids and red-rimmed eyes
Fear set this face to stone
        Make room for me
        I have dallied enough.

Remembering now that I have left love
tenderness kind touch of flesh far
in another land far in another time
Remembering now all beauty gone
as a dream goes
        Turn back delight
        Reach not to me.
This land a pock-marked harridan
brown-skinned furrowed with debauchery
flaunting a raddled face greystreaked
gaunt each empty eye a crater
where a lust burnt through.

This Summer morn a mockery.

Remembering this also
I have known mountains gold under the sun
I have trodden scree to bare a fern
mounted crest to meet dawn over sea
and this I know
I shall not die before her eyes
a man : a memory a legend that was life.
No more, no more.

Limbs strangely bent to mock the hurry of a start
a hand pointing the way . . . turn not,
evil athwart the path.
They blacken in the sun, scatter of a storm now past.

A sentinel walks unseen before this wood
flame where his footsteps fall and cloud.
He sleeps not.   The acres of the sky
burn bright and a lark publishes freedom
in a land of slaves, but lo !
what butchery within this wood
rending of flesh and red limbs crucified
on a tree ?

        Is there no end to murdering of man
be he Christ or ploughman ?   No.
Is death a joy to hold ?
These words betray.
Eyes countering mine smoulder and shine not,
say they this of me ?
I am dead to all I knew before.
Is there no end to this vast continent of day ?
No end but night.

Ride the great stallions of dismay
along the veins of other men ?
Silence that moaning boy
let him not cry again in the dark
he hath no hurt but fear.
And in this glade hearken
answer stand to your names.

They answer not
Their names are dead as they.

    This tree stained red
    the leaves were green
    now pale as we,
    rust not of steel
    upon this green

We have borne enough :
Let them be buried in their market-place.

VI

So that my song no answer brings
nor in the calm a whisper stirs
the leaves, no dawn to me
but waking-time and I bereft
betrayed their trust
                    for others move
to follow them
                    This not the song they wish to hear.

But men have died to give them place,
and they who live will one day sing
as I, will speak their sorrow once again,
but some will hear will sound a song
to lead the children into love
                    Whose children these?
                    Not theirs who died

O Mercy give us grace to live
O God send wisdom soon.

                              Ll. Wyn Griffith.

AUTHORS QUOTED

SOURCES

Advance from Mons, The, Capt. Walter Bloem (tr. G. C. Wynne), 4, 33, 79
Adventure, Maj.-Gen. Seely (Lord Mottistone), 567
Adventures in Turkey and Russia, E. H. Keeling, M.C., M.P., 443
And all for What ?, D. W. J. Cuddeford, 409
Army Quarterly, art. by Lieut. Kostlin, ix, 334 ; art. Canadian Battalion's War Diary, Oct. 1924,
     647 ; Random Reminiscences of an Ordinary Soldier in the Great War, 705
Assaut contre Verdun, L', E. Diatz-Retg., 234
At G.H.Q., Brig.-Gen. John Charteris, 191, 451, 456, 457
Australian Imperial Forces, Official History of, 383, 471
Avec Charles Péguy, Victor Boudon, 50, 68
Before Jutland, Admiral von Spee's last Voyage, Coronel and the Battle of the Falklands, Capt.
    Hans Pochhammer (tr. H. J. Stemming), 95
Belgium under German Occupation, Brand Whitlock, 203, 206
Black Monastery, Aladar Kuncz, 13, 631
Brass Hat in No Man's Land, A, Brig.-Gen. F. P. Crozier, 325
Breaking of the Storm, The, Capt. C. A. L. Brownlow, 38, 39, 41, 43, 45
Britain Holds On, Caroline E. Playne, 706
British Documents on the Origins of the War, 3, 5
Broadchalk (Three Personal Records), John Easton, 197
By Guess and by God, the Story of the British Submarines in the War, William Guy Carr, 161, 514
By Sea and Land, Lt.-Com. E. Hilton Young (Lord Kennet), 208, 214, 582
Campaign in Gallipoli, The, Maj.-Gen. Hans Kannengiesser (tr. Maj. C. J. P. Ball), 184
Campaign in Mesopotamie, The, 298
Canadian Battalion's War Diary, in *Army Quarterly,* Oct. 1924, 647
Captain Albert Ball, V.C., W. A. Briscoe and H. R. Stannard, 374
Carnet d'un combattant, Le, Louis Mairet, 226, 345, 346, 519
Carnets de Galliéni, Les, 69, 70
Case of Sergeant Grischa, The, Arnold Zweig (tr. Eric Sutton), 371, 427
C. E. Montague, a Memoir, Oliver Elton, 581
Collected Poems, Wilfrid Gibson, 377, 710
Collected Works of Patrick H. Pearse, 377
Cornhill Magazine, xxxviii, 93
Coronel and After, Paym.-Comm. Lloyd Hurst, 90
Cry Havoc !, Beverley Nichols, 307
De Liége à l'Yser, Capt.-Comm. R. de Wilde, 17
Desert Column, The, I. L. Idriess, 395
Diary of a Young Civil Servant, Victor Smith, 5
Diary of Otto Braun, 106, 225, 522
Disenchantment, C. E. Montague, 114, 648, 650, 718
Economic Consequences of the Peace Treaty, The, J. M. Keynes, 720, 721
Economist, The, 127
End of a War, The, Herbert Read, 703
Erlibnisse im Weltkrieg, Max Erzberger, 696
Escaping Club, The, A. J. Evans, 311, 367
Everyman at War, ed. C. B. Purdom, 137, 235, 425
Face à Face, Lieut. Jacques Péricard, 130
Falklands, Jutland and the Bight, Comm. the Hon. Barry Bingham, 268
Falsehood in War Time, Lord Ponsonby, 86
Fatalist at War, A, Rudolf Binding (tr. I.F.D. Morrow), 147, 566, 641
Field-Marshal Sir Henry Wilson, His Life and Diaries, Maj.-Gen. Sir C. E. Callwell, 81, 422, 565
Fighting at Jutland, The, H. W. Fawcett and G. W. W. Hooper, 272, 277, 288

755

SUMMARY OF CONTENTS

1914

1915